theCity

alan s. berger

City of Chicago Department of Human Services

theCity

urban communities and their problems

wcb

Wm. C. Brown Company Publishers   *Dubuque, Iowa*

Book Team

Ed Bowers, Jr. Publisher
Robert Nash Editor
David Corona Designer
Mary Heller Visual Research

Wm. C. Brown Company Publishers

Wm. C. Brown President
Larry W. Brown Executive Vice President
Lawrence E. Cremer Vice President, Director, College
  Division
Richard C. Crews Publisher
Raymond C. Deveaux National Sales Manager
John Graham National Marketing Manager
Roger Meyer Director, Production/Manufacturing
John Carlisle Assistant Vice President, Production
  Division
Ruth Richard Manager, Production-Editorial Depart-
  ment
David Corona Design Director

To Paula and Sheila, whose love, affection, encouragement, and support have made this book possible.

Contents

List of Tables

Preface

Many recent urban sociology textbooks have come close to abandoning the traditional concern of urban sociology, which is the community in urban society. Emphasis has shifted to individual adaptations to urban society or to characteristics of urban society. This book returns to an emphasis on the concept of community and integrates contemporary knowledge about local communities with an analysis of the nature and problems of urban society. This focus is sociologically sound, and, at least as important, it allows students to relate their own experiences to the analysis.

The theories and data needed to understand cities, communities, and urban problems are presented so that students with only a minimal background in sociology should be able to use this book. Complex theoretical issues are developed logically and clearly and are related to concrete examples. The materials and issues presented should be especially helpful to students working toward associate and baccalaureate degrees in such fields as urban studies, urban planning, and urban sociology.

Organization of *The City: Urban Communities and their Problems*

The framework adopted in this book views cities as large communities made up of smaller communities. They have grown and evolved from earlier settlements and less complex social systems. To understand the problems of communities within cities, and of cities as communities, is to understand their proper functions—what they are, how they are performed, and, especially, how they have evolved. The best way to understand contemporary situations and to prepare ourselves for future situations is to understand how we have arrived where we are. The best predictor of the future is the present; the next best predictor is the past. We will therefore look first to the past to find the seeds of contemporary situations and then trace how they grew.

But before we trace the evolution of social structures and social systems, we must define what they are and how they operate. They are, of course, ideas, not things, but are no less "real" than things. We are using some components of social structure and social systems as tools to analyze and understand the functioning of human society.

Chapter 1 sets the stage by describing the popular image of the urban crisis and by defining a city in such a way that the urban crisis may be analyzed in realistic terms.

In chapter 2 the basic concept of community is explained. Evolution of the community concept makes it clear that the communities found in contemporary cities are not communities in the classical or traditional sense. They have some characteristics of traditional communities and perform some communal functions, but because of the complexity and interdependence of contemporary urbanized, industrial society, these communities are unable to perform all the functions that our history and our heritage of communal concepts lead us to expect.

The third and fourth chapters trace the evolution of cities from their origins as temporary settlements at the dawn of history to their present form. Though the details have changed, the processes that created the first cities and shaped their social life have continued to the present day and are likely to continue into the future.

Chapters 5 through 7 provide data on the shapes of contemporary cities, the processes that have produced these shapes, and the character of urban population and its ways of life. This grounding is necessary for any informed discussion of the contemporary city and its problems. In chapters 8 through 14 some problems of American cities are analyzed. Chapter 8 describes the forces in contemporary society that have affected the ability of cities to control their own destiny. In chapters 9 and 10 two aspects of normative integration are considered: racial and ethnic relationships and political systems. In chapters 11 through 14 we examine the problems cities have performing their functions with respect to housing, transportation, health, pollution control, crime, and education.

Chapter 15 is a speculative and optimistic essay that draws on the materials in the previous chapters to look into the future of cities in the United States.

The organization of the book reflects my belief that it is better to learn key concepts and approaches to a body of facts than to learn a multitude of facts. Facts are important only insofar as they illuminate a topic under discussion. Thus the concept of community as expressed in different theories is discussed in some detail before the evolution of urban communities is traced. Ecological processes are discussed before the contemporary forms of cities and the forces that shaped them are analyzed. The reader is invited to make his or her own judgments about the usefulness of the various theories and models of urban evolution and ecological change in the light of personal experiences and the data presented in this book. Finally, a variety of urban problems are analyzed by means of the data and the theories developed in the first half of the book. Although the data and the problems are changing continuously, the concepts and the framework presented in this book should have lasting value for the interested reader. With these tools, he or she can analyze productively and critically other problems of urban society, present and future, and make informed choices about programs and policies.

Pedagogical Aids

A number of pedagogical aids are provided for the reader. Many chapters include examples of ideas being discussed, specially presented as visual inserts into the text. Besides a summary of its main ideas, each chapter has a glossary of words used in special ways and a bibliography. These words and references are gathered into a cumulative glossary and a complete bibliography at the end of the book. Empirical data, primarily in the form of tables, are provided where needed. Phenomena discussed in the text are concretely illustrated.

Acknowledgments

Writing a book such as this is a difficult task, one that could not be completed without the help and encouragement of many people. My wife Paula has contributed immensely to the clarity of the writing; my father provided many helpful suggestions; Mary Jo Broderick, Joanne Brown, Kay Carrillo, Rita McCarthy, Cathy Schaeffer, Roselle Silverman, Karen Sintic, and Bettye Wharton were invaluable in typing and assembling the various drafts of the manuscript. My students at Loyola have suffered through the development of different interpretations and presentations of the material and have provided valuable feedback. The Institute for Juvenile Research has offered a congenial atmosphere in which to work.

A special debt of gratitude is due to the reviewers, who were responsible for great improvement in the manuscript: James Beaudry, Parker Frisbie, Richard Hill, Nancy Loy, Harvey Marshall, William Martineau, Mario Renzi, and William Yancey. An even greater debt is owed to my editor, Bob Nash, who not only arranged for the reviews, but also encouraged me to keep working. Without him there would be no book. Naturally, any faults remaining are mine.

Alan S. Berger

This text, *The City: Urban Communities and Their Problems,* is accompanied by the following ancillary volume:

Instructor's Resource Manual / Test Item File

Part 1 **Theoretical and Historical Perspectives**

WELCOME! to the
48-4900 BLOCKS OF HARRISON STREET
PLEASE HELP US KEEP OUR BLOCKS SAFE
& BEAUTIFUL BY OBSERVING THE FOLLOWING
· KEEP OFF THE GRASS
· DO NOT DEFACE PROPERTY
· DON'T LITTER
· NO CAR WASHING OR REPAIRS ON STREET
· NO HORN BLOWING
· DON'T BLOCK DRIVEWAYS
· NO SPEEDING
· NO LOITERING
· CURB YOUR DOG
Thank You

1 Approaches to Cities and Their Problems

American cities have grown rapidly throughout most of our history because they have offered economic opportunities and a satisfying and varied life. Cities provide their residents with conveniences, services, and opportunities not available elsewhere. Until recently, the attractions and opportunities available to city dwellers far outweighed the disadvantages of urban life (Still, 1974; Davis, 1955:128-30).

In our older and larger cities this is no longer the case. They have begun to lose population, as well as businesses and industries; their housing stock is deteriorating; transportation and education are inadequate; racial and ethnic groups coexist in a state of tension; and crime and the fear of crime appear to be epidemic. Something seems to have gone terribly wrong, but nobody seems to know what that something is or how to correct it.

Despite all their problems, though, cities in the United States today are still the heart of our society. To understand their problems, it is necessary to understand the nature of cities, their social organization, and their structure. We can then also understand why people continue to live in cities, why major institutions remain in cities, and why cities are so important to the vitality of our society.

No single point of view or theory is adequate to explain the phenomenon and problems of cities and urban society. However, the development of an integrated point of view teaches us more about cities in the long run than merely listing facts or stating that cities and urban problems are too complex to understand.

The framework developed here is based on a set of concepts and a body of empirical data that can be used now and in the future. It will help the reader organize and understand existing data about cities and integrate new data as they become available. The framework rests on two major propositions: (1) that cities are special types of human communities and (2) that the forms of contemporary cities and urban societies evolved from earlier cities and societies.

As our cities have evolved, the local neighborhood has replaced the small town as the center of **communal attachments** and services. In the process of evolution, the nature of communities has changed. Local city neighborhoods are not very much like small towns, and the patterns of behavior and ways of life in cities suffer in comparison to people's recollections of life in small towns. According to the framework adopted in this book, one way to understand the problems of cities and city life is to analyze the functions that cities and neighborhoods as communities are expected to perform. Because our urban society has evolved from a small-town society in a relatively short time, we have expectations about communities based on nostalgic recollections of small towns. The unmet expectations about communal life and services in the city are a major source of urban problems. Another major source is the level of performance of **communal functions** (which will be defined in chapter 2)—the degree to which the performance of various functions is integrated within a given city and the degree to which it measures up to national standards.

The concepts and data that are crucial to the development and support of this framework will be explored in chapters 2 through 7. First, however, it is necessary to develop in greater detail the image of cities in contemporary society. This image dominates popular discussion of cities and their problems.

The Popular Image of Cities

The popular image of cities is based on a few very large urban centers, such as New York, Chicago, Detroit, Pittsburgh, and Los Angeles. Cities such as these, together with their surrounding suburbs, make up the major metropolitan areas of our country, but they are not typical of the social environments in which most urban residents live. The Bureau of the Census defines an **urban place** as one with a population of 2,500 persons or more and a *metropolitan area* as a city of 50,000 or more plus the socially and economically integrated surrounding counties (U.S. Bureau of the Census, 1971:xii-xiii). According to this definition, most Americans live in urban places. However, most urban places are not located in metropolitan areas. Still, the central cities of the largest metropolitan areas dominate the popular conception of cities (Glabb, 1963:286-317; Mizruchi, 1969:243-52; White and White, 1961:166-76; Hadden and Barton, 1973:79-119).

Americans have always held a somewhat negative view of cities and urban social life.[1] Thomas Jefferson once said, "The mobs of great cities add just so much to the support of pure government as sores do to the strength of the human body (1965:165)." As the number of large cities has increased from only 78 places of 50,000 or more in 1900 to 396 such places in 1970 (U.S. Bureau of the Census, 1975:11), the antiurban strain in American culture has not diminished. As our oldest and largest cities encounter more problems in the performance of their functions, the antiurban tradition helps to ensure the predominance of these problems in the popular image of urban areas.

Popularly, cities are seen as places of many skyscraper office and apartment buildings, bustling and crowded downtown areas, vast tracts of bleak slums, crowded subways and traffic jams, dirt, decay, crime, and vice. Few people think of cities in terms of orchestra halls, factories and industrial areas, museums, and individual homes on quiet streets. Yet cities have all these characteristics. No city has all positive or all negative attributes, nor does any city have all positive and negative attributes in equal degree.

The fact that our largest cities have grown and evolved from much smaller settlements has greatly influenced life in the city. Many kinds of people, migrating into the cities at different times, created much **heterogeneity** within each city and between cities. This heterogeneity makes it possible to talk about "the American city" only in the abstract. Cities differ in their racial composition, their industrial and economic bases, the types of ethnic and religious groups that inhabit them, the life styles that are dominant or even allowed, and their social and political structures—just as they differ in the intangible tone that seems to flavor or characterize each one. Most cities consist of many different ethnic and racial groups, people of different ages, different social levels, different stages in the life cycle, and different life styles. The business and commercial institutions of most cities range from small, family-owned grocery stores and cleaning establishments, profes-

The popular image of cities emphasizes such things as traffic jams, crowded subways, and bleak and often decayed industrial areas.

sional partnerships, and small companies to giant corporations, employing many thousands of people, who often are working in many different locations (Becker and Horowitz, 1973:243-51; Borgatta and Hadden, 1970:253-63; Duncan and Reiss, 1956). It is in this heterogeneity that the distinctive character of a city and many attractions of city life are found.

However, within the city much **homogeneity** can be found in individual neighborhoods (Schwirian, 1974; Park and Burgess, 1925). This, too, is part of the character and attraction of cities. This book will explore both the homogeneity and heterogeneity of cities. Both have developed as a consequence of evolution from small settlements into highly urbanized societies.

Despite their many internal and external differences, most cities have a great deal in common, too. Most have large populations, high population density, and many types of land use, and most must perform many communal services for the population.[2] These services include education of the young, care for the health and welfare of the old, provision of housing, transportation, water and other utilities, and **social control**.

The problems of the largest cities seem so overwhelming, so difficult to deal with, and so impossible of solution that it is often forgotten that not all cities are experiencing crises, let along crises of the same magnitude. The crises seem to be more pervasive and more severe in large cities. This may be because large cities have evolved further than small cities, and the crises occur only after a certain point in evolution has been reached.

Alternatively, the crises may result from the difficulties of life among very large, dense population concentrations, regardless of the city's stage of **evolutionary development.** Whatever the source of the problems, large cities seem beset by a greater variety of crises than small cities.

To understand the problems faced by our largest cities we must consider not only the positive and negative aspects of urban life, but also the nature of urban social systems and society.

Perspectives on Urban Society

Sociological study of the city has been dominated by three major perspectives, each of which has furthered our understanding of cities and urban social life (Reiss, 1970:27-37). We will consider them briefly to provide a basis for the analytic framework this book employs.

Cities as Small-Scale Societies

Probably the earliest of these three views is that the city is a small society, a concept that emerged from study of the history of cities. Starting with the Greek **polis,** city-states were the dominant form of urban life. The city-states of early Greece were not just cities, they were total societies. Much social history of cities is based on the assumption that, like the Greek city-states, cities were whole, although small, self-contained societies. This assumption can be seen clearly in the works of Max Weber (1958) and Henri Pirenne (1969), as well as in the more modern works on small American cities.

Viewing cities as small societies inevitably leads to the conclusion that cities are self-sufficient social organizations. The integration of the city with its surrounding **hinterland** was recognized, but the emphasis was on the dominance of the city over the hinterland. The implication is that the city controls its own destiny as well as the destiny of the hinterland. Decisions made in the city are important to the fate of both the city and the surrounding area. In contemporary society, however, the assumptions that control is lodged with the city and that the city has control over events inside and outside its own boundaries are open to considerable question. As will be seen in chapter 8, there are forces in the wider society that constrain the ability of a city to control its own destiny.

The concept of cities as small societies led to studies such as *Middletown* (Lynd and Lynd, 1929) and *Small Town in Mass Society* (Vidich and Bensman, 1958). Both studies begin with the belief that the city is a self-sufficient social system, and both end with the realization that much of what goes on within the city is determined by outside forces.

Both studies, and others too, have documented the city's loss of control over its own destiny to outside forces—forces that affect the total society.

This loss of control to outside forces has accelerated during the twentieth century, as the pace of social change has accelerated and as cities have accepted federal funds and the restrictions that have accompanied the funds. Just as small towns were affected by decisions made in large metropolitan centers, the large metropolitan centers have been influenced by technological, demographic, and social

changes beyond their control (Schmandt and Goldbach, 1969:473-98). Knowledge of these outside forces and their effects is vital to a city's ability to solve its own problems, but the forces themselves introduce elements into the social and political structures of the city that it cannot influence. In many ways the cities of today are controlled more by external than by internal forces. Once these external forces become dominant in the control of social processes of the city, to view the city as a small society is no longer appropriate. The city is not a self-sufficient social system; it is merely one component in a larger society.

Ecological Perspectives

A second perspective on the nature of urban society views the city as an accumulation of people in a spatially limited area. There are three aspects to this view (Reiss, 1970:27-37; Schwirian, 1974; Theodorson, 1961; Burgess and Bogue, 1964). One, generally called **human ecology**, deals mainly with how groups of people adapt to their environment. In part, this perspective is concerned with the spatial relationships between institutions, people, and their physical environment. This is important because, by knowing where different types of people and institutions are located and by discovering how these locations change over time, we can learn a great deal about how communities function and change. Second, the ecological view also focuses on the nature and development of behavior patterns related to adaptation to the city environment. And, third, the ecological view is concerned with how cities grow and attract populations and how the populations are distributed throughout the city.

It is assumed that behavior patterns, institutions, and modes of adapting to the physical and social environments are different in urban and nonurban areas. One classic ecological approach to the study of cities is to specify the distinctly urban behavior patterns and differentiate them from nonurban behavior patterns (Beers, 1957:698 ff.; Dewey, 1960:60-66; Duncan, 1957:35-45; Mann, 1970:38 ff.).

The three aspects of the ecological perspective are closely related. To summarize, the spatial location of people and institutions is related to how people and communities adapt to their physical and social environments. Human ecologists try to understand the institutional structures and behavior patterns that are distinctive to different spatial locations. They also study the way these behavior patterns and institutions serve as adaptations to the environment, both physical and social. How spatial distributions develop is a third matter of concern to human ecologists.

The City as a Community

A third perspective on urban society is the concept of the city as a special form of community. In a sense this perspective is closely related to the ecological perspective, which is also concerned with how communities adapt to their environment. The community perspective, however, focuses more on the social functioning of communities and especially on how differences in functioning affect the individuals who make up the community.

The community perspective views the city as a group of people who live in the same area and attempt, with varying degrees of success, to make social life possible. The community perspective emphasizes the study of urban modes of life and how they are affected by the nature and institutions of urban societies.

The term *community* has nearly one hundred different definitions (Hillery, 1955:111-123; Sutton and Munson, 1976), and thus must be used with considerable care. In chapter 2 a clear definition of community will be developed. However, a few tentative definitions of community are worth considering at this time, especially as they apply to the study of the urban community. Albert Reiss (1970:27-37) defines the community as an organized group functioning on the basis of residential location. Roland Warren (1972:9) defines the community as an organization of social units and systems responsible for carrying out the functions relevant to the locality in which they reside. If these two definitions are combined, they produce a working definition of a community that is of great help in the study of urban society.

The combined definition of **community** is a group of social units and systems organized on a residential basis to carry out the functions of the residential area. This definition permits us to consider the whole city as a residential area. It also requires us to look within the city for residential groups that perform similar functions on a much smaller scale—namely, the neighborhoods and local communities. In this way we may view the city as a relatively large-scale community, keeping in mind that it is also a collection of smaller communities. Employing this perspective in the study of functions carried out by both the total city and the communities that make up that city will enable us to develop a picture of the urban social system.

The Definition of a City

One major purpose of this chapter is to establish a definition of a city that we can use throughout the book. We will adopt the combined definition of an urban community stated above and integrate it with the ecological perspective. It is possible to conceive of the city as a spatially limited accumulation of people organized into residential areas that form the larger aggregate. Defining a city on the basis of the number of people who live in a given area implies the use of legally or politically defined areas in which people are counted. Such definitions are inherently inadequate for sociological study because urban ways of life and the influence of cities extend far beyond the legal boundaries of cities (Wirth, 1938:1-24). We need a definition that does not rely on legal or political boundaries, on the number of people living within these boundaries, or on the density of settlement within these boundaries. What is needed is a definition that includes both the local communities that comprise the city and the total community that is the city. Our definition cannot include precise limits for size and density of population, but it must take into account the size, density, and heterogeneous character of urban populations and the differences in their life styles.

An earlier view of the city as a small society in its own right—virtually complete and self-contained—is no longer possible. Society has itself grown in size, complexity, and internal interdependence. At the same time, the fate of any city within the society is fully integrated with the fate of the total society. More important, the behavior of individuals and the functioning of institutions within the city have become integrated with individuals and institutions within the society. It would be useful if our definition of a city took into account the necessity for integrating the functions of the city and its communities with the functions of the larger society.

In what may well be the single most influential statement on the nature of urban life, "Urbanism as a Way of Life," Louis Wirth (1938) not only noted the difficulties of defining a city on the basis of numbers, but also called attention to the factors that generated peculiarly urban life styles. Wirth argued that the size, density, and heterogeneity of urban populations were the primary causes of urban modes of behavior and must be included in any definition of a city.

The following definition incorporates these concerns: a **city** is a relatively large, dense, permanent settlement of heterogeneous individuals and groups of individuals organized to perform, or to facilitate the performance of, **locality-relevant functions** in an integrated manner and to ensure integration with the social system of which the city is a part.

This is a rather abstract definition, and it will require a good deal of work to apply it to concrete situations. It does focus attention on the crucial aspects of the city. In particular, it points up the necessity for understanding the behavior, activities, and institutions that have been established to carry out the functions of the city and its constituent communities. It requires that we understand the ways people live and interact both in their local communities and in the wider city society. The definition also focuses our attention on the ways in which the city coordinates the behavior, activities, and institutions that permit it to exist. Finally, it requires us to pay attention to the relationships between the city and the wider society. Our definition implies that some urban areas are more citified than others—some are larger, denser, more heterogeneous, and more integrated than others. Variations in these characteristics will affect the ability of the city and its constituent communities to carry out their locality-relevant functions; they also will affect the relationship between the city and the society as a whole.

Within this context, we can see that the current **crisis of the cities** is related to our expectations. It is our beliefs and feelings about communities and their functioning that lead us to describe our urban problems as a crisis. The largest cities are experiencing—and are perceived as being in—continual and critical crisis. Large cities, however, are a relatively new phenomenon. The first time an American city reached a population of one million was in 1880 (U.S. Bureau of the Census, 1975: 11). We do not really know how to make large cities function adequately. Our expectations are based on our experiences with much smaller settlements.

Our definition of a city should make it plain that many cities and urban neighborhoods *are* experiencing real difficulties in carrying out their functions. These difficulties do not all spring from romantic or idealistic notions of what cities and urban communities should do. Many are the consequences of the size and nature of modern industrial urban society.

Although the second half of the book is devoted to problems that cities face, we will now briefly sketch some problems and some positive aspects of city living. We can thus keep the contemporary situation of cities in focus while we first examine theories about social organization, then look to the evolutionary past of cities for understanding.

Images of the Urban Crisis

The urban crisis and the problems at the root of the crisis are so complex that no matter what the solutions to the problems may be about all that can be agreed upon is that vast sums of money and other resources will be needed to implement them. In fact, experts in urban affairs can agree about little else than the complexity of the crisis and the enormous cost of its solution. About the nature of the crisis and how to solve it, there are more theories than there are experts (Harris and Lindsay, 1972; U.S. Congress, September 1969-June 1970).

Despite all their problems, cities are essential to the continued existence of society as we know it. Cities are the centers of social and economic coordination and vitality. They create the environment in which a variety of economic forces can come together to keep the society functioning: financing, merchandising, labor, and production facilities are all found together only in the nation's cities. The largest banks are located in cities because that is where the most people and the largest institutions are. But people and institutions want more than banks in which to save their money; they want variety—in places to live, things to do, and goods and services to buy. It is circular but true to say that the many goods, services, and facilities available in cities attract people with wide-ranging interests, and, conversely, the people attract the variety of goods and services.

11

Cities create concentrations of cultural, social, and political activity as well as of economic power. Most major museums, symphony orchestras, opera and ballet companies, sports teams, and mass-media outlets are located in cities. Most of the critical political and economic decisions affecting all portions of society are made in the central cities of the largest metropolitan areas. Despite the loss of population in the central core of many major cities, large numbers of young adults continue to migrate there in search of jobs and opportunities for an independent, exciting life.

Some older, larger cities are experiencing declines in population and in available jobs, but other cities are growing. And even cities that are losing population and jobs in the central area are showing growth in their outlying **suburbs.** Although politically autonomous, the suburbs are functionally part of the city (Zimmer, 1975:23-91).

Despite problems of crime, pollution, inadequate education, housing, and transportation; despite racial tensions and conflicts; despite numerous political and economic crises—cities continue to dominate society. To a large extent, what happens in cities determines what happens throughout society. The crises of cities are thus the crises of society. No matter how complex the problems, we must understand them and seek solutions if we are to survive as a viable society for another two hundred years.

Physical and Social Decay

One of the unpleasant characteristics we associate with cities is a pervasive sense of physical decay, especially in the central core

The Urban Crisis: A Long-Range View

Within the circle of American scholars who have concerned themselves with the phenomenon of urbanization in the twentieth century, the theme of the irreversible decay of the central city has become virtually a canon law of conventional wisdom. The literature tends to accept as given that America's old core cities are irredeemably lost and that the only hope of the urban region is to save the inner suburb before it is too late. . . .

I am deeply troubled by the theme of inexorable decay. . . . How old is old? Newark, Jersey City, and New York are older than Milwaukee, but they are much younger than, say, Amsterdam, Copenhagen, Stockholm, Prague, and Zurich, not to mention Beirut and Jerusalem. Yet a case can certainly be made that many of those cities and their environs have much to recommend them today as places of residence and work over not only the older American metropolises but also their younger siblings.

In the inner city of Amsterdam, for example, old masonry structures abound to the extent that about 25 percent of the parcels contain buildings which date from before 1800, yet this area retains great economic vitality. In contrast Newark, for example, finds that twentieth-century skyscrapers are reverting to the city in lieu of overdue, unpaid taxes. At least one building has been demolished and replaced by a parking lot in order to minimize annual losses, and even recent housing stock (including some 1950 construction) is deteriorating to uselessness. Why?

In my view, age is not a terribly useful explanatory variable. To pursue the Amsterdam example, for instance, when the cities of the Netherlands were much younger, their situation seemed hopeless. By 1808 dwellings in Leiden were undergoing demolition and depopulation because the owners could not find paying tenants and meet their taxes.

Flagging trade balances, a national productivity-competition crisis, the collapse of the city, a permanent, demoralized welfare class—a culture of poverty—all of these elements were present. And what were the lucky few with means and options doing? Moving to the comfortable, landscaped suburban estates they had built in the waning days of prosperity.

The urban crisis has led to speculation that older American central cities are about to "die." In this excerpt, George Carey points out that a similar crisis occurred in Amsterdam in 1815 but that Amsterdam has survived. The similarity between Amsterdam's nineteenth-century urban crisis and the crisis being experienced today is striking.

These words carry with them a remarkable sense of *dèjá vu.* It does not take much imagination to conceive of a conference of distinguished urbanists meeting at—say—the University of Leiden in 1815 to contemplate the theme of "the aging metropolis." One can almost hear an imaginary theoretician, J. Houtvester, pointing out that in the process of Dutch urban land development a low-level steady state of decay was an immutable consequence of a glorious but profligate past of suburbanization and that any policy of public intervention on humanitarian but economically mistaken grounds would do more harm than good at this point. It would no doubt be considered tragic but inevitable that generations would have to suffer in adjusting to the new, lower-level equilibrium. Under the circumstances, it could not be helped that Dutch monied interests would disinvest from this barren urban arena.

Fortunately for the Dutch, it was a real William I who assumed a position of leadership at this juncture and not an imaginary J. Houtvester. William's policies led to massive public investment in urban infrastructure and ultimately to a late nineteenth-century revolution in land tenure. Today, partly as a result of this, Amsterdam is in immeasurably better circumstances than middle-aged Amsterdam was. And "at this point in time," as our public figures are wont to say, the old Dutch cities—horrified by the example of the young American cities—are resolved to avoid following in our footsteps.

Source George W. Carey, "Land Tenure, Speculation, and the State of the Aging Metropolis," *The Geographical Review* 66, 3 (July 1976):253-55.

of the city, which includes the central business district. We tend to think of cities (but not small towns or suburbs) as being physically dirty. We tend to project onto the entire city the image we have of decaying neighborhoods: piles of garbage on the sidewalks, dirt and litter scattered all around, abandoned cars, and abandoned buildings with boarded up windows and doors (National Commission on Urban Problems, 1972:6). Like many other problems that influence our image of the city, this is partially a problem of money and partially a problem of scale. Many cities are unable to afford the staff and equipment needed to remove the litter inevitably generated by large numbers of people confined to small areas. As for scale, the same problems may exist in small towns and suburbs, but they may not be as visible because the litter is less concentrated.

Urban social decay is often thought to be associated with the changing racial and economic character of the residential population of the city and its neighborhoods. Similarly, the downtown areas of major cities may decay as more affluent people move to the suburbs to live and shop at the newer and more luxurious suburban shopping centers. The shopping facilities of the downtown area may be forced to serve lower income populations who must, for economic reasons, remain in the city. Stores respond to these changes by carrying less expensive lines of merchandise and by cutting down on modernization and maintenance programs. Thus the downtown declines.

The same process is evident in the changing nature of downtown entertainment facilities. Legitimate theaters close as the theater-going public patronizes suburban dinner-playhouses. The films shown in downtown movie theaters become less oriented to the family and the general public and are of more limited interest. The downtown shopping area can no longer attract crowds at night, especially when office workers commute home to the outlying areas as soon as the workday ends. Even when middle- and upper-income housing is built close to the downtown area, these trends appear to continue, and the downtown continues to decay.

The decay of residential neighborhoods, like the decay of downtown areas, has a strong element of racism. Much of it is commonly attributed to the process of racially changing populations. As nonwhite residents move into a neighborhood and white residents leave, landlords often reduce maintenance and permit overcrowding in their aging buildings to maintain or increase profit. It must be noted that even before there were significant numbers of nonwhite residents in cities, changing ethnic residential patterns had much the same effect (Ward, 1974:457-75).

Segregated areas have existed as long as there have been cities, but in the contemporary metropolis the problems of racial and economic segregation have come together in a particularly unpleasant manner. The increased nonwhite population and its expansion into hitherto white neighborhoods have caused many white residents to flee the city. The relative poverty of the new occupants of these areas and the age of the physical structures have caused physical decay (Farley and Taeuber, 1974:541-49; Clemence, 1974:549-54). The changing racial composition of the neighborhood may not cause decay, but the

Decay of downtown areas follows much the same pattern in most cities.

association of racial change and neighborhood decline is immediately visible and thus often considered to be the only important factor. The whole process, of course, increases racial and economic segregation, which creates even more problems.

Crime in the city, for some people, is associated with the more general problems of decay and the changing racial composition of the population. The city is often considered to be the breeding ground for crime, violence, and juvenile delinquency. "Crime in the streets" traditionally has been considered an urban problem; more generally, vice is thought to center in urban areas (President's Commission on Law Enforcement and Administration of Justice, 1967:14-27, 35-37).

Crime, violence, delinquency, and vice are found in all areas of our society. In large cities there are more people and thus more criminal, delinquent, and violent events occurring. Again, because the scale is larger, people associate such behavior much more with the city than with the suburb or the small town.

Financing Urban Services

Among the most severe of city problems are those of financing basic services.[3] Primary among these services are education, transportation, welfare, and fire and police protection. Our largest cities suffer from a lack of financial resources, and their expenditures for education, transportation, police, and welfare programs severely strain their budgets. Lack of money, however, is not the only problem in these areas (Wilson, 1968:25-39). In many cases we simply do not know how to design a program or if a program can be designed that will accomplish what we want. In other cases the complexity of urban political realities and the interaction of competing interest groups make it difficult to design programs that will not make one part of a problem worse while improving another part.

In education, for example, cities must provide large populations with an extremely wide variety of services. Suburbs and small towns have neither the large populations to serve nor the need to offer the wide variety of services. For example, many cities provide educational services from kindergarten through college. Few small towns or suburbs attempt this much. The range of services and the diversity of the client population (in age, educational needs, and potential difficulties) magnify the educational problems of cities. Similarly, because small towns and suburbs are generally more compact than cities, they do not need extensive systems of public transportation; and because towns and suburbs serve smaller populations, they do not need as much equipment for the systems they do maintain.

The expensive solutions cities have devised to provide education, transportation, protection, housing, health, and welfare services for their citizens are a source of still further problems. As more affluent residents move to the suburbs, the taxes they pay and the wealth they generate move with them, and cities have increasing difficulty raising the funds needed to carry out programs (Kasarda, 1976:113-16). The urban residents who remain or move in often require expensive services and programs, but they require them because they cannot afford to pay for them. This dilemma is an important part of the popular image of the urban crisis: the very population movements that create the density and numbers which make costly programs necessary undermine the city's ability to pay for them.

City Government

Governments and political systems have the major responsibility for dealing with the problems of cities. These same governments and political systems, however, are also part of the unfavorable image of American cities. In the popular mind, big city politics are dominated by "machines"—corrupt political officials and patronage workers who are on the city payroll only to provide votes for the "bosses" on election day. At least since the day of the classic political bosses of the early twentieth century (Tweed in New York, Curley in Boston, Thompson in Chicago, Pendergast in Kansas City, and others in most major cities), and despite the changes that have occurred since, the image of urban politics is one of corruption and patronage pursued solely for personal gain and power (Harrigan, 1976:49-170; Cornwall, 1964:27-37, 93). Many people believe that there are no honest politicians and that this is why governments and political systems of cities are unable to solve urban problems.

Almost all cities share this popular image of urban crisis because large cities have dominated so much of our national life. We have been told for the past several decades that we are a nation of cities (Goldwin, 1966). But we are not yet a nation of metropolitan residents, and the metropolitan image is not

" 'I stick my fist in as far as it will go, and pull it out as full as it will hold. I stick to my friends, That's me!' There you have Tweed self-painted to the life."

appropriate to all cities. The problems just discussed usually are not central in the daily lives of metropolitan residents who live in suburbs or nonmetropolitan residents. The dominance of major metropolises in our national life, however, does mean that our lives are affected to some extent. Furthermore, even some central city residents live in neighborhoods in which they experience the problems to a lesser degree, and they see the problems as more manageable.

Medical Care

Within cities there are many areas that are poorly served by medical personnel and facilities. However, more people can obtain medical care in central city areas than in rural areas. There are hundreds of rural counties without a single doctor or clinic. Metropolises have thousands of doctors and clinics. They may not always be located where most of the people live, but in an emergency some form of care is available.

Job Opportunities

One major benefit of life in cities is the number and variety of available jobs. A city, more than a suburb or a small town, is an environment in which a person with virtually any kind of skill is more likely to have a chance to find a job. This is true for the unskilled as well as the skilled in manufacturing, finance, sales, and other services. The banks, insurance companies, and other types of commercial institutions concentrated in cities offer workers a large number of office jobs.

Metropolises often have large medical centers, but many rural communities do not have even one doctor. Similarly, a person with almost any kind of skill is more likely to find a job in a city than in a small town.

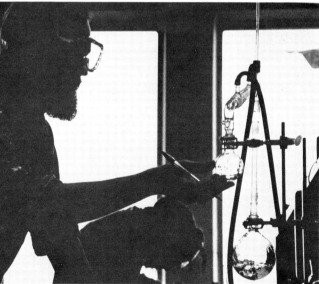

Cities especially offer women more concentrated occupational opportunities than other residential locations do. In part, jobs are concentrated in cities because many industries and offices must locate near other industries and offices to operate efficiently.

Another reason for the concentration of businesses in cities is that cities, more than small towns and suburbs, provide the municipal services on which these institutions depend. Although urban public transportation is not as good as it could be, it is better than that provided elsewhere. Thus, people can live almost anywhere in the city and commute to work in almost any other part of the city, particularly to the central business district. Stores, offices, factories, and other institutions can locate anywhere within the area served by the city's mass transit and road systems and know that a very large number of potential customers and employees can reach them. While the automobile has caused many problems for cities, it is still easier to commute by car within a city than from without. Large cities may not have all the parking facilities needed in either the central business district or the densely settled residential areas, but they have enough parking to make the automobile practical.

Other urban services—police and fire protection, banks, newspapers and other communication facilities, municipal and university libraries, research institutions, sanitation, public health clinics, shopping facilities—are available to workers and businesses in a city when they may not generally be available to those outside the city. These facilities make it advantageous for many businesses and residents to locate inside cities.

Heterogeneity of Urban Life

Heterogeneous neighborhoods offer various opportunities to the residents of the city. Every large metropolitan city has a variety of ethnic neighborhoods, neighborhoods dominated by young couples just starting their families or by older people finished with child rearing. There are neighborhoods of single persons, of families, of homosexuals. In some neighborhoods residents may be very wealthy or very poor. Each city resident is able to choose a neighborhood that offers the opportunities he or she most wants. Very poor residents have the least opportunity to choose the neighborhood they desire, but metropolitan central cities, unlike small towns and suburbs, are likely to have several areas in which low-cost housing and services are available. Thus, in large cities the elderly poor may not have to live in neighborhoods that are heavily populated by poor persons just beginning to raise families or by adolescents from poor families. Greater residential variety of every status level, ethnic composition, stage of life cycle, and life style provides the metropolitan central city resident with greater freedom of choice than that available to any suburban, small town, or even small city resident.

The size and heterogeneity of our largest cities means not only that there is a choice of places in which to live for all types of people, but also that there are enough people of each type living in the city to support services for that type of person. Small towns and many suburbs cannot support a store or a service that specializes in commodities or services that few people use. For example, only relatively large cities offer residents such services as piano tuning, violin or guitar repair, or electronic calculator or camera repair. In small towns there are usually not enough people using such services regularly enough to make them profitable. In a metropolitan area there may be several businesses performing each type of service.

The large population of the metropolitan city also makes possible the services and facilities that only a tiny fraction of the population will use occasionally. This is illustrated by the cultural facilities and activities available in cities of different sizes. It is no accident that live musical and theatrical performances, opera companies, museums, and art galleries are found mostly and in the greatest variety in the largest cities. Even though only a small proportion of the people in these cities avail themselves of these cultural opportunities, and an even smaller proportion use them regularly, there are enough people who do use them to maintain the institutions. Similarly, in large cities there are more nightclubs, movie houses, and other entertainment facilities. In the metropolis the heterogeneity of the population and the size of the different interest groups is sufficient to support all these activities. While a small town may support a single movie theater, a city can support scores of movie theaters. As a result, a wider choice of movies is available to the urban resident than to the small town resident.

The same principle applies to all the goods and services available in a large city. Large and expensive goods that are bought only rarely are generally available from a number of sources in a large city, for there are enough people buying them to support several stores.

The large population of a metropolitan area makes it possible for the city to support a variety of cultural facilities.

But in a small town or even in a suburb, there are not enough people continually making such purchases to support more than one store, if that, specializing in such goods. Similarly, large cities can support numerous mass media outlets: two or more morning and evening newspapers, a number of radio stations (and different types of stations—rock, news, classical music, variety, country and western), multiple television stations, and even neighborhood newspapers.

This range of goods and services makes it possible for diversity to flourish in the city. As a by-product of this diversity, the city dweller can maintain a high degree of individualism and privacy. The city is so large and heterogeneous that one can live the way one wishes without ever interacting with people who will object. Each individual can be as invisible as desired by taking advantage of the city's varied facilities.

This opportunity for individualism and privacy also has its negative consequences— isolation and alienation. The same factors that permit privacy also make it difficult for urban residents to become involved with one another and to overcome the barriers and reservations between individuals. In cities it is often difficult to meet people or to obtain the aid of strangers, and many people feel isolated and detached from the flow of social life. Thus, loneliness, isolation, and unhappiness are also characteristics of urban social life.

Although each neighborhood in the city is occupied by a group of relatively homogeneous people, there can be a great deal of difference among neighborhoods. In some there may be a high degree of social involvement between neighbors, while in others it may be understood that one leaves one's neighbors alone. This, too, contributes to personal freedom and individuality, and it also permits the development of different qualities of life.

Summary

As cities evolved, the urban neighborhood replaced the small town as the source of communal attachments and services. City neighborhoods, however, do not function like small towns—they are more anonymous and impersonal, and they cannot perform all the functions performed by the small town. Thus, the nature of community has changed in the city, and cities are perceived as being in a state of crisis partly because they do not provide the same psychological and emotional sense of community that small towns are supposed to have provided.

The popular image of cities is based on the largest metropolitan central cities, which are quite atypical of all American cities. This image, reflecting the American antiurban tradition, emphasizes the difficulties that large cities have in performing their functions. American cities, however, are not homogeneous, neither with respect to each other nor in their internal composition. Some perform many communal functions quite well, and some have many homogeneous neighborhoods that seem like traditional communities. The uniformly dismal popular image of cities does not accurately represent the real heterogeneity of the cities and their neighborhoods.

Cities have been studied as small-scale societies, as accumulations of people in a limited territory adapting to their environment, and as communities. In this book, the definition of a city combines the last two perspectives. A city is a relatively large, dense, and permanent settlement of heterogeneous individuals and groups of individuals organized to perform or to facilitate the performance of, locality-relevant functions in an integrated manner and to ensure the integration of the performance of these functions with the social system of which the city is a part. This definition implies the need to understand human behavior and institutions in the city in terms of spatial arrangements, characteristics, services needed, and functions performed.

The urban crisis can be understood as the difficulties cities have encountered in performing their communal functions. When cities are unable to maintain normative integration and social solidarity among the different segments of their population; when social control is ineffective; when city services, such as education, housing, health care, transportation, cultural and recreational activities, and employment are inadequate, then they are failing to perform their communal functions and are perceived as being in a state of crisis.

Because of their size and heterogeneity, and despite their difficulties in performing their functions, cities do provide facilities and services not available in smaller, less heterogeneous locations. Cities are centers of diversity, individualism, and personal freedom. Facilities and services that are of interest to only a small fraction of the population or that are used only rarely can flourish when the population base is large enough.

We are a nation of cities, despite the fact that a majority of our population lives outside metropolitan areas. The metropolis dominates not only our image of cities, but also the nature of our society. It is this domination that makes us an urban nation, a nation of cities. Urban problems may only reflect the failures of cities, or they may reflect the problems of society. Because the problems surface most frequently and most intensely in the largest cities, they are assumed to be urban in nature, and we know that they must be solved first in the largest urban settings.

Glossary

city a relatively large, dense, and permanent settlement of heterogeneous individuals and groups of individuals organized to perform, or to facilitate the performance of, locality-relevant functions in an integrated manner, and to ensure the integration of the performance of these functions with the social system of which the city is a part

communal attachments the attachment of the individuals who are part of a community to each other and to the community; the feeling of belonging to a community and the sense that physical and emotional needs are being met by the community

communal functions see locality-relevant functions

community a group of people living in the same area, within which they satisfy many of their needs. Traditionally there has been an intense and self-conscious identification with and an attachment to the group. In its traditional sense, community refers to a deep psychological and emotional relationship as well as a common residence. In contemporary society communities are more limited in scope and are the source of more limited attachments and identification; they are more likely to be primarily residential areas organized to perform communal functions

crisis of the cities (also **urban crisis**)   the collection of problems faced by cities in contemporary America. Problems include pollution, rising costs of city services as revenues decrease, crime, deterioration of housing, slums, inadequate educational and transportation systems, among others

eclectic approach   viewpoint composed of elements drawn from various sources or theories

ecology, human   a branch of sociology concerned with the ways in which human communities adapt to their physical and social environment; human ecology is often concerned with the spatial relationships, environmental relationships between institutions, people, and the physical environment

evolutionary development   growth characterized by continuous change from small to large, simple to complex, general to specialized

heterogeneity   the existence of differences among a population; a group possessing the characteristic of internal differentiation rather than similarity is heterogeneous

hinterland   the territory surrounding a settlement that depends on it for services and that provides raw materials, products, and workers for it

homogeneity   the opposite of heterogeneity; the internal similarity and uniformity existing among a population

housing stock   the total supply of available or existing housing in a given area

human ecology   see ecology, human

life cycle   the series of stages that an individual or a group goes through during its lifetime

locality-relevant functions   the functions that local communities perform. The most important are: (1) generating and maintaining normative integration among community members; (2) generating and maintaining social solidarity among community members; (3) providing the goods and services that community members need; (4) socializing community members to community norms;

(5) controlling the behavior of community members and others who are present; (6) providing a locale in which community members may interact and obtain mutual support (See chapter 2.)

metropolitan area   a city of 50,000 or more persons, plus the county containing the city and all counties socially and economically integrated with the central city, as defined by the U.S. Bureau of the Census and the Office of Management and the Budget

normative integration   the extent to which all components of a social system define the norms of the system in the same way and accept them to the same extent; also the degree to which the norms form a single, nonconflicting system

norms   social statements of right and wrong, proper ways of behaving and thinking; norms help to establish and maintain group cohesion

polis   a city that was also a state in ancient Greece

social control   control exercised by an organized group or community over the behavior of the residents and visitors to the group territory; control formally exercised by organizations, such as police and courts, and informally exercised by group members through social pressure

society   a group of people with a comprehensive set of roles and norms that provide for all of the needs of the people including culture and all other institutions needed for survival

suburb   a settlement within the boundaries of a metropolitan area that is not the central city of that area

urban crisis   see crisis of the cities

urban place   as defined by the U.S. Bureau of the Census, a place of at least 2,500 people

References

Becker, Howard S., and Horowitz, Irving Louis
1973   "The Culture of Civility: San Francisco." In
        *Cities in Change: Studies on the Urban Condi-
        tion,* edited by John Walton and Donald Carns,
        pp. 243-51. Boston: Allyn & Bacon, Inc.

Beers, Howard W
1957   "Rural-Urban Differences: Some Evidence from
        Public Opinion Polls." In *Cities and Society:
        The Revised Reader in Urban Sociology,* edited
        by Paul K. Hatt and Albert J. Reiss, Jr., pp.
        698-710. Glencoe, Ill.: Free Press.

Borgatta, Edgar, and Hadden, Jeffrey
1970   "The Classification of Cities." In *Neighbor-
        hood, City, and Metropolis,* edited by Robert
        Gutman and David Popenoe, pp. 253-63. New
        York: Random House, Inc.

Burgess, Ernest W., and Bogue, Donald J., eds.
1964   *Contributions to Urban Sociology.* Chicago:
        University of Chicago Press.

Clemence, Theodore
1974   "Residential Segregation in the Mid-Sixties." In
        Comparative Urban Structure, edited by Kent P.
        Schwirian, pp. 549-54. Lexington, Mass.: D. C.
        Heath & Company.

Cornwall, Elmer E., Jr.
1964   "Bosses, Machines, and Ethnic Groups." *Annals*
        353 (May):27-37, 93.

Davis, Kingsley
1955   "The Origin and Growth of Urbanization in the
        World." *American Journal of Sociology*
        61:430-37.

Dewey, Richard
1960   "The Rural-Urban Continuum: Real but Rela-
        tively Unimportant." *American Journal of
        Sociology* 66 (July):60-66.

Duncan, Otis Dudley
1957   "Community Size and the Rural-Urban Con-
        tinuum." In *Cities and Society: The Revised
        Reader in Urban Sociology,* edited by Paul K.
        Hatt and Albert J. Reiss, Jr., pp. 35-45. Glen-
        coe, Ill.: Free Press.

Duncan, Otis Dudley, and Reiss, Albert J., Jr.
1956   *Social Characteristics of Urban and Rural Com-
        munities, 1950.* New York: John Wiley & Sons,
        Inc.

Farley, Reynolds, and Taeuber, Karl
1974   "Population Trends and Racial Segregation
        Since 1960." In *Comparative Urban Structure,*
        edited by Kent P. Schwirian, pp. 541-49. Lex-
        ington, Mass.: D. C. Heath & Company.

Glaab, Charles N., ed.
1963   *The American City: A Documentary History.*
        Homewood, Ill.: Dorsey Press.

Goldwin, Robert A., ed.
1966   *A Nation of Cities: Essays on America's Urban
        Problems.* Chicago: Rand McNally & Company.

Gutman, Robert, and Popenoe, David, eds.
1970.   *Neighborhood, City, and Metropolis.* New
        York: Random House, Inc.

Hadden, Jeffrey K., and Barton, Josef J.
1973   "An Image That Will Not Die: Thoughts on the
        History of Anti-Urban Ideology." In *The Ur-
        banization of the Suburbs,* edited by Louis H.
        Masotti and Jeffrey K. Hadden, pp. 79-119.
        Beverly Hills, Calif.: Sage Publications, Inc.

Harrigan, John J.
1976   *Political Change in the Metropolis.* Boston: Lit-
        tle, Brown and Company.

Harris, Fred R. (Senator), and Lindsay, John (Mayor)
1972   *The State of the Cities: Report of the Commis-
        sion on the Cities in the '70s.* New York: Praeger
        Publishers, Inc. (for the National Urban Coali-
        tion).

Hatt, Paul K., and Reiss, Albert J., Jr., eds.
1957   *Cities and Society: The Revised Reader in Urban
        Sociology.* Glencoe, Ill.: Free Press.

Hawley, Amos A., and Rock, Vincent P., eds.
1975   *Metropolitan America in Contemporary Perspec-
        tive.* New York: John Wiley & Sons, Inc.

Hillery, George F.
1955   "Definitions of Community: Areas of Agree-
        ment." *Rural Sociology* 20, 2 (June):18-111-123.

Jefferson, Thomas
1965   *Notes on the State of Virginia.* Chapel Hill,
        N.C.: University of North Carolina Press.

Kasarda, John D.
1976   "The Changing Occupational Structure of the
        American Metropolis: Apropos the Urban Prob-
        lem." In *The Changing Face of the Suburbs,*
        edited by Barry Schwartz, pp. 113-36. Chicago:
        University of Chicago Press.

Lynd, Robert S., and Lynd, Helen M.
1929   *Middletown.* New York: Harcourt, Brace &
        World, Inc.

Mann, Peter H.
1970   "Descriptive Comparison of Rural and Urban
        Communities." In *Neighborhood, City, and
        Metropolis,* edited by Robert Gutman and David
        Popenoe, pp. 38-53. New York: Random House,
        Inc.

Mizruchi, Ephraim H.
1969   "Romanticism, Urbanism, and Small Town in
        Mass Society." In *Urbanism, Urbanization, and
        Change: Comparative Perspectives,* edited by
        Paul Meadows and Ephraim H. Mizruchi, pp.
        243-52. Reading, Mass.: Addison-Wesley
        Publishing Co., Inc.

National Commission on Urban Problems
1972   *Building the American City.* Washington, D.C.:
        Government Printing Office.

Park, Robert E., Burgess, Ernest W., and McKenzie,
Roderick D.
1925   *The City.* Chicago: University of Chicago Press.

Pirenne, Henri
1952   *Medieval Cities.* Princeton, N.J.: Princeton
        University Press.

President's Commission on Law Enforcement and Administration of Justice
1967   *Task Force Report: Crime and Its Impact—An
        Assessment.* Washington, D.C.: Government
        Printing Office.

Reiss, Albert J., Jr.
1970   "The Sociological Study of Communities." In
        Neighborhood, City, and Metropolis, edited by
        Robert Gutman and David Popenoe, pp. 27-37.
        New York: Random House, Inc.

Schmandt, Henry J., and Goldbach, John C.
1969   "The Urban Paradox." In *The Quality of Urban
        Life,* edited by Henry J. Schmandt and Werner
        Bloomberg, pp. 473-98. Beverly Hills, Calif.:
        Sage Publications, Inc.

Schwartz, Barry, ed.
1976   *The Changing Face of the Suburbs.* Chicago:
        University of Chicago Press.

Schwirian, Kent P., ed.
1974   *Comparative Urban Structure: Studies in the
        Ecology of Cities.* Lexington, Mass.: D. C.
        Heath & Company.

Siegel, Adrienne
1975   "When Cities Were Fun: The Image of the
        American City in Popular Books, 1840-1870."
        Journal of Popular Culture 9 (Winter):573-83.

Still, Bayard
1974   *Urban America: A History with Documents.* Lit-
        tle, Brown and Company.

Sutton, Willis, and Munson, Thomas
1976   "Definitions of Community: 1954 through
        1973." Paper presented at the meetings of the
        American Sociological Association, New York.

Taeuber, Irene B., and Taeuber, Conrad
1971   *The People of the United States in the Twentieth
        Century* (Census Monograph). Washington,
        D.C.: Government Printing Office.

Theodorson, George A., ed.
1961   *Studies in Human Ecology.* New York: Harper &
        Row.

U.S. Bureau of the Census
1971   *Census of Population: 1970, Number of In-
        habitants, United States Summary. Final Report
        PC(1)-A1,* (Washington, D.C.: Government
        Printing Office.

1975   *Historical Statistics of the United States, Col-
        onial Times to 1970. Vol. 1.* Washington, D.C.:
        Government Printing Office.

U.S. Congress, House Committee on Banking and Currency
1970   *The Quality of Urban Life.* Hearings before the
        Subcommittee on Urban Growth, 30 September
        1969 through 24 June 1970.

Vidich, Arthur, and Bensman, Joseph
1958   *Small Town in Mass Society.* Garden City, N. Y.
        Doubleday & Co., Inc.

Ward, David
1974   "The Emergence of Central Immigrant Ghettoes
        in American Cities: 1840-1920." In *Comparative
        Urban Structure,* edited by Kent P. Schwirian,
        pp. 457-75. Lexington, Mass.: D. C. Heath &
        Company.

Warren, Roland
1972   *The Community in America.* 2d ed. Chicago:
        Rand McNally & Company.

Weber, Max
1958   *The City.* New York: Free Press.

White, Morton, and White, Lucia
1961   "The American Intellectual Versus the American
        City." *Daedalus* 90 (Winter):166-79.

Wilson, James Q.
1968   "The Urban Unease: Community vs. the City."
        The Public Interest 12 (Summer):25-39.

Wirth, Louis H.
1938   "Urbanism as a Way of Life." *American Jour-
       nal of Sociology* 44, 1 (July):1-24.
Zimmer, Basil G.
1975   "The Urban Centrifugal Drift." In *Metropolitan
       America in Contemporary Perspective,* edited by
       Amos H. Hawley and Vincent P. Rock, pp.
       23-91. New York: John Wiley & Sons, Inc.

Suggested Readings

Banfield, Edward C. *The Unheavenly City Revisited.*
    Boston: Little, Brown, 1974. A controversial view of
    the nature of the urban crisis. Banfield argues that
    cities are better now than they have ever been before
    and that all they lack is the political will to do what,
    in Banfield's view, is necessary to eliminate their
    problems.
Goldwin, Robert A., ed. *A Nation of Cities: Essays on
    America's Urban Problems.* Chicago: Rand McNally,
    1966. A collection of excellent essays on the nature of
    the problems facing cities, and on the meaning of "A
    nation of cities."
Reiss, Albert J., Jr. "The Sociological Study of Com-
    munities." In *Neighborhood, City, and Metropolis.*
    New York: Random House, 1970. An excellent
    review of the variety of sociological perspectives that
    can be used to study communities and cities.
Wirth, Louis H. "Urbanism as a Way of Life."
    American Journal of Sociology 44, 1 (July
    1938):1-24. The classic sociological statement on the
    nature of cities and their effects on ways of life. This
    article is widely reprinted and can be found in many
    collections of readings.

Notes

1. In the latter part of the nineteenth century,
   however, the popular and mass media emphasized a
   much more positive view of cities than the antiurban image held and advocated by the intellectual
   segments of society. For a review of this perspective
   see Adrienne Siegel, "When Cities Were Fun: The
   Image of the American City in Popular Books,
   1840-1870," *Journal of Popular Culture* 9, no. 3
   (Winter 1975):573-83.

2. The nature of communal functions performed by
   cities is developed in chapter 2. See Roland Warren
   (1972) for an exposition of the nature of communal
   functions from a slightly different viewpoint but
   one that has strongly influenced the present work.
3. The financial crises faced by New York City in
   1975-77 have been widely reported and illustrate
   these service problems.

2 The Concept of Community

The **city** as a community is a relatively large, dense, permanent settlement of heterogeneous individuals and groups organized to perform locality-relevant functions in a manner that is integrated both within the settlement and with the wider society.[1] **Locality-relevant functions** can be carried out in different ways, and these variations have implications for the character of social life in the community.[2] This idea of community has evolved from earlier concepts, and to understand it, we must understand its evolution. It is important to trace these developments, because our communities—cities, suburbs, neighborhoods—are often evaluated on the basis of the extent to which they live up to our expectations. Such expectations are generated by the concept of **community** that is part of our cultural heritage.

The earliest known ideas of community developed before there were cities as we know them. Societies were smaller and less complex, and there were few large population centers. Society has changed radically since then. As society has changed, the intellectual notion of community has also changed, but not to the same extent. Earlier concepts of community focused on how people related to their society and to the groups that comprised that society. Such concepts emphasized the feelings that people had about each other and about their community. The **norms** that defined what communities *did*—the functions they performed—were less important than the norms that defined what communities *were*—the close interpersonal relationships between members of the same group. As society has become larger and more complex, ideas of community have focused more on what communities do. Despite the evolution of the idea

of community from one based on feelings and relationships to one based on functions, our earlier conception continues to shape our expectations of the ideal community. Understanding the evolution of the concept, even though earlier definitions do not apply directly to our society, should help us evaluate present-day communities.

Community Functions

The contemporary analytic concept of community is concerned with the ways communities perform or facilitate the performance of the following essential functions.

1. *Generating and maintaining normative integration among community members.* The community must have a set of norms that defines appropriate behavior patterns and values for its members. Furthermore, community members must agree on definition, interpretation, and legitimacy of these norms. For example, the activities that children and adolescents may engage in on street corners, the amount of pollution that is considered acceptable, the behavior that politicians exhibit while in office and during elections, and even the frequency with which houses are painted, lawns are mowed, and cars are washed are all influenced by community norms. The actions taken to regulate these behaviors and the values that such actions reflect are indications that these are norms. The degree of conflict of consensus over regulatory actions is indicative of the degree of **normative integration** in the community.

2. *Generating and maintaining social solidarity among community members.* Residents of a community must be able to identify

A sense of community depends on how well the community fulfills many functions. Providing access to goods and services, control of norm-violating behavior, and places where people may interact and obtain mutual support are just a few.

or feel some sense of **social solidarity** with the community. There must be some feeling among them that they are all from the same place. This feeling is most in evidence when people are traveling, as when two residents of Chicago encounter each other in New York, San Francisco, or Afghanistan. They are likely to ask each other about people they know, places they have been, and experiences they might have shared in an attempt to strengthen the bond between them, which results from their common solidarity with the city. In a city one is more likely to feel bonds of solidarity with one's neighbors than with residents of the city as a whole.

3. *Providing the goods and services that community members need.* Food, housing, medical care, clothing, and all other goods and services, including jobs, that are needed to support community life must be provided directly by the community or by other organizations. In an urban setting this means there should be a variety of retail outlets, such as supermarkets, drugstores, clothing and other specialty stores, as well as professional service outlets. Roads and mass transportation facilities are also needed to move people and goods throughout the city.

4. *Socializing community members to community norms.* New members of the community, both those who migrate there and those who grow up there, must be taught the norms of the community. Schools and the family must teach to its new members the community's distinctions between proper and improper behavior patterns and values. Communities must provide the institutional settings in which **socialization** may take place. Schools, for example, teach not only norms,

but also appropriate job skills, values, and behaviors that will permit the new member a choice of roles in the society.

5. *Controlling the behavior of community members and others who are present.* Violation of the community's norms is sanctioned, and the **sanctions** are most often imposed by formal agents of the community: the police, the courts, and religious leaders. Communities must organize formal agencies to detect and sanction norm-violating behavior, or they must provide channels for the informal control (through social pressures) of norm-violating behavior.

6. *Providing a locale in which community members may interact and obtain mutual support.* Members of a community must value interaction, support joint activities, and respond to each other in predictable ways. Clubs, voluntary organizations, and public meetings provide opportunities for interaction in modern societies. Much mutual support for members also comes through public welfare agencies and through private agencies that supplement public agency activities.

Not all communities perform all locality-relevant functions in the same way or to the same extent. Communities can be analyzed to see the degree to which they perform each function. These functions, especially in modern industrial societies, are allocated to specific roles and carried out by persons and institutions performing those roles. Associated with each role is a system of rewards and sanctions that ensures appropriate and effective role performance. As the complexity of the social organization increases, role definitions, role responsibilities, and the rewards and sanctions associated with role performance become more formal.

As social organizations and the tasks they perform become more complex and more highly specialized, it becomes more important to integrate the performance of community functions. It does no good, for example, to dispose of liquid wastes by dumping them into the source of the community's drinking water.

Communal Feelings

A community, however, is more than just a system of functions with its associated roles, rewards, and sanctions. It is people functioning and interacting, responding to each other individually and collectively. This interaction reinforces function-specific rewards with the more general rewards that come from simply participating. These general rewards are diffuse and not function specific; they are most often expressed as feelings of membership, belonging, and psychological identification, rather than as specific benefits (Warren, 1972:14, 138-42; Nisbet, 1966:47-48).

If membership itself is to be rewarding and sanctions are to be painful, community members must agree on what is valuable and what is painful. In other words, there must be a system of norms. Any social system (and a set of functional tasks, with an organization of roles and their associated rewards and sanctions, is a minimal definition of a social system) will have a set of norms associated with it (Parsons, 1960:250-79; Parsons, 1967:3-34). What distinguishes a community from other social systems is that the norm that makes membership gratifying is applicable (Nisbet, 1966:47-48). Membership in a community implies accepting all, not just some, norms of the community, at least in the traditional, normative concept of community.[3]

This ensures that the community generates a high degree of psychological identification among its members and that the community is an all-inclusive social system with a high degree of normative integration and social solidarity. The value attached to belonging to a community generates and maintains normative integration and social solidarity. Through these norms, each communal function is assigned to a specific role. Sanctions ensure that the roles are performed in accordance with the norms. Roles, norms, rewards and sanctions, and forms of social solidarity vary from community to community.

These variations in the levels and nature of normative integration and social solidarity have an impact on the nature of the community. It is not possible to understand the concept of community, and thus what a city is, without understanding how and why such variations occur and what the implications and consequences of these variations are.

At the core of the traditional conception of community is the great strength of the bonds among its members and between the members and the community. These ties are strong because of their emotional or affective content rather than their rational character, and the importance of maintaining them makes it clear that a critical function of communities is the generation and maintenance of high levels of social solidarity and normative integration. Much social and political thought of Western civilization since the middle of the nineteenth century has been concerned with how individuals have been tied to society (Nisbet, 1966: chaps. 2 and 3), that is, with the nature of social solidarity and normative integration.

Greek philosophers held that communities should be homogeneous. The medieval community was an extension of belief in divine right and well defined societal ties.

Classical Concepts of Community

Greek philosophers (Lindsay, 1950:128-68; Russell, 1945:108-19; McKeon, 1947:549, 552-55) argued that, to maintain social solidarity, communities should be composed of people with virtually identical values and beliefs. People who did not agree with communal values, or whose beliefs changed, were to be excluded. Social solidarity was to be generated and maintained by strict enforcement of homogeneity in political systems, socialization, and behavior. The Greek view of community colors our intellectual tradition and emphasizes the virtues—indeed the necessity—of homogeneous communities.

Medieval Conceptions of Community

Between the time of the Greek philosophers and the sixteenth century, the Western idea of community was importantly influenced by religious ideologies of the **medieval period.** The belief grew that the state was an entity created by divine law, rather than a natural outgrowth of people living together in families and villages, as Aristotle had thought. Because God or his representatives had established the social order and its modes of behavior, they were natural and inevitable. The feudal system of social organization required less **homogeneity** than the Greek system, for everyone had a specific place, specific duties (University of Chicago College History Staff, 1961a:1-43; 1961b:44-47), and well-defined societal ties originating in either divine or natural right.

The major social units of medieval society were guilds, monasteries, families, and villages. All these units were thought to have developed naturally. Each person's social position was determined naturally or divinely. Consequently, even to think of changing the social order placed a person outside of it, because solidarity was destroyed (University of Chicago College History Staff, 1961c:48-76; 1961d:77-83).

As a result, the community exerted great control over the daily lives of individuals, regardless of their position in the society. Their behavior was constrained by what was considered natural or right for a person to do in that position or role in society. In this essentially rural society, position was largely based on the individual's relationship to the land as a worker or owner. Only when commerce and industry began to develop were people able to break out of this restrictive structure.

In medieval society the community provided as many needs of daily life as possible for its members, regardless of social position—peasant, lord of the manor, priest or high church official, aristocrat, or guild merchant. Social security and welfare, help in times of need, indeed all of life was controlled by one's community, and this was viewed as the outgrowth of each person's divinely or naturally ordained position in the world.

Secular Reactions

Between A.D. 1500 and 1800, secular philosophers developed an alternative social theory. They sought a more rational image of society, one based on the image of humans as free individuals bound by their own choice to the community in specified and limited ways. Individuals and their personal characteristics, not their relationships to communities, would become the primary components of society. The philosophers did not view the traditional, communal forms of the Middle Ages, such as guilds, corporations, communes, and villages, as forms that were natural to human beings. A society acceptable to a social theorist of the sixteenth through the nineteenth century was based on individuals, not on community components. Society was a web of relationships that had been specifically willed at some time and that individuals could freely and rationally enter or leave through the exercise of their own efforts and intellect (Nisbet, 1966:48-49).[4]

The Social Contract: Thomas Hobbes and Jean Jacques Rousseau

Hobbes and Rousseau were among the first philosophers to view society as an organization that emerged out of the actions of humans.[5] Hobbes believed that before a social system existed, all men were naturally equal. In a state of nature, before there were governments, individuals attempted to preserve their own liberty while dominating others to the greatest extent possible. These desires are mutually incompatible; to reconcile them the natural situation of humans without a society or a community is the "war of all against all."

People avoid this natural state of interpersonal warfare by combining into communities subject to a central authority—a king or Leviathan. Hobbes argued that communities are brought into existence by a mythical **social contract,** the terms of which require all humans to submit to authority and to cooperate with one another. It is only this mythical contract that permits people to maintain social order. No form of social organization is natural; all such organizations are the result of rational thought and willed activity. When the terms of the mythical contract are recognized, social solidarity of the community results.

A century after Hobbes, Rousseau also wrote about a contract as the basis of the ties between the individual and society. Rousseau sought a form of association of individuals united by common interest—a form of community—that would protect and defend each individual with the total strength of the community and still leave the individual as free as if there had been no society. His answer, like Hobbes's, was the social contract.

The medieval community was based on the belief that there were natural or divinely established ties between individuals and between each individual and the community. Artificial contracts were unnecessary to maintain these ties and solidarities. Hobbes and Rousseau saw society as unnatural, held together only by a contract that bound individuals to each other and to society. The contract was the source of social solidarity, and without it there was neither normative integration nor solidarity.

The Consequences of the Social Contract

By the end of the eighteenth century, society was seen as a fabric of specifically willed relationships that spelled out both the nature of the social structure and the nature of social solidarity between individuals and society. An individual's ties to another individual and to society were specific and transitory, rather than general and permanent. Social solidarity was established and maintained by specific contractual relationships. A society based on a contract required neither the homogeneity of the Greek community nor the fixed positions of individuals found in the medieval community. Each person's relationship to society was determined by the contract. A person could change social position without violating the terms of the contract. An individual's ties to society were similar to, and reflections of, the ties between individuals.

Utilitarianism

During the nineteenth century, as Western societies industrialized, the need for a relatively large, readily available, and mobile labor force contributed to further redefinition of community and the nature of the individual's ties to society. Utilitarians, led by Jeremy Bentham and John Stuart Mill, argued that society emerged from rational self-interest. In a good society each individual is free to pursue happiness and self-interest. Thus personal and social mobility and freedom from strong ties to church, family, guild, and other communal organizations became desirable. Community became a purely rational, legal, abstract, impersonal, and contractually established form of social organization. As such, it generated **alienation, anomie,** estrangement, and loneliness—the failure of people to care about and for one another. The all-inclusive sense of community that characterized the classic tradition had been replaced by a set of limited relationships that permitted more personal freedom but increased interpersonal competition and weakened both social solidarity and ties between the individual and society (Russell, 1945b:773-82; Nisbet, 1966:51-54).

Ferdinand Tönnies: *Gemeinschaft* and *Gesellschaft*

Ferdinand Tönnies (1855-1936) described two ideal types of society—*Gemeinschaft,* corresponding to medieval society, and *Gesellschaft,* corresponding to industrialized society—and the process by which one is transformed into the other (Tönnies, 1957). Drawing on earlier analyses by Otto von Gierke (1841-1921) and Sir Henry Maine (1822-1888), Tönnies described several dimensions along which European society had changed.

The basis of social status changed from ascription to achievement; that is, the individual's position was becoming less dependent on membership in groups into which one was born and more dependent on the individual's achievement. Individuals were increasingly viewed as the basic units of society. As a result, legal systems increasingly recognized people as individuals with their own rights and responsibilities, rather than treating them solely as representatives of communal organizations. Individuals were granted a legal status independent of their membership in communities (Nisbet, 1966:72-73; McNeill, 1963:538-59). It is probably not possible to overemphasize the importance of this change. Among its consequences, the individual became a legitimate actor on the social scene,

social solidarity was weakened, and the development of mechanisms for bonding individuals to society became necessary.

Gesellschaft *As Process*

Tönnies developed the twin concepts of *Gemeinschaft* and *Gesellschaft* to describe societies, human relationships within those societies, and the transformation of society from one form to the other. The *Gesellschaft,* often translated as *society,* produced by this transformation is a form of social organization in which social relationships are characterized by high levels of individualism and impersonality. Relationships are contractual in nature and develop on the basis of will or interest.

In a *Gemeinschaft* society, social relationships are warm and personal, and there are strong ties among individuals and between the individual and the society. *Gesellschaft* develops out of *Gemeinschaft.* Human relationships grow impersonal, competition between individuals increases, and egoism and self-interest begin to dominate interpersonal relationships. When this happens, communal ties are weakened (Tönnies, 1957:33-35, 78, 239-59).

As the *Gemeinschaft* evolves into a *Gesellschaft,* social solidarity decreases, normative integration weakens, and the strong unions of the *Gemeinschaft* become mere associations. *Gesellschaft* is a process *and* a state of being. The focus on the twin terms *Gemeinschaft* and *Gesellschaft* is on the implications of and factors associated with different types of normative integration and forms of social solidarity (Nisbet, 1966:75; Tönnies, 1957:35-37).

Barn-raising with the help of a whole community is a traditional example of *Gemeinschaft* in action. It still occurs in some communities in the United States.

The Character of Gemeinschaft

Gemeinschaft is a harmonious working together of different units, producing a natural interchange. It is a community because all members exchange, of their own free will, assistance, relief, and services and are thus tied to one another and to the whole community. Interchange and association between individuals is real, resulting in intimate, private, and exclusive relationships. The *Gemeinschaft* members are like a family. Many aspects of life are shared completely, but only with other members of the group, and the closeness of the relationships has a familial quality (Tönnies, 1957:35-102). Further, as in a family, one belongs to a *Gemeinschaft* from the beginning of membership, or from birth.

An example of the intimacy of *Gemeinschaft* is the naturalness with which we use the language and know the folkways, mores, and beliefs of the society and the culture into which we are born. In a very real sense many religions aspire to be a *Gemeinschaft* of the whole human race.

Gemeinschaft is a form of social behavior and social organization in which the individual units are abstractions. The individuals have physical reality, but their nature can be understood only in the context of the community (Tönnies, 1957:35-37). By visualizing human relations in a *Gemeinschaft* as organic, we focus on the importance of relationships rather than individuals.

Gemeinschaft assumes that the individuals making up the community are homogeneous. There is a natural unity of wills and of behavior that is preserved despite the fact that the *Gemeinschaft* consists of individuals. This homogeneity has its origin in shared experiences and interactions that teach all members of the community to expect that others have had similar experiences. Thus solidarity and intimacy in the community are based on the knowledge that all members are likely to respond in similar ways to similar stimuli. This forms a strong social bond—a social solidarity. The ties from the individual to society are many, and each individual can count on the appropriate response from all other individuals who make up the community.

Contemporary examples of the solidarity and interpersonal reliance that characterize a *Gemeinschaft* can be found in well-trained military units, athletic teams, and to some extent groups that have gone through important life events or crises together.

In a *Gemeinschaft* members share a conceptual framework and understand each other's nature, relationship to the community, and position in the community. The members organize their lives to maximize the love, understanding, and intimacy that they all share. In turn, this maximizes social solidarity, strengthening the ties among members and between each member and the community (Tönnies, 1957:47-48).

Under these conditions, individualism and privacy are minimized. Everyone knows what one's friends, neighbors, and the other members of the *Gemeinschaft* will be doing and how they will react to stimuli. Interpersonal ties are so strong that each member of the *Gemeinschaft* can rely on every other member in times of need to provide the services and goods necessary to sustain life.

Levels of expressed and felt friendship and warmth are high, and frequently it is a comfortable, secure way of relating to one's society (Tönnies, 1957:49-50).

Contemporary social critics often espouse this way of life, especially so-called radicals who flee urban culture and civilization by establishing communes of various types in rural or urban settings. Clearly, from our analysis of community, what they are seeking is a *Gemeinschaft*-like existence. Everyone will belong, the society will be well integrated, and all members will experience strong feelings of solidarity. All aspects of life will be shared, and all activity will be common knowledge (Kanter, 1972; Melville, 1972). This form of communal organization, like medieval society, treats people as totalities—as abstract units. All life becomes intimate and private within the whole society, but also public to the community. There is little room for individuality.

The Character of Gesellschaft

Gesellschaft, like *Gemeinschaft,* has never really existed, except as an **ideal type** described by Tönnies. While *Gesellschaft* is a community, *Gesellschaft* is a society. In a *Gemeinschaft* individuals remain together, despite all the separating influences in their existence, because they are essentially united. In a *Gesellschaft,* however, despite all apparently unifying influences such as common locality, individuals behave as though they are essentially separate. In a *Gesellschaft* everyone is seen as an individual: isolated, atomized, alone, and working in competition with other people who share the living space (Tönnies, 1957:64-65).

As Tönnies pointed out, *Gemeinschaft* is an old form of human relationship, but *Gesellschaft* is a new name and (at the time he was writing) a relatively new phenomenon. Tönnies said, ''Whenever urban culture blossoms and bears fruit, *Gesellschaft* is its indispensable organ. Rural people know little of it.'' He went on to point out that rural life was praised because the *Gemeinschaft* is stronger there; *Gesellschaft* was seen as transitory and superficial.

Tönnies saw *Gesellschaft* as the end product of social change occurring in the mid-nineteenth century. It is a social system in which individuals do not naturally want to grant anything to anyone or produce anything for anyone, or altruistically to give up what they have. There is little sense of friendship, brotherhood, or identification, so there is little sense of community identity. When people give services or goods in a *Gesellschaft,* they give only for the sake of what they can receive (Tönnies, 1957:231-35).

The *Gesellschaft* is a rational, willed society that one can join or leave. One becomes part of a *Gemeinschaft* the way one becomes part of a family, brotherhood, or fraternity, but one joins a *Gesellschaft* as one joins a club or takes a job in a corporation. One joins a club, which is a less tightly knit, less permanent, less intimate organization, but one is taken in as a member of a fraternity, which is a much more tightly integrated, permanent, intimate organization.

In a *Gesellschaft* each individual strives for personal advantage; sharing and concern for others is minimal. Individuals relate to one another only to exchange goods and services.

Thus in a *Gesellschaft* the accumulation of real or tangible property clearly has higher priority than the development of close ties between individuals based on ideology, sentiment, or human values (Tönnies, 1957:79-82). The *Gesellschaft* is truly a contractual society based on utilitarian principles.

Contrasts Between Gemeinschaft *and* Gesellschaft

In a *Gesellschaft* the ties that bind individuals to one another and to the social system are much weaker than they are in a *Gemeinschaft*. The levels of faith and trust among the individuals making up the society, their ability to comprehend each other's reactions to stimuli, to predict and understand each other's responses, and to provide relief and assistance are much lower in a *Gesellschaft* than in a *Gemeinschaft*. Individuals in a *Gesellschaft* are much more isolated, individualized, atomized, and alienated than they are in a *Gemeinschaft*.

Max Weber: The Rationalization of Society

In many ways the work of Max Weber (1864-1920) adds richness and breadth to the work of Tönnies. Weber, like Tönnies, recognized a major transformation in society during the latter part of the nineteenth century. He used the term **rationalization** to describe the transformation of a society from a communal one that emphasized brotherhood, patriarchalism, and social action to achieve emotional-affective and traditional-conventional goals, to an associational and contractual one.

"An Idyll of Mr. Penn's Sylvania"

Berkeley, Calif.—I refuse to take it anymore. I refuse to see another television commercial or program in which the virtues of small-town life are practically deified.

What I fly in a fury about, is the mountain-top residence that American small-town life has risen to in the minds of urban consumers. Listen America: It just ain't so!

Six years ago, I spent the junior year of my high school days in a small (population 7,000) town in the middle of Pennsylvania. Simply beautiful country. A wide, slow-moving river curves around little Huntingdon. Many of the streets are still made of the original stone and brick.

Endless, deep woods surround the burg. If the mood should strike, you can pick up your sleeping bag, some matches, a can of beans and a canteen of water and walk-five minutes into a secluded spot with your dog, and gaze at the stars for the night.

The old Victorian and gingerbread houses on the narrow streets are shaded by tall trees, whose roots push up the sidewalk, creating the only danger to a late-night stroll around town. You know your neighbors and they know you.

Sounds just like the Waltons, doesn't it? Makes your stereotypical flannel-shirted youth want to jump into his old pickup truck and take his golden retriever named Cider out to where the living is "natural."

Let me tell you about that paradise.

When I first arrived in Huntingdon, I thought it would be wonderful. I was mildly disconcerted when I was "tracked" into a program of study and told to cut my hair. I protested but to no avail. My history teacher taught the class that Hitler lost World War II because God had put into his mind to open a two-front war. "God always takes things into His hands when events get too messed up on earth," he lectured.

I was soon being harassed by the student body and some teachers for objecting to such surprise. I was taunted and threatened because I once said marijuana should be legalized and the war in Vietnam was wrong. The favorite epithet slung at me was "faggot." Ostracized, I sat by myself daily when eating lunch.

Things got worse. No one would speak to me. I faced the constant threat of being slugged. I couldn't walk down a street without being threatened or having something thrown at me. I learned to avoid certain parts of town, like near the pool hall.

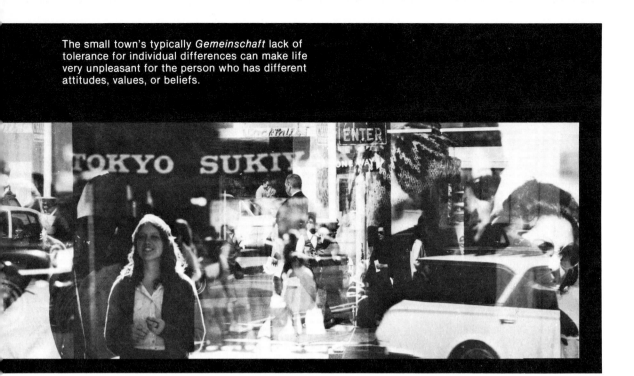

And all that fresh air! The biggest sport in Huntingdon is deer hunting. The first day of the season is an official school holiday. Almost the entire male portion of the student body doesn't return for a week. When the boys do trickle in, it's: "Did you get your buck? Got my eight-point. Shot him clean through the head!" Very organic.

One day, leaving a track meet in a distant town, I leaned out a bus window and flashed a peace sign to the opposing team. They instantly and unanimously chanted: "Faggot! Faggot!" I thought, "God, they're everywhere."

The day finally came when I was jumped from behind while running training laps around the track field. Three or four fists plunged into my sides and face. After the coach broke it up, they waited outside for me.

Black people were "niggers." Dissidents were subversives and the war a glorious crusade against Communism. If you were a real man, you drank so hard you threw up and passed out each weekend. Women were for sex and housework, plain and simple.

Ignorance, intolerance and persecution were the hallmarks of that idyllic setting, and I have learned from talking to others living in similar environments that it is the norm for almost all small communities.

Flying back to San Francisco at the end of the year was like coming into Jerusalem. Never before had the sprawl of lights, the stench of buses and cars seemed so good. Never before had I appreciated the sometimes bleak urban landscape. Now I know why people fled the farms when the cities rose. Like them, I'll never return to the country. It may look like a wonderful life in a TV commercial, but, thank you, I'll stay regular in the city.

Source Roland Dewolk, *New York Times,* February 20, 1977, p. E 15. © 1977 by The New York Times Company. Reprinted by permission.

In many ways the process of rationalization is similar to the process of *Gesellschaft*. Both describe a society changing in emphasis from affective relationships and traditional forms of authority to rational relationships and contractual forms of authority. In the rationalized society, emotional behavior and relationships based on feelings, traditions, or conventions are less legitimate than actions based on calculations and efficiency (Weber, 1961:218-29; Nisbet, 1966:79).

Weber illustrated what he meant by the rationalization of society by describing the historical process of social change that occurred as cities modernized. The earliest settlements were composed of groups that had associated for the accomplishment of common goals. The actors or social units in early society were not individuals but communities. The early cities were made up of tightly knit communities that embodied communal relationships and were legally indissoluble. Guilds, families, and other groups would associate on a rational basis, but this did not make the structure of each group any less communal. It simply made the city an association of communities.

Societies of the late medieval period through the nineteenth century (already having experienced some rationalization), were associations not of communities but of individuals. Individuals, not communities, paid allegiance to the city and to the social system that the city represented. Authority shifted from traditional allegiance to the leader to adherence to the rules of a rational bureaucracy. Individuals were tied to the city directly rather than through the groups to which they belonged (Nisbet, 1966).

As a result, the settlement became the focus and source of solidarity and thus became a community itself. The interpersonal relationships within the settlement became more associational than communal. The ties of brotherhood, intimacy, and affection were lacking. The ties among individuals and between individuals and the society were based on rational calculations of what was in the best interest of each individual.

This is the rationalization of social action and society. Cities became associations of individuals rather than associations of tightly knit communal groups. The bonds of solidarity became less personal, less affective, more individualistic, and more rational.

The unsolved problem in this analysis is, what holds society together under these conditions.

Émile Durkheim: Mechanical and Organic Solidarity

The problem of what holds a contractual society together was addressed by a number of thinkers who suggested a variety of theories. The analysis of Émile Durkheim (1858-1917) is the most complex and complete one we have on social integration and social solidarity.[6]

The Collective Conscience

For Durkheim the problem of social solidarity is the necessity of motivating individual commitment to the society and ensuring conformity to the expectations of its institutions (Parsons, 1967:10). Durkheim's solution is the **collective conscience,** which is the commonly held beliefs and sentiments of a society

(Durkheim, 1933:79). The collective conscience is not a definition of right and wrong, but rather the collection of fundamental values, articulated as beliefs and sentiments, and reflected in the norms, on which the society is based. Collective agreement on these values makes the establishment and institutionalization of norms possible, even in a highly differentiated society.

Durkheim's position is that the structure of a society or social system is not simply influenced by the pattern of normative culture that is institutionalized in the society, but *actually is* that pattern. It is internalized in the characteristics and personalities of the actors who make up the society. The value system of a society is that set of normative judgments made by the actors in that society. They define for that society what a good society is (Durkheim, 1933:79).

Ultimately then, the basis for the existence of any society is agreement on the nature of a good society. In utilitarian terms, the good society might be the one that maximizes happiness. Under another philosophy, the good society might maximize individuality, freedom, and mobility. A society might be most highly valued for meeting the needs of all its members, or for granting natural or divine dominance to some members, or for offering equality of opportunity to each person in seeking his or her own position in the society. It is agreement on questions as fundamental as these that establishes the basic value system of the society and thus the normative judgments for that society. These judgments, in turn, specify the normative expectations for performance of roles in the society.

The Forms of Solidarity

Mechanical solidarity results when members of the society have common goals supported by common values and, as in a *Gemeinschaft,* work to realize these values in a social context. The collective conscience is strong, and the ties of the members to the collectivity are strong. The beliefs about the nature of the world and the patterns of emotion that bind the individuals to the society and to each other are strong and shared. Especially strong are the commonly held beliefs that define legitimate behavior and action within the community (Durkheim, 1933:70-110). The **mechanically integrated society** is by definition a homogeneous society.

In contrast, **organic solidarity** occurs in societies in which a number of highly interdependent units or collectivities perform highly differentiated functions. This form of social solidarity is analogous to the functional solidarity occurring in living organisms; the whole is made up of a large number of specialized parts. The functioning of each part depends on the functioning of every other part, and none can continue to exist or to function without the existence and functioning of the others. Each component is carrying out a different function, but all components work together in the accomplishment of a single purpose (Durkheim, 1933:257).

This integration of units, with each unit carrying out its own purpose and at the same time participating in the functioning of the total organism, implies that not all needs of each individual in the collectivity can be satisfied by the individual's own activities. In a plant, for instance, the flowers have a structure different from that of the roots. But the flowers cannot blossom without the roots, the roots cannot collect nutrients without the leaves, and the plant wouldn't exist at all without these different organs.

The Basis of Changing Solidarity: Moral Density

When population is relatively small, it is possible for all individuals in a society to know one another personally rather than solely as occupants of roles. In such a society individuals can and do perform all functions necessary to the society. However, when the population increases to the point where everyone cannot and does not perform all social functions, the process of *Gesellschaft* begins. Society begins to rationalize, and not everyone can know everyone else.

> The division of labor develops . . . as there are more individuals sufficiently in contact to be able to act and react upon one another. If we agree to call this relation and the active commerce resulting from it dynamic or moral density, we can say that the progress of the division of labor is in direct ratio to the moral or dynamic density of society [Durkheim, 1933:257].

The growth of population and **moral density** are inseparably linked and lead to the **division of labor**, specialization of roles, and social differentiation. Increased differentiation allows individuals to specialize and to cooperate rather than to compete with one another, increasing productivity and supporting larger numbers of people.

The result, however, is a society composed of a heterogeneous rather than a homogeneous population. Social solidarity is generated by a web of interdependencies among people acting in various roles and institutions as a result of the division of labor. Organic solidarity does not ensure that the values of the members of the society will be homogeneous. However, the roles and norms will be sufficiently integrated to ensure that the functions of the society will be carried out (Durkheim, 1933:147-52, 251-70).

The division of labor necessitates a social system in which individuals are free to seek and achieve new roles and positions in society. The development of differentiated institutions requires mobility, especially in production and consumption (Durkheim, 1933:228-29, 329 ff.).

When position in society is not fixed, people can compete for position, producing the Hobbesian problem of potentially conflicting interests. Thus, the social contract is necessary in an organically integrated society to maintain social integration (Parsons, 1967:15).

The Institution of Contract

Durkheim agreed with Hobbes that the individual is secondary to the community, but he did not believe that a social contract could serve as the basis for social integration. In a homogeneous society the social contract would not be needed. In a complex society self-interest would not support enough integration and solidarity to keep a highly differentiated society together.

Durkheim argued that a social contract is not possible without a society that provides the basis for the contract. It is the society that defines what is and is not permissible in the contract, who can and cannot participate, and so on. Durkheim says, in effect, that social-contract thinkers did not push their concept to the limits of its logic. They assumed the existence of a contract as the basis for society but failed to realize that a prerequisite for such a contract is a society with a set of norms.

Society exists, in other words, not because there is a Hobbesian or Rousseauian contract, either real or mythical, but because the concept of the institution of a contract exists. A social contract is possible only when the norms underlying the **institution of contract** are already agreed on and in existence.

For the institution of the contract to exist, there must already be an agreement on the norms that make the institution possible. In other words, some form of society must exist before it is possible for the social contract to come into being. Durkheim's argument with the social-contract thinkers is based on this essential difference. Indeed, for a concept as subtle as the institution of contract to develop, and for the differentiated normative structure that is necessary to bring this concept into existence to develop, the society must be highly and organically integrated.

Maintaining Integration and Commitment

In contrast to the homogeneous, mechanically integrated society, the heterogeneous, organically integrated society is characterized by much less agreement about purposes, goals, and behavior. As a result, some members of a society may adopt goals or means that other members define as illegitimate or deviant. Thus heterogeneity of society builds in a potential for both freedom and deviance that is not found in a more homogeneous society.

Society must have at least minimum normative integration to exist. Society reinforces this integration and promotes performance of its functions by collective organs of goal attainment. The society can reinforce solidarity by rewarding participation in the society, especially productive participation; instead of punishing the nonproductive, society can reward the productive. Payment for participation, especially in the jobs that are vital to the society, reinforces integration and rewards productive performance.

To succeed in this positive approach to solidarity, the society must have norms defining the rights and obligations of its members. If rewards are to generate normative integration, all members of the society must believe that position in the economic system is determined by ability and desire, rather than by accident of birth. Achievement must be the *dominant* factor in the allocation of rewards, and members of society must earn their own rewards. Selected persons cannot be exempted and rewarded for reasons other than achievement without weakening the solidarity of society.

Freedom from the restrictions of ascriptive ties also is balanced and controlled by the normative structure, as are the rights and obligations of participation in the social system. This structure, tied to the roles and institutions of the society, defines the rights and obligations (and the limits) of each individual according to the institution in which he or she is participating.

Each institution has an unwritten contract with its participants, specifying the rights and obligations of the individuals and the institution. The interests of the society in ensuring that production will be carried out and functions will be performed are expressed in each of these contractual relationships. The contracts are not written, but are rather expressed as social norms. For example, when you go to work for an organization, you expect to be paid and you expect the working conditions to conform to some normative standard, regardless of whether these requirements are spelled out by law.

It was Durkheim's crucial insight that an organic society depends for its very existence on norms that differ from institution to institution. Because all the institutions are functionally interrelated, the norms are interrelated. The key to the stability of the society is ability of the norms to be interrelated in such a way that the functions of the society are carried out.

The Partial Community

The idea of an organically integrated, rational *Gesellschaft* evolved during the nineteenth century as society became increasingly urbanized and industrialized. Industrialization and urbanization produced societies so large in scale, so complex in organization, and so differentiated that forms of integration and solidarity were unlikely to be as strong and all-encompassing as they had been in earlier communities. Yet, as Tönnies pointed out, a longing for these earlier forms of community persisted. The ideal image of community with its close interpersonal relationships is based on the traditional concept. Robert Nisbet summarizes the traditional idea of community.

By community I mean something that goes far beyond mere local community. The word as we find it in much nineteenth and twentieth century thought encompasses all forms of relationship which are characterized by a high degree of personal intimacy, emotional depth, moral commitment, social cohesion, and continuity in time. Community is founded on man conceived in his wholeness rather than in one or another of the roles, taken separately, that he may hold in a social order. It draws its psychological strength from levels of motivation deeper than those of mere volition of interest, and it achieves its fulfillment in a submergence of individual will that is not possible in unions of mere convenience or rational assent. *Community is a fusion of feeling and thought, of tradition and commitment, of membership and volition* [Nisbet, 1966:47-48; emphasis added].

Community in this sense is expressive of our intellectual heritage but is unlikely to occur in contemporary society. We are not likely to find communities that have this character, especially in major urban centers, except under rare and remarkable circumstances. At best, we find **partial communities** performing some locality-relevant functions. At worst, we find neighborhoods striving to involve disinterested residents in community affairs. We find low levels of solidarity and normative integration. Community has become a word that describes small areas rather than ways of relating to people and to institutions. Community, as expressed by Nisbet, is what we search for and try to create, but rarely achieve.

Whole cities can be conceived of as communities only in a limited sense. Levels of solidarity, even among the residents of a small city, are low because personal knowledge of all residents is impossible. Many people we interact with, even on a daily basis, we know only in those roles in which we interact with them. We experience little solidarity and perhaps even less normative integration.

These difficulties of integration, severe even in a small city, are more extreme in a large city or a metropolis. We may describe ourselves as being *from* a city, but few city dwellers would say they are committed to or identify with the city in which they live. Politicians and city boosters may be exceptions. One reason for lack of commitment is the ever-present possibility of moving to another city. We do not want to develop an attachment that will be too painful to break should we move. Thus, the cities and the neighborhoods we live in do not begin to attract the degree of commitment or identification implicit in Nisbet's definition of community.

Contemporary Concepts of Community

Despite the low levels of our commitment to cities and neighborhoods, these local areas are frequently referred to as communities by their residents, and each is as much a community as is likely to be found in contemporary society. Traditional concepts of community continue to influence, if not dominate, our image of what a city or neighborhood should be like. It is necessary to develop a less inclusive concept of community that is more appropriate in contemporary society.

Because both cities and neighborhoods are residential localities, we can begin with Roland Warren's definition of a community as "that combination of social units and systems which perform the major social functions having locality relevance."[7] Communities, however, are abstractions. They do not act, except when their boundaries coincide with political jurisdictions and they become governments. Cities and neighborhoods are localities that facilitate to varying degrees the organization of individuals and institutions that perform locality-relevant functions and, as such, both may be considered communities. This notion of community is quite different from the traditional one. It is far less encompassing and is far less normative, cohesive, and affective. In comparison with the traditional community, the local community is only a partial community and a tool for analyzing behavior.

The view of community as an organization of social units performing or facilitating the performance of locality-relevant functions implies that there is continuity of individuals and institutions in the community. In some places individuals and institutions simply go about their own business, and the necessities of life are provided by various public and private agencies, but there is little community spirit. In other places large segments of the population may be involved in community affairs through the mechanisms of formal and informal voluntary groups, and neighbors may interact frequently, offering each other mutual support. In these places the community spirit is strong.[8]

Urban Community Functions

Six essential functions listed at the beginning of this chapter traditionally are performed or facilitated by communities. These are the locality-relevant functions defined by Warren that even partial communities must perform or facilitate. The manner and extent to which they are performed is critical to the existence of a community. Community functioning in cities can be examined from two perspectives: from the perspective of the city as a whole and from the perspective of each local community within the city.

The first two functions defined, and the two which Warren does not directly consider locality-relevant functions, are the most critical in the traditional view of community: the generation and maintenance of social solidarity and normative integration.[9] In a modern, industrialized, organically integrated society these functions have largely been taken over by the national society. The local community can provide at most an environment in which the norms are expressed and solidarity is experienced. The national society defines the general value system, sets many of the norms for role performance, and generally provides normative integration on a societal basis. For example, there are national standards for educational performance. Many laws regulating education apply at least statewide, and local community laws may not contradict them or set different standards. When local and national norms or laws conflict, the local community may not act independently, but must conform to the norms of the nation.

The third function of a community is providing the goods and services needed by community members. This is a function that cities and their constituent communities are more likely to perform. Industrial, commercial, wholesale, and retail facilities, as well as professional offices and government agencies, are the mechanisms for carrying out this function.

No community in our society may exist in isolation from the rest of society. A community can produce some of what it needs and import the rest. As part of a large city, many communities must import most of what they need. All goods and services must be distributed to all members of the community who consume them. The waste products, another form of production, must also be distributed to treatment facilities and disposed of. The community, regardless of its size, must make some provision for satisfying the material needs of the population. The production and distribution of goods and services for community consumption may be carried out by agencies of the community or by private institutions whose performance of these activities is facilitated by the community.

The fourth locality-relevant function of communities is socialization of the young— the training and education of a new generation of members who will carry on the community. To some extent this is the responsibility of the family, where children learn the social attitudes, values, and skills necessary to become members of the community. More specialized training in the social system, the roles that people perform, and the range of options open to individuals in the society, as well as the skills for performing in these roles, is carried out by the formal educational system. However, the most important socialization of individuals takes place within the family. The values and concepts that make the society and thus the community possible are internalized by the individual within the family. The community must provide the setting, the atmosphere, and the opportunity for this to occur if the community is to survive.

Communal functions stimulate interaction and thus a sense of cohesion
among members of a community.

Fifth, communities must exercise some social control over their members. While national norms and laws limit the authority of local communities to define legitimate behavior, many communities and cities do have their own standards. Furthermore, enforcement of laws is generally a local function. Communities can control, or attempt to control, many forms of public behavior not covered by national or state law as long as local norms do not contradict national or state norms. The members of the community can enforce these local standards informally by means of social pressure or formally by means of police or court action. The extent to which social pressure is effective varies from one community to another. Student dress codes, the regulation of books available in high school libraries, and the expectation that one will try to keep up with the Joneses are examples of norms that may be enforced at the local level. Setting of limits on behaviors, attitudes, or appearance is a means of ensuring a degree of homogeneity, and hence solidarity, in the community (Wilson, 1968:425-39). Some people may be offended or driven out by these controls, but they will be said to be "not our kind of people." In larger communities specialized institutions carry out enforcement functions. The police largely are responsible for formal control of social behavior, while religious leaders and judges exercise more normative control. All communities exercise some social control over their members, and they do so to ensure at least minimal solidarity. Their task, of course, is made easier when residents see both formal and informal social control as natural and legitimate.

Finally, communal functions include the provision of opportunities and outlets for social participation and mutual support. No community can exist without some participation and mutual support among its members. Lacking this, neighbors are a mere aggregation of people, not a community. The members must interact, and they must be able to help and support one another. Only in this way can there be a sense of cohesion, of attachment, and of shared solidarity and identity.

Variations in Community Functions

Obviously, neither neighborhoods nor cities carry out all six functions of a community, nor do they have to carry them out in the same way or to the same extent. In an urban society, local communities do not have the ability, administrative structure, or need to perform all these functions, and the tasks are passed on to specialized public and private organizations. Nevertheless, local areas that have some degree of community identity and feeling may facilitate the performance of, or even perform, some communal functions.

No community existing within a larger social structure can carry out its functions autonomously. To the extent that the community depends on the wider society for the goods and services it imports and exports, it must integrate its performance with that of the society. Warren refers to the ties between local communities and the wider society as vertical ties—extracommunity relationships that make the community and the wider society part of each other (Warren, 1972:53-94, 237-66). Both the vertical ties to extracom-

munity institutions and the horizontal ties between institutions within the community itself are related to the community's ability to perform its functions. When the horizontal ties are strong, it is easier for the community to socialize its members, to exert social control over them, and to provide for their mutual support and interaction. When the bonds between individuals and the community are weak (or when vertical ties are much stronger than horizontal ties), the community performs few communal functions. Formal mechanisms of social control, such as the police and the courts, are more frequently brought into play when horizontal ties are weak.

A crucial problem in urban society is how to foster the development of communal ties in neighborhoods and cities. The lack of communal feeling seems to be the source of the alienation and despair that people experience in city life.[10]

Community Ties to Society

The processes that have curtailed the ability of the community to perform its functions autonomously have been described by Max Weber, Ferdinand Tönnies, and Émile Durkheim as rationalization, *Gesellschaft,* and organic solidarity, respectively. All describe the transformation of social organization and life. As cities and urban institutions became more highly differentiated, so did the forms of association among the people. Life became increasingly impersonal and bureaucratic as the institutions in each city, town, or village developed links with similar institutions in other communities. Many government agencies and private businesses developed to fulfill many community functions, especially those of socialization (the school systems), social control (police and the courts), and mutual support (welfare and aid). Warren describes the process as follows:

> The "great change" in community living includes the increasing orientation of local community units toward extracommunity systems of which they are a part, with a corresponding decline in community cohesion and autonomy. As the relation of community units to state and national systems becomes strengthened, the locus of decision-making with regard to them often shifts to places outside the community. Decisions, policies, and programs of local units although they must conform in some respects to community norms, come to be formulated in centralized offices outside the community and come to be guided more by their relation to extracommunity systems than by their relation to other parts of the local community. Thus the ties between different local community units are weakened, and community autonomy, defined as control by local people over the establishment, goals, policies, and operations of local communities, is likewise reduced [Warren, 1972:53-54].

The vertical ties of the community to the outside world are rational and *Gesellschaft*-like. But within many communities traditional and *Gemeinschaft* qualities of life continue to exist. As a result, the communities come under continuing pressure to adapt to the structure of the cities that bind them to the wider society, or at least to act and behave in ways that are consistent with these ties.

As a result, local areas have become more closely integrated with the city, the metropolis, and the wider society. The cost for having done so is the inability of smaller communities to perform the full range of communal functions and to generate a sense of community.

The Community in the City

Within the city there are neighborhoods and groups that attempt to perform communal functions, to build social solidarity, and to maintain a sense of belonging. To some extent they are successful, but never totally because they are a part of the larger community, and must participate in the ongoing processes of the city and the nation. No local urban community and only a few independent towns and villages can ignore the processes of the larger society. These independent communities may attempt to defend themselves by building internal organizations that give them some power in negotiations with the political system. They may look inward for their activities, social controls, socialization practices, and mutual support and participation. But they also participate in the wider society. For example, they must pay taxes. Their land is taken for highways and schools. They have only limited control over where the roads go or what is taught in the schools. The prices of the goods and services they need are beyond their control, and they inevitably fail to provide independently for all needs of their residents.

Communities that exist within cities have been described in a variety of ways.[11] They perform only some community functions for only some of the people who live there, and they provide only a limited sense of social solidarity. Communities within cities are partial communities. Most major community functions have been taken over by larger social systems.

Nevertheless, there are islands or pockets in the city where people experience a high degree of social solidarity and a strong sense of community. In most instances these are older neighborhoods where mobility has been so low that a sense of continuity has developed. In other instances some central institution, such as a university, a hospital, a church, or an ethnic group, has been the focus for the development of social solidarity.

But even those sections of the city that are most highly integrated are not able to provide all resources for social life. The most communitylike local areas in cities have vertical ties to extracommunity institutions and must watch most of their members go elsewhere for jobs, entertainment, and even the necessities of life. For example, even if residents can satisfy all their food needs within the community, they cannot usually determine the kinds of food that will be available, the prices that will be charged, the nature of the packaging, or the rules and regulations that will govern the production, distribution, and quality of the food.

The most important community functions are the ones that even the most effective local area in a city can carry out only partially. The local community has only limited control over its schools. Educational policy is set at many different levels, and all policy must conform to the policy set at higher levels. Teachers are brought in, curriculum standards are set, and performance is judged not by the local community, but by city, state, and often federal standards. This is the case even in areas where there is so-called community control. As the community loses control over its schools, it cannot socialize its children as effectively in community traditions. In most major cities high schools serve more than one community, further weaning adolescents from their communities and orienting them to the wider society.

Wider orientation leads to participation in social activities outside the community, reducing the amount of interaction taking place within the community and strengthening ties with the wider society. As a result, solidarity and normative integration are reduced in the local community and increased in the wider society. The neighborhood or local area serves as a community only to those residents who have lived there a long time, which will be a small fraction of the population in our highly mobile society. To most people the local neighborhood is simply a place to live, not a community. Neighborhoods in the modern metropolis are at best only partial communities.

Urban neighborhoods, and even small towns outside metropolitan areas, were not designed to be partial communities. They evolved as a result of geographic and historical changes. This evolution did not occur in all places at the same rate. Thus vestiges of the past, present, and future coexist in one society. Some neighborhoods and small towns are contemporary versions of past social institutions. Some new towns today purportedly embody future forms of social organization.

Summary

We have traced the evolution of the concept of community. It began as a strong, all-encompassing normative system that defined how people living in a given area related to one another and to their social organizations.

It has become a set of functions that people living together must perform for themselves or ensure that other institutions perform. Community has become a way of analyzing local areas and their residents.

The contemporary concept of community may be used as a tool in the analysis of urban society. Cities, and the communities that make up cities, may be evaluated by the extent to which they perform their functions. By knowing how the concept has evolved, we are better able to judge the performances of cities and neighborhoods as communities.

Furthermore, because we have defined cities as special communities, our analysis has sensitized us to those aspects of community life that we should examine. We must focus on the ways cities and neighborhoods carry out locality-relevant functions that are crucial to their existence. We must also recognize the importance of normative integration and social solidarity as communal functions and the parts that homogeneity and heterogeneity play in the performance of these functions. This framework allows us to analyze the populations of cities and neighborhoods and to understand the role of racial and ethnic communities in urban society.

The critical role of normative integration and social solidarity also points us to an analysis of the performance of political systems in cities and their constituent communities. Similarly, our derivation of communal functions provides a framework for examining other aspects of urban life. The performance of urban society as a community may be evaluated by how well it provides essential goods and services, socializes the young, and controls social behavior.

To understand the modern metropolis and the functions that neighborhoods perform, we must know how cities developed into such large, complex organisms. The patterns of urban development have influenced not only the idea of community, but also the structure and shape of contemporary metropolises. Thus it is necessary to examine the history of cities.

Glossary

alienation as a state of society, feelings of detachment, isolation, and nonparticipation among members of a segment of the population; as an individual characteristic, feelings of powerlessness, isolation, meaninglessness, cultural estrangement, self-estrangement, and normlessness

anomie a state in which the individual feels that societal norms do not apply to the self; strictly defined, anomie, like alienation, is characteristic of a social system in which norms have lost their power to regulate behavior

city a relatively large, dense, and permanent settlement of heterogeneous individuals or groups of individuals organized to perform, or to facilitate the performance of, locality-relevant functions in an integrated manner and to ensure the integration of the performance of these functions with the social system of which the city is a part

collective conscience the commonly held beliefs and sentiments that are the fundamental values of a society

communal functions see **locality-relevant functions**

community a group of people living in the same area, within which they satisfy many of their needs. Traditionally there has been an intense and self-conscious identification with and attachment to the group. In its traditional sense, community refers to a deep psychological and emotional relationship as well as a common residence. In contemporary society communities are more limited in scope and are the source of more limited attachments and identification; they are more likely to be primarily residential areas organized to perform communal functions

contract, institution of   a set of norms that specifies the legitimate contents of agreements among members of society and the means by which these agreements can be reached and enforced

division of labor   the development of specialized occupational tasks. More generally the division of labor causes a task to be broken up into component tasks, each of which is performed individually

Gemeinschaft   a form of social organization characterized by close, intimate, and personal ties among a homogeneous social group. All members share the same reactions to stimuli and a common conceptual framework. Frequently, *Gemeinschaft* is translated into English as *community*

Gesellschaft   a form of social organization in which the individual is paramount. A rational, willed form of organization in which individuals are isolated and work for themselves, not for the group. Frequently, *Gesellschaft* is translated as *society*. Also describes the process of social change by which society is transformed from a *Gemeinschaft* to a *Gesellschaft*

heterogeneity   the existence of differences among a population; a group possessing the characteristic of internal differentiation rather than similarity is heterogeneous

homogeneity   the opposite of heterogeneity; the internal similarity and uniformity existing among a population

ideal type   a conceptual construct; a perfect example of something created logically, regardless of whether it exists or can exist in that form in the real world

labor force   the portion of the population that is employed or is looking for employment

locality-relevant functions   the functions that local communities perform. The most important are: (1) generating and maintaining normative integration among community members; (2) generating and maintaining social solidarity among community members; (3) providing the goods and services that community members need, (4) socializing community members to community norms; (5) controlling the behavior of community members and others who are present; (6) providing a locale in which community members may interact and obtain mutual support

mechanical solidarity   that form of social solidarity created by the similarity of the members of the group; social cohesion generated by individuals who engage in similar tasks with little social differentiation; a form of social solidarity that exists prior to the division of labor

mechanically integrated society   a homogeneous society that is integrated as a result of mechanical solidarity

medieval period   those years from the thirteenth to the sixteenth century in Europe when the feudal form of social and political organization dominated

moral density   the density of interaction between individuals and the relationships resulting from this increase; a function of population density with greater focus on relationships caused by increased population

normative integration   the extent to which all components of a social system define the norms of the system in the same way and accept them to the same extent; also the degree to which the norms form a single, nonconflicting system.

norms   social statements of right and wrong, proper ways of behaving and thinking

organic solidarity   that form of social solidarity created by the division of labor. Individuals engaged in different tasks are dependent on one another. Organic solidarity is created by the interdependence of various tasks in a common enterprise

partial community   a community that is not able to perform all locality-relevant functions; one that partially performs functions of a traditional community

rationalization   the transformation of a communal society into an associational, contractual society

role   a set of expected behaviors in a specific social status or setting

sanction   a penalty or denial of reward imposed on persons who violate social norms or a reward for appropriate behavior

social contract   according to Hobbes, a mythical contract requiring all members of a society to submit to the established laws and authority. A social contract is the basis of the submergence of individual desire and strength for the benefit of society. According to Rousseau, it is the basis of the ties between the individual and society

social control   control over the behavior of individuals and groups to ensure conformity with the norms

social solidarity   a feeling of membership in and identification with a group or a social system

socialization   the process of learning the norms, behaviors, and skills one must know to be a functioning member of society

utilitarianism   a philosophy that argues that society should be based on individual self-interest and that society thus emerges from rational self-interest

References

Durkheim, Émile
1933   *The Division of Labor in Society.* Translated by George Simpson. Glencoe, Ill.: Free Press.
1938   *The Rules of the Sociological Method.* Edited by George Catlin. Glencoe, Ill.: Free Press.
1951   *Suicide.* Translated by John A. Spaulding and George Simpson, edited by George Simpson. Glencoe, Ill.: Free Press.

Hobbes, Thomas
1909   *Leviathan.* Reprint of 1651 edition. New York: Oxford University Press.

Janowitz, Morris
1952   *The Community Press in an Urban Setting.* Glencoe, Ill.: Free Press.

Kanter, Rosabeth Moss
1972   *Commitment and Community: Communes and Utopias in Sociological Perspective.* Cambridge: Harvard University Press.

Kasarda, John D., and Janowitz, Morris
1974   "Community Attachment in Mass Society." *American Sociological Review* 39 (June):328-39.

Lindsay, A. D., tr.
1950   *The Republic of Plato.* New York: E. P. Dutton & Co., Inc.

McKeon, Richard, ed.
1947   *Introduction to Aristotle.* New York: Random House, Inc.

McNeill, William H.
1963   *The Rise of the West.* Chicago: University of Chicago Press.

Melville, Keith
1972   *Communes in the Counterculture: Origins, Theories, and Styles of Life.* New York: William Morrow & Co., Inc.

Nisbet, Robert A.
1966   *The Sociological Tradition.* New York: Basic Books, Inc., Publishers.

Parsons, Talcott
1937   *The Structure of Social Action.* New York: Free Press.
1960   "The Principal Structures of Community." In *Structure and Process in Modern Societies,* by Talcott Parsons. New York: Free Press.
1967   "Durkheim's Contribution to the Theory of Integration of Social Systems." In *Sociological Theory and Modern Society,* by Talcott Parsons. New York: Free Press.

Rousseau, Jean Jacques
1950   *The Social Contract and Discourses.* New York: E. P. Dutton & Co., Inc.

Russell, Bertrand
1945a *A History of Western Philosophy.* New York: Simon & Schuster, Inc.
1945b "Plato's Utopia." In *A History of Western Philosophy,* by Bertrand Russell. New York: Simon & Schuster, Inc.

Suttles, Gerald
1972   *The Social Construction of Communities.* Chicago: University of Chicago Press.

Tönnies, Ferdinand
1957   *Community and Society (Gemeinschaft and Gesellschaft).* Translated and edited by Charles Loomis. New York: Harper & Row for Michigan State University Press.

University of Chicago College History Staff, eds.
1961   *History of Western Civilization, Medieval Europe,* Topic V. Selected readings by the College History Staff. 2d ed. Chicago: University of Chicago Press.
  a. Power, Eileen. "Peasant Life and Rural Conditions, 1100-1500." From *The Cambridge Medieval History,* vol. VII, pp. 716-50. Cambridge: Cambridge University Press, 1932.
  b. "A Manor of the 13th Century, A.D. 1279." From *Translations and Reprints from the Original Sources of European History,* vol. III, no. 5, pp. 4-7. Philadelphia: University of Pennsylvania Press.
  c. Pirenne, Henri. "Northern Towns and Their Commerce." From *The Cambridge Medieval History,* vol. VI, pp. 505-27. Cambridge: Cambridge University Press, 1932.
  d. "Ordinances of the Gild Merchant." From *Translations and Reprints from the Original Sources of European History,* vol. II, no. 1, pp. 12-17. Philadelphia: University of Pennsylvania Press.

Warren, Roland
1972   *The Community in America.* 2d ed. Chicago: Rand McNally & Company.

Weber, Max
1961   "Types of Social Organization." In *Theories of Society,* edited by Talcott Parsons et al. New York: Free Press.

Wilson, James Q.
1968   "The Urban Unease: Community vs. the City." *The Public Interest* 12 (Summer): 25-39.

Suggested Readings

Baltzell, E. Digby. *The Search for Community in Modern America.* New York: Harper & Row, 1968. A short collection of papers focusing on the constraints that make traditional forms of community impossible in contemporary society.

Suttles, Gerald D. *The Social Order of the Slum.* Chicago: University of Chicago Press, 1968. Suttles describes a contemporary urban community and the ways in which it attempts to carry out its functions in a heterogeneous setting.

Warren, Roland. *The Community in America.* 2d ed. Chicago: Rand McNally, 1972. The best analysis of community currently available. While not focused on cities, this book provides an extended discussion of communal functions and their meanings.

Whyte, William F. *Street Corner Society.* Chicago: University of Chicago Press, 1943. A classic, and still the best, analysis of the nature of life in an urban community.

Notes

1. This definition was arrived at in chapter 1.
2. Roland Warren, *The Community in America,* 2d ed. (Chicago: Rand McNally & Company, 1972), pp. 9-14. The list of functions that follows is an adaptation of the set of functions developed by Warren.
3. The degree of acceptance of norms, of course, is variable. The degree of variation is one factor in the definition of some behaviors as deviant. *Community* is treated here as an ideal type for purposes of exposition.
4. The philosophical problems of the secular theorists were couched in terms of societies. Although Hobbes, Rousseau and the utilitarians were arguing about the philosophical and moral basis of society, their arguments apply directly and with equal force to less global communities.
5. The discussion of Hobbes is based on Russell, "Plato's Utopia," pp. 546-57; Parsons, *Structure of Social Action,* pp. 89-94; and Hobbes, *Leviathan.* The discussion of Rousseau draws upon Russell, "Plato's Utopia," pp. 695-99; and Rousseau, *Social Contract.*

6. Durkheim doesn't deal directly with community but rather with society. However, everything he says about society as a whole can be applied rather directly to the community. His concern with these topics runs through many of his works, notably *Suicide, The Division of Labor in Society,* and *The Rules of the Sociological Method.*

7. Warren, *Community in America,* pp. 9-10. Much of the following section draws on this very important work.

8. A community can be a mere residential aggregation in an area in which outside agencies perform critical services. A single institution—such as a school—can become a focal point for communal spirit. But in such cases, which appear to be common in urban settings, community integration and solidarities will be weak.

9. An extended discussion of locality-relevant functions appears in Warren, *Community in America,* pp. 167-208.

10. These feelings can also be caused in part by high mobility in modern society. See, for example, the way that length of residence strongly affects communal identity in John D. Kasarda and Morris Janowitz, "Community Attachment in Mass Society," *American Sociological Review* 39 (June 1974):328-39.

11. For example, as "communities of limited liability," in Morris Janowitz, *The Community Press in an Urban Setting* (Glencoe, Ill.: Free Press, 1952) or as "defended neighborhoods" or "contrived communities," in Gerald Suttles, *The Social Construction of Communities* (Chicago: University of Chicago Press, 1972).

3

The History of Cities

The historical perspective is critical to the study of cities, for the processes that continue to shape cities can be understood only if we observe their impact on cities in the past. Cities have developed and been formed by the forces of history, industrialization, technology, and the increasing division of labor.

We will consider only selected aspects of city history. There are rich traditions of city architecture and planning that we will not explore. Our discussion will focus on the effects of urban growth and development on social relationships that develop in cities, between cities, and around cities.

Prior to the Industrial Revolution in the nineteenth century, it had taken thousands of years for cities to evolve from primitive, relatively simple social systems to relatively developed, complex structures. Throughout the period, cities shared many features. We will not try to determine which settlements were cities and which were not, but rather we will distinguish in general terms between those settlements that grew into cities and those that did not. We are interested in the forces that permitted some settlements to develop into cities.

Settlements Prior to the Urban Revolution

The earliest permanent settlements were composed of so few people that they could hardly be called villages. Yet, throughout history, cities have eventually developed out of such settlements. In the United States, communities of barely a dozen dwellings have sometimes grown into cities of many millions.

Chicago, for example, was settled by a lone trapper in an Indian village. Other settlements have remained small towns, and still others disappeared. In southern Illinois, for example, there is a town named West Frankfort, but Frankfort, Illinois, is no more.

Most of the earliest settlements that developed before 10,000 B.C. were located in the Middle East in Sumer and Egypt. Remains of equally early settlements have also been discovered in China, Europe, and North America. During this early period, roving tribes rarely established permanent settlements. According to estimates, the land and social system could support populations ranging from .05 or .10 to 1.0 person per square mile, depending on the location (Childe, 1970: 111-18). The Pacific northwest coast of North America, with its abundant fish and fertile land, could support a full person per square mile. There are indications that winter settlements there had approximately thirty houses.

The Neolithic Settlement

Population expansion first occurred during the **Paleolithic** period between 10,000 and 8,000 B.C. At the beginning of the succeeding **Neolithic** period, settlements were small. The development of techniques such as irrigation that fostered food production rather than food gathering was vital to the growth of both population and settlements. These developments nearly doubled the number of people the land could support—up to nearly two persons per square mile (Davis, 1973:11; Childe, 1970:113).

This change presupposed three conditions: (1) enough natural resources to support the population; (2) the technology to exploit and transport the resources to the settlement; (3) the technology and social system to preserve, store, and distribute the resources once they were in the settlement.

The natural resources needed were land that was fertile enough to produce food for the population; wood, clay, and other building materials; and skins and fibers for clothes. Although today these needs seem simple, satisfying them was highly problematic and difficult during the transition from a hunting and gathering culture to a settled cultivation culture. Even when the land was fertile, people needed to know some techniques for cultivating and irrigating the land and harvesting the crops.

Irrigation and the transportation and preservation of food were basic problems. Harnessed animals or primitive barges were used to transport food from relatively distant fields to the settlements. During and after the trip the products of the fields had to be preserved and stored. Before the invention of irrigation, the people would rapidly exhaust the land and be forced to move, thus severely limiting the village size. Even with irrigation, Neolithic villages would reach the largest size that could be supported by farming the land around it, and the village would split up, forming more villages. Thus population growth was accompanied not by increases in the size and density of the population of the village, but rather by an increase in the number of villages, which kept the density relatively constant.

In Europe during this period, the typical village consisted of somewhere between sixteen and thirty single-room houses. The largest village known, Barkaer in what is now Germany, had fifty-two dwellings. The total population of such a settlement was between two hundred and four hundred persons (Childe, 1970:113).

The chief reason that settlements could not grow beyond this was the limited agricultural technology. Wheeled vehicles were unknown, so that the farthest farm had to be within walking distance of the settlement. Animals could pull sledges somewhat farther, but not much. Farming techniques were limited. Slash-and-burn farming—the cutting down of dead trees and the residue of the previous year's crop and the burning of them to clear the land for planting—was the most advanced agricultural technique available. Under these conditions villagers could develop only a minimal sense of permanence as residents, and each family was able to produce just enough food to support itself.

The Neolithic Social System

Before settlements could develop further, the social system had to become more complex. Development of this complexity required the division of labor, which in turn required specialization. However, for two reasons only minimal specialization could develop. First, no single village could produce enough excess food to support a craftsman who did not produce his own food; and second, the maintenance of village solidarity required a commitment to a common activity, so that, through cooperation, the people would produce enough food and shelter for all the villagers and defend each other against animals and against people from other villages.

This common commitment, or identity, had its basis in common activities and was supported by shared language, beliefs, and customs. At times several groups merged, and this mechanical solidarity was reinforced by common participation in religious rites and worship at ancestral shrines.

The division of labor in Neolithic culture began when some expert craftsmen approached the status of full-time professionals, devoting themselves to the production of tools and implements. But because the ability of a single village to support craftsmen was negligible, they would move from village to village, exchanging the tools and equipment they made for the food and shelter that they needed (Childe, 1970:113; Davis, 1970:120-30).

These craftsmen were no longer part of the social system of any village, and they were thus isolated from most of society. But their products were vital to society for food production. This primitive division of labor permitted people to develop a social system that ensured a dependable supply of food and even generated enough surplus to support a larger population.

The Earliest Cities

The first cities began to emerge in Mesopotamia, Egypt, and India in about 3,000 B.C. Advances in irrigation, in the breeding of farm animals, and in organized fishing, together with the development of wheeled vehicles and better river transportation, made larger settlements possible (Childe, 1970:111-18; Davis, 1973:11; Sjoberg, 1973:19-27; Cook, 1969:30).

These and other advances helped people produce enough surplus food to support full-time craftsmen and permitted the populations of early cities to engage in differentiated activities. However, these cities lasted only about 2,000 years. The technical and social progress that made their original development possible seems to have stopped, and the social structure that developed seems to have had a stultifying effect on future development. Although these settlements were quite possibly the first cities, they were eclipsed by later urban developments in Europe (Davis, 1970:122).

The changes that made the first permanent settlements possible brought about a revolution in the nature of human settlements and altered the organization of work and other social activities. Cooperation between individual farmers, the use of work teams, and the emergence of social roles for persons specializing in the collection, storage, and exchange of the surplus goods are examples of these changes.[1] The development of new social and economic relationships made it possible for more people to live in a single place. Farmers could raise more food than they could consume, creating a **social surplus,** and they could exchange a portion of their surplus for other goods. This allowed the population of settlements to grow not only larger, but also denser—to become cities.

(*Top*) The first cities began to emerge in Mesopotamia, Egypt, and India about 3000 B.C. (From "An Early City in Iran" by C. C. and Martha Lamberg-Karlovsky.

(*Bottom*) Invention of the wheeled plow helped make the social surplus.

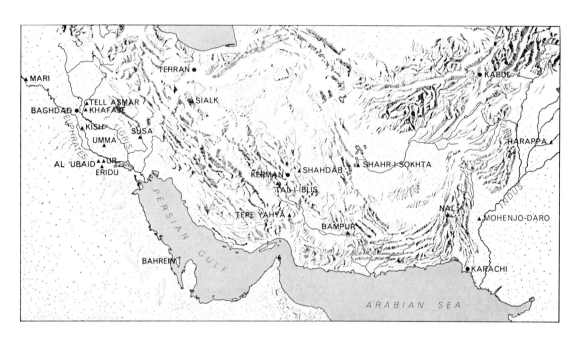

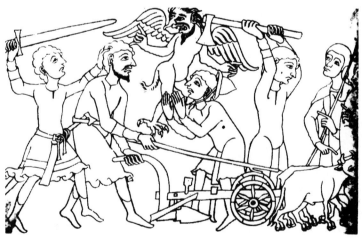

The Urban Revolution

The settlements in Europe signaled the beginning of what V. Gordon Childe has called the urban revolution. This was not a dramatic, violent, or sudden revolution. Social life and social structures changed gradually and naturally. Little by little human settlements grew from small, separate villages into large, integrated cities. And, as these changes took place, the populations grew.

It can be argued that populations increased first, causing the development of cities, but it seems more likely that without cities, larger populations could not have been supported. Population increases alone would not have brought about the development of the cities without some changes in technology and social structure (Davis, 1973:13-15).

Childe lists ten traits that distinguished early urban societies from nonurban societies (1970:116-18).

1. Urban settlements were large and more densely populated.
2. Cities supported full-time craftsmen.
3. Farmers produced a social surplus, some of which they turned back to the city society.
4. Cities built monumental public buildings.
5. Social surpluses were kept in central granaries owned or managed by priests.
6. Cities were the centers for recording and applying science.
7. Cities furthered the development of the predictive sciences.
8. Cities were centers for artistic advances.
9. Cities used imported raw materials.
10. Urban social organization was based on residence, not on kinship.

Table 3.1   The Size of Early Cities

City	Population	Size
Mohenjo-daro	20,000	1 square mile
Harappa	20,000	2 1/2 mile perimeter
Ur	5,000	220 acres
Erech	25,000	2 square miles

By these criteria, the first cities emerged in Mesopotamia, in the Tigris and Euphrates valleys, and in the Indus region about 3500 B.C. Table 3.1 shows the size and population of some early cities.[2] The total area of this region is about two-thirds the size of Texas. In about 1400 B.C., Tel el Amara was built as the capital city of the region. It was to have been a temporary capital, but it reached a population of forty thousand. Two hundred years earlier, in 1600 B.C., Thebes (the capital of Egypt) was described by Greek visitors as having a circumference of fourteen miles and the astounding population of nearly 225,000. Though much larger cities have developed since, there were no settlements that approached these sizes before 2000 B.C.

Initial Urban Developments

The first cities in history were larger, denser, and more differentiated than the villages that preceded them. The early cities were able to support full-time resident craftsmen for two reasons. First, the farmers in the surrounding area were able to produce more food than they needed—a social surplus. Second, the collection and distribution of the social surplus was coordinated by individuals who combined what are today religious, political, and economic roles. The social surplus freed these people from the need to grow their own food and allowed them to specialize. Much of the social surplus of the early city was collected as a religious tribute, or a **tithe**, to the divinity of the area, who shared it with his mortal representatives, the priests (Childe, 1970:116). This accomplished not only the religious goals of the community, but also ensured that the surplus agricultural production was imported to the city.

Uses of the Social Surplus

As the agricultural system began to operate more efficiently, the social surplus became large enough to support people other than religious leaders and craftsmen. Some resources were used in the construction of monumental public buildings, such as the temples that were built to honor the deity who had so generously provided for such extravagances. Early Sumerian cities, for example, were dominated by temples.[3]

The social surplus had to be large enough not only to build these structures, but also to staff and maintain them on a permanent basis. The surplus also had to make up for the food that the temple workers were no longer producing as agricultural workers. Some of these residents undoubtedly worked in the city for only a short period—a tithe of time. Others probably became permanent city residents, adding to the population, creating new social roles, increasing the division of labor and the social differentiation in the city, and making it even more necessary to have a dependable supply of food and goods from the surrounding area.

Monumental public buildings were constructed to provide for these workers and their families, as well as for the craftsmen and religious functionaries who were the original residents of the city. Public buildings included facilities for religious services, artisan workshops, and especially grain storage. Granaries were the city's insurance that, should agricultural production falter, there would still be enough food for its residents. Not all public monuments served as granaries. The Egyptian pyramids and the Mayan temples of Central America, for example, did not. But in Harappa the rampart protecting the city encircled the citadel, the palace of the ruler, the granary, and the dormitory for artisans (Childe, 1970:116-17; Mumford, 1961: 73-85). The inclusion of the granary and the artisans' residence within the ramparts made it clear that food and craftsmen were crucial to the city.

Social Organization

As Childe and Davis have pointed out (Childe, 1970; Davis, 1970, 1973), everybody living in the earliest cities depended for survival on the social surplus, which was by no means certain. As the process of collecting, storing, and distributing the surplus on which the urban standard of living depended became more complex, the functions of the deity's representatives became more differentiated. Although there was still a high degree of homogeneity in the society, which generated solidarity, different roles began to develop among the leaders and workers of the city.

Some of the solidarity-maintaining tasks that city leaders performed were assuring the population of continued fertility of the land, of the continued rising and setting of the sun, and of the equality of tithes. Although these now seem like simple tasks, three thousand or more years ago they were highly problematic. The fertility of the land and the rising of the sun were thought to be caused by the intervention of the gods in response to the pleas of the priests. The ability of the priests to reassure the people that these phenomena would reoccur on schedule reinforced the legitimacy of their rule and their claim on the tithe. Social solidarity also was strengthened, because it was felt that the rulers and the farmers were participating in a mutual enterprise.

To provide these reassurances the leaders of the city developed methods of counting and recording. Systems of arithmetic and geometry first appeared in the same areas of the Middle East in which some of the earliest cities were found. These systems made possible an increase in the size of the social surplus, which in turn led to the development of art forms centered around religious institutions and buildings.

With increases in both the social surplus and the division of labor, the city contained not only full-time craftsmen who could produce agricultural tools, but also specialists in religious and civil matters, art, transportation, and military affairs. In sum, an urban labor force grew up that was paid out of the social surplus by leaders or rulers who had, in turn, earned their share of the common store rather than grown it. Living in the city gave craftsmen access to a secure supply of materials, as well as a steady market. The craftsmen identified with the society of the city in which they lived rather than with the family, kin group, or village into which they had been born. They had exchanged one form of social solidarity for another.

In return for secure supplies, employment, and social solidarity, however, artisans became dependent on the temple, court, and ruling class of the city. They had become individual members of a labor force rather than members of a community, but their lives and their livelihoods were more secure.

Urban Development in the
Mediterranean Basin

The cities that developed in Greece and Rome followed the patterns seen in the cities of Mesopotamia, the Tigris and Euphrates valleys, and the Indus region.[4] However, these later cities, that were located around the Mediterranean Sea, extended and expanded on the earlier patterns.

The people of the Mediterranean Basin were able to explore distant areas and develop complex trade relationships because of several technological and social advances. They had reliable boats. Through the use of alphabets and coins they were able to exchange information and goods more efficiently. The labor force by this time was highly diversified. The ability to exchange goods with other areas allowed cities to support more and more people in a given area and to do it with fewer and fewer farmers. In the fifth century B.C., Athens alone supported from 120,000 to 180,000 people, while the populations of Syracuse and Carthage may have been slightly larger. However, the growth of these cities was limited by lack of adequate sanitary facilities and effective public health controls.

Disease was an ever-present threat, as was barbarian conquest. The state of agricultural knowledge and the social structure (Davis, 1970:124) still limited the size of the social surplus.

> Unfortunately, Greek civilization evolved in a region where only 20 percent of the land area could be cultivated, and this placed severe limits on food production. As the cities grew, their populations became increasingly dependent upon the imports of grain from outlying districts and provinces. As the demand for food grew, hills and mountains were laid bare of their forests. Few of those areas have recovered from the exploitive land practices prevalent during the golden years of the Greek empire [Cook, 1969:31].

While the cities of the Greek peninsula differed somewhat, they were but variations on a theme. Technically and socially these cities, although still limited, were more highly urbanized cultures than the earlier cities in the Indus Basin.

The conquest of Athens by the Romans ended the development of Greek cities and set the stage for the rise of Rome, the first society to take full advantage of urban social organization. None of the Greek cities was able to resist the onslaught of the Roman legions, although at the time of the Roman conquest, Rome was less urbanized than any Greek city. This soon changed, as the conquerors of a relatively urbanized society became urbanized in turn. More of Italy than of Greece could be cultivated, thereby creating a larger social surplus. This freed more people to live in cities and to work at other tasks, such as trade, military service, and administration. The technological inventions of Rome's military specialists, especially the development of roads, made possible the Roman empire. The ability to move men and goods quickly over long distances created a large **hinterland** around the city from which came the goods, the people, and the culture to support Rome and other cities of the empire (Davis, 1970:124).

Toward the end of Roman rule, the empire lost the vitality that had brought it to dominance. The social organization rigidified, and the city became unable to take advantage of the social and technological progress that it had made. Later emperors were constantly looking for enough food to feed Rome's large and demanding urban population, which is estimated by some historians to have been more than one million. There had been breakdowns in food production and in the social and political organization that imported food to Rome and distributed it (Cook, 1969:31-32).

The Fall of Urban Society

With the Fall of the Roman Empire about 400 A.D., urban civilization in Europe declined until the end of the Renaissance.

Italy, Gaul, Iberia, North Africa, Greece and Egypt were especially affected, and so were their cities. It has been estimated that Rome had about 350,000 people at the time of Augustus, 241,000 around 200 A.D., 172,600 about 350 A.D., 36,000-48,000 about 500 A.D., and only 30,000 in the 10th century. Cities of fairly considerable size had grown up elsewhere. Baghdad with an estimated population of 300,000 was the capital of the Caliphate Empire. Cordoba with 90,000 and Seville with 52,000 had risen in Moorish Spain. Constantinople with its 160,000 to 200,000 inhabitants was the pride of the Byzantine Empire [Cook, 1969:32].

(Top) The old Appian Way near Rome. Roads made possible the movement of goods, people, and culture which sustained urban populations of the Roman Empire.

(Bottom) St. Sebastian Interceding for the Plague Stricken City. (Reproduced by permission of Walters Art Gallery.) The plague was a factor in reducing urban populations during feudal times.

From the Fall of Rome to about the fifteenth century A.D., cities ceased to grow and even declined. During this period, the settlements that remained became far more self-sufficient but declined in population and commerce. Their social systems rigidified—social status, even occupations, became hereditary. Who your parents were, especially your father, was more important in determining one's position in society than was ability or achievement. This **feudal system** made political, social, and economic change difficult. Much of this period was taken up with feudal wars and conflicts—the content of much western political and social history. These were not wars over religious, social, or philosophical issues but rather wars to determine which hereditary leader would control which piece of land, its inhabitants and its resources. It took the philosophical revolution of Hobbes, Rousseau, and the utilitarians and the Industrial Revolution to initiate further change in society and cities.

In the fourteenth and fifteenth centuries European cities were relatively small—smaller than Rome had been and much smaller than they are now. Table 3.2 gives the sizes of several cities at different times during the feudal period. One reason for these relatively low figures was the **Black Plague** which began in 1348 and destroyed much of the European population. Before 1400, one third to one half of the people died of the plague (Langer, 1973:106-7). The rigidity of the social system and the loss of many technological advances made by the Romans—roads, viaducts, agricultural techniques—made recovery from the plague even more difficult.

Table 3.2   The Size of Cities During Period
             of Urban Decline*

Date	City	Population
1338	Florence	90,000
1377	London	30,000
1440	Frankfort	8,719
1442	Venice	190,000
1450	Nuremberg	20,000
1550	Paris	130,000-500,000

*Estimates reported in Davis (1970:124) and Cook
(1969:33).

The Preindustrial City

Cities remained essentially the same from the
time of the earliest cities until the Industrial
Revolution. The peasants who farmed the
hinterlands and provided the social surplus
were an integral part of the social system of
each city. While they had low status, they
were integrated into the urban social system,
at least in part, by religion (Sjoberg, 1970:167-
76), which provided a basically mechanical
form of social solidarity and integration.

The feudal, preindustrial city that emerged
during the Middle Ages had a fairly complex
social system that offered a variety of occupational roles that were maintained through a
complex hereditary status system. Essentially
independent, but somewhat integrated, political, religious, and economic subsystems
developed with specific functions. Each major
function carried out by the city led to the
development of an institution devoted to its
performance. Churches, shops, city halls, and
palaces were prominent features in the urban
landscape—signs of the social importance of
the institutions for which they stood.

The rigidity of the social system (Sjoberg,
1970; Weber, 1970:150-67) of the city was
reflected in its physical structure: the higher
one's social position, the larger and more im-
posing one's home or place of business—a
pattern that continues to this day. This devotion to monumental building was, perhaps,
helped along by the knowledge that status
would not evaporate over a short span of
time. A wealthy, prominent person knew with
a certainty that is not possible today that his
heirs would be wealthy and socially prominent, too, and would undoubtedly live in the
same place in the city. A large, impressive
house would thus be useful for several generations.

Although feudal cities were much larger
than earlier cities, their central problem was
much the same—that of maintaining a constant and dependable supply of food and
other necessities. Each city still depended on
its hinterlands to produce a social surplus, but
it solved the problem differently. The city
became a market and trade center where
goods were exchanged. Before this, cities had
relied heavily on religious or military-political
conquests to ensure the importation of vital
goods (Weber, 1970).

The Preindustrial City As a Market

Most cities of the Middle Ages, even those
that grew up around a central palace, fortress,
church, or monastery, had an area reserved
for a market. Farmers from surrounding areas
would meet there with tradespeople from the
city. There the traders, the lord of the area, or
other functionaries would collect and distribute the social surplus to the population.

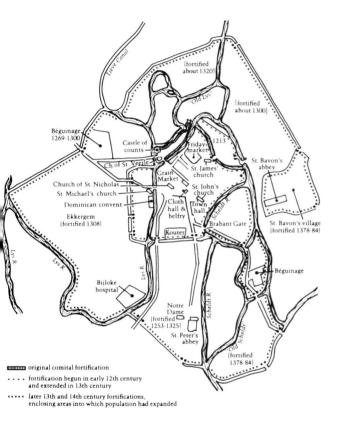

original comital fortification

fortification begun in early 12th century
and extended in 13th century

later 13th and 14th century fortifications,
enclosing areas into which population had expanded

The central market was the retail and commercial center, as well as the city's grocery store (Weber, 1970:151-52).

So critical was the market to the preindustrial city that Max Weber defined the preindustrial city as the location of continuous market activities. Because the market was active each day, both its operation and the supply of food and other raw materials were dependable. The exchange of goods did not depend on a periodic schedule.

> Thus we wish to speak of a "city" only in cases where the local inhabitants satisfy an economically substantial part of their daily wants in the local market, and to an essential extent by products which the local population and that of the immediate hinterland produced for sale in the market or acquired in other ways [Weber, 1970:152].

The market city was the natural prey of nonurbanized people who roamed through much of Europe and the West during the early feudal period. Barbarian conquest was a major threat to these cities. The citizens were protected mainly by a lord or prince whose estate and fortress provided the major market for goods produced by city residents (Weber, 1970:157-59).

Some cities during this period specialized in the manufacture of certain goods: tools, weapons, special forms of handicrafts, and clothes. Others specialized in political, religious, or educational services which residents exchanged for food and other necessities from other cities or from the hinterlands of various cities. The existence of money made such specialization possible. In the Far East,

Benares and Karbala were religious centers, while Peking was a political center. London, Paris, and Rome served similar functions in Western Europe (Weber, 1970:153, 154, 162-67).

Feudal Lords, Traders, and Landlords

In those cities protected by a lord of the manor, the relationship between the citizens and their lord was not simple (Weber, 1970; Sjoberg, 1970; Pirenne, 1961). In return for the patronage of his court and the protection of his fortress and men-at-arms, the lord of the manor received certain concessions from city residents. Citizens served in his militia and paid him taxes and rents. In many cases, the lord used some of his income to become part owner of some of the city's businesses.

Some cities developed without an attachment to a manorial estate, for instance, those at the intersections of trading routes. These were market cities, even more so than cities based on manorial estates. They facilitated the marketing of goods, provided the necessary inns and service facilities for the users of the routes. If necessary, there were workers and equipment to transship goods—transfer them from one form of transportation to another. Because these specialized cities were vital to commerce between distant areas, they were able to charge enough for their services to pay for the goods and services, including military protection, that they needed. Because their economic support came from all users of the transportation routes, not from a single estate, they could be independent and self-governing.

Other cities generated their own income from more diffuse sources than a single lord normally had access to. This produced a high level of internal solidarity, since there were few external and competing sources of loyalty. These sources of income included rents from lands, either in the city or in the hinterlands, taxes for performance of religious or political services, and trade with other cities. From its beginnings, Moscow was a city of economically powerful citizens who had large landholdings throughout Russia. The rent from these landholdings was not only the social surplus that made the city viable, but also the source of the economic power that made Moscow the center of Russian society. In China, the residents of Peking were mainly government officials and workers who depended on the economic activity of those officials. The Imperial Court located in Peking was important to the city, but the large number of government and court functionaries who resided permanently in Peking were more important economically to the residents.

The economic elite, regardless of its nature, supported craftsmen, artisans, and other urban workers. They thus fostered the development of the services they wanted to consume and added to their own economic power. In cities along trade routes, the economic power of the elite was based on their traffic monopoly and their ownership of strategically located property and facilities in much the same way that today's motel and gas station owners along interstate highways have monopolies. Operation of these facilities was vital, profitable, and provided employment for many urban residents. The owners became an urban aristocracy that drew its power from urban landholdings.

Skilled craftsmen working alone or in small groups were an important part of the economic base of pre-industrial cities.

Those preindustrial cities dominated by an economic elite relied for their economic vitality and even their continued existence on that elite. In successful cities, the elite consumed enough to keep the rest of the population employed, fed, and occupied in trade and commerce.

The economy of some preindustrial cities was based on the production of goods that were destined for territories outside the city. Skilled craftsmen working in small shops or **cottage industries** produced enough salable goods to enable the city to buy its food and raw materials from the hinterlands. As the profit from the sale of the manufactured goods grew, the producer city was able to support an increasingly large population.

Although many preindustrial cities had large populations, especially after the fifteenth century, city dwellers continued to represent a small percentage of the population of the society (Davis, 1970:124-25; Cook, 1969:34). For some cities the social surplus of food and other resources, such as building materials, cloth, and tools, needed to support the residents was limited. In turn, of course, the residents of most cities had only limited ability to produce in their homes and other workshops the materials they and the farmers needed.

Life in the Preindustrial City

Life in preindustrial cities was not easy. Though the rulers of the city tried to ensure that there would be a social surplus and that it would be available to city dwellers, the standard of living by contemporary standards was low. Even more so than in the villages, life in

the cities was short, dirty, and generally unhealthy. Whenever thousands or even hundreds of people lived in the same place, sanitation and public health became serious problems. The life span in the early city was short, and even the mildest disease was likely to be fatal. Diseases spread by poor sanitation, unhealthy living conditions, inadequate nutrition, and infection were all too common. Medicine was primitive, and there were few effective treatments for diseases. These medical problems limited the size of the city and the proportion of populations that could live in cities[5] (Cook, 1969:34-35). Indeed, throughout most of history, those living in the city have had shorter lives and been plagued with more disease and earlier death than those living outside the city. This has changed only in the twentieth century.

Technology, Social Organization, and the Growth of the Preindustrial City

Prior to the Industrial Revolution of the nineteenth century, the characteristics of cities remained essentially stable. Although they appear to have developed and grown inexorably and logically, though gradually, during this period, there were times, such as after the Fall of Rome, when growth did not take place, certain areas (the Indus and Nile basins) failed to continue their growth and apparently natural and inevitable processes did not occur. The forces that contributed to the growth and development of cities were technological and social-organizational. Both factors were and are highly interrelated.

Agricultural Technology

Prior to the urban revolution, and for much of subsequent history, agricultural yields were low and agricultural technology was primitive. Farming was hard, dirty, time-consuming manual labor. The individual farmer could produce enough for himself and a fraction of a person more—not enough to feed his whole family, let alone enough to tithe to the city. When all members of the farming family worked, there was a little left over—very little—which was the social surplus available to support the city. A great many farms and farm families were required for the support of even a small city. As we have seen, this limited social surplus restricted, in turn, the size of cities and the proportion of urban residents in the society.

One reason that agriculture was so underdeveloped was the low social status of the farmer. Leaders of early cities of the Indus and Nile basins developed certain sciences to a high degree and were able to predict natural occurrences such as floods and eclipses. Their scientific investigations were possible in part because there was a social surplus and scientists did not participate in raising food. They had become a privileged class. This made farming a role of low social status and constrained investment in agricultural technology (Davis, 1970:123).

Energy

In the Paleolithic and Neolithic settlements the only sources of energy were the muscles of people and animals. Until the Industrial Revolution farm productivity was limited by the lack of energy other than power provided

by these sources and by wind and water. Only
with the introduction of inanimate power
could farmers produce large surpluses. The
generation of inanimate energy made possible
the existence and growth of cities. Together
with social organization, energy production
altered the very nature of urban social life
(Sjoberg, 1970:164; 1973:26).

In the preindustrial city the lack of dependable inanimate power severely restricted the
city's physical and social character. The size
of most buildings was restricted by the difficulty of moving and raising heavy building
materials. The larger and higher the building,
the more difficult it became to handle the
materials. The residents of preindustrial cities
knew how to construct large buildings, but
they did not often choose to spend so much
available energy on such projects. The small
proportion of large, impressive, and beautiful
buildings that still enrich the European urban
landscape were exceptions. They were constructed slowly, some taking generations to
build.

Availability of power also shaped the physical and social structures of the city. Because
energy was scarce, streets were designed solely
for the passage of people—simple, narrow
walkways between buildings (Sjoberg, 1970:
168). Citizens lighted their way through public
plazas and streets with candles and torches.
Few commercial and social activities were carried out after dark.

Production was also limited by the sources
of power. Individual craftsmen or a master
craftsman and his apprentices worked alone
to produce goods in the preindustrial city.
Work was controlled by guilds or associations
of master craftsmen. Each individual produced a total product.

Transportation and Communication

With the exception of the early Roman empire, the size of cities usually was restricted by people's inability to transport even limited social surpluses over any great distance. During the Paleolithic and Neolithic eras, wheels were solid, heavy disks that added to the weight of the cart and reduced the payload that the cart could carry. On rivers, sailboats were clumsy modes of transportation—hard to steer and having small cargo capacities. Even during the feudal period, distances that could not be covered in a single day made communication and transportation difficult and undependable, limiting the size of the city.

Beyond the city limits lived tribes of people who wanted no part of the city and who resisted the encroachment of cities on their lands. Cities were unable to control or protect large areas. Distant settlements were highly autonomous and contributed little to the cities that supposedly controlled them (although at that time every little bit helped). Before 600 B.C. few cities were able to dominate large areas. Those cities that did control or even exert influence over a large area had to grant the subordinate areas much autonomy (Davis, 1970:123).

It was difficult to import heavy materials and ship bulk goods. One major means of transportation was the ocean-going vessel, which gave port cities great trade advantages. Food could be transported only limited distances, and transportation within cities was slow, difficult, and undependable. Animal-drawn carts cut ruts in the city's narrow passageways. During rains, the ruts often became so deep that carts were bogged down

and traffic came to a standstill. The animals that powered these carts polluted preindustrial cities at least as severely as the automobile pollutes our cities today. Natural pollution was no less an evil then than artificial pollution is now when it came to problems of health and environment (Mumford, 1961:216-17).

Spatial Arrangements

The cities of the preindustrial period were not as densely settled as contemporary cities, so many residents could grow some of their own food. The use of open spaces for gardens reduced some of the pressure on farmers to produce food for the cities, just as victory gardens in American cities during World War II reduced pressures on American farmers. Of course, the amount of land available and its productivity varied according to city size and density of settlement. By comparison with the contemporary city dweller who produces almost no food, the preindustrial city dweller was a semipeasant (Weber, 1970:154-55).

During the latter part of the medieval period, opportunities to raise food in the city were reduced. The open land that remained became the property of eminent citizens or the municipality itself and was farmed on behalf of the owner who got most of the produce. The individual who actually did the farming received only a small percentage of the output.

Segregation in the Preindustrial City

Most buildings in the preindustrial city, with the exception of public monuments, were not used for specialized purposes. People lived

and worked in the same building, a historical precedent that probably still influences our urban planning goals and our distaste for commuting to work. Because the whole family worked, and often worked in their home, distinctive occupational quarters, wards, and sections grew up in the city (Sjoberg, 1970: 169; Mumford, 1961:310; Sjoberg, 1973:22-23). Cabinetmakers lived and worked in one area, shoemakers in another, and tanners in yet another. These areas were not large, often being limited to a single street named for the principal activity of its residents.

The earliest cities were segregated on other bases. Ethnic groups were often concentrated in particular sections, and quarters or wards developed that were occupied almost exclusively by groups engaged in related trades or professions. This historic pattern persists today in some parts of our cities. The French quarter in New Orleans, the theater and garment districts in New York, North Beach in San Francisco, Rush Street in Chicago, and financial districts in almost every city are contemporary versions of these occupational quarters in preindustrial cities.

The center of the preindustrial city was the hub of its activities—the point most convenient to all other points. Those institutions and activities of highest status were located there. Having narrow streets and only foot or animal transportation limited mobility and made the central area the most expensive and desirable location in the city. Only people of high status could afford to live and work on such valuable land—the direct opposite of the contemporary urban pattern, the change being due at least in part to the availability of efficient and comfortable transportation.

The central portion did not dominate all spheres of urban activity. Indeed no single area, other than perhaps the manor or the marketplace, was dominant. The essential productive functions of the city were dispersed into the various quarters. The city occupied a much smaller area than that covered by most contemporary cities because transportation was so poor and protective walls could not encompass vast areas.

The Organization of Work

Apprentices who worked in the homes or shops of master craftsmen were recruited in accordance with **guild** regulations. There were no managers or middlemen in the production and delivery of goods. Orders were placed directly with the craftsmen who designed, produced, and delivered the goods.

Each guild set its own standards of workmanship, technique, and price. However, because goods were produced by hand, there was little standardization. Construction methods, size of product, and materials varied with the distinctive style and standards of each craftsman. No two pieces produced by a single craftsman, let alone those produced by different people, were identical. The finest, most durable goods produced during this period are now valuable antiques, while the goods of average quality were used up in daily living by those who purchased them.

Guild membership was an important stepping-stone to economic and social mobility. Being apprenticed to a guild member was one of the few avenues to a better life open to children of farmers or laborers. The surest way to become an apprentice was to be born to or adopted by a member of a guild.

Nonguild members often paid members to accept their children as apprentices. Family and ethnic ties also were important, as they still are in some unions, because selection of new guild members was based on ascribed characteristics rather than on achievement.

The guilds and kinship systems were integrated through this recruitment process. Religion, too, was tied in with work; each guild worshipped its own patron saint. Guilds also carried out communal functions such as providing social security for their members and dependents. While not comprehensive, some help was available through the guilds in times of sickness, unemployment, war, famine, and death. The guilds supplemented the communal functions of family, church, and village, and this provided a form of community not otherwise available (Sjoberg, 1970:168-70; Weber, 1970:156-62; Mumford, 1961:270-71).

Social Status and Mobility

Guilds were organized in status hierarchies running from apprentices to guild masters. Cities also had their status systems. Princes, lords, and members of the court formed the urban elite, a privileged class on which the city depended for its economic existence. The elite differed sharply from the masses. There was no middle class and little mobility from the masses to the elite.

The urban elite consumed a great deal in relation to the masses. Nothing could be produced in great enough quantity to satisfy any but the smallest elite. The number of elite roles was limited, and the society could not train large numbers of people for high-status positions. Without the advantage of elite status an individual was restricted to the lower classes.

The vast majority of urban residents were laborers, craftsmen, and semipeasants—the workers who produced the goods needed to keep the city functioning. Even lower in status were slaves, where slavery was practiced, beggars, burial workers, entertainers, and itinerant merchants. Some ethnic groups, notably the Jews, occupied outcast positions even lower than those of the lowliest city workers (Sjoberg, 1970:170-72; Weber, 1970:163).

In summary, status was predominantly ascribed on the basis of birth rather than won by achievement. Typically, one's status depended on one's father's position in urban society. Thus kinship and status were closely linked in the preindustrial city.

The Family

The family during the preindustrial era included several generations, and all family branches were closely linked physically, socially, and emotionally (Sjoberg, 1970: 171-72). Families were the basic social units. Through families and guilds, the essential forms of social solidarity were generated and maintained.

Because so much productive work was carried out in cottage or home workshops, a large family was an economic asset. The more able-bodied workers there were, the more work they could do and the more prosperous the family would be. A large number of workers, especially if they were spread out over several generations, assured older workers they would be supported in their old age by the younger members. Large families were a form of social security.

Most marriages were not marriages of love. Life was short, marriage partners were young, and parents made most of the arrangements for the young couple involved. When divorce occurred, it was not as likely as it is today to be accompanied by intense feelings or a sense of personal failure[6] (Sjoberg, 1970:167-76).

Sex Roles and Age-Grading

Sex and age differentiation in the preindustrial city was rigid. Women in the elite classes did little work outside the home. They supervised household staffs and carried out other domestic tasks. Women of the lower class had no household staffs. They did the household chores, raised the children, and worked in the family shops. These women engaged in far more activities than did women of the elite class.

Throughout society, women were considered subordinate to men, regardless of age. Women's roles, and especially their public behaviors, were rigidly controlled.[7] Only a few women were exempt from these restrictions because they occupied marginal jobs such as entertainer or prostitute. Peasant women who helped produce food for the society were also free from most sex-based restrictions.

One's age was an important mechanism for social control. The eldest male in the family was the patriarch who controlled the behavior of all family members. He was arbitrator in all disputes, and set all family policy. The eldest son was his father's heir apparent and the most privileged offspring. Other privileges within the family were determined by age. The older the adult, the greater the authority. All

adults had a higher status than the youths, who in turn dominated the children in the family (Sjoberg, 1970:172).

There was no stage in the medieval life cycle that resembled in any way what we call adolescence. After childhood, the individual became an adult, accepting all the rights and responsibilities of adulthood, particularly the roles of parent and producer of goods or services. Having no period of adolescence meant that there was no youth culture, no extended schooling, and no experimentation with different occupations. In one's early teens a young person married, began working, and soon became a parent, continuing the cycle. Life was so short, death so early, that early childbearing was necessary if some of the many children born were to survive infancy. This prevented problems of juvenile delinquency and premarital sexual activity that have been of such concern today.

Education

Among the elite, most learning took place in the home, where the male members of the family were trained to read and write. This training prepared them for their roles in government, religion, and the few institutions of higher education that there were. The workers did not need to be literate, for the means of production did not require literacy. Even the most skilled trades were taught by master to apprentice, a method that depended solely on observation and practice.

In fact, only a few roles occupied by members of the elite required literacy, so there was little need for books and other written materials. Cities were isolated from one

(*Left*) French carpenter and maid-servant, medieval period

(*Right*) Literacy and education were restricted to male members of the elite.

Evis par ce bzeuet que vantâce eſtoit le pzemiet maiſtre ſubalterne ozdonne par fauſſete ſi me pen ſay que la doctrine deuoit eſtre ſelon la pzpzieté des mai ſtres Lozs vertu ſarreſta la derrite aucuns eſcoliers Et auſſi feiz Je pour ouyr lire ce pzemiet chappitre qui eſtoit des declinoiſons côme diſoit le tiltre Adoncques maiſtre vantance po[2] peruenir a ſa lecture fiſt ſigne et ſilence aup eſcoliers Et Ilz comme bons diſciples tan toſt ſe teurent Et le maiſtre commença a lire et deiſt.

another; communication between them was restricted to messages sent by word of mouth or letters carried by traders who traveled from one city to another. Among the elite, traditions were passed on from generation to generation by written means, especially in religious institutions; among the masses traditions were transmitted by verbal means—through stories and songs (Sjoberg, 1970).

The elite used the same verbal techniques to transmit news, legends, and social norms to the masses. What the masses knew about their society was thus controlled by what was told to them by storytellers and folk singers who transmitted, in addition to their own repertoires, the information passed on to them by the elite.

Government and Social Control

City governments before the Industrial Revolution had far more restricted functions than contemporary city governments. The society-wide government (to the extent that one existed) was composed of all cities owing allegiance to a single elite and was mainly religious and political. It dealt with foreign relations and wars. Local city governments were responsible for collecting local taxes and tributes to the elite from foreign traders. These funds were used to build city buildings, to pay the city's contribution to the society-wide government, and to support the local police or militia. The local militia was used primarily to control outsiders. Internal social control was achieved by less formal means, such as public opinion, the teachings of the guild, and the family and religious institutions. These agencies ensured conformity in

behavior and homogeneity in belief and custom. It was not until the division of labor became more extensive that these mechanisms began to lose their effectiveness, and police and court systems became necessary. The institutions of a mechanically integrated *Gemeinschaft* were more than adequate to ensure that social norms would be followed during most of the preindustrial era.

Informal social control was reinforced by status. High-status individuals were quite visible, due to differences in their style of dress. They provided the behavior models and expressed the accepted attitudes and opinions for the masses. The models were not followed exactly, of course, but the general tenor of thought and behavior was sufficiently well communicated through the elite to set the tone of the society (Sjoberg, 1970:173). Status, combined with the other informal means of social control, helped to enforce the norms of the city and to strengthen social solidarity.

All strata of society were religious, and religious leaders had an obvious stake in controlling the social surplus and maintaining the structure of the society. During the feudal period the market function of the city was dominant. The fortress and the military forces of the lord of the manor protected the market. The lord's men also contributed heavily to market activity by purchasing goods. The economic power of the estate or the city elite multiplied as the purchase price was used in turn to buy other goods and to maintain the social surplus. Regulation of market transactions, even a primitive form of consumer protection, soon became functions performed by city governments (Sjoberg, 1970: 173; Weber, 1970:163-66).

Economic Policies

The city's economic policies emerged from the need to ensure a constant, dependable supply of food. Taxes collected by the city could be used to purchase food, to import food during times of reduced local production, and to finance the clearing and development of new farmlands. The marketplace in the city was the usual, but not the only, place in which foodstuffs were exchanged for goods. Because the market was so important to the city, the city's concern for the health of the market was paramount. Too many taxes or too high a tax rate would drive suppliers and craftsmen out. Too few taxes or too low a rate would not provide the city with enough revenue.

As the city began to regulate economic activities, its citizens—especially those with economic interests, such as guild leaders—began to participate in setting economic policies and regulations. It soon became traditional for urban residents to be represented in the making of regulations that influenced their interests (Weber, 1970:156).

As the urban market grew, the importance of land as a source of income, power, and social status decreased. Tradesmen, craftsmen, and merchants began to take part in regulating city economic activities, diminishing the role of princely landowners. The basis of elite status began to shift from noble birth and land ownership to money. The ensuing conflict between the traditional and the emerging elites led to the transformation of feudal cities into industrial cities.

Political Autonomy

The practice of allowing city tradesmen and craftsmen to be represented in economic policy-making activities marked the beginning of political autonomy for many citizens. Urban residents increasingly viewed themselves as citizens of the city rather than as members of the prince's estates. This led to partially autonomous urban communities that developed their own political and administrative arrangements independent of the lord of the estate. As this autonomy developed, cities became centers of personal freedom in a society that was otherwise tightly controlled.

As political and economic autonomy developed, princes began to demand laws requiring city residents to help support them and to pay for their protection from the incursions of barbarians. The residence of the prince was typically a fortified place large enough to house all the citizens in case of attack. Residents paid the prince in money or militia service.

This principle is illustrated by the mandatory garrison duty paid to English lords by people living on their land. For many years Roman fortresses guarded the English against the Celts. With the Fall of Rome this protection ended, but the northern tribes were still a threat to the English. Each resident of a borough, or fortified town, owed garrison duty to the lord or keeper of the shire (a larger unit including several boroughs). The lord, or keeper of the shire, in turn owed a certain number of armed men to the king in case of national emergency.

The City as a Source of Freedom

The usual signal that an urban community had won the first round of the struggle for freedom from feudal restraints was the granting of a charter. Charters varied in detail and were renewed, amended, and changed in various ways from time to time, but most of the major cities in those parts of Europe where feudalism existed had one kind or another by the thirteenth century. In the most general terms, a city or town charter granted the community concerned exemption from some or all feudal and agrarian regulations, which not only gave them the freedom necessary for their economic survival, but also placed them outside the sociopolitical framework of feudalism. The practical necessities of urban life led to townspeople enjoying "civil liberties" that people of a similar rank in rural society did not have. For example, most charters granted citizens the right to buy, sell, and bequeath their property as they pleased, limited only by the most nominal restrictions; they were allowed to hold fairs and markets at appointed times and to impose their own regulations on commercial activities; they had the freedom to travel about both inside and outside their home districts.

The privilege of greater freedom, an important by-product of the advent of city charters, heightened the townsman's sense of being "different" from his rural contemporaries; phrases such as "the air of the towns breeds freedom" were often used to express this special status. In many regions, by legal provision or by general custom, an escaped serf who lived in a town or city for a year and a day became a free man and was allowed the same privileges as all townspeople. The charter of Bologna, for example, stated that the people of the city had a right to be free, and the city also offered compensation to the owners of runaway serfs whom it placed on its own tax rolls as free individuals. This custom attracted some rural people to urban communities. It offered cities a means of expanding their labor resources, and it also meant that they generally attracted the better people in rural society—those with the wit and enterprise to escape and the adaptability to change their way of life. The successful runaway in effect had to work to support himself for a year in the urban community; this

The development of political autonomy on the part of medieval cities led to the development of individual freedom and civil liberties and emphasized the need for personal achievement as a means of attaining status.

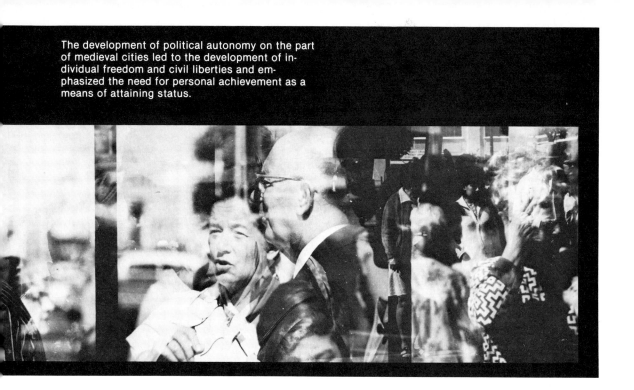

period of transition gave townspeople time to judge his worth. If he proved a useful and active addition, he would be accepted; if he proved to be idle or incompetent, he could be left to the mercy of pursuers, sent back home, or simply abandoned outside the walls and denied readmission. That mere acceptance into an urban community could transform a serf into a free man gave towns and cities a special place in the minds of contemporaries, both urban and rural.

Source Reprinted from *The Shaping of Urban Society,* by Janet Roebuck with the permission of Charles Scribner's Sons. Copyright © 1974 Janet Roebuck. Pp. 61, 68.

If garrison duty was the oldest form of civic duty in nonurbanized England, it was even more of a duty in urbanized areas. The real-estate and taxation policy made it possible for the wealthy to buy off their duty with hired men or monetary payments. As always, the poor served in the standing army or in garrisons (Weber, 1970:157-61).

In the process of establishing its independence, the city had to develop a political and social structure which could negotiate with the lord of the manor. Permitting the city to establish an internal government with the power of negotiation was a crucial concession on the lord's part. Political and judicial systems thus were born, bringing with them political and economic independence for the city. The lord of the manor was still an important source of funds and authority, but he no longer controlled all city institutions.

The city also began to develop its own forms of association and social solidarity apart from those relationships that tied residents directly to their lord. The city thus began to be a community in itself, not just an extension of the noble's court. The changes that took place in the preindustrial cities also changed the societies in which the cities were located. As cities became larger and more complex, the motivations needed to maintain citizen loyalty and participation became more complex.[8] This was partially reflected in the developing autonomy of the urban community. It was also reflected in the growth of personal autonomy and freedom, which attracted immigrants to the cities from throughout society. The aristocrats and religious leaders who valued the goods and power generated by cities were threatened by the changes that were based on achievement, social mobility, autonomy and personal freedom, and by the changes in the bases of social status needed to maintain cities. At the close of the preindustrial era the city was a center for freedom and innovation.

Summary

The modern urban revolution that began during the nineteenth century in Europe brought with it a society that was truly urbanized—a society in which the city dominated the social landscape even though most people lived outside the city. The city led in the development of new social, political, and economic forms that shaped the course of history (Davis, 1970:124-26).

The revolution begun then continues today. Since the nineteenth century, the world has become increasingly urban and has done so with increasing speed. Only recently, since the population has become predominantly urban, has the rate of urbanization slowed. But still the influence of the city continues to grow. The modern city is an outgrowth of the preindustrial city, transformed by industrialization and urbanization.

Each of these forces had its own impact, and each impact magnified and altered the impact of the others. We can conceptually dissect the effects of these forces and thus examine the process of transformation. We will see that the contemporary city was formed to a large extent by the nature of the preindustrial city. The forces and processes we have seen operating in the preindustrial city—the need for a social surplus, for a dependable food supply, for raw materials, labor, and social solidarity—continue to operate in the modern city.

The modern city is still integrated with its dependent hinterland, even though we now call this metropolitan dominance. The relationships between the major city and its hinterlands have become more complex, and the hinterland now often contains other cities, as well as farmlands. Contemporary industrial cities have far more complex internal social and physical structures than those found in preindustrial cities. However, certain patterns developed in the preindustrial city—such as wards or quarters, segregation on the basis of ethnic or occupational group, and local economic and social regulation—remain.

Urbanization is probably the most important force that has produced the modern city and its social patterns. Urbanization has had crucial consequences on the nature of cities and city life. There has been growth in the size of cities, growth in the proportion of the population living in cities, and numerous changes in urban life style. It no longer takes a massive rural population to produce the social surplus needed for cities; each farmer supports many city residents. As a result, most of the population can and does live in cities, contributing to the development of a truly urbanized society.

To understand the consequences of urbanization, we must examine modern developments and the internal physical and social structures of the city. We must look at the relationships between the city and the society. And, finally, we must come to understand how cities affect social life. What problems exist in the city as a result of its social structure? How are these problems manifested, and how does the city itself cause the problems?

Glossary

Black Plague also called the Black Death. A disease that swept Europe in 1348-50, killing at least a quarter of the population. Transmitted to man by fleas from black rats and other rodents. After the major attack, there were other outbreaks throughout Europe over the years. The last major outbreak occurred in 1665

cottage industry an early form of industrial production in which work was performed in the cottages of workers rather than in a central location, such as a factory

feudal system highly structured, hierarchical form of social organization characterized by ascribed social position, low social mobility, and status differentiation based on law as well as custom; rank was made evident by titles and symbols

guild a form of organization based on occupation and structured in the same way as the feudal society in which it occurred

hinterland the territory surrounding a settlement that depends on the settlement for services and that provides raw materials, products, and workers for the settlement

Neolithic period a period in early history from about 6000 B.C. to 3000 B.C.

Paleolithic period a period in early history ending about 6000 B.C.

social surplus goods produced in excess of the amount needed for survival by farmers and other workers in primary industries (hunting, mining, fishing) that thus becomes available for others in the society

tithe a proportion of all goods produced or of time spent working; a payment of money or work made to church, society, or the lord of the land

References

Adams, Robert McC.
1968   "The Evolution of Urban Society: Early Meso-
       potamia and Prehistoric Mexico." In *Urbanism
       in World Perspective,* edited by Sylvia F. Fava,
       pp. 98-115. New York: Thomas Y. Crowell Co.,
       Inc.

Childe, V. Gordon
1970   "The Urban Revolution." *Town Planning
       Review* 21, 1(April 1950):3-17. In *Neighborhood,
       City, and Metropolis,* edited by Robert Gutman
       and David Popenoe, pp. 111-18. New York:
       Random House, Inc.

Cook, Robert C.
1969   "The World's Great Cities: Evolution or Devolu-
       tion?" *Population Bulletin* (1960). In *Urbanism,
       Urbanization, and Change,* edited by Paul H.
       Meadows and Ephraim H. Mizruchi, pp. 29-51.
       Reading, Mass.: Addison-Wesley Publishing Co.,
       Inc.

Davis, Kingsley
1970   "The Origin and Growth of Urbanization in the
       World." *American Journal of Sociology*
       61(1955):430-37. In *Neighborhood, City, and
       Metropolis,* edited by Robert Gutman and David
       Popenoe, pp. 120-30. New York: Random
       House, Inc.
1973   "The First Cities: How and Why Did They
       Arise?" In *Cities: Their Origin, Growth, and
       Human Impact,* edited by Kingsley Davis, pp.
       9-19. San Francisco: W. H. Freeman & Com-
       pany Publishers.

Langer, William L.
1973   "The Black Death." *Scientific American* (Febru-
       ary 1964). In *Cities: Their Origin, Growth, and
       Human Impact,* edited by Kingsley Davis, pp.
       106-11. San Francisco: W. H. Freeman & Com-
       pany Publishers.

Mumford, Lewis
1961   *The City in History.* New York: Harcourt, Brace
       & World, Inc.

Pirenne, Henri
1961   "Northern Towns and Their Commerce." In
       *History of Western Civilization: Medieval
       Europe,* Topic V. Selected readings by the Col-
       lege History Staff, pp. 48-76. 2d ed. Chicago:
       University of Chicago Press. From *The Cam-
       bridge Medieval History,* vol. VI, pp. 505-27.
       Cambridge: Cambridge University Press, 1932.

Sjoberg, Gideon
1970   "The Preindustrial City." *American Journal of
       Sociology* 60 (March 1955):438-55. In
       Neighborhood, City, and Metropolis, edited by
       Robert Gutman and David Popenoe, pp. 167-76.
       New York: Random House, Inc.
1973   "The Origin and Evolution of Cities." *Scientific
       American* (September 1965). In *Cities: Their
       Origin, Growth, and Human Impact,* edited by
       Kingsley Davis, pp. 19-27. San Francisco: W. H.
       Freeman & Company Publishers.

Weber, Max
1970   "The Nature of the City." In *The City.* New
       York: Free Press, 1958. Reprinted in
       Neighborhood, City, and Metropolis, edited by
       Robert Gutman and David Popenoe, pp. 150-67.
       New York: Random House, Inc.

White, Lynn
1972   "Technology and Social Change." In *Social
       Change,* edited by Robert A. Nisbet, pp. 101-23.
       New York: Harper & Row.

Suggested Readings

Childe, V. Gordon. *Man Makes Himself.* New York:
    Mentor, 1951. A relatively brief review of the rise of
    civilization from an essentially anthropological-
    historic viewpoint. Chapter 10 deals with the urban
    revolution.

Pirenne, Henri. *Medieval Cities.* Princeton: Princeton
    University Press, 1952. The definitive work on the
    nature of social and economic organization in
    medieval cities.

Sjoberg, Gideon. *The Preindustrial City.* New York:
    Free Press, 1960. An extended discussion and analysis
    of the characteristics of preindustrial cities.

Weber, Max. *The City.* Martindale, Don, and
    Neuwirth, Gertrud, trans. and ed. New York: Free
    Press, 1958. One of the classic works in urban
    sociology. Weber's historic-sociological analysis of
    the nature of cities and their effects on society.

Notes

1. For an example of the changes in social organization of work and of whole communities that were required by the alteration of agricultural techniques, see White (1972:101-23). White discusses how farmers were forced to cooperate with each other and how village authority changed hands as a result of the invention of the moldboard plow. Similar changes in social relationships were undoubtedly required earlier in history by the invention of such techniques and products as irrigation, stock breeding, and wheeled vehicles.

2. The sizes of cities listed in table 3.1 and in the following paragraph are taken from Davis (1970: 122), Childe (1970:116), and Sjoberg (1973:19-27).

3. Central American cities that developed later and differently were also dominated by structures that appear to have been religious in function (Sjoberg, 1970:17). For an analysis of the differences between Mesopotamian and Mexican urban developments, see Adams (1968:98-115).

4. At about the same time that cities were evolving in Greece and Rome, other cities were evolving in Central America. Although many attempts have been made to show a connection between the two areas, no direct link has been found. The most interesting thing about the Central American cities is that they seem to have developed without the technological innovations that made more intensive agriculture in other areas possible. There is no evidence that these people knew about breeding of animals for a dependable supply of milk and meat or about metallurgical advances that would allow them to make plows. Indeed, these cities appear to have developed even without the wheel. This brings into question the idea that these technological innovations were necessary to the evolution of cities. However, because we do not have many details about the evolution of these cities, we will not abandon our line of thinking about the connection between technological innovation and city development. See, for example, Childe (1970:117-18), Sjoberg (1973:20-21), and Adams (1968:98-115).

5. Life expectancy appears to have been limited to about twenty years. See Mumford (1961:281-96).

6. Divorce involved civil, religious, and often political concerns especially among the nobility. Rarely did it center, as it does today, on personal characteristics, and especially not on feelings.

7. The highest level of segregation of women was reached in Korea, where women were permitted to be on the public streets only at times when men were not present. While this was an extreme form of sexual differentiation, it exemplified the type of role differentiation that existed in less stringent forms in most preindustrial cities (Sjoberg, 1970:172).

8. See the discussion of Durkheim, Tönnies, and Weber in chapter 2.

4 The Development and Nature of Urban-Metropolitan Society

Over time, definitions of urban populations and methods of collecting data about them have changed from era to era. Therefore, statistics describing the numbers of people and the proportions of populations living in urban areas are not totally reliable. However, they do give us a rough estimate of the extent of urbanization at various times in various societies. Table 4.1 indicates generally the levels of urbanization in England and the United States over the past two centuries.

Table 4.1 Degree of Urbanization, 1801 Projected to 2050

Society	Date	% of population living in places of at least 100,000 people	% of population living in cities of at least 20,000 people
England	1801	10.0	—
	1901	35.0	58.0
	1970	72.0	79.0
U.S.A.	1900	18.7	26.0
	1920	26.0	35.8
	1940	28.8	40.0
	1960	28.4	44.4
	1970	27.7	44.5
World	1970	24.0	37.0
	(2000)	(25.0)	(45.0)
	(2050)	(50.0)	(90.0)

Sources United States data for 1900-60 taken from Taeuber and Taeuber (1971:67). United States data for 1970 taken from U.S. Bureau of the Census (1975:19). In all years U.S. data refers to population of places of 25,000 or more rather than 20,000. English data for 1801 and 1901 from Davis (1955:430-37); world data and English (United Kingdom) data for 1970 from Davis (1969:Table A). (1970 data refers to population of places of 100,000 or more and to places defined as urban by individual countries.) World projections for 2000 and 2050 from Davis (1955:430-37). See also United Nations (1974).

Figures are also given for world urban populations in 1970, as well as estimates of future urban development around the world.

In 1801 the population of London, England, was 865,000, but only 10 percent of all people in England lived in cities of 100,000 or more. In 1901, 35 percent of the population lived in cities of 100,000 or more, which is triple the proportion of the previous century. Although London's population did not triple, the total urbanized population had increased over three times. In fact, by the beginning of the twentieth century more than half (58 percent) of the English population lived in cities of 20,000 or more. Half a century later, in 1958, the percentage of the population living in cities of 100,000 or more had not risen very much (only to 38 percent), but the percentage of the population living in cities of 20,000 or more had gone up from 58 percent to 69 percent. England was obviously in the vanguard of urbanization; the percentage of the population living in cities in England in 1801 (that is, 10 percent) was not reached elsewhere until fifty years later.

On a worldwide basis, since the beginning of the nineteenth century the percentage of the world's population living in cities of 20,000 or more has doubled every fifty years. Similar changes have occurred in the number of cities of 100,000 or more. In 1800 there were only 50 cities of 100,000 or more, in 1950 there were 900 such cities, and in 1957 there were 191 cities of a million people or more (Davis, 1955:124-26; United Nations, 1974:36).

Wood engraving *Ludgate Hill* by
Gustave Dore—a romanticized view
of the crush and bustle of 19th century London.

The World's Urban Populations

Few countries agree on the definition of an urban place or on how its boundaries are determined. Census techniques differ from country to country, and what may be urban in an agricultural country may not be urban in a highly urbanized country. For cross-national comparisons, the United Nations Population Division uses definitions in which each category is five times larger than the previous category (United Nations Bureau of Social Affairs, 1973:64-65):
The UN's minimum definition of an urban place as 20,000 persons is considerably larger and more restrictive than the definition used in many countries. The U.S. Bureau of the Census defines any place of 2,500 or more as urban. But the UN's definition is also applied more generously than the U.S. definition is, so that if a number of small places that are close together meet the size criterion, the combined population is counted as urban. This also means that if a large population center includes several smaller centers, the smaller ones are counted as part of the larger one. Thus if a suburb of 100,000 persons, which would constitute a **city** by UN definition, lies within a metropolis of 5 million persons, it would be counted only as part of a multimillion city.

Table 4.2   United Nations Definitions of Urban
              Areas

Population	Characterization
20,000 and over	Urban population
100,000 and over	City population
500,000 and over	Big city population
2,500,000 and over	Multimillion cities
12,500,000 and over	Metropolitan regions

Using these definitions, the UN estimated the world's urban population in 1960 to be 25 percent of the total population. The population living in **big cities** (those of one-half million or more) was about 12 percent of the world's population and about 47 percent of the world's urban population. Table 4.2 shows that in some parts of the world—North America and Oceania, for example—50 percent or more of the population lives in urban areas and almost a third lives in big cities. In East Asia, where only one-fifth of the population lives in urban areas, one-half of the urban population lives in big cities.

Although the regions with the highest percentage of urban population also tend to have the highest proportions of people living in big cities, this is not a universal rule. In Oceania, East Asia, and Latin America, where half or less than half of the population lives in urban areas, most urban residents live in big cities. These cities—for example, Calcutta—are urban in size but often are not urban in ways of life. This indicates that metropolitan areas can develop before a society is highly urbanized. Indeed, the growth of cities, even of large cities, is not the same as the **urbanization** of society.

Projections of Urban Populations

If urbanization continues at the rates that characterized the world population between 1800 and 1950, then 25 percent of the world's population will be living in cities of 100,000 or more by the year 2000. Fifty percent of the world's population will be living in cities of 100,000 or more by the year 2050. At these same rates of growth, 45 percent of the world's population by the year 2000 and 90

Table 4.3   Indicators of the World Urban Population

Region	1960 Urban (20,000 or more) as percent of total population	1960 Big city (500,000 or more) as percent of urban population	1970 Percent urban (by each country's own definition)	1975 Percent of total population in cities of million or more
World Total	25%	47%	36.7%	12.8%
Europe (excluding U.S.S.R.)	41	42	64.6	19.3
U.S.S.R.	Not available	Not available	56.6	9.2
North America	57	64	74.2	32.9
East Asia	20	54	26.5	12.9
South Asia	14	37	20.9	6.8
Latin America	32	52	56.7	21.9
Africa	13	30	21.5	5.5
Oceania	50	62	69.9	26.9

Source   United Nations Bureau of Social Affairs (1973:tables 4, 8, 9); United Nations (1974:33, 36).

percent by the year 2050 will be living in cities of 20,000 or more. These are projections based on past rates, not predictions, but if the past is any guide, the future urban population of the world will be this large.

If 90 percent of the world's population lives in cities of 20,000 or more, they are living in fairly dense settlements. Under such circumstances, little land can be cultivated, and there will be few farmers. It takes far more than 10 percent of today's world population to feed everyone.[1] For 90 percent of the population of the world to live in cities of 20,000 or more less than one hundred years from now, there will have to be a technological revolution in agriculture, if the remaining 10 percent is to feed the urban population.

The Growth of Urban Areas

Along with the increase in the percentage of population living in cities has come an increase in city size. That is, the urban population is growing because of increases in both the number of cities and the size of cities. Cities or metropolises of five to fifteen million people are a development of the twentieth century and are qualitatively as well as quantitatively different from smaller cities. Much expansion has been outward along the periphery of the city. **Suburbs** are growing faster than **central cities.** This has been the trend in London since about 1860 and in the United States since the beginning of the twentieth century (Davis, 1955:127-29).

As places grew larger, the forms of social organization and the sources of communal integration changed. A new concept had to be

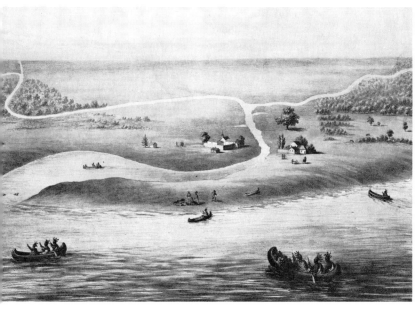

developed that took into account the increased size and scope of these populations and the new forms of social integration. This concept was the **metropolis,** a central city of 50,000 or more and the socially and economically integrated surrounding area (Duncan, 1957:34-45; Shyrock, 1957:163-70).

The metropolis is a conceptual entity that recognizes the difference between a city and the social influence that the city exerts over the people and the territory surrounding it. Neither a political nor a legal entity, the metropolis is a set of social relationships based on territory. The metropolitan community is the organization of people and institutions that perform or facilitate the performance of the communal functions that involve both the city and the surrounding area.

Although the U.S. Bureau of the Census distinguishes between metropolitan and nonmetropolitan areas and between the central city of the metropolis and the rest of the metropolitan area, it does not classify the different types of suburbs or distinguish between suburbs and rural areas that make up the metropolis. Since the metropolis is composed of the central city that gives it its name and all surrounding socially and economically integrated counties, there are many small towns, some large cities, and some rural areas included in the metropolis. The concept recognizes that all these areas—all towns, cities, and farms—are part of a single metropolitan community. They are dependent on one another, and therefore they are functionally and socially integrated with one another.

To understand the contemporary city, we must understand the areas within the metropolis that have variously been called belts, zones, or rings. The areas beyond the central city have social and ecological relationships to one another and to the central city. Regardless of how these outlying areas are conceptualized—whether as smaller cities, subsectors, zones, belts, or rings around the metropolitan center—they are consistent enough so that coherent areas can be identified (Schnore, 1970; Kish, 1954:388-98; Dobriner, 1970; Lineberry, 1975:1-9; Birch, 1975:25-35; Farley, 1976:3-38).

The Growth of the American Metropolis

The growth of **metropolitan areas** has been rapid and dramatic. Developments in technology, especially transportation, and in social structure have made these concentrations of large numbers of people possible. These same forces have also made the diffusion of metropolitan areas possible, not only by population growth but also by geographical growth and extension. The history of metropolitan growth is linked with improvements in living standards and wider choices of life styles and goods and services. For example, it is easier to live and work in a metropolitan area of 3 million people today than it was to live and work in a city of 500,000 in previous generations. Under current conditions there are more advantages and fewer disadvantages to living on the fringe of the city than there were only twenty-five to thirty years ago (Davis, 1955:128-30).

Early Twentieth Century Population Concentration

The movement of the rural population into urban areas was the most striking social change of the last decades of the nineteenth century and the first three decades of the twentieth century (McKenzie, 1957; Davis, 1955).[2] From 1800 to 1930 the percentage of the population classified as urban rose from 28 percent to 56 percent. The term *urban*, however, is ambiguous. The U.S. Bureau of the Census classifies as urban any settlement of 2,500 or more. Therefore, Kenilworth, Illinois, and Cooperstown, New York, as well as Chicago and New York City, are classified as urban places. More precise conceptions of the degree of urbanism can be derived from the size of the place in which people live. In truth, to understand urban life, we must view the city not only as a mass of people but also as a way of life. We should be interested in the development and spread of urban life.

The evidence is dramatic for urbanization, viewed as the concentration of population, during the first part of the twentieth century in this country. In the first third of the century the number of counties needed to include one-fourth of the country's population decreased from thirty-nine to twenty-seven, and the number of counties needed to include three-fourths of the population decreased from over one thousand to just over eight hundred. The population seems to have concentrated in areas of high density. In 1920, 265 counties had a density of one hundred or more people per square mile. In 1910 these counties had 45 percent of the country's total population and in 1930 nearly 53 percent.

Thus population growth took place in densely settled counties. These population concentrations tended to be within easy, daily access of a city of 100,000 or more and near a deep-water port (McKenzie, 1933; Davis, 1955; Taeuber and Taeuber, 1971:27-73). Urbanization and metropolitanization began to occur around large population concentrations that had access to raw materials by way of water. Subsequent development of metropolitan areas continued this pattern.

Causes of Metropolitan Development

During the first third of the twentieth century, technological innovations, especially in transportation, and the economic processes of our society contributed to the growth of the metropolis (McKenzie, 1933; Davis, 1955; Chinitz, 1964:4-12). These forces originally concentrated the population in the cities. They continue to influence metropolitan growth, but now by permitting the movement of the urban population into the suburbs and beyond.

Impact of steam. The impact of the Industrial Revolution on American cities shows how much industrialization depended on steam power. Steam-powered factories and railroad engines helped integrate the city and rural areas by making both production and distribution more efficient. The transportation of agricultural produce over long distances became feasible, enlarging the cities' supporting hinterlands. With the agricultural output of the world put at their disposal by steam-powered transport, cities could improve their standard of living and be assured of a dependable social surplus in times of need.

Within the city, steam led to great expansion of the industrial base and heavily influenced the spatial distribution of activities in the central city. Steam power required an enormous, continuous, dependable fuel supply, primarily coal. Steam plants had to be located near railheads or seaports where the imported coal was received. Steam power itself could not be transmitted far, and it was most efficiently generated and used in large, compact, central locations (National Resources Committee, 1937:29-30). This limited the distance from the port or transportation terminal that industrial plants could spread. Early American industrial cities developed in a centralized form partially because of the strong influence of steam power.

Impact of electricity. The steam engine was quickly supplanted by the electric engine and the internal combustion engine, but not before the spatial arrangement of American cities had been established. Electricity, like steam, is most efficiently generated in a central location, but, unlike steam, it may be efficiently transmitted over long distances. The city could deconcentrate, and manufacturing plants could be scattered over a relatively wide area and still have access to economical electric power.

Electricity is a quiet, clean, safe, and effective power source for local transportation. With the development of electricity, electric-powered trolley transportation systems within cities became possible. During the early 1900s, however, despite the potential of electric transportation systems for deconcentrating the city, electricity was used almost exclusively within the crowded central urban area. In this sense, the electric trolley continued the pattern of earlier steam-based systems. However, when electricity was used in communication (radio, telegraph, and telephone), it became instrumental in expanding city boundaries by reaching out into surrounding areas (National Resources Committee, 1937; Tobin, 1976:96-103).

Impact of the internal combustion engine. The invention of the internal combustion engine made both urban and rural transportation more flexible. The revolutionary change caused by the internal combustion engine was that the size, rate of growth, and spatial organization of cities came to reflect the general level of knowledge and technology throughout the world. City size, growth rate, and spatial organization no longer depended on local, particularly agricultural and ecological, factors. Through mechanization, agricultural production came to depend not only on local climate and soil conditions, but also on an industrial urban society that could produce the tools, fertilizer, and other goods used in agriculture and support the factories that would process raw agricultural products.

The motor vehicle was probably the most important factor in the spread and growth of metropolitan areas. It not only increased personal mobility, but also led to flexibility in short-distance bulk transportation. The automobile expanded city boundaries by reducing the social and physical isolation of people and small communities outside the city. When cars replaced horse-drawn vehicles or vehicles restricted to tracks, rural areas were brought within easy access of cities, and the urban population with its distinctive life styles began to move more quickly into rural areas (National Resources Committee, 1937:30-31; Tobin, 1976:101-5).

How urban development transformed
one sector of the Philadelphia
metropolitan area over the period of
a few years in the 1950s.

Technology and the Integration of the Metropolis

The metropolis is really a new social and economic organization. It is much more important and much greater in scope than the city because it brings together through transportation and communication the city and all its outlying areas. R. D. McKenzie made one of the earliest statements about the causes of metropolitan expansion:

> By reducing the scale of local distance the motor vehicle extended the horizon of the community and introduced a territorial division of labor among local institutions and neighboring centers which is unique in the history of settlement. The large center has been able to extend the radius of its influence. Its population and many of its institutions, freed from the dominance of rail transportation have become widely dispersed throughout surrounding territories. Moreover, formerly independent towns and villages and also rural territories have become part of this enlarged city complex. This new type of super community organized around a dominant focal point and comprising a multitude of differentiated centers of activity differs from the metropolitanism established by rail transportation in the complexity of its institutional division of labor and the mobility of its population. Its territorial scope is defined in terms of motor transportation and competition with other regions. Nor is this new type of metropolitan community confined to the great cities, it has become the communal unit of local relations throughout the nations [McKenzie, 1933:7].

Clearly, the high degree of mobility and versatility of the motor vehicle combined with the rapidity of communication, particularly by telephone, makes it possible for metropolitan subareas to specialize in certain functions—for example, residential, light commercial, heavy industrial, or service functions. These specialized areas are integrated with the metropolis, even those parts that are quite distant. Through speedy communication and flexible transportation, for example, a serviceman living at one end of a metropolis can be engaged to fix a dishwasher or repair a printing press at the other end of the metropolis. A person can live one place in a city and still work far from home in the same city.

In brief, the technological developments of the early twentieth century—automobile, radio, electricity, telephone—made possible the social and economic integration of widely dispersed areas and the existence of the metropolis as we know it. These innovations made possible the metropolitanwide performance and integration of locality-relevant functions (Hawley, 1971:208-10).

Technology and Spatial Organization

Rail transportation that is dependent on fixed routes and dependence on steam power required that factories and other establishments dealing in bulk goods be centrally located or concentrated on railroad routes or at port facilities. Only after the introduction of motor vehicles and electric power were industrial plants able to obtain supplies and ship products economically regardless of their physical location. Technology thus permitted the dispersion or deconcentration of manufacturing facilities, and made it possible for workers to live in places other than those directly on rail or trolley lines. The motor vehicle not only extended the area of the city, but also permitted the dispersal of its institutions over a much wider area (Chinitz, 1964:7-8; Dyckman, 1970:127; Tobin, 1976:101-9).[3]

Gin Lane by William Hogarth shows a seamy side of 18th century London. (Reproduced courtesy of The Metropolitan Museum of Art, Harris Brisbane Dick Fund, 1932.)

Before technology changed transportation, energy sources, and communication in cities, the metropolitan spatial organization had become relatively fixed. Workers lived near their places of employment, and heavy industry located near fixed transportation centers. As technology changed, these locational restraints weakened and a much freer spatial organization developed. Workers could commute, institutions could communicate, and heavy goods could be moved over great distances efficiently. Not all industry had to be concentrated in one or two districts. Few workers had to live near their jobs, and commercial establishments could be located farther from their clients. Because of technological progress, centers of several different types could become interdependent and function as a single metropolis.

Technology and Public Health

Medical technology also had a dramatic impact on urban growth. The novels of Charles Dickens depict in fiction the unhealthy conditions prevailing in many early English cities. The muckrakers described similar conditions in American cities. People died young, many in infancy. Infant mortality was estimated to have been as high as 180 deaths per thousand live births in New York in 1850 (Mumford, 1961:403-78; Palen, 1975:59; Taeuber and Taeuber, 1971:518; Davis, 1973:102).[4] Disease was common and often fatal, and sanitation was poor. The creation of sewer, sewage treatment, and water purification systems, along with advances in medical science, have made the city a much more livable environment.

The Dynamics of Metropolitan Population Growth

Until relatively recently, more people died in cities than were born there (National Resources Committee, 1937:68; Davis, 1973:102-4). This difference in birth and death rates appears to be characteristic only of societies that became urbanized at the time of the Industrial Revolution. Those societies that have urbanized more recently have grown by natural increase—more births than deaths. Many reasons have been offered for the urban birthrate having been lower than the death rate. One is that jobs available in cities require prolonged education and training, which leads to deferred marriage. This reduces the number of children born to each family. Another reason may be that the proportion of women participating in the labor force is larger in urban areas than in rural areas, reducing the number of women staying home to raise children (Taeuber and Taeuber, 1971:632).

In 1937 it was said that if U.S. cities were to continue to grow, their increased population would have to come from population shifts within the United States rather than from Europe (National Resources Committee, 1937:32). As foreign immigration was reduced, large numbers of rural residents from both the North and the South moved to cities, particularly northern metropolitan cities. As a result, for the first time substantial numbers of blacks were living in northern cities (Taeuber and Taeuber, 1971:749-812). At that time less than half the total population was rural, and the birthrate in rural areas was declining. The decline in rural birthrate in the thirties was taken as an indication that cities were influencing social behavior patterns far beyond their own boundaries and that differences between rural and urban areas were being reduced (Taeuber and Taeuber, 1971: 386-406; Dyckman, 1970).

The combination of declining birthrates and reduced foreign immigration meant that cities at the end of the first third of the twentieth century expected to grow more slowly. To an extent this was prevented by internal migration and a rise in the birthrate, especially after World War II. At the same time, however, cities have aged, and there has been a shift in the distribution of population, resulting in an increase in the number and size of settlements outside the central cities and a slowing of the growth of central cities.

Metropolitan Expansion

In recent decades there has been continual expansion in metropolitan populations as well as in the number of metropolitan areas.[5] Central cities, however, have accounted for a decreasing proportion of the population living in metropolitan areas. Both population growth and territorial growth have occurred within metropolitan areas, but outside the central cities. Rather than being a metropolitan society characterized by urban residents, we have become a metropolitan society characterized by suburban residents. By 1970 the number of people in metropolitan areas living outside the central cities exceeded the number of central city residents. Suburban residents are more urban than rural, and they participate in a society that is more urban than rural (U.S. Bureau of the Census, 1975:table 16; Dobriner, 1970; Dyckman, 1970; Fischer and Jackson, 1976:279-307).

As cities expanded beyond their earliest legal boundaries, they accumulated both population and area, which were integrated legally, socially, and economically into the city. This integration has been facilitated by better transportation and communication. Outlying population centers that were annexed to cities or developed as a result of urban growth continue to depend on cities for specialized services that no single suburb can provide for its citizens (National Resources Commission, 1937:31-33, 67-68; Dyckman, 1970).

These specialized functions include all those that require a large population base for economic viability. Large banks, specialized medical facilities, opera and theater companies, art museums, and shops dealing in expensive or rare items, as well as industries requiring a large labor force, rely on large populations. Modern technological innovations, such as the radio, telephone, mass circulation newspapers, and the automobile have made it possible for the metropolises to perform locality-relevant functions in an integrated fashion for an increasingly large geographic area. The city has begun to provide specialized functions for larger and larger areas, and as it has done so, it has drawn raw materials from a wider area. As it has grown, the city has developed more service functions (McKenzie, 1957; Chinitz, 1964; Schnore, 1970). These trends have produced an increase in the division of labor. This, as Durkheim pointed out, has increased the diversity of the population and thus increased the contrast between various segments of the population.

There are more cities today than there have been in the past. The contemporary city is larger and more complex than earlier cities, and the system of cities that dominate society is also complex. The number of cities, the size of cities, their internal complexity, and their importance to society are all aspects of urbanization and metropolitanization.

The Metropolis in Society

How and to what extent is the United States an urban or metropolitan society? Clearly, not everyone in the United States lives in a metropolitan area. Furthermore, it is not that the number of very large metropolitan areas is increasing or that existing areas are growing larger. Rather, large metropolitan centers are performing functions that are critical to society as a whole. Also the ways in which urban and metropolitan residents perform their functions, including the varied life styles they adopt, now strongly influence the behavior patterns of people who live outside urban and metropolitan areas. Finally, the problems of function performance faced by major urban centers influence the ability of all communities to carry out their own functions.

Cities and metropolitan areas have come to dominate society. To understand urban and metropolitan dominance we must first understand the various functions that cities perform, both for the areas immediately surrounding them and for the larger society. Much of our understanding of these functions is based on central place theory.

Central Place Theory

Thomlinson (1969:131-36) describes a **central place** as the source of goods and services for an area larger than itself. Centrality is not based on size alone, for some small communities are more important as central places than some large communities. A large, specialized mining or industrial city might perform only limited central place functions (Ullman, 1941: 853-64). Population is thus not an adequate measure of centrality. Better measures of central place are the number of central place functions carried out there and the extent of support for those functions.

Central place functions are those specialized financial and administrative tasks that direct, coordinate, influence, and facilitate all other activities in the city and its hinterland (Johnson, 1971:87-102). The central place lies at the **ecological center,** if not the geographical center, of the area—the place that is most accessible from all other parts of the area. It is thus the point at which activities dependent on interchange with or the support of the entire metropolis have the lowest transportation costs and are able to afford the high rents the central location entails. It is the prime location for the retailing and wholesaling of consumer goods, particularly credit, and it is the transportation and communication center for the metropolitan area.

Many central place functions consist of financial services. Traders exchange paper—money and credit, stocks and bonds, contracts and promissory notes. Here traders may invest in private and public businesses through the purchase of stocks and bonds. Here they may gain title to carloads of corn and soybeans or buy contracts for the purchase of corn and soybeans at some later date. In the central place, local banks seek services offered only by Federal Reserve and large metropolitan banks. Large insurance companies locate in the central city. The central place is the center of commercial functions for an entire

metropolitan area (Duncan, 1960; Lieberson, 1961:491-96).

Central place functions result from the centralization of specialized institutions produced by the division of labor that perform numerous supporting services for the financial institutions. These services include accounting, auditing, bookkeeping, legal counseling, insurance, management, promotion, and advertising. The institutions offering these services are usually located in the central place, because they depend on frequent and often face-to-face interaction to establish personal relationships and interpersonal trust. So important is this interaction in the performance of supporting services that those who offer these services compete strongly for space in the central place. Competition raises the cost of rents and gives rise to the very dense use of land that is so typical of the **central business districts** of metropolitan areas.

Central places in major metropolitan areas also have many retail establishments and sales and service outlets. Central places tend to account for a larger proportion of retail sales than would be expected solely on the basis of the number of retail establishments there (Johnson, 1971). This is because these retail establishments cater to the needs of individuals performing central place functions and are able to attract customers from throughout the entire metropolitan region. The population coming to the central place is large enough to support retail, commercial, and entertainment facilities that require a large population for support. The transportation and communication systems required by the central place make it possible for these establishments to attract their clientele from a large, widespread population.

Accurate, up-to-date information about all central place activities is needed by institutions of the central district and by the people who come there for business and pleasure. Thus, another activity that characterizes central places is the collection and dissemination of news. Current information about and for institutions of the central place is of interest throughout the society (Johnson, 1971).

The number and nature of central place functions performed varies according to the size of the city. Central place theory implies that larger cities perform more functions than do smaller places.[6] All cities perform some central place functions for their surrounding dependent territory. The central place functions carried out in larger cities, however, make up a larger proportion of all activities. The types and number of central place functions carried out in a city affect the city's social organization and the opportunities available there.

Types of Cities

Since the urban revolution, the primary urban function has been the provision of a marketplace. In addition, certain cities specialized in two major functions related to the transportation of goods and people.[7] First, some cities developed along transportation routes as trading locations. Second, and perhaps more important, were those cities that specialized in transshipment activities. At such points, goods are transferred from one mode of transportation to another or are processed or repackaged before being shipped on. For example, if goods must be transferred from an oceangoing vessel to a railroad car, workers are needed to perform these tasks. Residents who perform the services and provide the facilities will make up a specialized city. If, in addition to a change in mode of transportation, goods must be processed or repackaged before continuing on to market, more people and facilities will be needed in that location (Harris and Ullman, 1945:7-17).

Large populations supplying transportation facilities and services are not the only types of specialized cities. Cities have developed where natural resources are mined or extracted. In other localities, large populations have gathered to provide special social services—the vacation cities of Miami and Las Vegas, the political-administrative city of Washington, D.C., and the religious-political cities of Rome and Salt Lake City, for example.

A specialized industrial city develops when an industry within the city becomes the nucleus for many similar industries and related services. Industrial concentration provides a market for supporting services and related industries—supply facilities, machine shops, consultants, and other products and services. New companies spring up, for example, when individuals who know about the facilities and processes in the major industry attempt to start competing companies. The process of industrial concentration in a single industry will continue until the advantages of concentration are outweighed by business competition, as well as by the costs imposed by congestion and competition for land. The development of the nuclear instrumentation and electronics industries around Boston was based on the technical expertise of university professors teaching at schools in the area. The proliferation of chemical industries in the Southwest was based on the presence of personnel from oil companies located there. This industrial

A Case for the Central City—New York, 1967

The decision to build a new headquarters building for McGraw-Hill in New York City has been a long time in the making, and it came only after a comprehensive search and a careful weighing of many alternatives. . . . Ten years ago, we transferred some of our New York City operations—mainly clerical, circulation, and distribution—to Hightstown, N.J., where we own several hundred acres and have erected two office buildings and a book distribution center. Later, we built major book distribution centers near St. Louis and San Francisco. These decentralization moves turned out quite well. Yet, the more we explored the possibilities for our headquarters building, the more our thoughts seemed to turn to the advantages of remaining in New York City. Why?

The reason can be explained partly by statistics. New York is, of course, a city of superlatives—everything is the biggest, or tallest, or best. In a business sense, it simply has no rival. With Wall Street and the New York and American Stock Exchanges located here, it is the financial center of the country. It is also the corporate headquarters of the country, with some 150 of the top 500 companies located in Manhattan. The United Nations makes New York a world political center. More importantly, it is . . . the largest communication center in the world. There are 1,359 publishers of books, magazines, and newspapers located here, 146 news syndicates, and the headquarters of every national radio and television network. New York's 1,137 advertising agencies also make it the nation's advertising center—a fact not unimportant to anyone who publishes magazines.

The value of a central city location to an institution that performs central place functions is illustrated in this description of a publishing company's decision to remain in Manhattan.

But statistics are the smallest part of the story in making our decision. McGraw-Hill's principal assets are . . . talented, creative, imaginative people who make our books interesting, our magazines informative, and our information services useful and important. New York pulls these creative people to its core like a magnet. Part of the reason is that creative people find New York's overwhelming cultural atmosphere irresistible. As a result, a large percentage of the country's authors, editors, and artists are located here. And these are the kinds of people McGraw-Hill needs to be successful. The cultural pulls on these people abound throughout the city. The New York Public Library has 7.5-million books for research and browsing. The city has 700 art galleries to inspect, 48 classical music groups to hear, 40 museums to see, a spectacular and growing Lincoln Center, and a new "happening" almost every day. It has the excitement and environment which creative people thrive on. Whatever their needs or inclinations, they can better satisfy them in New York than anywhere else. . . .

It's true that New York has its problems. But we feel it has the strength, the permanence, and compelling desire to overcome its difficulties and keep it the Number One city of the world. So, we are betting on New York's long-term good future, and in our relatively small way, McGraw-Hill is going to stay here and help make that future.

Source Shelton Fisher, "Why Build in New York?" *McGraw-Hill News,* Nov. 30, 1967.

concentration pattern has developed mainly since World War II as industries and their supporting services have become more interdependent. Prior to the war most industrial cities, especially those outside the northeastern United States, specialized in a single industry (Harris and Ullman, 1945:7-17).

Today, even cities dominated by a single industry, like Detroit, an automobile-manufacturing city, have become increasingly involved with their hinterlands and the services they provide. Akron, Ohio, for example, has become part of Detroit's hinterland, specializing in automotive tire production.

As cities and their industries have grown, cities have had to assume administrative functions and provide facilities that permit industries to operate nationally and internationally. This is one important responsibility of the metropolis in today's society.

The Location of Cities

Cities are not randomly located. Visually, there is a definite spatial arrangement of cities, as seen on a map, and one may even see patterns of settlements developing on the basis of differences in size and internal population density. For the most part, cities are located in places that maximize their ability to generate a social surplus and to integrate their economic activities with the activities of the rest of society.

Although a pattern of city locations can be discerned, it did not develop by plan.[8] Accidents and incidents in history probably led to the founding of many cities. However, there seems to be an organizational principle underlying the pattern of urban locations—

the satisfaction of needs resulting from the social and economic activities that occur in cities. Cities seem to be located as close as possible to the sources of raw materials used by the city's major industries and to the people who consume the products of the city.

The first, if not the best known, theory of city location was Von Thunen's work on the isolated state published in 1826.[9] Von Thunen postulated that if all of a society were located on a flat plane without geographic features, the largest city would be located in the center of the plane, with smaller settlements located in concentric circles around it. Each circle would represent a different type of land use, and settlements would be smaller as the distance from the center increased. This theory applies to cities that are located on flat planes, such as the steppes of Russia, parts of Western Europe, and the American Midwest.

Other early theorists noted that both transportation routes and modes of transportation affected the location of a city. Kohl (in 1841) focused on transportation routes; Cooley (in 1894) emphasized transshipment points; Haig (in 1927) looked for causes of population concentration in the costs of transportation.

Christaller's Theory of the Location of Cities

Without a doubt the single most influential theory about the location of cities was formulated in 1933 by Walter Christaller (Ullman, 1941; Thomlinson, 1969:127-39; Hawley, 1971:221-22). Christaller's theory assumes, first, that a city performs its central place functions for the productive land that surrounds and supports the city. Christaller implies that the center develops and exists because the productive land needs essential services. Chicago, for example, would exist even without the Chicago River or Lake Michigan because the Midwest needs an urban center. Without the lake and the river, there would still be an urban center as large as the present Chicago, although it might be located elsewhere. Christaller's second assumption is that the urban center is located at the geographical center of the land it serves and that the land, in turn, serves as a tributary area for the city. The larger the city, the larger the tributary area that supports it and is, in turn, served by the central place.

If these assumptions are true, cities of different sizes will be scattered throughout a society. Each city will have tributary areas and service functions in direct proportion to its size. The smallest settlement will provide only limited goods and services, such as the things needed daily, while increasingly larger settlements will provide goods and services needed less frequently. The largest city, with the largest service and support area, will provide not only for the daily needs of its residents, but also for the very infrequent needs of residents and institutions in the entire tributary area. Food will be bought close to home, but rarely purchased commodities, such as freezers, refrigerators, and other major appliances, are likely to be purchased in large metropolitan areas. This is especially true of items such as pianos or violins that are purchased not only infrequently, but also by only a small proportion of the population (Berry and Garrison, 1958:84-85). The same reasons explain why professional sports teams are located almost exclusively in metropolitan areas.

All these theories assume that people and institutions make locational decisions (where to live, where to do business, how far to travel to make a purchase or engage in a given activity) on rational grounds. If this is the case, then transportation cost becomes an important factor (Thomlinson, 1969:131). The cost of commuting could determine where one buys a home or locates a factory or office building.

The assumption that locational decisions are made rationally led the early theorists to view cities as having circular tributary and service areas. Christaller observed that a model made up of circular urban territories leaves portions of an area unserved by any city, and he substituted overlapping hexagons for circles in the model. The largest central city provides central place functions for the entire area enclosed in the largest hexagon. The settlement at the center of each successively smaller hexagon performs fewer central place functions for the successively smaller areas covered by those hexagons. Of course, there are fewer large hexagons than small hexagons, and thus fewer large cities performing a full range of central place functions than there are small cities. Christaller showed that this model closely matched the actual distribution of population in southern Germany, and he claimed that the model applied to all Europe. In rural areas the central place functions of the smallest hexagon were performed by hamlets or towns. The next largest hexagon, which included several small hexagons, was a regional city. In successive stages, these hexagons form a pyramid, with the largest urban center at the top (Thomlinson, 1969:127-29; Berry and Garrison, 1958:83-84).

Theoretical shape of tributary areas. Circles leave unserved spaces, hexagons do not. Small hexagons are service areas for smaller places, large hexagons (broken lines) represent service areas for next higher rank central places. (Source: Redrawn from Edward L. Ullman, "A Theory of Location for Cities," *American Journal of Sociology* 46 [May 1941]. Printed by permission.)

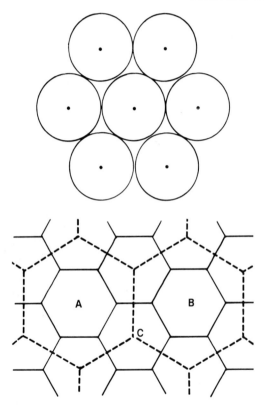

Subsequent theories of urban location, such as those of August Losch and of Harris and Ullman, have adopted Christaller's model of urban functioning and location. Although they disagree with Christaller over the number of levels, these theorists agree that the pattern or urban centers is determined by economic forces, trade areas, and the division of labor. There appears to be agreement, too, over the assumption that central place functions vary according to place size—large cities have more functions and cover wider tributary areas.

Contemporary Urban Location Theories

Contemporary urban location theorists, such as Walter Isard, continue to use Christaller's theory to explain relationships between industrial locations, market areas, land uses, trade patterns, and urban structure and location. Isard wrote, "An urban metropolitan region comes to comprise a hierarchy of strategic nodal sites classifiable by order and degree of dominance" (1956:11). The pattern of city sizes and locations indicates that the activities that take place within a city reflect not only the culture and economic activity of the city itself, but also the distance between cities and the characteristics of the productive areas served by each city.

Urban geographers such as Brian Berry offer an alternative approach to the study of urban location and the spatial distribution of cities. They seem to be more interested in the fact that there are fewer large cities than small cities than in questions of city location or forms of urban behavior (Berry and Garrison, 1958; Boyce, 1971; Alonso, 1971). Urban geographers suggest that the number of cities of each population size is determined by fac-

Table 4.4   A Theory of How Central Places are Related to Each Other in Size and Location

Central Place	Towns Distance Apart (Km.)	Population	Tributary Areas Size (Sq. Km.)	Population
Market hamlet	7	800	45	2,700
Township center	12	1,500	135	8,100
County seat	21	3,500	400	24,000
District city	36	9,000	1,200	75,000
Small state capital	62	27,000	3,600	225,000
Provincial head city	108	90,000	10,800	675,000
Regional capital city	186	300,000	32,400	2,025,000

Source   Edward L. Ullman, "A Theory of Location for Cities" *American Journal of Sociology* 46 (May 1941). Reprinted by permission.

tors such as the distribution of occupations, and thus the economic opportunities available; the dispersion needed to maximize effectiveness in locating and obtaining raw materials; the concentration needed to make the distribution of finished goods most efficient; or simply a probability process distributing cities over various size categories.

Central place theory seems consistent with the notion that there are regularities in the location and distribution of cities of various sizes. However, contemporary central place theorists no longer believe that cities occupy the center of their social space. One corollary of strict central place theory is that there is only one major or **primate city** surrounded by many smaller cities or preurban settlements. A primate city is a single large city in a society that otherwise has achieved a low level of urbanization. This pattern is usually not seen in industrialized societies, and this has led some theorists to criticize central place theory as applicable only to the period in which urban social systems and communities develop (Hawley, 1971:223-24).[10]

Hawley notes that central place theory does not require that one large city or metropolitan system dominate a multitude of small towns. There may be many large, interrelated cities performing central place functions. The primate city seems to occur in societies with a low level of industrial development, a history of colonial development, and low population density. Many developing countries (Asia, Africa, and Latin America) follow the primate city pattern. However, in industrialized societies, all cities perform some central place functions, and all geographic areas are fully served by urban institutions (Hawley, 1971: 224).

This critically important observation implies that an entire industrialized society is in some sense urbanized. If it can be demonstrated that all cities form a system, then all society is part of that system, even those portions that are not urban or metropolitan. Hawley implies then that, regardless of the validity of central place theory, there is a metropolitan hierarchy and that the metropolitan influence extends throughout the society, producing a metropolitan society.

The Metropolitan Society: A System of Cities

We have observed that American society is organically integrated and that all parts are functionally interdependent. Since the critical central place functions are performed in metropolitan areas, the interdependence of society means that the way those central place functions are performed affects what happens in all portions of society, no matter how remote they are from the metropolitan area.

In such a society metropolitan areas can be understood only when viewed as part of a system of metropolitan structures within the entire society (Schnore, 1970). Just as no part of the society is independent of the metropolitan system, no metropolis can be totally understood without understanding the system of which it is a part. Each type of city plays a different role in the system.

The Classification of Cities

As early as the fourteenth century, observers had noted that certain cities specialized in certain crafts, that different cities rested on different economic bases (Borgatta and Hadden, 1965, 1970:266-67), and that this led to interurban cooperation. In the 1930s Roderick McKenzie classified cities by their major industry. McKenzie distinguished between cities engaged in **primary industries** (mining and agriculture), in **secondary industries** (manufacturing), and in **tertiary industries** (commercial functions, such as banking, wholesaling, retailing, and other service functions) (McKenzie, 1933). In 1937 William Ogburn described seven types of cities based on their major economic and industrial activity. Ogburn's seven types were (1) trading cities, (2) factory cities, (3) transportation cities, (4) mining cities, (5) pleasure cities, (6) health resorts, and (7) college cities. Ogburn's criteria allowed him to construct a model of each type of city with which specific cities could be compared.

Duncan and Reiss classified cities on the basis of their regional location, economic activity, economic specialty, population size, and growth rate, among other factors (1956). In many ways their work paralleled Ogburn's, but it pointed more clearly to a hierarchy of cities and metropolitan areas. Duncan and Reiss not only demonstrated that some cities were more influential than others, but also how some cities and metropolitan areas within the hierarchy depended on others.

On the basis of the work of Duncan and Reiss, sociologists have attempted to rank large cities on the basis of their metropolitan characteristics and to list those cities that belong together at each level of the **metropolitan hierarchy.** Rupert Vance and Sara Sutker studied large southern cities and developed a composite index of metropolitan functions (1954:114-34). This index used such indicators of central place functions as amount or number of wholesale sales, business receipts, branch offices, bank clearings, and retail sales. The authors identified four degrees of metropolitan dominance: the regional capitals (Atlanta and Dallas), second order dominants in Duncan's hierarchy, third order subdominants (Houston, New Orleans, Memphis, Louisville, and Birmingham), and lower level subdominants with metropolitan characteristics.

111

Source: Redrawn from Rupert B. Vance and Nicolas J. Demerath (eds.), *The Urban South* (Chapel Hill: University of North Carolina Press, 1954), p. 133. Printed by permission.

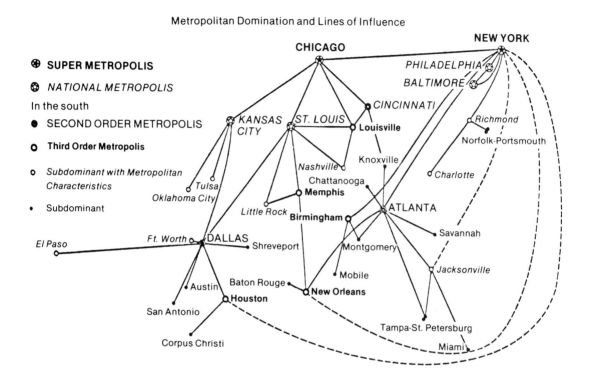

Metropolitan Domination and Lines of Influence

A Metropolitan Hierarchy

Such studies demonstrate not only the existence of a hierarchy of cities, but also the high degree of interdependence and interchange among cities. In 1960 Duncan further established the existence of a national hierarchy of metropolitan areas. He studied the national system of cities on the basis of bank loans, bank exchanges, and commercial and manufacturing activities in fifty-six metropolitan areas of 500,000 or more population. He identified five national cities at the top of the metropolitan hierarchy: New York, Chicago, Los Angeles, Philadelphia, and Detroit.

Each national city serves, and is served by, regional centers. The national cities coordinate the activities in the regional centers; the regional centers influence smaller cities, down to the smallest towns and villages. The influence of the national metropolis flows through the society by way of successively smaller and less dominant cities.

The studies of the metropolitan hierarchy have shown that no metropolis is independent of other metropolitan areas (Schnore, 1970). Furthermore, no single metropolis has complete control over its own financial or social activity because of its interdependence with all metropolitan areas (Lieberson, 1961:491-96).

Activities in small communities and even small cities are influenced by activities in regional centers that are then influenced by activities in national centers. The national centers are influenced not only by one another but also by the regional centers that coordinate the activities originating in the national centers.

The effects of a city's position in the metropolitan hierarchy are not limited simply to central place functions such as the bank data used to establish that position. A city's economic base and position in the metropolitan hierarchy influences the division of labor in the city. Cities with different industrial and occupational structures play different roles in the society, depending on their location in the metropolitan hierarchy (Galle, 1963:260-69). Galle classified metropolitan areas on the basis of type of manufacturing activity, major industries, and occupational distributions. Only those manufacturing cities that have a diversified industrial base and that carry out a large number of metropolitan functions have a strong relationship with their immediately surrounding territory. Cities manufacturing diversified products but carrying out few metropolitan functions offer fewer trading and financial services and are smaller. Cities manufacturing specialized products carry out few metropolitan functions for their immediately surrounding territories, but their products are consumed throughout the society, so their hinterlands are very diffuse.

Regional metropolitan areas with economic bases other than manufacturing activities dominate large and contiguous hinterlands.

Smaller, less dominant metropolitan areas tend to be those that are political rather than economic. Specialization in politics appears to come at the expense of industrial and commercial development. Wholesale trading, for example, is greater in regional metropolitan areas than in regional capitals.

Some Effects of Hierarchical Position

The position of a city in the metropolitan hierarchy not only affects the city's influence on society, but also affects the nature of the labor force within that metropolitan area. Regional metropolises, for example, have more white-collar workers than metropolises based on specialized or diversified manufacturing.

Because all society is more or less integrated with its metropolitan areas, society also has an impact on social activities, social processes, and behaviors within the metropolis. For example, society influences the relationship between occupations and local political processes in metropolitan areas. The nearer a city is to being a national or regional metropolis, the more widespread is its performance of central place functions and the larger the proportion of white-collar workers in its labor force. Workers in administrative, professional, and proprietary occupations tend to be politically active, but they do not necessarily agree with one another. This decreases the probability of agreement on policies and even on the form of political action. This may be why it is difficult to centralize political influence and power in large metropolitan areas (Rossi, 1960).[11] For example, the decision to fluoridate city water supplies has been more

Source: Adapted from Omer Galle, "Occupational Composition and the Metropolitan Hierarchy," *American Journal of Sociology* 69 (November 1963): 260–269.

The Metropolitan Hierarchy

National Metropolis

New York
Chicago
Los Angeles
Philadelphia
Detroit

Diversified Manufacturing with Metropolitan Functions

Boston
Pittsburgh
Saint Louis
Cleveland
Buffalo
Cincinnati

Diversified Manufacturing with Few Metropolitan Functions

Baltimore
Milwaukee
Albany—Schenectady—Troy
Toledo
Hartford
Syracuse

Specialized Manufacturing

Providence
Youngstown
Rochester
Dayton
Allentown—Bethlehem—Easton
Akron
Springfield—Holyoke
Wheeling—Steubenville
Charleston, West Virginia

Special Cases

Washington, D.C.
San Diego
San Antonio
Miami
Tampa—St. Petersburg
Norfolk—Portsmouth
Wilkes-Barre—Hazleton
Knoxville
Phoenix

Regional Metropolis

San Francisco
Minneapolis—St. Paul
Kansas City
Seattle
Portland
Atlanta
Dallas
Denver

Dually Classified Regional Capitals

Louisville
Birmingham
Indianapolis
Columbus
Richmond

Regional Capital

Houston
New Orleans
Memphis
Omaha
Fort Worth
Nashville
Oklahoma City
Jacksonville

easily made in areas where there are fewer managers, officials, professionals, and proprietors in the labor force. Hawley has found that the fewer managers, officials, and proprietors in the labor force the greater the success of urban renewal programs (1963:422-31). Thus, while certain economic and social characteristics permit larger metropolitan areas to exert a degree of control over the rest of society, these same characteristics may lead to greater difficulty in political decision making within the metropolitan area.

The Ecological Field

Because the influence of the metropolis on society is as extensive as it is and because the influence of society on life in the metropolis is equally great, metropolitan areas are perhaps best understood as occupants of particular niches in the **ecological field** that is society (Pappenfort, 1959:380). Pappenfort discovered that, among corporations located in Illinois with facilities located at more than one site, administrative headquarters tended to be located in the Chicago metropolitan area and manufacturing facilities tended to be located outside the metropolis. These findings would support the hypothesis that cities are part of a single national ecological system in which administrative and control functions are carried out in metropolitan areas.

This conclusion is further supported by studies showing that corporations employing 93 percent of the workers in this country have central offices located in metropolitan areas and that this concentration of administrative functions has been increasing (Hawley, 1971: 229). We see, then, that metropolitan areas perform central place functions not only for

their surrounding territories, but also for the entire nation. This is one way that metropolitan areas dominate society (Warren, 1972:243-66; Hawley, 1971:235-37).

Two ecological principles seem to be operating in our contemporary metropolitan society: interdependence and dominance. As society becomes increasingly interdependent, the metropolitan hierarchy becomes more important. A dominant position in the hierarchy gives a city vast influence over other cities in the hierarchy. However, as society has become more metropolitanized, even the most dominant metropolitan areas feel the constraint of forces beyond their control and have less freedom to act independently.

The Forms and Consequences of Metropolitan Domination

If we view society as a single, organically integrated system, we see that metropolitan areas perform critical central place functions of administration and coordination that extend throughout the society, thus influencing the behavior and the ability of other cities and towns to perform their own functions. The performance of central place functions lends a metropolitan character to the total society.

The economic activities of society are coordinated by large banks and other financial institutions located in metropolitan areas that influence economic behavior throughout society (Lieberson, 1961:491-96). These institutions have a national focus and even an international focus. All economic activities and functions are influenced in some way by their decisions. For example, major banks affect the functions of local government through the sale of tax-free municipal bonds, tax anticipation warrants, and other forms of local government financing. Without the cooperation of the major banks, local government agencies would be unable to provide a full range of public services.[12] Many state and private projects, such as road building, housing, and commercial developments, and personal credit depend on the financial decisions of major metropolitan financial institutions.

The prime lending rate established by major metropolitan banks affects the lending practices of local banks and their ability to make loans. Insurance companies, stock exchanges, commodities markets, and other financial institutions located in metropolitan areas also affect local financial conditions. Availability of credit throughout the system, for example, can affect the price that farmers must pay for fertilizer and ultimately affect the cost of food to the consumer. Because the flow of funds to local banks is directly influenced by actions of the major metropolitan financial institutions, the metropolis indirectly controls local activity. Actions taken in the metropolis can limit or expand the availability of funds for home building and commercial suburban developments in smaller communities.

The production, distribution, and consumption of goods and services must be centered in metropolitan areas, for only in these areas is there a labor force skilled enough and large enough to produce and a population large enough to consume the goods. Because of extensive transportation and communications systems, businesses and industries in metropolitan areas have a large and varied labor pool to draw on. Similarly, consumers in metropolitan areas have access to a wide selection of goods and services through these same systems.

For example, it is easier to hire educated clerks and secretaries in metropolitan areas because the large number of job openings attracts more people to the area. The metropolitan area thus tries to provide an adequate education for its youth to maintain a skilled labor pool that will keep employers in the area.

The purchase of large, expensive, relatively rare consumer goods is also easiest in a large metropolitan area. A large pool of potential purchasers is needed to support more than a single store carrying such goods. Therefore, there are likely to be more outlets for large, expensive, durable, or rare consumer goods in metropolitan areas than in smaller areas.

The development of many specialized services in such fields as law, medicine, and technology is possible only because the metropolis offers a large number of potential clients. For example, medical specialists who treat rare diseases or who offer highly skilled services need a large patient base to maintain their practices. Many cardiologists are needed to keep one cardiac surgeon busy enough to maintain a high level of skill in performing relatively rare operations. For each cardiologist, there must be many internists who examine patients and refer a few of them to a cardiologist. Therefore, only in a large metropolitan area will you find many cardiac surgeons.[13] Similarly, computer operations become more efficient if there is a large pool of computer users. Therefore, advanced computer facilities, technology, and skilled personnel are more likely to be found in metropolitan than in nonmetropolitan areas.

The large population of metropolitan areas makes a greater variety of cultural activities possible. Only the largest metropolitan areas can support symphony orchestras, choruses, opera companies, art museums, nightclubs, movies, and other forms of entertainment. Only a metropolis can support many radio stations catering to a variety of tastes. The same is true of professional athletic teams, although few metropolitan areas are able to support more than one team in a single sport.

The mass media—television, radio, and print—provide most news and entertainment on a nationwide basis. Network programming is designed to reach the largest possible audience, that is, the audience in metropolitan areas. Thus, most information, entertainment, and advertising is designed for, and reflects, metropolitan tastes and views.

One effect of centralizing news and entertainment media in cities and assuming a metropolitan audience is that metropolitan areas have great influence on life styles and tastes throughout society. Advertising, which profoundly influences tastes, life styles, and consumption patterns, is also metropolitan-oriented. National tastes in and preferences for cars, clothes, toothpastes, deodorants, food, drink, and many other products are at least influenced by the millions of dollars spent on advertising such products.

The metropolitan image of acceptable life styles, tastes, and behavior patterns thus is transmitted throughout the society by the mass media in the form of news, entertainment, and advertising. The entire society is therefore influenced by ways of life in the metropolis. What the media describe as popular in a metropolis may well become popular everywhere.

In summary, the metropolis influences virtually all aspects of social life in all portions of society, no matter how isolated physically a community may be from metropolitan areas. Some influence is easily detected and measured, as was the case with economic domination. Other influences are much more subtle and hard to quantify. Nevertheless, it is possible to see that metropolitan areas exercise domination throughout the society that influences the behavior of other communities and gives a metropolitan character to their social life on both the group and individual levels.

Not all mass media effects on metropolitan areas are positive. When problems develop in the metropolis and its institutions are unable to perform their communal functions, the mass media communicate throughout society images of alienation and isolation in city life.

The spreading of metropolitan mores, social styles, tastes, modes of interaction, norms, and behavior patterns throughout society by the mass media and by migration may well make futile contemporary attempts to determine whether there is a uniquely urban life style. The contemporary United States is truly an urban or metropolitan society.

Summary

We have traced the history of urban settlements from prehistory to the present. We have noted how both primitive settlements and contemporary metropolises depend on and serve their tributary areas. While goods and services may have changed, the relationship between the city and its hinterland has changed only in degree. Cities still need a social surplus; a city and its hinterland remain interdependent.

Modern forms of energy, transportation, and communication have altered the size of hinterlands and made the spatial organization of metropolises much more complex. The metropolitan society has extended its hinterland to the entire world. With this extension has come complex forms of metropolitan dominance. Where dominance once meant only military conquest and occupation, it now takes the form of economic, social, and cultural interchange. Cities and society are now interdependent.

Glossary

big city   defined by the United Nations as a city of 500,000 to 2.5 million persons

central business district   the ecological center of a city, the major business district where central place functions are performed for a city

central city   a city of 50,000 or more persons, or twin cities with a combined population of at least 50,000, that performs central place functions for a hinterland; the immediate hinterland is the metropolitan area named after the central city

central place   the source of goods and services for an area larger than itself

central place functions   the financial, administrative, and coordinating functions carried out for a city and its hinterland; also the functions that depend on access by a large population

city   defined by the United Nations as a place of 100,000 or more persons

ecological center   that area that is most accessible from all other places in the area, generally the location of the central business district

ecological field   the entire society as an environment to which cities, as communities, must adapt

metropolis   a central city of 50,000 or more persons that is socially and economically integrated with its surrounding area

metropolitan area   a city of 50,000 or more persons, plus the county containing the city and all counties socially and economically integrated with the central city, as defined by the Bureau of the Census and the Office of Management and the Budget

metropolitan hierarchy   the organization of metropolitan areas by rank according to their importance to the society and the functions they perform

primate city   a single large city in a society that has a low level of urbanization

primary industry   basic extractive industry—agriculture and mining—and the fabrication of materials used in manufacturing

secondary industry   manufacture of goods

suburb   a settlement within the boundaries of a metropolitan area that is not the central city of that area

tertiary industry   a service industry—the professions, commerce, the arts, and so on

urbanization   the process of populations moving from rural areas to cities; the extent of development of an urban society; the process by which individuals learn to live in an urban society

References

Acosta, Maruja, and Hardoy, Jorge E.
1972   "Urbanization Policies and Land Reforms in Revolutionary Cuba." In *Latin American Urban Research,* vol. 2, edited by Guillermo Geisse and Jorge E. Hardoy, pp. 167-77. Series edited by Francine F. Rabinovitz and Felicity M. Trueblood. Beverly Hills, Calif.: Sage Publications, Inc.

Alonso, William A.
1971   "A Theory of the Urban Land Market." In *Internal Structure of the City,* edited by Larry S. Bourne, pp. 154-59. New York: Oxford University Press.

Berry, Brian J. L., and Garrison, William L.
1958   "Alternate Explanations of Urban Rank-Size Relationships." *Annals of the Association of American Geographers* 48:83-91.

Birch, David L.
1975   "From Suburb to Urban Place." *Annals* 422 (November):25-35.

Borgatta, Edgar F., and Hadden, Jeffrey K.
1965   *American Cities: Their Social Characteristics.* Chicago: Rand McNally & Company.
1970   "The Classification of Cities." In *Neighborhood, City, and Metropolis,* edited by Robert Gutman and David Popenoe, pp. 253-64. New York: Random House, Inc.

Boyce, Ronald R.
1971   "The Edge of the Metropolis: The Wave Theory Analog Approach." In *Internal Structure of the City,* edited by Larry S. Bourne, pp. 104-12. New York: Oxford University Press.

Chinitz, Benjamin
1964   "City and Suburb: The Economics of Metropolitan Growth." In *City and Suburb: The Economics of Metropolitan Growth,* edited by Benjamin Chinitz, pp. 3-50. Englewood Cliffs, N.J.: Prentice-Hall, Inc.

Davis, Kingsley
1955   "The Origin and Growth of Urbanization in the World." *American Journal of Sociology* 61:430-37.
1969   *World Urbanization 1950-1970, Volume I. Basic Data for Cities, Countries, and Regions.* Rev. ed. Berkeley: University of California Institute for International Studies.
1973   "The Evolution of Western Industrial Cities." In *Cities: Their Origin, Growth, and Human Impact,* edited by Kingsley Davis, pp. 100-106. San Francisco: W. H. Freeman & Company Publishers.

Dobriner, William
1970   "The Growth and Structure of Metropolitan Areas." In *Class in Suburbia,* edited by William Dobriner, pp. 143-66. Englewood Cliffs, N.J.: Prentice-Hall, Inc., 1963. Reprinted in *Neighborhood, City, and Metropolis,* edited by Robert Gutman and David Popenoe, pp. 190-205. New York: Random House, Inc.

Duncan, Otis Dudley
1957   "Community Size and the Rural-Urban Continuum." In *Cities and Society,* edited by Paul K. Hatt and Albert J. Reiss, Jr., pp. 35-45. 2d ed. Glencoe, Ill.: Free Press.

1960   *Metropolis and Region.* Baltimore: The John Hopkins University Press.

Duncan, Otis Dudley, and Reiss, Albert J., Jr.
1956   *Social Characteristics of Urban and Rural Communities, 1950.* New York: John Wiley & Sons, Inc.

Dyckman, John W.
1970   "Socioeconomic and Technological Forces in Urban Expansion." In *Urban Expansion, Problems and Needs: Papers Presented at the Administrators' Spring Conference.* Washington, D.C.: Government Printing Office, 1963. Reprinted in *Neighborhood, City, and Metropolis,* edited by Robert Gutman and David Popenoe, pp. 439-59. New York: Random House, Inc.

Farley, Reynolds
1976   "Components of Suburban Population Growth." In *The Changing Face of the Suburbs,* edited by Barry Schwartz, pp. 3-38. Chicago: University of Chicago Press.

Fischer, Claude S., and Jackson, Robert Max
1976   "Suburbs, Networks, and Attitudes." In *The Changing Face of the Suburbs,* edited by Barry Schwartz, pp. 279-308. Chicago: University of Chicago Press.

Galle, Omer
1963   "Occupational Composition and the Metropolitan Hierarchy: The Inter and Intra Metropolitan Division of Labor." *American Journal of Sociology* 69:260-69.

Harris, Chauncey D., and Ullman, Edward L.
1945   "The Nature of Cities." *Annals* 242:7-17.

Hawley, Amos H.
1963   "Community Power Structure and Urban Renewal Success." *American Journal of Sociology* 68 (June 1963):422-31.
1971   *Urban Society.* New York: Ronald Press.

Isard, Walter
1956   *Location and Space-Economy.* Cambridge, Mass.: M.I.T. Press.

Johnson, Earl S.
1971   "The Function of the Central Business District in the Metropolitan Community." In *The Social Fabric of the Metropolis,* edited by James F. Short, Jr., pp. 87-108. Chicago: University of Chicago Press.

Kish, Leslie
1954   "Differentiation in Metropolitan Areas." *American Sociological Review* 19:388-98.

Lieberson, Stanley
1961   "The Division of Labor in Banking." *American Journal of Sociology* 66:491-96.

Lineberry, Robert L.
1975   "Suburbia and the Metropolitan Turf." *Annals* 422 (November):1-10.

Linsky, Arnold
1969   "Some Generalizations Concerning Primate Cities." In *The City in Newly Developing Countries: Readings on Urbanism and Urbanization,* edited by Gerald Breese, pp. 288-94. Englewood Cliffs, N.J.: Prentice-Hall, Inc.

McKenzie, Roderick D.
1933   *The Metropolitan Community.* New York: McGraw-Hill Book Company.
1957   "The Rise of Metropolitan Communities." In *Recent Social Trends,* Research Committee on Social Trends. New York: McGraw-Hill Book Company, 1933. Reprinted in *Cities in Society,* edited by Paul K. Hatt and Albert J. Reiss, Jr., pp. 201-13. 2d ed. Glencoe, Ill.: Free Press.

Mehta, Surinda K.
1969   "Some Demographic and Economic Correlates of Primate Cities." In *The City in Newly Developing Countries: Readings on Urbanism and Urbanization,* edited by Gerald Breese, pp. 295-308. Englewood Cliffs, N.J.: Prentice-Hall, Inc.

Mumford, Lewis
1961   *The City in History.* New York: Harcourt, Brace & World, Inc.

National Resources Committee
1937   "The Process of Urbanization: Underlying Forces and Emerging Trends." In *Our Cities: Their Role in the National Economy,* National Resources Committee, pp. 29-41. Washington, D.C.: Government Printing Office.

Ogburn, William F.
1937   *Social Characteristics of Cities.* Chicago: International Association of City Managers.

Palen, J. John
1975   *The Urban World.* New York: McGraw-Hill Book Company.

Pappenfort, Donnell
1959   "The Ecological Field and the Metropolitan Community." *American Journal of Sociology* 64:380-85.

Rossi, Peter H.
1960   "Theory and Method in the Study of Power in the Local Community." Paper given at the meetings of the American Sociological Association.

Schnore, Leo F.
1970   "Urban Form: The Case of the Metropolitan Community." In *Urban Life and Form,* edited by Werner Z. Hirsch. New York: Holt, Rinehart & Winston, 1963. Reprinted in *Neighborhood, City, and Metropolis,* edited by Robert Gutman and David Popenoe, pp. 393-414. New York: Random House, Inc.

Shyrock, H. S.
1957   "The Natural History of Standard Metropolitan Areas." *American Journal of Sociology* 63:163-70.

Smith, T. Lynn
1970   "The Changing Functions of Latin American Cities." *Studies of Latin American Societies,* pp. 372-89. Garden City, N.Y.: Doubleday & Co., Inc.

Taeuber, Irene B., and Taeuber, Conrad
1971   *The People of the United States in the Twentieth Century* (Census Monograph). Washington, D.C.: Government Printing Office.

Thomlinson, Ralph
1969   *Urban Structure.* New York: Random House, Inc.

Tobin, Gary A.
1976   "Suburbanization and the Development of Motor Transportation: Transportation Technology and the Suburbanization Process." In *The Changing Face of the Suburbs,* edited by Barry Schwartz, pp. 95-112. Chicago: University of Chicago Press.

Ullman, Edward
1941   "A Theory of Location for Cities." *American Journal of Sociology* 46 (May):853-64.

United Nations
1974   *Concise Report on the World Population Situation in 1970-1975 and Its Long-Range Implications.* New York: United Nations.

United Nations Bureau of Social Affairs, Population Division
1973   "World Population Trends, 1920-1960." In *Cities in Change,* edited by John Walton and Donald Carns, pp. 62-90. Boston: Allyn & Bacon, Inc.

U.S. Bureau of the Census
1975   *Statistical Abstract of the United States: 1975.* Washington, D.C.: Government Printing Office.

Vance, Rupert, and Demerath, N. J., eds.
1954 *The Urban South*. Chapel Hill, N.C.: University of North Carolina Press.

Vance, Rupert, and Sutker, Sara S.
1954 "Metropolitan Dominance and Integration." In *The Urban South,* edited by Rupert Vance and N. J. Demerath, pp. 114-34. Chapel Hill, N.C.: University of North Carolina Press.

Warren, Roland
1972 *The Community in America*. 2d ed. Chicago: Rand McNally & Company.

Suggested Readings

Davis, Kingsley. "The Origin and Growth of Urbanization in the World." *American Journal of Sociology,* 61(1955):430-37. The classic analysis of the growth of the urban population through the first half of the twentieth century.

Dobriner, William. "The Growth and Structure of Metropolitan Areas." In *Class in Suburbia*. Englewood Cliffs, N.J.: Prentice-Hall, 1963. An excellent discussion of the various components of the metropolitan area and of the sources of metropolitan development.

Klein, Maury, and Kantor, Harvey A. *Prisoners of Progress: American Industrial Cities 1850-1920.* New York: Macmillan, 1976. In chapter 5 is an excellent description of city expansion and the effects of technological developments on expansion.

National Resources Committee. "The Process of Urbanization: Underlying Forces and Emerging Trends." In *Our Cities: Their Role in the National Economy,* pp. 29-41. Washington, D.C.: Government Printing Office, 1937 (since widely reprinted). A comprehensive analysis of the roles of transportation, energy, and population redistribution on the growth of cities and on their spatial organization.

Schnore, Leo F. "Metropolitan Growth and Decentralization." *American Journal of Sociology* 63 (October 1957): 171-80. A description of the growth and development of metropolitan areas.

Schwartz, Barry, ed. *The Changing Face of the Suburbs.* Chicago: University of Chicago Press, 1976. A valuable collection of papers on suburban populations and their characteristics in the second half of the twentieth century.

Notes

1. The United Nations has estimated that only 25 percent of the world's population lived in cities of 20,000 or more in 1960. If only half of the rest were farmers, 37.5 percent of the world's population was required to feed the world (United Nations Bureau of Social Affairs, 1973:70).

2. See also the discussion of Wirth and Simmel in chapter 6 for a description of urban ways of living.

3. From the time before the mass adoption of the automobile comes the image of thousands of factory workers leaving their homes and walking in vast streams down the street to the factory gate. Such massive concentrations and "communities" of workers, once so critical to the development of unions, no longer exist, partly because of the automobile. Further, both natural obstacles, such as mountains, and the continuing effects of European rule altered these developments in Latin America. The freedom of movement that the automobile had provided in the United States was not achieved in Latin America until the airplane altered the time-distance ratio (Smith, 1970:27-28). There is a more detailed analysis of contemporary urban transportation in chapter 11 of this book.

4. There is a more detailed analysis of urban health problems in chapter 11 of this book.

5. The U.S. Census Bureau defines a metropolitan area as a central city of at least 50,000 plus the rest of the county containing that city and all surrounding, contiguous counties that are socially and economically integrated with the central city. See chapter 7 for a more extended discussion. By this definition, suburbs are those areas included in the metropolitan area that lie outside the central city.

6. See the discussion of the role of centrality in the theories of Christaller and Isard in Thomlinson (1969:125-31).

7. See the discussion in chapter 3.

8. There are some exceptions to this rule in societies that are currently developing and even in fully developed societies such as the United States. Cuba is attempting to alter the functions of specific cities to alter growth patterns. See Acosta and Hardoy (1972). Brasilia was deliberately planned and located to serve as a central place in the geographic center of Brazil. So-called new towns such as Reston, Virginia, and Columbia, Maryland, and many in Europe have been located in ways designed to maximize access to jobs and other urban facilities. But the ability to plan rationally the location of and to construct new cities in this manner is a very recent development.

9. See the discussion of this work in Ullman (1941: 853-64). Although not as frequently cited as later theories, the influence of Thunen's concept appears unmistakable.

10. Supporters of the concept of primate cities argue, with considerable justification, that in many developing societies, the primate city (one several times larger than the second largest city) provides many functions to the total society and is an important social center. See, for instance, Linsky (1969:288-94) and Mehta (1969:295-308).

11. New York City in the mid-1970s is a prime example of the difficulty of centralizing political power and influence. Elected political leaders, financial leaders, and union leaders all have different ideas about how the city should be run. Disagreements, leading to crises, are more common than agreements.

12. The example of New York is illustrative. In 1975 the Municipal Assistance Corporation was created to refinance the city's debt and provide operating funds controlled by bankers and stockbrokers. The corporation altered city employment patterns, changed the terms of city worker contracts, and forced a reduction in city services.

13. I am indebted to Dr. Jeffrey Schwartz for pointing this out to me.

5

The Internal Structure of the City and Metropolis

By today's standards most early cities were small and relatively homogeneous. Even so, they had wards or quarters that segregated people on the basis of occupation, social class, or ethnic background. During the early twentieth century, as new settlements appeared and expanded in the U.S., people began to distinguish between large cities and the smaller settlements around them. These settlements, called suburbs or satellite cities, often had some characteristics of a city, but because they depended on the central city, they could not be considered independent (National Resources Committee, 1937:29-41; Kish, 1954: 388-98; Schnore, 1970:393-414, 1957a:121-27; Dobriner, 1970:190-205). In recent years there has been a growing distinction between the city and the hinterland that provides most of the social surplus on which the city depends.

Contemporary cities, especially metropolises, are larger, more complex physically and socially, and more densely populated than earlier cities. It is easier to understand the modern city if we first study the spatial distribution of people and institutions and their activities. This is part of the subject matter of **human ecology.** Human ecology is the study of territorially based systems of which cities are a subset. Human ecology describes not only a community's spatial distribution, but also the processes that give rise to observable distributions and the relationships between a community and its physical and social environment (McKenzie, 1971:17-33; Burgess, 1967:47-62; Duncan and Schnore, 1959:132-46; Schnore, 1961:128-39; Hawley, 1971:11-12; Theodorson, 1961). We will first consider some theories about how the distributions of people, institutions, and characteristic ac-

tivities of the metropolis emerged. Then we will examine the spatial structure of cities and metropolitan areas. We will see how structure affects the sense of community in a city. We will learn about the processes leading to the development of areas that are relatively homogeneous on the basis of social characteristics, such as race, ethnic origin, social class, and life style. We will also investigate the forces that make the maintenance of homogeneity and community solidarity more difficult.

The critical assumption underlying the concept of a spatial structure is that people and institutions in a city or metropolitan area sort themselves into spatially homogeneous groups (Park, 1936:1-15; McKenzie, 1926:141-54; 1971:17-33; Burgess, 1967:47-62). If there were no homogeneity, it would not be possible to construct a coherent map of spatial distributions. The distinction between central city, suburbs, satellite cities, and rural fringes is enough to demonstrate that some sorting takes place. Within each major area of the metropolis, a more complicated but finer-grained sorting takes place.

Any map we create of the metropolis will be most useful if it does the following: accurately represents the spatial distribution of people, institutions, and activities; shows all subareas, each of which is more homogeneous than the total area; and identifies the basis for the homogeneity in each area. To such a map we will apply a variety of models of the internal shape of a city in light of what we know about urban development and change.

No city can be analyzed in isolation, because each city is part of a wider, highly metropolitanized society (Hawley, 1971:199-

240). The society itself is one element of the social environment to which the city must adapt.

Ecological Processes: The Development of Homogeneous Areas

There are two major reasons for beginning our analysis of urban spatial structure with the processes that produced the structure rather than with the observable form. First, we already have an idea of city structure from our earlier discussions of preindustrial and modern cities. Second, to understand the finer structural details we need some conceptual tools with which to probe developments and changes in urban spatial structure. With knowledge of processes of change we can examine the contemporary structure with greater precision. Knowing the kinds of persons, activities, and institutions that move from place to place in a metropolitan area and why they move will help us understand some dynamics of urban life. We will examine areas that are homogeneous to learn how that homogeneity developed. On these bases we will speculate about future changes in city structure.

People live, institutions exist, and activities take place in social and physical environments (Hawley, 1950; McKenzie, 1971; Bourne, 1971). The **social environment** is the people, their activities, and the social institutions that make up the community. This includes not only their physical presence and behavior, but also the attitudes and values they express.[1]

The **physical environment** is composed of both natural and man-made elements. Among the natural elements that affect human communities are weather (climate, earthquakes, tornadoes, rainfall, and so forth), topographical features (lakes, rivers, mountains, plains), and raw materials (minerals, forests, soil) (Hawley, 1950:chap. 2; Burgess, 1967:47-62). The man-made components of the physical environment include the equipment and techniques for using natural resources and for rearranging the physical landscape (skyscrapers and housing developments). Technology affects society's ways and means of agriculture, transportation (canals, airports), construction, manufacture, and communication. It also determines the type of energy available to the society (Nelson, 1969:198-207; McKenzie, 1971:17-33).

Social policies affect and are affected by relationships between the man-made and the natural environments. Housing patterns, for example, depend on available building technology and materials, energy, and economic and political policies regulating land use and mortgage monies. Social policies also affect transportation, communication, and economics throughout the community.

For most cities the natural environment is a given—a factor that can be influenced only minimally by man-made objects and social processes. Within the natural environment, the human community is subject to or influenced by the same ecological processes that affect plant communities.[2]

Communities originate in simple structures and become progressively more complex. As they grow, they are transformed from general structures to specialized structures—they shift from *Gemeinschaft* to *Gesellschaft,* from mechanical solidarity to organic solidarity. Furthermore, communities develop from centralized to decentralized structures (McKenzie, 1971:26-27). These three general ecological processes—simple to complex, general to specialized, centralized to decentralized—take place in stages as new components, such as new populations, new activities, and new institutions, are added to existing human communities.

Concentration and Deconcentration; Centralization and Decentralization

A city is shaped by four specific processes: **concentration, deconcentration, centralization,** and **decentralization.** The process of concentration is the piling up of people in an area. Population increase begins close to the center of the city, as successive waves of migrants seek housing close to major employment centers. New migrants increase the number of people in the area and the number of institutions that employ or serve the growing population. This increased concentration in turn produces outward movement— deconcentration—a phenomenon occurring in crowded areas as more people compete for the same land. Increased competition drives the price of land up and leads to intensive land use. Those low-income land users who can least afford to meet the competition move out.

Centralization, a process similar to concentration, is more than mere grouping around a central area. It is grouping with a central focus. For example, centralization occurs in a city where businesses are grouped around a particular point. Decentralization is the opposite process, that is, movement away from the central focal point and the shedding in general of the urban way of life (Thomlinson, 1969:152; Hawley, 1950:373-431).

American cities were originally highly concentrated and centralized as a result of the use of steam energy and relatively slow, inflexible means of transportation. Since World War II, however, American cities have deconcentrated rapidly and are continuing to do so. Deconcentration of cities has suburbanized society (Zimmer, 1975:23-91; Edel, Harris, Rothenberg, 1975:123-56).

Invasions

Urban populations grow either by an excess of births over deaths or by in-migration. In-migration of new types of residents to an existing community is called an **invasion** (McKenzie, 1971:22, 26, 28; Hawley, 1950: chap. 19). Changes in the social environment result when a community is invaded by people who differ from residents in social class, racial or ethnic background, or life-cycle stage. For example, the sudden influx of single persons or persons of an ethnic group not previously represented in the community may change the relationships among the components of the existing population. The social environment of a community may be altered by either allowing in or excluding a population with different values or attitudes. A change in land use can alter the social environment. For example, land that previously was too expensive for residential use may be made available for high-density dwellings or permission may be given to construct an industrial or commercial building in a previously residential area.

New components may be added to a community by changes in the physical environment. The climate and topography of an area are not likely to change, although humans can alter topography through techniques such as strip mining. But the discovery of oil, coal, or other natural resources can cause a change in patterns of land use.[3] A change in transportation can also modify the physical environment by opening new areas to settlement. Reducing the time it takes to go from one area to another alters their relative attractiveness to potential occupants (McKenzie, 1971:27; Nelson, 1969:76-77; Hawley, 1950). The introduction of mechanically powered boats encouraged settlement of river valleys in the Midwest. The motor vehicle had the same effect on cities.

A change in interaction between the physical and social environments can bring new components to a human community. Such is the case with the development of a new industry or with a new social policy. The opening of Siberia to scientific and cultural cities but not to agricultural cities is one example; the homesteading policies in the United States in the nineteenth century is another.

When environmental changes occur, the structure of the community continues to be modified until the changes stop and the new structure can stabilize (McKenzie, 1971:28). An invasion, then, may be a change in the use of land in a community or a change in the characteristics of its residents.

Invasions in both residential and commercial areas occur because competition forces occupants—institutions or individuals—of similar economic strength to move into areas of similar land values. At the same time invasion causes the concentration of activities, institutions, and populations that profit from being together. Institutions that can afford to pay a certain price for a certain amount of land will migrate to and compete for those parts of the city where the land is appropriately priced. Land in central business districts for which there is great competition will be densely occupied by those who can afford higher prices; outlying areas for which there is less competition will be less densely occupied by less affluent people and institutions. Some industries must pay a high price for location because they have to be close to another type of industry. For example, if a business depends on airline passengers or freight, it must pay the high price of locating near an airline terminal.

The stages of invasion. The initial stage of invasion is the attempt of a new type of occupant to enter an area (McKenzie, 1971:29-30; Hawley, 1950:400-401). The attack generally comes at the point of greatest mobility and thus least solidarity. The residents can either resist the invader, as they do when they invoke zoning laws to keep out occupants they consider harmful to the community, or offer inducements to the invader, as they do when they grant tax advantages to desirable businesses or institutions. The reaction to an invasion depends on both the community and the invader. A community with some solidarity can resist invasion more effectively than a community with little or no solidarity. The community may welcome the conversion of empty lots into a shopping center, but may oppose the conversion of a hotel or apartment building into a mental health shelter or a penal rehabilitation facility. In recent years even the taking of residential land for highways by government agencies has met with community opposition.

The next stage of invasion is development and displacement, generally characterized by much competition between the invader and the occupants of the area. The greater the solidarity and integration in the community, the greater its resistance to invasion and the more intense the competition (McKenzie, 1971; Hawley, 1950; 1971:102). Both the invader and the occupants of the community attempt to develop associations with other sources of power for protection against the opposing party. The invasion reaches a climax when the community establishes its **dominance** and the invader gives up or when the invading group establishes its dominance and is able, for the moment at least, to resist other invasions. The ecological process by which an invading group occupies a community and successfully establishes its dominance is referred to as **succession.**

The result of an invasion, successful or not, is a homogeneous area occupied either by the organized community that resisted invasion or by the successful invader. In either case, the community that emerges from the fray is characterized by a particular population, institution, or activity that gives it the strength to resist further invasions. This homogeneous area has been called a **natural area** by Burgess, McKenzie and other early members of the sociology department at the University of Chicago. McKenzie noted that natural areas based on similarities of race and linguistic background (a code phrase for European immigrant groups) were easy to detect but that other natural areas, based on more subtle characteristics such as age, sex, social class, and life style, were harder to detect (McKenzie, 1971:31).

McKenzie's colleague, Robert Park, described natural areas as follows:

The city plan establishes metes and bounds . . . and imposes an orderly arrangement . . . upon the buildings. . . . Within the limitations prescribed, however, the inevitable processes of human nature proceed to give these regions and these buildings a character which it is less easy to control. . . . Personal tastes and convenience, vocational and economic interests, infallibly tend to segregate and thus to classify the populations of great cities. . . .

Physical geography, natural advantages and disadvantages, including means of transportation, determine in advance the general outlines of the urban plan. As the city increases in population, the subtler influences of sympathy, rivalry, and economic necessity tend to control the distribution of population. Business and industry seek advantageous locations. . . . These spring up fashionable residence quarters from which poorer classes are excluded because of the increased value of the land. Then there grow up slums. . . .

In the course of time every section . . . of the city takes on something of the character and qualities of its inhabitants. . . . The effect of this is to convert what was at first a mere geographical expression into a neighborhood, that is to say, a locality with sentiments, traditions, and a history of its own . . . and the life of every locality moves on with a certain momentum of its own, more or less independent of the larger circles of life and interests about it [Park, 1925:4-6].

Later Park wrote:

Natural areas are the habitats of natural groups. Every typical urban area is likely to contain a characteristic section of the population. . . . In great cities the divergence in manners, in standards of living, and in general outlook on life in different urban areas is often astonishing. . . .

These are regions in the city in which there are almost no children, areas occupied by residential hotels, for example. There are regions where the number of children is relatively high: in the slums, in the middle-class residential suburbs. . . . There are regions where people almost never vote, except at national elections, regions where the divorce rate is higher than it is for any state in the Union, and other regions in the same city where there are almost no divorces. There are areas infected by boy's gangs . . . regions in which there is an excessive amount of juvenile delinquency and other regions in which there is almost none [Park 1926:11-12].

The causes of invasions. This view of invasions and of city structure is based in part on the assumption that a city is organized along its major routes of transportation. Any given city grew geographically as homes and businesses spread out from the center along transportation routes. As the city and its population enlarged, the number of services located at each intersection of transportation routes and the number of intersections increased. The largest number of intersections occurred at the social, though not necessarily the geographic, center of the city, because it was the most accessible, convenient location in the area and the place where there was greatest competition for space. Competition forced economically and politically weak residents out of the center and toward the edge of the city along the transportation routes (McKenzie, 1971:23-24, 27). A location at the social center of the city was economically valuable because it reduced transportation costs for travel to the largest number of other locations, thus helping to maximize profits.

As the city grew, the population became increasingly heterogeneous because of internal migration and heavy foreign immigration. Both foreign immigrants and native Americans, white and black, who migrated to cities first moved into the least expensive housing available. Typically these were centrally located residences abandoned by older, more affluent occupants who had lived there for some time but had moved outward as the central part of the city aged. The competition for residential space in the central city increased as the residential portions began to decay and the demand for land for commercial, industrial, and business facilities increased. Through a continuous series of invasions, the populations, shopping facilities, schools, churches, and other institutions in every area of the city were challenged by migrants (Nelson, 1969: 76; Burgess, 1967:47-62).

The Role of Values

Most ecological theory assumes that individuals and institutions respond rationally to the pressures of concentration, deconcentration, centralization, and decentralization. Rational economic calculations, either conscious or unconscious, also are assumed to guide community responses to competitive pressures and invading groups. However, other social values may affect land use in a particular area.[4] For example, one deeply held desire of American families apparently has always been to own a single-family detached home. This desire has affected the structure of cities, especially since World War II. Perhaps 15 million homes have been built, mostly in suburban, low-density residential areas (Nelson, 1969:76).[5] The building of residences in what were previously the hinterlands of central cities gave impetus to the decentralization of commercial and industrial institutions.

The desire to own single-family detached homes also influenced the economics of building and buying homes. Although it takes far less capital to rent an apartment or to buy part of a multiple-dwelling unit, the value of owning one's own home led to the devaluation of central city apartments and encouraged invasion of the hinterland. Perhaps the most telling example of the influence of values on the ecological structure of a city comes from Walter Firey's study of land use in central Boston (1945:140-48). The most economic use of land in any central city is not old churches, cemeteries, parks, and commons, but rather businesses, industries, and residences. However, the historical significance and sentiment attached to Boston's churches, cemeteries, and commons were important enough to the social solidarity of the community to explain their being maintained in an area of intensive commercial and governmental land use. Similar values underlie other uneconomic land uses, such as the Water Tower in Chicago, Washington Park in New York, and the sites of local historical importance in most cities.

Until recently, the Italians in the North End of Boston valued ethnic solidarity so highly they were able to resist invasions from more economically powerful groups. On the other hand, prejudice can cause people to abandon an otherwise economically secure community. If residents are highly prejudiced toward and highly fearful of invaders, they may flee from the area when a single representative of the invading group enters. This accounts for the success of blockbusting and similar tactics that change a community more rapidly than normal. Prejudice and ethnic solidarity can be more powerful than economics in determining which group will occupy a given area. Ethnic

segregation, especially when it develops naturally, as in natural areas, can be viewed as part of the community's adaptation to its social environment (Gans, 1962; Jacobs, 1961; Lieberson, 1963).

Classic Theories of City Structure

The ecological processes produce definable city areas with unique characteristics. Maps of these areas can be drawn to show their structure as if the theories on which they are based were totally true. Because no theory of human behavior completely reflects reality, these are generalized maps, conventionally called ideal-type maps. We now turn to the content of these maps and to the areas which they identify.

The Star or Axial Theory

The earliest theory of city shapes postulates a center from which the city spreads out along transportation lines in the shape of a star. The areas between transportation routes will eventually fill in but not before greater, more intensive development takes place along the main routes of transportation.[6] The star or axial theory applied best when transportation routes were fixed (by railway lines, rivers, and so forth), before there were many roads.

The invention of the automobile and of relatively inexpensive road-building techniques made cities look less like stars. However, major transportation routes continue to influence the shape of cities, as can be seen in current patterns of settlement—the areas around expressways and major roads are occupied before the areas in between are filled in. Due to widespread ownership of automobiles and flexibility of automobile travel, areas between major transportation routes fill in faster than they did during the first half of the twentieth century.

Obviously, transportation is an important factor in the spatial organization of cities. The star or axial theory describes city shapes quite accurately up to the time when the motor vehicle became ubiquitous. The flexibility of transportation routes and technological developments in motor vehicles, road building, and home building have made the axial theory less accurately descriptive of contemporary metropolitan areas.

Concentric Zone Theory

Although not the first, the **concentric zone** theory of Ernest W. Burgess is by far the best known and most influential theory of city structure (1967:47-62). The zonal theory incorporates concepts of process as well as shape, assuming continuous population growth as the motivating force in changing the shape of the city.[7]

According to the concentric zone theory, the city spreads out equally in all directions from its original center, producing circles of growth. Each growth period produces either a new zone at a greater distance from the center of the city or a change in land use in an existing inner zone. Each zone has its own land use, population, institutions, and activities. The theory assumes that the city has one center, that the city's population is heterogeneous, and that the economic base is a mixture of industrial and commercial businesses. Population growth leads to increasing economic competition for the highly valued space in the center of the city.

(*Top*) The impact of highways on development patterns, illustrated here by U.S. 89 in Arizona, has been rather extensively studied. But too little is done to analyze the potential impact of specific highways before they are constructed.

(*Bottom*) Diagram of concentric zone theory of city structure. (Source: Redrawn from Robert E. Park, Ernest W. Burgess, and Roderick D. McKenzie, *The City* [Chicago: University of Chicago Press, 1925]. Printed by permission.)

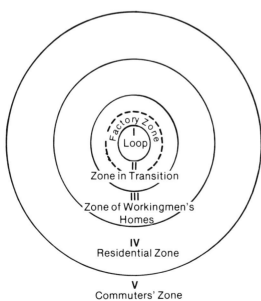

The central business district. At the center of the city is the first zone, the central business district. Physically, it is composed of department stores, high-fashion stores, office buildings, banks, hotels, theaters, and civic buildings. Most of the city's cultural activities take place here. Competition for land is intense, and land use is intensive. Activities that draw on and are based on the city's whole population are found here, for this is the focal point of transportation routes. The central business district is the downtown center for culture, commerce, business, and supporting facilities. It is the heart of the business and governmental activities of the city. The central business district, however, it not totally homogeneous. At the outer edge there is often a warehouse and wholesale area that serves the retail and commercial outlets at the center of the zone. Because wholesalers serve the central business district and not the city's total population, they need not attract as many individual customers. Therefore, they locate near their primary customers but in a less desirable part of the central city where competition is less intense.

The zone in transition. The second zone of the city is the **zone in transition.** Originally, this was a residential zone for the people who worked in the central business district. As the city expanded, the area was invaded by retail businesses, small manufacturing firms, and some warehouse and wholesale facilities from the outer edges of the central business district. These institutions had been forced outward by competition for space in the center. The homes in the zone of transition are among the oldest in the city and are deteriorating because of their age and the inability of residents to compete for the space with occupants from the encroaching central business district. The zone in transition is not homogeneous. Generally it has an inner factory belt close to the outer belt of warehouses in the central business district and an outer belt of declining neighborhoods and slums.

In the early twentieth century, the first generation of European immigrants to the cities found homes in the zone in transition. More recently, migrants from rural America, white and black, have settled here. Burgess described the zone as the location of "slums which housed poverty, degradation, disease, and underworld activities, crime and vice, the night club district"—a place occupied by artists and radicals, "all obsessed with the vision of a new and better world" [1967:55-56].

The zone of workingmen's homes. The third city zone is the zone of workingmen's homes. Here, low-rise apartments and small, closely spaced one- and two-family dwellings house the large labor force of the city. To this area the residents fleeing the invasions of the zone in transition escaped. Here, too, the second generation of immigrants and migrants moved—their first stop on the route to higher status suburbs.

The zones of better residences and commuters. Better residences make up the fourth zone. Relatively expensive apartment houses and detached homes on larger lots dominate in this area. Population density is lower here than in the zone of the workingmen's homes, and exclusive districts are found here. More accurately, it is a middle-class housing zone.

Beyond the better residence zone is the commuter zone. At the time Burgess was writing (in the 1920s), this was a suburban or satellite zone thirty to sixty minutes commuting time from the central business district. In the late 1970s, this zone has been incorporated into the city itself, and the commuter zone is now much farther from the center, although still only thirty to sixty minutes away by rapid transit or expressway travel. Burgess's commuter zone is perhaps best described as a ring of dormitory towns and suburbs—that is, areas with many residences but few other facilities.

Additional zones. Two additional zones lie beyond the commuter zone. One (in the 1920s) was an agricultural zone that overlapped the outer portion of the commuter zone and provided much of the local produce. Beyond that was the hinterland or fringe of the city, which might include independent settlements not completely integrated with the central city.

Criticisms of the Zone Theory

One criticism of the concentric zone theory is that is assumes the city is circular in shape around a single center (Nelson, 1969:78; Harris and Ullman, 1945; Thomlinson, 1969:145-46). Of course, not all cities are perfectly circular—Burgess recognized this. He argued that the circular city in his theory was an ideal type, in the same way that *Gemeinschaft, Gesellschaft,* and other social abstractions were ideal types (1967:51-52). Expansion by invasion is one force that would lead to a circular city, but the forces of concentration,

deconcentration, centralization, and decentralization also have an impact on the concentric shape of the contemporary city.

The concentric zone theory also is not universally valid. Sjoberg (1960:98-100) has demonstrated that the highest status persons in the preindustrial city lived in the most desirable location, which was the center of the city. Ecological studies of contemporary Latin American cities have indicated that the same pattern holds there: high-status persons live in the most desirable central sections of the city, which are surrounded by tenements and slums—a pattern opposite from that predicted by zonal theory. Differences in transportation and communication and the colonial origins of Latin American cities may explain these apparent discrepancies in living patterns. During the preindustrial era, living in the central city conferred high status. In Latin America the colonial "law of the Indies" required colonists to live in the city and prohibited natives from doing so. Only now is this law breaking down and only now are high-status persons seeking housing on the periphery of the city (Schnore, 1972:14-19).

Schnore has pointed out that the concentric zone pattern is more characteristic of commercial-industrial cities than of administrative cities; further, cities that exhibit a concentric zone structure developed under conditions that do not apply to cities developing today. Both the concentric zone pattern and the modifications of it observed in Latin America may be special cases of a more general, evolutionary pattern that has yet to be adequately developed (Schnore, 1965:347-98; Schwirian, 1974:10-11).

In modern Latin American cities, high status persons live in the central sections while tenements and slums occupy outlying areas—a pattern characteristic of preindustrial cities.

*Concentric Zones and the
Nature of Urban Life*

The concentric zone theory implies that urban ways of life are learned by migrants when they move into the inner city zones. The theory also implies that a certain amount of **social disorganization** is generated as invading groups come into conflict with current residents. That is, a breakdown in social control results in such problems as crime, delinquency, vice, and alcoholism. The extent of social disorganization is different in each zone. There is more disorganization in the **hobo zone** of the central business district or in the inner part of the zone in transition than in the outer part of the zone in transition or in more distant zones. Concentric zone theory would hold that social disorganization is a natural consequence of social life and change in the city and not an indication of either social or individual pathology (Schwirian, 1974:56-58).

The processes of city expansion and adjustment to city life naturally sort individuals, institutions, and activities into homogeneous or natural areas. These natural areas give shape and character to the city and make communities or partial communities possible. Within each city zone there is segregation based on ethnic origins, social class, life style, and stage of the life cycle. Segregation allows each individual to live in a homogeneous area that provides the basis for a community, while the city itself is made up of a wide range of different groups (Park, 1925:6-12; McKenzie, 1926:78). In other words, the city as a whole is heterogeneous, but its heterogeneity is a mosaic of homogeneous areas. Each zone has at least some potential for residential, in-dustrial, commercial, and institutional occupants, and many different activities can and do occur in each zone (Nelson, 1969:79-84). The natural areas become the locale of communal identification and are thus a form of adaptation to the city which makes at least partial communities possible.

The Sector Theory

The concentric zone theory considers different urban land uses (residential, commercial, industrial) but does not emphasize any single use. The **sector theory** of Homer Hoyt (1964:199-212) emphasizes the role of housing in determining city shape.[8] In Hoyt's theory there is a central business district, but the city is organized into pie-shaped wedges, not circular zones, extending out from the center. Once persons of a particular social status, owning homes at a given cost level, have occupied land in a portion of the central zone, that portion expands outward in a wedge, rather than spreading out equally in a circular pattern around the center. For example, if high-status homes were originally located toward the northwest of a city, more homes of this type would be built toward the northwest. The types of homes found in other sections would similarly expand outward in other directions. Better residential areas are generally found on high ground near lakes and rivers and along the fastest transportation routes. The wedge of homes with highest rental value is adjoined on both sides by wedges of homes of next highest value, and they in turn are bounded by areas of decreasing value.

The Multiple Nuclei Theory

The **multiple nuclei** theory assumes that there are several central business districts scattered throughout the modern metropolis, although the city is dominated by one main business district (Harris and Ullman, 1945). The picture of a wide area that includes several central shopping and business districts is particularly appropriate for cities that have grown by the consolidation of smaller, socially and economically integrated communities. Each nucleus is surrounded by concentric zones of the types described in concentric zone theory, leading outward to a hinterland that touches the hinterlands of adjoining central business districts.

The nuclei may have existed since the city began or may have developed as it expanded (Harris and Ullman, 1945). London, for example, began in the section called The City, now London's central financial district. London was separate from the city of Westminster, and there was open country between them. The present city of London simply grew up between and around the cities of London and Westminster. By contrast, heavy industry in Chicago was originally located near the present central business district (the Loop). Because of economic pressures, heavy industry migrated southward to the Calumet-Gary area where it formed the nucleus of a new city, which is now part of the Chicago metropolitan area.

Multiple nuclei theory offers numerous reasons for the development of an original central business district and the rise of separate nuclei (Harris and Ullman, 1945). The central business district may have begun as a city performing central place functions for a wide area; as a port city; as a facilities center along a transportation route; as an industrial center; or as an extractive center. Additional nuclei might be generated by different specialized activities. For example, business centers may grow up around rail, truck, or port facilities for intermetropolitan areas, or around power facilities that require large fuel storage areas. Some institutions, such as banks, law firms, insurance companies, and brokerages, band together and form a nucleus because they profit from being near each other. On the other hand, some enterprises detract from each other, such as heavy industry and high-status housing. In such cases, participants move far away from each other and may develop nuclei of their own.

Social Area Analysis

Social area analysis—and the closely related techniques of **factorial ecology** (factor analysis of population characteristics)—is a standardized method of categorizing urban areas based on the natural area concepts developed by Burgess and McKenzie (Shevsky and Williams, 1948; Shevsky and Bell, 1955; Thomlinson, 1969:154-57; Schwirian, 1974:10-12, 277-384). Social area analysis uses census data to identify populations with homogeneous characteristics. Several of these homogeneous groups located together in a city make up a natural, or social, area.

Social area analysis uses three categories of population characteristics: social rank (measured by occupation, education, and income of residents); degree of urbanization (measured by ratio of children to women,

Generalizations of internal structure of cities. The concentric zone theory is a generalization for all cities. The arrangement of the sectors in the sector theory varies from city to city. The diagram for multiple nuclei represents one possible pattern among innumerable variations.

(Source: Redrawn from Chauncy D. Harris and Edward Ullman, "The Nature of Cities," *The Annals of the American Academy of Political and Social Science* 242 [November 1945]. Printed by permission.)

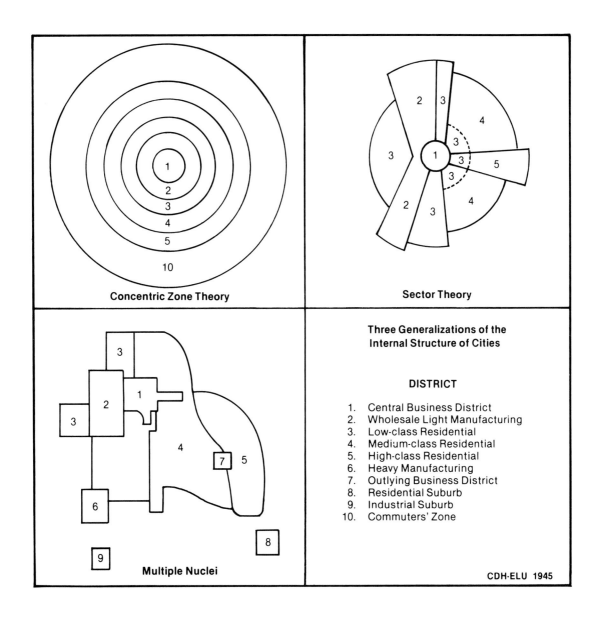

Concentric Zone Theory

Sector Theory

Multiple Nuclei

Three Generalizations of the Internal Structure of Cities

DISTRICT

1. Central Business District
2. Wholesale Light Manufacturing
3. Low-class Residential
4. Medium-class Residential
5. High-class Residential
6. Heavy Manufacturing
7. Outlying Business District
8. Residential Suburb
9. Industrial Suburb
10. Commuters' Zone

CDH-ELU 1945

percentage of working women, and percentage of single-family dwellings); and level of segregation (measured by percentage of members of a racial or ethnic group). Each census tract is ranked high, moderate, or low in each of the first two categories and either high or low on segregation, producing eighteen combinations. Each census tract falls into one of the eighteen types. A social area then is defined as a group of contiguous census tracts falling into the same type. So defined, one area of a city that ranks high on urbanization, segregation, and social rank may be compared with another area that is low on all these characteristics.[9]

Social area analysis has been criticized on a number of counts (Hawley and Duncan, 1957: 334-45). First, there is no link between such definitions of natural or social areas and any theory of city growth and development. Second, the characteristics used to measure urbanization do not seem to be appropriate. There is no immediately obvious reason why woman-to-child ratio, percentage of single-family homes, and percentage of working women should be used as measures of urban behavior. These may be the best census statistics available, but the theoretical link between these categories and urban ways of life is tenuous. These particular characteristics would seem to be better measures of an individual's stage in the life cycle than measures of urbanization in an area. Third, the use of census tracts as units of analysis may distort the identification of social areas because these may or may not be directly related to interaction patterns within the city. Despite these criticisms, social area analysis is a powerful tool in the study of urban behavior, as the works of Scott Greer and others illustrate

(Greer, 1962; 1972; Bell and Boat, 1957:391-98; Timms, 1971).

A final criticism of social area analysis is that it does not specify a shape for a city, as do the other theories of urban structure. Rather it is a technique for identifying urban areas that are homogeneous in limited ways. As a tool, however, social area analysis is compatible with various theories of urban structure and can be used to investigate their validity.

All the theories of city shape we have considered probably have some validity. In fact, a number of researchers have demonstrated that all theories of zones, sectors, and social areas taken together produce a more complete picture of urban structure than any one theory can (Nelson, 1969:80; Anderson and Egeland, 1961:392-99; Schwirian and Matre, 1974:309-23). Schnore suggests that no single theory is adequate because cities have urbanized and modernized at different times, under varying conditions, at different stages of technological development, and for the performance of various functions (1965:347-98). Each variation can lead to different patterns of development and different spatial arrangements within cities. Except for the multiple nuclei theory and social area analysis, theories of city structure were developed before automobile use and suburban living became widespread. The automobile and the suburb have changed the shape of cities, and it is unlikely that theories developed before World War II could explain either the shape of cities that have developed since that time or the changes in older cities that have occurred since then. To understand the contemporary metropolis, one must understand the shape and characteristics of suburbs.

139

Looking west along Madison Street from Oak Park Avenue, outside Chicago, 1903. Extension of trolley and bus lines beyond city limits, followed by roads, allowed the middle class to live outside the central city but still work inside it. (Photo courtesy of the Oak Park Public Library.)

The Shape and Characteristics of Suburbs

We have seen that the contemporary metropolis is a product of population growth, of improvements in transportation and communication, and an increasing division of labor (Chinitz, 1964; Dobriner, 1970; Schnore, 1970; 1957b; Kish, 1954; Tobin, 1976; Kasarda, 1972). Metropolitan structure is more complex than that of a city expanded to cover a larger area; the city's influence on behavior patterns extends far beyond its boundaries. The central city dominates the metropolis in critically important ways, but despite its complex internal structure, the central city is only part of the metropolis. The central city may not lie at the geographic center of the metropolis, but it is definitely at the social and economic center (Hoyt, 1964; Berry, 1965) and, according to Bureau of Census practice, gives its name to the larger area. The central city is surrounded by suburbs, satellite cities and towns, and other, less well-organized areas that make up one complex metropolitan structure (Schnore, 1957a; 1963; Lineberry, 1975; Birch, 1975; Singleton, 1973). The shape and organization of the metropolitan area reflect not only the forces that have been important in its development, but also the functions performed in various portions of the area.

The extension of trolley and bus lines into areas beyond city limits in the early 1900s, followed by extensive investments in roads and the widespread use of automobiles in the 1950s, made it possible for middle-class urbanites to live outside the central city but still work in the city (Dobriner, 1970:190-205; Chinitz, 1964:3-50; Dyckman, 1970; Tobin, 1976:99-111; Kasarda, 1976:128-29). Commercial and industrial organizations that did

The Role of Transportation in Early Suburban Growth

Just as the railroad affected the locations and functions of cities on a national scale, the street railway shaped their internal growth. From its crude beginnings with horse-drawn omnibuses to steam-power trolleys and later the electrified lines, mass transit moved urbanites faster and more efficiently. Every advance in transportation technology quickly outmoded its predecessor only to create new problems in construction, congestion, and pollution.

The most important effect of mass transit was its expanding the physical limits of the city. The street railway destroyed the compact "walking city" of colonial and preindustrial towns. Prior to about 1850 most towns were still intimate locales where street congestion involved nothing more than people on foot, on horseback, or in carriages. Most people lived near their place of work and could reach nearly any spot in the city in a thirty-minute walk. Few towns extended farther than two miles from their core, which usually nestled against some waterway.

During the 1820s the omnibus emerged as the first urban passenger carrier. Initially little more than enlarged hackney coaches, these wagons later resembled boxes on wheels with two lengthwise seats holding twelve to twenty people. They appeared first in the larger cities—New York, Boston, Philadelphia, New Orleans, Washington—where small businessmen, usually those already

in the livery or freight business, seized the initiative in establishing omnibus lines to tie the two most traveled parts of the city together.

For a five- or ten-cent fare, a passenger on the new urban transit line was treated to a slow ride which lurched through frequent stops, bumps, and jerks. He sat on unpadded benches and enjoyed little protection from the elements. Even though the fare was too steep for the masses, omnibuses drew heavy patronage from small businessmen and clerks, many of whom still went home for lunch. By the 1840s Boston had eighteen omnibus lines, of which twelve extended to outlying suburban communities. Despite its limitations, the omnibus speeded up the tempo of life, regularized transportation patterns, and launched the outward migration of wealthier people from the center of the city to the suburbs.

The era of the omnibus lasted scarcely a generation before the horse railway surpassed it in the 1850s. The horse railway, too, resembled a stagecoach, but utilized flanged wheels operating on iron tracks. The pioneer run of a horsecar in New York in 1836 also made history as the first horsecar accident. When its brake failed to catch, the second car smacked into the first car filled with city dignitaries. Fortunately, neither dignitaries nor horses were injured. Undaunted by the mishap, Mayor Walter Browne applauded the run as an event which "will go down in the history

The development of mass transit, at first powered by horses and later by electricity, made possible the physical growth of the city and the suburbs.

of our country as the greatest achievement of man."

No innovation in urban mass transit rivaled the application of electrical power. . . .

The electric cars moved along iron tracks in the street, drawing current from a central power source passed to the trains through overhead wires. The effect of a wire leading a car resembled that of a "troller"; soon the corruption of the word became universal and the new vehicles were dubbed "trolleys." Trolleys displaced horses so rapidly that by 1900 only 2 percent of the lines were horse-drawn, compared to 70 percent a decade earlier. By 1895, 850 lines embraced over 10,000 miles of electrified track. The new trolleys speeded up travel service to about twelve miles per hour and more in less congested areas. Their overhead wires cluttered the streetscapes of American cities and wreaked havoc during high winds and storms. . . .

All these achievements in the technology of transportation affected the physical growth of cities. The rural ideal retained its hold upon Americans even in the city, where its influence drove people toward the suburbs. Prior to the advent of mass transit lines, however, only the wealthy could maintain houses on the outskirts of the city. Once the pedestrian confines were broken in the 1850s, an outward migration com-

menced. Warner has painstakingly traced the development of Roxbury, West Roxbury, and Dorchester as bedroom satellites of Boston. Every stage of suburban development expanded the physical limits of Boston to house wealthy, middle-class, and lower middle-class expatriates from the city. Since all of the transit lines were privately built, the new suburbs alongside their tracks were the product of individual decision-making rather than coordinated social policy. . . .

Traction entrepreneurs enthusiastically promoted the flight to the suburbs. They found support among those who regarded the exodus as a boon for relieving congestion in the city's inner core. Adna Weber, the leading student of American cities in the nineteenth century, stated flatly, "it is clear that we are now in the sight of a solution of the problem of concentration of population." Weber advocated the extension of electrified transit lines and cheap fares because he saw in the rise of the suburbs "the solid basis of a hope that the evils of city life, so far as they result from overcrowding, may be in large part removed."

Source Reprinted with permission of Macmillan Publishing Co., Inc. from *Prisoners of Progress* by Maury Klein and Harvey A. Kantor. Copyright © 1976 by Maury Klein and Estate of Harvey A. Kantor.

not use land intensively also moved out of the central city and functioned efficiently in the surrounding area. New population centers developed around the metropolitan center, and previously existing population centers became more integrated with the city. When many middle-class families moved away from the center of the city (Schnore, 1972; Farley, 1976:15, 19), some shopping and service facilities followed them to the suburbs. These population centers, whether new or expansions of previous settlements, comprise the suburban ring around the city. They often remain politically independent, but they are socially, economically, and administratively dependent on the metropolitan center. Some suburban settlements are large and complex enough to act as cities in their own right; these serve as other nuclei in the metropolitan area. The central city continues to dominate the metropolitan area, however, because of its greater size and the critical social and economic functions that it performs for the surrounding cities (National Resources Committee, 1937; Schnore, 1965; Dyckman, 1970; Harris and Ullman, 1945; Dobriner, 1970; Berry, 1965; Masotti, 1975; Schwartz, 1976; Kramer, 1972).

The suburban ring, like the city itself, is internally differentiated. In areas close to the central city, land use and behavior patterns are more like those found in the central city; farther out, they become less typically urban (Kish, 1954; Zimmer, 1975:66-88). As distance from the central city increases, population density declines. Larger and older cities tend to be less compact than smaller or younger cities. Regardless of city size or age, density can increase only until the land is used

as intensively as technology and economics will permit. At some point, the land will be so built up that it will not be feasible to increase its utilization; there are suggestions that this point is approximately 30,000 persons per square mile (Berry, 1965:98-99; Zimmer, 1975:28-34; Thomlinson, 1969).

Suburban Rings

The suburbs are heterogeneous groups of people, institutions, structures, and communities, just as cities are. In an early study of heterogeneity, Leslie Kish analyzed social differentiation in suburban communities in zones around several cities. The population in each zone and the number of zones increased as the size of the metropolitan area, and particularly of the central city, increased. Inner zones, those close to the central city, were composed of suburbs that were two to six times as differentiated as those in outer zones. In this sense inner zones were much more urban than outer zones, which were much more homogeneous and more like small towns or nonurban places (Kish, 1954:388-98).

The heterogeneity and differentiation in suburbs close to the central city has important implications. In the central city and in the inner suburban zones, people can live almost anywhere they want to because they can get to and from work easily. In these areas one can choose one's neighbors without regard to one's place of work, which produces homogeneous communities within the central city and in zones immediately surrounding the central city. More distant suburbs are increasingly homogeneous—economically, occupationally, politically, and socially. The suburbs farthest from the central city hypothetically would have the greatest mechanical solidarity and a way of life resembling a *Gemeinschaft*.[10]

The cost of an increase in mechanical solidarity is a decrease in differentiation among suburbs and consequently a decrease in congenial areas, regardless of the kind of congeniality one is seeking. In communities along the fringe of the metropolis, social life and behavior patterns are similar. To find variety, one must move close to the central city.

We can summarize differentiation in the New York metropolitan area on the basis of a study by Hoover and Vernon (1962:1-20). New York is composed of three areas: the core, or central business district of New York, an inner ring, and an outer ring. The core includes Manhattan, the Bronx, Brooklyn, Queens, and Hudson County, New Jersey. It contains more jobs than people—65 percent of the metropolitan jobs but only 54 percent of the metropolitan population. Here the nonwhite population of the metropolis also is concentrated. Families who live in the core area may be either very wealthy or very poor, but the wealthy and the poor do not live in the same portions of the core. The inner ring of the New York metropolitan area is made up of six counties surrounding the core. It has slightly more population than jobs (30 percent of the population and 24 percent of the jobs), the reverse of the relationship in the core. As late as the second half of the twentieth century, nearly half the land was undeveloped. The outer ring covers three states and two and one-half million people. It has 16 percent of the population and 12 percent of the jobs, and is underdeveloped. The populations in the outer ring are relatively homogeneous and may be characterized as more *Gemeinschaft* than *Gesellschaft*.

Many analyses of suburban characteristics have concentrated on contrasts between the residents and institutions of the central city and those of the suburbs. In part this is due to the practice of the U.S. Bureau of the Census of presenting suburban data as a residual category (the portion of an urbanized area or standard metropolitan area outside the central city). Despite considerable heterogeneity in this category, an analysis of the data illuminates the nature of the contemporary suburb.

Suburbs differ markedly from central cities in racial composition, somewhat less markedly in socioeconomic composition, and to varying degrees in institutional characteristics and life styles.

Race

Evidence of the extent of racial segregation between cities and their suburbs is presented in chapter 7. (See tables 7.11-7.15.) Briefly, while blacks make up about one fifth of metropolitan central city populations, they constitute less than a twentieth of suburban populations. During the 1960s the black population grew faster than the white population in the suburbs, especially in large metropolitan areas. There were so few blacks living in the suburbs before 1960, however, that even a high rate of population growth left the suburbs less than 5 percent black in 1970.

Even when blacks are able to move to the suburbs, patterns of racial segregation that have characterized the central cities persist. In

Chicago the number of black suburbanites more than tripled between 1950 and 1970 (from 44,000 to 129,000), but the increase was highly concentrated in older industrial suburbs and a few new all-black, or nearly all-black, suburbs (Taeuber, 1975:90, 93, 95; Farley, 1976:28-32; Schnore, 1976:69).

Social Status

Evidence on city and suburban contrasts in socioeconomic status is somewhat ambiguous. In the early 1960s the socioeconomic status of suburbs was generally assumed to be higher than that of cities. Leo Schnore, however, demonstrated that, while this was true in older and larger urbanized areas, socioeconomic differences between city and suburbs declined and reversed in smaller, newer urbanized areas (1972:42-47).

During the 1960s the proportion of workers with high incomes, high levels of education, and high-status jobs increased in both cities and suburbs. However, the increase was greater in the suburbs than it was in the cities, and by 1970 suburbs nationally had a moderate-to-marked status advantage over their central cities (Farley, 1976:19; Glenn, 1973:67-69).

Like their city, the suburbs are segregated on the basis of socioeconomic status, with segregation greatest at the extremes. But suburbs are no more class-segregated within each race than is their central city (Farley, 1976:28-31). There are high-status suburbs and low-status suburbs. For example, in Chicago median income in the suburbs varied from over $42,000 in the highest status suburb (Kenilworth) to just over $10,000 in the lowest status suburb (Robbins) (Merridew, 1975).

Employment

The institutional structure of the suburbs changed between 1950 and 1970. In twenty years manufacturing jobs in suburbs increased by 94 percent. Of all manufacturing jobs available in metropolitan areas, the proportion of jobs available in suburbs increased from 36 percent to 53 percent. The loss of manufacturing jobs by central cities to suburbs was greatest in the larger and older urban centers of the Northeast and the upper Midwest. Southern and Western cities actually gained in manufacturing jobs.

Central cities of over one million population lost an average of 49,000 manufacturing jobs each in the 1960s. The reasons for these losses vary. Changes in production technology that favor spread-out, single-story, assembly-line processes made it difficult to build or convert buildings in the central city and more economical to build in less densely settled suburbs. Improvements in short-haul transportation—larger trucks, more expressways, better scheduling by carriers—and the availability of space for parking lots made suburban locations attractive. Business and industrial shipping schedules could be met, and commuting and parking problems for employees were less severe than they would have been in the central business district. Suburban governments improved their utilities (power, water, sewage), communications, police and fire protection, which attracted both residents and industrial plants (Kasarda, 1976:119, 125; Chinitz, 1964:22-29).

Although the movement of blue-collar jobs to the suburbs has been large, there has been some movement of white-collar positions as well, especially to suburbs of the older, larger, and more congested metropolitan areas of the Northeast. In 1960, 51 percent of the labor force in central cities were in white-collar occupations. By 1970 the suburban labor force was 51 percent white collar (Kasarda, 1976:118-19, 120-23). During the 1970s New York has begun to experience an outflow of corporate headquarters to suburbs in Connecticut (Kasarda, 1976:124; *New York Times,* 25 December 1975:42).

Age and Family Status

In most metropolitan areas, suburban residents are younger than city residents. Taken as a whole, white suburbanites are about five years younger than white city residents, but there is little age difference between black urban and black suburban residents. In large part these differences are due to differential rates of migration and family formation. The highest rate of suburban growth was found among persons thirty to forty years old— those people who are forming families and raising children. Suburban adults are more likely than city adults to be married and to have higher levels of fertility and thus more children (Farley, 1976:9-13; Glenn, 1973:62; Long and Glick, 1976:52). (See table 7.10.) These differences give some clues to the life styles that are likely to prevail in different residential locations.

Consumer Facilities

Retail merchants began to recognize the growth of suburban populations after World War II, although growth had begun as early as 1900. The accelerated growth in suburban

consumer services since 1950 has been as explosive as the population growth. Over 14,000 shopping centers have been built in suburban areas, and currently more than 50 percent of retail sales take place in these shopping centers (Kasarda, 1976:113). As early as 1958, more land was occupied by shopping centers than by all central business districts in metropolitan cities.[11]

Large regional shopping centers headed by major department stores offer a wide range of facilities similar to the retail facilities in many central business districts. There are relatively few such centers; most regional shopping centers cannot offer the variety in shops and prices offered by the central business district. Instead, there are many community shopping centers occupying smaller plots and offering less parking and more restricted facilities. Community centers usually are dominated by a small department store or discount store. Even smaller shopping centers of one to two acres are found not only in suburban areas, but also in residential sections of the central city. These are generally dominated by a supermarket or other convenience store (Nelson, 1969:81-82).

With the movement of more highly educated, highly paid workers to the suburbs, more physicians, lawyers, and dentists have opened offices there. Indeed, suburban populations, who because of their socioeconomic status use physicians and dentists more frequently, have drawn many physicians from the central city (Kasarda, 1976:124).

The Roles of City and Suburb in the Metropolis

The central city of a metropolis provides for the whole area the same central place functions of social, administrative, and economic coordination that the central business district provides for the city (Harris and Ullman, 1945; Nelson, 1969; Berry, 1965; Hoyt, 1964; Kasarda, 1976:114). Many of these functions involve an interchange of knowledge, skills, and information that is most effectively carried out face to face. The centrality of the city makes these interactions possible. Therefore, government offices, banks, newspapers, life insurance companies, legal offices, courts, and other institutions tend to concentrate in the center of the metropolis. Their central location increases efficiency and gives them maximum access to a skilled labor force (Johnson, 1971; Schnore, 1970; Smith, 1971; Chinitz, 1964). For example, a lawyer who is centrally located can quickly get to courts, government agencies, and insurance company offices. Informal communication would be much more difficult if these institutions were dispersed.

Most businesses and professional people still find that the advantages of locating in the central city outweigh the costs of competing for the land (Kasarda, 1976:114). The demand for the central office space has spurred further building in central metropolitan business districts in recent years. Many institutions now occupy land that earlier had been used less intensively and that had been cleared by urban renewal. This is true, for instance, of land developed by insurance companies in downtown Chicago. This use of land expanded the central business district and brought in a different type of occupant (Hoyt, 1964:88-89).

The central business district continues to provide retail and cultural services to the metropolis that require either a central location or a large population for support. Museums, art galleries, theaters, symphony orchestras, and opera companies, as well as specialized shops, depend on large metropolitan populations, for only a small segment of the population supports such institutions. Some of these services, most notably shops, have moved to the suburbs as populations there have grown (Burgess, 1967; Berry, 1965; Hoyt, 1964), but many are still found exclusively in the metropolitan center.

The Changing Location of Industry

Industries originally located in the central city were quickly forced out by more intensive land users who performed central place functions (Chinitz, 1964; Dyckman, 1970). Only selected industries have survived in the central business districts. These are usually small industrial firms that purchase services they cannot economically provide for themselves. Locating in the central business district brings these firms close to their suppliers and reduces the competitive disadvantage of small size. When the firm is large enough to fulfill its own service needs, it tends to move to the suburbs. In the central business district the small firm finds centrally located rental space, a readily available labor force that does not need to be transported or trained, and good transportation facilities for hire. The small firm can purchase these services without investing its limited resources in facilities. Similarly, the small urban firm hires legal,

Cultural institutions which depend on support from a small segment of large metropolitan populations tend to remain in the central city.

business, and banking specialists who provide services that the firm would find uneconomical to provide for itself. Similar small firms located in the central district can also share marketing facilities. These advantages are greater in unstandardized industries, such as the clothing industry, than in mass production industries that manufacture many identical items.

As an industrial firm begins to grow, it can no longer find economical rental space in the central district. It begins to provide its own transportation, and it needs parking, loading, and storage facilities. Its traffic problems become serious. As it gains interest in owning larger facilities, it considers moving away from the central city.

When older manufacturing firms move out, they may be replaced by new types of service offices or light manufacturing facilities, such as data processing firms or electronic assembly plants. However, competition in these new industries is so keen that they often do not make enough profit to pay high rents. This adds to the problems of maintaining service or manufacturing facilities in the central city.

As the physical facilities in the metropolitan center age, they become increasingly less attractive to industries (Chinitz, 1964; Dyckman, 1970; Hoyt, 1964). Fast communication and transportation between the central city and the suburbs begin to reduce the advantages of a central city location. So manufacturing industries, as well as population and retail facilities, have moved to the suburbs (Tobin, 1976). These movements have caused problems for the central cities. They are plagued by eroding tax bases, increasing costs, and losses in skilled labor force, residential population, and retail sales.

The functions performed in the central metropolitan city have changed during the twentieth century. Residential land use has become more intense, with more people living in a smaller area. Central-city land used for administrative, financial, legal, and other business offices has increased, partly because the metropolitan area they serve has increased. The zone in transition has become part of the central business district, and the manufacturing zone has expanded outward (Kasarda, 1976:114).

Land Use in the Metropolis

Metropolitan expansion was caused, at least in part, by lack of space in the central business district. Other factors in the expansion were urban population growth and the cycle of invasions and successions caused by competition for space. Competition also resulted in dense land use, particularly in the central business district, which led to traffic problems, especially for workers and business firms that needed parking, loading, and road facilities.

As intensive users occupied more central district land, previous occupants were forced farther out. Competition initiated residential invasions of previously vacant land in the metropolitan hinterland. Many families realized their dream of owning their own homes when federal policies after World War II vastly increased the development of suburbs. At the same time, the increased competition for central locations made plots for single-family homes more expensive than most people could afford. Thus the invasion of the urban hinterland was fueled by competition for central area land (Nelson, 1969;

Thomlinson, 1969:141-61; Hoyt, 1964; Dyck-man, 1970; Chinitz, 1964).

Despite the move to the suburbs, the residential density of the central city has not changed significantly. Populations that cannot afford low-density housing in the suburbs occupy old housing near the center of the city. This poorer population lives more densely (that is, more persons per room, more families per unit) than did previous residents. Furthermore, affluent populations in the city live more densely than before in large, high-rise buildings, and much high-density public housing has been built on abandoned land in the center of the city.

In the 1960s it was found that 77 percent of city land in forty-eight major metropolitan areas was in use (Niedercorn and Hearle, 1964:105-9). In a ten-year period, this proportion had increased significantly, and in cities that had not annexed unused and rural land areas, 86 percent of city land had been developed. These findings suggest that cities completely surrounded by incorporated places are using the land they have intensively and will be able to grow only by increasing density of land use or by annexing incorporated cities and towns.

In cities, slightly more than a third of the land is used for residences. Roads occupy a quarter or more of the land, and one-fifth more is given over to other public uses (administrative buildings, schools, parks, playgrounds, and cemeteries). In sum, land in the central cities is almost used up. Building more streets or expressways will increase the density of the land used for residential and commercial purposes, or it will force people and industries out of the city.

Summary

In general, the metropolitan area consists of a dominant central city and sometimes a few, scattered, subdominant cities. The dominant city and each of its subdominants is surrounded by a ring of settlements that are more urban than rural. Beyond the immediate ring is an outer ring of smaller, less urban places that gradually give way to rural countryside or to the hinterlands of other metropolitan areas.

Each zone of the metropolis has its own internal structure. That part of each successive zone that is closest to the central city is more complex, dense, and heterogeneous than other parts of the zone. The patterns of behavior, social institutions, and social structure in each ring are different. Structural characteristics embodied in the political, historical, economic, and educational institutions of each zone become increasingly differentiated as one gets closer to the dominant city or to the inner portion of the zone.

Performance of community functions also varies within each zone. While there is greater homogeneity in the outer zone, some functions are better performed by large, heterogeneous populations, such as those in the inner core and in the inner part of each zone.

Glossary

centralization the clustering of people and services at a central point, usually the point at which transportation lines converge; also the process by which such clustering occurs

concentration the ecological process by which increasing numbers of people and institutions locate in a given area, resulting in increased density

concentric zone   a band surrounding a central point; in sociology, zones of different populations and communities within a city; basis of a theory of city structure associated with Ernest W. Burgess

decentralization   the opposite of centralization; the dispersal of people and services from the central point in an area, usually after density of use has reached a high level

deconcentration   the opposite of concentration; the ecological process by which increasing numbers of people and institutions spread out from a central point, producing lower levels of density

density   number of persons per square mile; more generally, number of occupants of a given type over a standard unit of area (persons per square mile is population density; number of factories per square mile is density of industrial land use)

dominance   the controlling position—cities dominate their hinterlands, and within cities, a group may control use of the land in an area; the end result of ecological succession, as when one ethnic group becomes dominant in a neighborhood

ecology, human   the study of the ways communities and their components adapt to their physical and social environments; frequently, the study of spatial distributions of types of residents and institutions

factorial ecology   the study of population characteristics by means of statistical techniques (factor analysis); definition of areas in which populations have the same traits

hobo zone   that portion of the central business district occupied by transients and hobos

human ecology   see ecology, human

invasion   an ecological term for the process by which new types of occupants move into a community

multiple nuclei   structural characteristic of cities, especially cities developed after the invention of the automobile, in which several areas perform central place functions; several small central business districts, or one dominant district and several other central districts, in a city

natural area   a term developed by Ernest W. Burgess and his associates to describe the communities within cities; an area in which one group is dominant, a position established through the natural processes of invasion and succession; an area frequently characterized by ethnic homogeneity

physical environment   topography, climate, mineral and other resources of the area in which a community is located; also man-made elements for extracting natural resources and rearranging the physical landscape

satellite city   a city located within a metropolitan area that is neither totally independent of the central city nor restricted in function, as a suburb; frequently an independent city that has been engulfed by the metropolis

sectors   wedge-shaped areas of a city created by expansion away from the central business district; a term used by Homer Hoyt to describe the deconcentration of residences of approximately the same value; frequently used in contrast to zones

social area analysis   a technique for studying homogeneous areas of a city; social areas are defined on the basis of the income, urbanity, and ethnic segregation of the population

social disorganization   the existence of many personal problems among residents of an area caused by a breakdown in social control; generally, problems include crime, delinquency, vice, alcoholism, and the like

social environment   characteristics of the population and social system to which a community must adapt

suburb   a settlement within the boundaries of a metropolitan area that is not the central city of that area

succession   the ecological process by which an invading group occupies a community and successfully establishes dominance

zone in transition   the concentric zone surrounding the central business district; area characterized by warehouses, light manufacturing facilities, and so on, into which the central business district expands

References

Anderson, Theodore R., and Egeland, Janice A.
1961   "Spatial Aspects of Social Area Analysis." *American Sociological Review* 26, 3(June):392-99.

Bell, Wendell, and Boat, Marian D.
1957   "Urban Neighborhoods and Informal Social Relations." *American Journal of Sociology* 62:391-98.

Berry, Brian J. L.
1965   "Internal Structure of the City." *Law and Contemporary Problems* 30:11-119.

Birch, David L.
1975   "From Suburb to Urban Place." *Annals* 422 (November):24-35.

Bourne, Larry S., ed.
1971   *Internal Structure of the City.* New York: Oxford University Press.

Burgess, Ernest W.
1967   "The Growth of the City: An Introduction to a Research Project." *Publications of the American Sociological Society* 18 (1924). In *The City,* edited by Robert E. Park, Ernest W. Burgess, and Roderick McKenzie, pp. 47-62. Chicago: University of Chicago Press.

Chinitz, Benjamin
1964   "City and Suburb: The Economics of Metropolitan Growth." In *City and Suburb: The Economics of Metropolitan Growth,* edited by Benjamin Chinitz, pp. 3-50. Englewood Cliffs, N.J.: Prentice-Hall, Inc.

Dobriner, William
1970   "The Growth and Structure of Metropolitan Areas." In *Class in Suburbia,* edited by William Dobriner, pp. 143-66. Englewood Cliffs, N.J.: Prentice-Hall, Inc., 1963. Reprinted in *Neighborhood, City, and Metropolis,* edited by Robert Gutman and David Popenoe, pp. 190-205. New York: Random House, Inc.

Duncan, Otis Dudley, and Schnore, Leo F.
1959   "Cultural, Behavioral, and Ecological Perspectives in the Study of Social Organization." *American Journal of Sociology* 65:132-46.

Dyckman, John W.
1970   "Socioeconomic and Technological Forces in Urban Expansion." In *Urban Expansion, Problems and Needs: Papers Presented at the Administrators' Spring Conference.* Washington, D.C.: Government Printing Office, 1963. Reprinted in *Neighborhood, City, and Metropolis,* edited by Robert Gutman and David Popenoe, pp. 439-59. New York: Random House, Inc.

Edel, Matthew; Harris, John R.; and Rothenberg, Jerome
1975   "Urban Concentration and Deconcentration." In *Metropolitan America in Contemporary Perspective,* edited by Amos H. Hawley and Vincent P. Rock, pp. 123-56. New York: John Wiley & Sons, Inc.

Farley, Reynolds
1976   "Components of Suburban Population Growth." In *The Changing Face of the Suburbs,* edited by Barry Schwartz, pp. 3-38. Chicago: University of Chicago Press.

Firey, Walter
1945   "Sentiment and Symbolism As Ecological Variables." *American Sociological Review* 10:140-48.

Gans, Herbert
1962   *The Urban Villagers.* New York: Free Press.

Glenn, Norval D.
1973   "Suburbanization in the United States since World War II." In *The Urbanization of the Suburbs,* edited by Louis H. Masotti and Jeffrey K. Hadden, pp. 51-78. Beverly Hills, Calif.: Sage Publications, Inc.

Greer, Scott
1962   *The Emerging City.* New York: Free Press.
1972   *The Urbane View.* New York: Oxford University Press.

Harris, Chauncey D., and Ullman, Edward L.
1945   "The Nature of Cities." *Annals* 242:7-17.

Hawley, Amos H.
1950   *Human Ecology: A Theory of Community Structure.* New York: Ronald Press.
1971   *Urban Society: An Ecological Approach.* New York: Ronald Press.

Hawley, Amos H., and Duncan, Otis Dudley
1957   "Social Area Analysis: A Critical Appraisal." *Land Economics* 33:334-45.

Hoover, Edgar M., and Vernon, Raymond
1962   *Anatomy of a Metropolis.* Garden City, N.Y.: Doubleday & Co., Inc.

Hoyt, Homer
1964   "Recent Distortions of the Classical Models of Urban Structure." *Land Economics* 40, 2:199-212.

Jacobs, Jane
1961   *The Death and Life of Great American Cities.* New York: Random House, Inc.

Johnson, Earl S.
1971   "The Function of the Central Business District in the Metropolitan Community." In *The Social Fabric of the Metropolis,* edited by James F. Short, Jr., pp. 87-102. Chicago: University of Chicago Press.

Kasarda, John D.
1972   "The Theory of Ecological Expansion: An Empirical Test." *Social Forces* 51 (December):165-82.
1976   "The Changing Occupational Structure of the American Metropolis: Apropos the Urban Problem." In *The Changing Face of the Suburbs,* edited by Barry Schwartz, pp. 113-36. Chicago: University of Chicago Press.

Kish, Leslie
1954   "Differentiation in Metropolitan Areas." *American Sociological Review* 19:388-98.

Kramer, John, ed.
1972   *North American Suburbs: Politics, Diversity, and Change.* San Francisco: Boyd and Fraser Publishing Company.

Lieberson, Stanley
1963   *Ethnic Patterns in American Cities.* New York: Free Press.

Lineberry, Robert L.
1975   "Suburbia and the Metropolitan Turf." *Annals* 422 (November):1-10.

Long, Larry H., and Glick, Paul C.
1976   "Family Patterns in Suburban Areas: Recent Trends." In *The Changing Face of the Suburbs,* edited by Barry Schwartz, pp. 39-68. Chicago: University of Chicago Press.

McKenzie, Roderick D.
1926   "The Scope of Human Ecology." *Publications of the American Sociological Society* 20:141-54.
1971   "The Ecological Approach to the Study of the Human Community." *American Sociological Review* 30 (1924). In *The Social Fabric of the Metropolis,* edited by James F. Short, Jr., pp. 17-33. Chicago: University of Chicago Press.

Masotti, Louis H., ed.
1975   "The Suburban Seventies." *Annals* 422.

Merridew, Alan
1975   *Chicago Tribune,* December 18, sec. 7, p. 1.

National Resources Committee
1937   "The Process of Urbanization: Underlying Forces and Emerging Trends." In *Our Cities: Their Role in the National Economy,* by National Resources Committee, pp. 29-41. Washington, D.C.: Government Printing Office.

Nelson, Howard J.
1969   "The Form and Structure of Cities: Urban Growth Patterns." *Journal of Geography* 68:75-83.

Niedercorn, John H., and Hearle, Edward F. R.
1964   "Recent Land Use Trends in Forty-Eight Large American Cities." *Land Economics* 40:105-9.

Park, Robert E.
1925   "Suggestions for the Investigation of Human Behavior in the Urban Environment." In *The City,* edited by Robert E. Park, Ernest W. Burgess, and Roderick D. McKenzie, pp. 1-46. Chicago: University of Chicago Press.
1926   "The Urban Community as a Spatial Pattern and a Moral Order." In *The Urban Community,* edited by Ernest W. Burgess, pp. 3-18. Chicago: University of Chicago Press.
1936   "Human Ecology." *American Journal of Sociology* 42:1-15.

Schnore, Leo F.
1957a   "Satellites and Suburbs." *Social Forces* 36:109-27.
1957b   "Metropolitan Growth and Decentralization." *American Journal of Sociology* 63:171-80.
1961   "The Myth of Human Ecology." *Sociological Inquiry* 31:128-39.
1963   "The Social and Economic Characteristics of American Suburbs." *Sociological Quarterly* 4:122-34.
1965   "On the Spatial Structure of Cities in the Two Americas." In *The Study of Urbanization,* edited by Philip M. Hauser and Leo F. Schnore, pp. 347-98. New York: John Wiley & Sons, Inc.

1970   "Urban Form: The Case of the Metropolitan Community." In *Urban Life and Form,* edited by Werner Z. Hirsch. New York: Holt, Rinehart & Winston, 1963. Reprinted in *Neighborhood, City, and Metropolis,* edited by Robert Gutman and David Popenoe, pp. 393-414. New York: Random House, Inc.

1972   *Class and Race in Cities and Suburbs.* Chicago: Markham Publishing Co.

1976   "Black Suburbanization 1930-1970." In *The Changing Face of the Suburbs,* edited by Barry Schwartz, pp. 69-94. Chicago: University of Chicago Press.

Schwartz, Barry, ed.
1976   *The Changing Face of the Suburbs.* Chicago: University of Chicago Press.

Schwirian, Kent P.
1974   "Urban Models: An Overview." In *Comparative Urban Structure: Studies in the Ecology of Cities,* edited by Kent P. Schwirian, pp. 1-2. Lexington, Mass.: D. C. Heath & Company.

Schwirian, Kent P., and Matre, Marc
1974   "The Ecological Structure of Canadian Cities." In *Comparative Urban Structure: Studies in the Ecology of Cities,* edited by Kent P. Schwirian, pp. 309-23. Lexington, Mass.: D. C. Heath & Company.

Shevsky, Eshref, and Bell, Wendell
1955   *Social Area Analysis.* Stanford, Calif.: Stanford University Press.

Shevsky, Eshref, and Williams, Marilyn
1948   *The Social Areas of Los Angeles.* Berkeley: University of California Press.

Singleton, Gregory H.
1973   "The Genesis of Suburbia: A Complex of Historical Trends." In *The Urbanization of the Suburbs,* edited by Louis H. Masotti and Jeffrey K. Hadden, pp. 29-50. Beverly Hills, Calif.: Sage Publications, Inc.

Sjoberg, Gideon
1960   *The Preindustrial City.* New York: Free Press.

Smith, Larry
1971   "Space for the CBD's Functions." *Journal of the American Institute of Planners* 6. (1961). In *Internal Structure of the City,* edited by Larry S. Bourne, pp. 352-60. New York: Oxford University Press.

Taeuber, Karl E.
1975   "Racial Segregation: The Persisting Dilemma." *Annals* 422:87-96.

Theodorson, George A., ed.
1961   *Studies in Human Ecology.* New York: Harper & Row.

Thomlinson, Ralph
1969   *Urban Structure.* New York: Random House, Inc.

Timms, D. W. G.
1971   *The Urban Mosaic.* Cambridge, N.Y.: Cambridge University Press.

Tobin, Gary A.
1976   "Suburbanization and the Development of Motor Transportation: Transportation Technology and the Suburbanization Process." In *The Changing Face of the Suburbs,* edited by Barry Schwartz, pp. 95-112. Chicago: University of Chicago Press.

Tyron, Robert
1955   *Identification of Social Areas by Cluster Analysis.* Berkeley: University of California Press.

Wirth, Louis
1964   "The Scope and Problems of the Community." *Publications of the American Sociological Society* 37 (1933):61-73. In *Louis Wirth on Cities and Social Life,* edited by Albert J. Reiss, Jr., pp. 165-77. Chicago: University of Chicago Press.

Zimmer, Basil G.
1975   "The Urban Centrifugal Drift." In *Metropolitan America in Contemporary Perspective,* edited by Amos H. Hawley and Vincent P. Rock, pp. 23-91. New York: John Wiley & Sons, Inc.

Suggested Readings

Harris, Chauncey D., and Ullman, Edward L. "The Nature of Cities." *Annals* 242 (1945):7-17. The most clear-cut, straightforward description and comparison of models of city and metropolitan structure.

Park, Robert E.; Burgess, Ernest W.; and McKenzie, Roderick D. *The City.* Chicago: University of Chicago Press, 1925 (reprinted 1967). A collection of classic essays on the nature of urban structure and social life. One of the major statements of the contributions of the Chicago school of urban sociology.

Schwirian, Kent P., ed. *Comparative Urban Structure: Studies in the Ecology of Cities.* Lexington, Mass.: D. C. Heath, 1974. A collection of fifty readings on the ecological structure of cities and the uses of ecological analyses in the study of urban society.

Short, James F., Jr., ed. *The Social Fabric of the Metropolis.* Chicago: University of Chicago Press, 1971. A collection of articles with many outstanding contributions from the Chicago school of urban sociology. Should be used in conjunction with the work by Park, Burgess, and McKenzie.

Notes

1. The concern for the sociopsychological attributes of the individual is seen most clearly in the reaction to classical ecology. See, for example, the studies in Theodorson (1961).

2. This is the basic assumption of classical or orthodox ecologists. Most contemporary ecologists recognize that social and sociopsychological factors also influence human communities. See, for example, Hawley (1950:preface, chaps. 1, 3), Theodorson (1961:introductions to parts I and II), Wirth (1964), and McKenzie (1971:17-33).

3. An obvious example is the growth of cities around oil-producing areas of the Middle East and in Texas and Oklahoma. Similarly, cities in the western United States developed around mineheads. The internal structure of some cities, especially Los Angeles, has been altered by the discovery of oil.

4. Classical ecologists especially stressed the role of values. For examples of classical ecological thinking, see Theodorson (1961:3-76, 129-40, 144-50) and Schnore (1961:128-39).

5. This desire is nothing new (perhaps not even uniquely American), but combined with government financing and taxing policies after World War II, the improvements in transportation, and the rise in incomes, it has influenced the shape of the city. It is not possible to separate the effects of these factors.

6. Thomlinson (1969) attributes the origin of the star or axial theory to R. N. Hurd in 1903. Among the earliest discussions of this theory in American sociological thought is that of McKenzie (1971:27).

7. Examples of the use of this theory can be found in virtually all discussions of the internal shapes of cities. For example, see Berry (1965), Nelson (1969), Harris and Ullman (1945), Hoyt (1964), and Thomlinson (1969).

8. The sector theory was originally propounded by Homer Hoyt in 1939 on the basis of home rental data for 1930. See Thomlinson (1969:146-47) and Harris and Ullman (1945:243-44).

9. Robert Tyron (1955) uses complex mathematical techniques to obtain clusters of census tracts with similar demographic characteristics.

10. Kish (1954:397) phrases his conclusions in terms of homogeneity and integration, which we saw in chapter 2 to be characteristics of mechanical solidarity and *Gemeinschaft.*

11. The shopping centers occupied 52.5 square miles, while central business districts occupied 47.5 square miles (Hoyt, 1964). The development of a major shopping center can act as a nucleus that attracts new residential and commercial residents to an area.

6 Life Styles in the City and Suburbs

The expansion and growth of cities have altered the ways that people live, behave, and act toward one another. These changes have not occurred all at once, but their cumulative effect has been extensive. Because history has not provided us with any controlled experiments in city culture, we do not know whether the changes we observe are due to urbanization, population growth, industrialization, selective migration, or some combination of these factors. We do know that the pace of life in cities and the relationships among people and between people and institutions is markedly different from those in preurban settlements, contemporary small towns, and suburbs.

City residents, as compared with suburban and small-town residents, seem colder, more hurried, less interested and less willing to become involved in the affairs of others. Institutions and organizations in cities seem more distant from their customers and clients, harder to deal with, and much more bureaucratic than similar institutions in suburbs and small towns. Hospitals, pharmacies, supermarkets, fund-raising organizations, and churches, as well as governmental agencies, are examples of such institutions.

In urban politics the average citizen often feels isolated and excluded from political decision making. The image of the city "boss" or "city hall" as persons or seats of power, unreachable except through the use of contacts, stands in stark contrast to the image of small-town participatory democracy epitomized by the New England town meeting or the suburban assembly in the high school gym. Although the accuracy of both of these images is questionable, beyond doubt they

convey the common conception of differences in urban and small-town **life styles.**

Although common images suggest that one style characterizes life in large cities and another characterizes life in the suburbs and small towns, this is not so. If large cities could be described in a single term, that term would be heterogeneity. Cities, and even many suburbs, are occupied by so many different people and institutions, in pursuit of so many different goals that the dominant image is often one of chaos. Large cities are composed of many **natural areas** in which people exhibit vastly different life styles. In some parts of the city there are concentrations of single people in their twenties, sharing apartments, seeking mates, beginning independent lives away from home or college. Their way of life often finds organizational expression in bars, clubs, and voluntary associations designed to bring these young people together. In other parts of the city, residents are older, married, more permanently settled, and beginning to raise families. The organizations and institutions in these areas focus on families and children. Urban life styles, such as those based primarily on stage in the **life cycle,** differ along other dimensions as well. Ethnicity, race, and social class are major sources of differences in urban life styles. Sexual orientation and occupation also create homogeneous natural areas in cities.

Suburban life is generally thought to be far less variable than city life. Suburbs are commonly conceived of as communities of families who are homogeneous in class, race, and life-cycle stage. Their activities are thought of as family-centered—raising children, keeping the lawn trimmed, washing the car, and making repairs on the house. Social activities seem centered around block parties, coffee klatches, and neighborhood dinners. Like other myths, this concept is far too simple to be accurate. There is greater diversity in the suburbs than this image suggests. Apartment complexes where swinging singles or other groups predominate exist in suburbs as well as in cities. There are suburbs where family-centered activities and neighborhood-based social life are no more common than they are in some areas of the city.

Social Life in the Metropolis: Simmel and Wirth

The development of metropolitan social systems has had an extensive impact on urban social life. Both individual and collective behaviors have been transformed as people have adapted to life among large and highly heterogeneous populations. The obvious advantages of urban living—access to jobs, to diverse educational, recreational, and cultural activities, and to an increased range of goods and services—are offset by the disadvantages of high population densities—the lack of **primary relationships,** or frequent interpersonal contacts, and the multitude of problems lumped under the term the urban crisis.

The spread of metropolitan culture throughout the larger society has brought the relative advantages and disadvantages of the metropolis to cities and towns of all sizes. Nevertheless, one need not be an especially astute observer to see that social life in New York, Chicago, and other metropolitan centers is different from that in hundreds of small towns outside the metropolitan areas. The nature of social life in urban and metropolitan areas is one key to the nature of the modern metropolis and its problems.

During the first third of this century, Georg Simmel and Louis Wirth each analyzed urban social life and its impact on individual behavior and social structure. Simmel focused on the influence of urban social structures on the individual, while Wirth was more interested in observable regularities in social behavior. Although written more than thirty years ago, the analyses of both Simmel (1858-1918) and Wirth (1897-1952) have set the tone for much subsequent theory and research, and in many ways their studies are still the most illuminating we have.

Both Simmel and Wirth observed changes in individual personality and in social structures that they attributed to urban living. As these changes occurred, new urban life styles emerged that offered to the individual both new forms of freedom and new forms of isolation.

The City and Individualism

Simmel was concerned with the individual's ability to maintain individuality, autonomy, and self-concept in spite of the city's influence (Simmel, 1969). Simmel saw that changing concepts of community in the city increased people's ability to act as individuals rather than as parts of a social collectivity. The eighteenth-century utilitarians had seen the traditional structures of state, church, and community as restrictive and had called for more individualism and individual freedom. The nineteenth century and the Industrial Revolution brought functional specialization, which further altered concepts of community and made each individual more dependent on the work of other people (see chapter 2). Even before the assembly line was invented, factory

work and urban living had become highly routinized and mechanical. People had become like cogs in a machine that was the city, but they did not want to live that way. Simmel attributed the routinization of life to the interdependency of all people in an urban-industrial setting. Marx and other social philosophers blamed the alienation of urban-industrial life on the social and technological mechanisms of society. Simmel, however, attributed the alienation to nervous or **sensory stimulation,** intensified by a swift, uninterrupted bombardment of the individual by outside stimuli.

Urban Sensory Stimulation and Its Consequences

According to Simmel, the basic psychological characteristic of metropolitan residents is the ability to differentiate among many different stimuli. All people select and act on those stimuli that are immediately relevant.[1] The conscious effort required to differentiate between stimuli is greater in a metropolitan area than in a nonmetropolitan area, not only because there are more people, but also because each person interacts with more people of different types. In contrast to life in a small town, which is rooted in deeply felt, durable, emotional relationships, life in the metropolis is likely to be based on more fleeting, superficial relationships. Because more things change in the urban social environment, habits of response cannot become as deeply ingrained. Metropolitan residents use intellectual processes to protect themselves against exposure to large numbers of stimuli and to threatening discrepancies and currents in the external environment.

The complexity of social life in a metropolis requires residents to assign values to different goods and services on a colder, more intellectual basis than that used in smaller communities. It is not possible for a person to consider all individual characteristics of people and goods encountered in the city. The variety of characteristics and traits exhibited in a large, heterogeneous metropolitan area is so great that people must rely on summary characterizations and classifications or they would never get anything done. Therefore the intellectual processes of characterizing and classifying people, objects, and events on the basis of little information are necessary to reduce the number of stimuli to a manageable number of categories and to deal with each stimulus as a representative of a category or class rather than as an individual.

Urban Impersonality

People as well as things are seen and treated as representatives of classes or categories. They interact on the basis of the class or category to which they assign each other. A class defines what is common to all its members. This intellectual evaluation of people and goods emphasizes worth and cost rather than individual character and quality. As a result, the metropolitan resident is mainly concerned with the social and economic costs of relationships between individuals.

In small towns, suburbs, and perhaps even within neighborhoods of large metropolitan areas, there are small circles of acquaintances and friends among whom individual qualities and characteristics are important. For the most part, however, because metropolitan

Without a high degree of impersonal precision and coordination, the fabric of life in a metropolis would begin to break down.

residents must deal with large numbers of people and large numbers of social relationships, they deal with people primarily as role occupants. This leads to feelings of anonymity and to interpersonal contacts that are brief, cold, calculated, and relatively impersonal. People in metropolitan areas do not focus on the characteristics, attributes, and interpersonal relationships of people with whom they interact, but rather on the goal of the interaction. In many ways social life in the metropolis is analogous to relationships in physics, which are based on formulas; a person wearing the uniform of a police officer will be reacted to in the same way as are all police officers.

The need for coordination. Social life in the metropolis is so complex, but so interrelated, that a high degree of precision and coordination is necessary. Time, for example, is much more important in a metropolitan area than in a rural area. Simmel illustrated this point with a story about the effects of setting all watches in Berlin on different times. The result would be turmoil, for all organized activity would soon stop. Classes would not gather, people would miss trains, trains would run randomly and connections between them would be missed, people would appear in offices at different times, and the whole fabric of social life would begin to break down. Therefore, surface characteristics, such as punctuality, become important criteria for evaluating people in a metropolitan area.

The blasé metropolitan attitude. Dealing with people on the basis of superficial characteristics—treating them as representatives of

Anonymity and Impersonality in Urban Life

Tönnies is talking about what some sociologists describe as "primary" versus "secondary" relationships, or "organic" versus "functional" relationships. Having lived both as a villager and as an urbanite I know just what these terms mean. During my boyhood, my parents never referred to "the milkman," "the insurance agent," "the junk collector." These people were, respectively Paul Weaver, Joe Villanova, and Roxy Barazano. All of our family's market transactions took place within a web of wider and more inclusive friendship and kinship ties with the same people. They were never anonymous. In fact, the occasional salesman or repairman whom we did not know was always viewed with dark suspicion until we could make sure where he came from, who his parents were, and whether his family was "any good." Trips to the grocery store, gasoline station, or post office were inevitably social visits, never merely functional contacts.

Now, as an urbanite, my transactions are of a very different sort. If I need to have the transmission on my car repaired, buy a television antenna, or cash a check, I find myself in functional relationships with mechanics, salesmen, and bank clerks whom I never see in any other capacity. These "contacts" are in no sense "mean, nasty, or brutish," though they do tend to be short, at least not any longer than the time required to make the transaction and to exchange a brief pleasantry. Some of these human contacts occur with considerable frequency, so that I come to know the mannerisms and maybe even the names of some of the people. But the relationships are unifaceted and "segmental." I meet these people in no other context. To me they remain essentially just as anonymous as I do to them. Indeed, in the case of the transmission repairman, I hope I never see him again—not because he is in any way unpleasant, but because my only possible reason for seeing him again would be a new and costly breakdown in my car's gear box. The important point here is that my relationships with bank clerks and garagemen are no less human or authentic merely because we both prefer to keep them anonymous. . . .

Harvey Cox provides a vivid description of the nature of urban anonymity and impersonality in urban social relations.

Urban anonymity need not be heartless. Village sociability can mask a murderous hostility. Loneliness is undoubtedly a serious problem in the city, but it cannot be met by dragooning urban people into relationships which decimate their privacy and reduce their capacity to live responsibly with increasing numbers of neighbors. . . .

The small-town dweller, on the other hand, lives within a restricted web of relationships and senses a larger world he may be missing. Since the people he knows also know one another, he gossips more and yearns to hear gossip. His private life is public and vice versa. While urban man is unplugging his telephone, town man (or his wife) may be listening in on the party line or its modern equivalent, gossiping at the kaffee-klatsch.

Urban man, in contrast, wants to maintain a clear distinction between private and public. Otherwise public life would overwhelm and dehumanize him. His life represents a point touched by dozens of systems and hundreds of people. His capacity to know some of them better necessitates his minimizing the depth of his relationships to many others. Listening to the postman gossip becomes for urban man an act of sheer graciousness, since he probably has no interest in the people the postman wants to talk about. Unlike my parents, who suspected all strangers, he tends to be wary not of the functionaries he doesn't know but of those he does. . . .

Source Reprinted with permission of Macmillan Publishing Co., Inc. from *The Secular City* by Harvey Cox. Copyright © 1976 Harvey Cox.

classes and as role occupants rather than as individuals—leads to social life that is cold and calculating. Simmel described this as the **blasé attitude** characteristic of metropolitan residents. He concluded that city dwellers were blasé because of the overload of nervous stimulation caused by the frequency of interaction with so many different people and goods in the metropolis. A blasé attitude helps people overcome the inability to act as a consequence of attempting to discriminate between too many stimuli. To each other, and especially to people from small towns, blase urbanites appear to be cold, reserved, and heartless. This reserve helps the individual save face and hide one's full personality behind the roles one plays. It preserves individuality and protects the individual in the face of unexpected reactions or behaviors. Reserve also leads to feelings of alienation and mutual distrust. Metropolitan residents appear to be, and often are, indifferent to each other's needs and desires. This is why urban life is often described as atomized or alienated and why people fail to come to the aid of strangers in times of need or danger.[2] Urban social life and contacts are fluid, fleeting, and changing. People act in each other's presence, but they are strangers to one another and respond with mutual indifference. There is a positive side to indifference and reserve because we assume them to be mutual. We don't care who other people are or what they do, and they feel the same way about us. Consequently, people have a great deal of personal freedom in the metropolis.

The City As a Source of Freedom

Early cities and contemporary small towns are relatively small societies characterized by *Gemeinschaft.* Everybody knows everybody else, and there is little personal anonymity. Under such circumstances the individual does not develop unique or distinctive characteristics. The individuality and personal freedom, both social and psychic, available to members of an organically integrated *Gesellschaft* are rarely found in *Gemeinschaft* communities. Thoughts and behaviors must be homogeneous to maintain group solidarity.

In a mechanically integrated society or *Gemeinschaft* group solidarity is strong. With the loosening of social ties or bonds, individuals and groups of individuals may take positions that the total society would consider **contranormative**—think or act in ways that violate society's norms. Individuals and groups can do this because they are treated with great reserve. Their privacy is not invaded by other people, and they do not invade the privacy of others. Privacy and lack of attention are conducive to the development of individuality and a sense of personal, psychological freedom. Individuals are free to act, think, and feel as they please, with only general normative constraint.

Metropolitan styles of interaction also reduce the amount of petty personal prejudice—interpersonal dislike based on personal characteristics. (Prejudice based on group characteristics, such as racial or ethnic origin, is not reduced in the city.) Much small-town pettiness is dissipated in metropolitan interactions because relationships are based on social roles rather than personal characteristics.

Metropolitan residents don't care about or know about the personal behaviors and attitudes of others that normally generate interpersonal conflict, petty bickering, and prejudice in small towns. Life is so complex in the metropolis—there is so much to do, so many people with whom to interact—that most social contacts are extremely brief. Because social contacts are brief, contact must be direct and to the point. An individual attracts attention in these contacts by being distinctive. In the absence of distinctive personal characteristics and an immediate, recognizable purpose for interaction, people treat each other alike and evaluate each other on their surface characteristics.

In his analysis of social life, Simmel notes that small towns place certain constraints on individual behavior. These constraints are greatly reduced as the city becomes larger and as the number and frequency of social interactions increase. Urban residents have less time and energy to devote to each interpersonal contact. This promotes individual freedom and mobility, while weakening the bonds between the individual and society.

Urbanism As a Way of Life

Louis Wirth's analysis (1938) of urban life reformulated Simmel's theme in more sociological terms (Wirth, 1964:60-83; Sjoberg, 1964:127-60). Although the article appeared about forty years ago, Wirth's concepts continue to influence sociological thinking about social life in cities.

The Definition of a City

Wirth first attempted to define a city. He said that no definition based on size alone would be adequate, because any size one picks is arbitrary. The city is a legal-political entity and has legal boundaries. Definitions of a city based on size must use **census** data, which reflect administrative and political boundaries. Using a legal-political definition means having to assume that urban forms of behavior, interaction, and social organization cease abruptly at the city limits. This, Wirth observed, makes no sociological sense at all, for the city dominates an area much wider than its legal boundaries. Even in 1938, the city offered a full range of goods and services to people living both inside and outside the city limits. Thus the urban way of life, which is most typical of people living in the central city, extends well beyond the legal boundaries of the city. Therefore, studies of urban social life require a definition of the city that is based on something other than size.

Even a definition of city based on other criteria, such as population density, gives rise to the same objections. Whether a city is defined as a population settlement with a density of one person per square mile or ten thousand persons per square mile, the lives of people living well beyond the boundaries of the settlement will be influenced by it. Wirth was among the first to point out that the census counts people on the basis of where they live and sleep at night, rather than where they live and work during the day. The census is a nighttime **enumeration,** and the use of density as a census criterion can distort the findings.

The central city is a business district in which the urban way of life is clearly present. Yet people come to work there during the day and leave at night, reducing both the size and density of the population below that observed in other parts of the city. Therefore, population density is not a valid criterion for deciding what a city is or for analyzing urban ways of life.

However, any reasonable definition of a city must take into account physical size and population density, as well as variations in institutional structures and types of people living there. Wirth defined the city as

> a relatively large, dense, and permanent settlement of socially heterogeneous individuals. . . . The central problem of the sociologist of the city is to discover the forms of social action and organization that typically emerge in a permanent compact settlement of large numbers of heterogeneous individuals [Wirth 1964:66, 68].

Using this definition of a city and this concept of the urban sociologist's central problem, Wirth generated several hypotheses about urban life. Though subsequent research (Gans, 1962a; Lewis, 1965:441-503, 619-22) has shown them to need modification, these hypotheses have strongly influenced sociologists' thinking about social life in the city.

Wirth expected large, dense, heterogeneous cities to be more urban than small, less dense, homogeneous cities. Stated as a hypothesis, which has not been completely confirmed by subsequent empirical research, Wirth's idea is that as city size, density, and heterogeneity increase, ways of life among the population become more urban (Duncan, 1957:35-45; Dewey, 1960:60-66).

The Effects of Size: Heterogeneity and Secondary Relationships

Wirth pointed out that political and social thinkers have known since the time of Aristotle that an increase in population will affect interpersonal relationships in a society and the character of that society. The larger the population, the greater the variety among people. Thus size of city is one cause of urban heterogeneity. Heterogeneity itself is part of the definition of a city and has its own consequences, but size of city has consequences other than increased heterogeneity.

As urban population increases, the possibility that every resident will know every other resident decreases. According to Simmel (1969) and Max Weber (1958), this leads to individualized, **atomized relationships** between people. Because their contacts are so many and so fleeting, people in large cities interact mainly on the basis of role relationships, or what Weber called **secondary relationships**. Wirth refers to the **schizoid character** of the urban personality, by which he means that people living in urban areas know each other only as occupants of specific roles and reveal different aspects of their personalities in those different roles.

Although people in urban areas are free to express their individuality, the complexity of the city makes them dependent on others for the satisfaction of many basic needs, physical as well as social and psychological. Because most interaction among urbanites is through secondary relationships, they do not even know well the people on whom they depend.

In fact, outside of family contacts and immediate, primary relationships, each city dweller is dependent not on other specific individuals but rather on classes of people. The city resident engages in **segmental interaction**—that is, relates to others on the basis of role rather than on the basis of the personal characteristics of the individual filling that role. Social life in the city is characterized by secondary and even **tertiary relationships** between individuals. People interact in person, but their interactions are impersonal, superficial, transitory, and segmental. The people behind the counters at the stores where we shop are just people behind the counter. We know other people only in their roles as cleaners, postal carriers, police officers, supermarket clerks, and so forth. Simmel and Wirth came to the same conclusion: because social life in the city is the way it is, people do not deal with others in an open and trusting manner, but rather with reserve and with little personal knowledge of other people. They know little or nothing about the feelings of others.

The Effects of Density

Both Darwin and Durkheim pointed out that increasing specialization comes with increasing population density. Only with specialization can a given area support greater numbers of people. Simmel noted that close physical contact in cities due to density of population causes us to change the media through which we orient ourselves to our urban milieu. We no longer personally experience what is happening in the city; we learn about events, people, and problems from the radio, the television, and the newspapers.

As density increases, individuals who have no sentimental or emotional ties to each other increasingly live closer together. Sheer physical closeness increases the rate of interaction and, as Durkheim pointed out, leads to the division of labor and the development of organic forms of social solidarity. The consequences of these changes in the community become evident. The characteristics of *Gesellschaft* develop—a rationalized, organic society emerges (see chapter 2). Individuals compete rather than cooperate, and normative integration and social solidarity are weakened. As anonymity, reserve, and impersonality increase in relationships between individuals, these are few informal controls on social behavior. Formal controls and formal agencies of control are substituted for bonds of sentiment, emotion, or kinship. The substitution of institutional control for normative integration produces relatively high levels of loneliness, alienation, and anomie.

The Effects of Heterogeneity

Population size and density affect not only the character of the city and the social relationships within the city but the extent of heterogeneity in the city's population. Wirth pointed out that historically the city has been society's melting pot for people of different races and cultures, because the city tolerates differences and provides economic opportunities for all its residents. Differences in people are the basis of heterogeneity in the city. However, because different people must live close together in the city, they are forced to interact. This makes them less strange to one another and less different from one another.

In preurban society social status was relatively universally and unambiguously defined on the basis of long-term intimate knowledge of other persons. In a complicated, heterogeneous, differentiated urban society, individuals have few opportunities to judge from personal knowledge the social positions of persons with whom they interact. Consequently, urban residents rely on superficial attributes to judge the social status of others—their style of clothing, language, public behavior, and other visible signs (Form and Stone, 1957:504-14). The signs and symbols of status have different meanings to different groups and as a result may be interpreted differently. Thus status may be ambiguous and be defined differently by different groups.

High levels of physical and social mobility in the metropolis guarantee relatively rapid turnover in the membership of all urban groups. When city groups are defined on the basis of neighborhood, high turnover leads to segregation of each local area on the basis of characteristics other than place of residence. As an area becomes defined as the home of a particular group—people of like race, language, ethnic heritage, social or economic status, or life style—those who do not fit the general description tend to move out and those who do move in. The area becomes more segregated. Having only superficial characteristics to judge by, people who interact in a segmental way—that is, engage in secondary relationships—use these characteristics when choosing groups among whom they would like to live.

Effects on Social Organization

Wirth noted that increases in city size, density, and heterogeneity had consequences for the family, especially the extended family or kinship system. As traditional bonds of social solidarity disappear, particularly as secondary social relationships replace primary social relationships, the neighborhood loses strength as a source of social organization and control. Consequently, more aberrant, unfamiliar, and unusual behaviors begin to take place in the city, and residents lose confidence that others will behave consistently in accordance with a given set of norms. There is more normative differentiation, and far more deviance is tolerated.

As cities grow larger, institutions and voluntary groups arise to fill the needs previously satisfied by more extensive primary relationships. Clinics, churches, and government agencies provide the health care, religious counseling, and social and welfare services previously offered by the extended family, the kinship group, and other primary groups.

The urban individual, reserved and blase, relates in a segmented way in various isolated, voluntary groups. No single group has the individual's undivided allegiance. Because a person belongs to many different groups within the city, individual status and group identifications vary and are ambiguous. An individual may belong to an ethnic group, a particular occupational or educational group, a religious group, or any of a wide variety of voluntary associations—unions, veterans organizations, political action committees, study groups, recreational clubs, or cultural societies. Some individuals belong to many such groups. Wirth sees voluntary group membership as one source of sophistication and cosmopolitanism in urban life. The urban personality is expressed and developed through the status acquired in these voluntary groups.

In a large city it is almost impossible and very inefficient to appeal to individuals for political support or for any other commitment. Therefore, most appeals to urban residents are directed to them as members of organizations. The voluntary organization substitutes for the extended family, the neighborhood, or the community as a means of communicating with individuals.

Because of mobility and competing group affiliations, most voluntary social organizations in the city are volatile, fragile, and complicated. They do not offer to their members long-lasting bonds of solidarity among individuals or between the individual and the organization. Urban residents view these groups as undependable in times of crisis, so participation in them is inconsistent, length of membership is short, and levels of commitment are low.

Wirth concluded that urbanization breaks down the ties that bind the individual to society and to other individuals:

> In the face of the disappearance of the territorial unit as a basis of social solidarity we create interest units. Meanwhile the city as a community resolves itself into a series of tenuous, segmental relationships superimposed upon a territorial base with a definite center but without a definite periphery and upon a division of labor which far transcends the immediate locality and is worldwide in scope [Wirth 1964:68].

Wirth's theory, still by far the most influential theory of its kind, assumes that the three factors—population size, density, and heterogeneity—explain the nature of all urban social life. Wirth does not see even a **quasi-primary group** left in the city.[3] He argues that city life inherently destroys the primary group and primary relationships, throwing individuals out on their own as atomized human beings interacting in segmental ways.

Criticisms of Wirth's Theory

Wirth's theoretical speculations about the impact of population size, density, and heterogeneity on city social life was based on the early research of the Chicago school of sociology (Faris, 1967; Short, 1971). More recent research shows that atomization and isolation of individuals do not always occur as Wirth would have hypothesized. Groups living in so-called disorganized areas or slums exhibit high degrees of social organization and cohesion, as W. F. Whyte (1943), Herbert Gans (1962b), and Oscar Lewis (1965) and others have shown. Recent critics of Wirth (Fischer, 1972:187-242; 1975:71-73; Kasarda and Janowitz, 1974:328-39) have studied slums, ethnic ghettos, and public housing projects in large cities. They found that disorganized, isolated, atomized social relationships were not typical of life in these neighborhoods. Rather, close primary relationships appeared dominant.

Wirth's theory must be modified in light of these findings. Residents in some areas of the city may be able to maintain close personal ties with their neighbors. To the extent that they can isolate themselves from the rest of the city, they can create a **quasi-*Gemeinschaft*** by maintaining a communal identity and generating patterns of behavior that are warmer and more personal than either Simmel or Wirth would have predicted. However, residents are unlikely to extend these feelings and behaviors to persons who are not residents of the area or to those whom they visit in other areas of the city. Indeed, the city may be composed of numerous quasi-*Gemeinschaft*s that together interact as a *Gesellschaft*. Perhaps within each quasi-*Gemeinschaft* communal relationships predominate, but between different quasi-*Gemeinschaft*s relationships are cold, impersonal, and *Gesellschaft*-like. To the extent that urban residents engage in more extralocal than local area relationships, most urban social behavior, as described by Wirth, is *Gesellschaft*-like.

Viewing urban organization as many *Gemeinschaft* neighborhoods making up a *Gesellschaft* city does not prevent us from recognizing that in some areas different life styles, and even incompatible or socially deviant life styles, may dominate. Furthermore, such a situation would explain how residents can lose themselves in a city; by moving to a new area and adopting the appropriate social style, they assume a new identity. Historically, serfs, bondsmen, and peasants fled the countryside for the city, escaping the restrictions of their earlier life. Immigrants to this country did the same. Once assimilated enough to pass as Americans, they could move from their original neighborhoods to new ones. Similarly, slaves fleeing to northern urban centers from southern slave states prior to the Civil War could act as, and be treated as, freedmen. Both criminals and radical protestors in the

1960s and 1970s have demonstrated that the city still provides (as close as we are to 1984) at least some anonymity and isolation from those would act as Big Brother.

Anonymity, segmental interaction, and personal reserve are not encouraged in residents of small towns and suburbs. There are, of course, areas in the city where these characteristics also are not well tolerated (Gans, 1962b; Suttles, 1968; Whyte, 1943, 1957). Nevertheless, the city as a whole is a social arena in which the individual can be alone, anonymous, and free from constant observation by others. Individuals who follow one life style rarely bother fellow citizens who follow another. Each urban resident has great personal freedom because of the scale, density, and diversity of the urban social system.

City and Suburban Life Styles

One way to understand the life styles of cities and suburbs is to concentrate on their major differences, or apparent differences. During the 1950s and early 1960s many social commentators discussed the suburban explosion, the suburban life, and the suburban effect on national character. These commentators, depending on their philosophy and point of view, were either horrified or full of praise. The migrants to the suburbs were seen as living a distinctively suburban way of life that was characterized by concern for the family and for children, material consumption, status striving, a relatively high level of detachment from the wider society, and increased local involvement (Fava, 1956:34-38; Bell, 1958:225-47; Martin, 1956:445-53; Mowrer, 1958:147-64; Dobriner, 1958b:132-43; Seeley et al., 1972:116-36; Berger, 1972:5-18).

Subsequent research has given us reason to doubt that the patterns of behavior seen in the suburbs are due to suburban residence or even that there is a distinctly suburban way of life (Marshall, 1973:123-48; Fischer and Jackson, 1976:279-308). Rather, it has been suggested that particular types of people who shared certain values, attitudes, and ways of living moved to the suburbs (Gans, 1962a; Schnore, 1963:122-34; 1972). Their concentration in one area made their behavior more visible, but it was not a new form of behavior or a new way of life.

This explanation—**selective migration**—is just one of many that have been advanced to explain the suburban way of life. To a large extent the migration to the suburbs has been composed of relatively young families with small children who are white, middle-class, and upwardly mobile. They moved to the suburbs because there they could find the best house they could afford and a way of life that appealed to them.

A second explanation of suburban life styles stresses the life-cycle stage and class position of the migrants. It is argued that suburban residents do not differ significantly in life style from central city residents of the same class, and life-cycle stage (Marshall, 1973; Fischer and Jackson, 1976; Gans, 1962a; Schnore, 1963, 1972).

A third explanation is ecological: that the distance from the center of the city and the lower residential density of suburbs throws suburbanites on the resources of the family and the neighborhood for that short time when they are not working or commuting. Because the suburbs are so widespread and the central city is so distant, it is costly for people who live in suburbs to associate with people other than their neighbors and especially costly for them to use the facilities of the central city. The length of time it takes to commute to the central city forces suburban residents to spend their leisure time with their families or involved in local activities (Fischer and Jackson, 1976:297-308).

In summary, there does not seem to be a distinctively suburban way of life and only modest differences between urban and suburban life styles. These differences appear to be the result of the selective migration to suburbs of people with specific life-cycle stage, class, and sociopsychological characteristics; ecological factors of distance and density; and political independence from the city. Most likely, the differences are caused by a combination of these factors.

Family Orientation

One most commonly discussed attribute of suburban living is **familism**: a combination of beliefs, values, and behaviors centered on the nuclear family (Greer, 1973:149-70; Long and Glick, 1976:39-67; Marshall, 1973:123-48). While this attribute is commonly discussed, it does not reflect any striking differences between suburban and urban residents. When social class and life-cycle stage are similar for both groups, the differences between the two are quite small.

The image of suburban familism focuses on (1) more married couples having more children than urban couples do; (2) child-centered consumption patterns; (3) child-oriented reasons for moving to the suburbs (more space to play in, better schools, a better class of children to play with); and (4) greater involvement of parents, especially

mothers, in transporting children to school, to appointments with doctors and dentists, to music lessons, and to other children's houses. These characteristics give the impression that family life in the suburbs is much more close-knit and interdependent than family life in the city.

Children are only one component of the familistic image. The **nuclear family** in the suburbs acts more as a unit, partly because the home is designed to maximize family activity. The size and number of rooms and their uses (an eating nook in the kitchen, a family room or den), plus space for a patio or picnic and barbecue area outdoors, all help to make joint family activities more common in the suburbs than they are in urban apartments or detached homes in the city.

Employment may also influence familism. Because men are more likely than women to work outside the home, women become more involved than men in the familistic complex. This was especially true before suburban families commonly owned two cars.

Studies have shown that shared husband-wife activity, especially shared leisure-time activity, is not as common among blue-collar as among white-collar suburbanites. Therefore, familism may be a class phenomenon rather than a suburban phenomenon. Blue-collar wives in the suburbs, like blue-collar wives in the city, are more involved in home and family than in outside activities or in activities that they share with their husbands. Blue-collar suburban husbands, like their urban counterparts, are more involved in activities with other men outside the home and share less in family activities than do their wives. Thus, the apparent familism of the suburbs may reflect nothing more than a high concentration of

Although a street fair is characteristically urban and a back-yard barbecue characteristically suburban, there are few differences between urban and suburban life styles.

people who would exhibit familism wherever they lived. These traits are probably reinforced in the suburbs by distance from recreational facilities and by the design of suburban homes.

Neighborhood and Local Involvement

Suburban residents, especially housewives, seem to associate more with their neighbors than do urban residents. The difference between suburban and urban housewives is not great but it is consistent. In general, suburban residents spend more time with their neighbors and describe more of their close friends as neighbors than do city dwellers. They are more involved than city dwellers in local social activities and less involved in a wider circle of social action (Marshall, 1973; Fava, 1958:122-31; Dobriner, 1958b:132-43; Tallman and Morgner, 1970:334-48). Although some writers attribute this **localism** in the suburbs to demographic homogeneity (of age, race, class, life-cycle stage), others ascribe it to geographic isolation and ecological causes. Regardless of the reasons for it, this concentration in the suburbs of people who focus on their families and their neighborhoods has consequences for all suburban residents and institutions, especially the schools.

Maintaining Homogeneity in the Suburbs

Some city neighborhoods may be as homogeneous as suburban areas, but because they are part of the larger city, they cannot restrict participation in their institutions solely to neighborhood residents. Suburbs can impose such restrictions, and this is especially crucial in the schools.

One child-centered reason that people give for moving to the suburbs is the quality of the schools (Bell, 1958:225-47), and suburban residents want to maintain this quality. Parents highly value homogeneity of social class and guard their children's opportunities to interact exclusively, or at least predominantly, with other children of the same social class, who are likely to have the same values as their own. This exclusiveness is more possible in the suburbs than in the city. Because suburbs are politically independent, each tends to have its own school system, which can be attended only by residents of that suburb. Suburbs thus restrict participation in a way that city neighborhoods cannot.

The processes of growth and expansion that have produced homogeneous suburbs are probably not different in kind from the processes that have produced homogeneous natural areas in the central city. However, distance from the city and political independence allow suburbs to protect the homogeneity of their social life and of their schools. Protection is not absolute, of course, because the norms of the society do not favor exclusion on the basis of race, religion, income, national origin, and the like. Lacking other urban attractions, homogeneity of the schools and of social life may be critical elements in the continuing popularity of the suburbs.

Consumerism

The white-collar middle-class dominates in the suburbs, and many migrants there are upwardly mobile. As aspiring middle-class suburbanites, they are likely to purchase goods and services that offer visible evidence of their current financial success and their expectations. Thus the home and its furnishings symbolically indicate suburban residents' ability to live at least as well as their neighbors. The parent's accumulation of goods is extended to the children, who receive an unending supply of toys and other childhood status symbols, while the parents acquire for themselves an equally unending supply of furniture, appliances, cars, swimming pools, and so on (Seeley et al., 1972:116-36).

A Reassessment of City and
Suburban Life Styles

In an article that is now nearly as classic as Wirth's "Urbanism As a Way of Life," Herbert Gans (1962a) pointed out that many ways of life described as typical of the city or the suburbs were really typical of only portions of the city and suburbs. In his article "Urbanism and Suburbanism As Ways of Life: A Reevaluation of Definitions," Gans argued that most urban residents did not participate exclusively in impersonal, secondary *Gesellschaft*-like relationships that Wirth described as being universal in the city. Nor were suburban residents as tied up in their families and immediate neighborhoods as others had indicated. Rather, Gans maintained, in both suburb and city there was a mixture of life styles. In both locations individuals sought quasi-primary relationships in their immediate social environments. Suburban residents perhaps had greater opportunities to establish such relationships, especially with neighbors who shared their class, race, life-cycle stage, and other characteristics.

Types of Suburbs

The image of suburbia emerged as the suburbs emerged. These once new, almost totally residential areas subsequently developed along with the central cities, changing in character as a consequence (Schnore, 1957:109-21; 1958:26-44; Farley, 1976:3-38; Kasarda, 1976:113-36; Glenn, 1973:51-78). Many suburbs now have industrial parks, shopping centers, and other nonresidential institutions. The suburbanization of society during the 1950s and 1960s might just as accurately be called the urbanization of the suburbs. In the 1970s there is greater variation in types of suburbs and in styles of suburban living than ever before.

Residential density in the suburban areas is increasing as land becomes more valuable and more expensive than many home buyers can afford. Condominiums, townhouses, and cluster developments are being built in the suburbs (Bourne, 1971:321-28; Whyte, 1967: 462-77). Multiunit apartment buildings also are appearing. The physical design of these units will influence the life styles of residents. An apartment in the suburbs is not so different from an apartment in the city, although there may be more lawn around it. Furthermore, apartments in suburbs that offer business opportunities attract persons in an earlier life-cycle stage than that of residents who migrate there to live in detached homes and raise their children. Thus many apartment buildings in suburbia are attracting single persons who follow a different life style than that of earlier suburban residents.

Suburban living traditionally meant single-family homes on individual lots (*top*). The tradition was continued in Levitown, Pennsylvania in the 1950s (*right*). More recent suburban development often includes clustered and multi-family units surrounded by public open space (*bottom*).

Suburban areas have been categorized many different ways—as residential, industrial, or as satellite (once-independent cities encompassed by growing metropolitan or urbanized areas) (Schnore, 1957:109-21). As the institutional structures of suburbia have changed, their functions have changed. Since few suburbs are now limited to single functions, it seems inappropriate to classify them on this basis. Suburban areas are best analyzed in terms of population characteristics and distance from the central city.

Types of Suburbs

In pursuit of the suburban dream, Americans have precipitated one of the largest mass movements in history: during the past decade, the population of suburbia has grown by more than 15 million. According to the preliminary 1970 census reports, there are now 74.9 million people classified as suburbanites, a 25% increase over 1960. This surge has made suburbanites the largest group in the land, outnumbering both city dwellers and those who live in rural areas. So many Americans have already achieved the suburban goal that suburbia itself has undergone a mutation. Inevitably, the new migrants have undone the cliché image of an affluent, WASPish, Republican hotbed of wife swappers. In the suburban myth, all men are button-down commuters, swilling one martini too many in the bar car of the 5:32. Frustrated women spend their days driving from station to school to supermarket to bridge club. The kids are spoiled and confused. Families move regularly, as Daddy is transferred or climbs the corporate ladder.

A New Typology

That myth was nurtured in postwar fiction like Sloan Wilson's *The Man in the Gray Flannel Suit* and John Marquand's *Point of No Return;* it was caricatured by such writers as Max Shulman (*Rally Round the Flag, Boys!*) and Peter De Vries (*The Mackerel Plaza*), elaborated more darkly in John Cheever's *Bullet Park.* The stereotype was neither wholly wrong nor wholly accurate. But those who have taken the trouble to look carefully have recognized that suburbia has been steadily changing. Today the demographic realities are radically different from the cliché, a change that is clearly documented in a *Time*-Louis Harris survey of more than 1,600 suburban Americans in 100 different communities across the land.

What emerges from the survey is a picture of unexpected diversity, some contradiction and occasional surprise. Suburbanites are not primarily transients; more than half have lived for more than ten years in the same community. Suburbanites are not automatically Republicans; on the voting rolls, half are Democrats, a third Republicans. They are not enormously affluent; nearly half of suburban families have an annual income under $10,000, and one-third of them contain a union member. They are not primarily commuters; not many more than a third of the principal wage earners travel to the central city to work.

One reason the Harris results are at odds with the myth is that they are based on what the Census Bureau considers to be a suburb, which is, roughly, that part of a metropolitan area surrounding a central city with a population of 50,000 or more. That includes some unexpected territory.

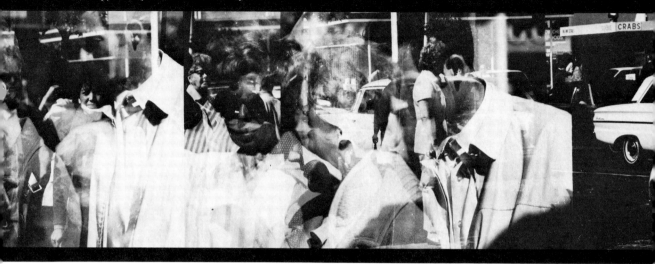

The myth of suburban homogeneity is contradicted by 1970 census data and by the results of surveys that indicate that a wide range of suburban types can be found. This excerpt from *Time* illustrates the variability in suburban residents and in the types of places in which they live.

Nassau County on Long Island is obviously suburban, reaching only 20 miles from Manhattan at its farthest point. Most Americans would also consider California's Marin County to be a suburb; many of its residents commute across the Golden Gate Bridge to San Francisco from upper-bohemian Sausalito, sophisticated Mill Valley or nondescript San Rafael.

But as the census sees it, suburbia also includes such unlikely terrain as Cascade County, around Great Falls, Mont.—lightly populated towns in flat, rolling wheat country—and Minnehaha County, surrounding Sioux Falls, S. Dak., mainly onetime farming towns that have increasingly become dormitory communities. Northwestern University Sociologist Raymond Mack says a suburb has only two distinct characteristics: proximity to a big city and specific political boundaries which result in local control of government. Most of the people whom Harris questioned do not even think of themselves as suburbanites. More often, they would say that they live in a small city, a town or even a rural area. Yet in the broader sense they are true suburbanites, living between city and countryside, geographically the middlemen between densely populated urban cores and the expanses of what remains of rural, small-town America.

Sociologists have made studies of single suburbs, or the suburbs of a single city, or of specific aspects of suburbia (such as politics or race), but they have never attempted a systematic nationwide classification of the types of towns that make up suburbia. Louis Harris and his polltakers set out to do just that for *Time*. "Our goal," he says, "was to examine suburban complexity and to find a systematic way of classifying suburban communities that would shed light on the real differences that exist within the wide and expanding belt between the cities and the small towns and farms."

Using a computer programmed to recognize patterns among the characteristics of suburbs covered by the survey data, the Harris staff discovered that the interplay of two particular factors—income level and rate of growth—can be used to classify suburbs in four groups. The result is a new four-way typology of American suburbia. Each kind of suburb has distinctive traits, though no single suburb precisely fits the Harris statistical model. The four composite types:

continued

Affluent bedroom. Of the four classes of suburb in the Harris catalogue, this is the only one that comes close to fitting the stereotypical conception. (And of the four categories, this is the only one in which a majority of residents even confessed to living in a suburb.) Even so, in towns of this type—New Canaan, Conn., Winnetka, Ill., and Atherton, Calif.—less than half of the breadwinners work in large cities. The Affluent Bedroom communities are tops in income, home ownership, proportion of professionals and executives. They contain increasing numbers of wealthy retired individuals, and they are 98% white, 61% Protestant, 3% Jewish. They are Republican (62% for Nixon in 1968. 24% for Humphrey). Few in the Affluent Bedroom admit to feeling "really bored and stuck out here"; most believe that their fellow townsmen truly enjoy suburban living. The Affluent Bedroom comes closest to Lewis Mumford's description of the historic suburb: "A sort of green ghetto dedicated to the elite."

Affluent settled. This type of suburb is not growing so rapidly as the Bedroom. It is more self-sufficient, even less of a dormitory for the central city. Here—the town of Fairfield, Conn., for example, or Huntington, L.I., or Arlington, Va.—the incomes may not be quite so high and there are slightly fewer homeowners. Protestants barely outnumber Catholics, though together they are a massive majority; only 6% are Jewish, double the proportion for Affluent Bedroom suburbs but hardly a significant minority. Here Nixon won—but only by 47% to 40%. The boredom quotient is higher; nearly half think that their community offers an inadequate range of things to do with leisure time.

Low-income growing. These are towns like Sylvania, Ohio, and Billerica, Mass., with sizable populations of skilled workers, most of whom earn their living close to home. This tends to be upward-mobile blue collar country, where incomes are substantially lower than in the affluent suburbs: only 9% of the residents earn $15,000 or more. Still, four out of five are homeowners. Protestants predominate even more than in wealthier suburbia: they make up 64% of the population, and there are practically no Jews. Most townspeople claim a Democratic political preference, but Nixon won handily here in 1968. Interestingly, the Wallace vote—11%—was no greater than in the Affluent Bedroom communities. Exactly half of the residents rate their town above average as a place to live in their state, but 16% say that many live there only until they can afford something better.

Low-income stagnant. This classification includes Cambridge, Mass., McKeesport, Pa., Joliet, Ill., and Bell Gardens, Calif. Of the four types, it has the highest proportion of nonskilled and service workers—janitors, firemen, waiters, long-shoremen, common laborers and the like— and the lowest proportion of commuters to the central city (34%). Here, on the average, 12% are black—although in some cases, as in East Orange, N.J., and Compton, Calif., blacks have become a majority. Residents register Democratic overwhelmingly, 63% to 28%, and generally vote that way as well. But even here, Nixon squeaked out a 1% margin three years ago. Understandably, those who live in Low-Income Stagnant communities say they enjoy their lives less than Americans in other types of suburb. They are most often bored (25%) and most likely to feel that they and their neighbors are only biding time until they can afford to move (21%). Even so, 39% rate their community as above average; only 10% consider it below average.

Searching for Space

For all the variables, suburbanites of all four types have much in common—not least the reasons they give for moving to the suburbs in the first place. For nearly half of all the suburbanites

Harris polled, the biggest single factor was the desire to have a home of their own. Next in order of importance came the search for a better atmosphere for the children (40%), a goal that they ruefully admit is not always realized. Suburban teen-agers are impressively unhappy with their surroundings; nearly three-fifths are "often bored," and 43% say that they would like to live somewhere else when they are no longer dependent on their parents. At least among the offspring of suburbia, the age of ecology has modified the urbanizing tradition that led their ambitious parents to the big city to seek their fortune. Of the kids who want to live elsewhere, more than half—54%—would prefer a more rural to a more urban setting. Says David Riggs, 16, of Virginia Beach, Va.: "By the time I'm out on my own, there will be too many people here. So I'll head for the open spaces."

Adult suburbanites often moved out of the city for the same reason; more than a third say that they were looking for "green, open spaces." Many also say that they came to the suburbs to find friends and neighbors more like themselves. "Life is slower out here," says Robert Pipp, 58, who lives in Lower Paxton Township, a suburban part of Harrisburg, Pa. Surprisingly few give negative reasons—the problems of the city: crime, racial tension, pollution—for getting out.

The statistics testify that, beyond a doubt, most adult suburbanites are happy with their lot. Fully 44% had no serious reservations at all about their neighborhoods, and the major complaints joined in by more than one in ten—high taxes, high cost of living—are problems that plague city dwellers at least as gravely. "Many people really enjoy living in the community" is a statement that 74% agree with; 67% also feel that there is a strong sense of neighborliness. There is always a possibility that such satisfaction may be feigned, a defense against the anxiety-ridden image of the suburbanite in contemporary fiction. Yet most insist that the friendliness of their neighbors is the one thing that has given them most satisfaction. Also important: community services, particularly good schools and convenient shopping. Most, in other words, have found what they were looking for. Once they have arrived, they do not look back. Two out of three say that their lives would scarcely be affected if, aside from working there, they would never again set foot in the central city. And even for work, the city is less and less important to suburbanites' lives; the number of those who work as well as live in the suburbs is sharply on the rise.

For all the increasing self-sufficiency and sense of satisfaction, there is a notably less cheery underside to suburban life. Many have found that suburbia shares the same problems as the cities, though possibly less severely.

Source Reprinted by permission from *Time,* The Weekly Newsmagazine; Copyright Time Inc. 1971.

Summary

In this chapter we have examined the effects of urban and metropolitan residence on human relationships. Size, density, and heterogeneity of population in an urban setting lead to secondary, relatively impersonal relationships between people; anonymity and alienation are more commonly experienced in urban settings than in small towns. Persons in cities must interact with so many people that they react to most people as representatives of a class rather than as individuals. Thus visible and often superficial cues become important determinants of how one is treated. But visual cues are not always reliable indicators of how others will react to a given stimulus, so people in urban settings often avoid or ignore strangers who might behave unpredictably. Also there are so many strangers in the city that interacting with all of them individually would not be possible. To people they don't know urban dwellers appear cold, distant, and unfriendly.

While the above description is generally accurate for the city as a whole, it is much less accurate when applied to natural areas of the city. The natural area or neighborhood is much more like a *Gemeinschaft,* and much closer personal relationships are possible there. The residents of a neighborhood tend to be more similar to one another than they are to residents of other urban neighborhoods, and it is possible to know them on a quasi-primary basis, especially in neighborhoods with residential stability.

Diversity of natural areas leads to diversity of life styles in the city. Some areas are dominated by an ethnic group; some are composed predominantly of stable families, while others are populated mainly by young adults who have not yet formed families. There are areas in which residents are homogeneous on the basis of other characteristics, such as sexual orientation or social class, or some combination of these characteristics. Local institutions, such as stores, restaurants, entertainment facilities, schools, and churches, reflect and support the life style of the population in the area. Mobility within the city allows residents of all areas to sample and participate in the life styles of areas different from their own. This freedom also makes it impossible for residents of a neighborhood to protect their own life style from others.

The people who live in suburbs and their activities are not noticeably different from the people and activities of the city. The suburban population does have a narrower age range than the city population, and their activities at this point in their life cycle are more important and dominant in the suburbs. These differences are reinforced by the residential architecture in suburbia. Suburban families are more isolated from distant contacts and are more focused on themselves and their neighbors. But the differences between urban and suburban life styles are differences of degree and not of kind. In neither case is there homogeneity of life style. In both city and suburbs there are areas in which the family predominates. There are also areas in both that are composed mainly of young, single adults interested in entertainment, parties, and evening social events. There are more young singles or married couples of this type in the city because there are more jobs for them there and more people like themselves.

Conversely, in the suburbs there are more young families who are interested in maintaining the quality of education and the homogeneity of the schools for their children.

Suburbs are most likely to be populated by middle-class whites. In the city, with more nonwhites and many different social classes, one may find neighborhoods of typical white middle-class families, but no single life style stands out in the city as starkly as the middle class stands out in the suburbs.

Glossary

atomized relationships   interactions between individuals who have few ties with each other and who participate in few, if any, group activities; a consequence of the breakdown of communal ties in a society

blase attitude   term used by Simmel to describe the effects of urban life; an attitude of having been exposed to everything and not reacting intensely to anything; detached and uninvolved

census   a complete enumeration, as distinct from a sample, of a population

consumerism   a devotion to consumption for its own sake, thought to be characteristic of upwardly mobile persons, especially those who live in or migrate to the suburbs; the continual purchase of unneeded goods

contranormative   against the norms; behaviors or beliefs that violate norms

enumeration   counting of the members of a group

familism   devotion to and concentration on one's immediate family; other social activity need not be forsaken, but the immediate family is much more important than the neighborhood or community

life cycle   the series of stages that an individual or a group goes through during its lifetime; among humans, the stages might be identified as infant, child, adolescent, young single adult, married adult without children, married adult with children, grandparent, elderly adult

life style   way of living characterized by dominant activities, attitudes, or beliefs

localism   greater participation in local activities than in activities of a wider sphere, such as the city or the society

natural area   a term developed by Ernest W. Burgess and his associates to describe the communities within cities; an area in which one group is dominant, a position established through the natural processes of invasion and succession; an area frequently characterized by ethnic homogeneity

nuclear family   the family composed of a husband and wife and their children, as distinguished from the extended family that includes other relatives, especially the parents of the husband and wife

primary relationships   social relationships based on frequent, direct, interpersonal contact; relating as total persons rather than as occupants of a single role

quasi-*Gemeinschaft*   a group that approximates a *Gemeinschaft* but is not completely based on primary relationships; alternatively, a group that aspires to be, but does not succeed in being, a *Gemeinschaft*

quasi-primary group   a group that aspires to have, but does not succeed in having, primary relationships between all members

schizoid character   (of urban personality) a term from Wirth describing the consequences of role-specific urban relationships that reveal different aspects of a person who is involved in different roles

secondary relationships   social relationships based on infrequent but direct interpersonal contacts; these are more likely than primary relationships to be specific to a given role or pair of role relationships

segmental interaction   interaction based on specific role relationships rather than on personal characteristics of the role occupants

selective migration   the movement of a specific group within a population from one location to another

sensory stimulation   a state occurring within the individual, produced by encounters with many different objects, each of which requires evaluation, recognition, and possible action

tertiary relationships   social relationships based on indirect contacts; totally role-specific interaction with no emotional content and little social content

References

Baltzell, E. Digby
1968   *The Search for Community in Modern America.* New York: Harper & Row Publishers, Inc.

Bell, Wendell
1958   "Social Choice, Life Styles, and Suburban Residence." In *The Suburban Community,* edited by William Dobriner, pp. 225-47. New York: G. P. Putnam's Sons.

Berger, Bennett M.
1972   "The Myth of Suburbia." In *North American Suburbs: Politics, Diversity, and Change,* edited by John Kramer, pp. 5-18. Berkeley: Glendessary.

Bourne, Larry S.
1971   "Apartment Location and the Housing Market." In *Internal Structure of the City,* edited by Larry S. Bourne, pp. 321-28. New York: Oxford University Press.

Dewey, Richard
1960   "The Rural-Urban Continuum: Real but Relatively Unimportant." *American Journal of Sociology* 66(July):60-66.

Dobriner, William, ed.
1958a   *The Suburban Community.* New York: G. P. Putnam's Sons.
1958b   "Local and Cosmopolitan as Contemporary Suburban Character Types." In *The Suburban Community,* edited by William Dobriner, pp. 132-43. New York: G. P. Putnam's Sons.

Duncan, Otis Dudley
1957   "Community Size and the Rural-Urban Continuum." In *Cities and Society,* edited by Paul K. Hatt and Albert J. Reiss, Jr., pp. 35-45. 2d ed. Glencoe, Ill.: Free Press.

Farley, Reynolds
1976   "Components of Suburban Population Growth." In *The Changing Face of the Suburbs,* edited by Barry Schwartz, pp. 3-38. Chicago: University of Chicago Press.

Faris, Robert E. L.
1967   *Chicago Sociology 1920-1932.* San Francisco: Chandler Publishing Company.

Fava, Sylvia F.
1956   "Suburbanism as a Way of Life." *American Sociological Review* 21:34-38.
1958   "Contrasts in Neighboring: New York City and a Suburban County." In *The Suburban Community,* edited by William Dobriner, pp. 122-31. New York: G. P. Putnam's Sons.

Fischer, Claude S.
1972   "Urbanism as a Way of Life: A Review and an Agenda." *Sociological Methods and Research* 1:187-242.
1975   "The Study of the Urban Community and Personality." In *Annual Review of Sociology,* vol. 1, pp. 71-73. Palo Alto, Calif.: Annual Review.

Fischer, Claude S., and Jackson, Robert Max
1976   "Suburbs, Networks, and Attitudes." In *The Changing Face of the Suburbs,* edited by Barry Schwartz, pp. 279-308. Chicago: University of Chicago Press.

Form, William H., and Stone, Gregory P.
1957   "Urbanism, Anonymity, and Status Symbolism." *American Journal of Sociology* 62:504-14.

Gans, Herbert J.
1962a   "Urbanism and Suburbanism As Ways of Life: A Reevaluation of Definitions." In *Human Behavior and Social Process: An Interactionist Approach,* edited by Arnold M. Rose, pp. 625-48. Boston: Houghton-Mifflin.
1962b   *The Urban Villagers.* New York: Free Press.

Glenn, Norval D.
1973   "Suburbanization in the United States since World War II." In *The Urbanization of the Suburbs,* edited by Louis H. Masotti and Jeffrey K. Hadden, pp. 51-78. Beverly Hills, Calif.: Sage Publications, Inc.

Greer, Scott
1973   "The Family in Suburbia." In *The Urbanization of the Suburbs,* edited by Louis H. Masotti and Jeffrey K. Hadden, pp. 149-70. Beverly Hills, Calif.: Sage Publications, Inc.

Hauser, Philip M.
1965   "Observations on the Urban Rural Dichotomies as Forms of Western Ethnocentrism." In *The Study of Urbanization,* edited by Philip M. Hauser and Leo F. Schnore, pp. 503-17. New York: John Wiley & Sons, Inc.

Kasarda, John D.
1976   "The Changing Occupational Structure of the American Metropolis: Apropos the Urban Problem." In *The Changing Face of the Suburbs,* edited by Barry Schwartz, pp. 113-36. Chicago: University of Chicago Press.

Kasarda, John D., and Janowitz, Morris
1974   "Community Attachment in Mass Society." *American Sociological Review* 39(June):328-39.

Lewis, Oscar
1965   "Further Observations on the Folk Urban Continuum and Urbanization with Specific Reference to Mexico City." In *The Study of Urbanization,* edited by Philip M. Hauser and Leo F. Schnore, pp. 441-503. New York: John Wiley & Sons, Inc.

Long, Larry H., and Glick, Paul C.
1976   "Family Patterns in Suburban Areas: Recent Trends." In *The Changing Face of the Suburbs,* edited by Barry Schwartz, pp. 39-68. Chicago: University of Chicago Press.

Marshall, Harvey
1973   "Suburban Life Styles: A Contribution to the Debate." In *The Urbanization of the Suburbs,* edited by Louis H. Masotti and Jeffrey K. Hadden, pp. 123-48. Beverly Hills, Calif.: Sage Publications, Inc.

Martin, Walter
1956   "The Structuring of Social Relationships Engendered by Suburban Residence." *American Sociological Review* 21:445-53.

Masotti, Louis H., and Hadden, Jeffrey K., eds.
1973   *The Urbanization of the Suburbs.* Beverly Hills, Calif.: Sage Publications, Inc.

Milgram, Stanley
1973   "The Experience of Living in Cities." *Science* 167 (March 13, 1970):1461-68. In *Cities in Change: Studies on the Urban Condition,* edited by John Walton and Donald Carns, pp. 159-76. Boston: Allyn & Bacon, Inc.

Mowrer, Ernest R.
1958   "The Family in Suburbia." In *The Suburban Community,* edited by William Dobriner, pp. 147-64. New York: G. P. Putnam's Sons.

Reiss, Albert J., Jr., ed.
1964   *Louis Wirth on Cities and Social Life.* Chicago: University of Chicago Press.

Schnore, Leo F.
1957   "Satellites and Suburbs." *Social Forces* 36:109-27.
1958   "The Growth of Metropolitan Suburbs." In *The Suburban Community,* edited by William Dobriner, pp. 26-44. New York: G. P. Putnam's Sons.
1963   "The Social and Economic Characteristics of American Suburbs." *Sociological Quarterly* 4:122-34.
1972   *Class and Race in Cities and Suburbs.* Chicago: Markham Publishing Co.

Schwartz, Barry, ed.
1976   *The Changing Face of the Suburbs.* Chicago: University of Chicago Press.

Seeley, John R., et al.
1972   "The Home in Crestwood Heights." In *North American Suburbs: Politics, Diversity, and Change,* edited by John Kramer, pp. 116-36. Berkeley: Glendessary.

Short, James F., Jr., ed.
1971   *The Social Fabric of the Metropolis.* Chicago: University of Chicago Press.

Simmel, Georg
1969   "The Metropolis and Mental Life." In *The Sociology of Georg Simmel,* translated by Kurt Wolff. New York: Free Press, 1950. Reprinted in *Classic Essays on the Culture of Cities,* edited by Richard Sennett, pp. 47-60. New York: Free Press.

Sjoberg, Gideon
1964   "The Rural-Urban Dimension in Preindustrial, Transitional, and Industrial Societies." In *Handbook of Modern Sociology,* edited by R. E. L. Faris, pp. 127-60. Chicago: Rand McNally & Company.

Suttles, Gerald
1968   *The Social Order of the Slum.* Chicago: University of Chicago Press.

Tallman, Irving, and Morgner, Ramona
1970   "Life Style Differences Among Urban and Suburban Blue Collar Families." *Social Forces* 48, 3:334-48.

Weber, Max
1958   *The City.* New York: Free Press.

Whyte, William F.
1943   *Street Corner Society.* Chicago: University of Chicago Press.

Whyte, William H.
1957   *The Organization Man.* New York: Doubleday & Company, Inc.
1967   "Cluster Development." In *Taming Megalopolis, Vol. I: What Is and What Could Be,* edited by H. Wentworth Eldredge, pp. 462-77. San Francisco: Anchor Press.

Wirth, Louis
1964   "Urbanism As a Way of Life." *American Journal of Sociology* 44, 1(July 1938):1-24. Reprinted in *Louis Wirth on Cities and Social Life,* edited by Albert J. Reiss, Jr., pp. 60-83. Chicago: University of Chicago Press.

Suggested Readings

Fischer, Claude S. *The Urban Experience.* New York: Harcourt Brace, 1976. Contains an empirical analysis of many hypothesized sociopsychological effects of urban life. Argues that urbanism has less effect on behavior than many theories predict.

Gans, Herbert J. "Urbanism and Suburbanism as Ways of Life: A Re-evaluation of Definitions." In *Human Behavior and Social Process: An Interactionist Perspective,* edited by Arnold M. Rose. Boston: Houghton-Mifflin, 1962. Argues that Wirth's theory of the effects of urban living on social life no longer applies, if it ever did.

Marshall, Harvey. "Suburban Life Styles: A Contribution to the Debate." In *The Urbanization of the Suburbs,* edited by Louis H. Masotti and Jeffrey K. Hadden. Beverly Hills, Calif.: Sage, 1973. A review of the literature on suburban life styles and the differences between urban and suburban life styles. Synthesizes a large body of empirical work.

Reiss, Albert J., Jr., ed. *Louis Wirth on Cities and Social Life.* Chicago: University of Chicago Press, 1964. A collection of Louis Wirth's most important papers edited by a noted scholar in the field. Perhaps the most accessible source.

Sennett, Richard. *Classic Essays on the Culture of Cities.* New York: Appleton-Century-Crofts, 1969. Contains classic essays by Wirth, Simmel, Park, and others on the nature of urban life.

Notes

1. For a contemporary discussion of the nature and consequences of urban sensory stimulation, see Milgram (1973:159-76).
2. See the example cited in Baltzell (1968:2). The incident on a New York street in which some thirty people watched a young woman being beaten and knifed to death without trying to help or even calling the police is an extreme but representative example of this blasé reserve.
3. Everett Hughes, a colleague of Wirth, pointed out that Wirth himself lived in a tightly knit ethnic neighborhood of Chicago that was essentially a primary group. See Short (1971:xxix).

7

The Population of Cities in the United States

To understand an urban society requires knowing with a high degree of reliability where people live, the types of places they live in, and other characteristics associated with residence. Particularly, we should know the size of the places where people live, the number of places of different sizes, and the extent to which people living in different places differ in their characteristics.

The major source of population data is the decennial United States census. The census primarily counts the population to determine governmental representation. Originally it was intended to determine representation in the U.S. Congress. In recent years census data have been used by state and local governments to determine the boundaries of their own representative districts. Within cities, wards and precinct boundaries have been altered on the basis of census data.

Because the census is used to determine political representation and district boundaries, data must be collected in a uniform manner. People are counted on the basis of where they are at a given time. On April 1 of every tenth year ending in zero people are counted in the place where they live or in their usual abode if they are away from home on this date. Thus residence, not legal address, voting address, or place of work, determines where one is counted.[1]

The Bureau of the Census uses its own definitions in collecting and reporting census data. It is easier and more efficient to learn these definitions as we examine the facts for information about the nature, extent, and character of the U.S. urban population.

The Growth of Urban Population and Places in the United States

Our exploration of the urban population begins with population growth. We will see how the increase in urban populations and urban places is reflected in the proportion of the population living in cities of different sizes. The relevant data are given in table 7.1. However, we must first understand the census bureau's definitions of place and urban.

Definition of Place

The census defines two types of **places:** incorporated and unincorporated (U.S. Bureau of the Census, 1971b:xi). Incorporated places are political units legally declared cities, towns, boroughs, and villages (except in certain states where these terms aren't used or have other meanings). Unincorporated places are closely settled population centers that do not have legal status or limits. The terms *incorporated* and *unincorporated* do not exhaust all the territory in the United States. Many people live in areas that the census bureau does not define as places—areas without a closely settled nucleus of residences. In other words, the people live scattered over relatively wide areas.

All places have either a legal corporate boundary or a boundary established by the census bureau. Therefore, a place ends at its legally defined boundary line, even if people's behaviors and interactions are unaffected by that line. For example, if the legal limit of an incorporated city lies along the middle of a street, and another city, town, or place begins at that line, all census bureau tables, which are organized by size of place, will list the two places separately. A suburb of 25,000 lying just across the street from a central city with a population of a half million will appear as a separate place in bureau documents, even though the people in the suburb shop, work, and play in the central city.

Definition of Urban

As of 1970, the census bureau defines urban population as the population of all incorporated and unincorporated places of 2,500 or more, and that portion of the population that lives in the densely settled fringe around urbanized areas. The part about the **urban fringe** in the definition is troublesome, and it is also the part that allows the census bureau to define places with fewer than 2,500 residents as urban. Places may be defined as urban if they fit any of the following descriptions: (1) small portions of land (normally less than one square mile) that have a population density of 1,000 or more inhabitants per square mile on the fringes of an urbanized area; (2) similar areas completely surrounded or enclosed on three sides by urbanized areas that are less than a mile apart; (3) outlying population districts that are no more than 1.5 miles from the main body of the urbanized area. Central cities of urbanized areas are places of 50,000 or more inhabitants (or twin cities with a total population of 50,000 or more, the smaller city having at least 15,000 people). Generally, an urban area may be defined as a place of 2,500 or more, or a densely populated area along the edge of a large city.

Urban Population and Places, 1790 to 1930

Even using the census bureau's generous definition of urban places,[2] we can see from table 7.1 that it was not until 1870 that one quarter of the U.S. population lived in places of 2,500 or more. By 1900 only a quarter of the population lived in places of 25,000 or more, and not until 1920, when the population became half urban, did a quarter of the U.S. population live in places of 100,000 or more.

The number of relatively large places of 100,000 or more doubled from seventeen to thirty-eight between 1880 and 1900, and almost tripled from thirty-eight to ninety-four between 1900 and 1930. The proportion of the population living in such places almost doubled, increasing from 28 percent to 56 percent between 1880 and 1930. Since 1930 the number of places of 100,000 or more has increased by about half from 94 to 156. During the same period, however, the number of places of more moderate size (25,000 or more) has nearly tripled from 377 to 916.

Recent Trends

The percentage of the population living in places of 100,000 or more has begun to decline, and the growth in the number of these large places has also slowed down. The population living in places of 100,000 or more dropped from 29.6 percent in 1930 to 27.7 percent in 1970. We must remember that these data are organized by place and that some large places are now surrounded by other urban places and cannot grow by incorporating

Table 7.1   The Historical Growth of Urban Population and Places in the U.S.

Date	Percent of Total U.S. Population			Number of Places		
	Urban	In Places of 100,000 or more	In Places of 25,000 or more	Urban	of 100,000 or more	of 25,000 or more
1790	5.1	— —	1.6	24	— —	2
1800	6.1	— —	2.4	33	— —	3
1810	7.3	— —	3.3	46	— —	4
1820	7.2	1.3	3.3	61	1	5
1830	8.8	1.6	4.1	90	1	6
1840	10.8	3.0	5.5	131	3	12
1850	15.3	5.0	8.8	236	6	26
1860	19.8	8.4	11.9	392	9	35
1870	25.7	10.8	15.2	663	14	52
1880	28.2	12.4	17.2	939	17	74
1890	35.1	15.4	22.2	1,348	28	124
1900	39.6	18.7	26.0	1,740	38	161
1910	45.6	22.0	31.0	2,266	50	229
1920	51.2	25.9	35.7	2,725	68	288
1930	56.1	29.6	40.1	3,179	94	377
1940	56.5	28.8	40.0	3,485	93	413
Previous urban definition						
1950	59.6	29.6	42.1	4,077	109	522
Current urban definition						
1950	64.0	29.4	41.1	4,764	107	486
1960	69.9	28.5	44.1	6,041	132	765
1970	73.5	27.7	44.7	7,062	156	916

Source   U.S. Bureau of the Census, *Census of Population, 1970: Number of Inhabitants, Final Report PC(1)-A1, United States Summary* (Washington, D.C.: Government Printing Office, 1971), table 7.

surrounding territories and populations. This is particularly true for the largest cities such as those with more than 100,000 population. The decline in population in places of 100,000 or more is also indicative of population movements from large central cities to outlying areas.

Table 7.1 illustrates the relatively rapid growth in urban population and urban places in the United States. It also suggests that the upper limit of growth may have been reached. More than half the population lives in places of less than 25,000 people. This has remained constant for the last thirty years. We are urbanites, but only a quarter of our population lives in places of 100,000 or more.

Table 7.2   The Growth of the U.S. Urban Population in the Twentieth Century (percent of total population)

Size of Place	1970	1960	1950 Urban Definition Current	Previous	1940	1930	1920	1910	1900
Urban									
1 million or more	9.2	9.8	11.5	11.5	12.0	12.2	9.6	9.2	8.4
500,000 to 1 million	6.4	6.2	6.1	6.1	4.9	4.7	5.9	3.3	2.2
250,000-500,000	5.1	6.0	5.4	5.4	5.9	6.5	4.3	4.3	3.8
100,000-250,000	7.0	6.5	6.4	6.6	6.0	6.2	6.1	5.2	4.3
50,000-100,000	8.2	7.7	5.9	6.0	5.6	5.3	5.0	4.6	3.6
25,000-50,000	8.8	8.3	5.8	6.5	5.6	5.2	4.8	4.4	3.7
10,000-25,000	10.5	9.8	7.8	8.4	7.6	7.4	6.6	6.0	5.7
5,000-10,000	6.4	5.5	5.4	5.2	5.1	4.8	4.7	4.6	4.2
2,500-5,000	4.0	4.2	4.3	3.7	3.8	3.9	4.1	4.0	3.8
less than 2,500	0.4	0.4	0.4	--	--	--	--	--	--
other urban	7.5	5.5	4.9	--	--	--	--	--	--
Rural									
1,000-2,500	3.3	3.6	4.3	3.6	3.8	3.9	4.5	4.6	4.3
under 1,000	1.9	2.2	2.7	2.7	3.3	3.5	4.0	4.3	3.9
other rural	21.3	24.3	29.9	34.1	36.4	36.4	40.4	45.5	53.1

Source   U.S. Bureau of the Census, *Census of Population, 1970: Number of Inhabitants, Final Report PC(1)-A1, United States Summary* (Washington, D.C.: Government Printing Office, 1971), table 7.

Table 7.2 focuses on the growth of urban population and the decline of rural population in the United States during the twentieth century. The shift of population from rural to urban places has been most dramatic. However, in 1970 the proportion of the population living in small towns (urban places of 5,000 or less) or in rural places of 1,000 to 2,500 is about the same as it was in 1900. The rural population lost to the cities came, for the most part, from other rural areas—those scattered locations that the U.S. Bureau of the Census does not even define as places. Other rural population declined from 53 percent to 21 percent from 1900 to 1970. Rural migrants and foreign immigrants fueled the expansion of U.S. cities in the twentieth century.[3]

Table 7.2 also shows that the proportion of the population living in very large places, those of one million or more, increased until 1930 and then steadily decreased until 1970, when it matched the proportion observed in 1910. Only 6.6 percent of the population lived in places of 500,000 to one million in 1970, but this is almost three times the proportion of population that lived in places of this size in 1900. Places of 5,000 to 500,000 persons were home to larger proportions of the population in 1970 than in 1900, but the differences are not as large as those seen in places of 500,000 to one million people.

With the exception of the dramatic decline in the proportion of population living in scattered rural areas, the distribution of population by place size in 1970 is similar to that in 1900. The population of the United States has increased from 73 to 203 million. Thus, 8.4 percent of those living in places of one million or more in 1900 equals 6.5 million persons, while 9.2 percent of those living in the same size places in 1970 equals 18.75 million—nearly three times as many persons (U.S. Bureau of the Census, 1971b:table 7). This increase in numbers of people is likely to affect urban social relationships.

As noted in table 7.2, the Bureau of the Census adopted the current definition of **urban place** in 1950. Persons living in places of less than 2,500, and even some persons not living in defined places, have been counted as urban since then. As a result, the urban population in 1970 included 7.9 percent living in urban places of fewer than 2,500 residents. So, while 9.2 percent of the U.S. population lived in places of one million or more in 1970, 7.9 percent lived in urban areas of 2,500 or less. There were nearly as many Americans classified as urban living in sparsely populated areas as there were living in large cities.

The pattern of growth and decline of large cities is partly a function of the Bureau of the Census's reliance on places. Some urban growth could have occurred by increases in population density, but it hasn't, and growth through annexation is no longer possible in large cities surrounded by incorporated suburban places. If the census data were organized according to social organization rather than legal boundaries, they would give us a different picture of urban growth patterns.

Data Organized to Reflect Social Organization

When it became clear that the current definition of urban was no longer adequate, the census bureau introduced two new concepts—**urbanized areas** and **standard metropolitan statistical areas** (SMSAs). Rather than trace the history of the development of these concepts,[4] let us consider the census bureau's definitions of the two terms.

Definition of an urbanized area. An urbanized area is a central city of 50,000 or more population and the closely settled surrounding territory (U.S. Bureau of the Census, 1971b: xii-xiii). The criteria that the census bureau uses to define closely settled surrounding territories are as follows:

1. Incorporated places of 2,500 or more.
2. Incorporated places of less than 2,500 that have a closely settled area of one hundred or more housing units.
3. Small tracts of land less than a mile square with populations of one thousand or more inhabitants per square mile.
4. Small tracts of land less than a mile square with populations of less than one thousand per square mile that (a) eliminate enclaves (areas completely enclosed by the city) or indentations (areas partially enclosed by the city) as seen on a map, or (b) act as links between outlying districts that lie no more than 1.5 miles away from the main body of the city and the city itself.

Relationship between urbanized area
and Standard Metropolitan Statistical
Area. Shaded areas are urbanized;
the heavy line defines the SMSA
boundary. (Source: U.S. Bureau of
the Census, *U.S. Census of Population: 1970. Number of Inhabitants,*
Final Report PC (1)–A 15 Illinois
[Washington, D.C.: Government
Printing Office, 1971], pp. 3, 70.)

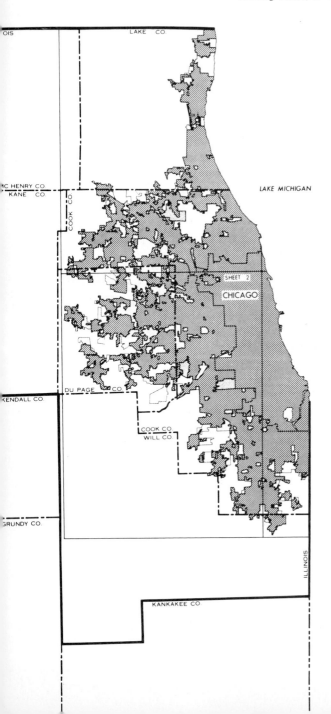

*Definition of a standard metropolitan statis-
tical area.* In contrast to an urbanized area,
an SMSA is a central city of 50,000 or more,
plus the *county* in which it is located and all
contiguous or surrounding counties that are
socially and economically integrated with the
central city (U.S. Bureau of the Census,
1971b:xii-xiii).

Two measures of social and economic integration for any given area are the proportion of the population engaged in agriculture
and, more important for this discussion, the
proportion working in the central city. In addition, integration is measured by inclusion in
the service areas of newspapers, department
stores, delivery companies, and similar enterprises.

*The relation of urbanized areas to standard
metropolitan statistical areas.* The urbanized area can be visualized as the physical city
as seen from an airplane, while the SMSA is
the metropolitan community (U.S. Bureau of
the Census, 1971b:xii-xiii). Urbanized areas
tend to be smaller than SMSAs, and in most
cases lie within SMSAs. Table 7.3 illustrates
the relationship between urbanized areas and
SMSAs. Note that twice as many people live
inside the SMSAs (139, 418, 811) as live outside them (63,793,115).

Almost all the people living within urbanized areas also live within SMSAs. Everyone living inside the central city of an urbanized area lives inside an SMSA, but 421,
985 people who live in central cities of urbanized areas do not live in the central cities
of SMSAs, and 112,885 people who live outside the central city of urbanized areas live inside the central city of an SMSA. Finally, 98

Table 7.3   Population Inside and Outside Urbanized Areas and Standard Metropolitan Statistical Areas: 1970

Location	Total	Inside SMSAs			Outside SMSAs
		Total	Inside Central Cities	Outside Central Cities	
United States	203,211,926	139,418,811	63,796,943	75,621,868	63,793,115
Inside urbanized areas	118,446,566	116,881,936	63,612,584	53,269,352	1,564,630
Inside central cities	63,921,684	63,921,684	63,499,699	421,985	
Outside central cities	54,524,882	52,960,252	112,885	52,847,367	1,564,630
Outside urbanized areas	84,765,360	22,536,875	184,359	22,352,516	62,228,485

Source   U.S. Bureau of the Census, *Census of Population, 1970: Number of Inhabitants, Final Report PC(1)-A1, United States Summary* (Washington, D.C.: Government Printing Office, 1971), p. xiii.

percent of the people who live outside of SMSAs also live outside of urbanized areas.

These data enable us to conclude that virtually all the population of urbanized areas (called *metropolitan districts* from 1910 to 1940—Goheen, 1971) live in SMSAs, and 53.7 percent of the residents of urbanized areas live in central cities of SMSAs. However, not all the central cities of urbanized areas are also the central cities of SMSAs, since nearly one-half million residents of central cities of urbanized areas live outside central cities of SMSAs. This last fact should help us realize that not all urban residents live in large cities. About a quarter of the population living in SMSAs lives outside urbanized areas—people who are not likely to be considered urban live in SMSAs but outside central cities.

The History of Metropolitan Concepts and Population

The U.S. Bureau of the Census has defined some variant of SMSAs since 1910 (Shyrock, 1957:163-70; Shyrock et al., 1973), but the definitions have not remained constant. Between 1910 and 1940 the census referred to metropolitan districts and defined them variously as cities of 200,000 or more persons (in 1910) to 50,000 or more persons (in 1940). At various times the definition was based on the incorporated central city, adjacent and contiguous minor civil divisions, or incorporated places with populations of 150 or more per square mile. The difficulty with this definition was that as size of central city population classified as metropolitan decreased, the proportion of the population classified as metropolitan increased, even though nothing else might have changed. This led to the creation in 1950 of **standard metropolitan areas** (SMAs), which are now known as standard metropolitan statistical areas (SMSAs).

With the creation of SMAs, the Bureau of the Census began to use county boundaries in defining metropolitan areas. Since counties change boundaries less frequently than cities, the boundaries were more likely to be constant. The census bureau also introduced the urbanized area concept in 1950. The current definition of urbanized areas is not unlike the definition of metropolitan district used by the bureau between 1910 and 1940, but it is somewhat more precise. The change in 1960 from SMA to SMSA emphasized the statistical criteria of social and economic integration with the central city that counties included in an SMSA had to meet and the statistical nature of the metropolis.

The geographic size of cities has also changed over time. Central cities have grown by annexation and incorporation, decreasing the number of places in metropolitan areas but increasing the size of some places. This raises the question: If a city grows in total population only because it annexes three suburbs, has there been population growth? The answer is both yes and no.

Tracing the history of metropolitan areas, and particularly the components of metropolitan areas, is extremely difficult. One solution is to use the definition of metropolitan area that was in use for each year being studied—data for 1910 would be studied in light of the 1910 definition; data for 1970, in light of the 1970 definition. This would recognize the social organization of each decade, but it would make the analysis of change almost impossible, since some places would disappear as they were annexed or incorporated into larger places. There would be no constant base for calculating change or the rate of change.

Another approach to the study of the history of metropolitan areas and population is to take the definition of metropolitan areas at a single point in time (generally the latest available) and trace the history of that area's population as far back as possible. However, there are many more metropolitan areas now than there were earlier. Tracing the history of metropolitan areas as currently defined through earlier censuses leads us to speak of metropolitan growth in areas that were not metropolitan until recently. It makes little sense to discuss as metropolitan the populations in counties that historically had no large central city and were not socially or economically metropolitan. However, by combining the techniques of census-by-census definition and constant areas we can draw some tentative conclusions about metropolitan growth.

Growth of Metropolitan Areas and Their Population

Table 7.4 shows that the number of metropolitan areas in the United States more than tripled between 1900 and 1973. At the same time, the percentage of the total population living in metropolitan areas more than doubled.

This table also shows that during the decade of the Great Depression, between 1930 and 1940, the rate of growth of metropolitan areas slowed dramatically. Only six new metropolitan areas developed in the thirties, while in the twenties and again in the forties the number of metropolitan areas increased by at least twenty. Metropolitan population also grew slowly during the depression decade, increasing by only 9.3 percent as compared with nearly 32 percent in the previous decade and 23 percent in the following decade. Since 1960, the rate of population growth in metropolitan areas has slowed again. Between 1960 and 1970 metropolitan areas and populations grew at their slowest rate in the twentieth century, with the exception of the depression decade.

Metropolitan areas have grown in several ways: by **natural increase** (more births than deaths), by **migration,** and by expansion of the central city. However, metropolises have not grown evenly throughout. The physical limits of central cities have changed, and much of the early population growth of metropolitan areas is accounted for by annexation of outlying areas to the central cities.

On the basis of the 212 SMSAs defined in 1960 (and using the boundaries established for them as of 1960), it is possible to trace the pattern of metropolitan growth in the United States from 1900 to 1970 (Taeuber, 1972). Table 7.5 shows that during the twentieth century the metropolitan population has grown faster than the total U.S. population. Central cities grew faster than their surrounding metropolitan areas until 1920. After 1920, areas outside the central cities grew faster.

Between 1960 and 1970, the 243 SMSAs defined in 1970 exhibited a pattern of differential population growth. Table 7.6 shows that while total population in 243 SMSAs increased by 16.6 percent from 1960 to 1970, central city populations increased by only 6.5 percent. However, almost all (6.4 percent) of the increase in the central cities was due not to **in-migration** or natural increase, but rather to annexation of new physical areas to the central cities (U.S. Bureau of the Census, 1971:table 39).

Table 7.4   Estimated Number and Population of Metropolitan Areas 1900-1973

Date	Number of Metropolitan Areas	% of Total Population	% Increase from Previous Date
1900	72	33.6	——
1910	95	39.6	41.5
1920	120	45.2	31.9
1930	142	51.2	31.6
1940	148	52.1	9.3
1950	168	56.1	23.1
1960	212	66.7	26.4
1970	243	68.6	16.6
7/1/73	253	72.8	2.3

Sources   1900-1940: Table presented by Hon. George Romney to Ad Hoc Subcommittee on Urban Growth, U.S. House of Representatives, Oct. 7, 1969. Attributed to U.S. Bureau of the Census, *Statistical Abstract of the United States: 1952* and *1969;* U.S. Bureau of the Census, *Current Population Reports,* Series P-25, 427; Donald J. Bogue, *Population Growth in Standard Metropolitan Areas, 1900-1950* (Housing and Home Finance Administration, 1963). Data for 1950-1970 calculated from the above and from the U.S. Bureau of the Census, *Census of Population, 1970 . . . Final Report PC(1)-A1.* Growth rates for 1950-1960 and 1960-1970 are based on areas as defined in 1970. The 1973 data are based on *Current Population Reports,* Series P-25, 537, "Estimates of the Population of Metropolitan Areas and Components of Change since 1970, 1974."

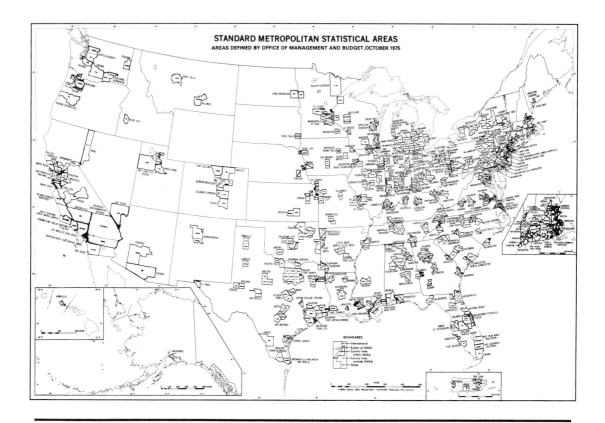

Table 7.5 Percentage Increase in Metropolitan Populations Since 1900 by Decades

	1910	1920	1930	1940	1950	1960	1970	SMSAs of 1960 and 1970
Total U.S.	21.0	14.9	16.1	7.2	14.1	18.8	13.3	13.3
Total SMSA	32.0	24.8	27.1	8.8	22.6	26.3	15.9	23.5
Central city	37.1	27.7	24.3	5.6	14.7	10.7	6.5	10.0
Outside central city	23.7	19.9	32.3	14.6	35.9	48.5	25.8	37.5
Non-SMSA	13.1	6.5	5.4	5.4	3.7	7.9	8.8	−4.1

Note: SMSAs are those defined for 1960 with the land area of 1960.

Source Irene B. Taeuber, "The Changing Distribution of the Population of the United States in the Twentieth Century," in Volume 5 of Commission Research Reports, *Population Distribution and Policy,* ed. Sara Mills Mazie, U.S. Commission on Population Growth and the American Future (Washington, D.C.: Government Printing Office, 1972), table 19.

Table 7.6   Metropolitan Population and Land
Growth, 1960-1970 (percent
increases)

	Total Population Change	Based on 1960 Corporate Limits	Due to Annexations
Total 243 SMSAs	16.6	16.6	
Central cities	6.5	.1	6.4
Outside central city	26.7	33.1	−6.5

Source   U.S. Bureau of the Census, *Census of Population, 1970: Number of Inhabitants, Final Report PC(1)-A1, United States Summary* (Washington, D.C.: Government Printing Office, 1971), table 39.

Metropolitan growth and particularly central city growth has decreased recently, while noncentral city growth has accelerated to nearly four times central city growth (table 7.5). For the first time this has produced equality of population distribution (table 7.7). Until 1970 more people lived inside than lived outside the central cities, despite the greater growth rate outside the central cities since 1920. The explanation for this seeming paradox is that a large number growing slowly, as in the central city population, produces a larger absolute increase than a small number growing fast, as in the noncentral city population. For example, a million dollars invested at 3 percent will produce $30,000 a year while a thousand dollars invested at 12 percent (four times the growth rate) will produce only $120. This example applies to the population inside and outside metropolitan areas. Because the

Table 7.7   Population of Metropolitan Areas in the Twentieth Century (percentage distribution)

Date	Total	Central City	Outside Central City	Non-SMSA
1900	41.9	26.0	15.9	58.1
1910	45.7	29.5	16.1	54.3
1920	49.7	32.8	16.9	50.3
1930	54.3	35.1	19.3	45.7
1940	55.1	34.5	20.6	44.9
1950	59.2	34.7	24.5	40.8
1960	63.0	32.3	30.6	37.0
1970	64.4	30.4	34.0	35.6
1970 (b)	68.6	31.4	37.2	31.4

Source   Irene B. Taeuber, "The Changing Distribution of the Population of the United States in the Twentieth Century," in Volume 5 of Commission Research Reports, *Population Distribution and Policy,* ed. Sara Mills Mazie, U.S. Commission on Population Growth and the American Future (Washington, D.C.: Government Printing Office, 1972), table 19; 1970 (b) calculated from U.S. Bureau of the Census, *Census of Population, 1970: Final Report PC(1)-A1, United States Summary* (Washington, D.C.: Government Printing Office), tables 17 and 33.

central cities started the century with 26 percent of the total U.S. population compared with less than 16 percent in metropolitan areas outside central cities, it has taken over two thirds of a century for the actual numbers of people to reach equality.[5]

So, we see, the United States is a metropolitan society in at least two senses— first, to the extent that cities perform communal functions and influence tastes and life styles throughout the society; second, about one third of the entire U.S. population and about one half of the metropolitan population lives in central cities. Not all central cities are large places, and many metropolitan residents do not live in densely populated centers. If we were a metropolitan society only in a statistical sense, our society might be more accurately described as a suburban metropolitan society than as an urban metropolitan society.

Contemporary Population Characteristics

As of 1970, our society had grown to 7,062 urban places in which 73.5 percent of the population lived. By 1974, nearly 73 percent of the population lived in 264 SMSAs (U.S. Bureau of the Census, 1975b:3, table A).

To understand urban and metropolitan populations we must look at data other than mere numbers of people and places. We will view the characteristics of people living in metropolitan and urbanized areas— characteristics that influence performance of communal functions and metropolitan behavior patterns and life styles.

Residential Location

Table 7.8 shows the 1970 U.S. population by size of place, inside and outside 243 SMSAs. The column headed *inside SMSAs* shows that 20.5 percent of the metropolitan population (or 28,635,135 people) lives outside population aggregates large enough to be called *places*. As we have already noted, a large portion of the metropolitan population lives in small population concentrations because of the census bureau's definition of *place*. Table 7.9 shows that 12 percent of the SMSA population is defined by the bureau as *rural* rather than *urban* (U.S. Bureau of the Census, 1975d:table 19). So, while we consider the metropolis the epitome of urban culture, we should not forget that many metropolitan residents live in either rural or small community settings within SMSAs.

Rural areas. More than one in ten metropolitan residents live in rural areas. This is because metropolitan areas are defined by county boundaries, and many counties that are socially and economically integrated with large central cities include rural areas. The Chicago SMSA is a good example. One can drive along the expressways in Cook County, the county that includes Chicago, and within a half an hour be driving past rolling farmland. The people living there may not even be listed as living in a *place,* as defined by the census, but they are classified by the Bureau of the Census as metropolitan residents. However, they are subject to urban influences. The shopping centers, newspapers, and other goods and services they enjoy are available because of the city. Their lives are dominated

Source U.S. Bureau of the Census. *Census of Population, 1970: Number of Inhabitants, Final Report PC(1)-A1, United States Summary* (Washington, D.C.: Government Printing Office, 1971), table 5.

Table 7.8   Population and Places Inside and Outside Standard Metropolitan Statistical Areas, 1970

United States Size of Place	All Places		Inside SMSAs		Outside SMSAs	
	Number	*Population*	*Number*	*Population*	*Number*	*Population*
Total	20,768	203,211,926	6,211	139,418,811	14,557	63,793,115
Inside places	20,768	144,747,761	6,211	110,783,676	14,557	33,964,085
Places of—						
1,000,000 or more	6	18,770,773	6	18,770,773	– –	– –
500,000 to 1,000,000	20	12,989,017	20	12,989,017	– –	– –
250,000 to 500,000	30	10,466,400	30	10,466,151	– –	249*
100,000 to 250,000	100	14,292,614	100	14,292,614	– –	– –
50,000 to 100,000	240	16,740,130	240	16,740,130	– –	– –
25,000 to 50,000	520	17,848,705	337	11,565,141	183	6,283,564
10,000 to 25,000	1,385	21,431,385	847	13,333,826	538	8,097,559
5,000 to 10,000	1,839	12,930,372	943	6,676,945	896	6,253,427
2,500 to 5,000	2,295	8,041,728	870	3,056,058	1,425	4,985,670
2,000 to 2,500	987	2,200,587	336	745,653	651	1,454,934
1,500 to 2,000	1,361	2,353,858	415	716,111	946	1,637,747
1,000 to 1,500	2,182	2,678,402	547	676,727	1,635	2,001,675
500 to 1,000	3,294	2,371,707	715	524,222	2,579	1,847,485
200 to 500	3,990	1,332,486	585	203,474	3,405	1,129,012
Less than 200	2,519	299,597	220	26,834	2,299	272,763
Outside places	– –	58,464,165	– –	28,635,135	– –	29,829,030
Cumulative summary:						
Places of—						
1,000,000 or more	6	18,770,773	6	18,770,773	– –	– –
500,000 or more	26	31,759,790	26	31,759,790	– –	– –
250,000 or more	56	42,226,190	56	42,225,941	– –	249
100,000 or more	156	56,518,804	156	56,518,555	– –	249
50,000 or more	396	73,258,934	396	73,258,685	– –	249
25,000 or more	916	91,107,639	733	84,823,826	183	6,283,813
10,000 or more	2,301	112,539,024	1,580	98,157,652	721	14,381,372
5,000 or more	4,140	125,469,396	2,523	104,834,597	1,617	20,634,799
2,500 or more	6,435	133,511,124	3,393	107,890,655	3,042	25,620,469
2,000 or more	7,422	135,711,711	3,729	108,636,308	3,693	27,075,403
1,500 or more	8,783	138,065,569	4,144	109,352,419	4,639	28,713,150
1,000 or more	10,965	140,743,971	4,691	110,029,146	6,274	30,714,825
500 or more	14,259	143,115,678	5,406	110,553,368	8,853	32,562,310
200 or more	18,249	144,448,164	5,991	110,756,842	12,258	33,691,322

*Population of that part of Oklahoma City outside the Oklahoma City SMSA in McClain County.

Table 7.9   Population Inside and Outside
SMSAs by Urban and
Rural Residence, 1970

	U.S. Total	Inside SMSA	Outside SMSA
Urban total	73.5	88.2	41.3
Central city	31.4	45.8	– –
Other urban	42.1	42.5	41.3
Rural total	26.5	11.8	58.7
Places of 1,000-2,500	3.3	1.1	7.9
Other rural	23.2	10.6	50.8

Source   U.S. Bureau of the Census, *Census of Population, 1970: Number of Inhabitants, Final Report PC(1)-A1, United States Summary* (Washington, D.C.: Government Printing Office, 1971), table 41.

by their proximity to Chicago. Their neighborhoods may be rural, but their life styles are heavily influenced by the social life, tax rate, and facilities of the city.

Metropolitan places.   Of the 6,211 places in metropolitan areas, fewer than half have a population of 5,000 or more. However, the 2,523 places in SMSAs with populations of at least 5,000 include more than three quarters of the total metropolitan population. Large cities of 5,000 or more, and particularly the large suburbs, which must be at least 49,999 people, since the central city of each metroplitan area is at least 50,000,[6] account for most of the metropolitan population. There are only 396 places of 50,000 or more in the United States, so these 6 percent of places within SMSAs must contain 52.5 percent of the SMSA population, or about one third of the total U.S. population.

Predominantly metropolitan and heavily concentrated in central cities, the U.S. population is nevertheless nearly as likely (21.3 percent to 27.8 percent) to live in other rural locations as to live in places of 100,000 or more people (U.S. Bureau of the Census, 1971b:tables 17 and 19). Table 7.9 showed that, while 88.2 percent of the SMSA population is urban, the urban population is nearly equally divided between the central cities and the rest of the SMSA. Most nonurban residents of the SMSA live in locations with fewer than one thousand persons (U.S. Bureau of the Census, 1971b:tables 17 and 19). The non-SMSA population is more rural than urban, but only by a slim margin (58.7 percent versus 41.3 percent), and most of this rural population is found in places of less than one thousand.

Gender and Marital Status

The urban population has a slightly higher proportion of women than the rural population (51.8 percent versus 50 percent). The percentage of women is highest (52.4 percent) in central cities of urbanized areas and lowest (49.7 percent) in rural areas of less than one thousand. Therefore, the **labor force** in urban areas is more likely to be composed of women than is the labor force in rural areas, because more women are available.

The larger number of women in central cities has implications for urban life styles, attitudes, tastes, and behavior patterns. Furthermore, not all central cities have the same proportion of women. Some cities, such as Washington, D.C., have a much higher proportion of women than of men. Such gender imbalances may well explain the existence in cities of singles bars and other institutions that facilitate heterosocial interaction. Women living in cities may be more prone to exhibit certain forms of behavior, such as initiating heterosocial interaction, working, and refraining from marriage, simply because there are more women in the population.

Among people fourteen years old and over, marriage is more common in rural than in urban populations. In urban areas marriage rates are lowest in central cities. This information, combined with data showing more single women than single men in central cities, implies that there is greater heterosocial competition among women for mates in central cities. This may explain the popularity of newspaper ads for opposite-sex roommates and computerized dating services in the city. In central cities, too, there is greater concern about crimes such as rape, mugging, and purse snatching. These data on gender and marital status help us see why the city must deal with the needs of women, and develop institutions designed to meet the needs of a relatively large, single female population.

The relatively low proportion of married persons living in central cities may be a cause or an effect of some isolation and alienation in urban life. People living in central cities marry less frequently than people living elsewhere, or they leave the city if they do marry. More single people of all ages live in central cities than anywhere else. This affects housing patterns. For example, single people rarely buy large homes. Since singles are more likely to rent than to buy, the marital status of a population implies a need for different types of housing according to residential location.

Similarly, gender and marital status will affect cost of housing and types of jobs available in the central city.

Fertility and Family Size

The **fertility ratio**—number of children born to women of child-bearing age—is lower in urban areas than in rural areas. Urban populations tend to grow more by in-migration than by natural increase. Within the urban population, however, fertility is higher in the suburbs than it is in central cities, reflecting the tendency of families with children to move to the suburbs. Thus people in the central city are more likely to be childless or to have fewer children than people in the suburbs. This is reflected in the higher cost of education in the suburbs and in the sizes, styles, and structural arrangements of homes. Homes in the city need not be as large as they are in the suburbs. A lower fertility rate means that central city women spend less time rearing children and have more years available to work than suburban women. Conversely, suburban women devote more years to child rearing and have fewer years available to work outside the home.

Only in urban areas of less than 10,000 is the fertility ratio much higher than it is in central cities. Suburban fertility rates lie somewhere between the two. But in no urban location does the fertility ratio even approach the rural fertility level. Higher fertility in cities of 2,500 to 10,000 may reflect greater emphasis on family relations. This may be why small cities do not support many non-family forms of entertainment, such as movie theaters and nightclubs. Higher fertility in the rural areas demonstrates not only the greater strength of the family, but also the continued need for children in the rural labor force.

Marriage rates and fertility levels are reflected in differences in family size (expressed as average persons per family) in populations living in places of different sizes. Rural families are larger than urban families (3.67 versus 3.53 persons per family) and are largest in rural areas of less than 1,000 persons. Unexpectedly, however, families are smallest not in central cities, but in medium-sized cities. This may be due to variations in the racial and religious compositions of different cities. The data also suggest that large central cities need more schools and other educational facilities than do cities of moderate size.

Family Structure

Rural families are more likely to have children under age eighteen than are urban families. Suburbia, on the other hand, is where families with children live. More families with children under eighteen live in suburbia (58.4 percent) than anywhere else. Families in rural areas of less than 1,000 are almost as likely as suburban families to have children under eighteen (55.8 percent), living at home.

The two-parent family is more common in rural areas than in urban areas (90 percent versus 85 percent). However, suburbia has more two-parent families (89 percent) than any other urban location, and even more two-parent families than rural places of more than a thousand persons (87.7 percent). The two-parent family is least common in central cities (81 percent). Children in two-parent families are most common in the suburbs, where the two-parent family itself is more likely, and least common in the central city. There are more female heads of families in the central city (15 percent). Only 9 percent of families are headed by a female in suburbia and only 7 percent in rural areas.

The sum of two-parent families and families headed by females is less than 100 percent, implying that families headed by males are 3 percent to 4 percent of all families. Since only about 12 percent of families are headed by females and 3-4 percent by males, about a quarter of all one-parent families are headed by males. This factor should be considered in discussions of the single-parent family as a social problem, particularly in terms of welfare costs. Table 7.10 indicates that only about half of the families headed by females have children under eighteen living with them. This percentage is almost the same as the percentage of two-parent families with children. Families headed by females are slightly more common in central cities than they are elsewhere, and half of these females have their own children living with them. Such families can be a problem if they need social and institutional support to provide food, shelter, care, and discipline for their children.

The Elderly

Approximately one in ten residents in both urban and rural areas is sixty-five years old or older. Within urbanized areas, there are more elderly people in central cities than in suburbs.

Elderly persons living in cities require special services from cities. The communal organization in relatively small urban places

Table 7.10   Type of Residence and Family Characteristics of Contemporary Population, 1970

	Percent Male	Percent Female	Persons over 14: Percent Married		Fertility Ratio*	Persons per Family	Percent of Families with Own Children under Age 18	Percent of Families with Husband and Wife	Percent of Husband and Wife Families with Own Children under 18	Percent of Families with Female Head	Percent of Female-headed Families with Own Children under 18	Percent Age 65 and Over
			Male	Female								
Total Urban	48.2	51.8	65.0	59.5	341	3.53	54.7	85.2	55.3	12.1	55.8	9.8
Urbanized areas	48.2	51.8	65.1	59.5	339	3.54	55.0	84.8	55.6	12.3	56.2	9.4
Central cities	47.6	52.4	62.5	56.1	336	3.48	52.0	81.2	52.1	15.8	56.6	10.7
Urban fringe	48.8	51.2	69.3	63.8	342	3.61	58.4	89.0	59.3	8.7	55.6	7.8
10,000 or more	48.4	51.6	63.0	58.1	336	3.47	53.8	84.8	54.2	11.6	54.6	10.8
2,500-10,000	48.2	51.8	66.5	60.6	363	3.49	53.6	86.9	54.3	10.7	52.7	12.2
Total Rural	50.0	50.0	67.7	66.7	387	3.67	55.4	90.0	56.6	7.3	49.5	10.1
1,000-2,500	48.1	51.9	68.5	62.0	376	3.48	52.2	87.7	53.1	9.8	49.8	13.6
Under 1,000	50.3	49.7	67.6	67.5	388	3.70	55.8	90.3	57.1	6.9	49.4	9.6

*Fertility ratio = children under five per 1,000 women ages 15 to 49 years.

Source   U.S. Bureau of the Census, *Census of Population, 1970: General Population Characteristics, Final Report PC(1)-B1, United States Summary* (Washington, D.C.: Government Printing Office, 1971), tables 47, 48, 54.

and in rural areas make it less likely that older persons will be isolated from their families and the community or detached from sources of social solidarity and support. Conversely, formal institutions in central cities must meet the social, physical, and emotional needs of the elderly in the absence of informal sources of support. Cities, more than smaller areas, must provide communal services to the elderly. Not only is the proportion of elderly persons in the population relatively high in large cities, but the absolute number is also large. This increases the welfare costs in large cities.

Racial Composition

The racial makeup of our cities and the existence of urban racial ghettos are persistent sources of tension in our society. Table 7.11 summarizes the racial distribution of population in urban and metropolitan areas. The black population is clearly concentrated in the central cities of urbanized and metropolitan areas. Both areas are 20.6 percent black compared with the national average of 11.1 percent black. Equally clear is the exclusion of blacks from the suburbs. The data in table 7.11 document the disproportionately large number of whites in suburban and rural areas and blacks in the central cities.

Table 7.11   Residential Location and Racial
Composition, United States,
1970 (percentage distribution)

Location	White	Negro	Other
Total U.S. population	87.5	11.1	1.4
Urban	86.2	12.3	1.5
Urbanized areas	85.6	13.2	1.5
Central cities	77.5	20.6	1.9
Urban fringe	94.3	4.7	1.0
Other urban	90.1	8.7	1.3
10,000 or more	89.3	9.4	1.3
2,500-10,000	91.0	7.8	1.2
Rural	90.9	7.8	1.3
1,000-2,500	92.2	6.3	1.4
Other rural	90.7	8.0	1.3
Metropolitan	86.5	12.0	1.5
Urban	85.5	13.0	1.6
Central city	77.5	20.6	1.9
Other urban	94.1	4.7	1.2
Rural	94.1	5.9	0.9
Non Metropolitan	89.6	9.1	1.3
Urban	89.8	9.2	1.0
Rural	89.5	9.0	1.5

Source   U.S. Bureau of the Census, *Census of Popula-
tion, 1970: General Population Characteristics, Final
Report PC(1)-B1, United States Summary* (Washington,
D.C.: Government Printing Office, 1971), table 48.

The pattern seen in table 7.11, however,
does not apply to all cities. Table 7.12 shows
that black concentration in the central city is
much more marked in the largest metropolitan areas, while the exclusion of blacks from
the suburbs in the largest SMSAs is no more
severe than that found in smaller SMSAs.

Table 7.12   Size of SMSA, 1970, and Black
Population Inside and Outside
Central City (percent)

Size of SMSA, 1970	Inside Central City	Outside Central City
3,000,000 or more	25.4	6.6
1,000,000 to 3,000,000	25.1	5.1
500,000 to 1,000,000	18.4	5.7
250,000 to 500,000	14.8	6.7
100,000 to 250,000	12.0	6.6
less than 100,000	7.7	6.7

Source   Irene B. Taeuber, "The Changing Distribution
of the Population of the United States in the Twentieth
Century," in Volume 5 of Commission Research
Reports, *Population Distribution and Policy*, ed. Sara
Mills Mazie, U.S. Commission on Population Growth
and the American Future (Washington, D.C.:
Government Printing Office, 1972), table 21.

Although the nation as a whole is 11.1 percent black, table 7.12 shows that the central
cities of the largest SMSAs (those of over a
million) have more than twice this proportion
of blacks. Cities of 100,000 to a quarter of a
million have almost the same proportion of
blacks as the nation as a whole. However,
black persons are less likely to live in the
suburbs of moderately large metropolitan
areas (500,000 to 3 million) than they are to
live in suburbs of larger or smaller cities.
Cities of less than 100,000 exclude blacks
from both the central city and the suburbs to
almost the same extent that suburbs of larger
metropolitan areas do. Regional variations in
these patterns are shown in table 7.13. (The
U.S. Bureau of the Census defines four
regions, each composed of several states:
Northeast, North Central, South, and West.)

Table 7.13   Region and Black Population Inside and Outside Metropolitan Central Cities (percent of population black)

Region	Inside Central City	Outside Central City
Total United States	20.6	5.9
New England	9.1	1.4
Mid Atlantic-coastal	23.9	6.0
Mid Atlantic–other	13.2	2.1
East North Central	24.6	2.9
West North Central	12.5	4.2
Appalachian	24.6	5.9
Del., Md., D.C.	57.9	7.9
Va., N. Carolina	30.8	13.6
Deep South	36.5	17.5
Florida	20.5	11.8
Texas, Oklahoma	16.2	6.5
Northern Mountain	4.8	1.9
Pacific Northwest	5.1	2.1
Calif. and Southwest	11.5	7.0

Source   Calculated from Irene B. Taeuber, "The Changing Distribution of Population in the United States in the Twentieth Century," in Volume 5 of Commission Research Reports, *Population Distribution and Policy,* ed. Sara Mills Mazie, U.S. Commission on Population Growth and the American Future (Washington, D.C.: Government Printing Office, 1972), table 21.

The central cities with the highest proportion of blacks are located along the Atlantic seaboard in Washington, D.C., and in the states of Maryland, Delaware, Virginia, and North Carolina, and in cities of the Deep South as a whole.

How did the central cities—especially the largest central cities—become so disproportionately black? Table 7.14 shows that throughout the twentieth century the black population has grown faster than the white population in central cities. Since the depression, the black suburban population has also increased faster than the white suburban population, although the disparity in the rate of increase that is seen in the central cities is not matched in the suburbs. Since there were so few blacks in both the central cities and the suburbs at the beginning of the twentieth century, the much higher black growth rates in three quarters of a century have produced central cities that are only 20 percent to 25 percent black and suburbs less than 10 percent black.

Central cities never recaptured the growth in white population that they exhibited prior to the depression. Overall growth of central cities slowed during the 1920s; table 7.14 shows that this slowing down was largely among the white population, rather than the black population. White population in central cities essentially stopped growing after 1930 and has declined since 1950. The black population has rebounded sharply from its low increases during the depression years, but the rate of growth has since slowed. Still, the black central city population has grown much more rapidly than the white population. In fact, the 1960-70 population growth rate (41.7 percent) among central city blacks was higher than any growth rate exhibited by central city whites at any time during the twentieth century.

Table 7.14   Racial Change in Metropolitan Areas in the Twentieth Century (percentage change)

Decade	Inside Central Cities		Outside Central Cities	
	White	Black	White	Black
1900-1910	36.2	46.3	25.2	19.3
1910-1920	24.7	93.7	39.0	33.7
1920-1930	25.9	107.8	67.4	77.9
1930-1940	4.2	27.6	17.1	20.8
1940-1950	4.4	74.2	42.3	62.3
1950-1960	−6.9	55.7	70.4	73.3
1960-1970	−7.6	41.7	24.7	57.6

Source   Irene B. Taeuber, "The Changing Distribution of Population in the United States in the Twentieth Century," in Volume 5 of Commission Research Reports, *Population Distribution and Policy,* ed. Sara Mills Mazie, U.S. Commission on Population Growth and the American Future (Washington, D.C.: Government Printing Office, 1972), page 89.

Rates of racial population growth between 1960 and 1970 varied by SMSA size. Table 7.15 shows that central city white population declined only in those SMSAs with more than 500,000 residents. The greatest decline took place in central cities of one to three million. In smaller SMSAs, with smaller proportions of blacks living in the central cities, the white population continued to grow, although not as fast as the black population. During the 1960s the black suburban population grew faster than the white population in SMSAs of more than a million; in smaller SMSAs the white suburban population grew faster than the black.

These differential growth patterns—the result of both differential fertility rates and differential in-migration rates in central cities and suburbs—have produced increased urban black populations, especially in the largest central cities. These same cities are the ones that exert the greatest influence on society's image of urban and metropolitan life, which in turn influences society's behavior toward cities.

Migration Patterns

Clearly, our society has become increasingly suburbanized. Growth rates of central cities, particularly among the white population, have slowed down in the largest SMSAs. This indicates that the whites are migrating from the central cities into the suburbs. However, white migration to the suburbs is not simply a racial matter. For example, between 1970 and 1974, of the 7.7 million whites moving to the suburbs, 40 percent of them moved to suburbs of cities other than the one in which they had lived—they went from Chicago to a suburb of Detroit, Boston, Atlanta, or some other SMSA central city. Meanwhile, 3.4 million whites reversed the trend, moving from suburbs to central cities (U.S. Bureau of the Census, 1975b:8).

Table 7.15   Racial Change in Metropolitan Areas, 1960-1970, by Size of SMSA* (percent change)

| | Inside Central City | | Outside Central City | |
	White	Black	White	Black
3 million or more	−7.6	41.7	24.7	57.6
1 to 3 million	−10.4	34.7	34.7	48.5
500,000 to 1 million	−6.5	27.7	34.6	20.7
250,000 to 500,000	11.9	29.8	11.9	0.5
100,000 to 250,000	9.6	18.4	23.6	8.8
less than 100,000	6.8	20.4	20.4	11.8
Total	−0.1	33.4	25.1	30.4

*1960 SMSAs, 1960 areas

Source   Irene B. Taeuber, "The Changing Distribution of Population in the United States in the Twentieth Century," in Volume 5 of Commission Research Reports, *Population Distribution and Policy,* ed. Sara Mills Mazie, U.S. Commission on Population Growth and the American Future (Washington, D.C.: Government Printing Office, 1972), page 90.

American cities have always attracted both foreign immigrants and rural migrants. Foreign immigration in the United States reached its peak from 1900-1910, when nearly 8.8 million persons arrived. Since that time, immigration steadily declined until 1965, when it began rising to an annual rate of about four hundred thousand, which is about half that observed during the first decade of the twentieth century (U.S. Bureau of the Census, 1975d:table 153).

Since most foreign immigrants settled in large cities, we would expect central cities to have a higher proportion of foreign-born residents. However, we would also expect that, because of upward mobility, children of foreign-born residents would be more likely to live in suburbs. Thus, suburbs should have nearly as many residents with foreign-born parents as cities have.

Table 7.16 shows that the proportion of foreign-born residents is more than twice as high in urban areas as in rural areas (5.8 percent versus 1.7 percent). The proportion of foreign-born residents is highest in central cities (7.5 percent) and decreases as one moves from the central city to the suburbs to the smaller urban places. Residents of urbanized areas are slightly less likely to be born of native parents than are residents of smaller urban places. Residents of urbanized areas are much more likely to have parents who were born abroad than are rural residents.

In sum these figures bear out our expectations that foreign-born residents and their descendants are attracted to city life. Certainly, the ethnic composition of central cities— ethnicity being provisionally defined as having been born in a foreign country or having parents who were born in a foreign country—

Table 7.16   Residence and Migration Status of the American Population, 1970

Nativity	Urbanized Areas				Other Places		
	Total Urban Population	Total	Inside Central Cities	Outside Central Cities	10,000 or more	2,500 to 10,000	Total Rural Population
Percent native	94.16	93.27	92.47	94.21	97.48	97.69	98.33
Native, of native parents	80.61	78.39	78.53	78.22	89.08	89.24	91.41
Foreign born	5.84	6.73	7.53	5.79	2.52	2.31	1.67
Residence: 1965							
Same house	51.31	51.73	51.06	52.52	48.20	51.50	57.55
Different house, same county	23.99	24.32	26.30	22.00	22.91	22.40	21.40
Different house, different county	18.38	16.32	14.10	18.94	22.41	20.24	16.15

Source   U.S. Bureau of the Census, *Census of Population, 1970: General Social and Economic Characteristics, Final Report PC(1)-C1, United States Summary* (Washington, D.C.: Government Printing Office, 1972), tables 97, 98.

is more heterogeneous than the ethnic composition of suburbs, smaller cities, and rural areas.

One measure of internal migrations of urban populations is the proportion of people who have lived in the same home for five years or more. This proportion is greatest in rural areas, where nearly 58 percent have lived in the same home for five years, and lowest in urban places of 10,000 or more that are not part of urbanized areas, where only 48 percent have lived in the same house for five years. People change homes within a single county in the central cities, reflecting moves from neighborhood to neighborhood within the city. They are more likely to cross county borders when they live in places of 10,000 or more outside urbanized areas.

Regional Variations

Metropolitan areas first developed in the Northeastern and North Central United States and grew by **in-migration** from foreign countries and from rural areas of the United States. Much internal migration to the north was from the South and included many blacks. This pattern has changed recently (see figure 7.3). The West and the South have experienced less **out-migration** and the Northeastern and North Central regions have experienced less in-migration. The patterns have in fact reversed, leading to net in-migration to southern and western regions. **Net migration** in the South alone took a great leap in the period from 1970-75. These patterns are most dramatically reflected in projections for metropolitan populations: by the end of the twentieth century the South is expected to

Inmigration, outmigration, and net migration for regions, 1965–70 and 1970–75. (Source: U.S. Bureau of the Census, *Current Population Reports,* Series P 20, No. 285 "Mobility of the Population of the United States, March 1970 to March 1975" [Washington, D.C.: Government Printing Office, 1975], p. 3.)

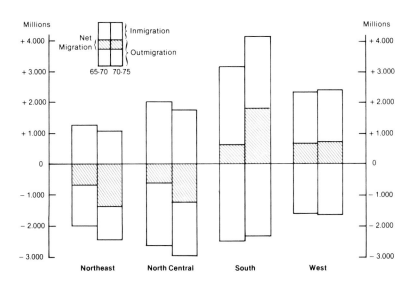

have the largest metropolitan population in the United States, and the West is expected to have as large a metropolitan population as the Northeast, which historically has always had the largest U.S. metropolitan population (U.S. Bureau of the Census, 1976:21; Pickard, 1972:138-41; U.S. Bureau of the Census, 1975a).

The newer metropolitan areas will experience the problems that older metropolitan areas have already experienced. New populations will need less expensive housing in the center of the city and improved mass transportation systems. Existing housing stocks will be old and inadequate. There will be problems of integrating older, more settled populations with the newer populations. In addition, declining population in older metropolitan areas abandoned by migrants will result in an excess of old, less desirable housing and a declining tax base.

Education, Occupation, and Income: Social Status

Educational attainments, occupational distributions, and income levels of different populations in urban areas partially characterize the labor force that can induce potential employers to locate in the city. These characteristics also partially determine the city population's need for various communal services.

The educational level of the population indicates the skills that the city can offer potential employers and the types of cultural and recreational facilities that residents of the city are likely to support. A city whose residents are highly educated may demand support for museums, symphony orchestras, opera companies, art galleries, and other cultural facilities and services. The occupational and income distributions of a city reflect the kinds of jobs available and the number of people who may need or who may provide city services. Occupational and income distributions affect not only the demand for social and other welfare services, but also the city's ability to carry out central place functions. Larger cities usually have more highly educated, professional people and are able to carry out many of the central place functions discussed in chapters five and six.

The suburbs of urbanized areas stand out as areas containing the most highly educated population. Presumably this is why suburbanites are most concerned with or devoted to schooling. Certainly, a large proportion of suburban taxes goes for maintaining school systems. The proportion of the population enrolled in school also is an indication of the level of demand among that population for provision of this essential, locality-relevant function. Table 7.17 clearly shows that the highest proportion of people over three years old who are enrolled in school live in the urban fringe. The median educational accomplishment among suburban residents is slightly beyond high school graduation, compared with less than high school graduation among rural residents and high school graduation throughout society. In the suburbs and in other urban places of 10,000 or more, nearly three out of four people have completed high school and one to three years of college. The proportion of persons actually completing college is highest in the urban fringe. Since the Bureau of the Census limits educational data to people ages sixteen to twenty-four, the proportion of people actually completing college or going on for more advanced training may be higher.

Labor Force Participation

More than three out of four men and nearly half the women in the United States age 65 and under are in the labor force. The proportion of working men and women in the population would be even higher if the age restrictions were lowered to 60 or to 55. Participation in the labor force is highest for men in the suburbs and highest for women in the central cities.

Table 7.17 displays selected types of occupations by place of residence. The urban fringe has the highest proportion of people employed in three categories: professional; technical and kindred workers; managers and sales workers. These occupations are likely to pay people well enough so that they can live in the suburbs and commute to work in the central city. Conversely, the central city has the highest proportion of women employed as clerical workers, reflecting the fact that people employed in such occupations often do not receive enough pay to work in the central city and live in the suburbs.

As might be expected, the highest median income is found among persons living in the suburbs. On the average, suburban families receive incomes of $2,200 (in 1970 dollars) more per year than the residents of central cities. Residents of smaller cities and rural areas make considerably less. Rural populations have the lowest income, since they grow some of their own food and the Bureau of the Census does not count it as income. Urbanized areas, especially central cities, have the highest proportion of people on public assistance (7 percent). Suburban welfare recipients are few. About one in twenty persons in smaller cities is on public assistance.

Table 7.17   Residence, Education, Occupation, Income, and Related Indicators of Social Status, 1970

	Urbanized Areas				Other Places		
	Total Urban Population	Total	Inside Central Cities	Outside Central Cities	10,000 or more	2,500 to 10,000	Total Rural Population
Percent enrolled in school (of population age 3-34)							
	54.5	54.7	53.0	56.6	54.5	53.5	53.5
Median years of school completed							
Males	12.2	12.2	12.0	12.4	12.2	12.0	10.7
Females	12.1	12.2	12.0	12.3	12.1	12.0	11.5
Persons 18-24 years							
Percent with 4 years of high school or 1-3 years college							
	68.4	67.9	66.3	70.0	72.2	67.3	59.6
Percent 4 or more years of college							
	6.9	7.3	7.3	7.4	5.8	4.8	3.6
Persons 16 years and over, percent in labor force							
Male	77.6	78.4	75.8	81.5	74.5	74.3	73.9
Female	43.1	43.6	44.5	42.5	42.3	40.6	36.0
Percent of workers in selected occupations							
Professional, technical, and kindred	16.2	16.5	15.2	18.0	15.8	13.8	10.6
Managerial	8.7	8.6	7.6	9.9	8.9	9.0	7.2
Sales	7.8	8.0	7.6	8.7	7.3	6.8	5.0
Clerical	19.9	20.9	21.6	20.2	16.5	14.7	11.9
Service	11.7	11.4	12.9	9.7	13.2	12.5	9.8
Median family income($)	10,196	10,618	9,519	11,771	8,817	8,487	8,071
Percent receiving public assistance income	5.4	5.4	7.2	3.4	5.0	5.4	5.2
Percent of families with income less than poverty level	9.0	8.3	11.0	5.2	11.3	12.2	15.2

Source   U.S. Bureau of the Census, *Census of Population, 1970: General Social and Economic Characteristics, Final Report PC(1)-C1, United States Summary* (Washington, D.C.: Government Printing Office, 1972), tables 99, 101, 102, 105, 106.

The proportion of families whose income falls below the poverty level (a measure established by the federal government and based on size of family, income, and the cost of living in urban and rural areas) is highest in rural areas and lowest in the suburbs. Central cities of urbanized areas and smaller cities have intermediate proportions of families living in poverty. As U.S. citizens, we should be absolutely horrified to learn that nine percent of all families in our society have incomes below the poverty level.

Summary

This relatively brief tour through urban population statistics and the history of urban population growth and migration has shown that the United States became half urban in 1920. At that time a quarter of the population lived in cities of 100,000 or more. Since then, the number of cities of this size has grown to 156 and the number of SMSAs to more than 270. But the proportion of population living in cities of 100,000 or more has begun to decline, as has the proportion living in metropolitan areas.

Many residents defined as metropolitan by the Bureau of the Census actually live in rural places. Although the United States is considered to be an urban society, only a small fraction of the people live in very large urban centers. The large cities grew by attracting foreign immigrants and native-born migrants from rural areas, largely from the South. The trend of immigration from rural areas to Northeastern and North Central metropolitan areas recently has reversed, and southern and western metropolitan areas are now growing faster than the older northern and eastern metropolitan areas. Suburbs and non-metropolitan areas are also growing faster than older, larger metropolitan central cities.

The characteristics of the urban population, as defined by age, gender, marital status, race, occupation, education, and labor force participation, determine the needs of urban populations for communal services. Cities must recognize and provide for concentrations of female, single, elderly, black, uneducated, and dependent persons.

Demographic data alone tell us almost nothing about the forces that have shaped the cities and caused their problems and needs. These data do reveal the dynamics of today's urban crisis and the characteristics of population that will determine the types of communal functions cities must perform for their residents.

Glossary

fertility ratio   number of children under five per 1,000 women ages 15 to 49

in-migration   migration of population into an area

labor force   the portion of the population that is employed, plus the portion that is unemployed and still job hunting (this excludes housewives, students, young persons, elderly persons, and those who are unemployed and no longer looking for work)

migration   the movement of people from one area to another

natural increase   the increase in size of population due to a greater number of births than deaths

net migration   the difference between in-migration and out-migration in an area

out-migration   migration of population away from an area

places   political units incorporated as cities, boroughs, towns, and villages (except in certain states where these designations do not refer to population centers), and certain unincorporated areas that have a dense nucleus of residences (Note: By this Bureau of the Census definition, some locations are not places.)

region   a combination of states defined by the U.S. Bureau of the Census; U.S. regions and states in each region are as follows:

Northeast
1. New England: Maine, Vermont, New Hampshire, Massachusetts, Connecticut, Rhode Island
2. Middle Atlantic: New York, New Jersey, Pennsylvania

North Central
1. East North Central: Ohio, Indiana, Illinois, Michigan, Wisconsin
2. West North Central: Minnesota, Iowa, Missouri, Kansas, Nebraska, South Dakota, North Dakota

South
1. South Atlantic: West Virginia, Maryland, Delaware, Virginia, Washington, D.C., South Carolina, North Carolina, Georgia, Florida
2. East South Central: Kentucky, Tennessee, Mississippi, Alabama
3. West South Central: Louisiana, Arkansas, Oklahoma, Texas

West
1. Mountain: Montana, Wyoming, Colorado, New Mexico, Arizona, Utah, Nevada, Idaho
2. Pacific: Washington, Oregon, California, Alaska, Hawaii

standard metropolitan area (SMA)   term used to describe the metropolitan community until the development of the standard metropolitan statistical area (SMSA) concept

standard metropolitan statistical area (SMSA)   term now used to describe and define the metropolitan community; SMSAs are designated by the Bureau of the Census and by the Office of Management and the Budget and consist of a central city of at least 50,000 persons, the county in which the central city lies, and all contiguous and adjacent counties that are socially and economically integrated with the central city

urban fringe   the portion of an urbanized area outside the central city

urban place   as defined by the U.S. Bureau of the Census, a place of at least 2,500 people

urbanized area   a central city of at least 50,000 persons, plus the densely settled area surrounding the city; in contrast to SMSA, an urbanized area is defined by population density rather than county borders; it is the physical community in contrast to the socioeconomic community of the SMSA

References

Goheen, Peter G.
1971 "Metropolitan Area Definitions: A Reevaluation of Concept and Statistical Practice." In *Internal Structure of the City,* edited by Larry S. Bourne, pp. 47-58. New York: Oxford University Press.

Pickard, Jerome P.
1972 "U.S. Metropolitan Growth and Expansion, 1970-2000, with Population Projections." In *Population Distribution and Policy,* edited by Sara Mills Mazie, pp. 127-82. U.S. Commission on Population Growth and the American Future, vol. 5 of Commission Research Reports. Washington, D.C.: Government Printing Office.

Shyrock, Henry S.
1957 "The Natural History of Standard Metropolitan Areas." *American Journal of Sociology* 63 (September): 163-70.

Shyrock, Henry S., et al.
1973 *The Methods and Materials of Demography.* Vol. 1. 2d printing, rev. U.S. Bureau of the Census. Washington, D.C.: Government Printing Office.

Taeuber, Irene B.
1972   "The Changing Distribution of the Population of the United States in the Twentieth Century." *Population Distribution and Policy,* edited by Sara Mills Mazie, pp. 31-108. U.S. Commission on Population Growth and the American Future, vol. 5 of Commission Research Reports. Washington, D.C.: Government Printing Office.

U.S. Bureau of the Census
1971a   *Census of Population, 1970: General Population Characteristics, Final Report PC(1)-B1, United States Summary.* Washington, D.C.: Government Printing Office.

1971b   *Census of Population, 1970: Number of Inhabitants, Final Report PC(1)-A1, United States Summary.* Washington, D.C.: Government Printing Office.

1972   *Census of Population, 1970: General Social and Economic Characteristics, Final Report PC(1)-C1, United States Summary.* Washington, D.C.: Government Printing Office.

1975a   "Mobility of the Population of the United States: March 1970 to March 1975." *Current Population Reports, Series P-20, 285.* Washington, D.C.: Government Printing Office.

1975b   "Social and Economic Conditions of the Metropolitan and Non-Metropolitan Population: 1974 and 1970." *Current Population Reports, Series P-23, 55.* Washington, D.C.: Government Printing Office.

1975c   *Historical Statistics of the United States, Colonial Times to 1970. Bicentennial Edition.* Vol. 1. Washington, D.C.: Government Printing Office.

1975d   *Statistical Abstract of the United States: 1974.* Washington, D.C.: Government Printing Office.

1976   "Population Profile of the United States: 1975." *Current Population Reports, Series P-20, 292.* Washington, D.C.: Government Printing Office.

Suggested Readings

Goheen, Peter G. "Metropolitan Area Definitions: A Reevaluation of Concept and Statistical Practice." In *The Internal Structure of the City.* New York: Oxford University Press, 1971. A valuable paper showing the history of the concept of the SMSA in theory and practice.

U.S. Bureau of the Census. *Statistical Abstract of the United States.* Washington, D.C.: Government Printing Office, annual. Published each year, this volume contains essential data on the population of the United States and many other relevant topics. The section "Metropolitan Area Statistics" contains data on population, housing, employment, and government by individual area.

Notes

1. Travelers are counted at their home addresses, but college students, members of the armed forces, and residents of institutions are counted where they are found. See Shyrock, et al., 1973:95-99.
2. We call this definition generous, because today 2,500 is a small town. When the census began, only a small proportion of the population lived in places of this size. See table 7.1.
3. Over 100,000 immigrants have arrived in the United States annually since 1845 with the exceptions of 1861, 1862, and 1931-1945. Most of these immigrants settled initially in cities (U.S. Bureau of the Census, 1975c:105-6). For a more extended discussion, see chapter 9.
4. Such a tracing can be found in Goheen, 1971:47-58.
5. We should note that, since the Supreme Court's one-man, one-vote ruling has been extended to the local level, this equality of population between the central city and the noncentral city in SMSAs is likely to have increasing political impact.
6. Some suburbs of very large central cities may be larger than 50,000, but this does not alter the argument.

DUNAGIN'S PEOPLE by Ralph Dunagin. (Reprinted by permission of Field Newspaper Syndicate.)

"WATCH FOR TRICKS IN THAT OFFER TO GIVE THE COUNTRY BACK TO THE INDIANS... THEY MIGHT WANT US TO TAKE THE CITIES, TOO."

The first seven chapters of this book introduced perspectives and analytic tools that can help us understand a wide variety of contemporary and future urban problems. The concept of community clarified the nature of neighborhoods, cities, suburbs, and metropolitan areas. It also identified a major source of our feelings about the failures of urban communities. We traced the evolution of cities from small settlements to modern metropolises, and we investigated changes in the nature of urban communities, in the communal functions performed by cities, and in the spatial organization of cities. The factors that have affected social and spatial organization in the city were seen to be changes in the wider society, such as population growth, changes in population characteristics, technological development, growth of the social surplus, and changes in the division of labor and the status system.

We saw that the city and its components can be viewed as communities attempting to perform communal functions. And we saw that change is evolutionary; that is, changes build upon one another, and the forces that affect a community's ability to perform communal functions at one time are likely to influence its performance at other times. We also considered ecological relationships. We learned that a community's performance of communal functions reflects its adaptation to the environment.

The second part of this book examines how cities in the United States perform some communal functions and analyzes some of their performance problems. An implicit assumption in Part 2 is that inadequate performance is a problem itself. Cities that perform fewer communal functions or perform them less effectively than other cities are less desirable places to live.

Chapter 8 suggests that three major sources of current urban problems are changing population characteristics, attitudes toward the city and urban life, and technology. The city cannot control these forces. Consequently, it must cope with their continuing challenges to its performance. Chapter 9 examines the problem of maintaining normative integration and social solidarity in the context of racial and ethnic diversity. Chapter 10 analyzes the political process as a form of organization to perform or facilitate the performance of communal functions.

Chapters 11 and 12 analyze specific aspects of the essential communal functions of providing and distributing goods and services. Chapter 11 is an overview of how cities provide housing, transportation, and health services to their residents. Chapter 12 looks at the ways in which cities deal with the by-products of human activities: liquid, solid, and airborne wastes. These two chapters not only describe specific problems facing cities but also provide models for understanding how cities deal with other problems of this sort.

Chapter 13 analyzes urban crime as part of the problem that cities have in performing the communal function of social control. In the same vein, chapter 14 analyzes education in the city as part of the problem that cities have in performing the communal function of socializing the young.

Chapter 15 forecasts prospects for the future of cities in the United States. Social scientists have begun to understand the trends that produced many urban problems, and they have identified other trends that may ameliorate these problems. There is good reason to expect that cities will be able to perform their communal functions more effectively in the future than they have in the past twenty-five years.

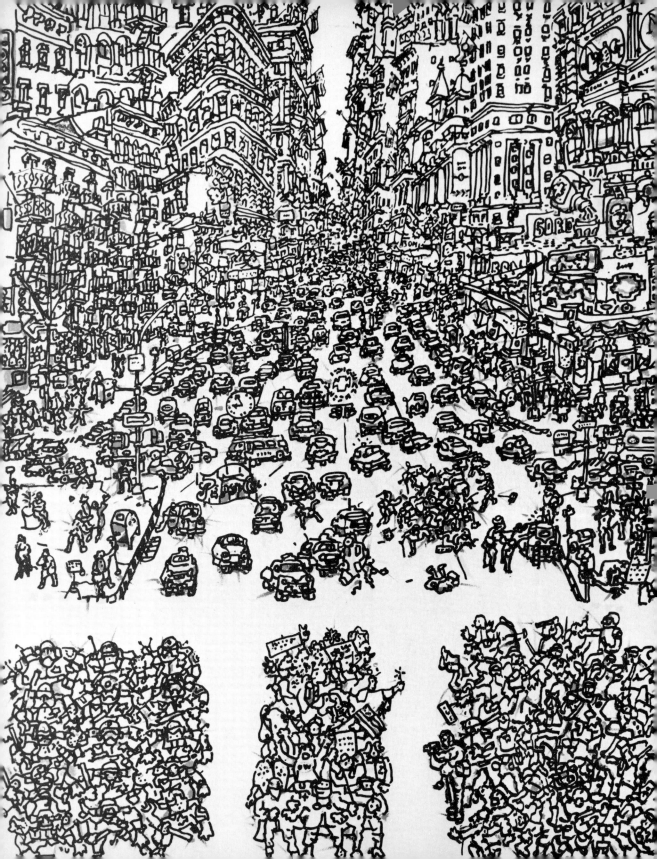

8

Cities Lose Control: The Roots of Urban Problems

Many forces that affect human behavior and the quality of life in a complex society are beyond the control of individuals, neighborhoods, cities, and metropolitan areas. For example, economic and technological developments in the United States or in the world may influence what happens in a city, but the city cannot control these forces. A city may lose jobs because there is no longer a market for goods produced by some of its industries. The market may disappear because of a worldwide economic recession. Or it may disappear because new technology enables other companies in other areas to produce more desirable or less expensive substitutes for those goods. The influence of "external forces" on urban areas and on their ability to cope with social problems can be seen most clearly when we examine some changes in small towns during the first sixty years of this century.

As in many small towns, the residents of Springdale, New York, in the mid-1950s felt their way of life was superior to life in large cities (Vidich and Bensman, 1958:30-46, 80-107). The pace was slower, the people knew one another, and few disturbing characteristics of urban life were in evidence. The residents of Springdale felt that they could enjoy the benefits of urban society from a distance without suffering any of its disadvantages.

Even though they lived far from a large city, the residents of Springdale interacted with representatives of the wider society. The farmers who provided the economic base of Springdale knew agricultural extension agents who were connected with the relatively cosmopolitan local agricultural college. Business leaders relied on distribution centers in large cities, and church groups relied on resources from religious organizations headquartered in large cities. Connections with the outside world, such as automobile dealers, traveling salesmen, and business agents, conferred resources and prestige on the Springdalers who came into contact with them, but these connections also brought the culture and attitudes of the urban society into Springdale. Outside influence was felt perhaps most critically in two areas: education and politics.

Springdale was proud of its ability to provide a high-quality education for its young people, but in doing so, it relinquished a large measure of control over what they were taught. To have an accredited high school that was eligible to send its graduates to a state agricultural college, Springdale had to accept the state's curriculum and hire teachers who had been educated outside of Springdale (Vidich and Bensman, 1958:174-201). To work in Springdale, the teachers had to live there, and they brought with them the norms, culture, attitudes, and values of the wider society.

Springdale's major political goal, like that of other small towns, was to provide as many services as possible and yet to keep local taxes low. Local political leaders and government officials had relatively little power. To provide necessary services, such as road maintenance and garbage and snow removal, they had to accept county, state, and federal facilities, subsidies, and services (Vidich and Bensman, 1958:115-17). These benefits kept taxes low and were provided at no monetary cost. The cost to Springdale was acceptance of the legitimacy of rules, regulations, and behaviors of outside jurisdictions and agents, even if there was a conflict with local values and decisions (Vidich and Bensman, 1958: 202-27). As a result, political decisions made in Springdale were basically limited to approving the actions of state and federal agencies.

The political dependence of Springdale led to a sense of psychological dependence. Indeed, the ability to generate local political power depended on one's connections with representatives of political power in the wider society. The ability to influence, or even to appear to influence, decisions of county, federal, and state officials was the major source of power. This was the central fact of political life in Springdale.

In addition, newspapers, magazines, and radio brought the metropolitan way of life and its culture to this small town. The mass media legitimated attitudes and values that, while typical of metropolitan residents, at times conflicted with attitudes and values of Springdale residents. Politically, culturally, economically, and socially, Springdale lost control over its own destiny. It became dependent on the outside world to make and carry out critical political and economic decisions and to provide the greater part of its cultural life.

Similar studies conducted in Muncie, Indiana, from 1925 to 1935 indicated even more dramatically that the same processes were taking place in middle-sized towns (Lynd and Lynd, 1929, 1937). Industrial plants that had been dominated by a single family and run without outside interference or influence for many years had to integrate with the national economic system. These national ties included contact with labor unions. Plant management could not continue to make decisions without

considering the welfare of the workers and national union policy.

Muncie residents believed in taking care of local problems locally, but during the depression of 1929-34 they were unable to care for residents who needed help. As a result, Muncie became dependent on the wider society for economic recovery programs and for financial and moral resources. The people of Muncie believed that they should not have needed this help, but they recognized that they did. Accepting help, however, meant accepting rules made by outsiders about the proper way to provide help.

The goals of education in Muncie did not conflict with the traditional values of the broader society. To provide the high-quality education that these values demanded, the city hired persons from outside Muncie as teachers. Often these teachers held values that were quite different from those of Muncie's citizens. They introduced new and disruptive ideas that led to changes in the town. Muncie not only lost its ability to control its economic and political life but also gave up some of its control over the socialization of its children.

Since the middle of the twentieth century, cities much larger than Muncie and Springdale have lost control in a similar manner. Small towns have lost effective political, economic, and social power to larger political jurisdictions. Some problems of large cities and metropolitan areas, such as poverty, pollution, racism, and lack of mass transportation, do not recognize political boundaries. The forces that generated these problems are national or international in scope. In the search for solutions, decision-making power has been taken by government agencies that cross city and metropolitan boundaries.

The ability of suburbs to maintain political control over activities within their boundaries is also being eroded. The federal government requires joint metropolitan planning and action in the areas of transportation, pollution control, and to some extent public housing and education. The same outside forces that affect the cities also influence the suburbs. In addition, the suburbs must integrate their activities with those of the dominant central city.

Roland Warren has suggested that all community systems are, to a greater or lesser extent, aspects of the wider society. He noted that in some units of community structure the **vertical ties** that go outside the community are stronger than the **horizontal ties** within the community (Warren, 1972:63-94, 161-66, 237-66). There is great similarity between Warren's position and the analysis presented here. The major difference is that in considering how cities and other communities have lost control over their own destiny, Warren places less emphasis on the control exerted by external agencies and general social forces over the local community.

In the following analysis we will see that there are other important factors that have helped to diminish local control. Among them are changes in **demographic structure** and technology and the increasing worldwide integration of social systems and cultures.

External Variables That Affect Cities

The forces that seem to be at the root of many urban problems are general, long-term trends in the society—trends that are beyond the control of any social institutions. The city has little control over these trends. Urban neighborhoods have even less control and often feel the problems more acutely.

Some of these trends are predominantly demographic. Others are related to the level of technology available to the society. Still other trends are the changing attitudes of the population and the society toward urban environments. And some trends are the result of the interaction of demography, technology, and attitudes.

Demographic Factors

The attractiveness of the city caused its population growth. However, cities have not deliberately adopted policies designed to attract migrants. The movement of population into urban areas is so well established and the legitimacy of personal mobility is so ingrained in our social system that cities cannot stop it. Even attempts to withdraw city services—especially welfare benefits—from recent migrants have failed to stop the movement of poor, rural residents into urban centers. This is one of the demographic factors beyond the control of cities.[1]

In chapter 7 we looked at the effects of urban life on fertility, birth and death rates, family size, and other features of population composition. These features are statistical representations of urban demography, but they are not "caused" by policies that cities establish. Even when urban policies, such as public health standards, have had an impact on the demographic characteristics of the urban population, much of the effect seems to result from general trends in the society.

The age and gender composition of the urban population is also beyond the control of the city. These characteristics help to determine the kinds of services that the city has to provide to its population. For example, the "baby boom" that followed World War II produced a rapid increase in the number of school-age children in the population in the 1950s. This demographic change required great expansion of urban school systems.

The changing age composition of the urban population also affects the housing supply needed by a city's residents. Recent increases in the proportion of young adults who are single or married but without children have created a demand for small and relatively inexpensive housing units. But if the bulge in this type of population is temporary it means that this type of housing is needed in large quantity for only a short time.

In education particularly, a temporary bulge in the age distribution at first demands that cities make expensive investments in certain facilities. Later the demand for these facilities may be dramatically reduced. But since the facilities exist, the city may have to pay for maintaining them for many years into the future, thereby reducing its ability to pay for programs to meet other needs.

The composition of a city's labor force also depends, at least in part, on the age and gender composition of the population as well as on social and cultural attitudes that affect women's participation in the labor force.[2] But the labor force may not mesh with the **labor market,** which is changing in central cities. Fewer unskilled or semiskilled workers are needed, and more clerical and skilled workers with a higher degree of education and training are required.[3] The biggest growth in the labor

The attractiveness of cities draws
people whether or not a city's
policies are designed to do so.

Social and cultural attitudes about
women's participation in the labor
force are changing.

market is in service industries that require workers with at least a high school education. With such changes in the labor market, the age, gender, and educational composition of the labor force can impose constraints on the city's ability to attract additional employers. As educational requirements increase and the proportion of blacks in the urban population increases, urban schools will have to provide a better education if future generations are to have a better chance of being employed than the current generation has had.

The issue of inferior schools in segregated neighborhoods will be a political controversy for years to come, particularly if segregation continues and schools in the central city do not improve. This issue is likely to be even more important in urban race relations in the future than it is at present.

The racial composition of the population is another demographic factor that cities cannot control. Chapter 7 reviewed statistical descriptions of the black population of cities and metropolitan areas. In chapter 9 we will examine racial and ethnic differentiation in cities. The discussion here is limited to some of the most important demographic aspects of urban race-related problems.

The rate of black migration to urban and metropolitan areas in the future is likely to decline, but the higher rate of natural increase of the black than of the nonblack population will lead to an increasing number and proportion of blacks in major urban centers. For example, the black portion of the population of Chicago grew by 35.7 percent between 1960 and 1970 (U.S. Bureau of the Census, 1975:867). At this rate the black portion of Chicago's population will double in less than thirty years.

The problems facing blacks as they attempt to gain political power will become more complex. Numbers will entitle them to power and first-class political citizenship, but if central city school systems fail to improve, the skills of young black people will not enable them to claim comparable economic power (Dyckman, 1963). Furthermore, to the extent that political and social changes allow blacks to move into the suburbs,[4] the political impact of the increasing black population in the central city will be diluted.

Finally, most people continue to want single-family detached homes, and increased affluence permits more people to contemplate buying such housing. Dense settlement in the central city means that such housing may be available only in the suburbs.[5] Since both social and geographic mobility are legitimate and valued in the society, the city cannot restrain the migration of affluent urbanites of any race to the suburbs. Unfortunately, these mobile members of the population may be the ones who are best able to make the city's labor force attractive to employers and add to the city's revenues through the taxes they pay. Their loss creates further problems for, but is beyond the control of, the city.

Technological Factors

Technology is also beyond the control or influence of the city. Economic historians, such as N.S.B. Gras, have argued that the mode of production and the nature of technology influence the level of urbanization (these arguments were analyzed in chapters 3, 4, and 5). We have seen that individuals and institutions originally chose their locations within

the city to minimize land and transportation costs. However, changes in the technology of communications and transportation have reduced the importance of transportation costs for raw materials and finished products. Furthermore, improved communications and a shift from locally generated power and heavy metals to long-distance transmission of electric power and lightweight synthetics have made central locations less critical for many industrial plants (Dyckman, 1970; Kasarda, 1976).

As the level of technology in the society increases, the labor force becomes more highly specialized. The consequence of increasing specialization in the labor force is further progress of the division of labor. As the division of labor progresses, the population becomes both more heterogeneous and more organically integrated (see chapter 2). The city has to cope not only with changes in production methods, in the materials used in production, and in the direct products of new technologies, but also with the social by-products of these changes. Examples of technological change in the past include production lines that require large single-level buildings, the increasing use of synthetic materials for clothing and building, air conditioning, expressways, high-rise buildings, new communications devices, and computers. Examples of the social by-products of these technological changes include the need for a better educated labor force, a vast reduction in the need for unskilled labor, the need for new industrial plants, the freedom of workers to commute long distances, a decreased tax base in the city, changes in police and fire protection tactics, and perhaps changes in building codes. In health care, for example, as new medical technologies develop, new medical occupations develop. Many cities have mobile intensive-care units, manned by paramedics, to aid accident and trauma victims. New medical technologies also prolong life for many older people and have helped to change the age structure of the society. Thus both the direct and the indirect effects of technological change have an impact on urban society.

Within the city, technological improvements in expressway design and traffic control have made it possible to get to any point from any other point in a relatively short time. Flexible routings for shipments of goods and rapid communications have made it less important for businesses to be centrally located. The change to lighter materials in much of manufacturing has reduced the ratio of weight to value, so that transportation is easier and cheaper (Dyckman, 1963; Kasarda, 1976; Hawley, 1971:80, 200, 242-44).

The decrease in the cost of transportation has to be understood as a decrease in the portion of income that is spent for transportation. Lower commuting costs have permitted more of the labor force and more employers to indulge their locational preferences (Dyckman, 1963; Kasarda, 1976; Schmandt and Goldbach, 1969:473-98). Where an individual works no longer determines where that person must live. For example, New York's office capacity has increased while its population has declined. The residential area of New York has increased fourfold since the nineteenth century because increased income and the decreased commuting costs have let people live farther from their work (Dyckman, 1963).

This ability to indulge residential preferences is part of the reason for the decay of areas in the central city. Improved transportation technology has made outward expansion of the city more economical than the redevelopment of aging and densely settled portions of the city.

Transportation and communication have affected the shape of the metropolis in ways that the city could neither foresee nor control. Other technological changes have also affected the city's ability to cope with its problems. Alterations in the technology of residential, commercial, and industrial construction have brought changes in the density of settlement and land use. The development of high-rise buildings that combine several types of land use is a notable example.[6] Changing technology in the fields of power generation for industry, residences, and transportation may alter energy demands in ways that we cannot now predict. But we can predict that such alterations will be beyond the control of cities and will have a direct effect on urban social patterns and urban life.

Attitudinal Factors

There have been many "golden ages" for the city, such as the Renaissance in Europe, but there have probably been more periods of urban chaos. In the fourteenth century the black plague killed more than half of the population of London. In more recent times urban rioting has been fairly frequent. There were draft protests in New York during the Civil War, police-labor clashes in Chicago and elsewhere in the 1930s, and race riots in several cities during the 1960s.

Sometimes improved transportation technology makes outward expansion of a city more economical than redevelopment.

In general, attitudes toward the city are paradoxical (Schmandt and Goldbach, 1969; White and White, 1961:166-79; Hadden and Barton, 1973:79-116). Metropolitan central cities are centers of intellectual, social, cultural, and industrial productive capacity and excitement. The same cities are also centers of great social failures: poverty, discrimination, violence, ineffective and unresponsive institutions, and the highest levels of social disorder we have experienced. The interdependence of life in the city brings together people with the highest and lowest levels of skills and a wide variety of talents and produces excitement, activity, and opportunity. The metropolis is also the arena in which the central city's political dominance is contested by the suburbs, where racial segregation is dominant, and where political power is fragmented. Cities appear to generate activism, excitement, and involvement, but they also generate a great deal of fear, alienation, withdrawal, and anomie (Mizruchi, 1969; Schmandt and Goldbach, 1969).

For many people the city is the source of different and thus threatening life styles, as was the case with Springdale and Muncie. Today the city is often thought of as the home of criminals, welfare recipients, persons living in poverty, ethnic groups who speak "strange" languages, and many other groups whose common characteristic is that their behavior cannot be predicted and is likely to be dangerous. Jokes about the dangers of city streets and the bizarre behavior of urban residents are common. Yet the attractions of the city are undeniable. There are more goods and services and cultural, economic, and social opportunities available in major metropolitan central cities than in any other place.

Clearly, attitudes toward the city are ambivalent. Cities are necessary to the type of society we have, but they are repulsive as well as attractive. Few people are much attached to cities. Nearly half the people responding to a recent poll reported that they preferred to live in a small town (Mizruchi, 1969; Schmandt and Goldbach, 1969; Boulding, 1968; Wilson, 1968). This preference reflects the heritage of small towns and their more communal orientation. It also reflects the realization that the city is the source of social, economic, and cultural power and innovation. It is unfortunate, but true, that it is not possible to have the best of both types of social organization. Many people attempt to combine the advantages of communal small-town life and the positive aspects of the city by living in suburbs that give them easy access to the city's economic, cultural, and social facilities (Schmandt and Goldbach, 1969).

The forces of demography, technology, and attitudes are societal or international in scope, and the city can neither influence nor control them or their effects. Cities thus face a variety of problems whose causes and solutions they have virtually no ability to master. The impact of these problems is complex, and it affects the city's ability to integrate its functions with the functions of the wider society.

Response to Lack of Control

Attempts to deal with urban problems generally occur in a political context. Local governments have most of the responsibility for facilitating or actually performing most urban and metropolitan administrative functions and for integrating the performance of these local functions into the wider society.

Even though many of the fundamental causes of urban problems lie in societal trends, there are many problems that have a local basis. Attempts to solve such problems are more likely to succeed, but organizing the metropolis to deal with local problems has been difficult. Many older metropolitan areas developed by spreading out and absorbing smaller political jurisdictions (see chapters 5 and 6). Depending on state, federal, and local laws, metropolitan areas can encompass several hundred political jurisdictions. This fragmentation of political organization complicates problem solving, and it is often considered a metropolitan problem in its own right.[7]

But local governments are not the only social units concerned with the performance of locality-relevant functions. A wide range of groups with varying amounts of political power are also concerned with urban problems and attempted solutions. Such groups include block and neighborhood groups, city-wide coalitions that focus on a single issue, and permanent organizations with broad constituencies and interests. The opinions of these groups and the resources they command can influence the policies of local governments. (Urban politics will be investigated in greater detail in chapter 10.)

In addition to problems of political organization, many cities are hampered by a shortage of revenues. The migration of the middle class to the suburbs is a major cause of this shortage. Cities rely heavily on real estate taxes for their revenues, and the home-owning middle class is the largest source of real estate taxes. These taxes are already high, and increasing them may send even more of the affluent residents to the suburbs. The imposition of other city taxes, such as sales taxes, payroll taxes, and taxes on stock transfers, have been shown to have the same effect: those who can best afford to pay the taxes migrate to the suburbs or to other cities that do not have such taxes. The result is a net loss of jobs and tax-paying residents by the city. Of the population that remains, many cannot afford to buy homes and pay real estate taxes, and they may need more and better services, such as police protection, sanitation, education, health, welfare, and public housing. It is tragic that the attempt to increase urban government revenues may reduce them at a time when the demand and costs for services are rising (Kasarda, 1976:115; Campbell and Dollenmayer, 1975:364-73).

Fiscal mismanagement is not exclusively to blame for the urban financial crisis. Federal taxation, housing, and transportation policies have made it possible for the suburbs to expand and draw population from the city while still utilizing city facilities and institutions. Better transportation and communications have made it possible to integrate the entire metropolis. As a result, individual and institutional ties to particular locations are reduced. But there has not been an accompanying integration of political authority across political boundaries within the metropolis (Haar, 1972:5; Friesma, 1969; Campbell and Dollenmayer, 1975). Minimal integration and coordination is often undertaken only because federal regulations require metropolitan planning and coordination before a program can be funded.[8]

Until recently, central cities were politically dominant in metropolitan areas, but this dominance has been reduced by the one man-one vote decisions of the Supreme Court.[9] Political representation has been increasingly distributed to reflect population distribution so that suburbs have a greater voice in metropolitan decision making. As a result, metropolitan areas have had to try to coordinate and integrate efforts to deal with urban problems such as pollution, mass transportation, housing, and poverty. The consequence is that both city and suburban governments have lost control over at least some of the resources needed to solve purely local problems.

The problem of urban organization has been called a problem of government and political systems (Schmandt and Goldbach, 1969). Many people argue that local political systems are no longer capable of dealing with the social and physical problems that constitute the urban crisis because they have been drained of the capacity to make decisions. Decision making, and thus power, has migrated to state and federal bureaucracies. Despite their loss of power, however, urban communities and urban governments are the major arenas from which solutions to some of the more pressing social problems must emerge. Many of these problems, such as poverty, unemployment, racial discrimination, and pollution, are national rather than urban. Traffic congestion, housing, residential segregation, crime, and public services are the types of problems that are more likely to be solved on a local level (Schmandt and Goldbach, 1969).

One response of cities to their lack of control over the forces that affect their destiny has been to recognize that the solutions to even local issues often require integration of several levels of government. National organizations of mayors, the establishment of Washington, D.C., lobbying offices by cities, and similar actions by local officials illustrate their recognition of this need. Of course, the enforcement of state, federal, and regional regulations to achieve integration of several levels of government is also a form of loss of local control to higher levels of government. And even when a city can act independently of other governments, the information on which it bases its decisions may be provided by "outside" experts and bureaucrats who rarely have local orientations or loyalties. Implementation of the decisions may also be left to these people.

The local community, then, is faced with a problem: the experts who know how to make the agencies and offices work and who have the expertise to solve problems do not have local orientations or loyalties. Decision making is invested in local political officials who depend on these "outside" experts and bureaucrats to provide information.

The democratic ambivalence in which power is both feared and required now has a metropolitan corollary where power is increasingly dispersed and brought in by two kinds of outsiders: the non-local officials and the non-civic antagonist. As cities became larger or leaner, the politics of bossism and bargaining gave way to bigger issues of alienation and "group mobilization" [Schmandt and Goldbach, 1969:489].

Until recently, Congress and most state legislatures were controlled by rural and farming districts. Philip Hauser points out that in 1960 the majority of the population in thirty-nine states lived in urban areas, but no state legislature had a majority of urban representatives. The Supreme Court's one man-one vote decision led to hopes for a more equitable distribution of power, but the balance of population is beginning to swing to the suburbs so that the impact of the decision will be to weight state legislatures not in favor of the cities but in favor of suburban and less urban areas (Hauser, 1971:15-21).

One factor that has inhibited the development of metropolitan government is the traditional American distrust of larger and more distant government. This distrust, combined with the political fragmentation of the suburbs and their growing political power, leads to an image of metropolitan government as large, distant, impersonal, and likely to be controlled by "somebody else," such as the central city (Schmandt and Goldbach, 1969). More often than not, voters reject metropolitan political integration.

The metropolitan area, however, is functionally integrated by economics, technology, and patterns of social life. Its problems are complex. They are made even more complex by the inability of the political system to deal with them in an integrated and coordinated fashion. Each political-legal unit of the metropolis has to deal with similar problems. No single political unit in the metropolitan area can perform all of the communal functions, and the heterogeneity of political units makes the integration of performance even more difficult. One response to heterogeneity

and political fragmentation has been the development of regional authorities and other forms of coordination, both formal and informal.

Homogeneity, Heterogeneity, and Partial Communities in Urban Society

Cities are composed of neighborhoods, and metropolitan areas are composed of cities and suburbs, each of which exhibits a relatively high degree of homogeneity. The metropolitan area as a whole, however, is quite heterogeneous. Any sense of attachment that residents of a city have is likely to be focused on the relatively homogeneous area they have chosen to live in rather than on the city as a whole. The heterogeneity and size of the city make it very difficult to develop a sense of attachment to it.

Citizens of the United States have traditionally believed that their political interests are best served by representatives with a limited constituency, such as a homogeneous neighborhood or community. Thus, the representatives of a heterogeneous metropolitan area's political jurisdictions (wards, townships, suburbs, and so forth) can have difficulty in agreeing on a uniform approach to a city's problems. Problems tend to be seen in a local context, not as reflection of underlying forces or problems that cannot be dealt with by a single neighborhood, community, ward, or other political subdivision. Political representatives attempt to protect and preserve the physical and social environment of the locality they represent. The cost of their doing so is a lack of city or metropolitan consensus that could facilitate the solution of some problems (Schmandt and Goldbach, 1969).

The focus on local norms and interests and the attempts to protect local norms produces conflict and ambivalence. Conflict is particularly obvious when local norms and interests differ greatly from those of the larger units, as they have in the cases of residential segregation, neighborhood schools, and expressway routing. Such conflict makes the development of a city or metropolitan community difficult. But external constraints, such as federal requirements for metropolitan planning and programs that cover entire SMSAs, have forced many local jurisdictions, against their will, to participate in regional agencies that include not only the central city but also the entire metropolitan area.[10] Central city officials no longer exercise complete control over the planning for their own city. And suburban residents and their representatives are no longer able to resist participating in programs with the central city. The establishment of integrated metropolitan programs requires agreement on policies and plans, and ultimately on norms that the communities of the city and suburbs rarely share.

Place-specific and Nonplace Functions

The push toward agreement on metropolitan norms has led to competition between functions that are place-specific and those that are independent of place. A **place-specific function,** such as providing housing, is one in which location is the central concern. A **nonplace function** is one that can occur anywhere and can be carried out in any location. Work is no longer a place-specific function, since virtually any occupation can be practiced in any portion of a metropolis. The neighborhood school is a place-specific institution, since it has a fixed location. Competition between place-specific and nonplace functions for control of metropolitan norms arises when place-specific and nonplace activities conflict. An example of such competition is found in the resistance of local residents to the construction of a nonplace institution, such as a **magnet school,** an **educational park,** or a hospital in their neighborhood. These essentially nonplace facilities attract residents of the entire city into an area, thereby threatening the identity and character of the area.

Residential areas tend to be homogeneous in life style and to generate place-specific institutions, such as schools and political organizations that reflect the norms of the area (Schmandt and Goldbach, 1969:chap. 5). Local control over these institutions is supposed to ensure that they carry out their functions in accordance with the local norms. However, most activities of people who live in residential areas are not place-specific. Much of their life is centered around their residence, but their work, social contacts, and professional contacts are increasingly being chosen without regard to location.[11] For some urban residents and neighborhoods, place-specific activities and functions are an increasingly small proportion of all activities and functions, but concern and fear about crime and deviant behavior is place-specific and appears to be increasingly important (Schmandt and Goldbach, 1969; *Chicago Tribune,* 6 May 1976, sec. 7:3).

In many ways urban and metropolitan problems are the result of the change from a society dominated by place-specific activities to a society dominated by nonplace activities.

Loss of Local Control to Metropolitan and Regional Agencies

St. Paul—Nobody elected John Boland to his job, and few in the Twin Cities area really know who he is or quite what he does. But probably no one has as much say about the way two million residents of the Middle West metropolitan area will live, work and play for the next generation.

Already the 39-year-old Mr. Boland and an unusual agency he leads have halted plans for a subway and jetport for the Minneapolis-St. Paul area. And soon, under a pioneering law passed by the Minnesota Legislature, they will draw up a plan telling local officials and developers what can and cannot be done with every square foot of the 3,000 square miles in the seven counties that make up the Twin Cities' metropolitan area.

The agency, the Metropolitan Council, is a powerful, unelected and somewhat resented shadow government, superimposed by the state over hundreds of municipalities. It is charged with containing helter-skelter suburban sprawl and with protecting the older suburbs and central cities from decay.

The council is at the forefront of a movement to bring metropolitan, or regional influence to bear on such concerns as pollution, water supply, waste disposal, transportation and health care—problems that usually do not respect city boundaries.

In recent interviews, officials in two North American metropolitan areas that do have regional authorities, Minneapolis and Toronto, emphasized that the change had come about only because the state government imposed it on reluctant local officials, jealous of their prerogatives and powers.

When the council was formed 10 years ago, developers were pushing back the cornfields, even though there were few sewer or water lines, and septic tanks were polluting wells and lakes. The council created a sewer system based on logical regional needs. Since then it has gradually acquired planning authority over such services as transit, pollution control, airports, parks, highways, housing and health care.

Regional planning agencies are beginning to exert control over the actions of city and suburban governments. This article is a recent report of a case in which a city and its suburbs lost some control over their planning to a metropolitan planning agency.

The cornerstone of the program is the "development framework," an "urban service line" drawn around 800 square miles where sewer lines and other facilities already exist and where development is encouraged. Outside the circle in the "rural service area," the preservation of agriculture is encouraged and "leapfrog" development is deterred by not providing sewers and other services.

To put sharper teeth in the plan, the Legislature recently passed the "Metropolitan Land Planning Act," probably the most sweeping legislation of its kind in the country. Under it, the council will provide local towns with detailed plans for sewers, highways, parks and mass transit until 1990, along with population projections. By 1980 each locality must respond with a comprehensive land-use plan consonant with the regional plan. . .

Some feel that the planners have been high-handed and that those on the fringes of the area face years of stunted growth. The residents of Scott County to the south, for example, feel they need a new bridge over the Minnesota River to get into Minneapolis, but they will not get it.

"We feel we are being hurt; we would like to have a little more control over our lives," said Robert Schmitz, a State Senator who represents mostly rural Scott and Carver Counties.

Others, though, have welcomed Metro. Josephine Nunn, a transplanted New Yorker who is Mayor of suburban Camplin, said the system had made her young town more aware of the need for planning. "We became very sophisticated very fast," she said. "After all, we don't want instant asphalt." But she too expressed a fear that Metro would become too powerful, a "big brother.". . .

Source Robert Reinhold, *New York Times,* March 8, 1977, p. 1. © 1977 by The New York Times Company. Reprinted by permission.

Residential patterns in cities are only part of the problem; another part is that many problems are society-wide, generated by forces that are not specific to a given place. The concept of community, especially as it is traditionally understood, depends on locality. When increasing proportions of urban populations are able to draw on the entire city or metropolis to satisfy their needs and when communal functions become less place-specific, the urban neighborhood tends to become a partial community. For example, when people have friends living throughout a city or metropolis rather than in the same neighborhood and when they shop, work, worship, and join clubs, unions, or other interest groups without regard to location, the neighborhood becomes less important as a source of community ties, attachments, and feelings.

The relative homogeneity produced by the ecological processes of invasion, competition, succession, and dominance ensures that some communal characteristics persist in at least some areas. As the ties of place are weakened, however, the neighborhood is increasingly replaced by the city or the metropolis as the setting where locality-relevant functions are performed.

The Paradox of Heterogeneity

Heterogeneity is one of the major reasons that the city is such an exciting place to live. There is at least one area in most large cities where almost any kind of function is performed and where any kind of activity can be found. A residential area characterized by a particular life style or by a particular ethnic, racial, or socioeconomic group can always be found.

And there are always areas dominated by industrial and commercial facilities, night clubs, and theaters. This produces a paradox: there is a great deal of heterogeneity in the city as a whole, but many areas in the city may be homogeneous. Some areas of the city are very successful in providing the goods and services and in carrying out the functions that are necessary to make urban life successful. Other areas are drastic failures.

The view that the city is a haven of heterogeneity and that most people who live in cities desire heterogeneity ignores this paradox. Many of the people who live in the homogeneous areas of the city may really want nothing more than to live in a noncosmopolitan, homogeneous neighborhood. The social diversity of the city may be attractive to people who view the city from a nonplace perspective. Other people who live in the city may really want and have relatively little diversity because they are tied to place-specific activities and life styles. Simply because the city as a whole is highly diverse does not mean we can assume that the typical urban resident wants diversity (Wilson, 1968).

Even city residents who desire diversity may not want all the kinds of diversity made possible by the heterogeneity of the city. They may want only a safe kind of diversity—a wide range of entertainment facilities, specialty shops, cultural facilities, ethnic shopping, and restaurants. Tolerance for diversity may be limited to the young and to persons of relatively high income and education who are least tied to place. But these persons are unlikely to desire the diversity that includes crime, vice, poverty, and segregation (Wilson, 1968).

Although a city as a whole may have a great deal of heterogeneity, many areas may be homogeneous.

The city is heterogeneous enough that behavior considered deviant or criminal by the residents of one area may not be frowned on by the residents of another. Different norms and values are dominant in different areas of the city. Public drinking, gambling, not keeping the lawn mowed, or even sitting on apartment stoops may be considered unacceptable behavior in some areas of the city and perfectly acceptable in other areas. Differences in local norms make it difficult to legislate for the entire city.

Urban residents who are predominantly single share many characteristics with those who are married and do not have dependent children. Neither group is concerned, for example, with schools. Both groups may be attracted to the same residential areas. In areas that contain a large proportion of families with young children, there will often be a relatively high degree of homogeneity in class background and ethnic origin. Even more frequently there will be shared concern for the educational system and for the conditions that are considered good for raising a young child. In areas where the residents are mainly people whose children are past school age, the dominant interests will be different. These different levels of concern for locality-based activities and functions arise out of the fact that similar physical and social environments are needed by persons who are in the same stage of the life cycle or who live similar life styles. Areas of the city that have appropriate facilities thus attract persons who have similar characteristics (Wilson, 1968).

Urban Neighborhoods

Analysis of the degree of homogeneity within neighborhoods and the degree of heterogeneity within the city reveals that the neighborhood is a partial community. The neighborhood appears to be the focus of community for most urban residents, especially those whose interactions are primarily place-specific. However, no urban neighborhood or suburb can be a full community, as the term was defined in chapter 2. Indeed, the forces discussed earlier in this chapter ensure that no city or metropolitan area can be a full community. The loss of local control and the helpless feeling of being buffeted by forces beyond the control of the institutions of the neighborhood, city, metropolis, and even the nation are probably more extreme for the neighborhood than for the city. Our unmet expectations for a sense of community seem to be at the root of many urban problems.

Even though neighborhoods generally lack the ability to fulfill most of the critical functions of a community, there are some exceptions. Many black neighborhoods, for example, provide the basis for a sense of identity. Similarly, and perhaps even more commonly, many old ethnic neighborhoods are able to provide a sense of identity, of social solidarity, and a high degree of normative integration. And some neighborhoods are dominated by an institution such as a university or church, which provides a focus of activity and may be able to provide a sense of community that would not be possible otherwise.

But in general, almost no neighborhood is able to provide anything like the spectrum of locality-relevant functions of a full community. And no neighborhood is able to provide

Sometimes an institution dominates the activity of a neighborhood, creating a sense of community. The University of Chicago occupies a substantial part of the Hyde Park section of Chicago and is the primary focus of activity in the community.

for the integration of its functions with the performance of the same functions in the wider society—partially because neighborhoods do not have governments that can provide the integration.

The neighborhood, as a surrogate for community within the urban or metropolitan area, is in many ways merely a residential aggregate and a focus for place-specific activity. However, since the neighborhood performs a few of the communal functions, it is a partial community. For most people, the neighborhood is the only community (Kasarda and Janowitz, 1974; Suttles, 1972). When the local neighborhood ceases to perform its communal functions, urban society fails. No one really expects the neighborhood to be a total society or to provide all communal functions, but we do expect it to provide and carry out place-specific functions. Its ability to perform its functions is what dominates the concerns of the residents (Kasarda and Janowitz, 1974; Suttles, 1972). The city as a whole is a social aggregate too large to deal with. What happens nearby and in the areas we are familiar with convinces us that the city is or is not working.

Because of this focus on the local area and on what occurs in it, residents who are home- or place-centered are concerned with maintaining the life style that attracted them to, and presumably dominates, the neighborhood. They are particularly interested in government actions that affect the ability of neighborhoods to perform place-specific functions. Characteristically, they are the residents who are the least mobile and who have the greatest financial and emotional investment in their neighborhoods. This investment is the source of their interest in governmental policies that affect "neighborhood control" and "neighborhood stability." Most critical in this respect are government activities that attempt to control deviance, provide place-specific services, and enhance or reduce the neighborhood's ability to exclude persons who have different life styles or who may be expected to have behavior patterns different from those of the residents. To the extent that a neighborhood can maintain its homogeneity and appearance, it expects to be able to maintain its social solidarity, normative standards, and thus its identity (Wilson, 1968).

Summary

From a variety of perspectives, we have seen that the concept of community, regardless of how expressed, seems to be critical to understanding the problems of life in urban and metropolitan society. Experts have told us for at least a decade that the urban crisis is a matter of overcrowded streets, lack of places to park, or the failure of mass transportation systems. They have also told us that the major problem of the city is the declining sales of retail establishments as suburbs attract a higher proportion of business, that cities' problems revolve around poor housing, poor education, or crime (Wilson, 1968) or around money for services, politics, or the inability of the poor to plan for the future (Banfield, 1974). However, viewing it as we have, we can see that these are merely manifestations of the loss of the sense of community and the ability of the community, the city, and the neighborhood to function as communities and to make life tolerable in an urban environment.

A common problem facing all societies at whatever stage of their development has been to devise and maintain a satisfactory sense of order in the fundamental sense of organizing and integrating human activities among the individuals and groups that share a common locality [Schmandt and Goldbach, 1969:474].

Classical urban theory recognized this problem by focusing on the city as a governmental agency responsible for establishing order and acting as an agent of social control to maintain order. Contemporary urban theory rejects this notion and views the city as a bureaucracy designed to provide services. The problems of the city are described in terms of administrative inefficiency (Schmandt and Goldbach, 1969:474). Viewed in this way, the central problem is to ensure that neighborhoods continue to function but that the city and the neighborhoods do not come into conflict with one another in providing the basic services.

Our perspective on urban problems is somewhat different. We see the essential problems of cities as their inability to provide communal functions on either a neighborhood or a city-wide basis. The difficulty with this perspective is that governmental solutions are not easily devised—if they are possible at all. Defining urban problems as rooted in a need for community, for a sense of normative integration, for the maintenance of neighborhoods, for the regulation of public behavior, and for the maintenance of social solidarity makes governmental policy and intervention virtually useless as a solution. Public opinion polls report a preference for living in small towns because most people seem to believe that it is easier to be self-governing and employ informal social sanc-

tions and controls to maintain normative integration and social solidarity in small towns than in large cities (Wilson, 1968).

This perspective has guided the selection of urban problems to be discussed in the remainder of this book. The remaining chapters are devoted to a discussion of problems of metropolitan areas, cities, and neighborhoods in performing their communal functions. The problems are analyzed or described in terms of their connection to the performance of the communal functions defined in chapter 2.

The most important, although perhaps the most problematic, functions of communities are maintaining a sense of identity and a degree of normative integration and social solidarity. One factor that has been notably effective in creating and maintaining normative integration and social solidarity in neighborhoods has been ethnic and racial homogeneity. However, this homogeneity has led to segregation, discrimination, and related problems for cities and metropolitan areas. The first urban problems to be described will be those that revolve around racial and ethnic problems in urban areas.

The major task of urban government and political systems is integrating the communal functions performed by neighborhoods, providing for the performance of functions that neighborhoods cannot perform, and integrating the performance of communal functions within the city with the performance of the same and related functions throughout the society. Furthermore, there is an important relationship between the functioning of urban government and the ability of cities to cope with other problems. The functioning of the political system—to the extent that it is responsible for making norms into laws, enforcing them, and providing a form of social integration—can also be a major urban problem. Conflict is built into the political system; therefore, attention is regularly drawn to it. Differences of opinion about the decisions made in the political system also provide a source of conflict.

Because the political system is so important to the performance of urban functions, we will consider urban politics after the analysis of racial and ethnic communities. Then we will turn to a consideration of urban functions performed partially by the urban government and partially by private institutions. These shared functions include providing for the housing, transportation, and health of the urban population. When these communal functions are not performed by the **private sector,** they must be performed by the **public sector.** The existence of the city is dependent on an adequate supply of housing, an adequate transportation system, and a healthy population. We will examine these communal functions and discuss how cities carry them out.

In a subsequent chapter, we will consider the impact that cities have on their physical environment. The density of settlement and the concentration of people and industry produces environmental pollution. Cities have little effective power to deal with these problems, which are of vital concern to their residents. We will examine the magnitude of urban pollution problems today and attempt to understand what cities are doing about them. We should note that pollution problems are related to other urban functions. Without industry, there would be much less pollution,

but there would also be no cities. Some environmental problems, such as water pollution, are related to both the size of the city and how the city performs its communal function of providing water.

Other problems are almost exclusively the responsibility of cities. Two of the most pressing urban problems today are controlling crime and providing an adequate education for the young. One of the city's communal functions is controlling behavior that violates norms. At the same time, however, the city's heterogeneity ensures that there is never total agreement on norms. In addition, there are factors in urban life that generate forms of behavior among some members of the population that other members want to see controlled. These problems will be considered in a chapter devoted to the definition, meaning, and level of crime in cities and in society.

Lack of agreement on norms is also involved in the educational problems of cities. The city has a communal responsibility to socialize the young. But because of the heterogeneity of urban populations there is little agreement on the content or methods of education that the schools should adopt. In consequence, many urban residents believe that public schools are not performing adequately. Many do not send their children to these schools. And they believe that inefficient schooling wastes resources. The urban educational system is a major urban problem.

Urban problems occur in the context of a highly interdependent and organically integrated society. Cities can no longer control the forces that cause their problems and influence their ability to cope with problems. Neither can they define adequate solutions.

Fiscal strategies employed in New York influence the ability of all cities to raise money for housing, transportation, education, and other functions. Industry in Indiana contributes to Chicago's air pollution problem. Supreme Court decisions affect hiring practices, law enforcement, the organization and content of urban and suburban schools, housing policies, and other communal responsibilities. Urban problems may be a consequence of the nature of urban social systems, but they more likely arise from an organically integrated society whose trends affect the cities' ability to perform their communal functions.

non-place functions urban functions that can be carried out in any location, such as the choice of friends, work locations, and occupation

place-specific functions urban functions that are centered on a specific place in an urban area; *place-specific* also refers to concern over behavior in an area where place is critical, for example, concern over the behavior of adolescents in a residential neighborhood

private sector private institutions such as business, industry, and privately financed and voluntary service groups

public sector government agencies and institutions

vertical ties the ties of individuals and institutions in a community to individuals and institutions outside that community

Glossary

demographic structure the composition of the population in terms of size, age, race, and other relatively fixed characteristics; demography includes the study of the distribution of these characteristics

educational park a large tract of land devoted to several schools of different types; elementary and secondary schools and often community colleges are located in the same place and share many facilities, such as gyms and libraries

horizontal ties the ties of individuals and institutions in a community to other individuals and institutions in the same community

labor market the demand for workers by the employing institutions of a community

magnet school a school organized to provide instruction in a particular subject matter or group of subjects; entrance is usually based on competition or on criteria such as a set of racial quotas, and the school draws its student body from an entire school district rather than from one area of the district

References

Banfield, Edward C.
1974 *The Unheavenly City Revisited.* Boston: Little, Brown & Company.

Boulding, Kenneth E.
1968 "The City as an Element in the International System." *Daedalus* 97, 4 (Fall):1111-24.

Campbell, Alan K., and Dollenmayer, Judith A.
1975 "Governance in a Metropolitan Society." In *Metropolitan America in Contemporary Perspective,* edited by Amos H. Hawley and Vincent P. Rock, pp. 355-96. New York: John Wiley & Sons, Inc.

Dyckman, John W.
1963 "Socioeconomic and Technological Forces in Urban Expansion." In *Urban Expansion, Problems and Needs: Papers Presented at the Administrators' Spring Conference.* Washington, D.C.: Government Printing Office. Reprinted in *Neighborhood, City, and Metropolis,* edited by Robert Gutman and David Popenoe, pp. 439-59. New York: Random House, Inc., 1970.

Friesma, H. Paul
1969 "The Metropolis and the Maze of Local Government." In *Urban Politics and Problems,* edited by H. R. Mahood and Edward L. Angus, pp. 409-25. New York: Charles Schribner's Sons.

Haar, Charles M.
1972   "Introduction: Metropolitanization and Public Services." In *Metropolitanization and Public Services,* edited by Lowdon Wingo, pp. 1-17. Baltimore: Resources for the Future.

Hadden, Jeffrey K., and Barton, Josef J.
1973   "An Image That Will Not Die: Thoughts on the History of Anti-Urban Ideology." In *The Urbanization of the Suburbs,* edited by Louis H. Masotti and Jeffrey K. Hadden, pp. 79-119. Beverly Hills, Calif.: Sage Publications, Inc.

Hauser, Philip M.
1971   "Whither Urban Society?" In *Cities in the '70s,* pp. 15-21. Washington, D.C.: National League of Cities.

Hawley, Amos H.
1971   *Urban Society.* New York: Ronald Press.

Hawley, Amos H., and Rock, Vincent P., eds.
1975   *Metropolitan America in Contemporary Perspective.* New York: John Wiley & Sons, Inc.

Kain, John F.
1970   "The Distribution and Movement of Jobs and Industry." In *The Metropolitan Enigma,* edited by James Q. Wilson, pp. 1-44. Garden City, N.Y.: Doubleday & Co., Inc.

Kasarda, John D.
1976   "The Changing Occupational Structure of the American Metropolis: Apropos the Urban Problem." In *The Changing Face of the Suburbs,* edited by Barry Schwartz, pp. 113-36. Chicago: University of Chicago Press.

Kasarda, John D., and Janowitz, Morris
1974   "Community Attachment in Mass Society." *American Sociological Review* 39(June):328-39.

Lynd, Robert S., and Lynd, Helen M.
1929   *Middletown.* New York: Harcourt, Brace & World, Inc.
1937   *Middletown in Transition.* New York: Harcourt, Brace & World, Inc.

Mahood, H. R., and Angus, Edward L., eds.
1969   *Urban Politics and Problems.* New York: Charles Schribner's Sons.

Meadows, Paul, and Mizruchi, Ephraim H., eds.
1969   *Urbanism, Urbanization, and Change.* Reading, Mass.: Addison-Wesley Publishing Co., Inc.

Mizruchi, Ephraim H.
1969   "Romanticism, Urbanism, and Small Town in Mass Society: An Exploratory Analysis." In *Urbanism, Urbanization, and Change: Comparative Perspectives,* edited by Paul Meadows and Ephraim H. Mizruchi, pp. 243-52. Reading, Mass.: Addison-Wesley Publishing Co., Inc.

Schmandt, Henry J., and Bloomberg, Werner, eds.
1969   *The Quality of Urban Life.* Beverly Hills, Calif.: Sage Publications, Inc.

Schmandt, Henry J., and Goldbach, John C.
1969   "The Urban Paradox." In *The Quality of Urban Life,* edited by Henry J. Schmandt and Werner Bloomberg, pp. 473-98. Beverly Hills, Calif.: Sage Publications, Inc.

Schwartz, Barry, ed.
1976   *The Changing Face of the Suburbs.* Chicago: University of Chicago Press.

Suttles, Gerald
1972   *The Social Construction of Communities.* Chicago: University of Chicago Press.

Tilly, Charles
1970   "Race and Migration to American Cities." In *The Metropolitan Enigma,* edited by James Q. Wilson, pp. 144-69. Garden City, N.Y.: Doubleday & Co., Inc.

U.S. Bureau of the Census
1970   "Trends in Social and Economic Conditions in Metropolitan and Non-Metropolitan Areas." *Current Population Reports, Series P-23, 33.* Washington, D.C.: Government Printing Office.
1973   *Graphic Summary of the 1970 Housing Census.* Washington, D.C.: Government Printing Office.
1975   *Statistical Abstract of the United States: 1974.* Washington, D.C.: Government Printing Office.

Vidich, Arthur, and Bensman, Joseph
1958   *Small Town in Mass Society.* Garden City, N.Y.: Doubleday & Co., Inc.

Warren, Roland
1972   *The Community in America,* 2d ed. Chicago: Rand McNally & Company.

White, Morton, and White, Lucia
1961   "The American Intellectual Versus the American City." *Daedalus* 90, 1 (Winter):166-79.

Wilson, James Q.
1968   "The Urban Unease: Community vs. the City." *The Public Interest* 12 (Summer):25-39.

Wilson, James Q., ed.
1970   *The Metropolitan Enigma.* Garden City, N.Y.: Doubleday & Co., Inc.

Suggested Readings

Advisory Commission on Intergovernmental Relations. *Improving Urban America: A Challenge to Federalism.* Washington, D.C.: Government Printing Office, 1976. A synthesis of research that emphasizes the roles of state, regional, and federal governments in dealing with the problems of the city.

Stein, Maurice R. *The Eclipse of Community.* Princeton: Princeton University Press, 1971. Describes several classic community studies, mainly in urban settings, and analyzes the loss of community.

Teska, Anona. "The Federal Impact on the Cities." In *Perspectives on Urban America.* Garden City, N.Y.: Doubleday, 1973. A valuable discussion of the intended and unintended consequences for cities of several major federal programs.

Vidich, Arthur, and Bensman, Joseph. *Small Town in Mass Society.* Garden City, N.Y.: Doubleday, 1958. A classic description of how a small town lost control over its own policies as it came into conflict with the wider society.

Notes

1. As the rural population declines, migrants tend to come from other cities. For a recent portrait of migrants to metropolitan areas, see Tilly, 1970:144-69.
2. Dyckman, 1970:439-59. The proportion of women who are considered to be part of the labor force has been increasing for several decades. Between the prime working ages (15-44), more than half of the women in the population participate in the labor force (U.S. Bureau of the Census, 1970:49).
3. In part, this is because manufacturing plants have been leaving the city, thereby reducing the number of unskilled or semiskilled jobs available in the city. Many of the workers continue to live in cities—they are unable to afford suburban housing—and this contributes to urban transportation problems. See U.S. Bureau of the Census, 1970; 1975:350; Kain, 1970; Kasarda, 1976.
4. Recent federal court decisions in Chicago have required that predominantly black public housing be built in white areas of the city or in the suburbs. These decisions and federal governmental regulations eventually ought to result in a deconcentration of the black population, but they are beyond the control of urban political or social systems. They offer another example of cities losing control over the forces that affect their destiny.
5. See, for example, U.S. Bureau of the Census, 1973:27, which shows three times as many single-family structures outside metropolitan central cities as within them.
6. The John Hancock Building in Chicago, for a few years the tallest building in the world, remains the tallest building devoted to retail, commercial, and residential uses. Several people reportedly live and work there and do most of their shopping without leaving the building.
7. For example, the Chicago SMSA has several hundred political jurisdictions. The problems of fragmentation (as well as competition) have at times been so severe that some areas have gotten no services from any jurisdiction. See also Dyckman, 1970; Friesma, 1969:409-25; Hawley, 1971:216; Campbell and Dollenmayer, 1975:363-64.
8. Much of this coordination and integration occurs in regional planning commissions or authorities. The New York Port Authority, Bay Area Rapid Transit Authority in San Francisco, and the Regional Transportation Authority in Chicago illustrate the role that such metropolitan planning agencies play.
9. For example, until the one man-one vote decision, two thirds of the members of the county board in Cook County, Illinois (which includes Chicago), were from Chicago even though the city had only a bit over half of the population. Now representation reflects the population distribution.
10. In the Chicago SMSA, the suburban areas voted against participation in a Regional Transportation Authority for fear they would be taxed to support Chicago urban transit. Nevertheless, the vote in Chicago was large enough so that the metropolitan transit organization was approved. As a result, the Chicago Transit Authority must include suburban needs in its planning.
11. The decreasing importance of place is probably class-linked. Members of the middle class and persons of higher status have the resources to free themselves from place in all aspects of life. The same cannot be said of members of lower classes. Thus, on an individual level, place may not be important to those who are able to function throughout the area of a city or metropolis. Those who cannot afford to travel are likely to find place-specific functions far more important. In a real sense, those who are detached from place can treat a city or metropolis as a community, while those who are not so detached are more likely to be limited to the community of the neighborhood.

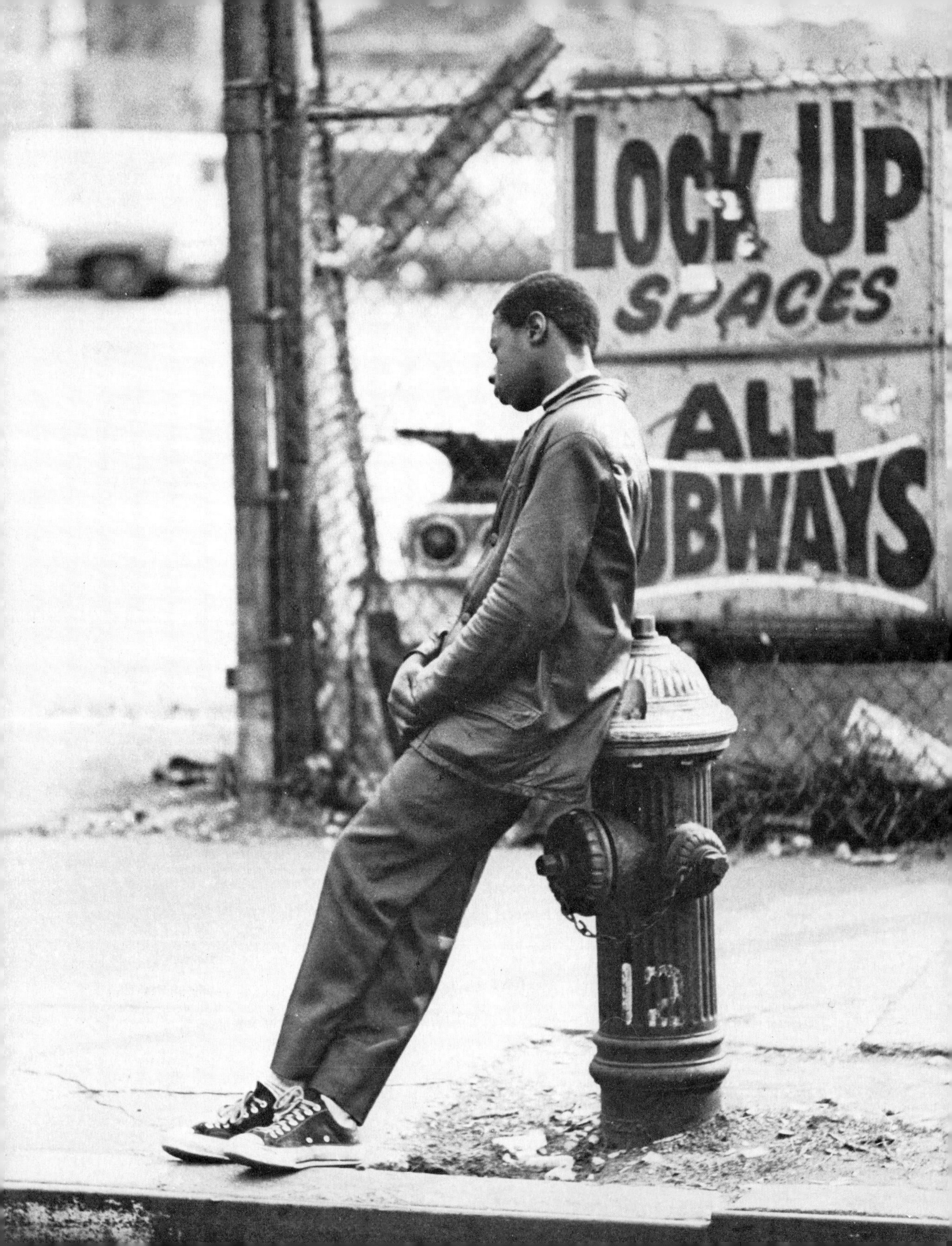
LOCK UP
SPACES
ALL

9

The Persistence of Racial and Ethnic Communities

The American city in the course of its history has continuously attracted new populations; foreign immigrants and rural Americans have moved into cities in vast numbers.[1] These migrants have contributed greatly to urban growth and the development and maintenance of many ethnically homogeneous neighborhoods in the city. Our review of ecological processes showed that people with similar characteristics tend to live close together. This phenomenon is perhaps most clearly seen in the residential patterns of urban in-migrants.

The positive effects of ethnically homogeneous urban neighborhoods are maximumization of social solidarity, interaction, and group identification and the maintenance of traditional cultures; negatively, the segregation of urban neighborhoods on the basis of race and/or ethnic origins encourages the development of **ghettos.** The **assimilation** of immigrants into American society has been more difficult than it would have been if the immigrants had been scattered throughout the city. The children have attended segregated and thus inferior schools, perpetuating the problems caused by ghetto residence. The immigrants have been forced to live in poor housing. However, many immigrant groups have broken out of this living pattern as a result of upward social **mobility,** and some urban ethnic ghettos are becoming social class ghettos instead.

In the past, **ethnic groups** have coexisted in the city, but ethnic coexistence has been at best problematic,[2] and it appears to be increasingly difficult to maintain as both the racial and social class characteristics of cities change. Currently it is questionable whether this coexistence can continue, as race, rather than national origin, becomes the basis of urban **ethnic identity.**

The ethnic and racial problems facing the contemporary city have been caused to a large extent by the rapid and massive movement of blacks and Latinos into the city (see chapter 7 for documentation of the size and speed of the black population movement). An optimistic assessment of contemporary urban ethnic and race relations is that the size and speed of this movement have strained the city's ability to assimilate these groups and perform its communal functions. This strain has caused special problems for earlier immigrants and their communities. Those who have not yet assimilated all the norms of the wider society or been assimilated into the city are now faced with increased competition. The ecological and social processes of cities have brought the **new ethnics** into competition with the **old ethnics** before assimilation of the old ethnics is complete and while new members are still beginning the process. The ethnics are competing for residential space, neighborhood dominance, jobs, and political representation and power. Residential contact and struggles over neighborhood dominance are most often the points of conflict between older and newer immigrants.

The major functions of the neighborhood include maintaining a sense of normative integration, social solidarity, and control over the public behavior of the residents. When people who "look different" move into an area, residents assume they will behave differently. Many people also assume that members of racial or ethnic minorities will not share the norms of the older residents of the neighborhood; consequently, they will behave differently. We must understand what is meant by (1) racial and ethnic groups and (2) the process of assimilation if we are to understand racial and ethnic relations in contemporary urban society.

Definitions of Ethnic and Racial Groups

Definitions of racial and ethnic groups are difficult to arrive at, particularly in terms that can be measured. As a result of intermarriage in this country, physical distinctions between ethnic groups have become blurred, and a unique ethnic or racial identity has become rare. Biological or genetic definitions of ethnicity or race are not very useful (Mack, 1968:55-61) because almost every characteristic, such as skin color, hair quality, nose shape, body size, and IQ varies more within biologically racial groupings than between groups.

Definitions of groups based on religion or national origin are also inadequate. Both attributes can be changed, either by an individual's act of will or by the political process that changes national borders. Other cultural characteristics provide a firmer basis for lasting ethnic identity.

Cultural Sources of Ethnicity

A definition based on identification with (or consciousness of membership in) a historic or cultural group having semi-*Gemeinschaft* characteristics is most useful. Such a group is more personal and permanent than a voluntary association but less personal and more extensive than a primary group based on family ties. The remembrance of a common homeland, a common history (mythic or real), and common cultural traditions, whether actually experienced by a person or not, can serve as the basis for membership in such a group. This leads to the identification of **nationality groups** as ethnic groups (Weber, 1961:305-9; Handlin, 1961:220-32; Yinger, 1961:247, 257-62; Glazer, 1954:158-73).

Thus an ethnic group is that group of people with whom group members find it easiest to enter into primary relationships. These relationships are made possible by consciously or unconsciously shared historic and cultural similarities, which reflect a common origin and lead to an expectation of shared norms, values, and behaviors.

Consciousness of kind, or consciousness of membership in a group, can be viewed as a sense of peoplehood, which perhaps began with historic ties and then fragmented as a result of various processes and events—geographic mobility, development of the nuclear family, **intermarriage,** and cultural assimilation into new nations. As a result, many people may have several possible ethnic identities. An individual's ethnic identity is a combination of other people's definitions of a person and that person's own choice from among all possible identities.

Milton Gordon (1964:26-30) proposes a model for ethnic identity. A person living in a particular nation can be a member of any one of a number of races, any one of a number of religions, and any one of a large number of groups based on national origin. The individual's ethnic identity depends on that attribute or combination of attributes that are most important to that person and on the attributes the society emphasizes in ascribing ethnicity. Thus a portion of the individual's choice of attributes is a result of social feedback. Choice is greatest when characteristics are not visible, as is most often the case for persons whose national origins are European. A white person named Jones has much more freedom to choose an identity than a visibly black person (even if the "black" characteristics are not very marked), because social feedback will limit the choices for the black person in ways that Jones will not experience. Thus, ethnic identity may be partially a matter of individual choice and partially a result of social definition based on appearance and behavior.

Sources of Urban Ethnic Diversity: Immigration

The greatest wave of immigration to American cities occurred in the nineteenth and early twentieth centuries (Yin, 1972:4; U.S. Bureau of the Census, 1975:97, table 153). Some immigrants, notably the Germans and Scandinavians, took up homesteads in the Midwest, but most settled in cities. More than a million Irish settlers who arrived between 1847 and 1854 and other immigrants in the early twentieth century who arrived after homesteads were no longer readily available gravitated to the cities. When immigrants did settle in cities, the ecological processes described in chapter 5 led many of them to settle in areas where there were already concentrations of people from the same place of origin (Vander Zanden, 1966: 27-31; McKelvey, 1963:63; Kramer,

1970:80-102). They did so for a number of reasons. Immigrants who did not speak English settled in areas of the city where their language was spoken. Chances were that friends or relatives who had immigrated earlier would be living in these areas, would have begun to establish themselves, and could help newer arrivals with jobs, housing, and language. The early immigrants soon developed their own natural areas in which they could maintain their cultural traditions and heritage. Later immigrants whose ethnic origins were visible were **segregated** into ghettos and not permitted to buy or rent homes in other areas of the city. The existence of natural areas, each with its own traditions, would eventually prove to be a source of both problems and benefits.

More recently migrants from rural areas of the United States and immigrants from Latin countries have followed the same pattern. They have settled in portions of cities where people from the same places had previously settled. Here they have found social contacts and help in assimilating the urban way of life.[3]

In the years of massive immigration (1851-1930),[4] an ethnic identity could both help and hinder the individual. Identification as a member of a particular ethnic group could help when members were able to provide jobs for their own or when the group dominated a particular occupation (as the Irish did the police force in early New York). An ethnic identity could also be a hindrance, as was clear from the signs in Boston and New York that announced "No Irish need apply." When immigrants were unable to speak English, job opportunities outside the ethnic community were limited.

Most immigrants to America during the nineteenth and early twentieth centuries settled in cities.

Ethnic Communities: Original Functions

Ethnic communities were psychologically comfortable places for immigrants to live, despite often poor physical conditions, because they provided the sense of peoplehood and belonging that made for high levels of solidarity and normative integration (Lopata, 1964:203-23; Kramer, 1970:51-75). The residents not only shared language and cultural traditions, but also reacted in similar ways to similar situations. Because of their common culture, they could understand and predict each other's behaviors at times of life's crises (birth, death, sickness, marriage, social disasters), as well as in the course of daily living. Even today many people, including those with only minimal ethnic identity, prefer to deal with doctors, dentists, lawyers, and funeral directors who share their ethnic identity. People with whom a person develops primary relationships (marriage partners, close friends) are often chosen on an ethnic basis because the individual can predict their reactions and understand their meanings and feelings. Social and geographic mobility as well as intermarriage are making it harder to identify those people with whom such relationships are possible (Gordon, 1964:70-81).

The maintenance of **enclaves** of cultural traditions and heritages, of a unique sense of peoplehood, also has some negative results, especially the dislike of those who do not share in the same sense of peoplehood. This attitude leads to stereotyping. Prejudice and **ethnocentrism** reinforce discrimination and resistance to intergroup contact and can result in intergroup hostility and enforced, rather than natural, segregation (Mack, 1968:3-52, 143-80; Rose and Rose, 1965:349-428).

The Assimilation of Ethnic Groups

As foreign immigrants and American rural migrants moved to the cities of the United States, they encountered both each other and urban society. For the first time (with the exception of Jews and American Negroes, for whom this was not a first-time experience) they became members of a minority group in the society in which they lived. To some extent members of all immigrant groups had to interact with one another, for they were competing for low-cost housing and jobs. They had to find both before they learned the norms of society and how to get along with people of different national or cultural traditions (Glazer, 1954; Gordon, 1964).

The process of normative and social integration of immigrants into society is called *assimilation.* The process involves learning to live with people who have different social and cultural traditions and who do not share a common identity.[5] The end result is a new sense of peoplehood based on the society into which one has been assimilated. The failure of assimilation is responsible for much intergroup conflict and hostility that we see in U.S. cities today.

The main function of assimilation is to increase the degree of normative integration and social solidarity among racial and ethnic groups. To the extent that assimilation succeeds, homogeneity, solidarity, and normative integration will be reduced within each ethnic community and increased among different ethnic groups. With full assimilation, ethnic minorities would disappear, for no group would have an identity different from any other group.

Table 9.1   The Assimilation Variables

Subprocess or Condition	Type or Stage of Assimilation	Special Term
Change of cultural patterns to those of host society	Cultural or behavioral assimilation	Acculturation
Large-scale entrance into cliques, clubs, and institutions of host society, on primary group level	Structural assimilation	None
Large-scale intermarriage	Marital assimilation	Amalgamation
Development of sense of peoplehood based exclusively on host society	Identificational assimilation	None
Absence of prejudice	Attitude receptional assimilation	None
Absence of discrimination	Behavior receptional assimilation	None
Absence of value and power conflict	Civic assimilation	None

Source   From *Assimilation in American Life: The Role of Race, Religion and National Origins* by Milton M. Gordon. Copyright © 1964 by Oxford University Press, Inc. Reprinted by permission. P. 71.

This is a major dilemma for ethnic groups that wish to live with other groups. Assimilation will lead to the disappearance of their ethnicity; maintaining ethnic identity may prevent them from living together.

Assimilation has proceeded unevenly, and consequently cities are composed of groups that share common norms to different extents.[6] There are still ethnic groups whose internal integration and solidarity are greater than the group's integration into the society. Members of such groups participate in society only to a limited extent. Many immigrant ethnic groups, especially the racially distinguishable ones, have not assimilated the norms of the city and society partially because they have been excluded by prejudice and discrimination. A common response to such exclusion is to stress the cultural and social heritage of one's own group.

The Development of Ideologies of Identification

Partially because of a desire to maintain their heritage and partially because of economic and ecological forces, older immigrant groups have maintained residential enclaves within the city, which has encouraged the development of ethnic identification (Kramer, 1970; Fellows, 1972). The black power movement is the major example of the development of racial identification and pride. This movement among blacks led to increasing awareness of ethnic identity among many other groups that migrated to American cities at the beginning of the twentieth century. As the new ethnics developed ideologies of pride and identification, partially as political strategies, the old ethnics responded in kind (Severo, 1972:70-75; Novak, 1971; Feinstein, 1971).

The aggressive ideology that developed out of the civil rights movement succeeded in channeling an increased proportion of society's limited resources to the most vocal ethnic groups. Older ethnic groups were forced to respond aggressively in competition for their share of society's goods and services.

Assimilation and Mobility

Assimilation into the wider society has been facilitated by social mobility. The rapid growth of the suburbs after World War II was a major means of social mobility and assimilation for white but not black populations. As federal benefits, especially from the **Veterans Administration** (VA) and the **Federal Housing Administration** (FHA) loans, became available, many members of older white immigrant groups moved from urban ethnic enclaves to the suburbs. Those left in the urban ethnic enclaves were the least mobile and least affluent members of white ethnic groups and the blacks and other racial minorities (Latinos, Indians) who were unable to move to suburbia.[7] The economic heterogeneity of urban ethnic enclaves and their ability to deal with the increasingly complex problems of the modern city have thus been reduced. Members of these communities must compete with emerging racial-ethnic groups, and they are the ones who are least well equipped to do so.

In the suburbs, the maintenance of ethnic traditions and culture has proven to be difficult. The residents who have come from urban ethnic enclaves have assimilated much of the American identity. Their communities have little ethnic character and are better described as homogeneous, American, and middle-class. Nevertheless, many suburban communities have some ethnic characteristics (Parenti, 1967:717-26; Gans, 1951:330-39). There is a full range of ethnic institutions—churches, temples, and voluntary groups—in suburbia. Ethnic segregation does exist, and the automobile makes it possible for group members to interact and reinforce their ethnic identity (Lieberson, 1962:673-81; Ringer, 1972:174-84).

Assimilation and Ethnic Homogeneity

Those people who moved from the old urban enclaves to the suburbs tended to be not only the most socially mobile but also the most assimilated—those who best knew the norms and behavior patterns of the wider society. The city thus remains a heterogeneous mixture of ethnic groups and a scene of great diversity. Each ethnic group has become more internally homogeneous, although the degree of homogeneity varies.

This internal homogeneity of the remaining urban ethnic groups is both economic and cultural, because those with more money and less commitment to the ethnic culture have moved out. Assimilation has reduced the sense of ethnic identity for many individuals, but not destroyed it, and has made the society as a whole more homogeneous.

Assimilation and Ethnic Heterogeneity

The new racial ethnics have had their social and geographic mobility greatly restricted by residential, educational, and occupational segregation, discrimination, and prejudice.

White Ethnics

I am born of PIGS—those Poles, Italians, Greeks, and Slavs, non-English-speaking immigrants, numbered so heavily among the workingmen of this nation. Not particularly liberal, nor radical, born into a history not white Anglo-Saxon and not Jewish—born outside what in America is considered the intellectual mainstream. And thus privy to neither power nor status nor intellectual voice.

Those Poles of Buffalo and Milwaukee—so notoriously taciturn, sullen, nearly speechless. Who has ever understood them? It is not that Poles do not feel emotion: what is their history if not dark passion, romanticism, betrayal, courage, blood? But where in America is there anywhere in a language for voicing what a Christian Pole in this nation feels? He has no Polish culture left him, no Polish tongue. Yet Polish feelings do not go easily into the idiom of happy America, the America of the Anglo-Saxons and, yes, in the arts, the Jews. (The Jews have long been a culture of the word, accustomed to exile, skilled in scholarship and in reflection. The Christian Poles are largely of peasant origin, free men for hardly more than a hundred years.) Of what shall the man of Buffalo think, on his way to work in the mills, departing from his relatively dreary home and street? What roots does he have? What language of the heart is available to him?

Let me hasten to add that the estrangement I have come to feel derives not only from a lack of family history. All my life, I have been made to feel a slight uneasiness when I must say my name. Under challenge in grammar school concerning my nationality, I had been instructed by my father to announce proudly: "American." When my family moved from the Slovak ghetto of Johnstown to the WASP suburb on the hill, my mother impressed upon us how well we must be dressed, and show good manners, and behave—people think of us as "different" and we mustn't give them any cause. "Whatever you do, marry a Slovak girl," was other advice to a similar end: "They cook. They clean. They take good care of you. For your own good."

Nowhere in my schooling do I recall an attempt to put me in touch with my own history. The strategy was clearly to make an American of me. English literature, American literature; and even the history books, as I recall them, were peopled mainly by Anglo-Saxons from Boston (where most historians seemed to live). Not even my native Pennsylvania, let along my Slovak forebears, counted for very many paragraphs. I don't remember feeling envy or regret: a feeling, perhaps, of unimportance of remoteness, of not having heft enough to count.

Since earliest childhood, I have known about a "power elite" that runs America: the boys from the Ivy League in the State Department, as opposed to the Catholic boys from Hoover's FBI who, as Daniel Moynihan once put it, keep watch on them. And on a whole host of issues, my people have been, though largely Democratic, conservative: on censorship, on Communism, on abortion, on religious schools. . . . Harvard and Yale long meant "them" to us.

We did not feel this country belonged to us. We felt fierce pride in it, more loyalty than anyone could know. But we felt blocked at every turn. There were not many intellectuals among us, not even very many professional men. Laborers mostly. Small businessmen, agents for corporations perhaps. Content with a little, yes, modest in expectation. But somehow feeling cheated. For a thousand years the Slovaks survived Hungarian hegemony, and our strategy here remained the same: endurance and steady work. Slowly, one day, we would overcome.

Yet more significant in the ethnic experience in America is the intellectual world one meets: the definition of values, ideas, and purposes emanating from universities, books, magazines, radio, and television. One hears one's own voice echoed back neither by spokesmen of "Middle America" (so complacent, smug, nativist, and Protestant), nor by "the intellectuals." Almost unavoidably, perhaps, education in America leads the student who entrusts his soul to it in a direction that, lacking a better word, we might call liberal: respect for individual conscience, a sense of social responsibility, trust in the free exchange of ideas and procedures of dissent, a certain confidence in the ability of men to "reason together" and to adjudicate their differences, a frank recognition of the vitality of the unconscious, a willingness to protect workers and the poor against the vast economic power of industrial corporations, and the like.

Unfortunately, it seems, the ethnics erred in attempting to Americanize themselves, before clearing the project with the educated classes. They learned to wave the flag and to send their sons to war. (The Poles in World War I were 4 percent of the population but took 12 percent of the casualties.) They learned to support their President—an easy task, after all, for those accustomed abroad to obeying authority. And where would they have been if Franklin Roosevelt had not sided with them against established interests? They knew a little about Communism, the radicals among them in one way, and by far the larger number of conservatives in another. Not a few exchange letters to this day with cousins and uncles

who did not leave for America when they might have, whose lot is demonstrably harder and less than free.

Finally, the ethnics do not like, or trust, or even understand the intellectuals. It is not easy to feel uncomplicated affection for those who call you "pig," "fascist," "racist." One had not yet grown accustomed not to hearing "Hunkie," "Polack," "Spic," "Mick," "Dago," and the rest. At no little sacrifice, one had apologized for foods that smelled too strong for Anglo-Saxon noses, moderated the wide swings of Slavic and Italian emotion, learned decorum, given oneself to education American style, tried to learn tolerance and assimilation. Each generation criticized the earlier for its authoritarian and European and old-fashioned ways. "Up-to-date" was a moral lever. And now when the process nears completion, when a generation appears that speaks without accent and goes to college, still you are considered pigs, fascists, and racists.

Racists? Our ancestors owned no slaves. Most of us ceased being serfs only in the last 200 years—the Russians in 1861. What have we got against blacks or blacks against us? Competition, yes, for jobs and homes and communities; competition, even, for political power. Italians, Lithuanians, Slovaks, Poles are not, in principle, against "community control," or even against ghettos of our own. Whereas the Anglo-Saxon model appears to be a system of atomic individuals and high mobility, our model has tended to stress communities of our own, attachment to family and relatives, stability, and roots. We tend to have a fierce sense of attachment to our homes, having been homeowners less than three generations: a home is almost fulfillment enough for one man's life. We have most ambivalent feelings about suburban assimilation and mobility. The melting pot is a kind of homogenized soup, and its mores only partly appeal to us: to some, yes, and to others, no.

Source Reprinted with permission of Macmillan Publishing Co., Inc. from *The Rise of the Un-meltable Ethnics* by Michael Novak. Copyright © 1971, 1972 by Michael Novak. Originally appeared in *Harper's* Magazine.

Consequently their assimilation into the wider society has been very limited. Because even the most assimilated and socially, economically, and educationally successful members of these groups have restricted opportunities to move to the suburbs (see chapters 5, 6, and 7), the areas of the city they occupy remain racially segregated but socioeconomically heterogeneous. In contemporary urban racial ghettos, people of diverse social statuses may be found living close to one another. There are ghetto residents who are socially and economically able to move out if they could find a place where they would be permitted to move (Kerner Commission, 1968:244; Grodzins, 1970:479-501). Unlike older ethnic enclaves that have become homogeneous on the basis of occupation, income, and education and have developed at least some political and normative solidarity, newer ethnic groups have had difficulty doing so. Members of older ethnic communities who no longer wished to live in the area or identify with the ethnic group were able to move away. Because of discrimination against the new racial minorities, those residents who no longer wish to live within the area and identify with or espouse the aspirations of the racial community cannot move away.[8] The difficulty that many black groups have experienced in organizing "the black community" is a reflection of this phenomenon. Heterogeneity based on class differences conflicts with the common bonds of racial identity. Social and economic heterogeneity within a geographic area makes political consensus and social organization difficult.

Another explanation for the socioeconomic heterogeneity of the new racial-ethnic groups is that they are subject to the same ecological processes that have operated in the city for all ethnic groups. These processes initially led to the concentration of new groups in particular parts of the city. Later, however, as assimilation occurred, the older ethnic communities deconcentrated and dispersed. This has not occurred among the racial minorities (Grodzins, 1970:479-88; Schnore, 1972:34-92).

Positive Consequences of Ethnic Homogeneity

Ethnic homogeneity has positive consequences for the city as a communal social structure and for the ethnic communities themselves. Homogeneous ethnic communities can support a variety of ethnic institutions that are much less likely to be found in more ethnically heterogeneous communities. Among these institutions are restaurants, specialty stores, newspapers, culture-maintaining institutions such as churches, parochial schools, and museums of national culture, and various civic groups. Because ethnic groups are relatively isolated, each group maintains its own institutions. These institutions not only add to the diversity, interest, and excitement of the city, but also provide a secure supply of leaders and activists who help ensure that urban communal functions are performed. Multiple and competing leaders, however, can be a source of urban conflict, political pressure, and tension, and they can generate political contests that may be advantageous or disadvantageous for their ethnic community and for the city.

Ethnic identity can persist in a city.

Diverse ethnic communities in the city also offer a collective identity for unassimilated individuals. Ethnic identity can persist even in the face of deconcentration and assimilation (Parenti, 1967), but it is not as strong as it is when members participate regularly in close-knit, formal institutions and interact informally with fellow members who live nearby. The homogeneous communities remaining after the more assimilated residents have moved out have strong communal bonds. For many nonassimilated persons such ethnic communal bonds are a vital anchor in the face of an alienated and alienating mass society.

Without internal homogeneity, the unique culture and sense of identity of an ethnic group would diminish as assimilation continued. Where there is great heterogeneity without assimilation, as is the case among nonwhites, the development of a common identity is much more difficult. The homogeneous ethnic community is closer to a mechanical form of solidarity, while the heterogeneous ethnic-racial community is closer to an organic form of solidarity.

Within the structure of post-New Deal coalition politics, the solidarity of urban ethnic groups has proven useful in the realm of political organization. In a mass society the successful politician works with organized groups (or their representatives) or with blocs of voters. The ethnic group, particularly the homogeneous ethnic group, is a potent power base from which to begin and maintain a political career. Of course, the politician must reward the group for its support with services, jobs, and other resources. In this sense, group solidarity produces positive results. Big-city politicians and political machines have relied heavily on ethnic group solidarity during much of the twentieth century (Dahl, 1961; Banfield and Wilson, 1963:80-100, 115-33; Cornwall, 1964:27-39; O'Connor, 1956). Such power can be abused, as it is when it leads to corruption, patronage, abuses, and lack of response to the voters' wishes. (Chapter 10 offers a more complete analysis of political machines and urban politics in general.)

In summary, ethnic homogeneity encourages informal social interaction. As a result, it is easier to develop and maintain local institutions focused on ethnic or national traditions and to maintain group norms. The relative compactness and homogeneity of the urban ethnic enclave make it possible to develop a sense of mechanical solidarity, a quasi-*Gemeinschaft,* and a strong sense of community among residents and between individuals and the group.

Negative Consequences of Ethnic Homogeneity

Competition among ethnic groups.   The existence of many homogeneous ethnic neighborhoods also has negative consequences for the city. These communities often compete with one another for goods, services, and political power. Just as some individuals develop ethnocentric attitudes that have behavioral correlates toward members of other ethnic groups (Williams, 1964:17-29), segments of society can develop ethnocentric attitudes and behaviors. These often become institutionalized in the policies of city governments, school systems, real estate brokers, and the like, and result in discrimination in housing, education, jobs, and the distribution of public goods and services. Thus homogeneous groups can give rise to institutions that foster prejudice, discrimination, and segregation. For example, many neighborhoods settled by foreign immigrants of the same ethnic group have been occupied continuously for several generations by unassimilated members of the group who have developed emotional attachments to the neighborhood. Their homes are their major financial and emotional investments and the focus for much of their social lives (Krickus, 1970:3-27). The residents of these neighborhoods have a sense of solidarity based on their homogeneity. Generations of living together have produced a form of *Gemeinschaft*. The residents tend to reject anybody who looks different and might have different standards of behavior.[9] This solidarity appears to be one major reason for resistance to the in-migration of people of different ethnic origins, and one major reason why public institutions, such as public housing, schools, and clinics, are located in areas where the people for whom the facilities are intended will be of the same ethnic identity as the residents.

Ethnocentrism and violence. Even without the institutionalized expression of ethnocentrism, the ecological processes of invasion, competition, and succession can lead to group competition for housing, jobs, goods and services, and political power, especially when the economy is not affluent. When such group competition is reinforced by individual and institutional ethnocentrism, it can become violent. Violence is particularly likely to occur when one ethnic group becomes convinced that others have combined to prevent it from obtaining a fair share of resources, or to take away resources won by generations of hard work.

Such violence is, unfortunately, all too common in American history. Lieberson and Silverman (1965:887-98) identified seventy-six race riots between 1913 and 1963. Grimshaw (1960:109-19) analyzed urban racial violence and determined that contested areas (areas in which racial groups were contesting for residential dominance or other uses) and the central business districts of cities were the major ecological locations of riots or incidents that precipitated riots. Table 9.2 lists some major incidents of interracial violence in the twentieth century (Lieberson and Silverman, 1965; Grimshaw, 1960; Kerner Commission, 1968:35-41, 532; Marden and Meyer, 1968: 339; Boskin, 1969; Baskin et al., 1972).

The occurrences of racial violence have had different causes and characteristics. Precipitating events have ranged from arrests to incidents of violence by a member of one racial group against a member of another. In many cases violent episodes that have included members of both races have been called race riots, even though group conflict has not been involved (Baskin, 1972:3).

Since 1970 many incidents of racial violence have accompanied attempts to desegregate northern urban school systems (for example, Detroit and especially Boston in 1974-76). Many incidents have occurred as schools have opened under court-ordered desegregation plans, especially those that included busing programs. The violence in Boston has occurred in sections that the Irish for generations have considered "theirs." The "forced" association in the public schools of their

Table 9.2   Major Occurrences of Racial Violence, 1908-1968

Date	City (or District)
1908	Springfield, Ill.
1917	East St. Louis
1919	Chicago
1921	Tulsa
1935	Harlem
1943	Harlem, Detroit, Los Angeles
1960	Greensboro, N.C.
1963	Birmingham; Savannah; Cambridge, MD.; Chicago; Philadelphia
1964	Jacksonville, Cleveland, St. Augustine, Jersey City, Elizabeth, Paterson, Harlem, Bedford-Stuyvesant, Philadelphia, Rochester, Chicago
1965	Selma, Watts, Chicago
1966	Watts, Chicago, Cleveland, and 15 others
1967	Detroit and 175 others
1968	Newark and 157 others

Many incidents of violence have accompanied attempts to desegregate schools by busing children.

children with children from black neighborhoods precipitated the violence. Even the threat of desegregation was enough to propel Louise Day Hicks, a leader of the antibusing movement, into political prominence in Boston in the early 1970s.

Anti-black prejudice and discrimination, especially in educational institutions and among the labor force, may be manifestations of the desires of older ethnic groups to keep blacks in disadvantaged positions and low-status roles and to deny them a fair share of society's resources (Blauner, 1969:393-408). On the other hand, the successes of the civil rights movement in the 1960s are seen by some older immigrant groups as the taking away of social advantages they worked for generations to earn—neighborhoods, jobs, social status— all the benefits they accumulated to pass on to their children.[10] These feelings lead to a cycle of conflict and redoubled efforts to maintain ethnocentric attitudes and behaviors. However, those who are left in the older urban neighborhoods are largely the unassimilated members of the ethnic community who are the ones most interested in ethnic institutions and the ones least skilled in organizing and obtaining support for these institutions.

Resistance to social change. Assimilation and out-migration of the most economically and educationally successful ethnic group members leaves the homogeneous urban ethnic community unprepared to cope with social change. While vulnerable to change, the community is relatively resistant to it. For example, community residents frequently do not understand that the functions of education have changed from merely providing basic

education in reading, writing, and arithmetic to preparation for life in a complex and continuously changing industrial society. Instead, they resist changes in the schools; they resist the introduction of new topics into the curriculum, and they often feel that schools are not performing their proper functions.

Members of ethnic groups may feel helpless and alienated as forces beyond their understanding or control produce changes in their schools and neighborhoods. As their assimilated members migrate out of the neighborhood, they are confronted with the immigration or invasion of new groups and institutions and changes in the composition, location, and curriculum of their schools. Communities bitterly resist federally mandated racial integration of the schools because it prevents them from controlling the socialization of the young—a critical communal function—and thus helps to break down the ethnic community. These communities, however, cannot afford to reject the federal aid that legitimates the regulations. The city's need for federal and state aid forces the city to work for integration against the ethnic community.

Exploitation of minority groups. Finally, minority groups, especially homogeneous, disadvantaged groups, are ripe for exploitation by members of older homogeneous ethnic groups. Old ethnics, abandoning central city areas to new ethnics, often keep control of some institutions that provide goods and services in the areas they have left. Those who practice economic, social, and political exploitation of the new ethnics become targets for violence during riots.

Segregation by Choice and by Imposition

Ecological processes have sorted out the urban population into neighborhoods of people with similar national or ethnic identities. Maintenance of these racially homogeneous neighborhoods seems due to other social forces as well as ecology. Rarely are the old ethnic neighborhoods in a city today referred to as ghettos, although earlier in the twentieth century they were quite clearly such (Wirth, 1964:85). Contemporary urban racial settlements are a new dimension in ethnic segregation. When we talk about ethnic neighborhoods today, it is assumed we are talking about race. The ethnic enclaves of the older European immigrants have been overshadowed by the black areas in major cities.

Major problems of cities today are those associated with racially segregated neighborhoods.[11] Two critical factors distinguish today's racially segregated neighborhoods from the earlier ethnic enclaves: first, the earlier ethnic enclaves were produced by ecological processes and maintained by unassimilated members of the group living there; second, racially segregated neighborhoods are not expected to change through assimilation or geographic mobility, as earlier ethnic enclaves did.

Black neighborhoods have been institutionalized in cities by the location of neighborhood schools, by real estate lending, rental, mortgage, and sales practices, and by the location of public housing in areas that are already black. Thus, black neighborhoods have been deliberately maintained by policy. The heterogeneity of black neighborhoods is generally not recognized. The image of pover-

Black neighborhoods have been institutionalized in cities by the location of neighborhood schools.

ty, crime, and lower-class life styles among blacks dominates, especially as black neighborhoods expand. The heterogeneity of class, education, occupation, and life style that characterizes black neighborhoods in metropolitan areas is lost or submerged in the overwhelming similarity of skin color (Erbe, 1975).

The development of urban racial segregation has been accompanied by the movement to the suburbs of assimilated older white ethnics.[12] This movement began at approximately the same time as the movement of the black people from the rural South to the metropolitan North. There may well be no causal relationship between these two movements; they may simply have started at the same time as a result of similar economic forces. Recently, migration to the suburbs has occurred even in metropolitan areas where the black population is too small to explain the suburban migration.

The size and rapidity of the black migration into central cities of metropolitan areas has overwhelmed urban populations and institutions. The older immigrant groups, the city's service system, the low-cost housing supply, and the areas abandoned by out-migrants are simply unable to accommodate such a rapid influx. The ecological invasion has been so large and so fast that the normal processes by which in-migrants are incorporated into the urban social system have proved inadequate. The migration of blacks to cities puts pressure on other groups living in low-cost housing areas in the central city. This leads to ecological invasions of city neighborhoods occupied by the unassimilated members of the older ethnic groups who are neither willing nor able to move to new ethnic enclaves in the city or suburbs previously established by assimilated group members.

The Black Urban Migration

To understand fully how black migration affected older ethnic communities and how racially segregated neighborhoods developed, it is first necessary to understand the magnitude of the migration. Northern metropolitan centers are now characterized by an urban society in which blacks are physically present but socially excluded. The movement of blacks out of the South has occurred largely in the twentieth century (Taeuber and Taeuber, 1971:55; U.S. Bureau of the Census, 1974:28, table 30). The extent of black migration can be seen in table 9.3. Before 1920, 85 percent of all blacks in the United States lived in the South, but as of 1960, this had been reduced to 61 percent, and by 1970 it was 47 percent. While the white population had begun moving west at the same time, the geographic redistribution of the white population was not nearly as massive as that of the black population.

Along with this migration from the South, there has been a dramatic increase in the size of the black population. In 1900 there were only about 8.8 million blacks in the United States, but in 1970 there were 20.5 million. While in 1900 there were only 880,000 blacks living outside the South, in 1970 there were 9.6 million blacks living outside the South.[13]

The black population not only migrated from the South to the North, but it also migrated to urban areas. In 1900 only 22.6 percent of the black population was urban,

Table 9.3   Population Location, by Race, 1900-1970 (percentage distribution)

	Northeast	Northcentral	South	West
White				
1900	30.9	38.5	24.7	5.8
1920	30.5	35.0	25.4	9.0
1940	29.2	32.7	26.8	11.3
1960	26.2	30.3	27.4	16.1
1970	25.0	29.1	28.4	17.4
Black				
1900	4.4	5.6	89.6	0.3
1920	6.5	7.6	85.2	0.8
1940	10.6	11.0	77.0	1.3
1960	16.0	18.3	60.7	5.7
1970	19.2	20.2	53.1	7.4

Source   Irene B. Taeuber, "The Changing Distribution of the Population of the United States in the Twentieth Century," *Population Distribution and Policy*, U.S. Commission on Population Growth and the American Future, vol. 5 of Commission Research Reports, ed. Sara Mills Mazie (Washington, D.C.: Government Printing Office, 1972), pp. 44-45.

compared with 39.6 percent of the total population; but in 1970 80.7 percent of the black population lived in urban areas, while 73.5 percent of the total population was urban.[14]

The nonsouthern black has always been more urbanized than the black population in general. In 1900 when 22.6 percent of the black population and 39.6 percent of the total population was urban, two thirds of the blacks living outside the South were urban residents. By 1970, when 80.7 percent of all blacks (and 72.5 percent of whites) were urban, more than 95 percent of nonsouthern blacks were urban (U.S. Bureau of the Census, 1972:table 85; Taeuber and Taeuber, 1971).

Thus, at the start of the twentieth century, American blacks were 90 percent southern and predominantly rural. By the mid-1960s, they were nearly half nonsouthern and largely urban, even metropolitan. By 1970 blacks were more urbanized and metropolitanized than whites, as 67.8 percent of whites but 74.3 percent of blacks lived in metropolitan areas (U.S. Bureau of the Census, 1974:table 30).

By 1970 the population in metropolitan areas of two hundred thousand or more persons was 14 percent black; in the central cities of these metropolitan areas, 23.9 percent were black, although outside the central city the black population was only 6 percent. The segregation in both central cities and suburbs is even more extreme in the twenty largest metropolitan areas. Together, these twenty SMSAs had 16.2 percent black residents, but the central cities were 29.2 percent black, while the areas outside the central city were only 5.9 percent black.[15]

As these data indicate, the black migration from the South was predominantly a migration to the central cities of metropolitan areas. At the same time, the white residents of metropolitan central cities were moving to areas outside the central city. Between 1960 and 1970 the white population of SMSAs decreased by 1.2 percent, while the black population increased by 36 percent. In the larger metropolitan areas, those of two hundred thousand or more, the central city white population decreased twice as fast (by 2.5 percent), while the black population increased slightly faster than the black population of all metropolitan areas (by 36.8 percent). Therefore, the black population of major cities is growing rapidly, both absolutely and in relation to the white population (U.S. Bureau of the Census, 1974).

Racial Ghettos

The ecological processes that shaped the population movement of the earlier urban immigrant groups also influenced the movement of blacks. Black migrants to the city, much like earlier immigrant groups, moved into sections of the central city where there was housing they could afford and where other blacks lived. This produced **black belts** that subsequently became ghettos. Unlike the early immigrants who were able to move out of their neighborhood enclaves as they became assimilated, the blacks have been almost totally denied both assimilation and out-migration. Although early immigrants often had to struggle against poverty and discrimination for one or two generations, they eventually overcame these hardships and took advantage of the educational and occupational opportunities that were available to them. Such opportunities for blacks have been restricted, making social mobility rare and keeping the average income of the black population low (the median income for white families in 1974 was $13,356; for blacks, $8,265) (U.S. Bureau of the Census, 1975:391). Blacks in metropolitan areas have been forced by lack of income or opportunity to stay in less desirable, concentrated locations (Kerner Commission, 1968:240-44).

Although the black areas of the city have been limited in size, the population of these areas has grown rapidly because of natural increase and continued in-migration. Even the original black migrants (like the foreign immigrants before them) were badly overcrowded when they first moved to the city. This overcrowding has increased, partially because of the economics of housing, but mainly because of the attitudes and responses of residents in other areas of the city that limit where blacks can move, even when they can afford it. Thus, the rate of geographic expansion of black areas has been slower than the rate of population increase, and these areas are dominated by the portions of the population that are growing fastest—the poor and recent immigrants. Because even socially mobile and economically successful blacks have been restricted to areas that are predominantly occupied by persons of low socioeconomic status, black neighborhoods and the black community are heterogeneous. Though some residents are assimilated into and participate in the wider society, most residents of black neighborhoods in our cities have not been educated for full social participation.

The concentration of blacks in the central city is evidence of one form of segregation—the segregation of central city and suburbs. There is also a high degree of segregation within the central city (Kerner Commission, 1968:240-44). How did this segregation develop and what maintains it? What are the current patterns of racial segregation in central cities?

The Development and Maintenance of Segregation

The number of blacks living in urban areas outside the South prior to World War I was so small that urban racial segregation was no problem. After World War I blacks migrated from the rural South to the urban North in such great numbers that resident populations reacted strenuously to the in-migrants, discriminating against them formally and informally, segregating them, and exercising strong control over their behavior and activities (Marden and Meyer, 1968:267).

Drake and Clayton's *Black Metropolis* is a classic study of segregation, written in 1945 and revised in 1962. It records the movement of blacks to Chicago during the 1930s and the development of white/black segregation there between the world wars. Drake and Clayton concluded that white people had extremely strong feelings against having blacks as neighbors and used both formal and informal means of social control to keep them away from white neighborhoods and in congested black neighborhoods. As early as 1920, white residents of Chicago had organized resistance to black population movements within the city and began taking active, violent steps to prevent the sale of homes outside the black belt to blacks. Even though the massive migration of blacks had not yet begun, there were forty-eight firebombings of homes sold to blacks between July 1917 and March 1921 (Drake and Clayton, 1962:64).

In addition to violence, whites used legal means, such as **restrictive covenants** and zoning ordinances, to maintain residential segregation. Restrictive zoning ordinances were effective until they were ruled unconstitutional in 1917. Restrictive covenants between individuals prevented homeowners from selling their houses to particular groups of people, generally blacks but also Jews. These covenants were not ruled unconstitutional until 1948 (Marden and Meyer, 1968:269).

Although public facilities in the North were generally not racially segregated, they were restricted. There was little legal school segregation in the North, but patterns of segregation based on residence were, and are, common. Similarly, public facilities that were shared by men and women were racially restricted. This often led to conflicts, especially on public beaches. Many methods of maintaining segregation in urban centers were informal. Even when laws requiring segregation were declared unconstitutional, segregation was maintained by turning facilities, even public facilities, into restricted membership clubs.

Prior to the migration of blacks from the South that began in the 1920s (see table 9.3), the relatively few blacks in northern cities had worked out fairly stable patterns of accommodation with the majority group. There were areas, however, in which the blacks were segregated and denied equality. For example, in Muncie, Indiana (the town that has become famous because of the Middletown studies of the Lynds) blacks were not permitted to join the YMCA, and there was a separate newspaper column devoted to black social gossip (Marden and Meyer, 1968:274). Southern black workers migrating to northern cities tended to disrupt patterns of racial accommodation. The southern portion of New Jersey showed a great deal more segregation than the northern portion, and the southern Negroes migrating to Illinois were subject to essentially the same caste system that prevailed in the Deep South.

As a result of overcrowding and poverty, the black neighborhoods in northern cities early became class ghettos as well as racial ghettos. These blighted areas were characterized by poverty, lack of facilities, antisocial behavior, pollution, exploitation, and a variety of other negative conditions (Marden and Meyer, 1968:275). The ghetto results from spatial segregation of minority groups into neighborhoods able to perform only a few, if any, communal functions.

The early black community in northern cities included churches, clubs, recreational facilities, and civic groups, that fit into established city patterns. Before the massive immigration following World War I, the black community was similar to other ethnic communities. Since then the older ethnic communities have begun to disappear as members have been assimilated into the wider society, but the black ghetto has remained and grown.

The Expansion of Ghettos

When overcrowding reached the point where more people simply could not be accommodated, the ghetto began to expand. Block by block the black population moved into nearby areas in which residents frequently exhibited patterns of residential mobility and overcrowding, educational attainment, unemployment, home ownership, and other socioeconomic characteristics similar to those of blacks. The first blacks who moved into middle-class white neighborhoods were themselves middle-class. Only later did other, less socially and economically successful blacks expand into the area as the white population left. Similarly, the first blacks to move into lower-class white areas were themselves lower-class (Grodzins, 1970:483).

Many white residents of threatened neighborhoods were barely able to afford to live in such neighborhoods. Many of them were old; inflation and increasing taxes made it financially difficult for them to maintain their homes. Having lived there for a long time, they often had emotional attachments to the neighborhood and to their homes, which represented the capital accumulation of one or two generations. Many residents interacted only with other residents and with those in charge of local institutions. They feared that if they moved they would enter an alien social environment, as indeed they would, where they would be isolated and alienated. Thus, they resisted the invasion of blacks vigorously and fought violently to control the area until it became clear that at least some blacks would succeed in moving into the neighborhood. When the proportion of nonwhite in-migrants reached a neighborhood's tolerance level, virtually all the whites in the neighborhood fled (Grodzins, 1970:484).

Ghettos, like early cities, have expanded from the center outward. The change in individual neighborhoods from predominantly white to predominantly black is rarely reversed. Once the population becomes substantially black, the neighborhood rarely remains integrated for long (Bradburn, Sudman, and Gockel, 1970:15-16). Even attempts to build public or private housing in these areas or to use urban renewal lands to promote racial integration have rarely altered these patterns.

Reasons for Neighborhood Change

Normal ecological processes. Neighborhood change is seldom rapid. Ecological invasion and succession can take several years. Because change generally occurs in areas of high residential mobility, blacks who move in by renting or buying vacant or for-sale dwellings cannot properly be said to be pushing out previous residents. As vacancies occur in low-income white areas, black families occasionally have the opportunity to move in. Some research has suggested that normal residential turnover, the desire for better housing, and cost factors can account for the transition of urban neighborhoods from white to black (Guest and Zuiches, 1971:457-67; Moltoch, 1969:226-37; McAllister, et al., 1971:445-56; Fishman, 1961:42-51). Blacks rent and move more frequently than whites and particularly within a city. Blacks are more likely than whites to be restricted to city, as opposed to suburban, areas because of economics and race. Therefore, normal ecological processes can result in a change in neighborhood racial composition. High levels of residential mobility in changing urban neighborhoods can be attributed to demographic and housing characteristics of those areas. There is little evidence of **white flight** to avoid blacks, either in anticipation of a racial change or as a consequence of such change.

Blockbusting and redlining. Real estate agencies and lending institutions can influence the composition of urban neighborhoods. **Blockbusting** is the tactic used by real estate agents to induce fear of racial change so that they can buy homes cheaply from white residents and resell them at inflated prices to

"Blockbusting" by real estate interests is believed to be responsible for some cases of rapid racial change of a neighborhood.

(*Top*) Whites typically believe that property values will deteriorate because blacks will not keep their property in good repair.

(*Bottom*) Closed parochial schools often signify racial change in a neighborhood.

blacks. Blockbusting has been implicated in some, though not in all, cases of rapid racial change (Moltoch, 1969:232). Some cities have attempted to reduce neighborhood fear of impending change by banning the posting of "For Sale" and "Sold" signs on houses (*New York Times,* 6 November 1976:26), but the effectiveness of this tactic is debatable. Some neighborhood leaders have charged that banks and other lending institutions have **redlined** (refused to loan money for home improvements or mortgages) to residents in neighborhoods they think are about to be ecologically invaded (*New York Times,* 26 May 1975:20).

Reasons for white resistance to black residents. A number of factors cause whites to resist the first black resident and to subsequently leave the neighborhood: prejudice, ethnocentrism, interracial conflict, and fear of loss of neighborhood status, to name a few. Whites typically believe that property values will deteriorate because blacks will not keep their houses and property in good repair; that blacks will engage in more disorderly behavior such as juvenile delinquency and crime; that educational programs and facilities will suffer.

The major variables affecting events in a particular neighborhood seem to be the strength of the whites' desire to move out, the strength of the blacks' desire to move in, the willingness of whites to purchase housing in interracial neighborhoods, the housing choices open to blacks in the city, and general price, income, and economic conditions (Marden and Meyer, 1968:319). The most definitive research indicates that housing values and neighborhood status will not decrease unless

As Blacks Move in the Ethnics Move Out

The signs were there, all right. The little photography studio on the corner of Harvey and 116th Street, where I had looked at the latest brides, their lips retouched deep red and eyebrows dark, was now a karate and judo school. A storefront church, Pilgrim Rest B. C., was on 93rd Street near Dickens. Protective grates guarded the front of Rosenbluth's, our local clothing store, whose recorded Santa Claus laugh had scared the patched corduroy pants right off me as a youngster. A public housing project rose from the mud. And in the streets there was a stillness.

As I drove back through my old neighborhood on the East Side of Cleveland last month, there was so little noise. No horns. At 8 o'clock in the evening, there were few cars on the street. There must have been more people walking around, but I remember only a handful at well-lit intersections. . . .

Living on Forest Avenue after the war and through the first half of the nineteen-fifties surely fulfilled all the dreams of the Slovak and Hungarian immigrants and their offspring. There was regular work nearby, the brick streets were clean, lawns were mowed and—except for some home-grown hooligans who might beat you up—it was safe. Blacks? Sure, we knew about blacks.

They were a growing mass of look-alikes who flooded in after the war to produce fantastic basketball teams at East Tech. They lived on the crumbling rim of the downtown area seemingly content to wallow in their poverty. They were at once out of mind and a dull pain that would surely trouble us more in days to come. . . .

The pastor, Father Michael Jasko, hasn't changed much over the years. He is 65 now, his hair still regally silver, his voice nasal and high. As he began to talk about his parish, it was obviously painful. The glory that was St. Benedict's, the optimism that had built a church with a seating capacity of 1,100, had faded.

"We had 2,000 families and 8,000 souls when you were here," he began. "Now it's 1,000 families and 3,000 souls, and most of them are pensioners. We stopped the Canteen [a weekly dance for teen-agers] 10 years ago and hoped to reopen it, but never did. We made $45,000 in a big year at the bazaar; last year we got $24,000. Novenas and other night-time services have been stopped. The old ladies of the church were getting beaten and robbed on their way to early mass, so we stopped those. Now the first mass is at 7 o'clock, except in the summer when we have the 5:30. Early this year, we're starting a drive to pay off the $95,000 owing on the church. If we don't do it now, we'll never be able to.

"We had a lot of trouble with school children being beaten, in fact the entire baseball team and their coaches were overrun by a gang of 30. I guess you heard about the eighth-grade girl who was raped by four boys from Audubon." I had, and Audubon, a public junior high school now almost entirely black though surrounded by a pre-dominantly white neighborhood, was the reason given by many people for the old neighborhood's current state. "We stopped most of the problem by starting school a half hour before Audubon and letting out a half hour before them. The children can be safely home before they get out. . . .

St. Benedict's School, which I had attended through the eighth grade, seemed to have changed little—the walls were still painted bland and restful beige and green, and the Blessed Virgin, who had looked out over us from her second-floor pedestal, was still standing firmly on the writhing serpent, though both he and she had been chipped and gouged over the years. But the appearance was deceptive.

While the 1,100 of us in the student body had been stuffed 50 or 60 to a classroom, there were now only 350 students scattered loosely about the school, and precious space was allotted to an audio-visual room and a library. The student body now includes 25 or 30 non-Catholics—I can't remember a single one in my day—and four blacks.

A lunchroom has been built because even those parents who live only a few blocks away won't allow their children to come home at noon. It is considered too dangerous. A thousand lunches are served free each month, and 400 more go at half price. The total price for those who can pay is 20 cents. . . .

Frank is an efficient man; he had outlined some things he wanted to tell me. A telephone booth on the corner of his street had been damaged so often that it was removed. A mail box had been burglarized on the day Social Security checks were to come. A doctor had installed a peep hole in his door and had gone to irregular office hours to thwart robbers. A mentally retarded boy whose joy was a paper route had to give it up after his collections were stolen and his papers thrown into the street. Somody's Delicatessen closed be-tween 2:30 and 4 each afternoon to avoid harass-ment from the Audubon students.

"In everything I've told you," he said, "I've not once mentioned race. It isn't race; it's law and order. We Slovaks are too trusting, too honest, too open. There was never trouble here just because blacks moved in. In Murray Hill, the Italians told the blacks they would kill any who

dared to move in. In Sowinski Park, the Polish pointed shotguns at them. That is not our way of life, but look what we are reaping now. Many people thought this neighborhood was a fortress, people are afraid to go out and those that must go out are prey.

"We didn't even know the Hungarians in our neighborhood, and we certainly weren't prejudiced against them. Slovaks come from a country that was a collection of small villages; there was no such a thing as national spirit. Here in America, the center was the church, and our people did everything within that church. The Slovaks have been occupied before, by Russians and Germans, by the Hungarians, and now we are being occupied by the robber, the rapist, the murderer. But this is by far harder to live with, the unknowingness of it all. I see two solutions to help the neighborhood; one is very short-term, the other long: Post a policeman every 150 feet to start. Then go to work on the sociological problems like giving these people a better education."

Frank's sister Ethel stopped by, as she often does. She lived on Manor, several blocks away, and had just sold her house at a $4,000 loss. She planned to move to the suburbs with her husband, a teacher, and their children. She flicked off her knitted cap, and—though she has a son ready to graduate from high school—looked like the lovely, shy, dark-haired girl she was 20 years ago. "One of the turning points for me was when I heard people were buying guns. I asked some of the women on the block and found three of them—just like that—who carry guns in their purses. Imagine, women who have never fired a gun in their lives carry one to go to the Pick 'n' Pay.". . .

"The 29th Ward is a ward in transition. That means whites move out, blacks move in, businesses close and everybody forgets about it until it's a slum, then Model Cities is supposed to rejuvenate it. We have 40 percent black, a lot of ethnics and a few WASP types on the upper edges, where we touch on Shaker Heights. We have people who are used to taking care of things by themselves and of living within their own world. My job is to bring them together for cooperation and let them know at the same time they don't have to go inviting each other over for supper. They can still be private people with their own traditions, but divided like this, they'll be eaten alive. Crime is up 25 or 30 percent, and

there's no reason why it won't go higher. Blacks are suffering, too, but they are used to it. The press on the ethnics is so strong, they want to kid themselves it's going to be O.K. tomorrow. So they wait and hope. Useless!''. . .

They are calling my neighborhood transitional, and it is not much fun to go home again. The old formula just doesn't seem to work any more and there are few people left who want to move along positive lines. So the ethnics continue to abandon the neighborhood, each saying he hates to go and he'll hate to come back in five or ten years when, as many of them say, it will be another Hough. Most major cities must have neighborhoods like it, neighborhoods that are being left to new immigrants who want to believe they have moved to Nirvana.

Source Paul Wilkes, *New York Times Magazine*, January 24, 1971. © 1977 by The New York Times Company. Reprinted by permission.

whites move en masse. It is only if the area becomes almost all black and poor that the undesirable effects of overcrowding begin and housing values deteriorate (Laurenti, 1960; McEntire, 1960:157-71).

All these processes result in central cities that are divided into white neighborhoods and black neighborhoods. Only a few communities have developed stable interracial living patterns (Hunter, 1975:540; Bradburn, Sudman, and Gockel, 1970).

Levels of Segregation

Most recent studies of racial segregation in major cities are based on the 1960 and 1970 censuses (Taeuber, 1964:42-50; Council on Municipal Performance, 1974:32-33). They found that segregation is so high and so universal among major cities that there is no point in trying to decide which city is not segregated. Virtually all metropolitan areas have segregation scores above 80, meaning that 80 percent of the black population would have to move into predominantly white census tracts to eliminate segregation. Research on ethnic segregation has shown that racial segregation is greater than segregation between immigrants and native-born persons or between persons of various class levels (Taeuber, 1964; Lieberson, 1963).

Racial and Ethnic Communities

The continuing segregation of ethnic groups from blacks and native whites and from each other facilitates the persistence of racial and ethnic communities. Some old ethnic communities perform some communal functions more completely than they perform others;

Table 9.4   Housing Segregation, 109 U.S. Cities, 1940-1970

City	How Many Non-Whites Would Have to Move?					
	1940	*Rank*	*1950*	*1960*	*1970*	*Rank*
Akron, Oh.	82.2	37	87.6	88.1	81.2	46
Asheville, N.C.	88.6	79	89.2	92.3	88.5	76
Atlanta, Ga.	87.4	68	91.5	93.6	91.5	98
Atlantic City, N.J.	94.6	105	94.0	89.2	86.9	70
Augusta, Ga.	86.9	66	88.9	93.0	93.3	107
Austin, Tx.	84.8	51	92.0	93.1	84.6	61
Baltimore, Md.	90.1	85	91.3	89.6	88.3	74
Beaumont, Tx.	81.0	26	89.6	92.3	89.7	86
Berkeley, Ca.	81.2	29	80.3	69.4	62.9	5
Birmingham, Al.	86.4	59	88.7	92.8	91.5	98
Boston, Ma.	86.3	58	86.5	83.9	79.9	43
Bridgeport, Ct.	78.8	11	74.4	69.7	71.7	17
Buffalo, N.Y.	87.9	72	89.5	86.5	84.2	60
Cambridge, Ma.	74.3	3	75.6	65.5	52.6	1
Camden, N.J.	87.6	70	89.6	76.5	67.4	7
Canton, Oh.	89.9	83	89.3	81.5	82.4	51
Charleston, S.C.	60.1	1	68.4	79.5	86.5	66
Charleston, W.V.	80.3	21	79.6	79.0	74.3	23
Charlotte, N.C.	90.1	85	92.8	94.3	92.7	104
Chattanooga, Tn.	86.5	60	88.5	91.5	89.9	88
Chester, Pa.	85.1	53	88.1	87.4	82.2	50
Chicago, Il.	95.0	107	92.1	92.6	88.8	79
Cincinnati, Oh.	90.6	91	91.2	89.0	83.1	54
Cleveland, Oh.	92.0	95	91.5	91.3	89.0	81
Columbia, S.C.	83.0	40	88.1	94.1	86.7	67
Columbus, Oh.	87.1	67	88.9	85.3	84.1	59
Covington, Ky.	80.6	22	85.0	87.8	86.9	70
Dallas, Tx.	80.2	20	88.4	94.6	92.7	104
Dayton, Oh.	91.5	93	93.3	91.3	90.1	90
Denver, Co.	87.9	72	88.9	85.5	77.6	36
Des Moines, Ia.	87.8	71	89.3	87.9	79.2	42
Detroit, Mi.	89.9	83	88.8	84.5	89.0	44
Durham, N.C.	88.2	77	88.8	92.7	87.5	73
East Chicago, In.	74.5	4	79.6	82.8	79.0	41
East Orange, N.J.	85.3	54	83.7	71.2	60.8	4
East St. Louis, Il.	93.8	103	94.2	92.0	76.8	31
Elizabeth, N.J.	75.9	6	76.1	75.2	75.5	27
Evanston, Il.	91.5	93	92.1	87.2	78.3	38
Evansville, In.	86.2	57	92.4	91.2	88.6	78
Flint, Mi.	92.5	97	95.3	94.4	81.7	47

Table 9.4   Housing Segregation, 109 U.S. Cities, 1940-1970, *continued*

City	How Many Non-Whites Would Have to Move?					
	1940	*Rank*	*1950*	*1960*	*1970*	*Rank*
Fort Worth, Tx.	81.3	30	90.4	94.3	92.6	103
Galveston, Tx.	72.2	2	78.3	82.9	77.4	34
Gary, In.	88.3	78	93.8	92.8	82.9	53
Greensboro, N.C.	93.1	102	93.5	93.3	91.4	97
Harrisburg, Pa.	87.2	68	89.8	85.7	76.2	29
Hartford, Ct.	84.8	51	84.4	82.1	77.4	34
Houston, Tx.	84.5	49	91.5	93.7	90.0	89
Huntington, W.Va.	81.6	31	85.8	88.8	85.9	65
Indianapolis, In.	90.4	89	91.4	91.6	88.3	75
Jacksonville, Fl.	94.3	104	94.9	96.9	92.5	102
Jersey City, N.J.	79.5	13	80.5	77.9	75.6	28
Kansas City, Ks.	90.5	90	92.0	91.5	84.7	62
Kansas City, Mo.	88.0	74	91.3	90.8	88.0	74
Knoxville, Tn.	88.6	79	89.6	90.7	89.6	85
Little Rock, Ar.	78.2	9	84.5	89.4	89.7	86
Los Angeles, Ca.	84.2	44	84.6	81.8	78.4	39
Louisville, Ky.	81.7	32	86.0	89.2	88.9	80
Macon, Ga.	74.9	5	77.1	83.7	90.2	91
Memphis, Tn.	79.9	16	86.4	92.0	91.8	100
Miami, Fl.	97.9	109	97.8	97.9	89.4	84
Milwaukee, Wi.	92.9	100	91.6	88.1	83.7	57
Minneapolis, Mn.	88.0	74	86.0	79.3	67.9	8
Mobile, Al.	86.6	62	89.4	91.9	91.0	95
Montgomery, Al.	86.8	64	90.5	94.7	93.2	106
Mt. Vernon, N.Y.	78.9	12	78.0	73.2	78.4	39
Nashville, Tn.	86.5	60	88.7	91.7	89.0	81
Newark, N.J.	77.4	7	76.9	71.6	74.9	24
New Bedford, Ma.	83.4	42	86.8	81.6	72.7	19
New Haven, Ct.	80.1	18	79.9	70.9	69.1	11
New Orleans, La.	81.0	26	84.9	86.3	83.1	54
New Rochelle, N.Y.	80.6	22	78.9	79.5	70.7	15
New York, N.Y.	86.8	64	87.3	79.3	73.0	20
Norfolk, Va.	96.0	108	95.0	94.6	90.8	93
Oakland, Ca.	78.4	10	81.2	73.1	63.4	6
Oklahoma City, Ok.	84.3	47	88.6	87.1	81.8	48
Omaha, Nb.	89.5	82	92.4	92.0	85.6	64
Pasadena, Ca.	84.2	44	85.9	83.4	75.0	26
Paterson, N.J.	79.8	15	80.0	75.9	70.3	14
Philadelphia, Pa.	88.0	74	89.0	87.1	83.2	56
Pittsburgh, Pa.	82.0	35	84.0	84.6	83.9	58

Table 9.4   Housing Segregation, 109 U.S. Cities, 1940-1970, *continued*

| City | How Many Non-Whites Would Have to Move? | | | | |
	1940	*Rank*	*1950*	*1960*	*1970*	*Rank*
Port Arthur, Tx.	81.7	32	91.3	90.4	87.0	72
Portland, Or.	83.8	43	84.3	76.7	69.0	10
Providence, R.I.	85.8	56	85.5	77.0	72.0	18
Richmond, Va.	92.7	99	92.2	94.8	90.8	93
Roanoke, Va.	94.8	106	96.0	93.9	91.8	100
Rochester, N.Y.	85.5	55	86.9	82.4	73.8	21
Sacramento, Ca.	77.8	8	77.6	63.9	56.3	3
St. Louis, Mo.	92.6	98	92.9	90.5	89.3	83
St. Paul, Mn.	88.6	79	90.0	87.3	76.8	31
San Antonio, Tx.	79.6	14	88.3	90.1	81.8	48
San Diego, Ca.	84.4	45	83.6	81.3	71.6	16
San Francisco, Ca.	82.9	39	79.8	69.3	55.5	2
Savannah, Ga.	84.2	44	88.8	92.3	91.2	96
Seattle, Wa.	82.2	37	83.3	79.7	69.2	12
Shreveport, La.	90.3	88	93.2	95.9	97.4	109
Springfield, Oh.	80.9	29	81.6	84.7	81.1	45
Tampa, Fl.	90.2	87	92.5	94.5	90.7	92
Terre Haute, In.	86.6	62	89.8	90.1	82.5	52
Toledo, Oh.	91.0	92	91.5	91.8	86.7	67
Topeka, Ks.	80.8	24	80.7	83.5	74.1	22
Trenton, N.J.	81.9	34	83.0	79.6	77.2	33
Tulsa, Ok.	84.6	50	91.2	86.3	76.4	30
Waco, Tx.	80.1	18	87.0	90.7	86.8	69
Washington, D.C.	81.0	26	80.1	79.7	77.7	37
Wichita, Ks.	92.0	95	93.3	91.9	85.0	63
Wilmington, De.	83.0	40	86.2	79.8	69.8	13
Winston Salem, N.C.	92.9	100	93.8	95.0	94.0	108
Yonkers, N.Y.	82.0	35	81.7	78.1	68.0	9
Youngstown, Oh.	80.0	17	83.5	78.5	74.9	24

Source   Annemette Sorenson, Karl E. Taeuber, and Leslie J. Hollingsworth, Jr., "Indexes of Racial Residential Segregation for 109 Cities in the United States, 1940 to 1970," *Sociological Focus* 8 (April 1975). The columns showing ranks were calculated by Council on Municipal Performance.

some ethnic communities perform more functions than others. In other words, the extent to which ethnic and racial neighborhoods were and are communities varies with different ethnic identities and different communal functions. In the present context we will generalize about ethnic communities, recognizing that we are ignoring much variability.

The Failure of Community: Decreased Solidarity

Ethnic communities that exist in urban areas today are clearly not much like the traditionally defined communities that existed in early urban society. By and large the remnants of the ethnic communities today perform only a few of the critical communal functions we have defined.

The most important of these functions are the generation and maintenance of communal identification, normative integration, and social solidarity. These functions, once performed extensively by immigrant ethnic communities, have been diluted, abandoned, or taken over by society as a whole.

One cause of abandonment of these functions is assimilation. As members of the ethnic group move out of the enclave, they participate less in the institutions and solidarity rituals of the group. However, some ethnic identity still exists among assimilated suburban ethnics. Even in the ethnic enclaves that remain in the city, the sense of identification and solidarity based on old cultural traditions has been weakened. Many members of the community with first-hand experience of the old country have died. In addition, many

otherwise unassimilated community members have internalized much of the American working-class and lower middle-class culture and thus have a less unique culture of their own.

As the mechanically integrated immigrant society has become part of the organically integrated larger society, community ties have begun to dissolve. Even in the face of an outside threat, such as invasion by new ethnic groups or urban renewal of their neighborhood, the old ethnics have been unable to generate much social solidarity. Particularly when faced with forces that appear to be beyond their control or even beyond the control of larger political units—population movements, transportation routing, technological change, the taking of land for redevelopment—ethnic communities have been forced to give up their urban territories.[16]

The Failure of Community: Socialization, Goods, and Services

As the ability of ethnic groups to perform their primary communal functions diminished, so their ability to perform other functions declined. With the development of public schools and the emphasis given to Americanization, the ethnic community lost its control over socialization of its members. Some communities attempted to maintain private or parochial schools that taught ethnic culture in addition to the socially required curriculum. However, as upwardly mobile community members moved out, the neighborhoods lost the financial base for these schools.

Ethnic communities once were able to provide a fairly wide range of goods and services for members. Most communities produced professionals (doctors, lawyers, funeral directors, real estate agents, dentists, and the like) who took care of community needs. Unfortunately for the ethnic community, this was the first step toward social mobility for these individuals. While some professionals stayed in the enclave, the more successful ones were assimilated and migrated to the suburbs. Those who remained had a stake in maintaining the status quo and furthered the development of ethnocentrism and resistance to the in-migration of new ethnics.

Many ethnic communities at one time supplied and distributed most of the commodities needed by their members during the course of daily life. Few facilities grew large enough on ethnic business alone to compete with chain stores and supermarkets, but they were successful enough until the ethnic population began moving away or developed chain-store buying habits in response to economic pressures.

The Community and Politics

The old ethnic communities generated substantial political power when their populations were larger and more cohesive. Integration and solidarity created dependable voting blocs that helped to ensure that the voice of the community would be heard when urban decisions were made. However, ties to the political structure also served as routes to social mobility and assimilation. Members of the ethnic community were rewarded with jobs for votes produced—the practice of patronage. Pressure to produce these votes led to a wide variety of abuses: city jobs with no duties, ghost voting, multiple voting, payments to vote "properly," and the like (Cornwall, 1964:27-37). Often political jobs were the first step to occupational success and assimilation. But generally patronage simply locked the jobholder into a particular class location. The city employee was no less affected by the pervasiveness of a class culture than any other employee, and a blue-collar city job was not particularly well paying in the long run.

As the ethnic communities have weakened, they have become less dependable as political blocs, and they have had a smaller, less commanding voice in decision making. On the other hand, the new racial groups have become larger, more visible, and more vocal political blocs. As a result, they have been gaining a voice and some political rewards, in terms of goods, services, jobs, and social and political influence.

Racial Communities and Communal Functions

Newer racial groups also live in neighborhoods that fail to perform communal functions. They fail not because residents have been assimilated, but rather because they have been excluded from participation in the wider society.

The exclusion of racial minorities produces a city of distinct systems and subcommunities. The possibility of integration and assimilation existed for early immigrant groups. But this has not been true for racial minorities. The failure to integrate blacks and whites—indeed, the existing anti-integration norms and support for those norms found on both sides of the racial barrier—leads to major problems for the city. There is general normative integration on some basic American values, but the exclusion of blacks from full participation and assimilation in society leaves the city broken into heterogeneous collectivities.

The racial problems of cities today have come about as a result of two failures of community. (1) Racial minorities have not developed a communal structure on which to base social solidarity and normative integration, as did the older European ethnic communities. (2) Cities have failed to provide a communal structure on which to develop social solidarity and normative integration across racial lines.

New racial neighborhoods, particularly black neighborhoods, have never really had a sense of community like the one that old ethnics had and lost. The traditions brought to the city by the black population were the traditions of postslavery rural America. Blacks have only recently begun to develop a sense of identity. American slavery lasted 250 years—longer than the French colonial empire lasted in Algeria or the British empire in Kenya. The pervasiveness of American racism has produced feelings of black cultural inferiority and white cultural superiority, making it difficult for blacks to generate their own valid and valued culture. Even today, blacks are torn between the desire to participate in the wider society and the desire to develop a unique community and identity. This conflict makes it even more difficult for them to develop communal institutions and to function as a community.

Members of old ethnic communities in the areas that the blacks have invaded still own apartment buildings, stores, and warehouses in the old communities and still dominate local political groups. They continue to provide goods and services, and in so doing they compete with and partially prevent the development of comparable black institutions and functions. These factors, combined with racial hostility toward them and the heterogeneity of their own population, have made the creation of community among blacks difficult.

The rate of black population growth has been so great that attempts to establish local or neighborhood communal institutions have been frustrated from the start. Public agencies, such as public aid and welfare, that developed during the depression, obviated the need of the black community to develop such institutions of its own. By appearing to make local community organizations unnecessary, public agencies have contributed to the difficulty of developing communal functions in the black community.

The segregation imposed on the black community has produced a heterogeneous population that by and large is considered by the wider society to be homogeneous. Segregation helps ensure normative differences will be expected whenever blacks come into contact with whites. These differences are expected to be so great and so critical that organic interaction cannot develop. The heterogeneity of the black population at the same time prevents it from developing a unified community with its own social solidarity and normative integration.

Other communal functions are also virtually impossible for the black community. Partially because of the level of poverty that characterizes many black areas, black institutions that can provide goods and services have not been developed. Nor have they been developed in those areas that are not very poor. Institutions, stores, warehouses, and manufacturing facilities are controlled by whites who had previously occupied the areas. They still fear that black participation in ownership will result in black control, especially in the area of politics. Therefore, black control of institutions in black areas is still denied and remains a dream that is yet to be realized.

Summary

Old ethnic groups and new racial groups in cities have come into violent conflict repeatedly in the twentieth century because they do not share common norms and are not participating equally in a single communal system. Race riots occurred in Detroit as early as 1942, and in 1919 there were race riots in twenty-six U.S. cities. During the 1960s and 1970s violence became even more pervasive, fifty-nine riots occurring between 1964 and August 1967, and hundreds more taking place in 1968 and later (Marden and Meyer, 1968:339; Baskin, 1972).

The remnants of old ethnic neighborhoods and the new racial ghettos are at best partial communities, unable to carry out many functions adequately. The failure of community in the city has serious implications for the way the city functions. Here we will discuss only those failures of community related to racial and ethnic interaction, hostility, and conflict.

The city, indeed the entire society, has been divided by race. It may be possible for blacks and whites to live out their entire lives with only minimal contact with each other. The Kerner Commission pointed out that our nation is moving toward two societies, one black, one white, separate and unequal (National Advisory Commission on Civil Disorders, 1968:1).

Our divided society rests partially on ethnocentrism, partially on racism (both individual and institutional), and partially on lack of contact between members of the two races, who do not know what behavior to expect from members of the other race. Consequently, the ecological and economic processes of the society are turning central cities black and suburbs white. Hostility and conflict accompany this transition, especially when central cities and suburbs must cooperate if they are to carry out their essential communal functions, such as schooling, housing, transportation, health, safety, and social control.[17]

It is more expensive to live in the suburbs than to live in the city. Housing and other goods and services are more expensive there. Therefore, only the relatively affluent will be able to migrate when the more central suburbs age and become less desirable and thus available to persons of lower economic status. Segregation will continue to prevent nonwhites from moving to the suburbs, with the possible exception of the older, industrial suburbs (see chapters 5 and 7).

The black population, if not the black institutions, will occupy more and more of the central city. Evidence of this can already be seen in the racial composition of cities and suburbs. Even the casual visitor to most central cities will quickly see that a large proportion of the shoppers and workers are black.

One reason for this is that black neighborhoods are only partial communities and do not provide all the goods and services needed by their residents. A single neighborhood is unable to support a full range of stores, forcing residents of black neighborhoods, more than any other urban dwellers, to use the central business district as their local shopping center. The convergence of transportation facilities in the central city and the availability of jobs there gives stores in the downtown area a large population to draw on.

As more affluent white urban residents move to the suburbs and transfer their shopping and entertainment loyalties and business there, the sales volume in the central business district declines. To compensate, stores in the central business districts begin to cater to black tastes and carry black-oriented merchandise. Movies and other entertainment facilities do the same. This draws a larger black population downtown, and often drives the local neighborhood stores out of business. This also reinforces the movement of whites to suburban facilities. The visible attributes of downtown shopping, office, and entertainment facilities begin to change. Theaters in the downtown areas find that they can attract large audiences only when they feature black films and plays. White residents who do not know what kind of behavior to expect from the blacks on the streets are afraid to shop among so many blacks and begin to avoid the downtown area after dark. Thus begins a vicious cycle that leads to increasing black and decreasing white utilization of central city

theaters, stores, and other facilities. The problem is a serious one for the city, because people have invested heavily in museums, theaters, and stores in the central business district. These facilities are now located in an area patronized by a population that has not been socialized to make heavy use of these facilities.

The economic and political elites of the city have invested too much there to abandon it. But the one-man, one-vote decisions of the courts, combined with the growing black population in the central city, has naturally led to demands for black political and economic control. As the suburban population begins to match in size that of the city, tensions in the realm of politics become particularly strong. Black control will be hollow if population changes leave the cities bankrupt and powerless. For example, Gary, Newark, and other cities that have elected black mayors have found only that the problems do not change. The white population will alter political boundaries as long as possible to maintain control over the black neighborhoods. When black leaders recognize these tactics for what they are, they will legitimately cry "foul." The older ethnics, fearful that black political leaders will ignore their needs even more than they have already been ignored, will respond to changes with violence and move as quickly as possible out of the city.

Racial and ethnic neighborhoods in cities today do not perform the functions expected of communities. Because they have performed better in the past and because all our traditions lead us to expect such performance, we resist the awareness that neighborhoods cannot do the job. We fight to maintain our illusions and thereby resist change in the neighborhoods and in even the central city. Our resistance takes the form of violent protests, abandonment, and political contests. For these reasons, racial tensions, hostility, and conflict are rife in the cities today. The current problems will be alleviated only when cities develop an overarching sense of normative integration and social solidarity that includes all ethnic and racial groups.

Glossary

assimilation   the merging of groups or individuals of one culture into a host society or culture; also the process of learning the norms and values of the culture into which one is moving

black belt   a somewhat archaic term, now used to describe the areas in northern cities into which black migrants from the southern United States moved

blockbusting   a technique used by real estate agents to accelerate the sale of houses by whites to blacks; the agent buys a house on an all-white block, resells it to a black family, and then tries to frighten other white residents into selling at low prices by telling them that blacks are moving onto the block

consciousness of kind   a conscious recognition that one shares attitudes, behavior patterns, and values with other people; the basis for ethnic identification and greater ease in establishing primary relationships

enclaves   areas of a city in which a single type of person or an ethnic group resides, or in which a single type of land use is dominant

ethnic group   a group with a common cultural tradition, generally based on national origin or race; a consciousness of kind

ethnic identity   defining oneself as a member of an ethnic group on the basis of self-perception and socially defined characteristics

ethnocentrism   looking on members of one's own ethnic group as inherently superior to all members of all other ethnic groups

Federal Housing Administration (FHA)   a federal agency that offers mortgage guarantees to builders and lenders so that potential buyers may purchase a home with an extremely small down payment

ghetto   an area of a city occupied exclusively by members of a single ethnic group; currently, the term connotes conditions of poverty, unemployment, and substandard housing

intermarriage   the marriage of two persons from different ethnic or racial groups

mobility   movement from one place to another; social mobility is movement within the socioeconomic hierarchy; geographic mobility is residential mobility

nationality group   a group that has migrated from one country to another, but whose group identification is based on the country of origin

new ethnics   ethnic groups that have recently migrated to the United States or to northern metropolitan cities; new ethnics are mainly blacks and Latinos

old ethnics   ethnic groups, mainly European, that migrated to the United States in the late nineteenth and early twentieth century, or earlier

redlining   the practice by lending institutions of drawing a line around areas of a city (usually in red ink) and refusing to grant home mortgages or improvement loans for dwellings within the area, regardless of the credit rating of the person who requests the loan; leads to the decay of the area, as it becomes virtually impossible for new residents to purchase homes or for existing residents to renovate or make major improvements

restrictive covenants   agreements, generally private but often legal, between buyers and sellers that prevented the sale of a house to members of specified groups, usually Jews or blacks

segregated   forced to live in specific areas or to use specific facilities on the basis of group characteristics

Veterans Administration (VA)   a federal agency that offers low-cost home loans to ex-service personnel

white flight   a phrase used to describe the migration of whites from one city area to another area or from the central city to the suburbs; connotes migration that involves large numbers of the white residents and takes place over a short period of time; a phenomenon that probably doesn't exist

---

References

Banfield, Edward C., and Wilson, James Q., eds.
1963   *City Politics.* New York: Random House, Inc.

Baskin, Jane A., et al.
1972   *The Long Hot Summer: An Analysis of Summer Disorders, 1967-1971.* Waltham, Mass.: Lemberg Center for the Study of Violence, Brandeis University.

Blauner, Robert
1969   "Internal Colonialism and the Ghetto Revolt." *Social Problems* 16, 4:393-408.

Boskin, Joseph
1969   *Urban Racial Violence in the Twentieth Century.* Encino, Calif.: Glencoe Press.

Bradburn, Norman M.; Sudman, Seymour; and Gockel, Galen
1970   *Racial Integration in American Neighborhoods.* Chicago: National Opinion Research Center.

Cornwall, Elmer E., Jr.
1964   "Bosses, Machines, and Ethnic Groups." *Annals* 353 (May):27-39.

Council on Municipal Performance
1974   "Housing Segregation: 109 Cities." *Municipal Performance Reports* 1, 5:32-35.

Dahl, Robert A.
1961   *Who Governs?* New Haven: Yale University Press.

Drake, St. Clair, and Clayton, Horace R.
1962   *Black Metropolis: A Study of Negro Life in a Northern City.* Rev. ed. New York: Harper & Row.

Erbe, Brigitte Mach
1975   "Race and Socioeconomic Segregation." *American Sociological Review* 40 (December):801-12.

Feinstein, Otto, ed.
1971   *Ethnic Groups in the City.* Lexington, Mass.: D.C. Heath & Company.

Fellows, Donald Keith
1972   *A Mosaic of America's Ethnic Minorities.* New York: John Wiley & Sons, Inc.

Fishman, Joshua A.
1961   "Some Social and Psychological Determinants of Intergroup Relations in Changing Neighborhoods." *Social Forces* 40, 1 (October):42-51.

Gans, Herbert J.
1951   "Park Forest: Birth of a Jewish Community." *Commentary* 2:330-39.
1962   *The Urban Villagers.* New York: Free Press.

Gitlin, Todd, and Hollander, Nanci
1970   *Uptown: Poor Whites in Chicago.* New York: Harper & Row.

Glazer, Nathan
1954   "Ethnic Groups in America: From National Culture to Ideology." In *Freedom and Control in Modern Society,* edited by Morroe Berger et al., pp. 158-73. New York: D. Van Nostrand Company.

Glazer, Nathan, and Moynihan, Daniel P.
1970   *Beyond the Melting Pot.* 2d ed. Cambridge, Mass.: M.I.T. Press.

Gordon, Milton
1964   *Assimilation in American Life.* New York: Oxford University Press.

Grimshaw, Allen D.
1960   "Urban Racial Violence in the United States: Changing Ecological Considerations." *American Journal of Sociology* 66 (September):109-19.

Grodzins, Morton
1970   *The Metropolitan Area as a Racial Problem.* Pittsburgh: University of Pittsburgh Press, 1958. In *Neighborhood, City, and Metropolis,* edited by Robert Gutman and David Popenoe, pp. 479-501. New York: Random House, Inc.

Guest, Avery M., and Zuiches, James J.
1971   "Another Look at Residential Turnover in Urban Neighborhoods." *American Journal of Sociology* 77, 3 (November):457-67.

Handlin, Oscar
1961   "Historical Perspectives on the American Ethnic Group." *Daedalus* 90, 2 (Spring):220-32.

Hunter, Albert
1975   "The Loss of Community: An Empirical Test Through Replication." *American Sociological Review* 40, 5 (October):537-52.

Kramer, Judith
1970   *The American Minority Community.* New York: Thomas Y. Crowell Co., Inc.

Krickus, Richard J.
1970   "White Ethnic Neighborhoods—Ripe for the Bulldozer?" *Middle America Pamphlet Series.* New York: American Jewish Committee.

Laurenti, Luigi
1960   *Property Values and Race.* Los Angeles: University of California Press.

Lieberson, Stanley
1962   "Suburbs and Ethnic Residential Patterns." *American Journal of Sociology* 67:673-81.
1963   *Ethnic Patterns in American Cities.* New York: Free Press.

Lieberson, Stanley, and Silverman, Arnold R.
1965   "The Precipitants and Underlying Conditions of Race Riots." *American Sociological Review* 30 (December):887-98.

Lopata, Helena Znaniecki
1964   "The Functions of Voluntary Associations in an Ethnic Community: 'Polonia.' " In *Contributions to Urban Sociology,* edited by Ernest W. Burgess and Donald J. Bogue, pp. 203-23. Chicago: University of Chicago Press.

McAllister, Ronald J., et al.
1971   "Residential Mobility of Blacks and Whites: A National Longitudinal Survey." *American Journal of Sociology* 77, 3 (November):445-56.

McEntire, David
1960   "The Housing Market in Racially Mixed Areas." In *Residence and Race,* edited by David McEntire, pp. 157-71. Berkeley: University of California Press.

McKelvey, Blake
1963   *The Urbanization of America, 1860-1915.* New Brunswick, N.J.: Rutgers University Press.

Mack, Raymond W.
1968   *Race, Class, and Power.* New York: D. Van Nostrand Company.

Marden, Charles F., and Meyer, Gladys
1968   *Minorities in American Society.* New York: D. Van Nostrand Company.

Moltoch, Harvey
1969   "Racial Change in a Stable Community." *American Journal of Sociology* 75, 2 (September):226-37.

National Advisory Commission on Civil Disorders (Kerner Commission).
1968   *Report of the National Advisory Commission on Civil Disorders.* New York: Bantam Books, Inc.

Novak, Michael
1971   "White Ethnic." *Harper's* (September).

O'Connor, Edwin
1956   *The Last Hurrah.* Boston: Little, Brown and Company.

Parenti, Michael
1967   "Ethnic Politics and the Persistence of Ethnic Identification." *American Political Science Review* 61, 3:717-26.

Ringer, Benjamin B.
1972   "Jewish-Gentile Relations in Lakeville." In *North American Suburbs,* edited by John Kramer, pp. 174-84. San Francisco: Boyd & Fraser Publishing Company.

Rose, Arnold, and Rose, Caroline B., eds.
1965   *Minority Problems.* 2d ed. New York: Harper & Row.

Schnore, Leo F.
1972   *Class and Race in Cities and Suburbs.* Chicago: Markham Publishing Co.

Severo, Richard
1972   "New York's Italians: A Question of Identity." *New York Times,* 8 November 1970. In *Minority Problems,* edited by Arnold Rose and Caroline B. Rose, pp. 70-75. 2d ed. New York: Harper & Row.

Suttles, Gerald
1968   *The Social Order of the Slum.* Chicago: University of Chicago Press.

Szymanski, Albert
1976   "Racial Discrimination and White Gain." *American Sociological Review* 41 (June):403-14.

Taeuber, Irene B., and Taeuber, Conrad
1971 *The People of the United States in the Twentieth Century* (Census Monograph). Washington, D.C.: Government Printing Office.

Taeuber, Karl E.
1964 "Negro Residential Segregation: Trends and Measurement." *Social Problems* 12:42-50.

U.S. Bureau of the Census
1972 *Census of Population, 1970: General Social and Economic Characteristics, Final Report PC(1)-C1, United States Summary.* Washington, D.C.: Government Printing Office.
1974 *Statistical Abstract of the United States: 1974.* Washington, D.C.: Government Printing Office.
1975 *Statistical Abstract of the United States: 1975.* Washington, D.C.: Government Printing Office.

Vander Zanden, James W.
1966 *American Minority Relations.* New York: Ronald Press.

Weber, Max
1961 "Ethnic Groups." In *Theories of Society,* edited by Talcott Parsons et al., pp. 305-9. New York: Free Press.

Whyte, William F.
1943 *Street Corner Society.* Chicago: University of Chicago Press.

Williams, Robin M.
1964 "Ethnocentrism." In *Strangers Next Door: Ethnic Relations in American Communities,* edited by Robin M. Williams, pp. 17-29. Englewood Cliffs, N.J.: Prentice-Hall, Inc.

Wilson, James Q.
1968 "The Urban Unease: Community vs. the City." *The Public Interest* 12 (Summer):25-39.

Wirth, Louis
1964 "The Ghetto." In *Louis Wirth on Cities and Social Life,* edited by Albert J. Reiss, Jr., pp. 84-98. Chicago: University of Chicago Press.

Yin, Robert K., ed.
1972 *The City in the Seventies.* Itasca, Ill.: F. E. Peacock Publishers, Inc.

Yinger, Milton J.
1961 "Social Forces Involved in Group Identification or Withdrawal." *Daedalus* 90, 2 (Spring):247-63.

Suggested Readings

Glazer, Nathan, and Moynihan, Daniel P. *Beyond the Melting Pot.* 2d ed. Cambridge, Mass.: M.I.T. Press, 1970. The classic study of ethnic groups (Negroes, Puerto Ricans, Jews, Italians, and Irish) in New York City. The patterns found in New York also generally describe these groups in other cities.

Kramer, Judith. The American Minority Community. New York: Crowell, 1970. An excellent study of ethnic communities and the effects of changing communal attachments on members of ethnic groups.

Myrdal, Gunnar. *An American Dilemma.* Rev. ed. New York: Harper & Row, 1962. The classic study of American society's treatment of blacks. Describes the pattern of race relations up to the middle of the twentieth century.

National Advisory Commission on Civil Disorders (Otto Kerner, chairman). *Report of the National Advisory Commission on Civil Disorders.* Washington, D.C.: Government Printing Office, 1968. (Also published by Bantam Books, Inc.) The report of the Kerner Commission on urban race relations in the mid-1960s is essential in the study of riots and subsequent developments in the black power movement. Additional data are available in a volume of *Supplemental Studies* (Washington, D.C.: Government Printing Office, 1968).

Novak, Michael. *The Rise of the Unmeltable Ethnics: Politics and Culture in the Seventies.* New York: Macmillan, 1972. An analysis of the old ethnics following the rise of the black power movement and the demise of the melting-pot model of racial and ethnic relations.

Notes

1. See chapter 7 for data on the population growth of cities. More detailed information on migration patterns is available in Taeuber and Taeuber, 1971:53-84, 117-28.
2. See, for example, the discussions of Irish-Italian conflict in Glazer and Moynihan, 1970:181-274. See also Whyte, 1942, and Gans, 1962.
3. This pattern is typical not only of blacks but also of rural whites. See, for example, Gitlin and Hollander, 1970.

4. In each decade during this time, two million or more immigrants arrived. Between 1901 and 1910, 8.8 million immigrants were admitted to the United States (U.S. Bureau of the Census, 1975:99).
5. Gordon discusses this in *Assimilation in American Life* and provides a number of theoretical models for understanding the process. The following discussion draws heavily on his work.
6. In Gordon's framework this is equivalent to saying that different ethnic groups have reached different stages in the assimilation process. See Gordon, 1964:71, for a chart of different stages.
7. Erbe (1975:801-12) describes a high level of socioeconomic segregation among the white population. This finding suggests that socioeconomic success is associated with moving away from the city. See also the discussions of suburbs in chapters 5 and 6.
8. Erbe (1975) demonstrates that the level of spatial segregation by socioeconomic status is lower among blacks than among whites.
9. Wilson, 1968:25-39. When members of a community are able to treat outsiders in a typically urban fashion, that is, "You mind your business and I'll mind mine," insiders and outsiders can coexist (see Gans, 1962). But when this is not possible, conflict and tension are generated (see Suttles, 1968).
10. See Krickus, 1970. The advances of the new ethnics are perceived as costs by the old ethnics, regardless of empirical evidence to the contrary. For example, see Szymanski, 1976. Nevertheless, the belief persists that discrimination aids whites.
11. This is not to say that racial segregation causes all or even most urban problems. However, it is associated with problems of crime, poverty, transportation, education, and politics. Segregation per se may be at the root of some of these, but it is clearly a major problem in its own right.
12. The near simultaneity of these movements has caused other problems, such as a decline in the real estate taxes needed to pay for urban facilities and services.
13. Calculated from data in Taeuber and Taeuber (1971) and the statistical abstract for 1974 (U.S. Bureau of the Census).
14. The 1900 data is from Taeuber and Taeuber (1971); the 1970 data is from U.S. Bureau of the Census (1974:tables 20 and 30).
15. Calculated from U.S. Bureau of the Census's statistical abstracts for 1974 (section 34).
16. For example, the Italian and Greek communities in Chicago were displaced by the construction of the University of Illinois Chicago Circle campus.
17. Riots, conflicts in schools, and interpersonal tensions in interracial contacts are seen as by-products of this transition. Poverty, unmet expectations, various deprivations, and individual pathology are all possible explanations. Our view is that much observable tension and conflict can be understood as the consequence of trying to determine whose "turf" the central city is. Old ethnics, the urban business elites, and whites in general are being displaced, not only from their residential neighborhoods, but also from the central city.

10 Urban Politics

City governments have a major share of the responsibility for the performance of almost all communal functions. They perform many functions directly and facilitate the performance of many others. Cities create agencies such as schools, police and fire departments, and sanitation departments. In addition, they regulate private agencies and establish laws that reflect social norms as city legislators and administrators see them.

To understand how urban communal functions are performed, it is necessary to realize that city governments are political entities. The political process by which cities make decisions may not be any different from the processes by which any organization makes decisions. There may be nothing distinctly urban about urban politics. But this does not make it any less important to study political processes in urban settings.

Political Structure and Process

In this chapter we will examine the political processes by which city governments arrive at those laws and regulations they will enact that will reflect the norms of the population. We will adopt two major perspectives (that may not be exhaustive or mutually exclusive) to gain a fairly comprehensive image of urban politics. From one perspective we will view the structure of politics and the distribution of power and influence. A second perspective will help us examine the process of obtaining and using political power and influence. Definitions of both power and influence will be developed.

The Structural Perspective

The structural perspective focuses on the existence and nature of a power elite—a very small group of politically influential persons in the city who are assumed to behave uniformly in political matters, come from the same social class position, and interact with each other. This perspective is exemplified in such works as the *Middletown* studies (Lynd and Lynd, 1929:413-34; 1937:74-101, 319-72), *Who Governs?* (Dahl, 1961), *The Power Elite* (Mills, 1959), *Community Power Structure* (Hunter, 1953), and (although it is only partially structural) *Political Influence* (Banfield, 1961). These and similar studies look for structural explanations, such as class or occupational position, for membership in a power elite or one of several power elites. The structural perspective is less concerned with the actual behavior of the elite than with their existence.

One variant on the structural perspective considers the effects of formal governmental practices on politics and government. Studies that adopt this perspective examine such factors as the **partisanship** of elections, the practice of holding local elections in nonpresidential election years, the differences between mayoral and city manager types of government, and urban-suburban political patterns. Another structural variant deals with the relationship between urban political structures and a city's demographic and social characteristics. A third variant on the structural perspective examines the formal properties and sources of power and influence that affect decision making. Although generally formal and theoretical, analyses that characterize this variant provide the basis for relating structure to process in political activities.

The Process Perspective

The process perspective, like the structural perspective, has a number of variants. Of common concern is decision making—how city governments reach and implement decisions. The process perspective focuses on how urban politics influences decision making and the involvement of various groups (ethnic, racial, citizen, official) in urban political matters. The structure of groups involved in urban politics helps us understand how decisions are made and how groups become involved. The processes of urban politics teach us how **political power** and **influence** are obtained, maintained, and used in decision making. Much of our knowledge of political processes comes not from academic studies but from journalistic accounts of politicians and political activities (Edwin O'Connor, 1956; Royko, 1971; Len O'Connor, 1975).

The structural perspective is mainly sociological; the process perspective stems from political science. By combining the two perspectives with journalistic accounts of political activity, we will develop a model of political power and influence that is essentially sociological, but is process-oriented. The characteristics of urban political power and influence and their use in the political process will help us understand daily urban politics.

Thinking about Political Power

Power can be defined in at least three ways: (1) from the point of view of the individual; (2) from the point of view of two individuals; and (3) as a social system (Clark, 1968: 48-81).

Individual power is simply the ability to achieve one's own goals. Other persons, their goals and relationships to the person with power, are irrelevant. The individualistic definition of power deals with the probability that a person in a social relationship will be able to fulfill his or her own desires regardless of resistance from other persons (Weber, 1947: 152). Such theories are not concerned with why the powerful person is likely to succeed.

The two-person concept defines power as a relationship between two individuals, one of whom is able to change an action, a belief, or some other characteristic of the other individual. Robert Dahl (1967:202-3) summarizes this conception as follows: "A has power over B to the extent that [A] can get B to do something B would not otherwise do." An extension of this definition makes it possible to differentiate power and influence. If person A does something so that person B changes an attitude, action, or belief, person A has influence over person B. If person A has the *capability* of influencing person B, person A has power over person B. Thus, power is *potential influence;* influence is the *utilization of power* to bring about actual change (Cartwright, 1959; 1965:4).

In a social system *power* can be defined as the potential ability of a person or a group of persons to select, to change, and to attain the goals of a social system. Influence is the actual selection of, or changing of, goals for the social system. Power is fixed in a particular social system, and it is not easily transferable among social systems (Clark, 1968:46-47). For example, Lyndon Johnson had a great deal of power as a senator and influenced many legislative decisions. He was less successful as president because his power was not easily transferable. Similarly, when a powerful member of the House of Representatives becomes a senator, it is difficult for him to take his power with him. Richard J. Daley, the late mayor of Chicago, had almost unlimited power in the city, but he was unable to obtain enough votes in the state legislature to override a governor's veto of a school-aid formula bill or to get a federal judge to release frozen revenue-sharing funds.

To analyze power and influence in a social system, we must examine the roles of individuals in that system. In many cases a person has power because of the role that is played (legislator, bank president, mayor, party leader, church leader). The analysis of power and influence focuses on the ability of the role occupant to regulate decisions by changing, altering, or otherwise controlling inputs to decisions.

Power is the potential ability to effect such changes. Therefore, power exists even when it isn't being used. Power is based on the belief of others that a person can cause change. In turn, this belief is based on the perception that a person can influence the choices, behaviors, or convictions of others. Influence is power used to bring about change in society. Influence is used when a choice must be made among alternative goals (Clark, 1968:46-47).

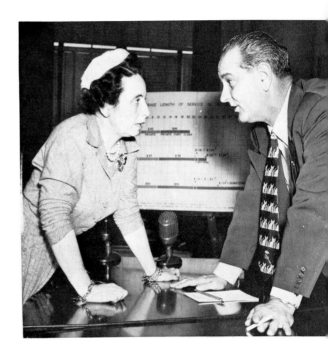

A power structure is the patterned distribution of power. The social systems perspective on power permits, but does not require, a power structure or a power elite. A structure may not exist—power may be diffused throughout the population. The study of political power structures from the social systems perspective is the study of the potential ability of persons to bring about change in a political system and of the sources of their ability. In contrast, a decision-making structure is the patterned distribution of influence, of actual alterations of decisions affecting the goals of the system.

Persons in social systems have the potential ability to change the decisions made in that system. Persons can influence the system, and even establish a stable, politically powerful role, by participating in the political process. They do this by accumulating and distributing resources that can be exchanged for changes in decisions about the goals of the social system.

The Source of Resources: Social Exchange

Exchange theory helps us understand how the accumulation and distribution of resources can generate and maintain political power (Gouldner, 1960:161-78; Blau, 1955, 1964; Homans, 1961). The theory argues that if social interaction is to continue, interacting parties must exchange something that each party values. The commodities that are exchanged can be information, knowledge, force, money, threats, flattery, deference, status, or anything else of value. Any exchange creates an imbalance that will eventually have to be balanced. If the exchange is not eventually balanced, interaction will cease when one party perceives the absence of reciprocity.

Exchanges are regulated by certain, almost universal norms. One such norm requires each person to participate in an exchange, especially when the exchange is initiated with no expectation of immediate reciprocal action. Another norm requires participants in a system to interact with other system members.

The forms and modes of **reciprocity** include returns of resources in the same medium that began the interaction; returns in a different medium of the same value; grants of deference to the person who initiated the interaction; promises of future reciprocity; and transfer of the need to reciprocate to a third participant whose exchange needs to be balanced. The first reciprocity mode is exemplified by friends who exchange dinner invitations with one another. In the second mode the exchange value of different media must be calculated—an afternoon's help in moving from one apartment to another is traded for pizza and beer. In the third mode, acknowledging the wisdom, knowledge, ability to govern, or superior ability of a colleague or a political leader, for example, may be sufficient reciprocity. A promise of returning a favor in some possibly undefined way in the future can serve as the exchange medium in the fourth mode. A vote cast now in return for the promise of another to vote as requested in the future leaves the exchange unbalanced, but the potential for restoring balance remains and is agreed on. Finally, an exchange may be reciprocated when one person agrees that another person is owed such-and-such but who has yet a third person who is in the first person's debt restore both balances. A legislator may say, ''I know I owe you a vote, but I cannot possibly vote for this bill. Another legislator owes me a vote, and I'll have him cast it for you.''

The precise balancing of reciprocal exchanges may or may not characterize all social interactions, but political life appears to be composed of interactions that are carefully reciprocated. Power is attained when a person is owed sufficient exchanges to enable that person to influence political decisions (Clark, 1968).

There are limits to the range and complexity of such exchange systems. It is difficult to calculate the exchangeability of resources. The value of what is being exchanged (money, speeches, votes, electoral endorsement, advice, deference) may not be easy to determine comparatively. The quantity of resources available in a given political system may be finite, and the persons in the system may not all agree on the nature and value of resources. When the consensus is lowest, the potential for conflict increases and disagreements result. Finally, there may be disagreement about the quantity of resources a person has available for exchange. This reduces that person's potential for obtaining favors (often votes) in the expectation that they will be returned.[1] For example, if people believe that a politician does not have the resources to fulfill campaign promises, they may be unwilling to support that candidate at election time.

Political Exchange

Mayors, legislators, other urban decision makers, and interest groups engage in exchanges to obtain support on issues, power, and influence. These exchanges are reciprocal; the media of exchange here are the commodities or resources needed to achieve systemic goals. Support on specific issues, speechmaking, political endorsements, votes, money, credit, knowledge, technical information, and alterations in laws or regulations are some of the commodities that are exchanged. These resources serve as **political capital**. Persons with large supplies of resources can maintain and use them by exchanging them with other persons, either in the expectation that they will be reciprocated or to obtain a specific goal. The urban political process can be thought of as a series of exchanges subject to the norms of the exchange process and to societal norms and values.

A skillful political leader accumulates many resources. He carefully calculates the value of the exchanges he makes with other persons in the system to maximize his return. For example, if a politician supports the position of an interest group or provides a service for that group (by closing a street for a block party, or having a street made one-way, or increasing the frequency of garbage pickups), the politician can expect support or votes from each member of the group on election day. From the point of view of the political leader, a single exchange has netted a great increase in resources (Clark, 1968). Naming a public building after an ethnic hero or constructing a new building in an ethnic neighborhood can be expected to produce votes from the members of that ethnic group. These political debts are resources that can later be converted into influence. The leader's ability to attain political goals is based on that person's capital—political resources exceeding the capital of nonleaders. The existence of this imbalance defines political power.

A supply of resources gives a leader some flexibility in following social norms. When a leader has enough resources and thus power, people close to the leader act in accordance with their perceptions of the leader's desires: city agencies give contracts to supporters of the mayor and make life difficult for opposing politicians. Post-Watergate revelations abundantly illustrate the operation of this process at the federal level. An extreme example of power and normative flexibility can be found in history. Henry II is reputed to have asked, when he was seriously provoked by Thomas a Becket, "Who will rid me of this man?" Without actually ordering Becket's death, he brought it about. He could not order Becket's death directly because the norms of the society prohibited it. He accomplished his aim by indirection and the implicit promise of an exchange.

Resources for Power

The possession of resources is the basis of power. We have not yet clearly defined the resources or commodities that are exchanged in the political process. The debts incurred in exchanges, or the perception of debts incurred, depend on the type of resources exchanged and the potential for conversion of such resources into influence. Clark (1968) suggests that the following commodities are the resources most generally used to attain and maintain political power and to influence specific decisions.[2]

1. *Money and credit.* These are perhaps the most important resources because almost all other resources can be purchased with them.

Thus money and credit can be directly converted to other resources, and their exchange value is clear. The supply of these resources, however, can be limited, and one may expend one's total supply.

2. *Control over jobs.* The ability to create jobs, to influence hiring decisions, and even to decide who among other political persons can fill available jobs is an important resource. Job control is the basis of political patronage and is critical during election campaigns. The exchange value of this resource can be readily estimated when it is exchanged with other politicians for other resources. The supply of exchangeable jobs is limited and may be controlled by outside factors, such as the condition of the national economy. Like money and credit, a politician's supply of available jobs can be totally expended.

3. *Control of the mass media (newspapers, television, and radio).* This resource allows the political leader to influence the attitudes and behaviors of the general public and other decision makers. Being selective about information that is released and favoring those media that cast the political leader in a favorable light minimize unfavorable publicity and potentially alter the positions taken by some institutions or groups. In an election campaign, control over the mass media gives a politician access to large voting blocs. Incumbent politicians can get more favorable attention from the media at press conferences and on releases than can challengers, especially in large, modern, industrial societies.

Estimating a political leader's holdings of mass media resources is difficult, as is estimating their exchange value. Control over the media can be converted to other resources, but quantities are exceedingly difficult to measure. Unlike money or credit and control over jobs, it may not be possible for a person to use up all of one's supply of this resource because the number of times one can obtain favorable publicity may be unlimited.

4. *High social status, popularity, other valued personal characteristics.* These attributes are political resources because many people look up to those who possess them. The endorsement of a position (or a person in an election campaign) by someone who is looked up to by many other people may translate into additional votes and other forms of support. The exchange value of this resource is difficult to calculate, but a political figure of high status cannot exhaust this characteristic. The value of endorsements by people with high social status or charisma may be eroded by overuse but never totally expended.

5. *Knowledge and specialized technical skills.* These are important resources when complex decisions must be made. Especially in large urban areas, where more specialized knowledge and technical skills are available, more decisions will be made on the basis of these resources. Knowledge and skills lend credence to a position or to one's choice of goal and thus increase the probability of its being implemented. As cities have become larger and more complex, election campaigns have become correspondingly complex. Political campaigns in metropolitan areas today depend less on personal contact and more on specialized skills and mechanical aids, such as telephone banks, computerized mailing lists, advertising, and the mass media. Access to these resources is important for political power.

Specialized knowledge and skills are available only from professionals from whom one can purchase these services. Thus the availability of these resources depends on the availability of money and credit and on the politician's willingness to spend for this purpose.

6. *Legal knowledge.* The ability to define, or to control the definition of, behaviors as legal or illegal is an important political resource. Legal means may be used to force political opponents off the ballot or stave off their challenges and to attack a politician's control of other resources. A federal court decision recently handed down in Chicago attacked the use of jobs as a power resource. Civil service workers must now be informed that they need not engage in political activities to keep their jobs.

7. *Subsystem solidarity.* When a group is highly integrated and has shared interests and responsibilities, the decisions of the leader are likely to be followed by all group members. Members of such subsystems will be willing to work hard for a position on an issue or a candidate endorsed by their leader. The subsystem may be a political party, a group of legislators, or a community organization. The backing of a subsystem that is high in solidarity is a political resource.

8. *The vote.* Control over the vote is the ultimate source of political power. When politicians believe that a particular individual has the ability to influence large numbers of voters, that person attains power. (This accounts for the value of personal attributes as power resources.) In this way community and ethnic leaders who control the votes of large blocs of followers become politically power-ful. It is this resource that gives local community organizations and their leaders influence over the decisions of public bodies.

9. *Access to community leaders.* The more access that community leaders have to each other and to political decision makers, the greater their ability to engage in political exchanges and thus to influence decisions or to use their resources. Access to other leaders is a power resource in itself. Leaders use such power to generate support for decisions they want to see implemented.

10. *Control of organizations.* This resource is related to control of jobs and subsystem solidarity, but it can be applied to independent groups, such as some liberal clubs in New York, the Independent Voters of Illinois, and the League of Women Voters. These organizations help a leader align mass support for a particular decision. During crucial election campaigns members of these organizations also help get out the vote and personally contact a large number of people.

11. *Control and interpretation of values.* Because political decisions must be made in keeping with societal values at both the local and national level, the control over interpretation of societal values is an important power resource. The Supreme Court, for example, interprets American law and thereby influences critical values throughout society.

None of these eleven resources is physically visible; it is difficult indeed to determine how many resources, or how much of each resource, a political figure has. In large measure an individual's power is determined by other people's perceptions of that individual's resources. Only by observing the uses of power can we make inferences about

The vote—and, therefore, control over it—is the ultimate source of political power.

the extent of a person's resources. Observation alone, however, is an inadequate gauge, as an individual may not use all available resources in a given situation. Thus, being perceived as a person with many resources may generate as much power as actually having those resources.

The Analysis of Urban Political Power

Power resources create and maintain political power and further political activity. Until the late 1940s, resources were most effectively accumulated and used by **political machines** and their bosses in large urban areas. Since the early 1950s, reformers have learned to accumulate resources and have successfully challenged the political machines in many cities. The use of power resources by reformers, better government groups, and emerging minorities, combined with alterations in the demographic structure of society and the increasing influence of state and federal governments on city politics, has altered the character of urban political systems (Harrigan, 1976:93-96).

Machines, Resources, and Political Power

The growth of immigrant populations in major cities was important in the development of political machines (Cornwall, 1964:27-39; Dahl, 1961:11-51). As immigrant populations grew large enough to offer significant voting support, they also became aware that they were entitled to a share of the jobs and services provided by the city and a voice in the administration of these services. At the same time cities began to provide more services, such as fire and police protection, social welfare assistance, and garbage collection. Politics rapidly became important in determining who provided these services and who received them. Jobs, welfare payments, Christmas and Thanksgiving baskets, and other favors or city services could be exchanged by members of the political party (or arranged for through city jobholders whose employment depended on doing such favors) for votes, election work, and the like. Political leaders could give lucrative contracts and franchises in return for election support, financial aid, control over jobs, and other resources as needed (Harrigan, 1976:49-90; Banfield and Wilson, 1963:chap. 9; Plunkett, 1967:266-72; Cornwall, 1964:27-39). Political parties could thus establish a large capital of resources that could be called on at election time to return the party and its leaders to office. The resources became virtually self-sustaining so long as no individual or group came along that was more talented in developing the resources.

Large immigrant populations were important to the development of political machines because they were not socialized to the norms of the society or the city. They often needed assistance from official agencies to obtain education, jobs, housing, welfare, and other necessities of life. Dealing with these official agencies led immigrants to identify the services with the politicians who provided them. When members of the ethnic-immigrant group were slated for political office, the identification became even stronger.

Faced with the need to vote—generally a new phenomenon—the immigrants voted for those who were either members of the group or politicians whose agencies had helped them. Intensive precinct work increased the machine's ability to control large numbers of votes. Thus political machines flourished, especially in large cities.

As the number and the voting potential of immigrants grew, many persons of higher status who had dominated politics began to withdraw. Disdaining competition for popularity and certain to lose, the groups that Dahl calls patricians and entrepreneurs departed from the urban political arena, leaving it to immigrants and their representatives in the political machine (Dahl, 1961).

Not all exchanges engaged in by machines and their representatives were as benevolent or as legal as those we have been describing. Graft, corruption, vote stealing, repeat voting, and voting in the names of dead or absent persons also helped keep political machines in power.[3] When these practices became too widespread and city populations became more sophisticated about their rights to obtain city services without contributing money, political work, or votes to politicians, the power or urban political machines began to decline.

With increasing regulation of city politics by state and federal governments came further reforms, and the power of political machines continued to diminish, although the machines did not totally disappear.[4] Interest in urban politics shifted to political decision makers in both the public and private sectors and to how their decisions were made. Both of these focuses employ, at least implicitly, the concept of resources as it has been developed in this chapter.

Who Makes Decisions? Power Structures and Power Elites

The social and economic positions of urban decision makers have been the subject of numerous studies, many of which assume that a power structure exists and that it consists largely of persons in specific, politically powerful social categories, such as bank presidents and corporation executives. The occupational and social positions of these persons supposedly provide them with the resources that generate their power and involve them in decision making. This approach also assumes that persons in these social categories behave similarly and that they all are maintaining or increasing their social advantage at the expense of the community, at least in their spheres of influence (Fisher, 1969:85-98).

Classic studies such as *Middletown in Transition* (Lynd and Lynd, 1937) and *The Power Elite* (Mills, 1959) have made these assumptions about persons in certain economic positions. Persons in positions of economic dominance in a community or nation were assumed to have influence in all kinds of decisions. The structural approach to analysis of urban politics assumes that position alone determines resources and power. All one needs to know to identify powerful persons is the socioeconomic structure of the city. A variant on this structural approach maintains that the reputation an individual possesses for having used power resources in the past determines membership in the urban **power elite** or power structure.

Plunkitt of Tammany Hall

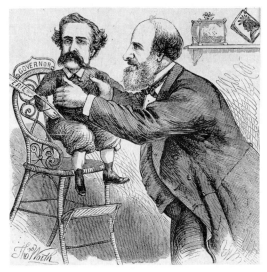

ONCE MORE

GRAND SACHEM. "There, my little man, you shall sit in your high chair once more, if you are a good boy, and mind me as you always have done. What will you have to play with? Your Stuffed Ballot Box or your Tammany Catechism?"

"**N**ow, I've told you what not to do; I guess I can explain best what to do to succeed in politics by tellin' you what I did. After goin' through the apprenticeship of the business while I was a boy by workin' around the district headquarters and hustlin' about the polls on election day, I set out when I cast my first vote to win fame and money in New York city politics. Did I offer my services to the district leader as a stump speaker? Not much. The woods are always full of speakers. Did I get up a book on municipal government and show it to the leader? I wasn't such a fool. What I did was to get some marketable goods before goin' to the leaders. What do I mean by marketable goods? Let me tell you: I had a cousin, a young man who didn't take any particular interest in politics. I went to him and said: 'Tommy, I'm goin' to be a politician, and I want to get a followin'; can I count on you?' He said: 'Sure, George.' That's how I started in business. I got a marketable commodity—one vote. Then I went to the district leader and told him I could command two votes on election day, Tommy's and my own. He smiled on me and told me to go ahead. If I had offered him a speech or a bookful of learnin', he would have said, 'Oh, forget it!'

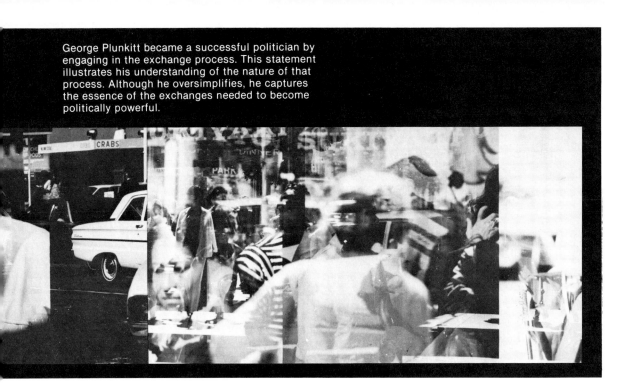

George Plunkitt became a successful politician by engaging in the exchange process. This statement illustrates his understanding of the nature of that process. Although he oversimplifies, he captures the essence of the exchanges needed to become politically powerful.

"That was beginnin' business in a small way, wasn't it? But that is the only way to become a real lastin' statesman. I soon branched out. Two young men in the flat next to mine were school friends. I went to them, just as I went to Tommy, and they agreed to stand by me. Then I had a followin' of three voters and I began to get a bit chesty. Whenever I dropped into district headquarters, everybody shook hands with me, and the leader one day honored me by lightin' a match for my cigar. And so it went on like a snowball rollin' down a hill. I worked the flat-house that I lived in from the basement to the top floor, and I got about a dozen young men to follow me. Then I tackled the next house and so on down the block and around the corner. Before long I had sixty men back of me, and formed the George Washington Plunkitt Association.

"What did the district leader say when I called at headquarters? I didn't have to call at headquarters. He came after me and said: 'George, what do you want? If you don't see what you want, ask for it. Wouldn't you like to have a job or two in the departments for your friends?' I said:

'I'll think it over; I haven't yet decided what the George Washington Plunkitt Association will do in the next campaign.' You ought to have seen how I was courted and petted then by the leaders of the rival organizations. I had marketable goods and there was bids for them from all sides, and I was a risin' man in politics. As time went on, and my association grew, I thought I would like to go to the Assembly. I just had to hint at what I wanted, and three different organizations offered me the nomination. Afterwards, I went to the Board of Aldermen, then to the State Senate, then became leader of the district, and so on up and up till I became a statesman.

Source From *Plunkitt of Tammany Hall* by William L. Riordan. Published by E. P. Dutton and reprinted with their permission.

This variant of the structural approach has been popular since the 1950s because it gives rise to testable hypotheses about who has power. The best known study is Floyd Hunter's *Community Power Structure* (1953), an investigation of the politics of charitable organizations in Atlanta during the 1950s. Hunter asked experts in different organizations who was most important when it came to getting things done in town. The study showed a high degree of consensus about the most influential persons in Atlanta. The forty most frequently nominated were taken to be the policy leaders, the power structure of the city. These people were mainly businessmen who were associated with one another, although there were cliques within the group. Hunter concluded that there was a single power elite dominated by members of the business community, although different structures prevailed, depending on the issue (Hunter, 1953; Walton, 1973).

Hunter's conclusions have affected many concepts of political power in American cities. The concepts of a local power elite and a power structure originated with this study. Similar studies have been conducted in other cities to validate or refute Hunter's conclusions.

The Decision-Making Process

In reaction to Hunter's work, some sociologists have tried to show that people from many social categories participate in urban political decision making. These studies have relied on observations of decision-making situations and analysis of social characteristics of the persons involved in the process (Dahl, 1961; Banfield, 1961). This difference in method may be one reason why conclusions about power structure differ so radically. Another explanation may be that types of persons with political power vary from city to city and from time to time.

Most decision-making studies have concluded that power in American cities is pluralistic. Different people have more or less power in different situations. The amount of power one has and uses depends on the situation and on the relationship of the person to the situation and to other participants in the situation. Different situations have different participants, so there is more than one urban structure.

Conclusion: Two Points of View

Here then are the two major trains of thought about political power in American cities. Researchers of a sociological bent—those who study people's structural positions and reputations for having power—tend to see a single urban power elite dominated by the city's economic elite. Those who view the question from a political science perspective—that is, observe decision making—tend to attribute power to different participants who exhibit different characteristics and behave differently on different issues. Evidence on community power leads to the conclusion that a power elite is less characteristic of cities of even moderate size than are groups of elites, each of which is interested in and influential in a single, restricted sphere of activity. Businessmen and lawyers whose primary activities depend on political decisions tend to be most heavily represented in these elites (Fisher, 1962; Bachrach and Baratz, 1962:947-52).

Stages in Decision-Making

Regardless of one's position, elitist or pluralist, one must recognize that power resources are used to influence decision making. Political decisions are made in several stages or steps (Clark, 1968; Munger, 1973). The first step is recognition that there is an issue to be decided. Political conflict may be prevented, or at least delayed, by preventing the recognition of issues. Consensus also prevents conflict but cannot be reached before the issue is recognized.

Recognizing an issue and bringing it to public attention requires control over the mass media, access to community leaders, and technical information. Urban political systems may have a threshold below which issues are not recognized. One may have to spend resources to generate enough political noise to bring an issue to the attention of decision makers. Political controversy is more likely in communities where more issues are brought to the attention of the public and the decision makers.

The second stage in decision making is the collection of information. Technical expertise is the crucial resource at this stage. Adequate information on available options—their consequences, implications, and costs—is vital if decision makers are to avoid unintended consequences and potential conflicts and embarrassments. Each party to the decision accumulates as much high-quality information as possible to strengthen a given position before proceeding to the next stage in the process.

The third stage is the formulation of policies. Each participant formulates a policy based on values, beliefs, desires, and information provided by the technical experts.

The fourth step is evaluation of all policies on the bases of technical information and any resources that participants may be willing to commit to obtain support for a given decision.

The fifth stage is the selection of a single policy. At this stage all participants use their resources to ensure enactment of the policy they favor. Only those resources in only those quantities deemed appropriate to the issue are used.

For example, residents of a neighborhood wish to undertake a program to ensure the continued vitality and attractiveness of their community. They invite community leaders, ward committeemen and -women, and aldermen and -women to meetings where the issue is presented. If residents hold enough meetings, write enough letters, and make enough speeches, the issue may be recognized. Other community groups then become involved. Each group collects information on various components of a renewal program. Various plans are developed: businessmen stress construction of facilities for stores and parking and favor reduced taxes; the PTA suggests additional school programs such as advanced courses and special classes in music, art, and science, and seeks a reduction in existing class sizes; minority groups oppose the removal of apartment houses that would lower population density because this would also lead to the construction of high-cost homes—a policy favored, however, by local real estate agents; block groups want one-way streets. Each group collects the best information it can to defend its plan and to highlight the shortcomings of other plans. All plans are then presented to a city urban renewal, community conservation, or other policy-making board. Each group makes promises, openly or privately, of future political support. Exchanges begin in earnest as each group marshals as many rational arguments and other resources as it can in support of its position. Allies are sought in return for promises of future support. Finally, the policy makers evaluate the alternatives and decide what to do. (They may decide to do nothing.) In some cases, decision makers will put off the question until competing groups reach consensus among themselves, but this action in itself is a form of decision making.[5]

The various resources of political power are used for different purposes at different steps in decision making. Some are more important at earlier stages, while others are more important in the later stages. Each political participant decides how much of which resources to use in each exchange. The allocation of power resources depends on how important the decision is to a participant.

One basis for assessing the importance of a particular decision is its cost in money to the social system. An alternative basis is the proportion of system resources that must be allocated for a given plan. Yet another basis is the number and social status of people and institutions that will be affected by the allocation or a change in allocation of city resources.[6]

There is no reason to assume that participants using the same modes of analysis will agree about the importance of a decision. A decision that is important to some people may be unimportant to others. Even those decisions that affect a large portion of the population may not cost much. For example, fluoridation of drinking water has been deemed important to a large proportion of many communities, but the costs are low. On the other hand, the rerouting of traffic or the building of an expressway or a shopping mall may be expensive, but it may affect a small proportion of the population and involve few city resources because the federal government supports much of the cost. The importance of a decision is thus a subjective evaluation, albeit a critical one, for it determines how deeply involved a participant becomes and how many resources that participant will commit in the decision-making process (Banfield, 1961:235-62, 324-41).

Constraints on the Use of Power

The distribution of power resources among political leaders, other participants in political processes, and the general public determines what can and cannot be done politically. If all resources were concentrated in the hands of a few (as would be the case if there were a single power elite or a political boss), the use of power would be relatively unconstrained. In contemporary society many power resources are relatively widely available. Thus a large number of groups have at least some power and can exercise at least some constraint over the use of power by political leaders (Banfield and Wilson, 1963:24-29, 243-60; Clark, 1968; Banfield, 1961:286-341). Citizen interest groups can draw attention to issues and bring about political decisions. The diffusion of power resources is a mixed blessing, however. While it permits citizens and special interest groups to participate in urban decision making, it also gives small, dedicated groups the means to prevent majority actions to which they are strongly opposed. Studies of fluoridation controversies have shown that small groups, through **polarization** of a community, can quite quickly bring about rejection of changes in policy or the adoption of new policies (Coleman, 1957; Crain, Katz, and Rosenthal, 1969). Small groups also have been able to generate great political controversy in local elections for membership on **Office of Economic Opportunity** (OEO), model cities, and community school boards.

Among other constraints on the use of political power in urban settings are those imposed by state and federal laws and by regulations governing the use of federal funds. These constraints apply equally, whether power resources are concentrated or diffused. Even a political leader with all the local power, is not free to carry out a policy that would contravene the norms, laws, or regulations of the wider society (Banfield and Wilson, 1963:74).

The Role of Interest Groups and Organizations

In no major metropolis can a political leader control all power resources. Too many individuals, groups, and organizations have at least some access to some resources and can initiate action, often as the result of invoking federal rules. Chicago is a good example. Richard J. Daley was as powerful a mayor as there has been in the 1970s—the last of the bosses, some say. Yet one Chicago police officer formed a group that brought suit in federal court against racial discrimination in police hiring practices. The result was the withholding of $150 million in federal revenue-sharing funds from the city (Dorf-

man, 1976:124). Other groups have blocked the building or rerouting of roads. Issue-oriented groups, neighborhood groups, and other citizen action groups have been able to influence decision making in the city.

Political decision makers in cities are also constrained by many nonpolitical institutions—business and voluntary organizations, charitable institutions, community action and neighborhood groups, and the like, each of which has some power resources. The positions adopted by voluntary agencies can operate in constraint or support of elected leaders (Van Til and Van Til, 1973:75-102).

These limitations on the use of political power indicate that the diffusion of resources among citizen groups participating in politics is neither romantic nor **dysfunctional** (Walton, 1973). Individuals and groups in increasing numbers are accumulating at least some power resources (at a minimum, their own votes and the votes of their friends) by forming groups of like-minded individuals and organizations. By establishing links with other organizations and pooling their power resources, these groups can have an impact on the political and decision-making processes (Aiken and Alford, 1970). The successes of the many groups that have generated resources and influenced decisions are eloquent testimony to the fact that you can fight city hall (Cox et al., 1970:209-301).

Political Controversy

Controversy occurs when groups cannot resolve an issue or reach a decision without involving a large segment of the population.

Many individuals, groups, and
organizations can initiate action.

Political resources are then expended to convince or to demonstrate to political leaders that one side will prevail. The most carefully studied controversies were those in the 1950s over fluoridation of local drinking water (Coleman, 1957; Crain, Katz, and Rosenthal, 1969; Kornhauser, 1973). The pattern of political controversy that emerged then is similar to that observed in subsequent political controversies. We study political debates and conflicts not to abolish them, but rather to understand them, so that communities and cities will not be torn apart when controversy occurs (Kornhauser, 1973).

The fluoridation decisions of the fifties went through all the stages of decision making. The issue was raised when dental research made it clear that adding fluorides to drinking water reduced cavities. Many cities adopted fluoridation outright, but in other cities the issue became controversial, and referendums were held.

On the fluoridation issue, as on many other issues (urban renewal, community participation in OEO community councils, and model cities planning), communities were polarized—on one side were prestigious residents with social, economic, and political power and on the other side were predominantly isolated individuals, community groups, and others who previously had not had much political power or prestige.

Powerful or prestigious participants in the controversies who were not primarily politicians were constrained from using all their resources or taking positions from which they could not retreat. The polarization of the community forced them to risk alienating large segments of the population. The cost of this risk outweighed the benefits of having their position adopted and made the spending of resources in its support very expensive. Such risks are particularly great when high-status persons advocate changes of policy. Hawley, for instance, found that cities with high proportions of managers, officials, and professionals had more difficulty approving innovative programs than did cities with low proportions of such high-status workers. There is much less risk in participation for persons of little prestige or low status. They have less at stake and fewer commitments to, or responsibilities in, the community (Crain, Katz, and Rosenthal, 1969; Kornhauser, 1973; Banfield, 1961; Hawley, 1963). They can thus spend more power resources, become more active in the decision-making process, and gain greater public attention with less risk to themselves and their position in the community. On the fluoridation issue, increased exposure and willingness to risk all on the part of persons with little prestige seems to have had the desired effect in some cities. People who did not usually vote turned out on referendum day and rejected the proposition.

Controversy increases voter turnout because of the interest generated by the controversy and because of the extra effort expended by partisans. The turnout is increased by voters who typically do not participate in elections. They are indifferent to issues that do not affect them personally and immediately. They have little interest in the larger society and do not participate heavily in voluntary organizations, such as clubs, churches, or unions. They tend not to understand changes taking place in society and in the world because they have few ties to organizations that mediate or interpret general social tendencies and realities to them. They are politically apathetic, but they can be mobilized by controversy. Because they are generally isolated and insulated from social change, their activity during a political conflict is not likely to be tempered by an understanding of the broader social issues involved. When persons who do not understand the consequences of political actions or programs are mobilized, they can go beyond the bounds of legitimate political conflict. Their participation can lead to violence and other disruptive behaviors (Kornhauser, 1959, 1973; Lipset, 1960:77-130).

Political controversy draws people from lower social, economic, and educational levels into the political process. These people are less strongly attached to the community and less likely to understand the norms that govern participation in community affairs. They are less likely to support the right of persons to express opinions with which they disagree, and they are more likely to believe in conspiracy theories of political action (Stouffer, 1955; Coleman, 1957; Kornhauser, 1973). Because of their social and economic position, their social ties are more likely to be to family and friends than to the community's institutional structure. They tend to be frightened by social change because they think it will impair their ability to maintain their own position in the community. Increased political participation thus reduces the ability of cities to develop and implement innovative programs such as fluoridation, model cities, and urban renewal (Aiken and Alford, 1970). Although political participation is highly valued in a democracy, participation does not always produce the desired results.

Loss of Local Control

Political power and decision making have become increasingly concentrated at the national level. As a consequence, there has been a loss of local autonomy and power and the citizen finds it harder to acquire information on which to evaluate political options. Persons with few ties to the local community know least about political decision making.

Because many decisions that affect local communities are made at the state and federal levels, people find it easier to believe those who say the decision-making process is controlled by evil outsiders who don't care about local residents. People who want to make the decisions that affect their own lives are frustrated by lack of local control and are easy prey for those who would generate conflict and opposition to change.

As it becomes increasingly difficult for people to control their own affairs or the affairs of their communities, the individual's allegiance to the local community decreases. The legitimacy of decisions made by the local community is lessened, as is the legitimacy of decision making and of the decision makers themselves.

Loss of control and legitimacy among local officials is most noticeable in large cities where even local decision makers appear to be anonymous, impersonal officials whom citizens cannot influence. The growing dominance of the suburbs may reverse this trend and increase community participation because many suburbs are smaller and more homogeneous than city communities. As leisure time increases, citizens may devote more energy to politics. However, state, federal, and possibly metropolitan decision-making bodies will continue to determine the availability and allocation of resources.

Urban communities engage in different political activities. Participation is highest when there is controversy, but many important decisions are made at higher levels of government that are beyond the control of the city. Within the city, political power resources are diffused widely—in most cities there are several power elites, each of which provides leadership in specific activities. Resources are diffused enough so that any group that wants to fight city hall can do so. Not all fights will be won (city hall wouldn't be city hall if it didn't have ample power), but the possibility exists. Virtually all groups in urban society that wish to participate in political exchanges can have some share in the decision-making process.

Summary

City governments are responsible for performing and facilitating the performance of communal functions. Because government is a political activity, the performance of communal functions is to some extent political. Urban politics can be studied from various perspectives. A combination of two viewpoints—the structural perspective that focuses on political participants and the identification of a power elite and the process perspective that focuses on decision making—seems most appropriate to the study of urban politics.

Political power is relevant only to the social system in which it exists. It is the potential ability of a participant or group of participants to select, change, or attain the goals of a social system. Influence is the utilization of this potential, and a power structure is the patterned distribution of power generated by political resources. Participants gain resources by engaging in social exchanges with other participants. According to exchange theory, interactions continue because each party exchanges something of value with the other. These interactions are governed by norms (part of the basic norms of all communities) that specify the conditions and terms of exchanges. One norm governing exchanges requires that participants continue to make exchanges or leave the system.

The forms and modes of exchange can vary. Repayment need not be immediate, although it is a debt that must be repaid eventually. Repayment also need not be in the same medium as the original exchange, although it must be of equal value. Deference, information, knowledge, attributed status, favorable recommendations, as well as money or other tangible goods, may be the media of exchange. The exchange value of many media is difficult to calculate, but approximations are routinely established to maintain the process.

The urban political system is a complex series of exchanges. Participants who are owed debts of exchange can cash in these debts for votes, assistance, or goods that help them attain or change system goals. Thus, to gain political power, a participant engages in exchanges with as many other participants as possible but defers repayment until it is needed. The number of debts owed to a participant is thus a measure of that participant's political power, for debts may be called in the process of choosing, altering, or attaining a system goal.

The resources that can be accumulated are diverse. They include money and credit, control over jobs, control over the mass media, high social status, knowledge and technical skills, control over the definitions and interpretations of the law, solidarity of subsystems, votes, access to influential community leaders, control over organizations, and control over interpretation of values. Among the most skilled users of power resources have been the leaders of political machines or organizations. In the past, political bosses took advantage of immigrants who came to the city unskilled in politics. They gave the immigrants goods and services in exchange for their votes at election time.

As immigrant groups grew large enough to have voting power, they also realized that they were entitled to more significant exchanges from the political leaders for whom they voted. Christmas and Thanksgiving baskets, although still expected, were no longer enough to ensure subsystem solidarity. Jobs, contracts, and franchises were also expected as part of the political exchange.

Political leaders, engaging in exchanges with influential community leaders as well as individual members of immigrant groups, developed large capitals of resources that they could use to keep themselves in office and attain other goals. By helping immigrants become socialized and by slating some of them for political office, machine politicians tied the ethnic groups to themselves. Not all exchanges were as benevolent as basketgiving at Christmas or Thanksgiving or welfare assistance or patronage jobs; threats, coercion, vote buying, and ghost voting also were used freely in the development of political power.

Many studies of urban decision making assume that power resources are distributed in a patterned way, creating a power structure dominated by the elite of the society. Membership in such elites is determined by occupancy of certain roles in business, finance, and government. These roles provide occupants with all the resources they need to attain and keep political power. While many studies identify city elites on the basis of the roles they occupy, others inquire among role occupants for the names of those who are most influential. Such studies often reveal a small number of people who occupy elite positions or who are reputed to be influential in getting things done. These people are considered the power elite. In contrast, studies of the decision-making process often reveal that a much larger number of people are involved from time to time in different situations, depending on the issue in question. Studies of the decision-making process often conclude that power is more diffuse than studies of political structure and of decision makers would indicate.

Decisions are made in several stages. At each stage appropriate power resources must be used to influence the course of decision making. The resources that are most appropriate at one stage are not necessarily the most valuable at another stage. Control over the mass media is more important at the first stage, which is issue recognition; knowledge and technical expertise are more important at the second stage, information collection; subsystem solidarity may be important as each participant formulates a preferred policy at the third stage, policy formulation; other resources are involved in the fourth stage, policy evaluation; and all resources may be involved in the final stage, the selection of a single policy.

Not all participants in decision making will evaluate the process in the same way, nor will they all evaluate their own commitment of resources to a particular policy and the commitments of others equally. The decision may not be equally important to all participants. Citizens affected by the decision may be few or many, and the costs of implementing options may be high for some participants and trivial for others. For these and other reasons, political participants may commit large or small portions of their available resources to influencing a given decision. Resource commitment also depends on how one evaluates the resources of other participants and how much of their power one believes they are likely to commit. A participant with relatively low political power can influence a decision if that participant commits a large portion of available resources to it and more powerful participants withhold many of their resources in opposition.

Power resources are widely available in urban society. Many individuals and groups have access to power resources and the ability to engage in exchanges with other persons or groups. This makes citizen participation in political life a reality and constrains the unbridled use of power by those with large capitals of resources. Groups that are issue-oriented and that do not care how much of their total store of resources they spend can often successfully fight city hall.

Glossary

dysfunction   the consequence of any behavior in a social system that hinders the stability, integration, or function performance of that system

exchange theory   the theory of social behavior that views interaction as exchanges between persons or institutions and that views social structures as patterns of exchange

influence   the act of selecting or altering social system goals

Office of Economic Opportunity (OEO)   a federal agency created during the War on Poverty that attempted to involve poor and disadvantaged urban citizens in decision making about programs for their benefit

partisanship   in relation to an election, the identification of candidates for elective office in terms of their political party affiliations

polarization   the division of a group into two diametrically opposed subgroups; in political terms, the division of a population into those in favor of and those opposed to a position

political capital   resources that can be spent in gaining power and influence

political machine   an organization of people with similar political interests who jointly accumulate and spend their political capital for their mutual benefit; frequently such an organization can accumulate sufficient capital to dominate decision making over a long period of time

political power   in a social system the potential ability to select, alter, or attain the goals of the system

power elite   a small group of politically influential people who behave uniformly in political matters; generally, the ones at the top of the power hierarchy who are assumed to have similar social characteristics and to interact with one another

reciprocity   the act of returning something of approximately equal value to a person who has given one something in the past; the objects exchanged may be goods, services, deference, votes, or anything else to which people attach value

References

Aiken, Michael, and Alford, Robert R.
1970   "Community Structure and Innovation: The Case of Urban Renewal." *American Sociological Review* 35:650-65.

Bachrach, Peter, and Baratz, Morton S.
1962   "Two Faces of Power." *American Political Science Review* 58 (December):947-52.

Banfield, Edward C.
1961   *Political Influence.* New York: Free Press.

Banfield, Edward C., and Wilson, James Q., eds.
1963   *City Politics.* New York: Random House, Inc.

Blau, Peter M.
1955   *The Dynamics of Bureaucracy.* Chicago: University of Chicago Press.
1964   *Exchange and Power in Social Life.* New York: John Wiley & Sons, Inc.

Cartwright, Dorian
1959   *Studies in Social Power.* Ann Arbor, Mich.: Institute for Social Research.
1965   "Influence, Leadership and Control." In *Handbook of Organizations,* edited by James G. March, pp. 1-47. Chicago: Rand McNally & Company.

Clark, Terry N.
1968   "The Concept of Power." In *Community Structure and Decision Making,* edited by Terry N. Clark, pp. 45-81. San Francisco: Chandler Publishing Company.

Coleman, James S.
1957   *Community Conflict.* New York: Free Press.

Cornwall, Elmer E., Jr.
1964   "Bosses, Machines, and Ethnic Groups." *Annals* 353 (May):27-39.

Cox, Fred M., et al., eds.
1970   *Community Organization.* Itasca, Ill.: F. E. Peacock Publishers, Inc.

Crain, Robert L.; Katz, Elihu; and Rosenthal, Donald
1969   *The Politics of Community Conflict: The Fluoridation Decision.* Indianapolis: The Bobbs-Merrill Co., Inc.

Dahl, Robert A.
1961   *Who Governs?* New Haven: Yale University Press.
1967   "The Concept of Power." *Behavioral Scientist* 2 (July):201-18.

Dorfman, Ron
1976   "Daley's Bluff." *Chicago* (April):124.

Fisher, Sethard
1969   "Community Power Studies: A Critique." *Social Research* (Winter 1962). In *Urban Politics and Problems,* edited by H. R. Mahood and Edward L. Angus, pp. 85-98. New York: Charles Schribner's Sons.

Gouldner, Alvin
1960   "The Norm of Reciprocity." *American Sociological Review* 25:161-78.

Harrigan, John J.
1976   *Political Change in the Metropolis.* Boston: Little, Brown and Company.

Hawley, Amos H.
1963   "Community Power and Urban Renewal Success." *American Journal of Sociology* 68 (June):422-31.

Homans, George C.
1961   *Social Behavior: Its Elementary Forms.* New York: Harcourt, Brace & World, Inc.

Hunter, Floyd
1953   *Community Power Structure.* Chapel Hill, N.C.: University of North Carolina Press.

Kornhauser, William
1959   *The Politics of Mass Society.* New York: Free Press.
1973   "Power and Participation in the Local Community." In *Cities in Change,* edited by John Walton and Donald Carns, pp. 389-98. Boston: Allyn & Bacon, Inc.

Lipset, Seymour Martin
1960   *Political Man.* New York: Doubleday & Co., Inc.

Lynd, Robert S., and Lynd, Helen M.
1929   *Middletown.* New York: Harcourt, Brace & World, Inc.
1937   *Middletown in Transition.* New York: Harcourt, Brace & World, Inc.

Mills, C. Wright
1959   *The Power Elite.* New York: Oxford University Press.

Munger, Frank J.
1973   "Community Power and Decision Making." In *Cities in Change,* edited by John Walton and Donald Carns, pp. 332-54. Boston: Allyn & Bacon, Inc.

O'Connor, Edwin
1956   *The Last Hurrah.* Boston: Little, Brown and Company.

O'Connor, Len
1975   *Clout: Mayor Daley and His City.* Chicago: Henry Regnery Company.

Plunkett, George Washington
1967   "How to Get a Political Following." In *Politics in the Metropolis,* edited by Thomas R. Dye and Brett W. Hawkins, pp. 266-72. Columbus: Charles E. Merrill Publishing Company.

Royko, Mike
1971   *Boss: Richard J. Daley of Chicago.* New York: E. P. Dutton & Co., Inc.

Stouffer, Samuel A.
1955   *Communism, Conformity, and Civil Liberties.* Garden City, N.Y.: Doubleday & Co., Inc.

Van Til, Jon, and Van Til, Sally Bould
1973   "Citizen Participation in Social Policy: The End of the Cycle." In *Cities in Change,* edited by John Walton and Donald Carns, pp. 75-102. Boston: Allyn & Bacon, Inc.

Walton, John
1973   "The Bearing of Social Science Research on Public Issues: Floyd Hunter and the Study of Power." In *Cities in Change,* edited by John Walton and Donald Carns, pp. 318-32. Boston: Allyn & Bacon, Inc.

Weber, Max
1947   *The Theory of Social and Economic Organization.* New York: Oxford University Press.

Whyte, William F.
1943   *Street Corner Society.* Chicago: University of Chicago Press.

Suggested Readings

Banfield, Edward C. *Political Influence.* New York: Free Press, 1961. A study of six decisions in Chicago and of the people, institutions, and social processes that affected the decision-making process.

Hawley, Willis D., and Wirt, Frederick M., eds. *The Search for Community Power.* Englewood Cliffs, N.J.: Prentice-Hall, 1968. An extensive collection of important papers on urban politics.

Klein, Maury, and Kantor, Harvey A. *Prisoners of Progress: American Industrial Cities 1850-1920.* New York: Macmillan, 1976. Chapter 10 contains an excellent discussion of the origins of political machines and the activities of political bosses. Chapter 11 describes the political reform in the early twentieth century.

Rakove, Milton. *Don't Make No Waves, Don't Back No Losers.* Bloomington, Ind.: Indiana University Press, 1976. Accurately subtitled an insider's view of the Daley machine, this highly readable, insightful analysis shows how a contemporary political machine and its boss gain and use power.

Notes

1. In *Political Influence* (1961), Edward Banfield analyzes a number of decisions made in Chicago. Although he does not employ exchange theory, the process described here can be seen operating in the cases he cites.
2. Edwin O'Connor in *The Last Hurrah* (1956), Len O'Connor in *Clout* (1975), and Royko in *Boss* (1971) give examples of how resources are used by urban political leaders. Banfield (1961) also shows how resources are employed.
3. Len O'Connor (1975). See also the report of these practices in Whyte's *Street Corner Society* (1943). During the early 1970s Chicago newspapers detailed these behaviors for about a week after each election.
4. For a review of the literature on the decline or the lack of a decline of political machines, see Harrigan, 1976:93-126.
5. Mayor Richard J. Daley of Chicago is often described as having made decisions this way. See Royko (1971); Len O'Connor (1975); Banfield (1961).
6. See Clark (1968). Banfield (1961), who sought to study "important issues," found that not all participants agreed on the importance of each issue. See also Bachrach and Baratz (1962).

11

Problems of Shared Communal Functions—Housing, Transportation, Health

Many communal functions are carried out by the city acting in the public interest. Police and fire protection and judicial and legislative functions are obvious examples. Many other functions are carried out jointly by the city and private institutions or individuals. Among these are provision of housing, transportation, and health care.

Ensuring a supply of adequate housing is one critical communal function that the city performs. But its role in providing housing is largely indirect. It actually provides only a small fraction of the housing for its residents. The city exercises its communal responsibility in this area most often by regulating the nature, quality, and location of housing through building codes, zoning laws, and the like. The city also must deal with the consequences of overcrowding and substandard or otherwise **inadequate housing.**

In transportation the city has the dual responsibility of providing for mass transportation and for private transportation. The city must maintain subways, buses, and other forms of mass transportation when private carriers will not. It must also regulate the use of private automobiles, coordinate vehicular traffic, and provide parking.

Urban health care is primarily provided by private physicians and hospitals. But the city has the responsibility of providing health care for persons who cannot afford private care. Furthermore, the city is responsible for protecting residents against certain infectious diseases to prevent epidemics. For that reason, the health functions of the city include responsibility for regulating, or at least monitoring, the quality of the water and air. In carrying out its health functions, the city is also respon-

sible for controlling food purity, preventing rodent and insect infestation, and otherwise regulating and controlling substances that can affect the health of residents.

In this chapter we will investigate the city's role in carrying out these functions. We will analyze the nature of each function, look at how problems are dealt with, and examine indicators of the city's success or failure in carrying out the functions. Solutions to the problems of function performance in these areas are few and far between. Improving performance is a most pressing problem for cities today. In this chapter, however, we will concentrate on describing the problems, because adequate analysis and evaluation of solutions would comprise a book at least as large as this one.

The City's Role in Housing

In recent years inadequate housing has become a major urban problem. Age, physical deterioration, costs, and the complex of problems we call **slums** have combined to produce both an inadequate supply of homes and a great number of inadequate homes in the cities. To understand urban housing problems, we must understand the city's role in housing and the definition of adequate housing.

The city provides little housing on its own. It sometimes participates in urban renewal and similar programs to encourage private construction, and it builds publicly owned housing for those who cannot afford to rent privately owned units. But its major role in housing is indirect. It regulates the density and location of housing through zoning laws, and it regulates the condition of existing and new housing through construction and safety codes. Many cities also regulate the services that landlords provide, including the amount of heat that must be provided during cold weather. And some cities regulate rents (Weiss, 1976; Frieden, 1970:170-225). Cities thus perform a limited number of housing communal functions directly, but by their real estate tax policies and other regulations they facilitate the performance of these functions by others.

The forces that affect the city's ability to perform its role in housing include how society defines adequate housing. This is important because changing definitions of adequacy can increase or decrease housing supplies. The rate of change in the size of the population also affects the city's ability to maintain an adequate supply of housing. A decrease in population may leave many units unoccupied, and rapid growth may produce a shortage of housing (National Commission on Urban Problems, 1972:67, 83). Changes in the composition of the population in terms of age, race, and family size also influence the demand for housing. Other factors that affect housing supply are changes in construction technology, the willingness of unions to allow modifications of building codes to take advantage of new technology, the age of the city and its housing supply, and the national supply of money and credit for construction, purchase, and rehabilitation of homes.

Objective descriptions of adequate housing often are based on the facilities available within a single housing unit, the structural characteristics of the unit, and the number of occupants. This is not a totally satisfactory definition because a unit that is adequate by these criteria may be subjectively inadequate because it is in an area of dilapidated structures (National Commission on Urban Problems, 1972:5-9). We should also recognize that all definitions of housing quality reflect cultural values. Other cultures, and even our own culture in earlier years, have employed many different standards of physical condition or occupancy in defining adequate housing. Feelings about the necessity of indoor plumbing and definitions of crowded conditions have varied with both culture and time (Schorr, 1970:709-11).

In the United States today, however, housing experts generally employ three measures to determine the adequacy of a house or apartment. First, each unit should have hot running water, a private toilet, and a bathroom. Second, the structure should be sound enough so that only routine maintenance is needed. Finally, the unit should have at least one room for each person in the household. A unit with less space is defined as overcrowded (Glazer, 1967:140-45).

Overcrowding is the most commonly used measure of housing conditions because it is measured by census and therefore provides the most complete coverage. Other definitions of overcrowding show how concepts of adequate housing can vary. In nineteenth century Britain, overcrowding was measured by the number of beds. A household that did not have at least one bed per person was overcrowded. In 1950 the American Public Health Association defined overcrowding in American homes on the basis of number of square feet per person. A single person needed 400 square feet, two people needed 750 square feet, and so on. Another definition is based on the number of bedrooms. Two people need one bedroom, three or four people need two bedrooms, and so on (Schorr, 1970).

Whatever definition we use, overcrowding is important because it is assumed—and there is some research to support the assumption—that overcrowded housing has negative physical and psychological effects on residents (Schorr, 1970; Frieden, 1970:171-72).

The Extent of Inadequate Housing

On the basis of structural condition, plumbing, and overcrowding, we can investigate housing adequacy in the United States today. Table 11.1 shows that inadequate housing is less common in metropolitan areas than in nonmetropolitan urban areas or in rural areas. And comparison of the data on housing in metropolitan central cities with that in their suburbs shows that it is wrong to think of cities as concentrations of inadequate homes and the suburbs as areas with little or no inadequate housing. Equal proportions of housing units in central cities and in suburbs lack some or all plumbing, and there are only small differences between cities and suburbs in the percentage of housing units that are overcrowded or otherwise substandard.

Despite the fact that the proportion of inadequate housing is about the same in cities and suburbs, because of ecological processes inadequate housing is more concentrated in cities than it is in suburbs. This concentration of inadequate housing and the dirt, disease, rodents, and other health hazards that accompany concentrations of homes with poor plumbing, garbage disposal, and sanitation facilities (National Commission on Urban Problems, 1972:1), is what makes some areas of cities slums. Slums are not individually inadequate homes; they are concentrations of such homes.

Thus, with the critical exception of slums, housing is not a more common problem in urban areas or even in metropolitan central cities than it is in rural areas or suburbs. Furthermore, 3.5 percent to 8.5 percent of inadequate housing units in central cities is enough to be a serious problem. If similar proportions of our population were to come down with a disabling disease, we would consider it an epidemic.

Table 11.1   Residence and Housing Conditions, 1970

Characteristics	Percent of Housing Units with Each Characteristic					
	SMSA, Central City	SMSA, not Central City	Urban, not SMSA	All Urban	Rural	All U.S.
Lacking some or all plumbing*	3.5	3.5	14.1	3.4	16.9	6.9
Less than one room per person*	8.5	7.1	9.2	7.6	10.1	8.2
Substandard structural condition**	5.1	3.4	14.2	4.6	15.5	7.4

Sources   *U.S. Bureau of the Census, *Census of Housing: 1970, Final Report HC(1)-A1, United States Summary* (Washington, D.C.: Government Printing Office, 1971), tables 1, 2. **Statistical Policy Division, Office of Management and the Budget, *Social Indicators, 1973* (Washington, D.C.: Government Printing Office, 1973).

Inadequate housing is more concentrated in metropolitan areas but more common in rural areas.

Source: Office of Management and Budget, *Social Indicators, 1973* (Washington, D.C.: Government Printing Office, 1973), Chart 6/1.

As a society, we have recognized inadequate housing as a serious problem. The housing supply has been improved dramatically since 1940, when more than 45 percent of the households lived in substandard units. By 1970 less than 10 percent of the households lived in substandard units (Statistical Policy Division, Office of Management and the Budget, 1973:190).

Characteristics of Occupants

Both home ownership and the race of the occupant are related to the adequacy of housing units. Units occupied by their owners are somewhat less likely to be inadequate than those occupied by renters. Race has a greater impact: units occupied by blacks (even owned units) are more likely to be inadequate than units owned and occupied by whites (see table 11.2).

Since more blacks (58.4 percent) than whites (34.6 percent) rent (U.S. Bureau of the Census, 1975:table 1226), a larger proportion of blacks than whites live in inadequate housing. Furthermore, since rental units are more likely to be overcrowded than are owned units, since blacks are more likely to rent than to own, and since many blacks, as new migrants to cities, are poor and able to rent only low-cost units, we may conclude that more blacks than whites are concentrated in poor, inadequate housing. Consequently, blacks suffer disproportionately from housing problems in urban areas. The urban housing problem is intimately tied to the racial problem (Kain, 1973:12-13).

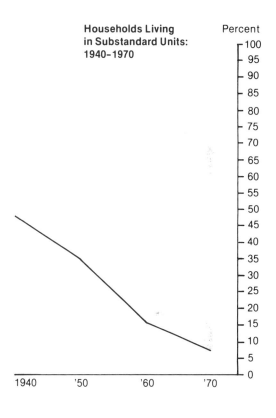

Households Living in Substandard Units: 1940-1970

Table 11.2   Occupancy, Race, and Housing Condition

Occupant	% of Units Lacking Some or All Plumbing	% of Dilapidated Units
All owner-occupants	4.5	1.5
White owner-occupants	3.8	1.3
Black owner-occupants	15.0	4.3
All tenants	8.3	3.9
White tenants	6.5	3.2
Black tenants	18.2	7.6

328

Source: Office of Management and
Budget, *Social Indicators, 1973*
(Washington, D.C.: Government
Printing Office, 1973), 193.

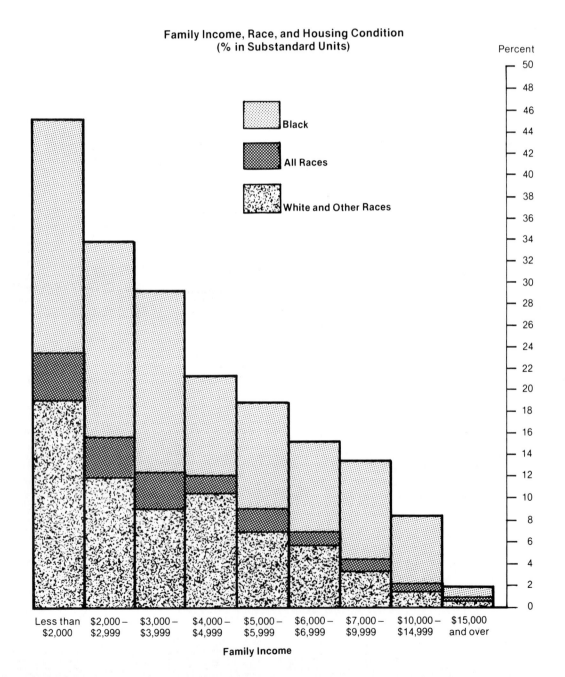

Family Income, Race, and Housing Condition
(% in Substandard Units)

The relationships between race and income and inadequate housing can be seen in the graph on page 328. Poor persons of all races are much more likely to live in inadequate homes than are affluent persons. At all income levels, however, blacks are more likely than members of other races to live in substandard housing units.

Housing and Values

The value placed on and the desire to own single-family detached homes partially fueled the migration of city dwellers to the suburbs. Only half of the housing in central cities is in single-unit structures. But 75 percent of the housing in suburbs, 83 percent of non-SMSA housing, and 88 percent of rural housing is in single-unit structures (U.S. Bureau of the Census, 1971a:tables 10, 21). Thus, regardless of condition, the housing available outside the central cities is more likely to be the kind of housing that is most valued in our society.

Apartments, despite the recent popularity of condominiums, are not where most people would live if circumstances allowed them to live elsewhere. Half of the housing in cities is in multiple-unit structures, which many people dislike. Life in such buildings appears to be incongruent with a basic American value, and this may be why cities are commonly perceived as concentrations of inadequate housing.

The Changing Housing Supply

The housing supply in cities is deteriorating even though fewer people live in substandard units now than in 1940. Between 1960 and 1970 the population increased by 19.7 percent, but the supply of occupied housing units increased by only 13.3 percent (U.S. Bureau of

The supply of housing in the central city is not growing as fast as the supply elsewhere.

FUTURE
SINGLE FAMILY HOMES

OPENING 1976

the Census, 1975:table 1225). Some factors behind the inadequate growth of the housing supply are the costs of building and operating housing and the costs that housing construction imposes on local government for sewer and water lines, roads, schools, and other municipal facilities.

During the 1960s more new housing was built in the suburbs (32.7 percent of all new units) and in nonmetropolitan areas (23.6 percent) than in central cities (18.5 percent). The supply of housing in the central city obviously is not growing as fast as the supply elsewhere. Furthermore, since much existing central city housing is older than suburban housing, it is more likely to be unstylish, unattractive, inadequately maintained, and in need of major repairs to the plumbing, wiring, and other major structural components. It is also more likely to be torn down. The supply of new housing has not kept up with demolitions. Urban renewal alone has demolished 404,000 units. Other federal programs have taken another 650,000. Between 1949 and 1967, only about 500,000 units of public housing were constructed (National Commission on Urban Problems, 1972:82-83).

Urban housing problems have been aggravated by discrimination and racial segregation. Blacks, the most rapidly growing segment of the population, have become concentrated in areas that contain the oldest and least adequate housing the city has to offer. Overcrowding in these areas has led to additional deterioration (National Commission on Urban Problems, 1972:56, 58). An area of deteriorated housing may be small in comparison with the city as a whole, but it can often be extensive, encompassing an entire natural area.

The Problem of Slums

The most widely used definitions of housing adequacy are based on evaluations of individual homes. But housing quality is strongly influenced by the physical and social context of the area in which it is located.

> When any reasonably intelligent person is looking for a house for himself and his family, he almost always asks for, or if the situation is favorable the real estate salesman offers, information about the availability of schools, churches, shopping facilities, parks or playgrounds, at least some centers of employment, and often about the location of buslines, hospitals, or clinics, or a branch library. Many prospective house buyers or renters also will check with friends or associates who live in the locality on the quality of the public schools, of the medical facilities and services, or the climate in race relations. Occasionally, an unusually thorough person will even investigate insurance rates on protection against fire and theft or statistics on crime or public health [National Commission on Urban Problems, 1972:56].

Defining Slums

These considerations allow us to define slums as areas in which inadequate housing is concentrated and in which communal functions are unavailable or inadequately provided. There are few private institutions—such as stores, churches, professional offices, businesses, and industry—to carry out communal functions. Public services are provided, but they are not enough to generate a sense of identification with the area. Normative integration, social solidarity, social participation, and mutual support among the residents are also lacking. All of these deficiencies are essential to the definition of an area as a slum.

Slums are undesirable places to live in, and the vast majority of residents would move out if they could afford to do so. In addition, people living near deteriorating areas often move to more desirable neighborhoods as soon as they can, a process that speeds the expansion of the slum. Slums are characterized not only by inadequate housing, but also by all the problems of poverty. As a result of inadequate communal functioning, slums suffer from increased deviance and crime, decreased informal social control, and inadequate socialization of the young (Schorr, 1970).

The Effects of Slums

For many years inadequate housing was thought to cause personal, family, and social disorganization as well as the pathologic behavior, disease, crime, and poverty found among slum residents (Frieden, 1970:171; Schorr, 1970; Ways, 1971:314-25). Government programs such as urban renewal, public housing, and model cities have been based on the assumption that the quality of housing alters the characteristics of the residents. Officials reason that if housing is improved, the lot of the inhabitants will also improve. Research has shown, however, that the relationship is not this simple (Frieden, 1970:172). Poor housing does have awful effects on both the city and the slum residents, but the problems found among slum residents cannot be eliminated just by improving the housing.

Effects on Residents: Health

The effects of slums on slum residents have been summarized by Alvin Schorr (1963:7-33). The relationship between poor housing and physical illness is known. Use of toilets and water facilities shared by many persons, inadequate food storage facilities, inadequate heating and ventilation, and crowded sleeping quarters can lead to acute respiratory infections and can help spread infectious diseases such as chicken pox, measles, and whooping cough among children. Some of the same factors can spread diseases of the digestive tract, such as typhoid, dysentery, and diarrhea, among children and adults. Age and poor maintenance in slum housing (for example, poor lighting, poor electrical wiring, broken steps, and crowded laundry facilities) can lead to many injuries. Ingestion of lead paint by children can cause mental retardation and death. Controlled statistical studies show that improved housing reduces the incidence of both illnesses and deaths.

Psychological Effects

Poor housing also affects the mental health of slum residents. It is often argued that poor housing is causally related to psychological problems (Frieden, 1970:1, 9). The evidence for the relationship, however, is not clear-cut. The effects tend to be reciprocal: people may develop psychological problems from living in slums, or people with psychological problems may have to live in slums.

Among the best-studied effects of slums on residents are the effects of overcrowding.[1] Crowded living conditions are thought to have a great impact on children. James S. Plant has proposed that crowded living conditions make it difficult to develop a satisfactory sense of self because close contact prevents the development of idealized images of adults (1930: 849-60; 1960:510-20).

Poor housing affects both the physical and mental health of its residents.

The most serious psychological effect of crowding, however, is on sexual behavior, according to Plant. Overcrowding is supposed to make it impossible for children to have illusions about sexual relationships and behavior. The eventual result is thought to be cynicism about relationships between men and women. Accounts of the sexual behavior of adolescents, both from former slum dwellers and from persons who have studied slum dwellers, suggest that children who see sexual activity become sexually active early in their lives. Other accounts suggest that crowded living causes repression of sexuality or treating sex as a physical activity remote from emotion. Among slum dwellers sex often is seen as a commodity that can be exchanged for something valuable—for example, a husband for a woman in a social setting where husbands are rare, or as payment for positive evaluations from others, or as a diversion when other recreational opportunities are lacking.

Overcrowding can also produce fatigue and irritation due to lack of sleep. And the lack of adequate play space in the home means that children may spend a lot of time away from home and away from adult supervision. This factor is thought to produce the correlation between poor housing and crime and delinquency. Rates of delinquent behavior are often reported to be higher in areas of cities where residents are poor and inadequate housing is concentrated. However, complex statistical analysis weakens these relationships. It appears that other factors may be more important than the quality of either the individual's housing or the housing in the neighborhood (Chilton, 1964:71-83; Polk, 1967:320-25; Lander, 1971:163-64).

The Use of Space

One characteristic that differentiates slum areas from middle-class areas is the use of space. In slums the common spaces—halls, streets, and parks—are considered part of the living space and are extensively and intensively used for social relationships. In contrast, space outside the apartments or homes in middle-class areas are only routes to get from one place to another and not places in which social interaction can take place. People are less likely to stand around or engage in interaction in public places. This difference may make it appear that social control is lacking in the slums and that there is much disorderly behavior. More likely, the difference reflects the inadequacy of space in the housing units (Fried and Gleicher, 1970:730).

Positive Effects of Slums

The use of the entire neighborhood as personal space makes it possible for the residents to develop satisfactions with the area that are independent of feelings about an individual dwelling unit. The residents feel they belong in the area. This feeling can increase community identification and has many positive communal values. The outside observer may not detect this feeling of community because the use of outside space may appear disorganized. Slum areas that many outside observers consider disorganized have been found to exhibit a high degree of social organization, and residents have been found to have positive feelings about their neighborhood (Suttles, 1968; Whyte, 1943; Fried and Gleicher, 1970).

From a middle-class perspective, slums may seem to be disorganized, uncomfortable, unfriendly places to live in, but it is not clear that all slum residents feel this way. This is not to say that all slum residents like all or even any characteristics of slums, but rather that some residents find positive aspects to living in densely settled neighborhoods with dilapidated, inadequate housing. This reaction may reflect a greater preference to be with people than is found among the middle class. Or it may reflect a preference for familiar neighborhoods, even with their physical disadvantages, to unfamiliar neighborhoods that may offer better housing (Schorr, 1963).

Overcrowded housing in slums may also reflect a high degree of familial integration. Several generations of a single family may share a dwelling because such intimacy is valued. Even so, such a situation can cause tension and stress, depending on the amount of space available and the way the space is divided. Many extended families prefer to have apartments with large kitchens and small living rooms, but most apartments in urban areas are not designed this way.

The Costs of Slums for the City

All forms of housing impose costs on cities. Obviously, when publicly owned housing is of good quality and low density, the costs are high. But the ultimate costs of cheaply built, sprawling developments, even those built by private developers, are huge. They involve increased pollution, fewer open spaces for public use, greater demand for public services, and a wide range of other economic and personal costs (Real Estate Research Corporation, 1974).

In slums, however, the direct and indirect costs to the city are even higher. Costs to the city and to slum residents have led many local and federal governments to try to eliminate slums. The magnitude of the costs that slums impose on the city were summarized by the National Commission on Urban Problems (1972:5-6).

Slums are expensive to city administrations. Normally, they reflect high welfare, police, and fire department activity. In other services, such as schools, garbage and trash removal, snow removal, street surfacing and repair, replacement of old and inadequate water and sewer lines, the slums, where additional expenditures are badly needed, are usually on the bottom of the priority lists (if they manage to get on the list at all) in competition with other city neighborhoods.

The concentration of low-income families places an inordinate burden on each central city to provide welfare services, expanded police protection, and other costly public services. Yet the departure of many middle- and upper-income residents and many industries to the suburbs weakens the central city tax base. The conversion of neighborhoods from middle-income to low-income occupancy, which occurs when slums expand, also reduces the prosperity of retail businesses, thereby further depressing the local tax base. So center cities experience a sharp rise in demand for revenue at the same time that their ability to produce revenue is either static or declining. The result can be, and sometimes is, death for a neighborhood or the slow strangulation of the city itself.

City services cost money. In 1962, the per capita expenditure of local governments averaged one-third more in metropolitan areas than elsewhere. However, the main reason for higher public expenditure in cities is that urban life requires public provision of some services that, under rural conditions, need not or cannot be supplied, like street cleaning, and public sewerage systems. Also cities call for increased intensity of other kinds of public services such as fire protection.

Few if any programs designed to eliminate slums, such as public housing, urban renewal, and model cities, have been notably successful. In part, their lack of success reflects inaccurate assumptions about slums and slum residents. These assumptions are reflected in the construction of inappropriate housing, that is, housing designed for the wrong life style. High-rise public housing prohibits the use of exterior space for social interaction, thereby requiring a change in behavior patterns of the residents. The internal arrangements are also often inappropriate. The kitchen layout is usually very small and efficient, but this arrangement is wrong when the kitchen is used as a major setting for social interaction. The residents' failure to adapt to their new physical surroundings may be part of the reason for the lack of informal social control in these structures.

Public housing also has failed to eliminate overcrowding. Much publicly supported housing offers fewer bedrooms per unit than are needed by most residents of deteriorated housing.

In general, there has been a lack of planning for anything but the construction of public housing. When slum dwellers are moved, they are often provided with housing but with little else. In building housing to replace slums, cities build as many housing units as they can per dollar, but they do not or cannot "waste" public funds on facilities such as stores, schools, offices for local professionals, or space for community organizations (although this tendency seems to be changing).

Federally aided housing programs have failed to eliminate slums, but they have helped to reduce the proportion of the population living in substandard housing units. More often than not, however, urban renewal programs have cleared slums without replacing them with homes that slum dwellers can afford. Rents in urban renewal areas increased from less than $60 a month before renewal to nearly $200 a month after renewal (Anderson, 1967:495).

The lack of knowledge about how to design public housing developments, the requirements of federal laws and regulations, and the economics of housing construction have all contributed to the city's loss of control over the solutions to housing problems and the problems of residents of inadequate housing.

The City's Role in Transportation

Modes of transportation played an important role in shaping the structure of cities (see chapter 6). The automobile and other motor vehicles were especially important in the expansion of the city, removing the limitations of fixed routes and leading to suburban sprawl (Gakenheimer, 1967:392-411). They have integrated the urban area by facilitating access to functionally differentiated individuals and businesses distributed throughout the city. City transportation systems aid in the performance of critical communal functions by integrating the spatial-ecological organization of the city with the division of labor (Greer, 1961:605-50; Gakenheimer, 1967). Transportation is a problem for most of the urban population, most obviously so in the **journey-to-work,** which is concentrated in twenty hours a week. The entire labor force experiences at least some problem at these times. People not in the labor force experience difficulties in getting from one place to another by public transportation or by automobile and in finding places to park. All these problems can be summed up as the failure of the transportation system to integrate adequately all portions of the city with all other portions, both physically and socially (Meyer, 1970:40-75). Expressways have aggravated urban transit problems because they have decreased public transportation's clientele and increased its need for subsidies at a time when the urban tax base is declining. Highways take valuable land from the tax rolls and make it easier for suburbanites to commute and thus avoid paying city real estate taxes (Meyer, 1970).

Transportation is one obvious city problem, and it has been an urban problem at least since the time of Rome. Inefficiency of transportation leads to loss of time, money, and jobs. In comparison with social welfare programs, transportation is often considered a luxury that can be given priority only when other, more pressing social problems are solved. However, because transportation is a major means of integrating the metropolitan community, it is linked to the performance of almost all other urban functions. The view that transportation is a luxury must be tempered with caution (Gakenheimer, 1967). For one thing, when public transportation is not available, the poor often find it hard or impossible to get from place to place, especially when low-cost housing is not located near places of employment.

Transportation is an integrative communal function affecting the ability of the city to perform many other vital functions. In the following section we will analyze urban transportation problems.

The Integrative Function of Urban Transportation Systems

A complex community such as a city or metropolis in which different areas (commercial, industrial, low-density residential, high-density residential, and so on) serve different functions requires functional integration if a cohesive, unified social system is to exist. Large cities or metropolitan areas can be functionally integrated only when distance presents few problems. Spatially differentiated functions are integrated by either communication or transportation. Transportation allows the continuous flow of goods, energy, and people throughout the society so that people who are widely separated can maintain their interdependence. Transportation integrates human activity through the exchange of products, information, goods, and services (Greer, 1961:626).

In the past, when the **space-time ratio** was high (when it took a long time to get from one place to another), factories and dwellings were close together. The construction of tenement houses and multistoried factories in the same area minimized the distance between work and home for many employees. Factories, of course, were also located close to their source of energy. The invention of the railroad changed the space-time ratio between cities but not within cities. Railroads made relatively long-distance commuting practical, but only when trains did not make many stops.

The space-time ratio within cities was altered when the horse and carriage was replaced by electric-powered streetcars and gasoline-powered trucks and automobiles. The streetcar and the automobile made it possible for people to commute to work from low-density residential districts in the city.

At first, the streetcar and the automobile increased the centralization of service facilities for dispersed residences, and the downtown flourished. The dense neighborhoods of the steam age became more congested in the age of the internal combustion engine. Most institutions located in the central city when they had had no choice. The internal combustion engine gave institutions and people the choice of locating farther from the central city (Greer, 1961:626). Improved transportation encouraged the spreading not only of residential areas but also of the service institutions and facilities used by people in these areas. Transportation thus integrated not only the city but also the entire metropolitan area by making possible the rapid circulation of people, energy, and goods.

Urban transportation systems have performed three major integrative tasks.

1. Getting people to and from work: the integration of home and work, which had been separated by the division of labor.
2. Moving goods, services, people, and energy supplies from one point in the city to another for business and commercial purposes: the integration of the interdependent activities of the city. Businesses and industries rely on prompt, efficient deliveries and shipments; consumers must travel from their homes to stores and shops. As the size of the city increases, routes become more complex, and transportation becomes even more vital.
3. Moving people for purposes other than business: the integration of social participation. People travel throughout the city, visiting friends and relatives and engaging in other recreations and leisure-time activities.

Transportation As a Network

All three integrative tasks are best understood in terms of a transportation network that facilitates access to goods, people, and energy anywhere in the city. We can specify the components that such a transportation network should have and analyze the characteristics, performance, and problems of existing transportation components.

Transportation Network Components

The components of a transportation network include routes, **modes of travel,** and supporting facilities. The routes are the streets, expressways, and rails for trains, streetcars, and subways. Routes can be on, above, or below the ground. The modes of travel include private cars, taxis, buses, trains, and streetcars. The supporting facilities include lighting, signs, parking spaces, traffic management and control devices, courts, laws, and regulations.

We must evaluate the components of such a network in terms of how well the three main integrative tasks of transportation are carried out. We also examine the performance of the transportation network in terms of its efficiency, costs (social and financial), and effects on other urban functions.

Characteristics of the Urban Transportation Network

Urban transportation networks are dominated by the automobile and the highway. In 1970 about 75 percent of all trips to and from work were made by automobile and only 20 percent were made by public transportation, most of these by bus. Nearly half as many trips to work in central cities were made by walking as by taking public transportation. Rail transportation accounts for only a small fraction of public travel. Railroads can provide efficient urban transportation only when a route is used by at least 25,000 riders. The need for this density of use on each rail route means that economically possible mass transit systems, using cars that run on rails, require **residential densities** similar to those found only in New York and Chicago (Meyer, 1970).

Improved performance of transportation networks.
With the geographic growth of cities and the development of much less densely settled suburbs, the use of urban transportation systems has slowly and steadily declined. This change is linked with both decreasing population in the central city and decreasing employment opportunities and business services, particularly in the central district.

Central business district employment determines the maximum **network capacity** needed in rush hours. Stable or declining central business district employment and increased transportation network capacity due to the building of expressways has improved the performance of urban transportation networks. Commuter trips today take less time than they did several decades ago. All modes of transportation have shared in this improvement, which is most dramatically demonstrated by a 30 to 40 percent reduction since 1940 in the time required to empty central business districts of both workers and shoppers at the end of the day (Meyer, 1970).

The problem of traffic congestion.
Despite improvement, there is still great dissatisfaction with almost all modes of urban transportation. The contrast between rush-hour congestion with its slow-moving traffic and the speed of both public and private travel at other times of day may explain some negative reactions. However, even with enormous investments in roads and public transportation systems, cities have been unable to eliminate traffic congestion.

The elimination of slow-moving traffic is not desirable for all urban systems. Service stations and other businesses often prefer to be located on streets that carry high volumes of slow-moving traffic for the trade that it generates. These businesses want travelers to stop and shop. Furthermore, the trip to work may be the only opportunity some drivers have to be alone or to listen to the radio. The slowness of rush-hour traffic also decreases the proportion of fatal accidents, although it increases the number of minor property-damage accidents.

The aggregate costs to society of accidents and automobile pollution are high, but individual drivers do not seem to consider these

Urban transportation networks are dominated by the automobile and the highway. But even with enormous investments in roads, cities have been unable to eliminate traffic congestion.

drawbacks serious. While accidents are frequent, most of them are minor, involving only property damage, which is generally covered by insurance (Greer, 1961). There has also been strenuous resistance to mandatory installation of both safety and antipollution devices on private cars. The costs of expanding our networks of streets and expressways to eliminate the congestion that takes place for twenty hours a week during rush periods would be far too high. The capital investment in roads, the loss of taxable property from city tax rolls, the social costs of dislocated neighborhoods and industry, and the increased need for downtown parking would be very high. Consequently, congestion is unlikely to be eliminated, and alternatives to the automobile must be considered (Dyckman, 1973:195).

Benefits of the automobile. To the user, transportation is a form of consumer goods purchased in light of the direct and indirect costs and benefits. The benefits of the automobile are that it is door-to-door transportation; it is private; its schedule is determined by the user (85 percent of those who get to work by car drive their own cars); it is generally safe from crime; it provides protection from the elements in bad weather. Many of the costs, as for streets and roads, streetlighting, and so on, are not borne directly by the consumer but are shared by all members of society. The consumer pays only direct operating costs—gasoline, oil, maintenance, insurance, and loss of capital. In terms of daily out-of-pocket costs and benefits, the average person thinks the automobile is the best value for the transportation dollar (Meyer, 1970:40-75). Mass transportation provides none of the benefits of the automobile and requires more daily out-of-pocket costs. Therefore, most people who can afford the initial investment in a car use it to get to work.

Inability of mass transportation to compete. Mass transportation, whether on buses, streetcars, subways, or railroads, operates on fixed routes. As residential density decreases and as the destinations of people going to work become more diffuse, there are not enough patrons to support **fixed route transportation** systems, and they become increasingly obsolete and expensive. Except in very densely settled cities, the capacity of rail-based transportation exceeds the number of people who live close enough to the stops to use this means of transportation. This problem is aggravated as the work locations spread farther from downtown terminals of the system; thus rail-based systems cannot work at peak efficiency (Dyckman, 1973). Mass transportation systems cannot compete with the automobile in providing door-to-door service. If they make enough stops to approximate door-to-door service, they become slow and unprofitable (Meyer, 1970; Greer, 1961).

It should be apparent that problems of overutilization of roads and underutilization of mass transportation facilities are related both to the type of vehicle used (car versus train, streetcar, bus) and to the routes available. These problems are a consequence of the density of urban residential areas, the relative centralization of work locations, and the standardized workday (Meyer, 1970; Greer, 1961).

Some Consequences of Transportation Characteristics

Change in courtship patterns. The widespread use of the automobile has resulted in a net gain in personal mobility, but the automobile has had many anticipated and unanticipated consequences for its users and the society. For example, it caused a dramatic change in the courtship patterns of the American population and in the relationships between adolescents and their parents. The mobility and privacy that the automobile provides were at first widely deplored and viewed with horror. Now that we have become an automotive society, the effect of the automobile on courtship, privacy, and morality is no longer a major social problem (Meyer, 1970; Greer, 1961).

Decreased values of older areas. By opening outlying areas of the city to settlement and use, the automobile has decreased the relative value of the older residential, commercial, and industrial structures in the center of the city. The older residential areas have become less attractive, and the older multistoried office buildings, lofts, and other industrial space in the city are unable to compete with modern single-story factories, stores, warehouses, and office buildings in suburban districts. Congestion in the older streets of the central city, caused by the use of the private automobile for commuting, has handicapped the central business district by making it increasingly difficult to use trucks or other vehicles for business purposes (Meyer, 1970).

Financial difficulties of mass transit systems. The automobile is such an attractive alternative to contemporary mass transportation systems that few people choose to use these systems when they do not have to. As a consequence, mass transit systems are generally in financial difficulty and have had to raise fares (and thus lose more riders) or reduce service. Were mass public transportation to disappear completely, however, cities would be choked by cars. The streets would be totally overcrowded and impassable; parking would be unavailable; the competitive position of the central business district would deteriorate further.

The institutions of the central city want to maintain their accessibility to the vast marketplace of the metropolitan area. The merchants and employers of the central city want their customers and workers to have easy, rapid, inexpensive transportation to the central business district. Suburban institutions do not have the same interest in maintaining mass public transportation because private transportation brings their customers and employees to them. Suburban shopping centers do not want public transportation centered on the central business district because it would encourage customers to abandon the suburban shopping centers for the downtown shopping facilities (Greer, 1961; Dyckman, 1973).

Many suburban residents feel they are being doubly taxed when asked to support mass transportation—taxed to provide transportation for people who do not use cars and taxed to provide roads for their own cars. Americans spend more on automobile transportation than they do on doctors, religion, charity, telephone, radio, television, furniture, electricity, gas, books, magazines, and newspapers combined. They clearly value their automobiles and do not want to be taxed to support other means of transportation. The problem for those who champion public transportation is that the public is choosing what it wants and getting what it chooses, although it is getting other things it doesn't want, such as accidents and pollution.

The complex interdependency between the urban transportation network and the physical obsolescence of the buildings and other structures in the inner city—lofts, streets, sidewalks, parking facilities, and so on—poses serious problems. The city was designed for a different set of transportation technologies. It may be necessary to alter both to modernize either successfully. In doing so, the social costs to the city—such as the cost of increasing the rapidity of movement between suburb and downtown, leading to an exodus of population from the city to the suburbs—must be included (Greer, 1961).

Types of use problems. Three factors affect the problems of vehicle types and routes used in urban transportation.

1. There is a collection problem. Fixed-route mass transit systems are unpopular, which leads to the use of the automobile. This problem arises largely from the low density of most residential areas and a diffusion of urban workplaces made possible by the automobile.
2. There is a delivery problem. This problem is similar to the collection problem. It arises from the fact that the central business district has increased in size, and a single transportation terminal in the downtown area is no longer adequate because many people work more than a convenient walk from any single terminal.
3. There is a **peak use** problem. Standardized working hours concentrate a high proportion of transportation volume in a small period of time. This leads to congestion on the roads and in mass transit vehicles during peak-use hours and the underutilization of these facilities at other times, which produces high operating costs (Greer, 1961; Meyer, 1970; Dyckman, 1973).

Problems of Performance, Efficiency, and Cost

The performance and efficiency of urban transportation networks are lowest when movement is slowed by congestion. There is no convincing evidence that congestion occurs frequently outside of rush hours or that it is getting worse. In fact, with the shift of workplaces and residences to the edges of urban areas, the proportion of trips made from decentralized residential areas to the central business district may have decreased somewhat (Gakenheimer, 1967).

Because the average travel time for the journey-to-work has been reduced, why is there so much talk about a transportation crisis? First, we have unmet expectations about higher traffic speeds during nonrush hours. Second, despite vast expenditures on transportation systems designed to support the central business district, suburban property values have increased more rapidly than have inner-city values. Many businesses performing central place functions have discovered that it is no longer necessary to put up with central business district traffic congestion (Meyer, 1970).

One way to evaluate the efficiency and performance of urban transportation systems is in terms of their effects on the conservation of cities as we have known them. From this perspective, the issue in transportation is one of centrality: the existence of a viable, efficient downtown or the creation of a diffuse, sprawling city. Reliance on the automobile for the bulk of trips to work has a destructive effect on the downtown area: space is used for automobile traffic and parking; land is removed from the tax rolls; congestion results; and residential and central business district functions are dispersed (Dyckman, 1973).

The dispersion of the urban population is likely to continue and even accelerate. Present modes of transportation, especially those on fixed routes, will become outmoded. Cities will be so large that cars or other personal and flexible means of transportation will be needed to get around the city. Proposals for traffic improvement include the restriction of vehicles to particular lanes, controlled timing and access, and the use of technological devices to increase the efficiency of the use of automobiles or other personal transportation modes (Dyckman, 1973).

The costs of present transportation systems are felt throughout the entire society. A large fraction of the labor force works directly in the transportation industry, particularly in the automobile industry. Much of the economy depends directly or indirectly on the automobile industry. A substantial proportion of state and federal taxes goes to maintain highways, streets, and roads. The economic costs of adapting cities to the automobile are also high: more and wider streets, more parking, more expressways, increased access routes, more personnel and material for the control of traffic, as well as increased highway building. All this is expensive in terms of capital investment and land and property taken off the tax rolls.

The private automobile also imposes incalculable costs in human suffering. In 1974 there were over twenty-three million traffic accidents involving automobiles, which caused nearly five million injuries and forty-six thousand deaths. The economic loss came to over thirty million dollars, but the physical pain and emotional suffering that these accidents caused, which appear necessary correlates of travel by automobile, cannot be calculated (U.S Bureau of the Census, 1975: table 964).

The urban transportation system, heavily dependent on the automobile, is largely responsible for the depletion of natural resources. The oil embargo of 1973-74 showed what happens when petrochemicals become more expensive and less readily available. The use of mass transportation increased seven to eight percent as a result of the oil embargo (*New York Times,* 30 December 1974:39). Despite temporary changes in availability, world oil reserves are running out. As oil becomes more scarce and more expensive, some people who now live in the suburbs may move to the downtown, changing both the social character and economic status of the inner city. This may also lead to a resurgence of interest in urban amenities, such as theaters and museums, much like that shown in New York City during the oil embargo (*New York Times,* 21 February 1974:1).

In 1974 there were over twenty-three million traffic accidents involving automobiles.

Without modern medical advances, the city would have remained "such a death trap that urban growth would probably have stalled in the later nineteenth century."

The City's Role in Health Care

Cities have always been unhealthy places to live in. They have been regularly devastated by plagues, such as the Black Plague and epidemics of typhoid, typhus, and cholera (Langer, 1973:106-11; Mumford, 1961:217, 290-93, 467-68, 473-78). Lack of sanitation, of knowledge of the need for pure water, and of the ability to dispose safely of garbage and solid wastes resulted in the rapid spread of infectious diseases. The combination of dense population and undeveloped medical knowledge caused many urban health problems. Until the twentieth century, life was short even for those who survived the first year. The death rate during the first year of life was very high, reaching 25 percent in a hospital in Paris in the 1830s (Roebuck, 1974:135).

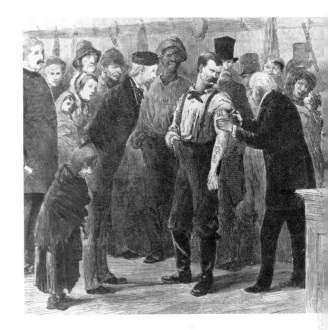

With the development of modern medicine in the twentieth century, cities learned that to protect the health of their populations and to reduce the death rate, they would have to undertake a series of actions, or functions. Without these actions the city would have remained "such a death trap that urban growth would probably have stalled in the later nineteenth century" (Roebuck, 1974:135). The functions included provision of safe drinking water, sewage control, refuse removal, regulation of slaughterhouses, and quarantining of persons with infectious diseases. As medical knowledge increased, the number of health-related functions performed by cities also increased. At present, the city's role in health care is not limited to regulation of activities that pose a direct threat to health; it also includes provision of health care through municipally supported hospitals, clinics, and other facilities and personnel.

We can understand the role cities play in health care by examining health care activities and the available data on the health of the urban population. Most contemporary urban health care involves provision of a safe environment and healthful conditions and facilities, and regulation of behavior that might be detrimental to health.

The major health care function of cities is to ensure the availability of personal health care. Cities act to keep people healthy, or to help ill people recover their health, by making it possible for physicians and hospitals to function. We use data describing the location of physicians and hospitals and data on the health of the population to evaluate the success of cities in carrying out their health functions.

Although the health care system in American cities today is far from ideal, contemporary urban Americans live longer and are healthier than their predecessors (Roebuck, 1974:188). The health of even those who are racially and economically disadvantaged is considerably better than that of even the most advantaged Americans of a century ago (Richmond, 1970:5-38; Stewart, 1970:39-64). It is clear, however, that high-quality medical care is not equally available to the whole urban population (Ribicoff, 1971:12-19). The poor, the nonwhite, and in some respects the nonurban are less healthy than white, nonpoor residents of cities. The health of Americans who live in cities could be better than it is; to some extent we have the knowledge, although perhaps not the will, to make it better. In large measure this is the so-called crisis in American health care.

Modern medical and public health knowledge and its implementation in urban health functioning have virtually eliminated some health hazards that formerly contributed heavily to death rates (Stewart, 1970). Dysentery and cholera, the primary waterborne diseases, have been eliminated by water processing and chlorination (Roebuck, 1974; Stewart, 1970). Concerns about water quality standards now focus on topics and pollutants other than those that cause diseases directly (see chapter 13). With the exception of the common cold and the multiple and changing varieties of influenza, many infectious diseases have been controlled by vaccination programs. Cities often require children entering public schools to be vaccinated against a wide range of diseases and provide free vaccinations if the family cannot afford them (Stewart, 1970).

Cities also regulate other behaviors that can damage health. They attempt to control pollutants that have negative effects on health, and through various regulatory agencies are attempting to eliminate from the environment lead paint and other heavy metals that can cause poisoning and permanent damage. Cities inspect food and food handling facilities in retail outlets and restaurants to ensure purity, cleanliness, and safety. Cities also take action against a variety of sources of industrial pollution that affect the quality of health in urban areas. Cities acted to control industrial smoke emissions, for example, when it became clear that only sunlight (or special artificial lamps) could prevent rickets. Elimination of the heavy layers of smoke that characterized the early industrial city has eliminated this disease that was widespread in early nineteenth-century London and other European cities (Loomis, 1973:112-22; McDermott, 1973:132-40).

The Health of the Urban Population

Indicators of the health of populations are difficult to obtain: not all sickness is treated, not all treatment is recorded, and not all recorded treatments are statistically compiled. Therefore it is difficult to measure how many people have been sick in a given period. One general indicator that is universally recorded is the death rate—an unambiguous measure of health status. The specific death rate most widely used is infant mortality rate. The death rate of infants less than a year old is a sensitive indicator of other health conditions, especially the general health of the infant and the mother during pregnancy (Stewart, 1970). In addition to death-rate data, some evidence of the general health of the American population is available from surveys conducted since 1957 by the National Center for Health Statistics (Health Resources Administration, 1974).

Infant Mortality Rates

In the United States in 1972, the infant mortality rate was 18.5 per 1,000 live births. Fifteen other countries of the world had a lower rate (Health Resources Administration, 1975b:table 7.2 and 7-75; Richmond, 1970:11; Stewart, 1970:43). Infant mortality in the United States, however, was not constant and varied according to socioeconomic conditions. The rate was higher in urban places of ten thousand or more people than in smaller places (19.1 versus 17.7 per 1,000 live births). It was also higher in nonmetropolitan counties than in metropolitan counties, but in both metropolitan and nonmetropolitan counties the infant death rate was higher in the urban than in the rural portions. The highest infant death rate occurred in the urban portions of nonmetropolitan counties where 21 of 1,000 live births died. Other factors related to infant mortality rates in the United States were race, income, and residence in the poverty areas of a major city (Health Resources Administration, 1975b, 1975a:table C).

Nonwhites are concentrated in urban areas, particularly metropolitan urban areas, and also are disproportionately represented among the poor portions of our population. The nonwhite infant mortality rate in the United States in 1972 was 27.7 deaths per 1,000 live births, while the white infant mortality rate was only 16.4. Within cities the infant death rate is much higher in poverty areas than in nonpoverty areas, and in both areas the nonwhite infant death rates are much higher than the white infant death rates (Health Resources Administration, 1975b, 1975a:table C). In summary, the infant mortality rate in the United States is higher in cities than outside cities; it is particularly high among nonwhites and in poverty areas. The higher urban infant death rate is a reversal of the pattern that prevailed in the United States until 1920 (Stewart, 1970:44).

These data indicate that cities are not providing as good health care as is available outside cities. The distribution of infant death rates by race and urban-rural residence within metropolitan areas suggests that poverty and race are significantly related to the location and utilization of health care facilities. A large part of the crisis in American health care, to the extent that there is a crisis, can be accounted for by deficiencies in the availability of health care facilities rather than deficiencies in the quality of health care that can be made available.

Before discussing health care delivery systems, we will examine data on ecological distributions of sickness and death to see if they show the same patterns shown by infant death rate.

Sickness

Data on sickness among the American population comes from surveys conducted by the National Center for Health Statistics, which has been measuring the health of the American population since 1957. Long-term changes in public health are impossible to assess because the studies started so recently. We do know, however, that numerous diseases that historically have caused much sickness and death among urban populations no longer do so. These are mainly infectious diseases like measles, polio, smallpox, diphtheria, and whooping cough. Deaths from these diseases are rare today. Other infectious diseases, such as the common cold and influenza, are not yet preventable by inoculation. Large-scale vaccination and inoculation programs, combined with the invention of sulfa drugs in 1935 and antibiotics in 1940 and after, have reduced deaths and sickness caused by infection and led to prolonged life (Stewart, 1970; Roebuck, 1974: 188).

Despite these advances in controlling communicable diseases, urban populations are still not as healthy as nonurban populations, especially nonmetropolitan populations. Controlling communicable diseases is more important where population density and interaction density are greatest.

Levels of health are lowest in central cities of metropolitan areas; residents of central cities have more days of restricted activity per person per year, more days of being restricted to bed, more days lost from work, more acute conditions, and more surgical treatments than residents of areas outside central cities. These rates are higher in large SMSAs (both cities and suburbs) than in smaller SMSAs (National Center for Health Statistics, 1974:12).

Metropolitan residents see doctors and dentists more frequently than do nonmetropolitan residents, perhaps because services are more easily available; within metropolitan areas, suburban and central city residents have about the same average number of visits yearly. However, the proportion of suburban residents who make more than one trip a year to both doctors and dentists is larger than the proportion of central city residents who do (National Center for Health Statistics, 1974: 12).

Because levels of health are lower in central cities than in suburban areas, and because central city residents have more acute conditions and more surgical treatments, we would expect them to see physicians more frequently. The fact that suburban residents are more likely to visit medical personnel more than once a year leads us to wonder whether doctors and dentists are located where they are most needed.

Death

We have already seen that the infant death rate varies according to racial and social characteristics and residence. These characteristics also affect the death rate of persons beyond their first birthday. Again, we will be concerned not only with variations in rates between urban and nonurban areas and between metropolitan and nonmetropolitan areas, but also with variations in death rates between areas inside cities, particularly between poverty and nonpoverty areas.

In 1970 the crude death rate (the death rate that is not adjusted for the age distribution of the population) was higher in urban areas than in the balance of the United States (1003.99 versus 920.84).[2] However, the crude death rate was higher outside metropolitan counties than it was within SMSAs (1069.10 versus 919.48 per 100,000 population). But both within and outside metropolitan areas the crude death rate was higher in urban than in nonurban portions. In other words, more people die in urban than in nonurban areas, and the difference is not due to the size of the population.

The causes of death varied by where people lived. Infectious diseases caused relatively few deaths, but they were slightly more likely to have been the cause of death in urban areas than in rural areas, especially in urban areas within metropolitan areas. This fact is likely due to the density of the urban population, which facilitates the transmission of infectious diseases. Heart and other **cardiovascular diseases** were the leading causes of death and were more common in urban than in nonurban areas. Almost 80 percent of the deaths due to the thirty-four leading causes of death were caused by heart diseases. Finally, influenza, **hypertension,** and ulcers are more common causes of death in urban than in nonurban portions of the United States. This is to be expected because hypertension and

ulcers are diseases that may result from the more intense interaction and faster pace of urban life, as suggested by Wirth and Simmel.

As with infant mortality, the death rate for adults living in poverty areas is higher than for those living in nonpoverty areas. This difference is found for almost all causes of death from illness (Health Resources Administration, 1975b:table 7.9; U.S. Bureau of the Census, 1971b:tables 4, 5; Appel, 1970:157).

To summarize, the city historically has been an unhealthy and dangerous place to live in, and while the absolute levels of risk have been dramatically reduced, people living in metropolitan areas today are less healthy than those living in less developed portions of the country. Poor health is most likely to be found in the urban portions of metropolitan areas. Death rates are higher in urban than in nonurban areas and especially in the urban portions of metropolitan areas. The poverty areas of cities exhibit higher rates of impaired health and higher death rates than do nonpoverty areas.

Mental Health

Concern for the effects of cities on the psychological well-being of their residents goes back to the analyses of Simmel and Wirth (see chapter 6). Both described the effects of cities on personal adjustment and interpersonal interaction in negative terms. More recently, attention has focused on more specific indicators of mental health than those employed by Simmel and Wirth, who were concerned with alienation, reserve, and other general personality characteristics. Research

Adult mental health first admission
rates, Chicago. (Source: Leo Levy
and Louis Rowitz, *The Ecology of
Mental Disorders* [New York:
Behavioral Publications, 1973], p.
74.)

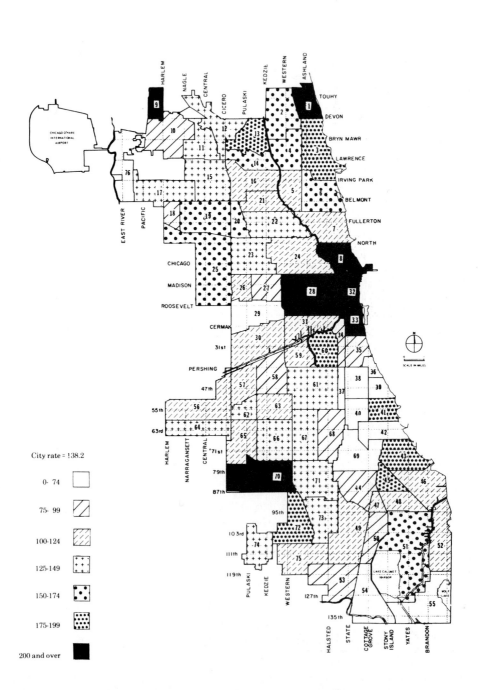

City rate = 138.2

0- 74	
75- 99	
100-124	
125-149	
150-174	
175-199	
200 and over	

in the last few decades has employed projective tests, mental hospital admission and readmission rates, as indicators of adjustment and disorganization in the examination of levels of impaired mental health in specific areas of cities (Clausen and Kohn, 1954:140-51; Faris and Dunham, 1939; Srole et al., 1975; Levy and Visotsky, 1969:255-69; Levy and Rowitz, 1973).

Despite difficulties in definition and measurement, rates of first admission to mental hospitals are now generally employed as a measure of public mental health. Many mentally ill persons, especially those of high social status, obtain their treatment from private physicians and are either never hospitalized or are admitted with a nonpsychiatric diagnosis. Thus the extent of mental illness may be biased toward overestimating the number of poor or low-status persons who are mentally ill. If higher admission rates are observed in low-status areas of cities, some portion of this finding may be due to this bias.

Urban residents, especially those in large cities, do appear to be admitted to mental institutions at a higher rate than do residents of small cities or rural areas (Wanklin et al., 1955:103-16). Within cities, rates of first admission vary by location. Overall first admission rates are higher at or near the core of the city than they are at greater distances from the city center (Levy and Rowitz, 1973:74). The ecological distribution of mental illness follows the pattern to be expected from the analyses of Simmel and Wirth.

Schizophrenia, the most common mental illness, is clearly distributed ecologically. However, the high incidence of schizophrenia statistically overwhelms the fact that other diagnoses, such as manic-depressive, have other distributions. In fact, there is a tendency for manic-depressive patients to reside in urban areas of high socioeconomic status (Levy and Rowitz, 1973:80). This finding is exactly the opposite of the result we would expect because of the reporting bias which underestimates admissions of high-status residents. We therefore have greater faith in findings that mental illness is ecologically distributed.

Because levels of poor health, both physical and mental, and the death rate vary by rural-urban location and by ecological distribution within cities, we must examine the health care delivery system to understand how cities perform their health-related functions.

The Health Care Delivery System and the City

The **health care delivery system** consists mainly of hospitals and physicians. Other components are health care personnel, public clinics, pharmacies, and so on. This section presents the distribution and availability of hospitals and physicians by residential location throughout the society and by types of areas within cities.

Physician Distributions

On a national basis there is one physician for every 750 people, but there is considerable variation from state to state and from region to region. In the northeastern states there is one physician for each 568 residents (and in some states one to 280 people), while in southern states there is only one physician to 1,400 people (Appel, 1970:144; Glazer, 1972: 160).

Metropolitan areas have more than their proportionate share of physicians: 73 percent of the United States population in 1972 lived in SMSAs, but 85 percent of the total patient-care physicians, 83 percent of physicians practicing in private offices, and 85 to 97 percent of physicians practicing in hospitals were located in metropolitan areas (Roback, 1973). As a consequence, nonmetropolitan areas may not have enough medically trained personnel. In nonmetropolitan portions of the country, the physician-to-population ratio is 70 or fewer physicians per 100,000 population; some isolated rural counties in the United States that had 3.2 percent of the population in 1970 had only 1.5 percent of the physicians (Glazer, 1972:160). Many rural areas and small towns are unable to maintain or even attract a single physician. Newspapers and national television programs periodically report the heroic efforts and generous offers that some small towns make to attract a physician, often without success (Fahs and Petersen, 1968:1200-1211; Wainwright, 1970:47-50). There are even magazines for doctors in which small towns seeking physicians can advertise. The reasons that many small towns and rural areas have difficulty attracting physicians are many and complex. Most medical training takes place in metropolitan areas, and modern medicine requires both expensive facilities and access to specialists. A large population is needed to support such facilities and to offer specialists enough patients to maintain their skills (Rourke, 1971:151; Roebuck, 1974:189). Like most professionals, doctors like to be in personal contact with other professionals. They like to know and to have feedback from the specialists to whom they refer their patients. A town that can support only one doctor cannot provide this opportunity.

Because physicians are overrepresented in metropolitan areas, we cannot conclude that all metropolitan areas (or that all areas within a metropolis) are equally provided with physicians. The metropolitan areas that have the most physicians are those that are the largest, have the most hospital facilities, and above all have the most medical training facilities. The life styles on the two coasts also attract physicians away from the Midwest. Physicians are especially drawn to the more comfortable areas of the West Coast (Marden, 1966:290-300; DeVise, 1973:141-51).

Perhaps even more obvious than the difference between metropolitan and nonmetropolitan areas in number of physicians is the fact that within metropolitan areas medical facilities are far from evenly distributed. Physicians in private practice are found in nonpoor areas of cities and increasingly in the suburban portions of SMSAs rather than in the central city. For example, Chicago lost nearly 3,000 family practice (that is, general practice) physicians between 1950 and 1974. At the same time the total number of physicians in the Chicago SMSA increased from 9,270 to 13,060. Poverty areas of the central city lost physicians to the suburbs, and new physicians located in the suburbs. Suburbs were increasingly well supplied with physicians while the city was experiencing a net loss of physicians (Merridew, 1975). The location of physicians is affected by such factors as proximity to a medical school and number of hospital beds available in the SMSA. The availability of office space near hospitals, or near major transportation routes, is also important in determining location within an

SMSA (Joroff and Navarro, 1971:428-38; Kaplan and Leinhardt, 1973:406-15).

The racial composition of an area within an SMSA also affects the distribution of physicians. All types of physicians tend to avoid heavily black areas, specialists more so than general practitioners. Specialists are not as frequently consulted by residents who are of low average education. Most physicians are white, and they may not wish to encroach on the "territory" of black physicians. However, there is relatively little evidence on these matters.

Hospital Distributions

The joint effects of poverty, the scarcity of private physicians in poor areas of the city, and the distances to offices of private physicians have made hospital facilities the predominant source of medical care for the urban poor (Health Resources Administration, 1974:12). Residents of SMSA central cities receive a much larger proportion of their physician care in hospital clinics and emergency rooms than do other Americans.

Much health care provided to the urban poor in hospitals, clinics, and other inpatient facilities is paid for either by Medicare-Medicaid, public aid, or the city as owner and operator of the hospital where treatment takes place. New York City, for example, has eighteen municipal hospitals that give medical services to two million persons annually (most of them poor, old, or both). These facilities handle 90 percent of the emergency cases in the city and half of all outpatient care. This costs the city $1 billion per year (*New York Times,* 22 October 1975:1). While other cities are not as generous, they follow the same general pattern. These municipal hospitals serve increasing proportions of the urban population as a result of the migration of physicians and middle-class residents to the suburbs. The concomitant rise in the cost of medical care, particularly hospital care, has seriously handicapped the ability of hospitals to provide adequate care. City hospitals are older and have less up-to-date facilities and equipment. Staffs find it increasingly difficult to provide high-quality medical care in the face of decreasing revenues from financially pressed city governments and the increasing reluctance of third parties to insure health care for the urban poor. Users of municipal hospitals, county hospitals, and other public facilities have complained of long waits, impersonal treatment, bureaucratic inefficiency, and less than humane care by medical staffs (Ribicoff, 1970; Glazer, 1972).

Summary of Health Care Problems

There seems to be a dichotomy between the poor and the nonpoor and the urban and the nonurban in the kind of medical care they receive in our society. The nonpoor, particularly those who live in the suburbs, have a wider choice of private practitioners, medical specialists, and modern hospital facilities than do the poor. The poor, living in central cities of SMSAs, rely on hospital clinics that have neither the staff nor often the up-to-date facilities to provide the kind of individual attention that private physicians can. Urban health care clearly poses a serious problem for society. The costs of health care are going up, seemingly uncontrollably, while the quality of health care among city residents has stagnated, as reflected in higher infant and other

Tchula, Miss., One of 1,600 Towns in Nation Looking for a Doctor

Tchula, Miss.—Tchula, like many other small towns around the country, is looking for a doctor.

By the end of the month, Ronald W. Brass, Christine Klasen and Joji Kappes, the three physicians placed in this poverty-bound delta town by the Federal National Service Corps, will complete a two-year tour of duty and will leave to continue their medical training.

Next January, Dr. Howard J. Hoody, a family physician from Sioux Falls, S.D., who was recruited by the three doctors, plans to join the corps and set up practice in Tchula's clinic.

For the intervening six months, however, the clinic has found no doctor.

None of 278 physicians being placed by the National Health Service Corps this year have chosen to work in Tchula. And officials of the corps have not assigned a doctor here, although they can do so in some circumstances.

Two candidates for the corps have visited the Tchula clinic, but if neither chooses to work there the clinic will be closed, says David E. Gorrison, director of the clinic.

If the clinic is closed Tchula would lose some of its attraction for Dr. Hoody, who expects to be working there with another doctor. Moreover, the closing of the clinic, now the town's third largest industry, would have a severe economic effect on the area—even if the closing were only temporary.

The National Service Corps, which places doctors in areas with fewer than one doctor per 4,000 population, says there are 1,600 federally designated communities with the same or similar physician problems as Tchula.

To alleviate the problems, towns such as Tchula face in attracting doctors, Congress is considering if it should require all American medical school graduates to serve in a community needing doctors in repayment for the substantial Federal subsidies that go to their education.

Others, especially physician groups, would rather let the corps handle the problem.

The corps gets its doctors, dentists, nurses and other health workers, for the most part, by giving scholarships and loans to students in return for later service. These scholarship students must take assignments or repay the money. Some elect to repay.

The program's director, Dr. George P. Tolbert, and its former director, Dr. Edward Martin, prefer the assignments to be voluntary.

To send doctors to places they would prefer not to be, they believe, "estranges" the doctor and the community and does not serve the long-range goal of the corps. According to Dr. Martin, that goal is to get doctors to stay permanently in the places to which they are assigned.

356

The shortage of physicians in small towns, especially those located in poor or rural areas, is still severe. The federal national service corps is able to help some of these towns, but both the towns and the physicians have difficulty adjusting to one another.

The voluntary system has worked well, Dr. Tolbert said. There are now 520 corpsmen in 340 mostly rural communities around the country, and 40 percent of those corpsmen are settling in them.

Tchula, however, has not been that lucky, and those who now use the clinic are waiting to see if they must again spend more money on transportation to distant doctors offices than for health care.

Part of a Chronic Problem

The crisis in Tchula is a case history of the chronic problem of getting the country's best educated, highest paid professionals—doctors— to its poorest, least developed and most needy communities.

While organizations such as the National Health Service Corps have improved the general outlook for these communities, they have left unresolved problems, as illustrated by Tchula.

Tchula, in west-central Holmes County, is a town whose population of 1,800 is 85 percent black and whose median family income is $3,089 a year, most of it earned from work on the cotton and soybean plantations that are the economic mainstay of the region.

The remnants of old South racism abound in Tchula. Physicians in other towns in Holmes County still keep separate black and white waiting rooms in violations of Federal law. The public schools, which were burned down rather than desegregated, have been rebuilt, but they are 100 percent black. Whites attend private academies.

The average length of schooling in the community is 8.4 years—two years lower than the state average, which is below the national average.

Plantation families live for the most part in dilapidated shacks first inhabited by their slave ancestors: Two or three rooms furnished with wall-to-wall beds, bare light bulbs, outdoor plumbing.

Reminder of Slave Days

These families file into the Tchula clinic with slips from their plantation owners, authorizing medical care for a host of problems, worse than those found in most inner city populations.

One family, for example, came to the clinic with nausea and diarrhea.

It was discovered that the family's well and outhouse were near one another and a drought had caused wastes to seep into the water supply.

Drs. Brass, Klasen, and Kappes—all in their late '20s, all 1973 graduates of the University of Southern California—chose to practice together in Tchula, where the town's sole doctor died in 1971.

The beginning was not easy for them, however. They argued with many townspeople, who opposed their integrated waiting room, their communal living arrangement, and their failure to join the church.

"Many in the town, didn't want anything to do with the government," explained John Edgar Hays, a cotton farmer who is the community liaison between the clinic and the town Board of Aldermen, of which he is a member. "They thought it was socialized medicine."

In time, however, the townspeople got used to the doctor's ways. And the doctors hired Mr. Garrison, set up a fee schedule and placed the clinic on a sound business footing. At first the doctors had refused to charge fees, a stance that prompted some difficulties.

The doctors hired and trained eight workers, who are among the highest paid in a town of low pay scales. They applied for and received grant money to expand the facilities and to recruit a dentist, Dr. Russell Kearneu of nearby Yazoo City. The clinic has also attracted a private, part-time optometrist, Dr. Allen Findley, who sees patients two days a week.

A new pharmacy opened next door to the clinic, which has created two more jobs and has, according to the mayor, Lester Lyons, brought the town an appreciable increase in sales tax revenue.

The town is gaining in population and has new, small businesses opening up in New South tradition. But the doctors do not come.

Source Nancy Hicks, *New York Times*, June 21, 1977, p. 20. © 1977 by The New York Times Company. Reprinted by Permission.

he doctor won't be in today
or tomorrow

Surgoinsville, Tennessee, hasn't had a doctor since 1965. That's when the community's only doctor died. Day after day, Surgoinsville's modern medical clinic stands empty, useless.

What do 5,000 Surgoinsville residents do when they get sick? They drive a long way. And wait a long time.

Surgoinsville's clinic faces a lot of empty tomorrows. If you can help Surgoinsville find a doctor, write today for more information on the clinic, the people, and the resources in Surgoinsville.

SICK

Surgoinsville, Tennessee 37873

death rates. More urban residents are relying on the city directly or indirectly for medical care. They complain bitterly when the care they receive is less than adequate, which it often is if adequacy is judged on the basis of speed of treatment, respect accorded the patient, and quality of treatment. The poor and minority group members of society who use public urban health care systems exhibit lower levels of health and much higher death rates because of restricted access to much of the health care system. Seventy-one percent of all patient-care physicians in SMSAs are in private practice in their own offices, leaving few to practice in the hospitals (Roback, 1973). The physicians who practice in hospitals are predominantly residents and interns completing their training, who have to fill the gap in health care caused by the dearth of private, office-based physicians in the city. While metropolitan areas have an oversupply of physicians, hospitals, medical schools, and the like, their distribution within the SMSA seems to be out of balance with the need for their services, especially in poor areas of the city.

Summary

Cities are currently experiencing problems in performing, or in facilitating the performance of, their functions in the areas of housing, transportation, and health. Many solutions have been proposed—so many, of such variety, and with so little testing of results that an adequate analysis of them would require a more extensive discussion than would be possible here. However, the discussion of the nature and sociological character of the problems presented here should provide a basis for analysis of proposed solutions as they arise.

Providing housing for residents is an important communal function of cities. Cities, however, perform this function only to a limited extent: most housing is provided by private sources. The city's role is limited to regulating the kind of housing provided, inspecting housing units for safety and compliance with city codes, dealing with problems caused by concentrations of poor housing, and ensuring an adequate supply of housing. The quality of housing has improved in recent years, and cities have maintained this quality at least as well as suburbs and rural areas.

Housing adequacy and supply are closely linked to both race and income; poor and black urban residents, especially those who do not own their own homes, are much more likely than others to live in inadequate housing. Urban homes, unlike homes outside the city, are less likely to be single-family units, and the supply of urban homes is no longer growing as rapidly as the number of families seeking them. As the age and family size of the population change, the supply of urban dwellings will become even less well matched with the population seeking housing.

Many urban housing problems are caused by slums, concentrations of overcrowded and inadequate housing units. The slums cause physical and psychological health problems for their residents. Slum dwellers cannot support private providers of goods and services, and they require many more services than those living in other areas.

Transportation has altered the shape of the city and allowed the integration of the metropolis. The automobile, however, imposes high costs on the city: it causes pollution and accidents, requires expensive parking, highway, and regulatory facilities, and fails to provide satisfactory transportation for large numbers of people.

Most urban trips are made by automobile; it is private and convenient. Consequently roads are clogged, costs to the individual and society are high, and mass transportation is inefficiently used. The high density of riders needed to make rail-based transit systems efficient rarely occurs, and buses do not seem to be a satisfactory alternative to the automobile. Attempts to provide integrated metropolitan transportation often meet with resistance because of different interests of city and suburban residents, different travel needs of different groups, and the high costs of mass transportation systems.

With the development of modern medical and public health knowledge, cities have become healthier places to live in. Death rates in cities historically have been very much higher than those in rural areas, but this difference has been dramatically reduced in the twentieth century. Urban infant and adult death rates are still, however, somewhat higher than those found outside cities. Poverty and the concentration of poor people in areas of cities where health care delivery systems are inadequate are partially responsible. Rates of impaired physical and mental health are higher in cities than in nonurban areas.

Medical personnel are concentrated in metropolitan areas. But in sections where the need is greatest, most care is provided by clinics and hospital emergency rooms. Despite its shortcomings, some care is available in most areas of a metropolis. Rural areas, in contrast, often have difficulty attracting any medical personnel and resources.

Cities face tremendous interrelated problems in performing their communal functions. In many cases the problems are caused by forces beyond the control of any single city, and solutions will have to emerge on a societal scale. Until solutions are developed, housing, transportation, and health will continue to be major urban problems. Our ability to continue as an urban society depends on how well our cities perform their communal functions in the future.

Glossary

cardiovascular diseases   diseases of the heart and circulatory system

family formation   the creation of new families by marriage

first admission   the first time a person is admitted to a hospital, particularly as it applies to mental health; subsequent admissions for the same illness are not counted, but subsequent admissions for different illnesses are counted as a new first admission

fixed route transportation   means of transportation that operate on routes that cannot vary, especially on tracks, but also on rivers

health care delivery system   the system that provides health care, including such components as physicians, nurses, hospitals, pharmacists, offices, and so on

hypertension   a circulatory disease, often called high blood pressure, which can be fatal; stress and diet contribute to its development

inadequate housing   generally housing that needs major repairs, lacks some or all plumbing, and is overcrowded; all characteristics need not be present to make a single unit inadequate, and units that have none of these characteristics can also be considered inadequate if they are located in an area with many inadequate units

infant mortality rate   the number of children under one year of age who died in a given year, divided by the total number of live births in that year

interaction density   the number of interpersonal contacts in a given area in a given period of time; this number must increase as population density increases

journey-to-work   the journey from one's home to one's work location and back again

mass transit   means of transportation for carrying large numbers of people in a relatively small number of vehicles: subways, commuter railroads, buses; frequently, but not always, publicly owned

mode of travel   the type of vehicle used in travel—car, bus, train, subway

multiple-unit structures   buildings that contain more than one dwelling unit, such as apartment houses, townhouses, and duplexes

network capacity   in transportation terms the maximum capacity of the transportation system

overcrowding   in housing, less than one room per person in a dwelling unit (statisticians express the measure as 1.01 or more persons per room); the figure is based on current values in the United States

peak use   the maximum use of a transportation network; generally observed during the hours of the journey-to-work

residential density   the number of residents living in an area, divided by the physical size of the area in square miles or square kilometers

rickets   a bone disease, found mostly among children; commonly thought to be a dietary deficiency disease caused by lack of vitamin D, but in fact an air pollution disease caused by lack of exposure to sunlight

slum   a concentrated, densely settled area where housing is inadequate, residents are poor, and communal functions are lacking. Some observers have said that social disorganization and pathological behavior are common in such areas, but others consider slums to be highly organized and have pointed out that the behavior of slum residents is based on values that are very different from the middle-class values of most social scientists

space-time ratio   the distance traveled, divided by the time it takes to travel

---

References

Anderson, Martin
1967   "The Federal Bulldozer." In *Urban Renewal: The Record and the Controversy,* edited by James Q. Wilson, pp. 441-508. Cambridge, Mass.: M.I.T. Press.

Appel, James Z.
1970   "Health Care Delivery." In *The Health of Americans,* edited by Boisfeuillet Jones, pp. 141-66. Englewood Cliffs, N.J.: Prentice-Hall, Inc.

Calhoun, John B.
1963   "Population Density and Social Pathology." In *The Urban Condition: People and Policy in the Metropolis,* edited by Leonard J. Duhl, pp. 33-44. New York: Basic Books, Inc., Publishers.

Chilton, Ronald J.
1964   "Continuities in Delinquency Area Research: A Comparison of Studies for Baltimore, Detroit, and Indianapolis." *American Sociological Review* 29 (February):71-83.

Choldin, Harvey
1976   "Crowding and Pathology: Los Angeles, 1970." Paper presented at meetings of the American Sociological Association.

Clausen, John A., and Kohn, Melvin L.
1954   "The Ecological Approach in Social Psychiatry." *American Journal of Sociology* 60 (September):140-51.

DeVise, Pierre
1973   "Physician Migration from Inland to Coastal States." *Journal of Medical Education* 48 (February):141-51.

Dyckman, John W.
1973   "Transportation in Cities." *Scientific American* (September 1965). In *Cities: Their Origin, Growth, and Human Impact,* edited by Kingsley Davis, pp. 195-206. San Francisco: W. H. Freeman & Company Publishers.

Fahs, Ivan J., and Petersen, Osler J.
1968   "Towns without Physicians and Towns with Only One: A Study of Four States in the Upper Midwest." *American Journal of Public Health* 58, no. 7:1200-1211.

Faris, Robert E. L., and Dunham, H. Warren
1939   *Mental Disorder in Urban Areas.* Chicago: University of Chicago Press.

Fried, Marc, and Gleicher, Peggy
1970   "Some Sources of Residential Satisfaction in an Urban Slum." In *Neighborhood, City, and Metropolis,* edited by David Gutman and Robert Popenoe, pp. 730-45. New York: Random House, Inc.

Frieden, Bernard J.
1970   "Housing and National Urban Goals: Old Policies and New Realities." In *The Metropolitan Enigma,* edited by James Q. Wilson, pp. 170-225. Garden City, N.Y.: Doubleday & Co., Inc.

Gakenheimer, Ralph A.
1967   "Urban Transportation Planning: An Overview." In *Taming Megalopolis, Vol. I, What Is and What Could Be,* edited by H. Wentworth Eldredge, pp. 392-411. Garden City, N.Y.: Doubleday & Co., Inc.

Glazer, Nathan
1967   "The Effects of Poor Housing." *Journal of Marriage and the Family* 29, no. 1 (February):140-45.

1972   "Paradoxes of Health Care." *The Public Interest* (Winter, 1971). In *The View from Below: Urban Politics and Social Policy,* edited by Susan S. and Norman J. Fainstein, pp. 159-74. Boston: Little, Brown and Company.

Greer, Scott
1961   "Traffic, Transportation, and Problems of the Metropolis." In *Contemporary Social Problems,* edited by Robert K. Merton and Robert A. Nisbet, pp. 605-50. 1st ed. New York: Harcourt, Brace & World, Inc.

Health Resources Administration, National Center for Health Statistics
1974   *Health Characteristics by Geographic Regions, Large Metropolitan Areas, and Other Places of Residence: United States 1969-70.* Washington, D.C.: Government Printing Office.

1975a   *Selected Vital and Health Statistics in Poverty and Nonpoverty Areas of 19 Large Cities, United States 1969-71.* Washington, D.C.: Government Printing Office.

1975b *Vital Statistics of the United States. Vol. II, Mortality, 1972.* Washington, D.C.: Government Printing Office.

Joroff, Sheila, and Navarro, Vincente
1971 "Medical Manpower: A Multivariate Analysis of the Distribution of Physicians in Urban United States." *Medical Care* 9, 5(September 10):428-38.

Kain, John F.
1973 "What Should America's Housing Policy Be?" *U.S. Department of Commerce, Economic Development Administration Program on Regional and Urban Economics,* Discussion Paper 82 (December 27).

Kaplan, Robert S., and Leinhardt, Samuel
1973 "Determinants of Physician Office Location." *Medical Care* 11, 5(September 10):406-15.

Lander, Bernard
1971 "Towards an Understanding of Juvenile Delinquency." In *Ecology, Crime, and Delinquency,* edited by Harwin L. Voss and David M. Petersen, pp. 161-75. New York: Appleton-Century-Crofts.

Langer, William L.
1973 "The Black Death." *Scientific American* (February 1964). In *Cities: Their Origin, Growth, and Human Impact,* edited by Kingsley Davis, pp. 106-11. San Francisco: W. H. Freeman & Company Publishers.

Levy, Leo, and Rowitz, Louis
1973 *The Ecology of Mental Disorder.* New York: Behavioral Publications, Inc.

Levy, Leo, and Visotsky, Harold M.
1969 "The Quality of Urban Life: An Analysis from the Perspective of Mental Health." In *The Quality of Urban Life,* edited by Henry J. Schmandt and Warner Bloomberg, pp. 255-68. Beverly Hills, Calif.: Sage Publications, Inc.

Loomis, W. F.
1973 "Rickets." *Scientific American* (December 1970). In *Cities: Their Origin, Growth, and Human Impact,* edited by Kingsley Davis, pp. 112-22. San Francisco: W. H. Freeman & Company Publishers.

McDermott, Walsh
1973 "Air Pollution and Public Health." *Scientific American* (October 1961). In *Cities: Their Origin, Growth, and Human Impact,* edited by Kingsley Davis, pp. 132-40. San Francisco: W. H. Freeman & Company Publishers.

Marden, Parker G.
1966 "A Demographic and Ecological Analysis of the Distribution of Physicians in Metropolitan America." *American Journal of Sociology* 72:290-300.

Merridew, Alan
1975 "Doctors Seeking Greener Suburb Pastures, Flee City." *Chicago Tribune* (November 20).

Meyer, John R.
1970 "Urban Transportation." In *The Metropolitan Enigma,* edited by James Q. Wilson, pp. 40-75. Garden City, N.Y.: Doubleday & Co., Inc.

Mladenka, Kenneth R., and Hill, Kim Quailie
1976 "A Reexamination of the Etiology of Urban Crime." *Criminology* 13, 4(February):491-506.

Mumford, Lewis
1961 *The City in History.* New York: Harcourt, Brace & World, Inc.

National Commission on Urban Problems
1972 *Building the American City.* Washington, D.C.: Government Printing Office.

Plant, James S.
1930 "Some Psychiatric Aspects of Crowded Living Conditions." *American Journal of Psychiatry* 9, 5(March):849-60.
1960 "Family Living Space and Personality Development." In *A Modern Introduction to the Family,* edited by Norman W. Bell and Ezra F. Vogel, pp. 510-20. New York: Free Press.

Polk, Kenneth
1967 "Urban Social Areas and Delinquency." *Social Problems* 14, 3(Winter):320-25.

Real Estate Research Corporation
1974 *The Costs of Sprawl, Executive Summary.* Washington, D.C.: Government Printing Office.

Ribicoff, Abraham
1971 "The Healthiest Nation Myth." *Saturday Review* 53 (22 August 1970). In *The Nation's Health,* edited by Stephen Lewin, pp. 12-19. New York: The H. W. Wilson Company.

Richmond, Julius B.
1970 "Human Development." In *The Health of Americans,* edited by Boisfeuillet Jones, pp. 5-38. Englewood Cliffs, N.J.: Prentice-Hall, Inc.

Roback, G. A.
1973 *Distribution of Physicians in the United States, 1972, Vol. II, Metropolitan Areas.* Chicago: American Medical Association Center for Health Services Research and Development.

Roebuck, Janet
1974 *The Shaping of Urban Society.* New York:
Charles Scribner's Sons.

Rourke, Anthony J.
1971 "Small Town Doctor Needs More Than an Office," *Modern Medicine* 117, 5(November):151.

Schorr, Alvin L.
1963 *Slums and Social Insecurity: An Appraisal of the
Effectiveness of Housing Policies in Helping to
Eliminate Poverty.* Washington, D.C.: Government Printing Office.
1970 "Housing and Its Effects." In *Neighborhood,
City, and Metropolis,* edited by David Gutman
and Robert Popenoe, pp. 709-11. New York:
Random House, Inc.

Schwirian, Kent P., ed.
1974 *Comparative Urban Structure: Studies in the
Ecology of Cities.* Lexington, Mass.: D. C.
Heath & Company.

Srole, Leo F., et al.
1975 *Mental Health in the Metropolis.* Torchbook
enlarged edition, Book 1. New York: Harper &
Row.

Statistical Policy Division, Office of Management and
the Budget
1973 *Social Indicators, 1973.* Washington, D.C.:
Government Printing Office.

Stewart, William H.
1970 "Health Assessment." In *The Health of Americans,* edited by Boisfeuillet Jones, pp. 39-64.
Englewood Cliffs, N.J.: Prentice-Hall, Inc.

Suttles, Gerald
1968 *The Social Order of the Slum.* Chicago: University of Chicago Press.

U.S. Bureau of the Census
1971a *Census of Housing, 1970: Final Report
HC(1)-A1, United States Summary.* Washington,
D.C.: Government Printing Office.
1971b *Census of Population, 1970: Number of In-
habitants, Final Report PC(1)-A1, United States
Summary.* Washington, D.C.: Government
Printing Office.
1975 *Statistical Abstract of the United States: 1975.*
Washington, D.C.: Government Printing Office.

Wainwright, Loudon
1970 "Dilemma in Dyersville." *Life* (May 29):47-50.

Wanklin, J. M., et al.
1955 "Factors Influencing the Rate of First Admission
to Mental Hospital." *Journal of Nervous and
Mental Disease* 121:103-16.

Ways, Max
1971 "How to Think about the Environment." In
Metropolis in Crisis, edited by Jeffrey K. Hadden et al., pp. 314-25. Itasca, Ill.: F. E. Peacock
Publishers, Inc.

Weiss, Theodore S.
1976 "On Removing $300 Plus Rental Limits." *New
York Times* (March 12).

Whyte, William F.
1943 *Street Corner Society.* Chicago: University of
Chicago Press.

Suggested Readings

Davis, Kingsley, ed. *Cities: Their Origin, Growth, and
Human Impact.* San Francisco: Freeman, 1973. A
collection of readings from *Scientific American* that
contains eleven articles on health and transportation,
and others on race relations, origins of cities, and
cities in developing countries.

Duhl, Leonard J., ed. *The Urban Condition.* New
York: Basic Books, 1963. A collection of articles
dealing with health, housing, and other urban problems. Considerable attention is paid to mental health.

Lewin, Stephen, ed. *The Nation's Health.* New York:
H. W. Wilson, 1971. A collection of speeches and articles describing health problems in a metropolitan
nation.

National Commission on Urban Problems. *Building the
American City.* Washington, D.C.: Government
Printing Office, 1968. The report of the commission
deals mainly with housing problems, slums, and the
factors that cause them. It presents the most comprehensive treatment of these problems available,
together with a large body of supporting evidence.

Notes

1. Studying the effects of overcrowding is difficult. The usual statistical definition of overcrowding is 1.01 or more persons per room. These data come from the Bureau of the Census and are reported widely. To analyze population density, the population of a given area is divided by the number of square miles in that area. These data also come from the census, but they are less widely available. Two measures of crowding need not produce the same results. Population density can be very high in a neighborhood of luxury high-rises, in which none of the units is crowded. For research articles analyzing crowding and density and their consequences, see the studies reported in Schwirian, 1974:141-214; Calhoun, 1963:33; Choldin, 1976; Mladenka, 1976: 491-506.

2. The rates reported in this discussion have been calculated from data in Health Resources Administration, 1975b:table 7.9, and U.S. Bureau of the Census, 1971b:tables 4, 5.

12 Problems of the Physical Environment

The growth of large, dense cities has made it increasingly difficult to provide urban residents with pure water to drink, clean air to breathe, and safe, efficient removal of the by-products of urban production, distribution, and consumption. These problems are in part a function of city size and in part a function of the level of industrialization in cities. Not all urban pollution is related to industry; transportation and population density account for some. Environmental problems have become of increasing concern. Society is becoming ever more knowledgeable about environmental pollution and its sources.

Many environmental problems of the city are complex and highly interrelated. For example, due to the high proportion of land used for highways and roads and the density of urban settlement, much land in urban areas is covered over and will not absorb rainwater, especially during storms. As a result, runoff pollutes the sources of drinking water. Another severe problem in cities is the removal and disposal of abandoned cars.

The physical environment has an impact on urban social structure, organization, and behavior. It is equally true that social organization and structure can affect the physical environment. The quality of drinking water, the methods used to maintain its quality, the pollutants dumped into water supplies and the pollutants spewed into the air, and the disposal of liquid and solid wastes all affect the physical environment of cities. The social structure and organization and the division of labor within a city partially determine how and to what extent it will pollute the environment.

Environmental problems are not limited to cities. Rural areas are also sources of pollution. The by-products of power production, agriculture, mining, and other rural activities affect urban areas just as urban pollution affects rural areas. Societal factors such as the quantity of energy produced, the means of energy production, the technology used in all human pursuits, the size and density of settlements, and the level of industrialization all contribute to the level of pollution everywhere. The interaction of the social and physical components of environment is one factor in human ecology; pollution is a major example of such interaction.

Factors affecting the levels of pollution are by and large beyond the control of cities. The sources of pollution for a given city may be outside that city. In many cases federal and state laws regulate public and private activities with regard to pollution. In other cases there is considerable dispute about what should be done and who should pay for it, with industrial groups opposing any actions that might be costly and environmentalists demanding them. Much of the time, however, cities enforce federal and state regulations and initiate local actions to clean up their environment. Cities may even have to take actions that they don't want to take, such as banning or discouraging the use of automobiles in the central business district, when federal regulations call for pollution control, as in the case of meeting air quality standards.

In this chapter we will consider some crucial environmental problems facing cities: maintenance of a clean water supply for drinking and other uses, removal of liquid and solid

Environmental problems are not
limited to cities.

wastes, and control of air pollution. Other environmental problems, such as preservation of open spaces, prairies, and forests; reduction in noise levels; control of the use of pesticides; and preservation of historic buildings and landmarks will not be considered here.

Water and Water-Related Problems

Cities are faced with two major water management problems. First, they must provide water that is suitable for drinking, recreational, and industrial use. Second, they must treat and dispose of liquid wastes, as well as regulate the sources of these wastes.

In theory it is possible to separate the activities of purifying water and removing liquid wastes, but in practice the activities are closely related. The disposal of liquid wastes (sewage) has often contaminated water sources. However, the federal government provides construction grants for water supply and sewage treatment plants, but not for plants that would serve both functions (de Torres, 1972: 87).

Water Supplies

Providing water for the city is almost totally a city function. Except for New Haven and Indianapolis, municipalities provide the water in all major metropolitan areas (de Torres, 1972:87). This function has a long history, beginning with the Roman aqueducts. A source of pure water was located at some distance from the city and piped to its users. While construction methods and materials have changed, this means of ensuring an adequate pure water supply is still very common.

Many cities are located on large bodies of fresh water and thus do not have to seek water from distant sources to make sure it is fit to drink. The city of Chicago, located on Lake Michigan, early in its history built pumping stations far out in the lake to avoid the pollution along the shore and brought lake water to central treatment and filtration plants before distributing it to users.

Cities not located beside adequate sources of fresh water must import water, often from considerable distances. Even some cities located beside large bodies of fresh water must import their supplies because the local water is not fit to drink and purification would be too difficult or expensive.

In 1965, New York City experienced a major water shortage. Reservoirs in upstate New York that held city water supplies were close to empty, and rainfall was inadequate to replenish them. Emergency pumping stations were built on unpolluted sections of the Hudson River to alleviate the shortage that caused restaurants to stop serving water, firefighters to reduce critical water pressures, and industries to curtail some activities.

A dependable supply of water is critical to the existence of a city. New Yorkers have proposed nuclear-powered desalination plants and other technological solutions, all of which have proven to be more expensive than piping water by gravity flow from sources one hundred or more miles away (Wolman, 1966:165). Cities in southern California, which normally has a drier climate than New York State, experienced no water shortages between 1965 and 1977 because of an extensive aqueduct system. The drought of 1976-77, however, caused severe water shortages in all the Pacific states and led to restrictions on the use of water in many areas. Chicago diverts 2,073,600,000 gallons of water per day from Lake Michigan for residents of Chicago and many of its suburbs (*Chicago Tribune,* 28 August 1975; Eisenbud, 1972:158). But approximately two million people in the Chicago SMSA still depend on ground wells for their water. Population density affects groundwater wells, and wells in the Chicago SMSA now show signs of becoming undependable. As the population in the area increases and groundwater supplies fail, more water will have to be diverted from Lake Michigan, an act that will require the agreement of all cities, states, and counties bordering on the lake, or other sources of pure water must be developed.

Problems of Water Supply

Whatever its source, water requires the use of aqueducts or treatment plants, both of which are extremely expensive. Los Angeles is supplied water through a 440-mile-long aqueduct. New York City, to alleviate the shortages of the mid-1960s, also built a long aqueduct. The cost of bringing water to the city through the aqueduct was about fifteen cents per thousand gallons.

Filtration plants, such as the one used in Chicago, require large capital investments for plant, pumping stations, and water mains. Aqueducts tend to be less costly, since neither treatment plants nor water mains are needed and water can be distributed by feeder lines off the main aqueduct. A project to pump Chicago water to the suburbs where wells are drying up would require construction of a water main 10 feet in diameter and 46,000 feet long at an estimated cost of more than $75 million. Despite the high costs of water mains, a central community water system is more efficient than either wells or truck delivery when population density is over one thousand persons per square mile (approximately 1.25 acre residential lots). Only at lower densities, which are rarely found in central cities, can well water or water that is bottled or trucked in compete in cost with water from central systems.

Even in rural areas, wells are fast becoming inadequate as sources of water. The Farmers Home Administration has spent nearly $2 billion in the past decade to replace over six thousand failing community wells with central systems. The new systems provide a more constant supply of better quality water than was available from either wells or commercial sources—and at a lower cost. An unanticipated consequence has been the spread of urban residential developments along these water mains, which were originally installed to keep rural communities viable (*New York Times,* 18 November 1975:1).

Basically, central water systems are more efficient at higher population densities because of economy of scale. There is little difference in the initial cost of installing a large water main or a small water main; the ditch for one is not much more expensive than the ditch for the other. But with more people using the system, the cost of the larger pipe is spread over more taxpayers. As centrally supplied water becomes available, the population using it grows, and settlements become larger and denser. As population size and density increase, more land is covered up and can no longer absorb rainfall. The groundwater supplies on which wells depend dwindle. Dense populations thus destroy wells as dependable water sources, while increasing the efficiency of centralized water distribution.

Water distributed by a centralized system must first be made fit to drink. The water sources that cities use and the treatment that they give the water varies. As has been noted, New York City obtains its water by aqueduct from upstate. Cities in Southern California also are supplied by aqueducts bringing water from less arid areas several hundred miles away. Chicago and other cities around the Great Lakes filter and purify lake water. The diversion of water from one place to another or from a common source often provokes social conflict. Disputes about how much water Chicago diverts from Lake Michigan have been settled by the U.S. Supreme Court and by international treaties with Canada. The quantity of water taken from northern California and parts of the Southwest for the city of Los Angeles and for agricultural lands in southern California has resulted in legal conflicts and occasionally in sabotage of water mains.

The major concern about sources of urban drinking water is the purity of the source. Water obtained from large bodies of water, such as the Great Lakes, is often contaminated by various wastes—municipal sewage, industrial discharges, urban storm runoffs, and runoffs from agricultural land on which pesticides have been used. To minimize contamination of drinking water, state and federal governments have recently begun requiring the treatment of all liquid wastes before discharge. Fluid wastes may now be discharged only with a federal-state permit certifying compliance with treatment standards or promising compliance by a specified date (*New York Times,* 15 March 1976:1).

Sewage and Related Problems

It is generally assumed that drinking water is safe if two rules are observed in the process of liquid waste disposal and water distribution. First, liquid wastes must be treated before they are dumped into anyone's source of drinking water. Second, before water is distributed, it must be disinfected by chlorination. This second action is so important that a federal act has been proposed that would authorize the government to (1) develop drinking water standards; (2) intervene in the case of a health emergency; and (3) ensure adequate supplies of chlorine for disinfecting water (Environmental Protection Agency, 1975:150-51).

Until the early 1960s, treating sewage was the exception rather than the rule; the assumption was that water had an almost unlimited ability to cleanse itself of wastes. Dirty water was seen as a sign of progress and economic prosperity, particularly in the northeast and around the Great Lakes, two areas that have the longest histories of urban and industrial growth (Abend, 1971:333-40). The consequences of this belief can be seen in Lake Erie.

That water cannot purify itself of what man adds to it first became clear in 1963 with the publication of Rachel Carson's landmark book *Silent Spring.* This book and others that

Chicago and Its Suburbs Compete for Water

Illinois may ask the United States Supreme Court next year to allow more Lake Michigan water to be diverted in order to avert a suburban water shortage according to a state official.

Several growing suburbs, particularly in eastern Du Page County and northwestern and southern Cook County, face general water shortages, some within 15 years, the Illinois State Water Survey and the Northeastern Illinois Planning Commission [NIPC] say.

Short-term shortages and quality problems plague some suburbs already.

Paradoxically, the region is water-rich, bordering on "virtually limitless" supplies in Lake Michigan. This causes men like Richard A. Pavia, Chicago commissioner for water and sewers, to steam about "the absurdity" of the situation.

Nearly two million people in the six-county metropolitan area now depend on wells for their water. The dolomite and underlying deep sandstone aquifers which supply nearly 90 percent of their groundwater are being "mined."

That is, the water is being pumped from the aquifers up to three times faster that it is able to recharge naturally. The water table in the deep sandstone is lowering as fast as 13 feet a year.

This requires deeper wells which entail higher drilling and pumping costs. As they go deeper, some wells are expected to run into brackish water, in turn requiring reverse osmosis or distillation plants to make it drinkable. . . .

However, Lake Michigan supplies more than 80 percent of the region's domestic water needs. The City of Chicago pumps from the lake to supply itself and 84 suburbs. Another 14 water supply systems in Cook and Lake counties draw water from the lake.

In June, 1967, after 45 years of interstate fighting, the Supreme Court ruled that 3,200 cubic feet per second was the most water Illinois could divert from Lake Michigan for all purposes. [A cubic foot contains 7.481 gallons].

The battle started in 1900 when the Metropolitan Sanitary District of Greater Chicago reversed the flow of the Chicago River, from into the lake to away from it and into the Des Plaines and Illinois Rivers toward the Mississippi River.

Other Great Lakes states argued that Illinois wasn't entitled to Lake Michigan water because it didn't help fill the lake. They said Chicago's "great water steal" deprived them of navigational, industrial, power generation, domestic, and recreational uses of their water.

Since the 1930s, Illinois has diverted about 3,200 cubic feet per second for domestic, industrial, navigational, and wastewater dilution pur-

The problems of supplying water to a large metropolis are complex. Chicago and its suburbs have an unlimited water supply in Lake Michigan, but technical, economic, legal and political problems must be solved before the water becomes available.

poses. And since then about 1,700 cubic feet per second of that have been used for public water supply.

Acting on the recommendation of its special master, Albert B. Maris, the court in 1967 said it was the State of Illinois' responsibility to allocate the 3,200 cubic feet per second for all purposes. That was more than eight years ago.

For most of this year Berry Tucker, an adviser to the Illinois Department of Transportation's Division of Water Resources, has been holding allocation application hearings for various suburbs.

He said he expects to finish the hearings next January, and hopes allocation orders can be issued in April. The hearings are being held as adversary proceedings, with applicant communities' testimony subject to challenge by other applicant communities.

In June, 1973, Lake County Circuit Court voided the state's first tentative allocations, made on a first-come first-served basis, because the state failed to follow proper administrative procedures.

Tucker said some 182 communities have applied for lake water allocations. About 100, he said, already receive water diverted from the lake. The others are pumping well water and want lake water.

The 182 communities have applied for a total of 3,426 cubic feet per second, Tucker said.

"This [excess over the Supreme Court's limit] means that somebody is not going to get all they are asking for, or some may not get any of what they are asking for," said Tucker.

A key part of the Supreme Court ruling said that any additional lake water needed to meet future domestic needs could be obtained only after "all feasible means reasonably available" had been used to improve water quality in the Sanitary and Ship Canal and "conserve and manage" the region's water resources "in accordance with the best modern scientific knowledge and engineering practice."

Tucker said Illinois would consider going back to the Supreme Court "if we feel there is a reasonable chance of success."

Gerald Seinwill, assistant director of the Division of Water Resources, said more scientific and consultant work needs to be done before the state could ask to have the case reopened.

"I would say there are at least even odds that we will need to request a change in Maris [the 1967 Supreme Court ruling], if not right now, as soon as we get our facts together," said Seinwill.

He said he would not expect a request to reopen the case until late 1976.

Some observers say that to convince the court that it is husbanding its present Lake Michigan water efficiently Illinois would have to show a

373

sound regional water plan for Northeastern Illinois.

As yet there is no regional water plan. NIPC has produced a regional water supply report intended as a data base for preparing any regional water supply scheme.

It points out that the region doesn't face any acute water shortage, and says the "major obstacles to improved water management and allocation are judged to be legal, economic, institutional, and political, rather than technical."

Current laws on groundwater "are inadequate and outdated," according to NIPC. "They tend to encourage indiscriminate use and therefore are not conducive to the optimum management of the water resources."

Further, says NIPC, there is a proliferation of separate and independent water supply systems [some 397 in the six-county area]. They were built haphazardly and contribute to the problems of urban sprawl, says NIPC.

The disadvantages of the present arrangements include poor coordination, conflicts and competition, duplications of effort, inefficient use of financial resources, shortages of trained manpower, lack of economies of scale, and crisis-oriented approaches, says NIPC.

Alternatives include establishing a metro water authority, expanding Chicago's role, establishing a suburban water authority, and bringing about greater county involvement, the agency has suggested.

NIPC's experts say an extra diversion of 500 cubic feet per second from the lake would more than meet the region's forecast water needs.

Chicago water and sewers commissioner Pavia, and others, say that if the hearings which led to the Maris rulings were held today Illinois would be allowed to divert far more than 3,200 cubic feet per second.

In the 1960s, Lake Michigan was at low levels, while now it is so high that millions of dollars worth of shore line erosion damage is done each year. The lake level fluctuates in something like 10-year cycles.

"It's an absurdity that we have water shortages 15 miles from Lake Michigan, the largest supply of good quality fresh water in the world, while the lake is so high it's doing so much damage," Pavia said.

"It's almost unbelievable," he continued. "There are no engineering or technical problems in providing the water. There is no logic in the Maris decision when you consider that 240,000 cubic feet per second goes out of the Great Lakes to the Atlantic."

Pavia said it would be "criminal to ask people to use the Des Plaines River or Fox River when Lake Michigan's high-quality water is nearby."

NIPC's chief engineer, Joseph A. Smedile, points out that a "substantially greater diversion by Illinois would, in fact, have only minimal effects on [Lake Michigan] water levels."

Smedile cited a 1974 report to the International [U.S.-Canadian] Joint Commission by its Great Lakes Levels Board, which said:

• Natural forces, such as rain and snow, evaporation and wind, are the main factors influencing Great Lakes water levels.

• The Great Lakes are mainly self-regulating.

• While the Illinois diversion currently lowers Lake Michigan-Huron levels by 2.75 inches, water diverted into Lake Superior by Canada for hydroelectric power generation [5,000 cubic feet per second] raises the Lakes Michigan-Huron levels by 4.5 inches.

A 500 cubic foot per second increase in diversion would cause the water level in Lake Michigan and Huron to drop less than half an inch over 15 years, he said.

Source Alan Merridew and Casey Bukro, *Chicago Tribune,* Aug. 28, 1975. Reprinted, Courtesy of the Chicago Tribune.

followed pointed out that damage to the environment, especially to water, can be irreversible. As a result, numerous environmental problems have come to public attention. When it was realized in the early seventies that phosphates in laundry detergents could damage water supplies, many cities banned the sale of these laundry products. As a result, water quality dramatically improved (Environmental Protection Agency, 1975:288).

According to the Federal Water Pollution Control Act, by 1977 all municipalities must provide secondary treatment of wastewater before it is discharged. Secondary treatment plants pump air or oxygen through liquid wastes after they have settled. Settling removes most solid wastes from sewage, leaving only dissolved organic materials. Oxygen combines with dissolved organic materials, rendering them chemically and organically harmless. Pumping oxygen or air through the waste speeds up the process. The amount of organic material in water is measured by the biological oxygen demand (BOD) of the water. Secondary treatment reduces the BOD by 80 to 95 percent, leaving the water pure enough to drink (Abend, 1971). However, secondary sewage treatment facilities are expensive to construct. Construction costs for a national system of comprehensive secondary treatment plants were estimated at more than $24 billion in 1974 (Environmental Protection Agency, 1975:145). Expensive as it is, secondary treatment will not solve all problems of polluted water supplies, because untreated sewage comes from sources other than city sewers.

Sewage treatment facilities are expensive to construct.

Sources of Sewage and Pollution

Municipal sewage systems are the major source of liquid wastes entering sources of drinking water. Sewage is collected from homes, businesses, and industries, and flows to treatment plants or dumping stations through underground pipes. About 45 percent of the sewage collected by these systems comes from homes and commercial sources, and 30 percent from industries (Abend, 1971; de Torres, 1972:87). Before these wastes can be dumped into water sources, they must be treated by plants constructed in accordance with the requirements of the Federal Water Pollution Control Act.

Runoff from major storms aggravates the pollution of water sources and remains a major problem, even in areas that already perform secondary sewage treatment. Between 40 and 80 percent of BOD wastes receiving treatment come from overflowing sewers, storm sewers, and similar sources (Environmental Protection Agency, 1975:481; Eisenbud, 1972:160). Runoff problems are caused by the density of land use in urban areas that reduces the ability of the ground to absorb water during major storms. This water collects on streets and runs into the sewers, which overflow and overtax treatment facilities. Since it is neither practical or economical for the city to construct sewers large enough to absorb this unusual amount, the excess is allowed to go untreated into the lake or other source of drinking water. The larger the city, the more the overflow and the greater the damage done to the water supply.

Toward Some Solutions

Legislation is being passed to improve water quality in the future. Many municipalities are already acting to ensure sewage treatment; almost 78 percent of Americans have been served by sewer systems since 1973. Where there are no sewers, liquid wastes are mainly treated in septic tanks that work well when population density is less than 2,500 persons per square mile (approximately half-acre residential lots).

Almost all sewer systems provide at least primary treatment, which allows solids to settle and produces discharge water fit for industrial, and some recreational, uses. But only 64 percent of the population served by sewers have their wastes given what will soon be mandatory secondary treatment. As a result of both population growth and failure to expand treatment facilities, the BOD in sewage discharged from municipal systems has remained constant at 8.6 million pounds a day since 1957 (Environmental Protection Agency, 1975:144-45).

The estimated total investment in physical plant alone for sewage treatment that will be required of cities if they are to meet 1977 federal drinking water quality standards approaches $61 billion dollars (Environmental Protection Agency, 1975:144-45).

The operating costs of these facilities will be shared by cities and industrial users who produce liquid wastes. Industries must also remove the most dangerous pollutants from their wastes before they add them to municipal sewage systems. All users of municipal treatment facilities that have been constructed with federal aid are required to pay their share of treatment costs (Environmental Protection Agency, 1975:144-45).

The United States has enough water to meet its needs at least through the twenty-first century (Wolman, 1966:165). The problems of water supply are problems of distribution and quality caused by two centuries of inattention to the effects we were having on our water.

The Problems of Garbage and Solid Waste

Just as cities must treat and dispose of liquid wastes, cities must also remove and treat solid wastes produced by inhabitants. Ideally, solid wastes are treated in such a way that raw material components can be recovered and reused. Solid waste disposal is one aspect of the communal function of production, distribution, and consumption of goods. Because much solid waste produced by cities is food garbage (Stewart, 1972:36), which breeds rodents, insects, and disease, the communal responsibility for dealing with solid wastes is also part of the communal responsibility for protecting health.

Three major sources of garbage and other solid wastes are household activities, littering on public streets, and industrial activities. A large part of solid wastes comes from homes—the remnants and uneaten portions of meals and food material left in bottles, cans, wrapping papers, or plastics. Other household wastes are wrapping materials, large quantities of paper, dirt, and dust, and diverse items being disposed of or junked. Members of our throwaway, disposable society litter the streets with all kinds of junk, trash, bottles, papers, and cans. A particularly serious form of litter is abandoned automobiles. Industrial solid wastes come in almost infinite variety.

Much, if not most, of these wastes are transported by private companies to municipal disposal facilities.

The Magnitude of the Problem

Disposal of so much garbage and solid waste—not to mention the waste of the unrecovered material—is an extremely serious urban problem. New York City produces more than twenty-one thousand tons of refuse daily (Eisenbud, 1972:163). American society runs on paper: newspapers, books, magazines, and advertising circulars, plus business, industrial, commercial, and government forms that must be filled out in duplicate, triplicate, and quintuplicate! This paper, however necessary, comprises 45 percent of all municipal solid wastes. In the United States, we use 450 pounds of paper per person per year, more than many other industrialized nations—inhabitants of Sweden and Canada use 300 pounds each per year and the Chinese only 6 (Still, 1972:133). Although about one third of used paper is reclaimed, the rest is disposed of by dumping, burning, or other means. Equally staggering is the disposal problem posed by the fifty billion beverage and food cans, the thirty billion bottles and jars, and the sixty-five billion plastic, metal, and glass caps that are discarded annually (Still, 1972:133).

New construction and the demolition of older structures in urban areas produces large quantities of solid wastes. In Los Angeles, five thousand tons a day of material from demolished buildings goes into landfills (Still, 1972:133). Since 1965, New York City has required construction and demolition industries to cut and solidly pack their debris in standard

More than seven million car and truck bodies are junked every year, and urban Americans annually throw away as much as a ton of materials per person.

sizes so that it can be used for landfill and so that rats cannot live in it. This practice reduced the weekly number of truckloads transported to landfills from 485 to 331 (Still, 1972:133).

More than seven million car and truck bodies are junked every year. In New York City, about one thousand cars and trucks are abandoned on the streets each week. This steel rusts on our streets and in junkyards, reducing the reclamation value of the metal and contaminating our physical environment. Disposal of automobiles is more difficult for modern cities than was disposal of animal carcasses for earlier cities (Still, 1972:133).

All these materials—food scraps, junk and litter, industrial wastes, paper, construction debris, and automobiles—add up to an enormous pile of solid wastes in and around cities. Wastes are dirty and contain substantial quantities of organic materials that attract rodents and pests, and cause disease. It has been estimated that urban Americans annually throw away as much as a ton of materials per person at a total cost of $4 billion, or $21.50 per person (American Public Works Association, 1970:10). Garbage and litter in these quantities contributes to the image of our cities as dirty places.

The disposal of waste materials is primarily an urban municipal responsibility. It is not a new problem: In 1866 the New York Metropolitan Board of Health said:

The time has come when manure heaps, slaughterhouses, fat and bone boiling establishments, glue manufacturers, outdoor unsewered privies, and all kinds of occupations and nuisances cannot much longer be tolerated within the built up portions of New York or Brooklyn [Still, 1972:130].

In 1914 the New York Board of
Health removed nearly fifteen thousand horse bodies.

In that same year, the city chased out a
large number of cowbarn and piggery owners
and instituted regular garbage pickups. The
problem of removing animals that die or are
killed in the city has continued almost until
the present day. In 1914 the New York Board
of Health removed nearly fifteen thousand
horse bodies, two thousand steer bodies, a
variety of mule, deer, monkey, and camel
corpses, and the bodies of nearly sixty thousand dogs and cats. The last city outhouses to
be outlawed in a major metropolitan area
were thirty of them in Trenton, New Jersey, in
1956 (Still, 1972:130). Improved disposal of
solid wastes is not solely responsible for the
increase in life expectancy from forty-five to
seventy-five years or for the virtual elimination of yellow fever, cholera, typhus, measles,
and other diseases in cities, but it has helped.
Although the numbers of outhouses and animal carcasses found in the city have been
dramatically reduced and slaughterhouses
have improved their pollution control, Americans have, with characteristic ingenuity,
replaced these solid wastes with vast quantities
of paper, glass, metal, plastic, and abandoned
automobiles.

Collecting Solid Wastes

The process of collecting solid wastes varies
according to technology and population density. By and large, the process of collecting
solid wastes has remained primitive. Normally, regular collections are made from homes
and businesses in the city and wastes are taken
to a disposal site (Stewart, 1972:138; Abend,
1971:363). As the city grows, more collection routes are added, because each collection
crew can make only so many pickups per day.

When the physical area is large, collection crews must either transfer the contents of their full trucks to a larger container or drive individually to the waste disposal site. As population density increases, trucks fill up faster, and more trucks or more frequent transfers to larger containers are required. At the same time, population density forces the city to dispose of wastes at sites farther and farther from the city. Other variables, such as temperature, influence the speed at which solid wastes rot, and determine the length of time solid wastes can remain in trucks, in transit, or undisposed of (de Torres, 1972:101-2).

There have been only a few advances in the technology and efficiency of collecting solid wastes. The in-sink home garbage disposal reduces a considerable portion of solid wastes to liquid wastes, reducing bulk as well as potential health hazards. The transformation of solid wastes into liquid wastes, however, may tax the capacity of city sewage systems. Home trash compactors make it possible to store larger quantities of solid wastes in smaller volumes and reduces the potential for rodent infestation. Compact packages of wastes may extend the life of landfill sites, although compacted wastes can generate concentrations of gases in the process of chemical decomposition and possibly lead to hazardous explosions (Abend, 1971:358-64; Stewart, 1972:139-40).

Finally, the use of **containerized bins** for solid wastes has speeded up and mechanized the collection of solid wastes from many commercial institutions.

We should note that, where solid waste collection is a municipal service, total mechanization and increased efficiency may not be a desired goal. Old-fashioned collection techniques require more workers and provide municipal officeholders with a pool of jobs to be distributed among their constituents as patronage.

The Treatment of Solid Wastes

Solid waste by-products of urban life are disposed of by open dumps, sanitary landfill, and incineration. The dumping of solid wastes into water has been stopped because of its effects on water quality. Even disposal methods currently used are potentially polluting. Incineration can pollute the air and runoff from sanitary landfills can pollute the soil and groundwater. The dilemma is to dispose of solid wastes economically but safely.

Both state and city governments have taken responsibility for the handling of solid wastes. State governments are responsible for many regulations governing the disposal of solid wastes, while cities are directly responsible for providing local collection and disposal services (de Torres, 1972:101-2).

There is no agreement among cities or municipal officials as to the character or amount of collection service that should be provided. Communities have different standards of sanitation and appearance and varying attitudes as to the division of the work between the householders and the collection forces. The residents of some cities insist on healthful and attractive conditions and demand prompt and complete refuse removal. They do not want refuse containers on streets at any time, will not permit waste materials to accumulate on public or private lands, and will not tolerate conditions that menace public health. In other communities, the citizens apparently place a much lower value on sanitation and orderliness. The people in some communities are unwilling to do any of the work of preparing refuse or setting it out on collection days for removal; in others, the citizen will do part of the work or accept part of the responsibility in order to keep the cost as low as possible [American Public Works Association, 1963:187-88].

Open Dumps

As recently as 1965, 30 to 40 percent of cities with populations of 5,000 or more used open dumps to dispose of solid wastes. While this is the least expensive disposal method when the land is available, open dumps have a number of serious disadvantages: they pollute the air and water around them; encourage the breeding of rodents and insects; contribute to the spread of disease; and can be an odor nuisance to people who live nearby (de Torres, 1972). The U.S. Public Health Service recommends open dumps for low population densities—between 1,000-2,500 persons per square mile. In such communities, collection services are unnecessary; citizens can simply be instructed to take their wastes to the dump (de Torres, 1972). As the population density increases, solid waste collection systems become more economical, just as the use of open dumps begins to present problems.

Sanitary Landfill

A slightly more expensive disposal method is sanitary landfill, which costs from $1 to $3 per ton (Abend, 1971:361-63). Wastes are dumped in open pits and covered with earth daily to discourage odors, insects, and rodents. Where land is available, sanitary land-

fill is effective and economical. Landfill requires large areas of cheap, otherwise unused land, the collection of wastes and transportation to the site, and men and machines at the site to pack the wastes and spread the dirt cover.

New York City has used dumps and sanitary landfills since colonial times. Eleven percent of the present area of New York City has been created by landfill methods (Eisenbud, 1972:163). But as a city grows larger in both population and geographic area, land becomes more expensive, and appropriate sites for dumping solid wastes become harder to find. Some early landfill sites are now inside densely settled suburbs, and the largest available landfill area in New York City is now completely filled. Thus the solid wastes must be transported farther and farther from the city, increasing both land and transportation costs. Most major metropolitan areas will continue to use sanitary landfills until the method becomes economically unfeasible, but in Chicago, New York, and Los Angeles disposal by landfill is already a severe problem (Bukro, 1975). An alternative is to create artificial hills by mounding up solid wastes instead of plowing them under. Mount Trashmore in Evanston, Illinois, is such a hill, used now for winter sports (Abend, 1971:361-63).

Incineration

Incineration prior to disposal in landfills can reduce the bulk of solid wastes by 90 percent and extend the life of landfill sites considerably. However, high operating costs offset this advantage of incineration to some extent.

Where land is available, sanitary landfill is an effective way to dispose of waste. When filled, such areas can be used for recreation, as in Jackson, Mississippi (*bottom*).

By means of sanitary landfill, the City of Evanston, Illinois created a 45-acre park out of a former clay pit. It includes a hill for skiing, complete with rope tow and snow-making equipment.

An experimental plant operated by the Commonwealth Edison Company in Chicago is burning garbage to generate electricity.

The major drawback of incineration is its potential for polluting the air. Some gaseous by-products of incineration are so corrosive that they destroy the furnace, stacks, and furnace-cleaning equipment itself (Abend, 1971). Municipal incinerators are generally equipped with devices to trap and clean stack gases, but the devices are both expensive to install and difficult to maintain. Nevertheless, in major metropolitan areas incineration appears to be the method of choice for dealing with solid wastes. New York City handles about 21,000 tons of refuse a day, of which 7,000 tons are incinerated and compacted before being sent to a landfill site (Eisenbud, 1972). Chicago incinerates all but 30,000 tons of the more than 1 million tons of solid wastes that it produces yearly (*Chicago Tribune,* 18 December 1975).

Some cities recover part of the costs of constructing and operating incinerators by building in excess capacity, which they then sell to smaller, surrounding communities (de Torres, 1972). Even with large, efficient incinerators, costs can be as high as $3 to $10 per ton. Another way of reducing the costs of incineration is to recover and use the energy released by burning refuse. Instead of using coal or oil, an experimental plant operated by the Commonwealth Edison Company in Chicago is burning garbage to generate electricity.

Burning refuse has a heat value of 5,000 **BTUs** per ton. This heat can be recovered at a cost of $.80 per million BTUs, giving garbage approximately the same heat value as a barrel of oil, which cost $4.50 in 1975. As oil costs continue to rise, garbage could conceivably be used as fuel for stationary power plants and thus make the United States more indepen-

Air pollution, as in St. Louis, is largely beyond the control of central cities, metropolitan areas, and even whole regions.

dent of outside energy sources. Three cities have already built such energy recovery systems, and several others have similar systems in advanced planning stages—a hopeful sign for the future (Environmental Protection Agency, 1975:132-35).

Problems of Air Quality and Pollution

Many forces that affect air quality—technology, industrial concentrations, and the wind—are largely beyond the control of cities. The control of air pollution and air quality is an urban function only to the extent that local rather than state or federal governments carry out the regulations. Federal regulations cover automobile and some stationary sources of pollution, but the primary responsibility for establishing and enforcing air quality standards falls to state and local agencies (Abend, 1971:343-44). This is particularly true within the city, where local traffic patterns and the adequacy of mass transportation facilities can dramatically alter the nature and amount of air pollution. However, the impact of federal standards for stationary sources of air pollution should not be underestimated. The Environmental Protection Agency has suggested that much improvement in urban air quality is due to the forced construction of power plants away from urban areas (1974:262). However, as a result, rural air quality has been degraded.

Air pollution is largely beyond the control of central cities, metropolitan areas, and even whole regions because much of it takes the form of extremely light particles or gases that can be carried great distances. Unless standards are imposed over a wide geographic

(*Top*) Pittsburgh. (*Bottom*) New York.

area, no city can have anywhere near complete control over the quality of its air. Chicago, for example, suffers from air pollution originating in Indiana. Lawsuits were necessary to force cities and industries in neighboring states to comply with air quality standards, so that Chicago could begin cleaning up its air.

Control of air pollution is complicated by the fact that much of it is a by-product of the generation of power required to run an industrialized society. Unless precautions are taken, burning coal or oil to generate power on a large scale produces a great deal of smoke or gaseous air pollution. Thus cities must strike a balance between power requirements and pollution control.

City problems with air pollution have a long history. Burning coal was prohibited in England by royal proclamation in 1306; coal smoke was considered a grave health hazard, and one man was executed for disobeying the law (Council on Municipal Performance, 1974:3). However, three centuries later, burning coal was a matter of course in London (Cole, 1973:39).

The Magnitude of the Problem

According to Environmental Protection Agency estimates (1975:262, 267, 274, 276), in 1970 the amount of the four most common types of gases (**carbon monoxide, sulfur dioxide, nitrogen oxides,** and **hydrocarbons**) and of particles suspended in the air came to 209 million tons. Almost half of this total, 100 million tons, was carbon monoxide—enough to create a blanket of this gas seven feet deep over forty cities the size of Chicago.

Air pollution is predominantly but not completely an urban problem.

Air pollution is, for the most part, an urban phenomenon which occurs when the air's capacity to dilute pollutants is overburdened. Population, industrial growth and high dependence on single-passenger motor vehicles cause new gaseous and particulate emissions to complement, interact with, and further complicate the traditional smoke and soot [Council on Municipal Performance, 1974:3].

Air pollution affects the health of residents in small cities as well as large cities (Linton, 1972:140-41). However, the severity of the pollution problem and the extent of public dissatisfaction with air quality increases as city size increases. The problem is, in fact, more severe in large cities, and it is perceived as being more severe by the people who live in large cities (Elgin, 1974:97, 99).

In addition to negative effects on plants and the quality and appearance of buildings and machinery, the kinds of air pollution experienced in urban areas have severe consequences for human health: respiratory illness, vision problems, aggravation of existing health conditions, emphysema, and death (Abend, 1971:346).

William Harvey documented the health effects of air pollutants in 1635 (Harvey, 1907, pp. 209-10). He performed an autopsy on "Old Parr," a poor country man who had died of "peripneumony" after coming to London to be presented to the King because he was a healthy man at age 152. Harvey believed that "the cause of death seemed fairly referable to . . . change of air which through the whole course of (Parr's) life had been inhaled of perfect clarity." He termed London's air "heavy"—and "insalubrious" because of sulfurous coal burning.

A few years later, John Evelyn, diarist and practical horticulturalist, was so incensed at the "fuliginous and filthy vapour" in London that he submitted his famous 1661 pamphlet, *Fumifugium, or the Smoke of London Dissipated,* to Charles II. Evelyn wrote that London's air pollution corrupts "the Lungs and disorders the entire habit of their bodies; so that *Catharrs, Phthisicks, Coughs* and *Consumptions* rate more in this city, than in the whole Earth besides" [Council on Municipal Performance, 1974:3].

Medical expenses due to pollution have been estimated at about $18 billion annually. In New York City during the 1970s, the annual costs of medical care, building maintenance, cleaning, and so on, have been estimated at $620 per family (Breckenfeld, 1970:12), and for large urban areas the cost is thought to average $65 per person per year (Eisenbud, 1972). Finally, airborne allergenic agents, such as those that cause hay fever, affect approximately 8 million people. Allergies cost around $65 million in medicine and the loss of about 25 million workdays annually in the 1960s. They may cause more health impairment over the years than any other form of air pollution, yet no controls have been developed for them (Eisenbud, 1972).

Health is most severely endangered by abnormally high concentrations of polluted air in localized areas. The Council on Municipal Performance (1974:4) documents five such episodes:

1930, Belgium, the Meuse River Valley—an air inversion caused sixty deaths.

1943, Los Angeles—photochemical smog was first noted.

1948, Donora, Pennsylvania—six thousand people were sick, twenty deaths resulted from an air pollution episode.

1952, London—four thousand deaths (there were other air pollution episodes in London in 1956, 1957, and 1962).

1963, New York City—405 deaths attributed to air pollution.

The widespread public recognition that air pollution can damage health and even kill people has led to regulation of air pollution—a royal decree in London in 1306 may have been the first antipollution law, but U.S. cities have regulated smoke emissions since 1881. By 1923, twenty-three of the twenty-eight cities with populations over 200,000 had smoke abatement programs. Federal Environmental Protection Agency pollution regulations are now in effect for all agencies that use federal funds or engage in federal programs. In addition, the 1970 Clean Air Act set national standards for air quality that the states were supposed to implement by 1972. However, these standards have not been met in the allotted time because of numerous variance grants (Council on Municipal Performance, 1974).

The prospects for control of air pollution are brighter than the prospects for control of water pollution. Air pollution can be and is being controlled at its source. Control is more practical than trying to clean dirty air, and those responsible for air pollution can be identified and required to stop polluting. Most air pollution control problems can be solved by installing devices that clean up smoke emissions. However, sources of air pollution are increasing, as is the complexity of the problem. The automobile is a major source of carbon monoxide pollution, but our attempts to control automobile emissions have produced other pollutants that are equally harmful (Abend, 1971).

About half the suspended particulate matter polluting the air comes from industrial sources.

Suspended Particulate Matter

Suspended particles are drops of oil, water, acid, dirt, and dust that are small or fine enough to stay in the air. About half of these pollutants come from industrial sources, mainly stationary power-generating facilities; small amounts come from transportation and from solid waste disposal facilities (Council on Municipal Performance, 1974:8-9; Abend, 1971). A fraction of **suspended particulate matter** comes from street sweeping and leaf burning.

The sources of suspended particles in urban air vary according to the industrial-commercial character of the city. In New York City, the largest single source of suspended particles is space heating equipment used in thirty thousand apartment buildings burning No. 6 residual fuel oil (Eisenbud, 1972:163). The familiar sight of black smoke curling above an apartment building is the result of improper burner operation—a significant contributor to air pollution in New York. The second largest source of particulate matter in that city is its seventeen thousand apartment house incinerators that were built between 1947 and 1967 to dispose of solid wastes. They continue to operate and to emit solid particles into the air (Eisenbud, 1972:163).

The larger particles emitted by fuel-burning power generators settle in the immediate vicinity of the source, and while they are annoying, they are not as dangerous to health as the small particles that stay suspended in the air. Particles suspended in the air primarily affect the nasal and respiratory systems and lead to chronic bronchitis and asthma. Although causality has not been established, the rate of death from gastric cancer is twice as high in

cities that have high levels of suspended particulate matter as in cities with low levels. In some cities the levels of particulate matter in the air were so high that the Federal Aviation Authority required extensive equipment alterations for safe operation of aircraft. Autopsies on people who lived and died in New York City and in other polluted cities have revealed particles in the lungs. Particulate matter is suspected of having carcinogenic properties (Abend, 1971; Council on Municipal Performance, 1974:6-7).

Suspended particles are controlled by strict standards on smokestack emissions. Both wet (water and other liquids) and dry (electrostatic) control mechanisms are used to trap the particles carried in smoke. While highly effective, these devices are costly, and owners of facilities that cause pollution frequently resist demands to install them.

During the 1960s the level of air pollution in urban areas was reduced by approximately 25 percent. The quantity of suspended particles was reduced from 110 to 82 milligrams, but this is still above the recommended level. Improvement in air quality that has occurred is attributed not to emission controls or cleaning devices, but rather to the building of new power-generating facilities outside major urban population concentrations (Abend, 1971; Council on Municipal Performance, 1974; Environmental Protection Agency, 1975:262).

Sulfur Dioxide

Sulfur dioxide (SO_2) is a gas produced when coal and fuel oil are burned. More than 75 percent of the SO_2 polluting the atmosphere is produced by power-generating sources, about 20 percent by other industries, and about 2 percent by transportation sources. Space heaters produce some sulfur dioxide, but not as much as industrial processes and power plants (Abend, 1971; Council on Municipal Performance, 1974:7).

Sulfur dioxide primarily affects the health of individuals with lung or heart problems. It was the major cause of death during the air pollution disasters in Donora and London (Abend, 1971). Even in healthy individuals, SO_2 can irritate the eyes, nose, and throat and eventually injure the tubes leading to the lungs, which makes breathing difficult and puts a burden on the heart. When levels of SO_2 in the air rise above .19 parts per million (ppm), hospital admissions and emergency room visits for upper-respiratory infections increase. Among the long-term effects of exposure to SO_2 are respiratory diseases that can bring on depression and apathy in emphysema victims already in hospitals.

Sulfur dioxide and other sulfur oxides turn to acids when wet. When such acids settle on limestone, marble, slate, or mortar, these building materials begin to dissolve. Exposure to sulfur oxides in the air can fade rayon, cotton, and nylon textiles, and can stunt the growth of trees and crops (Council on Municipal Performance, 1974).

If fuel with a low sulfur content (1 to 3 percent) is used, problems are virtually eliminated. Sulfur dioxide emissions also can be controlled by collection systems installed in tall chimneys. The collected sulfur is reclaimed and sold, thereby reducing the cost of pollution control. However, if the tall stacks are not equipped with collection devices, SO_2 is released into the upper atmosphere, where it is converted into sulfates. These pollutants can be detected hundreds of miles from their source and can damage plant and animal life. Some sulfates detected on the East Coast, which are suspected of having originated at power plants in the Midwest, produce a rain that is acidic enough to damage soil and plants, deplete watersheds, and reduce the utility of wells and other pure water sources. During the 1960s the level of sulfur dioxide in the air declined by about 50 percent, mainly because power-generating sources were moved away from urban population concentrations (Council on Municipal Performance, 1974:14; Environmental Protection Agency, 1975:267).

Hydrocarbons

Hydrocarbons are compounds of carbon and hydrogen released into the air from unburned fuels—oil, natural gasolines, and coal. The primary source of hydrocarbons is the internal combustion engine. A secondary source is leakage from stored industrial chemicals and cleaning supplies, particularly solvents. Of an estimated 26.4 million tons of hydrocarbons in the air, 61 percent comes from transportation, 24 percent from industry, and only 2 percent from power generation (Abend, 1971; Council on Municipal Performance, 1974:11).

Most hydrocarbons are not known to be dangerous; some, however, are suspected of causing cancer. By and large, hydrocarbon emissions from automobiles can be controlled by improving the efficiency of the engine, cleaning the exhaust gases, and changing carburetion and crankcase design (Abend, 1971). Most hydrocarbon emissions from automobiles can be controlled by the same changes that reduce carbon monoxide emissions.

Nitrogen Oxides

Nitrogen oxides under certain atmospheric conditions can produce smog. About half of the nitrogen gases come from stationary heating sources, both industrial and residential. Nitrogen oxides are formed when any fuel is burned and combines with oxygen in the air to form nitrogen dioxide, a lethal gas. Automobiles are the major source of nitrogen dioxide, and power-generating plants run a close second. Approximately twenty-two million tons of nitrogen oxide are emitted into the air each year. The long-term effect of exposure to small levels of nitrogen oxide (.02 ppm or more) is impaired respiratory function. Emission of nitrogen gases may be controlled by modifying the combustion process, by substituting other sources of fuel, and by passing gases containing nitrogen oxide over catalysts. These controls have not yet proven effective; the Environmental Protection Agency estimates that total nationwide emissions in the last three decades have at least quadrupled (Abend, 1971; Council on Municipal Performance, 1974:12; Environmental Protection Agency, 1975:276; Linton, 1972:142).

Carbon Monoxide

Carbon monoxide is a lethal gas, produced when fuels containing carbon are burned. Over 100 million tons a year are put into the air, virtually all from automobiles (Council on Municipal Performance, 1974:10; Environmental Protection Agency, 1975:274). The effects of carbon monoxide depend on its concentration, which is a function of the density of generation and the air flow. Urban streets and expressways, surrounded by tall buildings, have a poor air flow and in some spots, concentrations get high enough to be dangerous.

The effects of low-level exposure to carbon monoxide are well known: loss of motor coordination, dizziness, headaches, and, finally, death. The fatal level is estimated to be 80 ppm. Federal standards for air quality have been set at 9 ppm. Along busy roads in cities concentrations regularly reach over 50 ppm. The level inside a car in a traffic jam can reach 370 ppm for short periods of time.

Carbon monoxide is controlled by better tuning of engines, improved traffic flow, and highways designed to enhance air flow.

Summary

The total energy used in the United States in the 1970s *per person* is equivalent to the strength of about five hundred human slaves (Ways, 1971:314-25). This energy availability not only has produced a great increase in personal mobility, but also allowed American industry to build and maintain cities that, while they are not the most densely settled in the world, produce a high level of wasteful congestion. The congestion results not from the number of people per square mile, but rather from the energy sources and materials that surround all individuals. Even our farmers, whose operations are highly mechanized and who use great quantities of energy, put more pressure on the environment than do Chinese farmers who use far less artificial energy and material (Ways, 1971).

Source: Adapted from U.S. Department of the Interior, *Mining and Minerals Policy,* 1973 (Washington, D.C.: Government Printing Office), p. 18.

U.S. Annual Requirements for New Materials per Capita, 1972

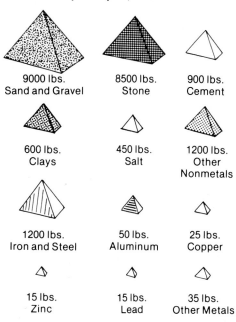

9000 lbs. Sand and Gravel	8500 lbs. Stone	900 lbs. Cement
600 lbs. Clays	450 lbs. Salt	1200 lbs. Other Nonmetals
1200 lbs. Iron and Steel	50 lbs. Aluminum	25 lbs. Copper
15 lbs. Zinc	15 lbs. Lead	35 lbs. Other Metals

Plus

7800 lbs. Petroleum	5000 lbs. Coal	5000 lbs. Natural Gas	1/20 lb. Uranium

To Generate

Energy Equivalent to 300 Persons Working Around the Clock for Each U.S. Citizen

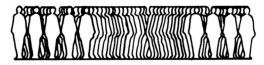

U.S. Total Use of New Mineral Supplies in 1972 Exceeded 4 Billion Tons

Apparently, we do not yet know how to reduce or eliminate the undesirable side effects of technology on our cities and societies. We have no models for future social design that will help us avoid negative effects on the environment. We cannot, however, retreat from technology. Were we to reduce our use of energy and material to avoid negative effects, we would produce a society that is not as liveable as our present one. Some people suggest that we can avoid negative impact by going back to a nostalgic or romantic past and by giving up unnecessary technological devices. We have unnecessary technological devices, but we would have to give up a great many of them to take ourselves back to the point where we would not damage the environment. We would have to go back more than a century. In the 1870s the American buffalo had already been destroyed, the eastern forests had been eliminated, and the colonial cities were badly degraded. A retreat to the technology of that time would produce a median standard of living below today's poverty level. We would have to close almost all colleges and high schools, give up automobiles, trucks, planes, and social services. Elderly people would not live as long and those who did would not be cared for as well as they are today (Ways, 1971). Thus, sheer practicality forces us to seek an alternative to retreat from technology. We may have to invent new, less environmentally destructive technologies. We may have to think of individuals as individuals and not as members of a group, and we may have to rethink and restructure numerous technological innovations if we are to maintain our standard of living without destroying our environment. Until a more general solution is found, we will continue to employ makeshift solutions, such as moving stationary pollution sources farther from population concentrations and installing expensive pollution-control devices in automobiles and smokestacks.

Glossary

aqueduct   a pipe, often not completely covered and running along the ground or on stilts above the ground, that carries fresh water from its source to the population that needs it; originally, the water source had to be higher than the settlement being served so that gravity would maintain water flow through the pipes; pumps are now used to supplement gravity flow

biological oxygen demand (BOD)   a measure of the organic activity in water supplies; the higher the BOD, the higher the bacterial content of the water, which makes it unfit for use

BTU   British Thermal Unit—a measure of heat energy in a substance; the amount of energy needed to raise the temperature of one pound of water one degree Fahrenheit

carbon monoxide   a tasteless, odorless, colorless gas that is a by-product of combustion of materials containing carbon; fatal in high concentrations; its most common source is the automobile

chlorination   the process of adding chlorine to water supplies to kill bacteria and to make the water safe to drink

containerized bins   large refuse disposal bins that can be winched aboard trucks and carried directly to disposal sites; a much faster way of collecting large quantities of solid wastes

desalination   the removal of salt from ocean water to make it drinkable

hydrocarbons   a by-product of the combustion of carbon-containing materials; a common air pollutant

nitrogen oxide   a by-product of burning fuels that can combine with oxygen in the air to produce a lethal gas

primary treatment   a method of treating water that allows solid particles to settle; the result is water that can be used for some recreational purposes and most industrial processes, but not for drinking

runoff   water that cannot be accommodated by urban sewage systems and that runs off into sources of water supply during heavy storms; also, the water that cannot be absorbed into the ground in areas where most of the ground is paved

sanitary landfill   the process of filling in swamps, dumps, mine pits, quarries, and other areas with solid wastes and covering each day's collection with a layer of earth; prevents or minimizes problems of rodent infestation and odor

secondary treatment   a form of treating water by forcing either air or oxygen through the liquid wastes to accelerate biochemical reactions that remove biological materials; the water that results is safe to drink

SO_2   chemical symbol for sulfur dioxide, a by-product of burning sulfur-rich fuels, such as certain coals or oils; a major source of air pollution

sulfur dioxide   see SO_2

suspended particulate matter   particles of dirt or liquid small enough to be suspended in the air; particles in dust and mists produced by fuel combustion, street sweeping, and other causes

References

Abend, Norman A.
1971   "The Urban Environment." In *Exploring Urban Problems*, edited by Melvin R. Levin, pp. 322-79. Boston: Urban Press.

American Public Works Association
1963   Cited in *Performance of Urban Functions,* U.S.
       Advisory Commission on Intergovernmental
       Functions. Washington, D.C.: Government
       Printing Office.
1970   *Municipal Refuse Disposal.* Chicago: Public Ad-
       ministration Service.

Breckenfeld, Gurney
1970   "Environmental Protection Devices." *Planning
       1970: Selected Papers from the American Society
       of Planning Officials National Planning Con-
       ference.* Chicago: American Society of Planning
       Officials.

Bukro, Casey
1975   "Garbage Dumps Fill Up at 'Crisis' Rate."
       Chicago Tribune (December 18).

Cole Lamont C.
1973   "Man and the Air." In *Man and the Environ-
       ment,* edited by Wes Jackson, pp. 35-43. Du-
       buque, Ia.: Wm. C. Brown Company Publishers.

Council on Municipal Performance
1974   "City Air." *Municipal Performance Reports* 1,
       5:3-31.

de Torres, Juan
1972   *Government Services in Major Metropolitan
       Areas.* New York: The Conference Board, Inc.

Eisenbud, Merril
1972   "Environmental Protection in the City of New
       York." In *The City in the Seventies,* edited by
       Robert K. Yin, pp. 152-64. Itasca, Ill.: F. E.
       Peacock Publishers, Inc.

Elgin, Duane
1974   "Environmental Quality and City Size." In *City
       Size and the Quality of Life,* by Duane Elgin et
       al., pp. 97-114. Washington, D.C.: Government
       Printing Office.

Environmental Protection Agency
1975   *Environmental Quality: 1974.* Washington, D.C.:
       Government Printing Office.

Linton, Ron M.
1972   "Breathing." In *The City in the Seventies,* edited
       by Robert K. Yin, pp. 140-44. Itasca, Ill.: F. E.
       Peacock Publishers, Inc.

Stewart, George R.
1972   "Garbage." In *The City in the Seventies,* edited
       by Robert K. Yin, pp. 136-40. Itasca, Ill.: F. E.
       Peacock Publishers, Inc.

Still, Henry
1972   "Littered Land." In *The City in the Seventies,*
       edited by Robert K. Yin, pp. 130-36. Itasca, Ill.:
       F. E. Peacock Publishers, Inc.

Ways, Max
1971   "How to Think about the Environment." In
       Metropolis in Crisis, edited by Jeffrey Hadden et
       al., pp. 314-25. Itasca, Ill.: F. E. Peacock
       Publishers, Inc.

Wolman, Abel
1966   "The Metabolism of Cities." In *Cities,* edited by
       Scientific American editors, pp. 156-74. New
       York: Alfred A. Knopf, Inc.

Suggested Readings

Abend, Norman A. "The Urban Environment." In *Exploring Urban Problems,* edited by Melvin R. Levin,
pp. 322-79. Boston: Urban Press, 1971. An excellent
review of urban pollution problems and what is being
done about them.

Council on Environmental Quality. *Environmental
Quality.* Washington, D.C.: Government Printing Office, annual. This yearly report provides definitive
data on the composition and quantity of pollution in
our environment. In many volumes recent data are
compared with data reported earlier to show changes
that have taken place.

Yin, Robert K., ed. *The City in the Seventies.* Itasca,
Ill.: F. E. Peacock Publishers, Inc., 1972. This book
contains several abridged articles on environmental
pollution that are not available elsewhere.

13 Functional Problems: Crime

The President's Commission on Law Enforcement and Administration of Justice has reported that crime was second only to race relations as the most frequently cited social problem in America (1967b:49, 50-51). By 1977, crime ranked first (Nelson, 1977). The crimes that bother most people are those that result in personal, brutal violence, those that make us afraid to walk on the streets at night and to take advantage of city facilities and amenities (President's Commission on Law Enforcement, 1967b; 1967a:14). Most people think this type of crime is more common now than in the past, but this belief is not totally correct. As early as 1784, New York City frequently was the scene of murders, drug abuse, robberies, and infanticides. Lynching and **vigilantism** have been part of our tradition as long as America has existed as a country (Lane, 1976:1-13).

In the nineteenth century, the relationship between crime and urban life was decried by such astute observers of our nation as Thomas Jefferson, Benjamin Rush, and Alexis de Tocqueville (Glaab, 1963:51-63, 286-317).

The President's Commission on Law Enforcement summarizes the history of crime in the United States as follows:

> There has always been too much crime. Virtually every generation since the founding of the Nation and before has felt itself threatened by the spectre of rising crime and violence.
>
> A hundred years ago contemporary accounts of San Francisco told of extensive areas where "no decent man was in safety to walk the street after dark; while at all hours, both night and day, his property was jeopardized by incendiarism and burglary." Teenage gangs gave rise to the word "hoodlum," while in one central New York City area, near Broadway, the police entered "only in pairs, and never unarmed." A noted chronicler of the period declared that "municipal law is a failure . . . we must soon fall back on the law of self-preservation."
>
> "Alarming" increases in robbery and violent crimes were reported throughout the country prior to the Revolution. And in 1910 one author declared that "crime, especially its more violent forms, and among the young is increasing steadily and is threatening to bankrupt the Nation."
>
> Crime and violence in the past took many forms. During the great railway strike of 1877 hundreds were killed across the country and almost 2 miles of railroad cars and buildings were burned in Pittsburgh in clashes between strikers and company police and the militia. It was nearly a half century later, after pitched battles in the steel industry in the late thirties, that the Nation's long history of labor violence subsided. The looting and takeover of New York for 3 days by mobs in the 1863 draft riots rivaled the violence of Watts, while racial disturbances in Atlanta in 1907, in Chicago, Washington, and East St. Louis in 1919, Detroit in 1943 and New York in 1900, 1935, and 1943 marred big city life in the first half of the 20th Century. Lynchings took the lives of more than 4,500 persons throughout the country between 1882 and 1930. And the violence of Al Capone and Jesse James was so striking that they have left their marks permanently on our understanding of the eras in which they lived [1967b:22-23].

In the second half of this century, the notion that the rate of crime is rising has been reinforced by the annual **Uniform Crime Report** (UCR) of the FBI, which provides nearly all the data we have on crime in America. Despite the great care that goes into compiling these reports, statistical complexities make it difficult to conclude reliably that crime has actually increased by any specific amount.

The crimes that bother most people
are those that result in personal,
brutal violence.

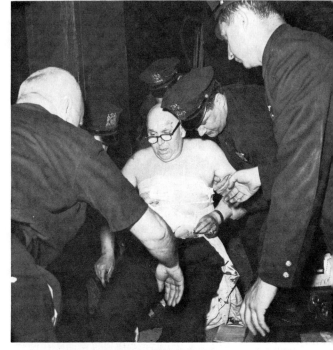

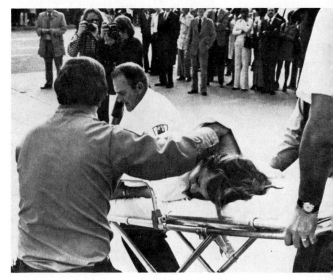

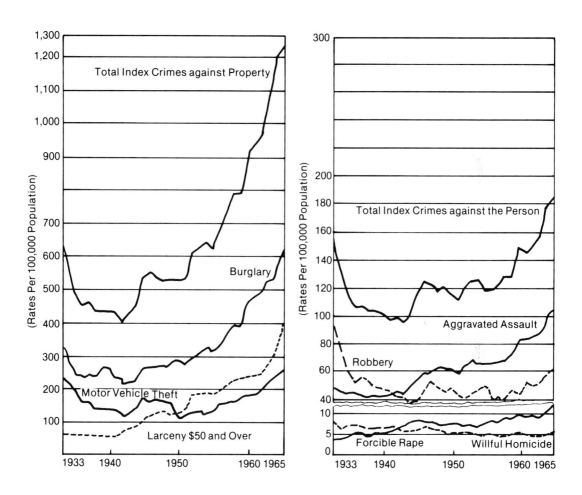

(*Left*) Reported crimes against property, 1933–1965. (*Right*) Reported crimes against the person, 1933–1965. (Source: President's Commission on Law Enforcement and Administration of Justice, *Task Force Report, Crime and Its Impact: An Assessment* [Washington, D.C.: Government Printing Office, 1967].)

It is commonly assumed that the rate of crime is much higher in big cities than in small cities, in central cities than in suburbs, and in urban areas than in rural areas. Support for this assumption is given in table 13.1. However, the total crime rate is slightly higher in medium-sized cities (100,000 to a million) than in cities of a million or more. Although the **violent crime** rate rises regularly with city size, the rate of **property crime** is higher in medium-sized cities than in larger cities.

The reasons for these variations in crime rate statistics are not clear. They may involve differences in the proportions of crimes that become known to the police, differences in police reporting practices, differences between urban and rural residents, or differences in urban and rural ways of life (Wolfgang, 1970: 280-81; Wilson, 1968:25-39). The character-

istic of urban life that is most likely to be related to differential crime reporting is the lack of communal control over the behavior of individuals and reliance on impersonal criteria and modes of law enforcement. Informal modes of social control exercised in small towns permit many crimes to be handled outside the police reporting system, and thus outside the Uniform Crime Reports (Wolfgang, 1970:296). We must understand the definition of crime and the nature of crime reporting before we can understand the role that cities play in relation to crime.

The Definition of Crime

Durkheim (1938:66-67) pointed out that all societies have some crime and, although it is regrettable, it is a normal part of social life. Because societies are complex, the strength of the collective conscience varies from individual to individual and group to group (Cohen, 1966:12). Not everyone in a society interprets all norms in the same way or follows all norms totally. There is always some norm-violating behavior. When a city, like most modern American cities, is made up of various racial and ethnic groups, each of which follows its own traditions, two factors increase the potential for the violation of society's collective sentiment. First, different groups may have different interpretations of the norms and follow traditions that conflict with another group's traditions or with those of society as a whole. As a result, behavior that some groups may consider normal other groups or the laws of society may define as criminal. Second, the attachment of some groups to societal norms may not be as strong as that of other groups, or it may be based on

Table 13.1 Crime Rate by Size of City, 1975
(rate per 100,000 population rounded)

Size of City	Total Index Crimes	Violent Crime	Property Crime
1 million or more	7,630	1,420	6,210
500,000-1 million	8,814	1,013	7,801
250,000-499,999	8,414	910	7,504
100,000-249,999	7,669	632	7,068
50,000-99,999	6,361	451	5,910
25,000-49,999	5,591	343	5,248
10,000-24,999	4,763	268	4,496
Under 10,000	4,112	232	3,881
Suburban areas*	4,614	289	4,324
Rural areas	2,229	177	2,045

*City and suburban police agencies in SMSAs; excludes central cities. Suburban cities also included in data for size groups.

Source *Uniform Crime Report: 1975:*table 14.

different interpretations of the collective sentiments. Thus, some groups may behave in ways they think are in accord with collective sentiments when in actuality their behaviors are defined by society as criminal (Sellin, 1971:395-99).

In complex societies, **deviance** can also emerge when a behavior is approved under some circumstances but not under others. For example, betting is legal in state lotteries or in church bingo games but not with bookies or on the numbers. Sexual flirtation by females is appropriate in some settings, but not in others; the same is true for sexual aggressiveness by males. As we shall see, cultural dilemmas like these can provoke deviance and crime, particularly when norms dictate that an individual behave in a particular way in some settings but not in others, or employ only selected means to attain particular goals (Lemert, 1971:30-43).

Robert K. Merton, in his classic essay "Social Structure and Anomie" (1957:131-60), described how emphasizing the attainment of particular goals without giving equal emphasis to appropriate means to those goals can lead to deviance and crime. In American society, for example, there is great pressure to accumulate money—but considerably less pressure to do so only in legitimate ways. In a city where most people do not know much about other people or about the source of their money, the means by which wealth has been obtained is less important than the fact that one has it.

The emphasis on success in obtaining money can encourage illegitimate means of obtaining it—sharp business practices, cheating, bribery, and so forth, are available and are used by some segments of the population.

Only recently has the extent of the use of illegitimate means by businesses and high-status individuals become even partially known, and it is likely that much **white-collar crime** goes unnoticed and undetected. In the lower strata of society individuals and small businesses are pressed to succeed financially but have few opportunities to do so legitimately. The result is considerable pressure and a marked tendency toward illegitimate means of achieving financial success.

According to Merton's formulation, the pressures for financial success are equal in all strata of society, but the opportunities for legitimate gratification are more limited in the lower strata of society. The result is more frequent and more obvious deviant behavior and crime among groups of lower status. Those in the upper strata have more opportunities to achieve socially approved goals legitimately. Therefore they are not as likely to be involved in crime and deviance.

Merton identifies five different adaptations or responses to social pressures, according to degree of acceptance of goals and means. As table 13.2 shows, the conformist accepts both

Table 13.2   Adaptations to Social Pressure

Mode of Adaptation	Cultural Goal	Institutionalized Means
I. Conformity	+	+
II. Innovation	+	−
III. Ritualism	−	+
IV. Retreatism	−	−
V. Rebellion	±	±

Source Reprinted with permission of Macmillan Publishing Co., Inc. from *Social Theory and Structure*, rev. ed., by Robert K. Merton, p. 140. Copyright © 1957 by The Free Press, a Corporation.

goals and means and is thus not deviant. The innovator accepts the goals of society but develops new modes for achieving them. In the upper strata of society, this can lead to illegitimate business practices—for example, a conspiracy to fix prices so that all participants realize a high level of profit. In the lower strata of society adaptation of means to maximize profits often leads to individual or organized crime. In the third adaptation, the ritualist accepts reduced goals and makes enough to get by, but does not engage in either hard work or crime to succeed. Deviance generated by this adaptation is generally not criminal, but those adapting ritualistically deviate to the extent that they accept relative lack of success. The retreatist manifests escapist behavior, such as use of drugs and withdrawal from society. Other forms of deviance may become necessary to support this life stance, but the basic attitude of the retreatist is that neither the goals nor the legitimate means of attaining them are worthwhile. The rebel reacts to society with hostility, frustration, and resistance. Young people in the sixties became frustrated with the structure of society and attempted to both succeed and to change the social structure. In reaction to the Vietnam War, they exhibited behaviors that many older people considered both deviant and criminal.

This framework allows us to define deviance as behavior contrary to the norms or rules of the group—a violation of communal or societal norms (Cohen, 1966:12; Becker, 1971:21-25). Although this definition is useful, it does not cover all possible cases, because there are many ambiguities in norms as well as in situations and in the rules for applying norms in a given situation. An individual, for example, can be a member of several groups—racial, occupational, voluntary—each of which has norms, some of which conflict (Becker, 1971; Lemert, 1971). Furthermore, frequency of deviance can affect the definition of an act or an actor as deviant or criminal. Some acts are deviant if they are performed at all, while others are not considered deviant until they have been repeated so often that sanctions are invoked by society or by individuals themselves who recognize their deviance.

From this definition, several important characteristics follow. First, for there to be deviance or crime, there must be a community that invokes norms against the behavior in question (Cohen, 1966:2). Second, to the extent that an action occurs in violation of norms because of normative ambiguity, cultural conflict, or lack of legitimate means to socially approved goals, social control will be more difficult (Lemert, 1971; Merton, 1957). Furthermore, since much deviance is created by the situation itself, prevention or control of deviance virtually amounts to preventing the occurrence of situations in which norms are ambiguous (Lemert, 1971) or in conflict.

In a heterogeneous city, the prevention and control of deviant behavior are exceedingly difficult. In an urban society composed of many partial communities, the potential for ambiguity and conflict is heightened, especially during periods of great social change, such as the in-migration of new population groups or the changes brought on by industrialization and urbanization.

Defining deviance as the failure to abide by the norms of the community, which in turn are integrated with the norms of the wider society, leads us to the following conclusions. First, no behavior is universally criminal or deviant. Second, as is the case with all norms, the community will impose sanctions on the violator. Third, the nature of the sanction and the ability of the community to apply it are highly variable. Both depend on such factors as the strength and clarity of the norms, their interpretation, the degree to which the norms of the community and the society are integrated, and the acceptance of norms governing both goals and means as equally legitimate and compelling. Finally, the community's norms and sanctions must be defined as legitimate by the wider society. Some sanctions that a community might wish to impose—the death penalty, for example—might be defined as illegitimate by the wider society or might be applicable only in certain cases, such as the murder of a police officer or a prison guard. If the community is to sanction norm violators, it must first be able to detect, identify, and apprehend those who violate norms.

Deviance as described here applies to many types of behavior, including crime, delinquency, mental illness, political protest, and lack of academic achievement. Our consideration of deviance in the urban setting will be limited to criminal deviance, that is, behavior that violates criminal law at all levels.

Measuring Crime

Crime, once considered characteristic only of big cities, is spreading throughout society—into suburbs, small towns, and rural areas.

This may reflect the metropolitanization of society, as discussed in chapters 4 and 5; the increased migration of lower-status and blue-collar central city residents[1] to the suburbs and their consequent urbanization; increased normative ambiguity or conflict; or the fact that, as society urbanizes, partial communities become less able to perform their social control function.

The extent of crime and the increase in the crime rate must be viewed with an understanding of how crime is measured. Table 13.1 shows the extent of serious property and violent crime, but does not define them. To calculate changes in the crime rate, an operational definition must be employed. **Serious crimes** are defined by the FBI as criminal homicide, forcible rape, robbery, aggravated assault, burglary, larceny, and motor vehicle theft (Kelley, 1975:6).

We will look at how data on these crimes are collected and measured, what is known about the spatial distribution of crime between and within cities of various sizes and types, and how crime relates to the ability of cities to carry out their communal function of crime control.

Measurement Problems: Counting Crimes

We have only two sources of data on the extent of crime in the United States, neither of which is totally satisfactory. The best known source, which until recently was the only source, is the FBI Uniform Crime Report (UCR), published annually and available from the U.S. Government Printing Office. The UCR compiles data from police departments on offenses and known offenders.

Recently, the Law Enforcement Assistance Administration and the Bureau of the Census have begun large surveys on the extent to which urban populations and businesses have been victimized by crime. Serious deficiencies in both of these sources make it difficult to pinpoint the actual amount of crime and how crime rates differ from place to place and from time to time.

Assuming that criminal acts could be unambiguously defined, measurement becomes a simple matter of counting accomplished and attempted crimes. However, the difficulty of defining crime is shown in the following questions. If a man goes into a bar or a supermarket in which there are twenty patrons, pulls out a gun and robs them, how many crimes have been committed: one or twenty? If in the course of a robbery the victim is shot or knifed, is the crime robbery or assault? If an attempted robbery is thwarted, should the attempt be counted in crime statistics?

The Uniform Crime Reports count only the most serious offense in each instance of accomplished or attempted crime (Reiss, 1971: 542). Thus, in the example of the victim who is knifed in the course of a robbery, only the robbery, which is more serious than aggravated assault, would be listed. Since each offense against property (robbery) is counted only once, the robbery of twenty people in a supermarket is counted as one rather than twenty criminal acts.

In addition to problems of counting and classifying incidents, some complaints of known crimes are not entered into the statistical reporting system. If the truth of the complaint cannot be established through evidence or witnesses, the police may decide

there is no way to determine that a crime has occurred. And the crime, no matter how serious, does not appear in the statistics. For this reason, white-collar crimes like embezzlement, fraud, and crimes against consumers, as well as the activities of organized crime rings, are not adequately reported (Reiss, 1971). Other crime is never reported to the police because it is considered too trivial, is concealed by the offender or the victim, or is in violation of federal agency regulations and thus is not a police matter. Stock fraud, embezzlement, and many corporate crimes are federal violations. Fornication, incest, sodomy, nonsupport, seduction, rape, desertion, tax evasion, gambling, weapons possession, and shoplifting are violations that may not be detected or reported, so statistics do not reflect their actual rate of occurrence (Wolfgang, 1970:280, 544-45).

Burglary, larceny of over $50, and automobile theft normally account for 85 percent of all acts included in the FBI Serious Crime Index (Kelley, 1975:6). Thus only changes in the number of these crimes against property have an impact on the UCR serious (index) crime rate. Only two other acts, aggravated assault and robbery, are of any significance in the crime index, and they do not contribute significantly to the total amount of serious crime.

Offenses considered less serious than those included in the UCR index (i.e., kidnapping, arson, or assault and battery) are somewhat arbitrarily excluded from public discussion of serious crime. Furthermore, all index crimes are considered equal in the calculation of the crime rate—a robbery of $5 is counted as one serious crime and so is one murder (Kelley,

1975:6). These ambiguities have existed as long as we have collected these data, and thus, even if we could define "serious" crime, we do not know whether it has increased, whether the crimes included are the same or different, or even whether the officially reported counts are an unbiased estimate (President's Commission on Law Enforcement, 1967a:21-22).

Calculating the Crime Rate

The FBI calculates the crime rate by dividing the number of offenses that police departments report by the total population. Aside from the fact that we do not know how complete or representative the numbers of crimes reported are, the total population may well not be the best figure to use in the calculation (Reiss, 1971:537-47). There is a differential probability of being exposed to particular crimes, depending on age, race, gender, and so forth. For example, it makes no sense at all to calculate the rate of automobile thefts by dividing the number of automobiles reported stolen in a given year by the total number of people in the country. Not all people have automobiles; some have more than one. Dividing the total number of automobile thefts by the total number of automobiles registered would be better. Similarly, in the case of rape, it makes no sense to divide the total number of reported rapes by the total number of people. At the very least, the total number of rapes should be divided only by the number of women. This would approximately double the rape rate reported in crime statistics!

An adequate calculation of crime rate (Reiss, 1971:541), would be based only on the population exposed to the crime, would reflect the means used in gathering the data, and would allow persons to assess realistically their chances of being victimized by that type of crime.

The Extent of Crime

In 1975, there were just over five serious crimes per 100 inhabitants in the United States. More than 90 percent of these crimes were property crimes, the majority burglary or larceny-theft. Table 13.3 shows the actual number and the rate per 100,000 inhabitants of serious crimes in 1975 as well as the changes in both rate and number since 1960. When compared with 1960, violent crime increased 199.3 percent—somewhat more than property crime (178.1 percent), but this trend seems to have tapered off since 1970.

These data suggest a continuous increase in the rate of crime, but if crime rates are traced back as far as possible (to 1933), this is not the case. In fact, the crime rate declined between 1933 and 1942, and only since then has it risen continuously. The actual *amount* of the increase cannot be stated precisely.

Despite the difficulties of determining the absolute rise in crime, data in the Uniform Crime Reports clearly show relatively more crime occurred in major metropolitan areas than in rural areas or nonmetropolitan cities. Even though more criminal acts occur in large cities (those over one million), the rate of increase of both violent and property crime is lower there than in smaller cities.

Table 13.3   National Crime, Rate, and Percent Change

Crime Index Offenses	Estimated Crime 1975		Percent Change over 1974		Percent Change over 1970		Percent Change over 1960	
	Number	*Rate per 100,000 Inhabitants*	*Number*	*Rate*	*Number*	*Rate*	*Number*	*Rate*
Total	11,256,600	5,281.7	+ 9.8	+ 8.9	+39.0	+32.6	+232.6	+179.9
Violent	1,026,280	481.5	+ 5.3	+ 4.4	+38.9	+32.5	+255.8	+199.3
Property	10,230,300	4,800.2	+10.3	+ 9.4	+39.0	+32.6	+230.5	+178.1
Murder	20,510	9.6	− 1.0	− 2.0	+28.2	+21.5	+125.1	+ 88.2
Forcible rape	56,090	26.3	+ 1.3	+ .4	+47.6	+40.6	+226.3	+174.0
Robbery	464,970	218.2	+ 5.1	+ 4.3	+32.9	+26.8	+331.2	+263.1
Aggravated assault	484,710	227.4	+ 6.2	+ 5.4	+44.7	+38.0	+214.1	+164.1
Burglary	3,252,100	1,525.9	+ 7.0	+ 6.1	+47.5	+40.6	+256.6	+200.0
Larceny-theft	5,977,700	2,804.8	+13.6	+12.7	+41.5	+34.9	+222.2	+171.1
Motor vehicle theft	1,000,500	469.4	+ 2.4	+ 1.6	+ 7.8	+ 2.8	+204.8	+158.5

Source   Clarence Kelley, *Crime in The United States (Uniform Crime Report)*. (Washington, D.C.: Government Printing Office, 1975) p. 11.

Table 13.4   Crime Rate by Area, 1975 (rate per 100,000 inhabitants)

Crime Index Offenses	Total U.S.	Metropolitan Areas	Rural	Other Cities
Total	5,281.7	6,110.5	1,997.2	4,437.2
Violent	481.5	580.8	167.3	269.1
Property	4,800.2	5,529.7	1,829.9	4,168.1
Murder	9.6	10.6	8.1	5.5
Forcible rape	26.3	31.3	12.0	13.5
Robbery	218.2	284.0	23.5	57.8
Aggravated assault	227.4	254.9	123.7	192.2
Burglary	1,525.9	1,747.9	785.9	1,103.3
Larceny-theft	2,804.8	3,195.6	941.6	2,849.2
Motor vehicle theft	469.4	586.2	102.4	215.5

Source   Clarence Kelley, *Crime in The United States (Uniform Crime Report)*. (Washington, D.C.: Government Printing Office, 1975), p. 11.

Table 13.5   Trends in Crime 1973-74, 1974-75 by Population Group (percentage change)

Population Group (Size of City)	Total Crime		Violent Crime		Property Crime	
	'73-74	'74-75	'73-74	'74-75	'73-74	'74-75
1 million or more	9.9	6.3	8.1	1.1	10.3	7.6
500,000 to 1 million	4.4	8.8	10.4	5.2	15.0	9.3
250,000-499,999	13.4	7.6	9.5	4.5	13.9	8.0
100,000-249,999	15.1	7.6	10.4	3.3	15.5	7.9
50,000-99,999	18.6	9.0	13.9	7.8	19.0	9.1
25,000-49,999	19.7	8.8	16.4	4.4	20.0	9.1
10,000-24,999	21.2	10.5	15.4	9.3	21.5	10.6
Under 10,000	22.2	11.0	10.6	7.9	23.0	11.2
Suburban areas*	20.1	9.7	15.3	6.7	20.5	9.9
Rural areas	20.3	8.0	6.1	5.0	21.8	8.2

*City and suburban police agencies in SMSA, excluding central cities; suburban cities also included in data for size groups.

Source   Clarence Kelley, *Uniform Crime Report,* 1974, 1975: table 10.

Differential Crime Rates

The reasons for these surprising findings are not clear. Part of the explanation may be differential police reporting practices or the tendency of residents to consider some crimes more worthy of police attention than others. Crime reporting, in general, is getting better, but may have improved more dramatically in small cities, which have historically needed more improvement, than in large ones. Improved police **command control** and better information processing systems make it more likely that previously unreported property crimes in medium-sized cities now appear in police reports. Also, citizens are using police services more often than before. For example, blacks in our society are becoming more likely to report crime to police, as part of the overall "equal treatment" they have been seeking.

Crimes against blacks can no longer be ignored, as might have been the case in the past. Second, as urban residents increase their use of homeowners' and renters' insurance, the proportion of reported thefts will probably increase so that insurance claims can be filed. This may be more typical of medium-sized cities than of very large cities.

Another factor in small versus large city crime rates may be that people who used to migrate to large cities now seek out smaller metropolitan areas.

The changing age distribution of the population in cities of different sizes may also be implicated. Young people are more likely to commit crimes than older people, and in recent years the proportion of people ages 14 to 21 in the population is increasing, especially in the suburbs.

As for the general increase in serious crimes, one neglected factor in differential rates may be inflation. Five years ago many bicycles cost less than $50, and bicycle theft was not an indexed crime. Today, bicycles easily cost over $50, making theft of one larceny (over $50) and reportable as a serious crime. Finally, part of the apparent increase in number of crimes may be the increase in opportunities to commit crimes. Americans have become more careless with their property, and other Americans have greater mobility to commit crimes. It is unlikely, however, that these factors alone account for the increase in reported crime (Reiss, 1971:537-63).

Unreported Crime

The number of crimes known to police departments does not represent all offenses committed. This has been documented through surveys in which people and businesses were asked how often, and in what ways, they had been victims of crime. Table 13.6 shows the proportion of crimes not reported to police by respondents in a national **victimization survey,** as well as their reasons for remaining silent. The most common reasons for not reporting a crime are that the victim wanted to keep it a private matter or that they did not want to harm the offender. In many cases, victims felt the police would not be effective, or would not want to be bothered, even if they knew about the crime. In sum, "although police statistics indicate that there is a lot of crime today, they do not begin to indicate the full amount" (President's Commission on Law Enforcement, 1967a:18).

Victimization surveys show that the actual amount of crime in the United States is several times that shown in the Uniform Crime Reports. Critically, the ratio is not the same for all types of crime. The UCR includes only 50 percent of robberies committed, and there are 3.5 times as many rapes committed as are reported to the police. Automobile thefts are reported 89 percent of the time, more often than any other type of crime except those that result in death, which are always recorded by the police. Sixty-five percent of robberies and aggravated assaults are reported, and only 58 percent of burglaries. Other crimes are reported to authorities even less frequently (President's Commission on Law Enforcement, 1967a). If these reporting rates vary by city size and are lower in very large cities than they are in smaller cities, this would help explain lower rates of reported property crimes in the largest cities.

Victimization studies began in 1967 and are now being conducted continuously under the generic name of National Crime Panel Surveys by the Bureau of the Census and the Law Enforcement Assistance Administration (Law Enforcement Assistance Administration, 1975). These surveys are not fully comparable with the UCR statistics because of differences in definitions, cities, and crimes included. Still, they continue to show a much greater incidence of crime in major cities than the UCRs and may become our most reliable source of data on crime, especially in metropolitan areas.

In general, the rate of serious crime varies by size of city. The crime rate is lower in cities of one million or more persons than in cities of 100,000 to a million people, but this is

Table 13.6   Victims' Most Important Reason for Not Notifying Police[a] (in percentages)

Crimes	Percent of Cases in Which Police Not Notified	Reasons for Not Notifying Police				
		Felt It Was Private Matter or Did Not Want to Harm Offender	Police Could Not Be Effective or Would Not Want to Be Bothered	Did Not Want to Take Time	Too Confused or Did Not Know How to Report	Fear of Reprisal
Robbery	35	27	45	9	18	0
Aggravated assault	35	50	25	4	8	13
Simple assault	54	50	35	4	4	7
Burglary	42	30	63	4	2	2
Larceny ($50 and over)	40	23	62	7	7	0
Larceny (under $50)	63	31	58	7	3	[b] ...
Auto theft	11	20[c]	60[c]	0	0[c]	20[c]
Malicious mischief	62	23	68	5	2	2
Consumer fraud	90	50	40	0	10	0
Other fraud (bad checks, swindling, etc.)	74	41	35	16	8	0
Sex offenses (other than forcible rape)	49	40	50	0	5	5
Family crimes (desertion, nonsupport, etc.)	50	65	17	10	0	7

[a]Willful homicide, forcible rape, and a few other crimes had too few cases to be statistically useful, and they are therefore excluded.

[b]Less than 0.5%.

[c]There were only 5 instances in which auto theft was not reported.

Source   President's Commission on Law Enforcement. *Task Force Report: Crime and Its Impact.* (Washington, D.C.: Government Printing Office, 1967), p. 18.

| Table 13.7 | Comparison of Survey and UCR Rates (per 100,000 population) | | |

Index Crimes	NORC Survey 1955-66	UCR Rate for Individuals 1965[a]	UCR Rate for Individuals and Organizations 1965[a]
Willful homicide	3.0	5.1	5.1
Forcible rape	42.5	11.6	11.6
Robbery	94.0	61.4	61.4
Aggravated assault	218.3	106.6	106.6
Burglary	949.1	299.6	605.3
Larceny ($50 and over)	606.5	267.4	393.3
Motor vehicle theft	206.2	226.0	251.0
Total violence	357.8	184.7	184.7
Total property	1,761.8	793.0	1,249.6

[a]"Uniform Crime Reports," 1965, p. 51. The UCR national totals do not distinguish crimes committed against individuals or households from those committed against businesses or other organizations. The UCR rate for individuals is the published national rate adjusted to eliminate burglaries, larcenies, and vehicle thefts not committed against individuals or households. No adjustment was made for robbery.

Source   President's Commission on Law Enforcement. *Task Force Report: Crime and Its Impact.* (Washington, D.C.: Government Printing Office, 1967), p. 17.

because there are fewer property crimes in cities of over a million. Violent crimes, however, increase as city size increases.

Whatever the source, the evidence seems clear: the larger the city, the higher the rate of violent crime; with the exception of cities over a million, the higher also the rate of property crime. There is considerable evidence that there is something about cities that encourages criminal acts.

Crime-Producing Characteristics of Cities

What is it that causes higher crime rates in larger rather than smaller cities, in central cities rather than smaller suburbs, and in cities rather than rural areas? At the beginning of this chapter, we discussed the potential of cultural conflicts and ambiguous norms for generating deviance and crime. Aside from this, some differences in crime rates are undoubtedly due to differences in reporting practices. But a third factor must be considered. Crime is undoubtedly connected with the narcotics, gambling, prostitution, and other commercialized vice activities that are more common in big cities (McLennan and McLennan, 1971:256; Wolfgang, 1970:276).

Throughout history, cities have been described as places of debauchery and poor moral conditions, while rural areas have been praised for their encouragement of virtuous living. Hesiod wrote about the corruption of Greeks who lived in cities, and in the fourteenth century, Ibn Khaldun compared city dwellers with nomads and described the latter as much less depraved and wicked than urban residents (Clinard, 1964:237-45).

In contemporary America, so-called adult bookstores and massage parlors are concentrated in large cities. Boston has its "Combat Zone," where sexually explicit movie houses are found; New York City has its "porno" houses and bookstores around Times Square; and Detroit was forced to use zoning legislation to control similar businesses there. The high levels of crime associated with such areas reinforce the association between immorality and crime in cities (*Time,* 5 April 1976:58-63; *New York Times,* 12 November 1976:B1, B3).

While commercial vice is also found in small towns, there are not enough customers to make the effort profitable on a large scale. Furthermore, in such areas, these operations are more visible and thus subject to strong **informal social control** and sanctions. In a small town or rural community, minor and even fairly major offenses can be handled without resort to official police action, which results in fewer recorded crimes (Dinitz, 1973:10).

Urban life, as described in chapter 6, implies a high degree of **formal control,** more than likely control provided by distant bureaucrats and impersonal officials, which consequently has less impact on the individual than social pressure from neighbors. In large cities, police are most often strangers, known to, and knowing, the people they deal with only as role occupants. Likewise, victims are more likely to be seen as impersonal—and insured (Wolfgang, 1970:296-98).

When density, spatial mobility, ethnic and class heterogeneity, and anonymity of the city are combined with poverty, physical deterioration, poor education, unemployment, and a wide range of other negative characteristics, it is logical to assume that urban life generates lawlessness and deviance, especially among its most deprived citizens. These assumptions have not been proven, but they support the belief that the cumulative effects of urban life produce violence and crime. An important corollary is that since these conditions are not present to the same degree in small towns, the incidence of crime there will be less (Danziger, 1976:291-96). In summary there is considerable theoretical justification for and empirical evidence to support the conclusion that life in cities may generate more crime and violence than life in smaller, less urbanized places.

The Distribution of Crime in Cities

Anyone who has ever lived in or visited a city knows that some sections are more dangerous than others. It is not easy to pinpoint why this is true. Much of what we know about the ecological distribution of crime within cities has emerged from studies of city areas in relation to crime rates. Robert Park (1926:11-12) and Ernest Burgess (1925:143, 152-53) studied the incidence of deviance in Chicago by mapping locations where known delinquents and criminals lived. Deviants were concentrated in core areas of the city, characterized by high levels of social disorganization. However, the studies of Park and Burgess were based on police or court statistics (not totally unbiased data) and may not accurately reflect the distribution of crime in the city.

The Chicago School of sociologists, notably Shaw, McKay, and their colleagues, also found that certain crimes and deviant behavior were concentrated in specific city areas.[2]

The inner zones of the city, Zones 1 and 2, were most often the scene of crimes and deviant behaviors such as robbery, mental illness, suicide, prostitution, and vagrancy. As the distance from the center of the city increased, the number of persons processed by the criminal and juvenile courts for criminal or deviant behaviors declined. Alcoholism and white-collar crimes show different patterns and become more common in the zones farther from the center of the city.

In the last two decades ecological studies of crime and delinquency have become increasingly sophisticated. **Census tract** computer tapes and modern research survey techniques are used to relate the social characteristics of small areas to rates of delinquency and thus to test theories of crime and delinquency.

The conclusions of the Chicago School of delinquency research, and of later researchers in the same tradition, can be summarized as follows: (1) rates of delinquency decrease as distance from the center of the city increases; (2) zones with high rates of truancy also exhibit high rates of serious delinquency and adult crime; and (3) areas of the city with high rates of delinquency were characterized by physical deterioration and population decline, but high population density, economic insecurity, transiency, conflicting social norms, and an absence of constructive community organizations. Furthermore, areas with a high rate of delinquency and crime during one decade have shown similar rates of crime and delinquency in subsequent decades, regardless of changes in the ethnic or racial composition of the area. In Chicago, areas that in one generation were Italian and in another generation became black had essentially similar rates of crime and delinquency in both generations. Thus crime is not caused by ethnic or personal characteristics, but rather by social organization.

These findings can be interpreted in a number of ways. Miller (1958:5-19) stresses the fact that concentrations of lower-class families in an **ecological niche** can produce pressures that generate youth gangs and delinquency. Cloward and Ohlin (1960) suggest that the ecological areas of a city will differ in the opportunities they offer for behaving in legitimate and illegitimate ways. In those areas with few legitimate and many **illegitimate opportunities** and role models, delinquency and crime will be more common. Cohen (1955) argues that the social class characteristics of an area are *the* factors, or, at least, very important factors, in producing high rates of delinquency and crime.

Polk (1967), Quinney (1964), Lander (1971), and Chilton (1964) all disagree with Cohen. They contend that other factors, such as race, proportion of homeowners, and other indicators of anomie in neighborhoods, are more important. But statistical analyses suggest that these factors are not related to socioeconomic characteristics. On the other hand, studies that rely on adolescents' reports of their own behavior also throw into question the link between socioeconomic status and delinquency (Akers, 1964:38-46; Empy and Erickson, 1966:546-54; Short and Nye, 1958: 296-302; Institute for Juvenile Research, 1976).

There are more clear-cut explanations of delinquency in theory than there is empirical evidence to support them. It is generally agreed, however, that the ecological structure of the city is related to delinquency (Polk, 1967:281) and that some areas in the city will have higher rates of crime and delinquency than the city as a whole. The finding of the Chicago School that it is the characteristics of the city area rather than of its residents that contribute to delinquency is also generally accepted. As such, areas that are poor, densely settled, or experiencing a transition in types of residents have the potential for trouble. Most critically, areas with few voluntary social agencies working with citizens to establish and strengthen community norms and to integrate the normative structure with the structure of the wider society are the ones that will experience the highest overall rate of crime.

The Response of Cities and Urban Residents to Crime

Urban residents perceive the extent of crime and its increase with reasonable accuracy. While an incomplete understanding of the problem and a good deal of sensationalized reporting (*Time,* 30 June 1975:10-24) can exaggerate the problem, people are afraid of crime, and in four high-crime precincts sampled in Boston and Chicago, 20 percent of the population wanted to move to safer neighborhoods. Fully half of those living in high-crime areas reported that they stay off the street at night, and 60 percent of them have taken steps to protect themselves with dogs, locks, guns, and so on. National Crime Commission surveys show that 37 percent of the population in the United States keep firearms in their homes for self-defense (Reiss, 1971:559). In recent years, "city

paranoia'' has been less confined to metropolitan centers than before; even at city fringes and within suburbs, there are fewer areas where one can walk safely at night, and still fewer areas with generally low crime rates (Reiss, 1971:559).

People are most concerned about crimes accompanied by senseless personal violence—a sudden attack by a stranger, a mugging or purse snatching that is accompanied by a physical struggle (President's Commission on Law Enforcement, 1967a:14). The fear of such a crime is widespread and real, but the possibility of being a victim is not particularly high. For every 100,000 Americans, fewer than five hundred such crimes are reported each year to the police (see table 13.3). Another five hundred go unreported, for a total of one such crime per one hundred people. However, the speed and impact of television reporting makes people more aware of these crimes, even if the number of offenses remains fairly constant.

Official rates of crime are rising moderately, partially because of better, more centralized record keeping and command systems and increased willingness of citizens to report crime. In addition, the proportion of young people in the population is greater, and youths have always engaged in more crime than adults have. Thus, simply on the basis of numbers, the chance of an offense being committed within a given area is increasing. It is possible that at least part of the increased crime rate in the United States over the past twenty-five years does not reflect moral decay or decreased normative integration, but rather the increase in the size of the age group having the highest probability of committing crimes.

Victims and Offenders

Much of the fear of crime is a fear of senseless violent, personal attack by a stranger. Given the extent of racial tensions (see chapter 9), the specific fear in major metropolitan areas is that of violent crimes committed by members of one race against members of another race. In fact, official statistics show that this type of crime is relatively rare. A study of six hundred criminal homicides in Philadelphia showed that in only thirty-six cases was the victim of a different race from that of the offender. Of the thirty-six victims, half were white and half were black (Wolfgang, 1970:294-95).

According to the National Crime Panel (Law Enforcement Assistance Administration, 1975:table c), in crimes of personal violence other than murder, offenders and victims were strangers in about 66 percent of the incidents. Applying this percentage to the rate of violent crime (corrected for unreported crime), there are only about .7 attacks of violence by strangers per 100 persons. The chances of being murdered by a stranger are even less. In 1975, only one-third of all murders occurred in the course of a felony (and this includes all police killed in the line of duty). The other two-thirds of murders occurred during family arguments, as the result of a romantic triangle, or in other instances in which the victim knew the killer (Kelley, 1975: 19).

Thus, despite the great fear of violence by strangers, a substantial proportion of personal attacks are committed by persons known to the victim. Half of such crimes are not reported to the police because the victim does not want to harm the offender (President's Commission on Law Enforcement,

Neighborhood Cop of the Block Program

In quiet times, the police officers patrolling a corner of the Bedford-Stuyvesant section of Brooklyn have taken to dropping in at the homes of residents for a few minutes of friendly talk.

Most of the policemen are white and most of the residents are black and they say the visits have brought some startling revelations.

"You find out that these people are the same as other people," said Detective Joseph Cunningham. "They want the same things you want."

Talking about the policemen, Una Squires, a retired social worker who lives on Putnam Avenue, said, "You begin to see them as individuals.". . .

The melting of ugly stereotypes in this community of 56,000 that less than four years ago was rolling with social tension has come about, the police and the residents say, in a strikingly simple manner: people just started talking to one another. . . .

Now There's Help

Sgt. Meere said it is difficult to measure the impact of the "Cop of the Block" program on the rate of crime. He said department statistics show a marked decline in homicides, rapes, robberies and burglaries in the precinct in the last five or six years and "we'd like to think we've contributed to that."

Almost every officer now seems to remember some instance when his friends on the block have helped him.

Police Officer Ferdinand J. Guerra recalls the day when several teen-agers held back a crowd and yelled, "Stay back, let Freddy do his job," as he broke up a knife fight. . . .

Officer Lionel Feldman, who grew up in Bedford-Stuyvesant, said he lost sight of a gunman he was chasing after a grocery stick-up one afternoon and a woman at a window pointed to the building the man had entered. Inside, Officer Feldman said, another resident showed him the exact apartment where the gunman was hiding.

"Before, people would tell you they didn't want to get involved," Officer Feldman said. "They felt it was your job and your job alone."

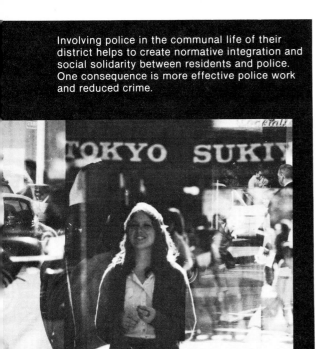

Involving police in the communal life of their district helps to create normative integration and social solidarity between residents and police. One consequence is more effective police work and reduced crime.

Another bonus of the program, the police say, has been improved morale. Officer Rudolph, for example, feels people respect him "as a person, not just a uniform" now that they know him. And Officer Guerra says he gets a special thrill when someone on the block introduces him to an outsider as "our" policeman. "I tell you," he said, "it does something for the policeman. It does something for me.". . .

"It breaks away some of the myths," said Detective Volpe. "The men find out that all black people aren't stick-up men or rip-off artists and the women aren't all prostitutes."

Source Joseph B. Treaster, *New York Times,* January 29, 1975, Section 2, page 1. © 1975 by The New York Times Company. Reprinted by permission.

1967a:18). The level of violent crime will probably not abate until these percentages, and the reasons for them, are altered—that is, until fewer acquaintances harm each other and victims report such crimes more frequently.

Urban Attempts to Control Crime

Dealing with most crimes is a local matter. Even though there has been a trend toward increased federal involvement in all matters of government, there are few federal statutes that regulate the behaviors we have been discussing. The federal role is basically limited to record keeping, financial and technical aid, and the enforcement of federal laws against crimes such as bank robbery and kidnapping and all those crimes that involve the crossing of state lines.

The control of crime is a local community function. Given the magnitude of the problem and the limited resources that cities have, what can be done about crime? The typical response has been to try anything and everything to prevent people from ever committing a crime or from becoming repeat offenders, and to deal with those persons who have engaged in multiple offenses (Wolfgang, 1970:299).

Preventing people from ever committing crimes seems almost impossible. As we have seen, nobody knows for certain what causes crime or if these factors can ever be totally controlled.[3] And, a good proportion of offenses (especially crimes of violence) are committed by persons who know their victims. Formalized means of preventing crime such as strengthening community institutions, pro-

The solution to crime lies not in more formal controls but in strengthening the norms of urban communities.

viding street workers, or increasing police personnel and coverage are not likely to affect the incidence of these crimes.

Other forms of social control have been proposed—faster processing through the criminal justice system or more certain and severe punishment of criminals (Wheeler, Cottrell, and Romasco, 1970:428-43; van der Haag, 1976:133-41). But again, since so many crimes are committed by and against friends and acquaintances, often the offender is not apprehended. Only 18 percent of property crimes and 45 percent of violent crimes are cleared by arrests (Kelley, 1975). If the offender is not caught, speedier processing and more certain punishment cannot serve to reduce crime.

Crime Control As a Communal Function

One way of viewing crime is as a reflection of the clarity and universality of the norms of the community. The higher rate of crime in large cities would be a function, then, of norms that are neither as universal nor as clear as they are in small towns, where the sense of shared values is strong. Given that so many offenses occur because of basic disagreement on standards of behavior, it is suggested that even the most severe sanctions will not prevent or reduce city crime. When neighborhoods, cities, and the partial communities that make up a city have lost their sense of community, they are unable to socialize their members to community or societal norms (Wilson, 1968). At this point, there are no informal controls to prevent crime against friends, let alone strangers. Once the sense of community is lost, people with an interest and competence in maintaining norms and social solidarity leave the area, which increases the demand for more formal means of control. But such controls, embodied in criminal law and enforcement agencies, have not proven effective in conflicts between friends or disagreements over intangible standards of public behavior. The failure to control such conflicts and the resulting behavior really is the failure of the sense of community.

Thus, the solution to the problems of crime lies not in more formal controls, more severe sanctions, or faster processing of the few criminals who are apprehended, but in the strengthening of the norms of urban communities and the integration of these communities with the wider society.

Summary

In our concern over what appears to be an exceedingly high rate of crime, especially in urban areas, we often forget that crime and deviance have apparently always been present in urban societies. The heterogeneity of urban populations makes it difficult to have uniform attachment to or interpretation of norms. This leads to patterns of behavior that some people define as criminal, and that others define as not criminal. Our cultural belief in financial success by any means reinforces low levels of normative integration.

Measuring the extent of crime and defining and counting criminal acts have proven to be exceedingly difficult tasks. The crime rate is calculated by the FBI on the basis of the reports of crimes known to police departments. Studies of rates of victimization among the population have suggested, however, that not all crime is known to the police. Far more offenses occur than are reported, and the ratio of crimes committed to crimes reported varies by the type of offense and, perhaps, by size of city.

According to police data in the Uniform Crime Reports, the rate of violent crimes is higher in large cities, but the rate of property crimes is higher in medium-sized cities (100,000 to a million) than in cities of over one million people. In general, there is more crime of all types in metropolitan areas than in nonmetropolitan areas, and more in cities than in rural areas. Difficulties of precise measurement of crimes make more detailed analyses of differences in crime rates highly tenuous.

A number of theories have been advanced to explain urban crime, including the reliance on formal rather than informal means of control; the heterogeneity of the population; the density and mobility of the population, and so on. Whatever the explanation, it is also known that different areas of cities are characterized by different levels of juvenile and adult crime. Again, the reasons for these ecological variations have not been established, although the fact of variation is generally accepted.

Crime control has taken many forms, from massive police patrols to attempts to deal with underlying causes. The position taken here is that the underlying cause of crime involves lack of normative consensus throughout the city and inability of the partial communities that make up the city to control the behavior of either their own residents or those residing nearby. Until the partial communities develop a higher degree of normative integration among themselves and with the wider society, we will have to rely on formal means of control that can never be as effective as normative integration, informal social control, and a sense of social solidarity.

Glossary

census tract   a small unit of a city area used as an enumeration district; the population of the tract is kept between three thousand and six thousand by alterations in boundaries; the smallest area for which a great deal of information is generally available from the census; also a unit used for administrative purposes

command control   in police work, the control exercised by persons at high levels in the police department over operations of the entire force

deviance   violation of community or societal norms (the specific behaviors vary from community to community); deviance may occur when subgroup norms conflict with norms of the larger society

ecological niche   a location within an ecological structure in which a particular mode of adaptation to the environment dominates

formal control   the control of social behavior by institutions and their representatives, in contrast to control by means of social pressure, socialization, and other noninstitutional means

illegitimate opportunities   the chances available in an area for a person to make money by violating norms and the presence of persons in that area who will train others in the use of these opportunities

index crimes   offenses listed in the index of serious crimes used by the Uniform Crime Reports—criminal homicide, forcible rape, robbery, aggravated assault, burglary, larceny, and motor vehicle theft

informal social control   the control of social behavior by noninstitutional means, such as internalization of norms, social pressure exerted by other community residents, or voluntary groups responding to particular events or under particular circumstances

property crime   acts involving theft or destruction of another's property in which the property owner is not personally harmed; examples are burglary, larceny, motor vehicle theft

serious crimes   by FBI definition, criminal homicide, forcible rape, robbery, aggravated assault, burglary, larceny, motor vehicle theft; note that crimes such as kidnapping, arson, and embezzlement are not included

Uniform Crime Report (UCR)   the FBI's system for counting and reporting crimes; using a standard set of definitions, participating police departments report to the FBI all known crimes, arrests, and the characteristics of the people arrested

victimization survey   a technique developed in the late 1960s to supplement the Uniform Crime Report; samples of the population are asked if they had been crime victims; results showed that more crimes occurred than had been reported to police

vigilantism   the practice of citizens banding together without legal sanction to take action against crime

violent crime   crimes of coercion against the person; often involving injury or death; as defined by the FBI in the UCR, aggravated assault, robbery, forcible rape, homicide, etc.

white-collar crime   crime committed by white-collar workers—those in salaried or professional positions; embezzlement, stock fraud, and corporate crimes such as price fixing are examples

References

Akers, Ronald L.
1964   "Socioeconomic Status and Delinquent Behavior: A Retest." *Journal of Research in Crime and Delinquency* 2, 1:38-46.

Becker, Howard S.
1971   "The Outsiders." In *The Criminal in Society,* edited by Leon Radzinowicz and Marvin Wolfgang, pp. 21-25. New York: Basic Books, Inc., Publishers.

Burgess, Ernest W.
1925   "Can Neighborhood Work Have a Scientific Basis?" In *The City,* edited by Robert E. Park, Ernest W. Burgess, and Roderick McKenzie, pp. 142-56. Chicago: University of Chicago Press.

Cartwright, Desmond, and Howard, Kenneth I.
1966   "Multivariate Analysis of Gang Delinquency I: Ecologic Influences." *Multivariate Behavioral Research* 1 (July):321-71.

Chilton, Ronald
1964   "Continuities in Delinquency Area Research: A Comparison of Studies for Baltimore, Detroit, and Indianapolis." *American Sociological Review* 29 (February):71-83.

Clinard, Marshall B.
1964   "Deviant Behavior, Urban-Rural Contrasts." In *Metropolis: Values in Conflict,* edited by C. E. Elias et al., pp. 237-45. Belmont, Calif.: Wadsworth Publishing Co., Inc.

Cloward, Richard A., and Ohlin, Lloyd E.
1960   *Delinquency and Opportunity: A Theory of Delinquent Gangs.* Glencoe, Ill.: Free Press.

Cohen, Albert F.
1955   *Delinquent Boys: The Culture of the Gang.* Glencoe, Ill.: Free Press.
1966   *Deviance and Society.* Englewood Cliffs, N.J.: Prentice-Hall, Inc.

Danziger, Sheldon
1976   "Explaining Urban Crime Rates." *Criminology* 14, 2 (August):291-96.

Dinitz, Simon
1973   "Progress, Crime, and the Folk Ethnic." *Criminology* (May):3-21.

Durkheim, Émile
1938   *The Rules of the Sociological Method.* Edited by George Catlin. Glencoe, Ill.: Free Press.

Empy, Lamar T., and Erickson, Maynard L.
1966   "Hidden Delinquency and Social Status." *Social Forces* 44, 4:546-54.

Fitzpatrick, John J.
1976   "Psychoanalysis and Crime: A Critical Survey of Salient Trends in the Literature." *Annals* 423 (January):67-74.

Glaab, Charles N., ed.
1963   *The American City: A Documentary History.* Homewood, Ill.: Dorsey Press.

Gordon, Robert A.
1971   "Issues in the Ecological Study of Delinquency." *American Sociological Review* 32 (1967):927-44. In *Ecology, Crime, and Delinquency,* edited by Harwin Voss and David M. Petersen, pp. 227-59. New York: Appleton-Century-Crofts.

Hirschi, Travis, and Rudisill, David
1976   "The Great American Search: Causes of Crime." *Annals* 423 (January):14-22.

Institute for Juvenile Research
1976   *Youth and Society in Illinois.* 7 vols. Chicago: Institute for Juvenile Research (offset).

Kelley, Clarence
1974   *Crime in the United States (Uniform Crime Report) 1974.* Washington, D.C.: Government Printing Office.
1975   *Crime in the United States (Uniform Crime Report) 1975.* Washington, D.C.: Government Printing Office.

Lander, Bernard
1971   "Towards an Understanding of Juvenile Delinquency." In *Ecology, Crime, and Delinquency,* edited by Harwin L. Voss and David M. Petersen, pp. 161-75. New York: Appleton-Century-Crofts.

Lane, Roger
1976   "Criminal Violence in America: The First Hundred Years." *Annals* 423 (January):1-13.

Law Enforcement Assistance Administration, U.S. Department of Justice
1975   *Criminal Victimization Surveys in the Nation's Five Largest Cities.* Washington, D.C.: Government Printing Office.

Lemert, Edwin
1971   "Deviance and Social Control." In *The Criminal in Society,* edited by Leon Radzinowicz and Marvin Wolfgang, pp. 30-43. New York: Basic Books, Inc., Publishers.

McLennan, Barbara N., and McLennan, Kenneth
1971   "Public Policy and the Control of Crime." In *Exploring Urban Problems,* edited by Melvin R. Levin, pp. 564-75. Boston: Urban Press.

Merton, Robert K.
1957   "Social Structure and Anomie." In *Social Theory and Structure,* edited by Robert K. Merton, pp. 131-60. Rev. ed., Glencoe, Ill.: Free Press.

Miller, Walter, B.
1958   "Lower Class Culture as a Generating Milieu of Gang Delinquency." *Journal of Social Issues* 14, 3:5-19.

Nelson, Wade
1977   "Crime Our No. 1 Concern." *Chicago Daily News,* 5 April 1977:1.

Park, Robert E.
1926   "The Urban Community as a Spatial Pattern and a Moral Order." In *The Urban Community,* edited by Ernest W. Burgess, pp. 3-18. Chicago: University of Chicago Press.

Polk, Kenneth
1967   "Urban Social Areas and Delinquency." *Social Problems* 14, 3 (Winter):320-325.

President's Commission on Law Enforcement and Administration of Justice
1967a   *Task Force Report. Crime and Its Impact: An Assessment.* Washington, D.C.: Government Printing Office.
1967b   *The Challenge of Crime in a Free Society.* Washington, D.C.: Government Printing Office.

Quinney, Richard
1964   "Crime, Delinquency, and Social Areas." *Journal of Research in Crime and Delinquency* 1 (July):149-54.

Reiss, Albert J., Jr.
1971   "Assessing the Current Crime Wave." In *Exploring Urban Problems,* edited by Melvin R. Levin, pp. 537-63. Boston: Urban Press.

Sellin, Thorsten
1971   "Conflicting Norms." In *Culture, Conflict and Crime,* edited by Thorsten Sellin. New York: Social Science Research Council, 1938. Reprinted in *The Criminal in Society,* edited by Leon Radzinowicz and Marvin Wolfgang, pp. 395-99. New York: Basic Books, Inc., Publishers.

Shaw, Clifford, and McKay, Henry D.
1967   *Juvenile Delinquency and Urban Areas.* Chicago: University of Chicago Press.

Shaw, Clifford; Zorbaugh, Harvey; McKay, Henry D.; and Cottrell, Leonard S., Jr.
1929   *Delinquency Areas.* Chicago: University of Chicago Press.

Short, James F., Jr., and Nye, F. Ivan
1958   "Extent of Unrecorded Juvenile Delinquency: Tentative Conclusions." *Journal of Criminal Law, Criminology, and Police Science* 49:296-302.

van der Haag, Ernest
1976   "No Excuse for Crime." *Annals* 423 (January):133-41.

Wheeler, Stanton; Cottrell, Leonard S., Jr.; and Romasco, Anne
1970   "Juvenile Delinquency: Its Prevention and Control." In *Delinquency and Social Policy,* edited by Paul Lerman, pp. 428-43. New York: Praeger Publishers, Inc.

Wilkes, Judith A.
1967   "Ecological Correlates of Crime and Delinquency." In *Task Force Report. Crime and Its Impact: An Assessment,* President's Commission on Law Enforcement and Administration of Justice, pp. 138-56. Washington, D.C.: Government Printing Office.

Wilson, James Q.
1968   "The Urban Unease: Community vs. the City." *The Public Interest* 12 (Summer):25-39.

Wolfgang, Marvin
1970   "Urban Crime." In *The Metropolitan Enigma,* edited by James Q. Wilson, pp. 270-311. Garden City, N.Y.: Doubleday & Co., Inc.

Suggested Readings

Crime in the United States. Washington, D.C.: Government Printing Office, annual (also known as Uniform Crime Reports). This is the FBI's annual report on crime. Other than victimization studies, the UCRs are the only source of data on crime in the United States.

Jacobs, Jane. *The Death and Life of Great American Cities.* New York: Random House, 1961. Jacobs points out that urban life and the physical design of neighborhoods affect the safety of people on the streets.

Reiss, Albert J., Jr. "Assessing the Current Crime Wave." In *Exploring Urban Problems,* edited by Melvin R. Levin. Boston: Urban Press, 1971. A comprehensive analysis of the FBI's Uniform Crime Reports and its measurement problems, together with an analysis of current data.

Voss, Harwin, and Petersen, David M., eds. *Ecology, Crime and Delinquency.* New York: Appleton-Century-Crofts, 1971. A collection of many important articles on the relationship between crime and the city, including many studies on the nature of crime itself.

Wilson, James Q. "The Urban Unease: Community vs. the City." *The Public Interest* 12 (Summer, 1968). An analysis of the loss of community in the city and the city's inability to control social behavior.

Notes

1. For the impact of this population group on juvenile crime, see Walter B. Miller, "Lower Class Culture as a Generating Milieu of Gang Delinquency," *Journal of Social Issues* 14, 3 (1958).
2. Shaw, Zorbaugh, McKay, and Cottrell, 1929. More recent studies have verified their findings: Shaw and McKay, 1967; Cartwright and Howard, 1966:321-71; Polk, 1967:320-25; Lander, 1971:161-75; Chilton, 1964:71-83; Quinney, 1964:149-54; Wilkes, 1967:138-56; Wolfgang, 1970:277.
3. Explanations for criminal conduct include the personality of the offender (Hirschi and Rudisill, 1976:14-22; Fitzpatrick, 1976:67-74), as well as characteristics of the offender's social system (for example, theories of differential association, strain, legitimate vs. illegitimate opportunity, labeling, and control).

14 Educational Problems of Cities

In the United States most public elementary and secondary school systems are organized on the same territorial basis as cities and suburbs. That is, each city and suburb has its own school system. It is true that many suburbs as well as less densely settled areas have consolidated school districts, and many large cities have administrative subdivisions. But these exceptions do not affect our basic analysis of the educational problems of cities.

Sources of Urban Educational Problems

Virtually all large cities and even some older suburbs in major metropolitan areas are currently having difficulty defining and performing one critical communal function: socializing the young. As society has industrialized and grown in size and complexity, school systems have taken over most of the **socialization** function from the family. City schools now have primary responsibility for socializing the young to society, to the urban social system and its institutions, and to the roles that the students will occupy as adults. When city schools fail to perform their socialization function adequately, dissatisfied parents move their families to the suburbs in search of a better education for their children. (See the discussion on suburban migration in chapter 5.) This population movement further contributes to the decline of the middle class in the central city, the financial problems of the city, and the difficulties of the school system.

In contemporary society education is the major route to occupational success. If the schools fail to educate students adequately, it is reasonable to assume that students will not qualify for good jobs as adults. This is espe-

cially important as an increasing proportion of students in city schools come from poor, disadvantaged, or lower class homes. For earlier urban residents, public education was a major means of **social mobility.** When the schools fail to educate, this route is closed. There are few alternative routes, especially for the poor who cannot afford private or parochial schools. The apparent failure of the public schools can be interpreted by parents as an indication that their children are never going to achieve a better life than they now have. This interpretation can lead to anger, frustration, hopelessness, and rage, and manifest itself in intense concern about urban public schools. The perception that schools are failing has an immediate impact on the character of communal life in the neighborhoods. When it is perceived that all schools in a city are failing, the negative impact is felt by the entire city, and the city is seen as failing.

Defining the Goals of the Socialization Function

Defining socialization goals and thus the tasks of the school system is difficult. Professional educators who run urban school systems traditionally say that schools should prepare students for life as citizens of a democracy in a complex society and provide them with the intellectual skills needed to hold jobs (U.S. Commission on Civil Rights, 1967:73; Havighurst and Levine, 1967:326; Sizer, 1970:349, 365). There is, however, incontrovertible evidence that large portions of the urban school population are learning neither the needed job skills nor the attitudes and values that lead to adequate functioning as informed citizens of a complex industrialized democracy (Passow, 1971:4, 5; Coleman et al., 1966: 274-75; U.S. Department of HEW, 1973:158; U.S. Commission on Civil Rights, 1967:13, 14, 74; Dye, 1969:89-100; Sizer, 1970:343; Green, 1974:262-63).

Preparing students for jobs.   If children are to be prepared for roles as productive members of society, they must be taught the intellectual skills they will need on the job as adults. Exactly what those skills are is difficult to define, as the nature of the labor force is continually changing and at an increasingly rapid rate. There is general agreement that reading and basic computational skills are critical in all fields. But how much training in science, geography, history, and other subjects do students need to hold jobs in the next decade? In vocational training, how can students be prepared for jobs that may not now exist and not be prepared for jobs that may no longer exist when they enter the work force? How can students who do not plan to go to college be prepared for occupational success in both the short term and the long term? These are questions that school curriculum planners face. There are no clear-cut answers, and as budgets become increasingly restricted, school boards have difficult choices to make. The skills taught today tend to be those that were needed for occupational success and mobility when teachers, administrators, and school board members were receiving their education; they usually are not the skills that students will need when they enter the job market. The intellectual content of educational curricula becomes increasingly irrelevant to students who are aware of these job market changes. Many students therefore view all education as irrelevant and think very little of disrupting the process. They feel alienated and often become discipline problems for the school.

Preparing students for citizenship.   The preparation of students for life as citizens of a democracy includes socializing the students to the norms of society. However, our society's norms are in the process of critical examination and flux. Because we currently accept a **pluralistic model** of society, a wider variety of values, cultures, and traditions is valued (Gordon, 1964:84-132 and chap. 9). There is no single set of norms that can be taught to all children uniformly.

At the same time that the pluralistic model of society is gaining legitimacy, various national laws and regulations accompanying grants of federal funds to local school districts are requiring homogeneity of socialization and equal population representation in all educational units supported by those funds. Therefore, there is competition over which model of society young people should be socialized for. Factions cannot agree about which option—integration and homogeneity or local community control and difference—is "right." Federal laws and regulations support a melting-pot or Anglo-culture model of society. Many local groups are unwilling to support such a model, preferring instead a more heterogeneous and diversified pluralistic model. These groups control local educational funds and the hiring of teachers. They nominate, elect, or serve on school boards, and they attempt to control curriculum.

Urban school systems, like the cities themselves, have lost control over their ability to perform their critical functions. As a consequence of changes in the occupational structure and in the relationships between groups that make up the society, schools are unable to define precisely what their function is and what they should teach. Urban schools must also cope with student populations whose characteristics are changing, with financial limitations, and with problems of integrating their function with the norms of the wider society.

Changes in Student Population Characteristics

Urban and suburban school systems have no influence or control over the nature or size of the school-age population, which is changing in two major ways. In many cities, the racial composition of the school-age population is changing from predominantly or exclusively white to either (1) white and nonwhite or (2) predominantly nonwhite. At the same time, the average socioeconomic status of students in both city and suburban schools is declining as lower status groups migrate to the suburbs, leaving cities increasingly populated by the lowest status groups.

A second major change affecting school systems is a decline in enrollment as the result of a declining birth rate. (See chapter 7 for a discussion of population trends.) Because most state and federal school funding is based on average daily enrollment, fewer students mean less outside revenue for local schools. Changes in age distribution in the school population also leave schools with faculty

Urban school-age population is changing from predominantly white to predominantly nonwhite. And enrollment is declining as the result of a declining birth rate.

members who have **tenure** and often belong to unions, but who were trained and hired earlier to teach students of a different age group.

School systems must also adapt old educational programs and introduce new programs for the new student population, and they must make these alterations even as costs increase faster than revenues.

Fiscal Problems

As the population of school-age children declines, schools will be closed and faculties reduced. These changes anger parents who may have moved to a particular suburb or neighborhood because of the local school. School closings also mean that children will have to be bused for reasons other than racial integration to distant schools (*New York Times,* 18 November 1975). This, too, can be a shock to parents who may have invested in expensive homes and are prepared to pay relatively high real estate taxes to support better than average local school systems.

Many schools were built after World War II in response to the baby boom. Many of those that were designed as elementary schools are no longer needed because there are fewer children entering school. The bonds issued to raise money to build these schools must still be paid off, and the buildings must still be maintained. These unusable physical facilities then continue to be a drain on local school resources. A faculty of tenured and unionized teachers trained and hired for a student population of a different age distribution is an expense that must be met annually even if schools need fewer lower grade teachers and more upper grade teachers. Some school districts have had to fire teachers for this reason.

Schools are supported by local property taxes and by state and federal funds. A number of states have limited the amount of property tax local jurisdictions may levy for schools, and several federal court decisions have declared that local property taxes are unconstitutional as a means of supporting schools. Furthermore, **school districts** may not have the same boundaries as other political jurisdictions. Residents may have approval power over local tax levies, but they frequently have little control over school funding. To the extent that funds come from state or federal governments, rules and regulations about racial integration, gender segregation, and educational programs are determined outside the school district. When outside agencies place limits on local tax contributions to schools, this puts a ceiling on the amount of money available to school districts, a ceiling that suburbs are more likely than cities to have reached. The limit equalizes the resources that city and suburban school districts may spend in education. Many suburban residents object because they want to invest more in education (*New York Times,* 30 December 1974).

Problems of Integrating the Socialization Function

In dealing with their many problems the schools must also integrate their efforts with the norms of the wider society. School systems must observe state and federal laws and regulations that constrain the school systems in carrying out their socialization function. The integration of socialization with other functions means integrating educational content,

The Roles of Education

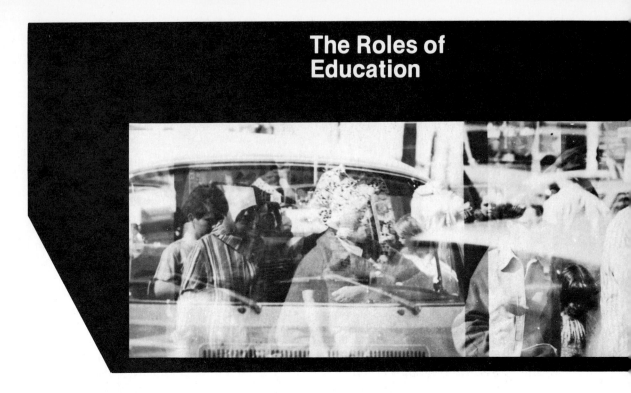

Educator. Baby-sitter. Counselor. Trainer. Instructor of the handicapped. Companion. Motivator. In a phrase, ersatz parent.

This, more and more, is becoming the role of the school in the nation's central city. But ersatz parents are costly. High-income families who might otherwise help carry the burden of providing them have fled to suburban communities, often paying their taxes instead to less needy, better-heeled school districts. In their place have come greater numbers of low-income, minority groups with larger broods.

The problems that sprawl showers on urban education thus tend to fall more heavily on the central city that is left behind in sprawl's outward dash than upon newly created suburbs. True, new communities need schools and the staffs to man them; older metropolitan areas, on the other hand, have both schools and, at least to start off with, the staffs to man them. But the means to build new schools and provide them with the finest of staffs are not lacking in the relatively affluent suburb. For the most part, in fact, those funds have been summoned with relative ease despite the outcries and the attention they have brought.

Moreover, the suburban child typically is the benefactor of an educational resource far more vital to education than those money can buy: concerned parents capable of providing the strongest motivation and all the trappings to go with it, from private study space and well-chosen books to provocative conversation at the dinner table, an occasional evening at the theater, or a Sunday afternoon in the museum.

But the most serious of all schooling challenges to the community are not likely to be found in the suburbs at all. They lie, rather, in the deteriorating areas of the central city with its highly limited means and growing needs. Here, a catalog of welfare functions is thrust upon school systems to meet the needs of underprivileged youngsters who must be fed before they can be taught and assured before they can be interested, of teenagers who lack the diligence or wherewithal to acquire the learning so vital for secure employment in an increasingly automated economy, and of adults who do not themselves understand the uses of education, much less desire its assiduous acquisition by their youngsters.

Schools have difficulty performing their functions because these functions are hard to define. In some schools it is necessary to provide supplementary programs to overcome barriers to learning.

Along with their own particular handicaps, school systems in the central city, as well as those in the suburbs, are being weighted more heavily with new responsibilities. Beyond their original objectives of instilling five "R's"— reading, 'riting, 'rithmetic, the ability to reason, and a sense of responsibility—the nation's public schools are expected today to combat all manner of handicap, mental as well as physical, social as well as economic. In addition, they are being called upon to raise educational levels to meet the challenges of scientific achievements in the race for space and nuclear supremacy, to cope with the complex demands of world leadership, properly channel the use of lengthening leisure, and otherwise equip an amorphous electorate for a better understanding of complex political, economic, and sociological change.

Any effort to raise the educational level of low-income minority groups must inevitably come to grips with a wide range of difficulties. As Robert L. Baker, Director of Secondary Education for the St. Louis Public School District, puts it: "These children don't get discussion of world affairs at the dinner table. They're just told to shut up.

Some of them come to class so hungry in the morning, they can't absorb anything unless they're fed first." In some instances, the school system is doing exactly that. But its undertakings also extend well beyond the breakfast platter. One extracurricular program, for instance, attempts to raise aspirations of "culturally deprived" youth by taking them to concerts, getting them part-time jobs that will sharpen their appreciation of the value of education, and otherwise attempting to fire ambitions.

Source Mitchell Gordon, *Sick Cities*, Baltimore: Penguin, 1963, pp. 219, 220, 221, 236.

integrating the norms and values that agree with society's model of its own structure, and assuring that funds are spent and children are taught in accordance with the norms and values of the society. In contemporary America the most difficult integrative problem has been organizing urban school systems so that they do not discriminate against members of minority groups (Hogan, 1974:413). (See chapter 9.) This problem reflects the larger problems that society is having with racial and ethnic communities.

Racial Problems and Urban Schools

The basis of many urban school problems today is the continuing debate about the goals of socialization. This debate has largely been caused by the presence of racial and ethnic communities in our cities and the failure of schools to socialize children of all racial and ethnic origins to academic competence or to citizenship equally well. Nor do urban schools instill positive self-concepts in or motivate members of different ethnic groups equally

Table 14.1   Extent of Elementary School Segregation in 75 School Systems

	% of Blacks in 90 to 100% Black Schools	% of Blacks in Majority-Black Schools	% of Whites in 90 to 100% White Schools		% of Blacks in 90 to 100% Black Schools	% of Blacks in Majority-Black Schools	% of Whites in 90 to 100% White Schools
Mobile, Ala	99.9	99.9	100.0	East St. Louis, Ill	80.4	92.4	68.6
Tuscaloosa, Ala	99.6	99.6	100.0	Peoria, Ill	21.0	86.9	89.6
Little Rock, Ark	95.6	95.6	97.1	Fort Wayne, Ind	60.8	82.9	87.7
Pine Bluff, Ark	98.2	98.2	100.0	Gary, Ind	89.9	94.8	75.9
Los Angeles, Calif	39.5	87.5	94.7	Indianapolis, Ind	70.5	84.2	80.7
Oakland, Calif	48.7	83.2	50.2	Wichita, Kans	63.5	89.1	94.8
Pasadena, Calif	None	71.4	82.1	Louisville, Ky	69.5	84.5	61.3
Richmond, Calif	39.2	82.9	90.2	New Orleans, La	95.9	96.7	83.8
San Diego, Calif	13.9	73.3	88.7	Baltimore, Md	84.2	92.3	67.0
San Francisco, Calif	21.1	72.3	65.1	Boston, Mass	35.4	79.5	76.5
Denver, Colo	29.4	75.2	95.5	Springfield, Mass	15.4	71.9	82.8
Hartford, Conn	9.4	73.8	66.2	Detroit, Mich	72.3	91.5	65.0
New Haven, Conn	36.8	73.4	47.1	Flint, Mich	67.9	85.9	80.0
Wilmington, Del	49.7	92.5	27.3	Minneapolis, Minn	None	39.2	84.9
Miami, Fla	91.4	94.4	95.3	Hattiesburg, Miss	98.7	98.7	100.0
Tallahassee, Fla	99.7	99.7	100.0	Vicksburg, Miss	97.1	97.1	100.0
Americus, Ga	99.3	99.3	100.0	Kansas City, Mo	69.1	85.5	65.2
Atlanta, Ga	97.4	98.8	95.4	St. Joseph, Mo	39.3	39.3	91.3
Augusta, Ga	99.2	99.2	100.0	St. Louis, Mo	90.9	93.7	66.0
Marietta, Ga	94.2	94.2	100.0	Omaha, Nebr	47.7	81.1	89.0
Chicago, Ill	89.2	96.9	88.8	Newark, N.J	51.3	90.3	37.1

well. The largest and most segregated minority group is the blacks (see chapter 9). Segregation of blacks in cities and in specific areas of cities has produced racially segregated neighborhood schools. As a result urban school systems are racially segregated and treat black and white pupils very differently.

Extent of Racial Segregation in Urban Schools

Most data on the extent of racial segregation in urban schools has been developed since the mid-1960s. Two studies commissioned by the federal government have been especially important in developing data on racial problems and differences in urban schools: *Equality of Educational Opportunity,* known as the Coleman Report (Coleman et al., 1966), and *Racial Isolation in the Public Schools* (U.S. Commission on Civil Rights, 1967).[1] Both studies (the second relied on the findings of the first) documented the very high level of racial segregation in public schools in the United States. Regardless of how segregation

	% of Blacks in 90 to 100% Black Schools	% of Blacks in Majority-Black Schools	% of Whites in 90 to 100% White Schools		% of Blacks in 90 to 100% Black Schools	% of Blacks in Majority-Black Schools	% of Whites in 90 to 100% White Schools
Camden, N.J	37.0	90.4	62.4	Providence, R.I	14.6	55.5	63.3
Albany, N.Y	None	74.0	66.5	Columbia, S.C	99.1	99.1	100.0
Buffalo, N.Y	77.0	88.7	81.1	Florence, S.C	99.1	99.1	100.0
New York City, N.Y	20.7	55.5	56.8	Sumter, S.C	99.0	99.0	100.0
Charlotte, N.C	95.7	95.7	94.7	Knoxville, Tenn	79.3	79.3	94.9
Raleigh, N.C	98.5	98.5	100.0	Memphis, Tenn	95.1	98.8	93.6
Winston-Salem, N.C	88.7	95.1	95.6	Nashville, Tenn	82.2	86.4	90.7
Cincinnati, Ohio	49.4	88.0	63.3	Amarillo, Tex	89.6	89.6	98.3
Cleveland, Ohio	82.3	94.6	80.2	Austin, Tex	86.1	86.1	93.1
Columbus, Ohio	34.3	80.8	77.0	Dallas, Tex	82.6	90.3	90.1
Oklahoma City, Okla	90.5	96.8	96.1	Houston, Tex	93.0	97.6	97.3
Tulsa, Okla	90.7	98.7	98.8	San Antonio, Tex	65.9	77.2	89.4
Portland, Oreg	46.5	59.2	92.0	Richmond, Va	98.5	98.5	95.3
Chester, Pa	77.9	89.1	37.9	Seattle, Wash	9.9	60.4	89.8
Harrisburg, Pa	54.0	81.3	56.2	Milwaukee, Wis	72.4	86.8	86.3
Philadelphia, Pa	72.0	90.2	57.7	Washington, D.C	90.4	99.3	34.3
Pittsburgh, Pa	49.5	83.8	62.3				

Note: Percentages shown in this table are for 1965-66 school year, except for Seattle, Wash. (1964-65), Los Angeles, Calif. (1963-64), and Cleveland, Ohio (1962-63).

Source   Adapted from U.S. Commission on Civil Rights, *Racial Isolation in the Public Schools* (Washington, D.C.: U.S. Government Printing Office, 1967), pp. 4-5.

was measured, the vast majority of black students were found in segregated schools. Although these reports were done in the mid-1960s, there is evidence that high levels of segregation have continued to the present time (Coleman et al., 1975:38; Dye, 1969). Segregation in twenty-two large cities studied by Coleman from 1968 to 1973 generally increased, so that the average black pupil attended schools with only 2 percent to 39 percent white students.

Equalization of Funding by School Systems

These studies, and many subsequent ones, documented the fact that many predominantly black urban schools were drastically short-changed in resources by urban school boards. These schools had fewer books per student in their libraries, less laboratory equipment, less well-trained and less well-paid teachers, fewer special programs, and buildings that were old and in poor condition.

In response to these findings and to keep their federal funds, urban school systems have altered their funding practices and support payments in accordance with federal court rulings and administrative regulations. Only in this way can they integrate the performance of their function with the norms of society and at the same time keep their federal aid. Programs instituted to correct past practices are designed to ensure that the schools attended by minority pupils are funded at the same levels as schools attended by majority pupils and that the proportions of majority and minority pupils in the schools are the same as those prevailing in the population (Dye, 1969; Coleman et al., 1966; Green, 1974:258-59).

Effects of Segregation on Student Achievement

The Coleman Report concluded, however, that it was not the differences in resources that affected student achievement, but rather the characteristics of the students and their backgrounds. Because race and socioeconomic status are statistically correlated in contemporary society, schools that are heavily black or all black are also likely to be composed of students from poor homes. Regardless of race, students are not likely to do well in a school made up of students whose parents are poor and unable to provide a home environment that supports and encourages academic achievement. When students from such schools are dispersed into schools whose students come from higher status homes, they enter an educational environment that can counteract the effects of the poor home environment. When black students are enrolled in majority white schools, the educational achievement of the black students tends to rise (Coleman et al., 1966:325; Crain, 1970; Crain, 1974; Jencks and Brown, 1975; St. John, 1970). Schools will have to cope with the effects of racial and socioeconomic segregation so long as blacks are segregated residentially and school populations are based on neighborhoods and therefore segregated.

The solution to many critical problems in urban education lies in the adoption of policies that will somehow counteract the negative effects of segregation on student achievement. The solution, of course, must be considered in light of federal laws and regulations requiring equality of opportunity.

Equality has been interpreted to mean equality of resource distribution and of racial representation in all schools in a school district. Urban schools have adopted two major approaches to meet these requirements: **integration** and **community control**.

Integration As a Solution to School Racial Problems

A number of strategies have been proposed for integrating the public schools within a district (Dye, 1969; Hogan, 1974). These include open enrollment, paired black and white schools, magnet schools that attract students from all over the city, educational parks, closed circuit TV between schools, and **busing** to equalize racial distribution. With the exception of busing programs, which have caused widespread discontent and even violence, these strategies have had little success in desegregating urban schools. In fact, since the Brown vs. the Board of Education decision in 1954, the extent of urban school segregation has changed very little (Dye, 1969; U.S. Commission on Civil Rights, 1967).

Strategies other than busing have failed for the following reasons:

1. At least some whites would rather move out of cities or to other locations within a city than send their children to schools with a large percentage of black students (Coleman, 1975; Green, 1974; Rubin, 1972:1-23).

2. Strategies, however successful, have been unable to keep up with the growth of the black population in cities (due to both migration and natural rates of increase). The continued concentration of the black population in cities has increased the proportion of children in city schools who are black (U.S.

Commission on Civil Rights, 1967:19; *New York Times,* 18 June 1971; U.S. Bureau of the Census, 1975:table 2).

3. While large numbers and proportions of black students in a school system do not make school integration impossible, they do make it difficult. Small programs will no longer work. As the percentage of black enrollment increases, the percentage of white students who will have to be involved in integration programs also increases. This increases the potential for political controversy over the integration plan and the probability that at least some parents will protest.

Busing for School Integration

Because of the concentration of blacks in the cities and their relative exclusion from the suburbs, successful school integration in most major metropolitan areas will require busing across city-suburban political boundaries. Black students will have to be bused to white schools, and white students will have to attend predominantly black schools. Busing large numbers of children from school to school is the most controversial contemporary desegregation method (Green, 1974; Hogan, 1974; Armour, 1972:90-126).

Probably the best known legal and political controversy associated with busing occurred in Detroit (Green, 1974; Hogan, 1974). As a result of declining white student enrollment, a federal judge ruled in 1972 that the Detroit schools would have to bus pupils from city to suburban schools and from suburban to city schools to achieve desegregation (Stevens, 1976:40). This ruling was overturned in 1974 by the Supreme Court. The problem remains:

School busing programs have caused widespread discontent and even violence.

how can city schools be desegregated when large proportions of the student bodies are black? Some school systems have tried voluntary cross-district busing programs, for example, the METCO Program in Boston (Armour, 1972). However, these programs have not affected many students. One reason for the cross-district busing controversy is that many white children involved are those whose parents moved to the suburbs to avoid city schools.

The concept of desegregation upon which busing is based is that the racial distribution of students in each school must be at least approximately the same as the racial distribution in the school system. This definition of integration leads directly to a system of quotas to ensure proportional representation of all minority groups in each school. The extent of student movement needed to achieve equal distributions can be measured by the same index of dissimilarity used to measure residential racial segregation (see chapter 9).

Unlike the other desegregation strategies, school busing programs affect large portions of the urban community. The whole city, even the whole metropolitan area, may be affected. Unlike urban renewal, model cities, or construction programs, busing programs are not limited to a few neighborhoods or to minority neighborhoods, but may affect white neighborhoods and suburbs as well. It has been charged that busing plans cause or accelerate white migration to the suburbs (Coleman et al., 1966; Coleman, 1974:3-12). Racial integration of schools within a city, but not within the whole metropolis, is often cited as an explanation for the migration of whites to the suburbs, but the evidence to support this argument is at best ambiguous and contradictory (Jackson, 1975:21-25; Wisenbaker, 1976: 17-26).

Resistance to Busing and the Effects of Busing

A number of explanations can be advanced for the resistance to busing, and to other intracity desegregation plans. Racism is one. White parents' fear that their children will be subjected to violence in school is another, although more black than white students have been victims of violence during the initial stages of busing. A third explanation is that the white neighborhoods and suburbs involved are inhabited by people who have recently adopted the pluralistic model of society and feel pride in their ethnic identities. To maintain this ethnic pride, they want each group to have its own schools and teach its own heritage and traditions. They reject the homogeneous melting-pot model of society and resist efforts to enforce homogeneity in the schools and dilute ethnic identities. While the immediate result of ethnic and racial groups mixing is heterogeneity, its long-run effect is homogeneity rather than pluralism. Persons who want to maintain their ethnic identities resist pressure to adopt the melting-pot model taught to children in public schools. They want their children to be educated with "their own kind," and race is simply one difference that they see their children being taught to ignore. It appears that ethnic mixing of any type—not simply racial mixing—would be resisted by those people who object to busing. This hypothesis or supposition is without empirical support, but it is worth testing.

Busing is a highly visible manifestation of the loss of control by neighborhoods and cities over performance of their communal functions.

Busing is also a highly visible manifestation of the loss of control by neighborhoods and cities over performance of their communal functions. Busing is generally the last resort in attempts to integrate the schools and is generally ordered by federal courts. The local population feels forced, and is "forced," by federal regulations to desegregate schools by busing (Hogan, 1974; Green, 1974). Local norms pertaining to the socialization of children are overridden when they come into conflict with societal norms.

The effects of busing on student academic achievement and on communities that are involved are still being widely and hotly debated (Armour, 1972; Pettigrew et al., 1973:88-118; Coleman, 1974; Coleman et al., 1975; Jackson, 1975). Part of the debate concerns the extent to which busing has raised the achievement of black students bused to white schools and reduced (or not) the achievement of whites bused to black schools or attending schools to which black pupils are bused. Another part of the debate concerns the extent to which busing programs limited to central cities have prompted whites to flee to the suburbs. The evidence on all sides in these debates is ambiguous and conflicting. David Armour (1972) and James Coleman (1974) have suggested that the effects of busing on achievement are minimal, and Coleman has suggested that whites do flee central cities that have busing programs. There are more studies, however, that show that busing does not have this effect (Bosco and Robin, 1976:263-75; Giles, Cataldo, and Catlin, 1975:85-92; Giles, Catlin, and Cataldo, 1974:493-501; Lord and Catau, 1976:275-95; Wisenbaker, 1976:19-27). Census reports

show that about 9.7 million persons moved from central cities to suburbs between 1970 and 1975, but that 38 percent of these migrants moved to suburbs of other central cities, implying that at least this much migration was for reasons other than avoiding school desegregation (U.S. Bureau of the Census, 1976:table 1).

What is beyond debate, however, is that busing proposals and their implementation can cause intense controversy and even large-scale violence within the city, the metropolitan area, and the nation. The controversy and riots in South Boston from 1974 to 1976 are an example of the violence that the implementation of busing proposals can cause. The controversy in Detroit in the early 1970s over the proposals to bus Detroit children to schools in the suburbs, and the controversy in Richmond, Virginia, when similar plans were made, illustrate the spread of the problem from the central city to entire metropolitan areas. Like other forms of political conflict, busing controversies quickly polarize cities and affect other political issues. The question of busing has even had an influence on local, state, and federal elections. George Wallace's candidacy for president in 1968 and 1972 seemed to be partially a consequence of passions aroused by busing debates.

Community Control As a Solution to School Racial Problems

An alternative to the integration approach is known by the generic term *community control*. It is designed not to desegregate schools but to ameliorate the effects of segregation in urban schools. To a large extent the community control strategy is based on research findings that a positive **self-concept** and a **sense of mastery** are strongly related to student achievement (Pettigrew, 1968:73-74; Coleman et al., 1966:22, 275-89; U.S. Commission on Civil Rights, 1967:204). Community control advocates reason that if schools can be organized and run so as to enhance the students' self-image and sense of mastery, the negative effects of student background associated with poverty and minority group membership may be overcome (Gittell et al., 1972:chap. 11; Fantini, Gittell, and Magat, 1970:228-51; Ornstein, 1974:39-57).[2] The term community control applies to a wide range of programs with various definitions of community and of control. These programs include such measures as (1) administrative decentralization within districts that have grown very large, (2) the legal dissolution of large school districts, and (3) the granting of legal control over school policies to locally elected boards. Under some community control programs, central school boards merely listen to parental complaints and suggestions. Ideally, however, under any community control program, parents have some say-so about the methods and the goals of socialization carried out in the local schools.

The desire for community control emerged in the late 1960s and sprang from several sources (Gittell et al., 1972:chap. 1; Carmichael and Hamilton, 1967; Billings, 1972: 277-78).

1. The failure of the major urban educational systems to provide meaningful racial integration in the early 1960s caused many black and other minority group leaders to abandon integration as a strategy or goal (Carmichael and Hamilton, 1967; Fantini, Gittell, and Magat, 1970:94-95; McCoy, 1969; Banks, 1972:266-67).

2. The failure to achieve school integration (and racial integration generally), the growth of the black power movement, and the recognition that the pluralistic rather than the melting-pot concept was the appropriate model for intergroup relationships in the United States led to the demand for local (neighborhood or community) control of the schools. Local control would ensure an education that included socialization to the culture of the local area. This education could be provided only if the local culture, traditions, language, and life style were recognized by the school system as legitimate and valid.

3. This line of reasoning was supported by major federal studies (*Equality of Educational Opportunity* [Coleman et al., 1966] and *Racial Isolation in the Public Schools* [U.S. Commission on Civil Rights, 1967]), which pointed out that **neighborhood context** and the child's sense of mastery were probably the most important factors related to academic achievement (Pettigrew, 1968; Coleman et al., 1966:22, 275-89; U.S. Commission on Civil Rights, 1967:204).

4. Many people came to the conclusion that, without meaningful racial integration of the schools, minority academic achievement could be accomplished only if poor and minority group students were taught in schools controlled and staffed by the poor and minority groups. Only in this way would the schools be able to provide adequate role models for children to follow. As teachers and school administrators, poor people and minority group members would provide the students with models of success and mastery

in a complex urban society. The teaching by such a staff would be understandable and relevant to the students, encouraging and facilitating their learning. The teaching would be in the language of the children, both linguistically and conceptually. The students would see that "their type of people" could successfully use power to gain control of and run major urban institutions. All this would facilitate the development of positive student self-images and improve their educational achievement.

5. Community control of the schools is attained through the use of political power. Community control, once attained, becomes a power base for urban ethnic and racial minority groups and thus helps to ensure cultural pluralism.

In summary, community control over local urban schools, as an alternative to desegregation, is preferred by many persons. Communities that choose this alternative tend to favor the pluralistic model of society and bring themselves into conflict with the norms of the wider society. Under community control the school system performs its function independently in the hope of overcoming the deficiencies of larger urban school systems.

Community Control and Decentralization of Urban Schools

Community control is also a means of reducing the number of schools administered by an urban school system bureaucracy. In the first few decades of this century, school centralization was seen as a means of eliminating waste and inefficiency, partisan influence, corruption, and a lack of professionalism in school systems (Scribner and O'Shea, 1974:380). Local urban school boards, often based on wards, were replaced with centralized boards that separated policy making and administration. Professional, administrative, and educational leadership and nonpartisan school boards were designed to ensure the efficient operation of urban schools. In the period between 1932 and 1970, the number of school districts in the United States shrank from 127,000 to 18,000, with a consequent increase in the size of each district and in the size and the complexity of the bureaucracy needed to administer it (Scribner and O'Shea, 1974; U.S. Department of HEW, 1973).

As the bureaucracy grew, it became more distant from local communities and more difficult to control. Administrative decentralization or the creation of subdistricts, zones, or regions within enlarged school districts became imperative if students and parents were to have any influence over the schools. By 1974 almost all school districts of 100,000 or more students had some form of decentralized administration or control, while only two thirds of those districts with 50,000 to 100,000 students had decentralized, most of these since 1967 (Ornstein, 1974:5-10). Much decentralization took place not because of local community power demands, but because persons involved in managing American public education now believe that decentralized school systems are more attractive than large centralized school systems. Many school districts seem to have passed the point at which large size is economical, making decentralization not only politically but economically compelling. Furthermore, many professional educators feel that smaller school districts are likely to be better school districts. They argue that the ideal size for a school district is twenty to thirty thousand students or less.[3]

The New York Experiment in Community Control

Although some community control over school policies is found in many areas, neighborhoods have legal control over local schools only in New York City and Detroit. Elsewhere, citizens perform advisory and informational functions, but control is vested in locally elected or appointed school boards. Among the reasons that community legal control over schools is not more common is that improvements in student achievement have not been demonstrated (Scribner and O'Shea, 1974:387; Ornstein, 1974:40-45). Another reason is that political controversy that has accompanied the granting of local control has been intense. In the New York experiment, the benefits were apparently outweighed by the effects of political controversy generated by the experiment (Ornstein, 1974:49-57; Scribner and O'Shea, 1974:394-400).

The New York experiment was the result of minority demands that the schools do something to alleviate both lack of achievement among minority pupils and segregation in the public schools. Although the majority of public school students in New York City came from minority groups, a majority of voters electing school board members were white. It was the white majority, not the minorities, that had access to and power over the city school board (Ornstein, 1974:49-57; Scribner and O'Shea, 1974:394-400). Consequently, the city school board was relatively unresponsive to minority complaints about segregation and relative achievement and operated the local schools as part of a large, centralized bureaucracy that was highly resistant to change.

Mayor John Lindsay was persuaded by the proponents of community schools and community control to initiate (with Ford Foundation support) an experiment in community control (Ornstein, 1974:40-45). The proponents argued as follows.

First, the schools have all-black student bodies. Giving control to blacks would lead to quality education for black children and youth. The problems of New York City schools were due to racism in the schools. If the schools were to provide teaching, administrative, and other jobs for blacks, they would drive out the racism and improve the quality of the education (Ornstein, 1974:40-41).

Supporters argued that the solution to ghetto problems required special knowledge available only to those who lived in the community. Therefore the solution to the problems of ghetto schools would come only if the schools employed ghetto residents. In this sense, community control was advocated as a form of grass-roots democracy, the equivalent of suburban school boards (Ornstein, 1974:42-43).

Finally it was argued that if the local school was controlled by local residents who had the power to hire and fire, the local residents would be able to hold the professionals who ran the schools accountable for the education their children received. The teachers would then not only improve education by innovation and reform but would also enhance the local community's culture and its pride in that culture (Ornstein, 1974:44-51).

The experiment provided for locally elected school boards that controlled the curriculum, personnel, and budget in three experimental schools. Local school boards were to administer the local schools in a fashion integrated with the general policies of the central school board. The local school boards quickly came into conflict with citywide institutions whose concerns extended beyond the locally relevant concerns of the community. The teachers' union and the city school board did not expect the locally elected school boards to violate the city's teacher contract by firing tenured teachers and hiring local residents to replace them, but that is exactly what the local boards did. When the local boards took these actions and experimented with new forms of teaching that they hoped would rapidly improve achievement scores, political conflict in the New York City school system and in the city as a whole quickly followed. The teachers' union protested the violation of the city's contract with them, and the resulting strike closed all schools in the city for seven weeks.

The New York experiment resulted in a fairly high degree of local citizen participation in the election of the local school boards. There was some evidence that the achievement scores of students in the experimental schools did not decline as fast as the achievement scores of students in nonexperimental schools. The conflict generated by the experiment was more political than educational.[4] The locally elected school boards' policies conflicted with the policies of the systemwide school board. This conflict raised fundamental questions about community control. There is no clear evidence whether community control can or cannot make the educational establishment provide more effective education or be any more responsible or accountable to the local community than a centralized school board.

Appraisal of Community Control

The extent of political conflict over issues involved in community control can hardly be overemphasized. Indeed, whether the movement toward community control is an educational movement or a political movement is open to some debate. In the New York experiment the welfare and education of the pupils seems to have come second to the political purposes of the community leaders who emphasized racial awareness, imposed racial quotas on hiring, and hired less qualified people to replace those fired. These practices call into question the legitimacy of the entire local control and urban decentralization movements (Ornstein, 1974:39-40).

Despite conflicts, most metropolitan districts have decentralized and implemented some form of community participation, if not complete control. The arguments for community control rather than participation, however, have not convinced many legislators or administrators of school districts. Community leaders outside New York City seem aware that community control can, instead of improving the nature of schools, increase racial segregation and hostility, and it cannot achieve what its advocates have claimed for it.

Community control of the schools assumes that maintaining and socializing children to the homogeneity of a small area will constitute a better education. This is true only if the society in which the child will live is homogeneous. But contemporary society is not by and large homogeneous. Society has decided that racial integration of the schools is desirable. Given the concentration of blacks in the central cities and their relative exclusion from the suburbs, integration can be accomplished only if city and suburbs have a single, nondiscriminatory and nonterritorially-based school system. This goal is in direct conflict with the characteristics of community control.

Because so many problems faced by cities (pollution, transportation, housing, health, crime) are metropolitan in character, there is an increasing tendency to deal with these problems on a metropolitan basis even if political integration is not employed in the solution. The movement toward community control of schools is in opposition to this tendency and thus appears unlikely to succeed in the long run.

Summary

The socialization of children to urban society and their preparation for roles as citizens, including inculcation of skills for occupational success and upward mobility, is a critical urban function. However, urban schools are having difficulty defining the curriculum and the social norms to be taught and in organizing themselves to perform their functions in a manner that is integrated with the norms of the wider society. In addition, urban schools are faced with changing characteristics of their student bodies and with changing models of society. The effects of these changes are seen most dramatically in the attempts of urban school systems to cope with the continuing problems of racial and ethnic communities.

Educational segregation caused by residential segregation has produced conflict in urban schools. Desegregation plans of many types have been proposed; the most controversial and bitterly resisted procedure has been the busing of students to achieve racial integration. Busing is based on the assumption that integration is the same as achieving proportional representation of all races in all schools. Its effects on student achievement, on white out-migration, and on community life are still hotly debated.

Plans advocating local community control of the schools are based on the belief that minority students can receive a higher quality education if their schools are controlled and staffed by members of their minority group. It is argued that community control will improve student self-concept and sense of power and mastery over the environment, outcomes that have been shown to be related to educational achievement.

Administrative problems associated with the increasing size of urban school districts have also hindered function performance. In many cases, attempts to decentralize the school districts have been made in response to demands for community control. Many of these programs have been associated with political controversy and other problems. Such programs, however, potentially reduce the levels of bureaucracy and make urban schools more responsive to the needs of the community.

The problems of urban schools seem insoluble until society reaches greater agreement about its norms and values. Schools will not be able to define their function and develop the means to perform that function in a manner that is integrated with the performance of other functions until the society decides what its overall structure should be. As long as some groups believe that American society is a melting pot and others believe it is culturally pluralistic, the schools will be unable to solve either their racial and ethnic problems or their problems of norm definition and socialization.

Glossary

busing   the transporting of students from one school to another to achieve racial balance; however, most students are still bused to school simply because they live too far from school to walk there

community control   a form of school administration that gives residents of the community the power to decide on curriculum and all administrative matters, including the selection of teachers and the spending of funds; in recent years, it has been used as an alternative to racial integration of the schools

integration   racial integration of schools; achieving approximately equal proportions of white and nonwhite children in each school or school district

neighborhood context   the social characteristics of the neighborhood in which the school is located; refers specifically to the value placed on educational achievement by the parents of children who attend the neighborhood school and the transmission of this value to the students

pluralistic model   a theory of society that states that each subgroup of society should maintain its own identity and cooperate with other subgroups in determining the nature of the total society

school district   in cities overall, the administrative district that controls the schools; within cities, the district or area from which a school draws its students; in many suburban and rural counties, consolidated districts that include many incorporated places; large cities may have several administrative subareas that are larger than single school districts but that taken together do not comprise the entire city

self-concept   the mental picture and evaluation that one has of oneself; thinking well or poorly of one's own character or ability to function

sense of mastery   an individual's sense of ability to master the environment and to accomplish one's goals

socialization   the process of learning the norms, behaviors, and skills one must know to be a functioning member of society

social mobility   a change in the social status of an individual; or a change in social position by a family or group member of one generation from that held by a member of the preceding generation; upward mobility is an increase in social status, downward mobility a loss in social status

tenure   the right of a person to hold a job until retirement unless one is found guilty of incompetence or malfeasance; tenure protects individuals (usually teachers) from being fired because they hold unpopular attitudes or beliefs and frequently protects them even against being fired for reasons of low budget or administrative reorganization

References

Armour, David
1972   "The Evidence on Busing." *The Public Interest* 28 (Summer):90-126.

Banks, James A.
1972   "Imperatives in Ethnic Minority Education." *Phi Delta Kappan* 53:266-67.

Billings, Charles E.
1972   "Community Control of the School and the Quest for Power." *Phi Delta Kappan* 53:277-78.

Bosco, James J., and Robin, Stanley S.
1976   "White Flight from Busing? A Second, Longer Look." *Urban Education* 11, 3 (October):263-75.

Carmichael, Stokely, and Hamilton, Charles
1967   *Black Power.* New York: Random House, Inc.

Coleman, James S.
1974   "Recent Trends in School Integration." *Educational Researcher* (July-August):3-12.

Coleman, James S., et al.
1966   *Equality of Educational Opportunity.* Washington, D.C.: Government Printing Office.

1975   *Trends in School Segregation 1968-1973.* Washington, D.C.: The Urban Institute.

Crain, Robert L.
1970   "School Integration and the Occupational Achievement of Negroes." *American Journal of Sociology* 75, 4 (January):593-606.

1974   "School Integration and the Academic Achievement of Negroes." *Sociology of Education* 44 (Winter):1-26.

Dye, Thomas R.
1969   "Urban School Segregation: A Comparative Analysis." *Urban Affairs Quarterly* 4 (December 1968):141-65. In *The Politics of Urban Education,* edited by Marilyn Gittell and Alan G. Hevesi, pp. 89-100. New York: Praeger Publishers, Inc.

Fantini, Mario; Gittell, Marilyn; and Magat, Richard
1970   *Community Control and the Urban School.* New York: Praeger Publishers, Inc.

Giles, Michael; Cataldo, Everett F.; and Catlin, Douglas S.
1975   "White Flight and Percent Black: The Tipping Point Re-examined." *Social Science Quarterly* 56 (June):85-92.

Giles, Michael; Catlin, Douglas S.; and Cataldo, Everett F.
1974   "The Impact of Busing on White Flight." *Social Science Quarterly* 55 (September):493-501.

Gittell, Marilyn, et al.
1972   *Local Control in Education.* New York: Praeger Publishers, Inc.

Gordon, Milton
1964   *Assimilation in American Life.* New York: Oxford University Press.

Green, Robert L.
1974   "Northern School Desegregation. Educational, Legal, and Political Issues." In *Uses of the Sociology of Education, the 73rd Yearbook of the National Society for the Study of Education,*

Part II, edited by C. Wayne Gordon, pp. 213-73. Chicago: University of Chicago Press.

Havighurst, Robert J., and Levine, Daniel V.
1967   "The Quality of Urban Education." In *The Quality of Urban Life,* edited by Henry J. Schmandt and Warner Bloomberg, pp. 323-54. Beverly Hills, Calif.: Sage Publications, Inc.

Hogan, John C.
1974   "Law, Society, and the Schools." In *Uses of the Sociology of Education, the 73rd Yearbook of the National Society for the Study of Education, Part II,* edited by C. Wayne Gordon, pp. 411-47. Chicago: University of Chicago Press.

Jackson, Gregg
1975   "Reanalysis of Coleman's 'Recent Trends in School Integration.' " *Educational Researcher* (November):21-25.

Jencks, Christopher, and Brown, Marsha
1975   "The Effects of Desegregation on Student Achievement: Some New Evidence from the Equality of Educational Opportunity Survey." *Sociology of Education* 48 (Winter):126-40.

Lord, J. Dennis, and Catau, John
1976   "School Desegregation, Busing, and Suburban Migration." *Urban Education* 11, 3 (October):275-94.

McCoy, Rhody
1969   "Introduction." In *Diary of a Harlem School Teacher,* edited by J. Haskins, pp. xi-xiii. New York: Grove Press, Inc.

Ornstein, Allen C.
1974   *Race and Politics in School/Community Organizations.* Pacific Palisades, Calif.: Goodyear Publishing Co., Inc.

Passow, A. Harry
1967   *Toward Creating a Model Urban School System.* New York: Teachers College Press.

1971   "Urban Education in the 1970s." In *Urban Education in the 1970s,* edited by A. Harry Passow, pp. 1-45. New York: Teachers College Press.

Pettigrew, Thomas F.
1968   "Race and Equal Educational Opportunity." *Harvard Educational Review* 38:66-70.

Pettigrew, Thomas F., et al.
1973   "Busing: A Review of the Evidence." *The Public Interest* 29 (Winter):88-118.

Rubin, Lillian
1972   *Busing and Backlash.* Berkeley: University of California Press.

Scribner, Jay D., and O'Shea, David
1974   "Political Developments in Urban School Districts." In *Uses of the Sociology of Education, the 73rd Yearbook of the National Society for the Study of Education, Part II,* edited by C. Wayne Gordon, pp. 380-408. Chicago: University of Chicago Press.

Sizer, Theodore B.
1970   "The Schools and the City." In *The Metropolitan Enigma,* edited by James Q. Wilson, pp. 342-66. New York: Doubleday & Co., Inc.

St. John, Nancy
1970   "Desegregation and Minority Group Performance." *Review of Educational Research* 40 (February):111-33.

Stevens, William K.
1976   "Detroit Facing Court Ordered Busing of 21,000 Students Remains Calm." *New York Times* (January 4):40.

U.S. Bureau of the Census
1975   "School Enrollment: Social and Economic Characteristics of Students, October 1974." *Current Population Reports, Series P-20.* Washington, D.C.: Government Printing Office.

1976   "Mobility of the Population of the United States March 1970 to March 1975." *Current Population Reports, Series P-20, 285.* Washington, D.C.: Government Printing Office.

U.S. Commission on Civil Rights
1967   *Racial Isolation in the Public Schools.* Washington, D.C.: Government Printing Office.

U.S. Department of Health, Education, and Welfare, Office of Education
1973   *Digest of Educational Statistics.* Washington, D.C.: Government Printing Office.

Wisenbaker, Joseph
1976   "Desegregation and White Flight: A Case Study." *Educational Research Quarterly* 1, 2 (Summer):17-27.

Suggested Readings

Jencks, Christopher, et al. *Inequality: A Reassessment of the Effect of Family and Schooling in America.* New York: Basic Books, 1972. A review and reanalysis of a large body of data on the effects of schools on occupational attainment and income inequality. Concludes that school quality and other school factors are less important than family characteristics.

Ornstein, Allen C. *Race and Politics in School/Community Organizations.* Pacific Palisades, Calif.: Goodyear, 1974. The first two chapters review various means of school organization in metropolitan areas. Included is an analysis of community control and racial quotas as an organizational alternative.

Pettigrew, Thomas F., and Green, Robert L. "School Desegregation in Large Cities: A Critique of the Coleman 'White Flight' Thesis." *Harvard Educational Review* 46 (February 1976):1-53. A review and critique of Coleman's thesis that desegregation of city schools causes whites to move to the suburbs in large numbers, especially when desegregation is achieved by busing. The article includes a reanalysis of Coleman's own data, as well as data from other sources, and comes to very different conclusions.

U.S. Commission on Civil Rights. *Racial Isolation in the Public Schools, Volume I.* Washington, D.C.: Government Printing Office, 1967. A comprehensive analysis of the nature of public school segregation based on data collected from many different sources. The basic source document for the study of school segregation. Subsequent reports by the commission describe specific desegregation programs.

Notes

1. The Coleman study documents both inequality of resource distribution and inequality of socialization.
2. Community control programs have other purposes as well. Ornstein (1974) reviews the evidence and argues persuasively that community control of schools is simply a strategy for obtaining local political power and jobs.
3. Havighurst and Levine (1967) recommended twenty-five to thirty thousand; the Bundy Report to New York's Mayor Lindsay in 1967 recommended twelve to fourteen thousand; Passow (1967) recommended twenty thousand (cited in Ornstein, 1974:10). See also Scribner and O'Shea, 383; Ornstein, 1974:15-17.
4. See description and analyses of the New York experiment in Ornstein, 1974; Fantini, Gittell, and Magat, 1970; Gittell et al., 1972; Scribner and O'Shea, 1974.

15 The Future of Cities: Some Speculations

Cities developed, grew, and came to dominate modern industrial society because they were the most efficient way of meeting certain human needs. They performed critical communal functions for the society in which they were located and, as communities, gave their residents considerable individual freedom. In the last quarter of the twentieth century many cities began to have great difficulty performing their communal functions.

Some observers think that the problems of cities and city neighborhoods are so severe that cities may die out altogether (Baer, 1976). Don Martindale states:

> The modern city is losing its external and formal structure. Internally it is in a state of decay while the new community represented by the nation everywhere grows at its expense. The age of the city seems to be at an end [1958:62].

Pessimism about the future of very large, old central cities is certainly justified. In cities like New York, Boston, Detroit, Pittsburgh, Trenton, Gary, and Chicago, residential neighborhoods are deteriorating and being abandoned; industrial plants and corporate headquarters are moving to suburbs (DeVise, 1976:350). The remaining population is poor and needs many municipal services. The city's tax base is shrinking, and there are fewer jobs available.

The inability of cities to cope with all these problems is the urban crisis. Cities are described as sick and even dying, as though their problems were analogous to physical illness in human beings. The analogy is strengthened because the symptoms, which we do not know how to cure, are most severe in the oldest cities. When old people have incurable

illnesses, so the argument goes, they die. Thus, the argument continues, old cities with seemingly incurable problems are going to die. Since they are going to die and since society has only limited resources to spend on cities, we should emulate medical practitioners and use resources only where they are likely to save the patient: in neighborhoods and cities that are not beyond saving (Cannon, 1977: 35-39).

Many cities are deteriorating and decaying because they no longer have the resources or power to deal with their problems. The expansion of cities into metropolitan areas, the interdependence of all metropolitan areas, and the emergence of an integrated national, and sometimes even international, community has both limited the ability of cities to take effective action and created many city problems. The growth of functionally integrated metropolitan areas has brought about the migration of people and institutions; their mobility has been facilitated by the development of national and international business and commercial institutions and has led to national rather than local identifications. The age of the city may be ending, but we must ask if cities are dying or if they are just being transformed.

Urban Transformations

Decaying urban areas are nothing new in our society's history; populations have moved and industries have changed locations as long as there have been cities. But until relatively recently there have been new populations and new industries ready to invade the vacated space. In fact, such invasions frequently began before residents were ready to leave.

451

Now there are frequently no new populations or institutions competing to occupy the vacated land.

One major exception to this generalization is that cities do have reservoirs of poor, disadvantaged, and minority citizens who are willing to occupy residential areas of better quality than the ones they live in. These populations, however, frequently cannot afford to buy or maintain higher-quality housing. So when they begin to invade higher-quality areas, many residents leave to avoid losing their investments. Furthermore, in large central cities there are few people left to occupy areas abandoned by the poor. This creates pockets of decay and abandonment within central cities.

The same process occurs in urban industrial, retail, and commercial areas. Businesses occupying the oldest, least modern, and least efficient locations look for more desirable sites. When they relocate, no new businesses rush in to occupy the area.

The traditional pattern of urban invasion and succession has been broken because there are no new invaders. In the past, groups and institutions in invaded areas moved outward, first to outer portions of the city and then to the suburbs. Three major factors contributed to the outward movement of populations and institutions. First, the growing affluence after World War II, combined with a growing population and an increase in family size, accelerated the growth of the suburbs. Second, the development of efficient, economical transportation and communication systems furthered the functional integration of the entire metropolis and offered families and institutions their choice of location, essentially without regard to costs. As a result, space for homes, businesses, and industries was less costly in the suburbs than in the central city. Finally, contemporary immigrants to metropolitan areas have been affluent enough to avoid locating in the least desirable portions of the central city (U.S. Bureau of the Census, 1977a). These factors have altered the traditional pattern that once made the central business district and the residential areas with best access to the central business district the most sought after locations.

The future of many American cities depends on the strength of these factors. If traditional patterns of invasion and succession are destroyed, there is ample reason for pessimism. If traditional patterns hold or if new, potentially positive forces develop, there may be grounds for optimism. In this chapter we will speculate about the future of cities and some forces that shape them.

Changing Family Patterns

One major force behind the migration of the urban populations to the suburbs has been a desire for a better life for one's children. A higher status peer group, more space in which to live and play, and better schools have all been used as explanations for the migration to the suburbs. However, since the beginning of the 1970s, the structure of the population has begun to change. The rate of population growth has slowed—fewer persons are getting married, and those who do marry are having fewer children or no children (U.S. Bureau of the Census, 1975, 1976, 1977b, 1977c).

If these family patterns persist for the next several decades, they may dramatically reduce the appeal of the suburbs and increase the appeal of central cities for substantial portions of the population. Furthermore, if these patterns coincide and interact with other changes in the social environment, such as those accompanying the energy crisis, they will further reduce the attractiveness of suburban living and increase the attractiveness of the central city. In this section we will concentrate on possible effects of changing family patterns.

The Family and Suburban Growth

Suburbs grew and drew population from central cities because they offered a way of life that was and is centered on the nuclear family. Suburban homes and activity patterns emphasized family living and activities that included both children and parents. Mothers, in particular, were deeply involved, although often only as chauffeurs, in the daily lives of their children. Homes in the suburbs were larger and designed to provide adequate living and play space for children as well as parents.

Because suburban residents were child-centered and demanded high-quality educational facilities, suburban governments invested heavily in their school systems. Since many early suburbs were primarily residential, suburban governments also enacted zoning regulations to shut out most heavy industries and other forms of business and commerce. As a result, the burden of supporting the school systems fell mainly on residential real estate taxpayers.

There are a few business and commercial facilities, including recreational facilities such as restaurants, theaters, and movie houses thinly scattered throughout the suburbs. Many are located in small commercial areas or in shopping centers. More business and commercial facilities have developed in outlying areas in recent years, usually in newer suburbs that lie at relatively great distances from the central city and often in industrial or office "parks" that are designed to maintain the residential character and low density of the suburbs. There are not many of these park developments in the suburbs, and they are not a major source of tax revenue, though they do help reduce the residential real estate tax burden.

Education

Changing family patterns have already begun to affect education. As the population of school-age children declines, the need for school facilities also declines and the cost of school facilities increases. A decline in average daily enrollment reduces state aid to local school districts and increases the local tax burden.

As the number of children in families decreases, fewer families may be willing to assume the high costs of suburban living. Families with several children often find that suburban real estate taxes, high though they are, are lower than costs of tuition for their children in urban private or parochial schools. However, tuition for one child in a private or parochial school is lower than the suburban real estate tax. As more families have fewer children, tuition costs (plus the lower central city real estate taxes) may be lower than real estate taxes in the suburbs. American families may have to reevaluate the quality of education in suburban schools versus that in central city schools in deciding where to live.

Another factor in education is the possibility that racial integration may come to the suburbs. If this happens, and especially if integration is accomplished by city-suburban integration of schools, many people may choose to send their children to private schools. Those who do will not be anxious to pay both private school tuition and suburban real estate taxes to support suburban schools, especially since most private schools are located in central cities.

Thus private schools, which until now have been unable to compete with "free" tax-supported suburban schools, may be able to do so in the future, especially as an increasing proportion of families have only one child to send to school. Furthermore, if fewer middle-class families migrate to the suburbs, the presence of more middle-class students in urban public schools may increase the quality of education provided there. The fact that most urban elementary schools are located within walking distance of the homes they serve may increase their attractiveness as energy costs increase. Car pools, bus trips to school, and school bus programs will become more costly, further enhancing the value of local schools. High population density means that more students will be able to walk to school in the central city.

In summary, changing family patterns, the likelihood of increased energy costs, and the possibility of racial integration all suggest that suburban school systems may lose some of their advantage over central city schools.

Housing

Changing family patterns are likely to have their greatest impact on the housing market. Suburban homes and lots are generally larger than homes and lots in the city because the families attracted there were larger. As a result, the suburban household required the full-time care of the wife. As families become smaller and as the proportion of mothers employed outside the home on a full-time basis increases (Hayghe, 1975), the burdens of maintaining the suburban home will inevitably increase. Suburban homes may become less desirable than smaller homes or apartments available in the central city.

The cost of both new and existing homes increased in the 1970s, especially in suburbs. If these trends continue, it will become increasingly difficult for new families to purchase their first home in the suburbs. Federal agencies (FHA and VA) that have traditionally aided in the purchase of suburban homes are becoming less active in the suburbs as more governmental attention is paid to housing problems of the central city and as the size of the armed forces declines.

The distances that must be traveled in the suburbs, compared with the distances traveled in the central city, to shopping, schools, work, friends, and entertainment are high. If both parents work, but not at the same place, commuting costs are likely to be expensive, and the cost of maintaining a large home, especially if both parents work full time, will also be high.

These facts suggest that contemporary suburban housing and the suburban life style may become less attractive than they are now to an increasing proportion of the population.

However, this lessened attraction will be felt only if there is more attractive alternative housing available. Such alternatives are likely to be high-density developments that are located close to institutions performing a wide range of communal functions. Such developments could be created in many places: in the central city, in the suburbs themselves, and in new areas beyond the densely settled portions of the metropolis. Creating such developments in existing suburbs or in the fringes of urbanized areas will change the character of these areas and make them into small cities. These small cities will have the disadvantage of continuing to be dependent on the central business districts of major metropolitan areas for the performance of their central place functions. They will also lack converging transportation routes and populations large enough to support the development of entertainment and cultural facilities found in the central business districts of major metropolitan cities today.

An alternative that avoids some of these problems is the development of new residential areas in abandoned portions of the central city. The creation of "new towns" or "suburbs in the city" on abandoned residential or industrial land is a modification of urban renewal and independent "new town" programs. Previous attempts have not been successful, but the problem has become more acute and more land is now available for redevelopment. At the same time, changing family patterns may make in-city developments more feasible than they have been in the past. If they are designed to take into account changing family patterns, city developments may be more successful than they have been in the past.

If suburban housing stock does lose favor with American families, such a decline is more likely to occur among the moderately affluent than among the very rich or the very poor. One major source of buyers for existing suburban homes may be the black middle class, which until now has been mainly excluded from suburban areas. Middle-class blacks are still having more children than the national average and are likely to want more rooms and larger homes than the white population. This fact, perhaps more than changing racial attitudes, may help break down the barriers that have thus far kept the suburbs predominantly white.

Remember, too, that traditionally the most desirable and highest status residences are located in the center of the city. Changes in family patterns may result in a return to historically dominant patterns.

The Effects of Energy Costs

Since the invention of the automobile, the low cost of energy for transportation has made this factor unimportant in decisions about where to locate. Without the automobile and the highway system built around it, the suburbs would never have developed, cities would never have spread out, and the population would be far more concentrated. Problems of decay and abandonment in the central city would be much less severe, if they existed at all.

As energy becomes more expensive and as fuel for automobiles becomes scarce, problems associated with transportation to and within the suburbs are likely to become more severe than they have ever been before.

Energy problems will affect the central city, but greater density and reliance on mass transportation will alleviate the problems to some extent.

It is possible, of course, that an alternative to gasoline fuel for automobiles and trucks will be developed before the world's petroleum resources are depleted. Whether such an alternative will offer as fast and comfortable transportation as the gas-fueled automobile is another question, and one that cannot be answered. Some form of mass transportation may replace the private automobile. Such a development would have great impact on the suburbs.

Suburban Mass Transit

One alternative to the private automobile is mass transit. Suburban residents, however, are emphatically unenthusiastic about buses and trains. The low density of the suburbs severely limits the usefulness of trains within the suburbs, and between the suburbs and the central city. Developing bus and trolley systems throughout the suburbs would require not only large capital investments but large operating staffs. Furthermore, such buses and trolleys tend to be slow and relatively inconvenient for persons shopping, visiting friends, and commuting to work.

To construct an adequate bus, rail, or trolley system that would interconnect the suburban areas of a metropolis or link the suburbs with the central city would require that a large investment be made before the system went into operation. If the system were to go into operation shortly after the costs of operating a car became prohibitive, investments would have to be made while people could still afford their automobiles. It would be difficult to obtain political support for public financing of such a system. The prospects for a greatly expanded suburban mass transit system, even in the face of the increased costs and reduced supplies of automobile fuel, seem dismal.

Commuting and the Journey-to-Work

The increased costs of commuting, within the suburbs or between a suburb and a central city, will increase as the costs of fuel increase. Most commuting is currently done by a single person in a single car. As fuel becomes scarce, this pattern will become increasingly difficult to maintain. Even if it were possible to establish an adequate bus or bus/train system for traveling from the suburbs to the central city, few potential suburban residents would find the increased travel time acceptable. People may choose to live in the city rather than commute from the suburbs by bus, or by a combination of transportation modes. Part of the reason that suburban residents have been willing to spend so much time commuting by automobile has been the quality of the life their children lead in the suburbs. Will suburbanites settle for a commute as long or longer under less comfortable conditions on mass transportation when there are fewer children in the family? Under these circumstances, the central city might be attractive as a residential location, especially for white-collar workers employed in the central city.

The Utilization of Suburban Facilities

As the costs of transportation in private automobiles rises, and as mass transportation becomes increasingly necessary, people will find it more expensive, more time-consuming, and more difficult to use suburban shopping centers and facilities. Shopping centers, the major source of goods in the suburbs, are based on the private automobile. As the use of the automobile declines, will these centers continue to thrive?

The low density of suburban areas means that distances between homes and between homes and other facilities is relatively great. As the costs of travel increase, or as the modes of travel become less comfortable and less convenient, the difficulty of utilizing the facilities of the suburbs will increase. It will be harder, for example, to get to the supermarket in the local area without a car; it will be more difficult to get to the pharmacy, the doctor, the dentist, or even to the school. Furthermore, as more mothers of school-age children go to work and become tied to work and transportation schedules, it will be harder for them to drive the children to and from appointments and educational and social activities.

As the number of children per family decreases, the lower density of the suburban areas means that there will be fewer children in any given neighborhood for other children to play with. Children's demands for transportation are thus likely to increase at the same time that transportation is becoming more difficult and costly.

The low-density, detached, single-family home characteristic of the suburbs is less energy efficient than apartment buildings or even single-family homes in more densely settled areas. As fuel costs increase, the costs of heating and cooling homes in the suburbs will become more burdensome more rapidly than the costs of heating and cooling in the central city.

Finally, the lower density of the suburbs means that entertainment facilities are more spread out and more distant. The cost of entertainment will increase as the cost of travel to these facilities, if it is available, increases.

As the energy crisis becomes more severe, suburban residents are also likely to encounter increased difficulty in utilizing central city facilities. Access to facilities in the central city will be reduced by the costs and lack of availability of transportation.

Residents of the central city, however, will not suffer from the energy crisis to the same extent. The greater density of the central city means that all sorts of facilities are closer to one's residence. Further, the density of the city population means that mass transit facilities can operate efficiently. Thus scarcity of gasoline or an increase in its cost will not be as difficult for central city residents.

The Suburbanization of Business and Industry

Since the development of the suburbs and with the increasing problems of the central cities, many industries and businesses moved from central cities to suburbs. Heavy industry was the first to move, and in recent years some critical institutions such as corporate headquarters along with their support facilities have begun to move to the suburbs of the oldest SMSA central cities. Whether this pattern of migration continues or reverses is critical to the future of both the city and the suburbs.

If the pattern continues, central city facilities will continue to decline and the suburbs will continue to grow vigorously. It is important to recognize that heavy industry and central place functions moved to the suburbs for different reasons. Industry moved because of its need for space and to avoid the congestion of the central city. Central place functions have moved to avoid problems of crime, congestion, and taxes, and frequently to follow the residential movements of many workers.

Heavy industry will probably not move back to the central city unless large enough tracts of abandoned land can be made available at prices that are at least as low as those for land in currently undeveloped portions of the suburbs. However, some industries such as steel production that depend on adequate bulk transportation by either boat or train are unlikely to move to areas where such facilities are not available. In general, industries for which transportation is important are the most likely ones to be lured back to central city locations.

The Central Business District and the Future of the City

The central business district has been crucial in the development and growth of cities, primarily because of the performance of cen-

tral place functions there. Consequently, the vitality of the central business district will be absolutely vital to the future of cities. Unless cities remain the centers of entertainment, culture, government, business, and commerce, they will be unable to maintain a position of dominance in the social organization of our society.

In the third quarter of the twentieth century many older major metropolitan business districts have begun to experience an outmigration of many facilities. Not only have central cities lost blue-collar jobs, but many corporate headquarters have moved into suburban office buildings and suburban office park developments (DeVise, 1976). Suburban shopping centers have drawn a considerable portion of the retail sales business from the central business districts, and many professionals who provide support services to corporations, stores, and other institutions have moved to the suburbs. If these trends continue, two consequences are likely: the suburban areas in which city facilities locate will become far more urbanized and develop into central business districts, and the central city will continue to decline.

The extent to which these trends can and will continue, however, depends on the central place functions performed and changing conditions. The critical aspect of central place functions that will determine the continuation of these migrations is the need for face-to-face interaction. Any suburb that would replace the central city as the central business district would have to duplicate all the facilities of the central business district: banks, insurance companies, law offices, government agencies, department stores, private clubs, accounting firms, and so forth. The business district of the suburb would have to be large enough to provide office space for all these facilities and would have to be the focus of enough routes of transportation to bring in the work force, the clients, and the customers. Such a development would obviously violate most suburban zoning regulations and would not only be resisted by suburban residents but would be very costly.

A dispersed central business district, such as one spread out over several suburbs in a metropolitan area, would be possible if the need for face-to-face interaction was not critical. However, in the face of rising transportation costs, few developers are likely to try to attract vital institutions to diffuse suburban locales. Some companies may move, but the majority of institutions that perform central place functions are not likely to leave the city so long as it exists. The major banks that must deal with the Federal Reserve bank, the newspaper and other mass media headquarters, the major department stores, the professional offices of accounting and legal firms, and similar institutions are not likely to migrate to the suburbs so long as their functioning depends on being accessible to people from all over the metropolis—and indeed from all over the nation—and on their ability to engage in face-to-face interaction with their customers and clients.

Many corporations have moved to the suburbs to avoid the crime in some central cities and to find shopping and other facilities, more space, and locations closer to the homes of employees and corporate presidents (Whyte, 1976). If the trends in family patterns and energy costs have the expected consequences, these factors are likely to favor the central city in the course of the next twenty or twenty-five years. More white-collar employees are likely to settle in cities than in suburbs. This will make the central city the location closer to home for a larger proportion of the work force; the greater availability of mass transportation in the central city together with the converging transportation routes in the central business district will make commuting easier and increase accessibility to more customers and clients.

If cities are able to stem and even reverse the tide of out-migration by institutions that perform central place functions, the effects are likely to be felt in a number of areas. Central business district retail sales, which have declined in the past decades, are likely to increase. In part, this will be due to the increasing working population in the central business district and in part it will be due to the return of the middle-class residents to the city. Further, city tax receipts will increase as the land in the city becomes more desirable, and this will relieve urban fiscal problems. Instead of being a drain on the city's resources, the land in and around the central business district will once again become valuable; the central business districts may need to expand, becoming a new type of invader in areas surrounding the central business district.

Since many abandoned areas in the central cities have been located fairly close to the central business district, these are likely to be the areas that are invaded. Abandoned commercial and industrial property on the fringes of the central business district will be a major source of land on which to build new office buildings and planned urban residential developments.

Invasions in abandoned areas of the city will have a dramatic impact on urban social life. Probably it will be felt most strongly in the neighborhoods occupied by the city's poor and minority populations. While abandoned areas will be the first areas acquired by the invaders, the slums and other poor and minority neighborhoods located on the fringes of these areas will thereby become more attractive to developers and potential residents. Redevelopment is likely to force the poor to migrate from the areas in which they now live.

In the past the groups forced out of areas around the central business district have moved to other areas in the central city. The groups that are likely to be forced to move in the coming decades are the poor blacks and Latinos. Unless racial attitudes change, there will be relatively few places for them to move. They may be able to move into central city areas now occupied by the black middle class and into the suburbs.

The central city areas are not large enough to accommodate all those who will be displaced by redevelopment. In addition, those moving from the redeveloped areas will have to compete for central city areas with more affluent persons moving back into the city. Many homes in the central areas are relatively small and inappropriate for large families. The suburbs with their large homes may become more accessible to the black middle class and even to relatively poor portions of the population.

Given the migration of industries to the suburbs, there may be a migration of blue-collar families, especially minority families, to the suburbs. If federal rent supplements and FHA-type financing programs are developed to encourage these movements, there will be a large-scale rearrangement of population in and around metropolitan central cities.

The very poorest people in the population will not be able to move to suburban homes, but as more affluent and working-class minority members move into the suburbs, the resistance to public housing developments may diminish. As the private homes in the suburbs become less attractive to the middle class, their costs may decrease and the character of the occupants may change.

The consequence of these developments is not likely to be a dramatic short-term change in racial balance between the suburbs and the central city. The poor and minority groups will live closer to the location of the blue-collar jobs, while the middle class will live closer to their white-collar and professional jobs. Both groups will benefit from reduced commuting times and distances and from increased access to housing that they find most desirable.

By-products of these changes would be improvements in the city's financial position and deterioration in the financial position of many suburbs. In addition, the political power of ethnic minorities would be diffused as group members relocate in several suburbs rather than in constricted areas of the central city.

In the short run the political power of blacks and Latinos in the central city will increase; indeed, black mayors have already been elected in several cities. If more central city black residents migrate to the suburbs in the future, the potential for electoral victories based solely on race will diminish in the central city.

Summary

We have speculated about the future of American cities. Many forces that have shaped cities in our history have been beyond the control of the city, and this condition is likely to continue. Until relatively recently, these forces concentrated population and institutions in the center of cities. But since the invention of the automobile, low-cost energy and population growth have led to deconcentration and decentralization of city residents and institutions. The car, the development of extensive highway systems, inexpensive gasoline, and housing policies based on the desire of Americans for single-family detached homes have led to the formation and growth of suburbs.

In the future these factors are likely to change, and their effect on the city is likely to change. The decline in the proportion of people who marry, the decline in size of the family and the population, and the increasing cost of scarce energy supplies are likely to make suburban residences and life styles less attractive and central city residences and life styles more attractive.

These changes suggest that there is a limit to which central place function institutions can migrate to the suburbs. Investments in facilities and institutions that perform central place functions have already been made in the central city and would be exceedingly difficult to duplicate. Not only can a single suburb not afford to duplicate these functions, but even to do so would change the character of the suburb.

The reversal or modification of suburbanization of cities will be felt in all areas of city life. Virtually all communal functions will be affected by the return to the city of small, affluent families that in the past have migrated to the suburbs. In addition, the changing costs of energy are likely to have widespread consequences. Problems of maintaining racial and ethnic communities will be different, although no less important than they are today. Politics in the city and suburbs will probably not change, although issues and practices may change. Housing problems will be different, especially if cities try to take advantage of planned unit developments. Transportation, health, pollution, crime, and education will all continue to be problems, although the problems will change as the city and suburbs change.

The prognosis for American cities is optimistic. Revitalization of cities is not likely to be smooth or to take place in all cities at the same pace. Some cities may not be revitalized, if they are unable to perform their communal functions adequately or if they are unable to develop programs or to take advantage of the trends we have analyzed. Residents of many American cities, especially the newer, smaller metropolitan cities, currently have higher incomes and higher educational levels than residents of their suburbs (Harrigan, 1976). These cities will undoubtedly continue to prosper. Older, larger central cities will benefit from changing family patterns and increased energy costs.

The future of American cities is not determined. We have suggested that cities will remain or become even more vital and attractive places to live than they are now. The American city will continue to dominate society. The age of the city may have ended, but the age of urban society may just be dawning.

References

Baer, William C.
1976   "On the Death of Cities." *Public Interest* 24 (Autumn):3-20.
Cannon, Donald S.
1977   "Identifying Neighborhoods for Preservation and Renewal." *Growth and Change* 8, 1:35-39.
DeVise, Pierre
1976   "The Suburbanization of Jobs and Minority Employment." *Economic Geography* 52, 4:348-62.
Harrigan, John J.
1976   "A New Look at Central City-Suburban Differences. *Social Science* 51, 4:200-209.
Hayghe, Howard
1975   "Marital and Family Characteristics of the Labor Force, March 1975." *Monthly Labor Review* (November 1975). In *Special Labor Force Report 183.* Washington, D.C.: Government Printing Office.
Martindale, Don
1958   "Prefatory Remarks: The Theory of the City." In *The City* by Max Weber. Translated and edited by Don Martindale and Gertrud Neuwirth. New York: Free Press.
U.S. Bureau of the Census
1975   "Some Recent Changes in American Families." *Current Population Reports, Series P-23, 52.* Washington, D.C.: Government Printing Office.
1976   "Fertility History and Prospects of American Women: June 1975." *Current Population Reports, Series P-20, 288.* Washington, D.C.: Government Printing Office.
1977a   "Geographical Mobility: March 1975 to March 1976." *Current Population Reports, Series P-20, 305.* Washington, D.C.: Government Printing Office.
1977b   "Marital Status and Living Arrangements: March 1976." *Current Population Reports, Series P-20, 306.* Washington, D.C.: Government Printing Office.
1977c   "Population Profile of the United States: 1976." *Current Population Reports, Series P-20, 307.* Washington, D.C.: Government Printing Office.
Whyte, William H.
1976   "End of the Exodus: The Logic of Headquarters City." *New York,* September 20, 1976:88-99.

Suggested Readings

Baer, William C. "On the Death of Cities." *The Public Interest* 24 (Autumn, 1976). A pessimistic appraisal of the future of cities. Argues that nothing we can do can save our cities, so we should invest only in cities with relatively few problems.

Goldfield, David R. "The Limits of Suburban Growth." *Urban Affairs Quarterly* 12 (September 1976). Analyzes patterns of settlement in suburban Washington, D.C. and argues that either higher density, planned unit development, or central city resettlement is likely to occur.

Mazie, Sara Mills, ed. *Population Distribution and Policy.* U.S. Commission on Population Growth and the American Future, Vol. 5 of Commission Research Reports. Washington, D.C.: Government Printing Office, 1972. The most comprehensive collection of research reports dealing with population characteristics. Includes the data needed to study the future composition and distribution of the American people.

Glossary

alienation as a state of society, feelings of detachment, isolation, and nonparticipation among members of a segment of the population; as an individual characteristic, feelings of powerlessness, isolation, meaninglessness, cultural estrangement, self-estrangement, and normlessness

anomie a state in which the individual feels that societal norms do not apply to the self; strictly defined, anomie, like alienation, is characteristic of a social system in which norms have lost their power to regulate behavior

aqueduct a pipe, often not completely covered and running along the ground or on stilts above the ground, that carries fresh water from its source to the population that needs it; originally, the water source had to be higher than the settlement being served so that gravity would maintain water flow through the pipes; pumps are now used to supplement gravity flow

assimilation the merging of groups or individuals of one culture into a host society or culture; also the process of learning the norms and values of the culture into which one is moving

atomized relationships interactions between individuals who have few ties with each other and who participate in few, if any, group activities; a consequence of the breakdown of communal ties in a society

big city defined by the United Nations as a city of 500,000 to 2.5 million persons

biological oxygen demand (BOD) a measure of the organic activity in water supplies; the higher the BOD, the higher the bacterial content of the water, which makes it unfit for use

black belt a somewhat archaic term, now used to describe the areas in northern cities into which black migrants from the southern United States moved

Black Plague also called the Black Death. A disease that swept Europe in 1348–50, killing at least a quarter of the population. Trans-mitted to man by fleas from black rats and other rodents. After the major attack, there were other outbreaks throughout Europe over the years. The last major outbreak occurred in 1665

blasé attitude term used by Simmel to describe the effects of urban life; an attitude of having been exposed to everything and not reacting intensely to anything; detached and uninvolved

blockbusting a technique used by real estate agents to accelerate the sale of houses by whites to blacks; the agent buys a house on an all-white block, resells it to a black family, and then tries to frighten other white residents into selling at low prices by telling them that blacks are moving onto the block

BTU British Thermal Unit—a measure of heat energy in a substance; the amount of energy needed to raise the temperature of one pound of water one degree Fahrenheit

busing the transporting of students from one school to another to achieve racial balance; however, most students are still bused to school simply because they live too far from school to walk there

carbon monoxide a tasteless, odorless, colorless gas that is a by-product of combustion of materials containing carbon; fatal in high concentrations; its most common source is the automobile

cardiovascular diseases diseases of the heart and circulatory system

census a complete enumeration, as distinct from a sample, of a population

census tract a small unit of a city area used as an enumeration district; the population of the tract is kept between three thousand and six thousand by alterations in boundaries; the smallest area for which a great deal of information is generally available from the census; also a unit used for administrative purposes

central business district the ecological center of a city, the major business district where central place functions are performed for a city

central city   a city of 50,000 or more persons, or twin cities with a combined population of at least 50,000, that performs central place functions for a hinterland; the immediate hinterland is the metropolitan area named after the central city

central place   the source of goods and services for an area larger than itself

central place functions   the financial, administrative, and coordinating functions carried out for a city and its hinterland; also the functions that depend on access by a large population

centralization   the clustering of people and services at a central point, usually the point at which transportation lines converge; also the process by which such clustering occurs

chlorination   the process of adding chlorine to water supplies to kill bacteria and to make the water safe to drink

city   a relatively large, dense, and permanent settlement of heterogeneous individuals and groups of individuals organized to perform, or to facilitate the performance of, locality-relevant functions in an integrated manner, and to ensure the integration of the performance of these functions with the social system of which the city is a part; defined by the United Nations as a place of 100,000 or more persons

collective conscience   the commonly held beliefs and sentiments that are the fundamental values of that society

command control   in police work, the control exercised by persons at high levels in the police department over operations of the entire force

communal attachments   the attachment of the individuals who are part of a community to each other and to the community; the feeling of belonging to a community and the sense that physical and emotional needs are being met by the community

communal functions   see **locality-relevant functions**

community   a group of people living in the same area, within which they satisfy many of their needs. Traditionally there has been an intense and self-conscious identification with and an attachment to the group. In its traditional sense, community refers to a deep psychological and emotional relationship as well as a common residence. In contemporary society communities are more limited in scope and are the source of more limited attachments and identification; they are more likely to be primarily residential areas organized to perform communal functions

community control   a form of school administration that gives residents of the community the power to decide on curriculum and all administrative matters, including the selection of teachers and the spending of funds; in recent years, it has been used as an alternative to racial integration of the schools

concentration   the ecological process by which increasing numbers of people and institutions locate in a given area, resulting in increased density

concentric zone   a band surrounding a central point; in sociology, zones of different populations and communities within a city; basis of a theory of city structure associated with Ernest W. Burgess

consciousness of kind   a conscious recognition that one shares attitudes, behavior patterns, and values with other people; the basis for ethnic identification and greater ease in establishing primary relationships

consumerism   a devotion to consumption for its own sake, thought to be characteristic of upwardly mobile persons, especially those who live in or migrate to the suburbs; the continual purchase of unneeded goods

containerized bins   large refuse disposal bins that can be winched aboard trucks and carried directly to disposal sites; a much faster way of collecting large quantities of solid wastes

contract, institution of   a set of norms that specifies the legitimate contents of agreements among members of society and the means by which these agreements can be reached and enforced

contranormative   against the norms; behaviors or beliefs that violate norms

cottage industry   an early form of industrial production in which work was performed in the cottages of workers rather than in a central location, such as a factory

crisis of the cities   (also **urban crisis**) the collection of problems faced by cities in contemporary America. Problems include pollution, rising costs of city services as revenues decrease, crime, deterioration of housing, slums, inadequate educational and transportation systems, among others

decentralization   the opposite of centralization; the dispersal of people and services from the central point in an area, usually after density of use has reached a high level

deconcentration   the opposite of concentration; the ecological process by which increasing numbers of people and institutions spread out from a central point, producing lower levels of density

demographic structure   the composition of the population in terms of size, age, race, and other relatively fixed characteristics; demography includes the study of the distribution of these characteristics

density   number of persons per square mile; more generally, number of occupants of a given type over a standard unit of area (persons per square mile is population density; number of factories per square mile is density of industrial land use)

desalination   the removal of salt from ocean water to make it drinkable

deviance   violation of community or societal norms (the specific behaviors vary from community to community); deviance may occur when subgroup norms conflict with norms of the larger society

division of labor   the development of specialized occupational tasks. More generally the division of labor causes a task to be broken up into component tasks, each of which is performed individually

dominance   the controlling position—cities dominate their hinterlands, and within cities, a group may control use of the land in an area; the end result of ecological succession, as when one ethnic group becomes dominant in a neighborhood

dysfunction   the consequence of any behavior in a social system that hinders the stability, integration, or function performance of that system

eclectic approach   viewpoint composed of elements drawn from various sources or theories

ecological center   that area that is most accessible from all other places in the area, generally the location of the central business district

ecological field   the entire society as an environment to which cities, as communities, must adapt

ecological niche   a location within an ecological structure in which a particular mode of adaptation to the environment dominates

ecology, human   a branch of sociology concerned with the ways in which human communities adapt to their physical and social environment; human ecology is often concerned with the spatial relationships, environmental relationships between institutions, people, and the physical environment

educational park   a large tract of land devoted to several schools of different types; elementary and secondary schools and often community colleges are located in the same place and share many facilities, such as gyms and libraries

enclaves   areas of a city in which a single type of person or an ethnic group resides, or in which a single type of land use is dominant

enumeration   counting of the members of a group

ethnic group   a group with a common cultural tradition, generally based on national origin or race; a consciousness of kind

ethnic identity   defining oneself as a member of an ethnic group on the basis of self-perception and socially defined characteristics

ethnocentrism   looking on members of one's own ethnic group as inherently superior to all members of all other ethnic groups

evolutionary development   growth characterized by continuous change from small to large, simple to complex, general to specialized

exchange theory   the theory of social behavior that views interaction as exchanges between persons or institutions and that views social structures as patterns of exchange

factorial ecology   the study of population characteristics by means of statistical techniques (factor analysis); definition of areas in which populations have the same traits

familism   devotion to and concentration on one's immediate family; other social activity need not be forsaken, but the immediate family is much more important than the neighborhood or community

family formation   the creation of new families by marriage

Federal Housing Administration (FHA)   a federal agency that offers mortgage guarantees to builders and lenders so that potential buyers may purchase a home with an extremely small down payment

fertility ratio   number of children under five per 1,000 women ages 15 to 49

feudal system   highly structured, hierarchical form of social organization characterized by ascribed social position, low social mobility, and status differentiation based on law as well as custom; rank was made evident by titles and symbols

first admission   the first time a person is admitted to a hospital, particularly as it applies to mental health; subsequent admissions for the same illness are not counted, but subsequent admissions for different illnesses are counted as a new first admission

fixed route transportation   means of transportation that operate on routes that cannot vary, especially on tracks, but also on rivers

formal control   the control of social behavior by institutions and their representatives, in contrast to control by means of social pressure, socialization, and other noninstitutional means

Gemeinschaft   a form of social organization characterized by close, intimate, and personal ties among a homogeneous social group. All members share the same reactions to stimuli and a common conceptual framework. Frequently, *Gemeinschaft* is translated into English as *community*

Gesellschaft   a form of social organization in which the individual is paramount. A rational, willed form of organization in which individuals are isolated and work for themselves, not for the group. Frequently, *Gesellschaft* is translated as *society*. Also describes the process of social change by which society is transformed from a *Gemeinschaft* to a *Gesellschaft*

ghetto   an area of a city occupied exclusively by members of a single ethnic group; currently, the term connotes conditions of poverty, unemployment, and substandard housing

guild   a form of organization based on occupation and structured in the same way as the feudal society in which it occurred

health care delivery system   the system that provides health care, including such components as physicians, nurses, hospitals, pharmacists, offices, and so on

heterogeneity   the existence of differences among a population; a group possessing the characteristic of internal differentiation rather than similarity is heterogeneous

hinterland   the territory surrounding a settlement that depends on the settlement for services and that provides raw materials, products, and workers for the settlement

hobo zone   that portion of the central business district occupied by transients and hobos

homogeneity   the opposite of heterogeneity. The internal similarity and uniformity existing among a population

horizontal ties   the ties of individuals and institutions in a community to other individuals and institutions in the same community

housing stock   the total supply of available or existing housing in a given area

human ecology   see **ecology, human**

hydrocarbons   a by-product of the combustion of carbon-containing materials; a common air pollutant

hypertension   a circulatory disease, often called high blood pressure, which can be fatal; stress and diet contribute to its development

ideal type   a conceptual construct; a perfect example of something created logically, regardless of whether it exists or can exist in that form in the real world

illegitimate opportunities   the chances available in an area for a person to make money by violating norms and the presence of persons in that area who will train others in the use of these opportunities

inadequate housing   generally housing that needs major repairs, lacks some or all plumbing, and is overcrowded; all characteristics need not be present to make a single unit inadequate, and units that have none of these characteristics can also be considered inadequate if they are located in an area with many inadequate units

index crimes   offenses listed in the index of serious crimes used by the Uniform Crime Reports—criminal homicide, forcible rape, robbery, aggravated assault, burglary, larceny, and motor vehicle theft

infant mortality rate   the number of children under one year of age who died in a given year, divided by the total number of live births in that year

influence   the act of selecting or altering social system goals

informal social control   the control of social behavior by noninstitutional means, such as internalization of norms, social pressure exerted by other community residents, or voluntary groups responding to particular events or under particular circumstances

in-migration   migration of population into an area

integration   racial integration of schools; achieving approximately equal proportions of white and nonwhite children in each school or school district

interaction density   the number of interpersonal contacts in a given area in a given period of time; this number must increase as population density increases

intermarriage   the marriage of two persons from different ethnic or racial groups

invasion   an ecological term for the process by which new types of occupants move into a community

journey-to-work   the journey from one's home to one's work location and back again

labor force   the portion of the population that is employed, plus the portion that is unemployed and still job hunting (this excludes housewives, students, young persons, elderly persons, and those who are unemployed and no longer looking for work)

labor market   the demand for workers by the employing institutions of a community

life cycle   the series of stages that an individual or a group goes through during its lifetime; among humans, the stages might be identified as infant, child, adolescent, young single adult, married adult without children, married adult with children, grandparent, elderly adult

life style way of living characterized by dominant activities, attitudes, or beliefs

localism greater participation in local activities than in activities of a wider sphere, such as the city or the society

locality-relevant functions the functions that local communities perform. The most important are: (1) generating and maintaining normative integration among community members; (2) generating and maintaining social solidarity among community members; (3) providing the goods and services that community members need; (4) socializing community members to community norms; (5) controlling the behavior of community members and others who are present; (6) providing a locale in which community members may interact and obtain mutual support

magnet school a school organized to provide instruction in a particular subject matter or group of subjects; entrance is usually based on competition or on criteria such as a set of racial quotas, and the school draws its student body from an entire school district rather than from one area of the district

mass transit means of transportation for carrying large numbers of people in a relatively small number of vehicles: subways, commuter railroads, buses; frequently, but not always, publicly owned

mechanical solidarity that form of social solidarity created by the similarity of the members of the group; social cohesion generated by individuals who engage in similar tasks with little social differentiation; a form of social solidarity that exists prior to the division of labor

mechanically integrated society a homogeneous society that is integrated as a result of mechanical solidarity

medieval period the years between A.D. 500 and 1500 in Europe when the feudal form of social and political organization dominated

metropolis a central city of 50,000 or more persons that is socially and economically integrated with its surrounding area

metropolitan area a city of 50,000 or more persons, plus the county containing the city and all counties socially and economically integrated with the central city, as defined by the Bureau of the Census and the Office of Management and the Budget

metropolitan hierarchy the organization of metropolitan areas by rank according to their importance to the society and the functions they perform

migration the movement of people from one area to another

mobility movement from one place to another; social mobility is movement within the socioeconomic hierarchy; geographic mobility is residential mobility.

mode of travel the type of vehicle used in travel—car, bus, train, subway

moral density the density of interaction between individuals and the relationships resulting from this increase; a function of population density with greater focus on relationships caused by increased population

multiple nuclei structural characteristic of cities, especially cities developed after the invention of the automobile, in which several areas perform central place functions; several small central business districts, or one dominant district and several other central districts, in a city

multiple-unit structures buildings that contain more than one dwelling unit, such as apartment houses, townhouses, and duplexes

nationality group a group that has migrated from one country to another, but whose group identification is based on the country of origin

natural area a term developed by Ernest W. Burgess and his associates to describe the communities within cities; an area in which one group is dominant, a position established through the natural processes of invasion and succession; an area frequently characterized by ethnic homogeneity

natural increase   the increase in size of population due to a greater number of births than deaths

neighborhood context   the social characteristics of the neighborhood in which the school is located; refers specifically to the value placed on educational achievement by the parents of children who attend the neighborhood school and the transmission of this value to the students

Neolithic period   the period of man's prehistory from about 6000 to 3000 B.C.

net migration   the difference between in-migration and out-migration in an area

network capacity   in transportation terms the maximum capacity of the transportation system

new ethnics   ethnic groups that have recently migrated to the United States or to northern metropolitan cities; new ethnics are mainly blacks and Latinos

nitrogen oxide   a by-product of burning fuels that can combine with oxygen in the air to produce a lethal gas

non-place functions   urban functions that can be carried out in any location, such as the choice of friends, work locations, and occupation

normative integration   the extent to which all components of a social system define the norms of the system in the same way and accept them to the same extent; also the degree to which the norms form a single, nonconflicting system.

norms   social statements of right and wrong, proper ways of behaving and thinking

nuclear family   the family composed of a husband and wife and their children, as distinguished from the extended family that includes other relatives, especially the parents of the husband and wife

Office of Economic Opportunity (OEO)   a federal agency created during the War on Poverty that attempted to involve poor and disadvantaged urban citizens in decision making about programs for their benefit

old ethnics   ethnic groups, mainly European, that migrated to the United States in the late nineteenth and early twentieth century, or earlier

organic solidarity   that form of social solidarity created by the division of labor. Individuals engaged in different tasks are dependent on one another. Organic solidarity is created by the interdependence of various tasks in a common enterprise

out-migration   migration of population away from an area

overcrowding   in housing, less than one room per person in a dwelling unit (statisticians express the measure as 1.01 or more persons per room); the figure is based on current values in the United States

Paleolithic period   the period of man's prehistory ending about 6000 B.C.

partial community   a community that is not able to perform all locality-relevant functions; one that partially performs functions of a traditional community

partisanship   in relation to an election, the identification of candidates for elective office in terms of their political party affiliations

peak use   the maximum use of a transportation network; generally observed during the hours of the journey-to-work

physical environment   topography, climate, mineral and other resources of the area in which a community is located; also man-made elements for extracting natural resources and rearranging the physical landscape

places   political units incorporated as cities, boroughs, towns, and villages (except in certain states where these designations do not refer to population centers), and certain unincorporated areas that have a dense nucleus of residences (Note: By this Bureau of the Census definition, some locations are not places.)

place-specific functions   urban functions that are centered on a specific place in an urban area; *place-specific* also refers to concern over behavior in an area where place is critical, for example, concern over the behavior of adolescents in a residential neighborhood

pluralistic model   a theory of society that states that each subgroup of society should maintain its own identity and cooperate with other subgroups in determining the nature of the total society

polarization   the division of a group into two diametrically opposed subgroups; in political terms, the division of a population into those in favor of and those opposed to a position

polis   a city that was also a state in ancient Greece

political capital   resources that can be spent in gaining power and influence

political machine   an organization of people with similar political interests who jointly accumulate and spend their political capital for their mutual benefit; frequently such an organization can accumulate sufficient capital to dominate decision making over a long period of time

political power   in a social system the potential ability to select, alter, or attain the goals of the system

power elite   a small group of politically influential people who behave uniformly in political matters; generally, the ones at the top of the power hierarchy who are assumed to have similar social characteristics and to interact with one another

primary industry   basic extractive industry—agriculture and mining—and the fabrication of materials used in manufacturing

primary relationships   social relationships based on frequent, direct, interpersonal contact; relating as total persons rather than as occupants of a single role

primary treatment   a method of treating water that allows solid particles to settle; the result is water that can be used for some recreational purposes and most industrial processes, but not for drinking

primate city   a single large city in a society that has a low level of urbanization

private sector   private institutions such as business, industry, and privately financed and voluntary service groups

property crime   acts involving theft or destruction of another's property in which the property owner is not personally harmed; examples are burglary, larceny, motor vehicle theft

public sector   government agencies and institutions

quasi-*Gemeinschaft*   a group that approximates a *Gemeinschaft* but is not completely based on primary relationships; alternatively, a group that aspires to be, but does not succeed in being, a *Gemeinschaft*

quasi-primary group   a group that aspires to have, but does not succeed in having, primary relationships between all members

rationalization   the transformation of a communal society into an associational, contractual society

reciprocity   the act of returning something of approximately equal value to a person who has given one something in the past; the objects exchanged may be goods, services, deference, votes, or anything else to which people attach value

redlining   the practice by lending institutions of drawing a line around areas of a city (usually in red ink) and refusing to grant home mortgages or improvement loans for dwellings within the area, regardless of the credit rating of the person who requests the loan; leads to the decay of the area, as it becomes virtually impossible for new residents to purchase homes or for existing residents to renovate or make major improvements

region a combination of states defined by the U.S. Bureau of the Census; U.S. regions and states in each region are as follows:

Northeast
1. New England: Maine, Vermont, New Hampshire, Massachusetts, Connecticut, Rhode Island
2. Middle Atlantic: New York, New Jersey, Pennsylvania

North Central
1. East North Central: Ohio, Indiana, Illinois, Michigan, Wisconsin
2. West North Central: Minnesota, Iowa, Missouri, Kansas, Nebraska, South Dakota, North Dakota

South
1. South Atlantic: West Virginia, Maryland, Delaware, Virginia, Washington, D.C., South Carolina, North Carolina, Georgia, Florida
2. East South Central: Kentucky, Tennessee, Mississippi, Alabama
3. West South Central: Louisiana, Arkansas, Oklahoma, Texas

West
1. Mountain: Montana, Wyoming, Colorado, New Mexico, Arizona, Utah, Nevada, Idaho
2. Pacific: Washington, Oregon, California, Alaska, Hawaii

residential density the number of residents living in an area, divided by the physical size of the area in square miles or square kilometers

restrictive covenants agreements, generally private but often legal, between buyers and sellers that prevented the sale of a house to members of specified groups, usually Jews or blacks

rickets a bone disease, found mostly among children; commonly thought to be a dietary deficiency disease caused by lack of vitamin D, but in fact an air pollution disease caused by lack of exposure to sunlight

role a set of expected behaviors in a specific social status or setting

runoff water that cannot be accommodated by urban sewage systems and that runs off into sources of water supply during heavy storms; also, the water that cannot be absorbed into the ground in areas where most of the ground is paved

sanction a penalty or denial of reward imposed on persons who violate social norms or a reward for appropriate behavior

sanitary landfill the process of filling in swamps, dumps, mine pits, quarries, and other areas with solid wastes and covering each day's collection with a layer of earth; prevents or minimizes problems of rodent infestation and odor

satellite city a city located within a metropolitan area that is neither totally independent of the central city nor restricted in function, as a suburb; frequently an independent city that has been engulfed by the metropolis

schizoid character (of urban personality) a term from Wirth describing the consequences of role-specific urban relationships that reveal different aspects of a person who is involved in different roles

school district in cities overall, the administrative district that controls the schools; within cities, the district or area from which a school draws its students; in many suburban and rural counties, consolidated districts that include many incorporated places; large cities may have several administrative subareas that are larger than single school districts but that taken together do not comprise the entire city

secondary industry manufacture of goods

secondary relationships social relationships based on infrequent but direct interpersonal contacts; these are more likely than primary relationships to be specific to a given role or pair of role relationships

secondary treatment a form of treating water by forcing either air or oxygen through the liquid wastes to accelerate biochemical reactions that remove biological materials; the water that results is safe to drink

sectors   wedge-shaped areas of a city created by expansion away from the central business district; a term used by Homer Hoyt to describe the deconcentration of residences of approximately the same value; frequently used in contrast to zones

segmental interaction   interaction based on specific role relationships rather than on personal characteristics of the role occupants

segregated   forced to live in specific areas or to use specific facilities on the basis of group characteristics

selective migration   the movement of a specific group within a population from one location to another

self-concept   the mental picture and evaluation that one has of oneself; thinking well or poorly of one's own character or ability to function

sense of mastery   an individual's sense of ability to master the environment and to accomplish one's goals

sensory stimulation   a state occurring within the individual, produced by encounters with many different objects, each of which requires evaluation, recognition, and possible action

serious crimes   by FBI definition, criminal homicide, forcible rape, robbery, aggravated assault, burglary, larceny, motor vehicle theft; note that crimes such as kidnapping, arson, and embezzlement are not included

slum   a concentrated, densely settled area where housing is inadequate, residents are poor, and communal functions are lacking. Some observers have said that social disorganization and pathological behavior are common in such areas, but others consider slums to be highly organized and have pointed out that the behavior of slum residents is based on values that are very different from the middle-class values of most social scientists

SO$_2$ chemical symbol for sulfur dioxide, a by-product of burning sulfur-rich fuels, such as certain coals or oils; a major source of air pollution

social area analysis   a technique for studying homogeneous areas of a city; social areas are defined on the basis of the income, urbanity, and ethnic segregation of the population

social contract   according to Hobbes, a mythical contract requiring all members of a society to submit to the established laws and authority. A social contract is the basis of the submergence of individual desire and strength for the benefit of society. According to Rousseau, it is the basis of the ties between the individual and society

social control   control exercised by an organized group or community over the behavior of the residents and visitors to the group territory; control formally exercised by organizations, such as police and courts, and informally exercised by group members through social pressure

social disorganization   the existence of many personal problems among residents of an area caused by a breakdown in social control; generally, problems include crime, delinquency, vice, alcoholism, and the like

social environment   characteristics of the population and social system to which a community must adapt

social mobility   a change in the social status of an individual; or a change in social position by a family or group member of one generation from that held by a member of the preceding generation; upward mobility is an increase in social status, downward mobility a loss in social status

social solidarity   a feeling of membership in and identification with a group or a social system

social surplus   goods produced in excess of the amount needed for survival by farmers and other workers in primary industries (hunting, mining, fishing) that thus becomes available for others in the society

socialization   the process of learning the norms, behaviors, and skills one must know to be a functioning member of society

society a group of people with a comprehensive set of roles and norms that provide for all of the needs of the people including culture and all other institutions needed for survival

space-time ratio the distance traveled, divided by the time it takes to travel

standard metropolitan area (SMA) term used to describe the metropolitan community until the development of the standard metropolitan statistical area (SMSA) concept

standard metropolitan statistical area (SMSA) term now used to describe and define the metropolitan community; SMSAs are designated by the Bureau of the Census and by the Office of Management and the Budget and consist of a central city, the county in which the central city lies, and all contiguous and adjacent counties that are socially and economically integrated with the central city

suburb a settlement within the boundaries of a metropolitan area that is not the central city of that area

succession the ecological process by which an invading group occupies a community and successfully establishes dominance

sulfur dioxide see **SO₂**

suspended particulate matter particles of dirt or liquid small enough to be suspended in the air; particles in dust and mists produced by fuel combustion, street sweeping, and other causes

tenure the right of a person to hold a job until retirement unless one is found guilty of incompetence or malfeasance; tenure protects individuals (usually teachers) from being fired because they hold unpopular attitudes or beliefs and frequently protects them even against being fired for reasons of low budget or administrative reorganization

tertiary industry a service industry—the professions, commerce, the arts, and so on

tertiary relationships social relationships based on indirect contacts; totally role-specific interaction with no emotional content and little social content

tithe a proportion of all goods produced or of time spent working; a payment of money or work made to church, society, or the lord of the land

Uniform Crime Report (UCR) the FBI's system for counting and reporting crimes; using a standard set of definitions, participating police departments report to the FBI all known crimes, arrests, and the characteristics of the people arrested

urban crisis see **crisis of the cities**

urban fringe the portion of an urbanized area outside the central city

urban place as defined by the U.S. Bureau of the Census, a place of at least 2,500 people

urbanization the process of populations moving from rural areas to cities; the extent of development of an urban society; the process by which individuals learn to live in an urban society

urbanized area a central city of at least 50,000 persons, plus the densely settled area surrounding the city; in contrast to SMSA, an urbanized area is defined by population density rather than county borders; it is the physical community in contrast to the socioeconomic community of the SMSA

utilitarianism a philosophy that argues that society should be based on individual self-interest and that society thus emerges from rational self-interest

vertical ties the ties of individuals and institutions in a community to individuals and institutions outside that community

Veterans Administration (VA) a federal agency that offers low-cost home loans to ex-service personnel

victimization survey a technique developed in the late 1960s to supplement the Uniform Crime Report; samples of the population are asked if they had been crime victims; results showed that more crimes occurred than had been reported to police

vigilantism   the practice of citizens banding together without legal sanction to take action against crime

violent crime   crimes of coercion against the person; often involving injury or death; as defined by the FBI in the UCR, aggravated assault, robbery, forcible rape, homicide, etc.

white flight   a phrase used to describe the migration of whites from one city area to another area or from the central city to the suburbs; connotes migration that involves large numbers of the white residents and takes place over a short period of time; a phenomenon that probably doesn't exist

white-collar crime   crime committed by white-collar workers—those in salaried or professional positions; embezzlement, stock fraud, and corporate crimes such as price fixing are examples

zone in transition   the concentric zone surrounding the central business district; area characterized by warehouses, light manufacturing facilities, and so on, into which the central business district expands

References

Abend, Norman A.
1971 "The Urban Environment." In *Exploring Urban Problems,* edited by Melvin R. Levin, pp. 322–79. Boston: Urban Press. [12]

Acosta, Maruja, and Hardoy, Jorge E.
1972 "Urbanization Policies and Land Reforms in Revolutionary Cuba." In *Latin American Urban Research,* vol. 2, edited by Guillermo Geisse and Jorge E. Hardoy, pp. 167–77. Series edited by Francine F. Rabinovitz and Felicity M. Trueblood. Beverly Hills, Calif.: Sage Publications, Inc. [4]

Adams, Robert McC.
1968 "The Evolution of Urban Society: Early Mesopotamia and Prehistoric Mexico." In *Urbanism in World Perspective,* edited by Sylvia F. Fava, pp. 98–115. New York: Thomas Y. Crowell Co., Inc. [3]

Aiken, Michael, and Alford, Robert R.
1970 "Community Structure and Innovation: The Case of Urban Renewal." *American Sociological Review* 35:650–65. [10]

Akers, Ronald L.
1964 "Socioeconomic Status and Delinquent Behavior: A Retest." *Journal of Research in Crime and Delinquency* 2, 1:38–46. [13]

Alonso, William A.
1971 "A Theory of the Urban Land Market." In *Internal Structure of the City,* edited by Larry S. Bourne, pp. 154–59. New York: Oxford University Press. [4]

American Public Works Association
1963 Cited in *Performance of Urban Functions,* U.S. Advisory Commission on Intergovernmental Functions. Washington, D.C.: Government Printing Office. [12]
1970 *Municipal Refuse Disposal.* Chicago: Public Administration Service. [12]

Anderson, Martin
1967 "The Federal Bulldozer." In *Urban Renewal: The Record and the Controversy,* edited by James Q. Wilson, pp. 441–508. Cambridge, Mass.: M.I.T. Press. [11]

Anderson, Theodore R., and Egeland, Janice A.
1961 "Spatial Aspects of Social Area Analysis." *American Sociological Review* 26, 3 (June):392–99. [5]

Appel, James Z.
1970 "Health Care Delivery." In *The Health of Americans,* edited by Boisfeuillet Jones, pp. 141–66. Englewood Cliffs, N.J.: Prentice-Hall, Inc. [11]

Armour, David
1972 "The Evidence on Busing." *The Public Interest* 28 (Summer):90–126. [14]

Bachrach, Peter, and Baratz, Morton S.
1962 "Two Faces of Power." *American Political Science Review* 58 (December):947–52. [10]

Baer, William C.
1976 "On the Death of Cities." *Public Interest* 24 (Autumn):3–20. [15]

Baltzell, E. Digby
1968 *The Search for Community in Modern America.* New York: Harper & Row Publishers, Inc. [6]

Banfield, Edward C.
1961 *Political Influence.* New York: Free Press. [10]
1974 *The Unheavenly City Revisited.* Boston: Little, Brown & Company. [8]

Banfield, Edward C., and Wilson, James Q., eds.
1963 *City Politics.* New York: Random House, Inc. [9, 10]

Banks, James A.
1972 "Imperatives in Ethnic Minority Education." *Phi Delta Kappan* 53:266–67. [14]

Baskin, Jane A., et al.
1972 *The Long Hot Summer: An Analysis of Summer Disorders, 1967–1971.* Waltham, Mass.: Lemberg Center for the Study of Violence, Brandeis University. [9]

Becker, Howard S.
1971 "The Outsiders." In *The Criminal in Society,* edited by Leon Radzinowicz and Marvin Wolfgang, pp. 21–25. New York: Basic Books, Inc., Publishers. [13]

Becker, Howard S., and Horowitz, Irving Louis.
1973 "The Culture of Civility: San Francisco." In *Cities in Change: Studies on the Urban Condition,* edited by John Walton and Donald Carns, pp. 243–51. Boston: Allyn & Bacon, Inc. [1]

Beers, Howard W.
1957 "Rural-Urban Differences: Some Evidence from Public Opinion Polls." In *Cities and Society: The Revised Reader in Urban Sociology,* edited by Paul K. Hatt and Albert J. Reiss, Jr., pp. 698–711. Glencoe, Ill.: Free Press. [1]

Bell, Wendell
1958   "Social Choice, Life Styles, and Suburban Residence." In *The Suburban Community,* edited by William Dobriner, pp. 225–47. New York: G. P. Putnam's Sons. [6]

Bell, Wendell, and Boat, Marian D.
1957   "Urban Neighborhoods and Informal Social Relations." *American Journal of Sociology* 62:391–98. [5]

Berger, Bennett M.
1972   "The Myth of Suburbia." In *North American Suburbs: Politics, Diversity, and Change,* edited by John Kramer, pp. 5–18. Berkeley: Glendessary. [6]

Berry, Brian J. L.
1965   "Internal Structure of the City." *Law and Contemporary Problems* 30:11–119. [5]

Berry, Brian J. L., and Garrison, William L.
1958   "Alternate Explanations of Urban Rank-Size Relationships." *Annals of the Association of American Geographers* 48:83–91. [4]

Billings, Charles E.
1972   "Community Control of the School and the Quest for Power." *Phi Delta Kappan* 53:277–78. [14]

Birch, David L.
1975   "From Suburb to Urban Place." *Annals* 422 (November):25–35. [4, 5]

Blau, Peter M.
1955   *The Dynamics of Bureaucracy.* Chicago: University of Chicago Press. [10]
1964   *Exchange and Power in Social Life.* New York: John Wiley & Sons, Inc. [10]

Blauner, Robert
1969   "Internal Colonialism and the Ghetto Revolt." *Social Problems* 16, 4:393–408. [9]

Borgatta, Edgar F., and Hadden, Jeffrey K.
1965   *American Cities: Their Social Characteristics.* Chicago: Rand McNally & Company. [4]
1970   "The Classification of Cities." In *Neighborhood, City, and Metropolis,* edited by Robert Gutman and David Popenoe, pp. 253–63. New York: Random House, Inc. [1, 4]

Bosco, James J., and Robin, Stanley S.
1976   "White Flight from Busing? A Second, Longer Look." *Urban Education* 11, 3 (October):263–75. [14]

Boskin, Joseph
1969   *Urban Racial Violence in the Twentieth Century.* Encino, Calif.: Glencoe Press. [9]

Boulding, Kenneth E.
1968   "The City as an Element in the International System." *Daedalus* 97, 4 (Fall):1111–24. [8]

Bourne, Larry S.
1971   "Apartment Location and the Housing Market." In *Internal Structure of the City,* edited by Larry S. Bourne, pp. 321–28. New York: Oxford University Press. [6]

Bourne, Larry S., ed.
1971   *Internal Structure of the City.* New York: Oxford University Press. [5]

Boyce, Ronald R.
1971   "The Edge of the Metropolis: The Wave Theory Analog Approach." In *Internal Structure of the City,* edited by Larry S. Bourne, pp. 104–12. New York: Oxford University Press. [4]

Bradburn, Norman M.; Sudman, Seymour; and Gockel, Galen
1970   *Racial Integration in American Neighborhoods.* Chicago: National Opinion Research Center. [9]

Breckenfeld, Gurney
1970   "Environmental Protection Devices." *Planning 1970: Selected Papers from the American Society of Planning Officials National Planning Conference.* Chicago: American Society of Planning Officials. [12]

Bukro, Casey
1975   "Garbage Dumps Fill Up at 'Crisis' Rate." *Chicago Tribune* (December 18). [12]

Burgess, Ernest W.
1925   "Can Neighborhood Work Have a Scientific Basis?" In *The City,* edited by Robert E. Park, Ernest W. Burgess, and Roderick McKenzie, pp. 142–56. Chicago: University of Chicago Press. [13]
1967   "The Growth of the City: An Introduction to a Research Project." *Publications of the American Sociological Society* 18 (1924). In *The City,* edited by Robert E. Park, Ernest W. Burgess, and Roderick McKenzie, pp. 47–62. Chicago: University of Chicago Press. [5]

Burgess, Ernest W., and Bogue, Donald J., eds.
1964   *Contributions to Urban Sociology.* Chicago: University of Chicago Press. [1]

Calhoun, John B.
1963   "Population Density and Social Pathology." In *The Urban Condition: People and Policy in the Metropolis,* edited by Leonard J. Duhl, pp. 33–44. New York: Basic Books, Inc., Publishers. [11]

Campbell, Alan K., and Dollenmayer, Judith A.
1975 "Governance in a Metropolitan Society." In *Metropolitan America in Contemporary Perspective,* edited by Amos H. Hawley and Vincent P. Rock, pp. 355–96. New York: John Wiley & Sons, Inc. [8]

Cannon, Donald S.
1977 "Identifying Neighborhoods for Preservation and Renewal." *Growth and Change* 8, 1:35–39. [15]

Carmichael, Stokely, and Hamilton, Charles
1967 *Black Power.* New York: Random House, Inc. [14]

Cartwright, Desmond, and Howard, Kenneth I.
1966 "Multivariate Analysis of Gang Delinquency I: Ecologic Influences." *Multivariate Behavioral Research* 1 (July):321–71. [13]

Cartwright, Dorian
1959 *Studies in Social Power.* Ann Arbor, Mich.: Institute for Social Research. [10]
1965 "Influence, Leadership and Control." In *Handbook of Organizations,* edited by James G. March, pp. 1–47. Chicago: Rand McNally & Company. [10]

Childe, V. Gordon
1951 *Man Makes Himself.* New York: Mentor. [3]
1970 "The Urban Revolution." *Town Planning Review* 21, 1 (April 1950):3–17. In *Neighborhood, City, and Metropolis,* edited by Robert Gutman and David Popenoe, pp. 111–18. New York: Random House, Inc. [3]

Chilton, Ronald J.
1964 "Continuities in Delinquency Area Research: A Comparison of Studies for Baltimore, Detroit, and Indianapolis." *American Sociological Review* 29 (February):71–83. [11, 13]

Chinitz, Benjamin
1964 "City and Suburb: The Economics of Metropolitan Growth." In *City and Suburb: The Economics of Metropolitan Growth,* edited by Benjamin Chinitz, pp. 3–50. Englewood Cliffs, N.J.: Prentice-Hall, Inc. [4, 5]

Choldin, Harvey
1976 "Crowding and Pathology: Los Angeles, 1970." Paper presented at meetings of the American Sociological Association. [11]

Clark, Terry N.
1968 "The Concept of Power." In *Community Structure and Decision Making,* edited by Terry N. Clark, pp. 45–81. San Francisco: Chandler Publishing Company. [10]

Clausen, John A., and Kohn, Melvin L.
1954 "The Ecological Approach in Social Psychiatry." *American Journal of Sociology* 60 (September):140–51. [11]

Clemence, Theodore
1974 "Residential Segregation in the Mid-Sixties." In *Comparative Urban Structure,* edited by Kent P. Schwirian, pp. 549–54. Lexington, Mass.: D.C. Heath & Company. [1]

Clinard, Marshall B.
1964 "Deviant Behavior, Urban-Rural Contrasts." In *Metropolis: Values in Conflict,* edited by C. E. Elias, et al., pp. 237–45. Belmont, Calif.: Wadsworth Publishing Co., Inc. [13]

Cloward, Richard A., and Ohlin, Lloyd E.
1960 *Delinquency and Opportunity: A Theory of Delinquent Gangs.* Glencoe, Ill.: Free Press. [13]

Cohen, Albert F.
1955 *Delinquent Boys: The Culture of the Gang.* Glencoe, Ill.: Free Press. [13]
1966 *Deviance and Society.* Englewood Cliffs, N.J.: Prentice-Hall, Inc. [13]

Cole, Lamont C.
1973 "Man and the Air." In *Man and the Environment,* edited by Wes Jackson, pp. 35–43. Dubuque, Ia.: Wm. C. Brown Company Publishers. [12]

Coleman, James S.
1957 *Community Conflict.* New York: Free Press. [10]
1974 "Recent Trends in School Integration." *Educational Researcher* (July-August):3–12. [14]

Coleman, James S., et al.
1966 *Equality of Educational Opportunity.* Washington, D.C.: Government Printing Office. [14]
1975 *Trends in School Segregation 1968–1973.* Washington, D.C.: The Urban Institute. [14]

Cook, Robert C.
1969 "The World's Great Cities: Evolution or Devolution?" *Population Bulletin* (1960). In *Urbanism, Urbanization, and Change,* edited by Paul H. Meadows and Ephraim H. Mizruchi, pp. 29–51. Reading, Mass.: Addison-Wesley Publishing Co., Inc. [3]

Cornwall, Elmer E., Jr.
1964 "Bosses, Machines, and Ethnic Groups." *Annals* 353 (May):27–39. [1, 9, 10]

Council on Municipal Performance
1974 "City Air." *Municipal Performance Reports* 1, 5:3–31. [12]

1974   "Housing Segregation: 109 Cities." *Municipal Performance Reports* 1, 5:32–35. [9]

Cox, Fred M., et al., eds.
1970   *Community Organization.* Itasca, Ill.: F. E. Peacock Publishers, Inc. [10]

Crain, Robert L.
1970   "School Integration and the Occupational Achievement of Negroes." *American Journal of Sociology* 75, 4 (January):593–606. [14]
1974   "School Integration and the Academic Achievement of Negroes." *Sociology of Education* 44 (Winter):1–26. [14]

Crain, Robert L.; Katz, Elihu; and Rosenthal, Donald
1969   *The Politics of Community Conflict: The Fluoridation Decision.* Indianapolis: The Bobbs-Merrill Co., Inc. [10]

Dahl, Robert A.
1961   *Who Governs?* New Haven: Yale University Press. [9, 10]
1967   "The Concept of Power." *Behavioral Scientist* 2 (July):201–18. [10]

Danziger, Sheldon
1976   "Explaining Urban Crime Rates." *Criminology* 14, 2 (August):291–96. [13]

Davis, Kingsley
1955   "The Origin and Growth of Urbanization in the World." *American Journal of Sociology* 61:430–37. [1, 3, 4]
1969   *World Urbanization 1950–1970, Volume I. Basic Data for Cities, Countries, and Regions.* Rev. ed. Berkeley: University of California Institute for International Studies. [4]
1973   "The Evolution of Western Industrial Cities." In *Cities: Their Origin, Growth, and Human Impact,* edited by Kingsley Davis, pp. 100–106. San Francisco: W. H. Freeman & Company Publishers. [4]
1973   "The First Cities: How and Why Did They Arise?" In *Cities: Their Origin, Growth, and Human Impact,* edited by Kingsley Davis, pp. 9–19. San Francisco: W. H. Freeman & Company Publishers. [3]

de Torres, Juan
1972   *Government Services in Major Metropolitan Areas.* New York: The Conference Board, Inc. [12]

DeVise, Pierre
1973   "Physician Migration from Inland to Coastal States." *Journal of Medical Education* 48 (February):141–51. [11]

1976   "The Suburbanization of Jobs and Minority Employment." *Economic Geography* 52, 4:348–62. [15]

Dewey, Richard
1960   "The Rural-Urban Continuum: Real but Relatively Unimportant." *American Journal of Sociology* 66 (July):60–66. [1, 6]

Dinitz, Simon
1973   "Progress, Crime, and the Folk Ethic." *Criminology* (May):3–21. [13]

Dobriner, William
1958   "Local and Cosmopolitan as Contemporary Suburban Character Types." In *The Suburban Community,* edited by William Dobriner, pp. 132–43. New York: G. P. Putnam's Sons. [6]
1970   "The Growth and Structure of Metropolitan Areas." In *Class in Suburbia,* edited by William Dobriner, pp. 143–66. Englewood Cliffs, N.J.: Prentice-Hall, Inc., 1963. Reprinted in *Neighborhood, City, and Metropolis,* edited by Robert Gutman and David Popenoe, pp. 190–205. New York: Random House, Inc. [4, 5]

Dobriner, William, ed.
1958   *The Suburban Community.* New York: G. P. Putnam's Sons. [6]

Dorfman, Ron
1976   "Daley's Bluff." *Chicago* (April):124. [10]

Drake, St. Clair, and Clayton, Horace R.
1962   *Black Metropolis: A Study of Negro Life in a Northern City.* Rev. ed. New York: Harper & Row. [9]

Duncan, Otis Dudley
1957   "Community Size and the Rural-Urban Continuum." In *Cities and Society,* edited by Paul K. Hatt and Albert J. Reiss, Jr., pp. 35–45. 2d ed. Glencoe, Ill.: Free Press. [1, 4, 6]
1960   *Metropolis and Region.* Baltimore: The Johns Hopkins University Press. [4]

Duncan, Otis Dudley, and Reiss, Albert J., Jr.
1956   *Social Characteristics of Urban and Rural Communities, 1950.* New York: John Wiley & Sons, Inc. [1, 4]

Duncan, Otis Dudley, and Schnore, Leo F.
1959   "Cultural, Behavioral, and Ecological Perspectives in the Study of Social Organization." *American Journal of Sociology* 65:132–46. [5]

Durkheim, Émile
1933   *The Division of Labor in Society.* Translated by George Simpson. Glencoe, Ill.: Free Press. [2]

1938   *The Rules of the Sociological Method.* Edited by George Catlin. Glencoe, Ill.: Free Press. [2, 13]

1951   *Suicide.* Translated by John A. Spaulding and George Simpson, edited by George Simpson. Glencoe, Ill.: Free Press. [2]

Dyckman, John W.
1970   "Socioeconomic and Technological Forces in Urban Expansion." In *Urban Expansion, Problems and Needs: Papers Presented at the Administrators' Spring Conference.* Washington, D.C.: Government Printing Office, 1963. Reprinted in *Neighborhood, City, and Metropolis,* edited by Robert Gutman and David Popenoe, pp. 439–59. New York: Random House, Inc. [4, 5, 8]

1973   "Transportation in Cities." *Scientific American* (September 1965). In *Cities: Their Origin, Growth, and Human Impact,* edited by Kingsley Davis, pp. 195–206. San Francisco: W. H. Freeman & Company Publishers. [11]

Dye, Thomas R.
1969   "Urban School Segregation: A Comparative Analysis." *Urban Affairs Quarterly* 4 (December 1968):141–65. In *The Politics of Urban Education,* edited by Marilyn Gittell and Alan G. Hevesi, pp. 89–100. New York: Praeger Publishers, Inc. [14]

Edel, Matthew; Harris, John R.; and Rothenberg, Jerome
1975   "Urban Concentration and Deconcentration." In *Metropolitan America in Contemporary Perspective,* edited by Amos H. Hawley and Vincent P. Rock, pp. 123–56. New York: John Wiley & Sons, Inc. [5]

Eisenbud, Merril
1972   "Environmental Protection in the City of New York." In *The City in the Seventies,* edited by Robert K. Yin, pp. 152–64. Itasca, Ill.: F. E. Peacock Publishers, Inc. [12]

Elgin, Duane
1974   "Environmental Quality and City Size." In *City Size and the Quality of Life,* by Duane Elgin et al., pp. 97–114. Washington, D.C.: Government Printing Office. [12]

Empy, Lamar T., and Erickson, Maynard L.
1966   "Hidden Delinquency and Social Status." *Social Forces* 44, 4:546–54. [13]

Environmental Protection Agency
1975   *Environmental Quality: 1974.* Washington, D.C.: Government Printing Office. [12]

Erbe, Brigitte Mach
1975   "Race and Socioeconomic Segregation." *American Sociological Review* 40 (December):801–12. [9]

Fahs, Ivan J., and Petersen, Osler J.
1968   "Towns without Physicians and Towns with Only One: A Study of Four States in the Upper Midwest." *American Journal of Public Health* 58, 7:1200–1211. [11]

Fantini, Mario; Gittell, Marilyn; and Magat, Richard
1970   *Community Control and the Urban School.* New York: Praeger Publishers, Inc. [14]

Faris, Robert E. L.
1967   *Chicago Sociology 1920–1932.* San Francisco: Chandler Publishing Company. [6]

Faris, Robert E. L., and Dunham, H. Warren
1939   *Mental Disorder in Urban Areas.* Chicago: University of Chicago Press. [11]

Farley, Reynolds
1976   "Components of Suburban Population Growth." In *The Changing Face of the Suburbs,* edited by Barry Schwartz, pp. 3–38. Chicago: University of Chicago Press. [4, 5, 6]

Farley, Reynolds, and Taeuber, Karl.
1974   "Population Trends and Racial Segregation Since 1960." In *Comparative Urban Structure,* edited by Kent P. Schwirian, pp. 541–49. Lexington, Mass.: D. C. Heath & Company. [1]

Fava, Sylvia F.
1956   "Suburbanism as a Way of Life." *American Sociological Review* 21:34–38. [6]

1958   "Contrasts in Neighboring: New York City and a Suburban County." In *The Suburban Community,* edited by William Dobriner, pp. 122–31. New York: G. P. Putnam's Sons. [6]

Feinstein, Otto, ed.
1971   *Ethnic Groups in the City.* Lexington, Mass.: D. C. Heath & Company. [9]

Fellows, Donald Keith
1972   *A Mosaic of America's Ethnic Minorities.* New York: John Wiley & Sons, Inc. [9]

Firey, Walter
1945   "Sentiment and Symbolism as Ecological Variables." *American Sociological Review* 10:140–48. [5]

Fischer, Claude S.
1972   "Urbanism as a Way of Life: A Review and an Agenda." *Sociological Methods and Research* 1:187–242. [6]

1975   "The Study of the Urban Community and Personality." In *Annual Review of Sociology,* vol. 1, pp. 71–73. Palo Alto, Calif.: Annual Review. [6]

Fischer, Claude S., and Jackson, Robert Max
1976   "Suburbs, Networks, and Attitudes." In *The Changing Face of the Suburbs,* edited by Barry Schwartz, pp. 279–308. Chicago: University of Chicago Press. [4, 6]

Fisher, Sethard
1969   "Community Power Studies: A Critique." *Social Research* (Winter 1962). In *Urban Politics and Problems,* edited by H. R. Mahood and Edward L. Angus, pp. 85–98. New York: Charles Scribner's Sons. [10]

Fishman, Joshua A.
1961   "Some Social and Psychological Determinants of Intergroup Relations in Changing Neighborhoods." *Social Forces* 40, 1 (October):42–51. [9]

Fitzpatrick, John J.
1976   "Psychoanalysis and Crime: A Critical Survey of Salient Trends in the Literature." *Annals* 423 (January):67–74. [13]

Form, William H., and Stone, Gregory P.
1957   "Urbanism, Anonymity, and Status Symbolism." *American Journal of Sociology* 62:504–14. [6]

Fried, Marc, and Gleicher, Peggy
1970   "Some Sources of Residential Satisfaction in an Urban Slum." In *Neighborhood, City, and Metropolis,* edited by David Gutman and Robert Popenoe, pp. 730–45. New York: Random House, Inc. [11]

Frieden, Bernard J.
1970   "Housing and National Urban Goals: Old Policies and New Realities." In *The Metropolitan Enigma,* edited by James Q. Wilson, pp. 170–225. Garden City, N.Y.: Doubleday & Co., Inc. [11]

Friesma, H. Paul
1969   "The Metropolis and the Maze of Local Government." In *Urban Politics and Problems,* edited by H. R. Mahood and Edward L. Angus, pp. 409–25. New York: Charles Scribner's Sons. [8]

Gakenheimer, Ralph A.
1967   "Urban Transportation Planning: An Overview." In *Taming Megalopolis, Vol. I, What Is and What Could Be,* edited by H. Wentworth Eldredge, pp. 392–411. Garden City, N.Y.: Doubleday & Co., Inc. [11]

Galle, Omer
1963   "Occupational Composition and the Metropolitan Hierarchy: The Inter and Intra Metropolitan Division of Labor." *American Journal of Sociology* 69:260–69. [4]

Gans, Herbert J.
1951   "Park Forest: Birth of a Jewish Community." *Commentary* 2:330–39. [9]
1962   *The Urban Villagers.* New York: Free Press. [5, 6, 9]
1962   "Urbanism and Suburbanism as Ways of Life: A Reevaluation of Definitions." In *Human Behavior and Social Process: An Interactionist Approach,* edited by Arnold M. Rose, pp. 625–48. Boston: Houghton-Mifflin. [6]

Giles, Michael; Cataldo, Everett F.; and Catlin, Douglas S.
1975   "White Flight and Percent Black: The Tipping Point Re-examined." *Social Science Quarterly* 56 (June):85–92. [14]

Giles, Michael; Catlin, Douglas S.; and Cataldo, Everett F.
1974   "The Impact of Busing on White Flight." *Social Science Quarterly* 55 (September):493–501. [14]

Gitlin, Todd, and Hollander, Nanci
1970   *Uptown: Poor Whites in Chicago.* New York: Harper & Row. [9]

Gittell, Marilyn, et al.
1972   *Local Control in Education.* New York: Praeger Publishers, Inc. [14]

Glaab, Charles N.
1963   *The American City: A Documentary History.* Homewood, Ill.: Dorsey Press. [1, 13]

Glazer, Nathan
1954   "Ethnic Groups in America: From National Culture to Ideology." In *Freedom and Control in Modern Society,* edited by Morroe Berger et al., pp. 158–73. New York: D. Van Nostrand Company. [9]
1967   "The Effects of Poor Housing." *Journal of Marriage and the Family* 29, 1 (February):140–45. [11]
1972   "Paradoxes of Health Care." *The Public Interest* (Winter, 1971). In *The View from Below: Urban Politics and Social Policy,* edited by Susan S. and Norman J. Fainstein, pp. 159–74. Boston: Little, Brown and Company. [11]

Glazer, Nathan, and Moynihan, Daniel P.
1970   *Beyond the Melting Pot.* 2d ed. Cambridge, Mass.: M.I.T. Press. [9]

Glenn, Norval D.
1973   "Suburbanization in the United States since World War II." In *The Urbanization of the Suburbs,* edited by Louis H. Masotti and Jeffrey K. Hadden, pp. 51-78. Beverly Hills, Calif.: Sage Publications, Inc. [5, 6]

Goheen, Peter G.
1971   "Metropolitan Area Definitions: A Reevaluation of Concept and Statistical Practice." In *Internal Structure of the City,* edited by Larry S. Bourne, pp. 47-58. New York: Oxford University Press. [7]

Goldwin, Robert A., ed.
1966   *A Nation of Cities: Essays on America's Urban Problems.* Chicago: Rand McNally & Company. [1]

Gordon, Milton
1964   *Assimilation in American Life.* New York: Oxford University Press. [9, 14]

Gordon, Robert A.
1971   "Issues in the Ecological Study of Delinquency." *American Sociological Review* 32 (1967):927-44. In *Ecology, Crime, and Delinquency,* edited by Harwin Voss and David M. Petersen, pp. 227-59. New York: Appleton-Century-Crofts. [13]

Gouldner, Alvin
1960   "The Norm of Reciprocity." *American Sociological Review* 25:161-78. [10]

Green, Robert L.
1974   "Northern School Desegregation. Educational, Legal, and Political Issues." In *Uses of the Sociology of Education, the 73rd Yearbook of the National Society for the Study of Education, Part II,* edited by C. Wayne Gordon, pp. 213-73. Chicago: University of Chicago Press. [14]

Greer, Scott
1961   "Traffic, Transportation, and Problems of the Metropolis." In *Contemporary Social Problems,* edited by Robert K. Merton and Robert A. Nisbet, pp. 605-50. 1st ed. New York: Harcourt, Brace & World, Inc. [11]
1962   *The Emerging City.* New York: Free Press. [5]
1972   *The Urbane View.* New York: Oxford University Press. [5]
1973   "The Family in Suburbia." In *The Urbanization of the Suburbs,* edited by Louis H. Masotti and Jeffrey K. Hadden, pp. 149-70. Beverly Hills, Calif.: Sage Publications, Inc. [6]

Grimshaw, Allen D.
1960   "Urban Racial Violence in the United States: Changing Ecological Considerations." *American Journal of Sociology* 66 (September):109-19. [9]

Grodzins, Morton
1970   *The Metropolitan Area as a Racial Problem.* Pittsburgh: University of Pittsburgh Press, 1958. In *Neighborhood, City, and Metropolis,* edited by Robert Gutman and David Popenoe, pp. 479-501. New York: Random House, Inc. [9]

Guest, Avery M., and Zuiches, James J.
1971   "Another Look at Residential Turnover in Urban Neighborhoods." *American Journal of Sociology* 77, 3 (November):457-67. [9]

Gutman, Robert, and Popenoe, David., eds.
1970   *Neighborhood, City, and Metropolis.* New York: Random House, Inc. [1]

Haar, Charles M.
1972   "Introduction: Metropolitanization and Public Services." In *Metropolitanization and Public Services,* edited by Lowdon Wingo, pp. 1-17. Baltimore: Resources for the Future. [8]

Hadden, Jeffrey K., and Barton, Josef J.
1973   "An Image That Will Not Die: Thoughts on the History of Anti-Urban Ideology." In *The Urbanization of the Suburbs,* edited by Louis H. Masotti and Jeffrey K. Hadden, pp. 79-119. Beverly Hills, Calif.: Sage Publications, Inc. [1, 8]

Handlin, Oscar
1961   "Historical Perspectives on the American Ethnic Group." *Daedalus* 90, 2 (Spring):220-32. [9]

Harrigan, John J.
1976   "A New Look at Central City—Suburban Differences." *Social Science* 51, 4:200-209. [15]
1976   *Political Change in the Metropolis.* Boston: Little, Brown and Company. [1, 10]

Harris, Chauncey D., and Ullman, Edward L.
1945   "The Nature of Cities." *Annals* 242-17. [4, 5]

Harris, Fred R. (Senator), and Lindsay, John (Mayor).
1972   *The State of the Cities: Report of the Commission on the Cities in the '70s.* New York: Praeger Publishers, Inc. (for the National Urban Coalition). [1]

Hatt, Paul K., and Reiss, Albert J., Jr., eds.
1957   *Cities and Society: The Revised Reader in Urban Sociology.* Glencoe, Ill.: Free Press. [1]

Hauser, Philip M.
1965   "Observations on the Urban Rural Dichotomies as Forms of Western Ethnocentrism." In *The Study of Urbanization,* edited by Philip M. Hauser and Leo F. Schnore, pp. 503–17. New York: John Wiley & Sons, Inc. [6]
1971   "Whither Urban Society?" In *Cities in the '70s,* pp. 15–21. Washington, D.C.: National League of Cities. [8]

Havighurst, Robert J., and Levine, Daniel V.
1967   "The Quality of Urban Education." In *The Quality of Urban Life,* edited by Henry J. Schmandt and Warner Bloomberg, pp. 323–54. Beverly Hills, Calif.: Sage Publications, Inc. [14]

Hawley, Amos H.
1950   *Human Ecology: A Theory of Community Structure.* New York: Ronald Press. [5]
1963   "Community Power Structure and Urban Renewal Success." *American Journal of Sociology* 68 (June):422–31. [4, 10]
1971   *Urban Society.* New York: Ronald Press. [4, 5, 8]

Hawley, Amos H., and Duncan, Otis Dudley
1957   "Social Area Analysis: A Critical Appraisal." *Land Economics* 33:334–45. [5]

Hawley, Amos H., and Rock, Vincent P., eds.
1975   *Metropolitan America in Contemporary Perspective.* New York: John Wiley & Sons, Inc. [1, 8]

Hayghe, Howard.
1975   "Marital and Family Characteristics of the Labor Force, March 1975." *Monthly Labor Review* (November 1975). In *Special Labor Force Report 183.* Washington, D.C.: Government Printing Office. [15]

Health Resources Administration, National Center for Health Statistics
1974   *Health Characteristics by Geographic Regions, Large Metropolitan Areas, and Other Places of Residence: United States 1969–70.* Washington, D.C.: Government Printing Office. [11]
1975   *Selected Vital and Health Statistics in Poverty and Nonpoverty Areas of 19 Large Cities, United States 1969–71.* Washington, D.C.: Government Printing Office. [11]
1975   *Vital Statistics of the United States. Vol. II, Mortality, 1972.* Washington, D.C.: Government Printing Office. [11]

Hillery, George F.
1955   "Definitions of Community: Areas of Agreement." *Rural Sociology* 20, 2 (June):18, 111–23. [1]

Hirschi, Travis, and Rudisill, David
1976   "The Great American Search: Causes of Crime." *Annals* 423 (January):14–22. [13]

Hobbes, Thomas
1909   *Leviathan.* Reprint of 1651 edition. New York: Oxford University Press. [2]

Hogan, John C.
1974   "Law, Society, and the Schools." In *Uses of the Sociology of Education, the 73rd Yearbook of the National Society for the Study of Education, Part II,* edited by C. Wayne Gordon, pp. 411–47. Chicago: University of Chicago Press. [14]

Homans, George C.
1961   *Social Behavior: Its Elementary Forms.* New York: Harcourt, Brace & World, Inc. [10]

Hoover, Edgar M., and Vernon, Raymond
1962   *Anatomy of a Metropolis.* Garden City, N.Y.: Doubleday & Co., Inc. [5]

Hoyt, Homer
1964   "Recent Distortions of the Classical Models of Urban Structure." *Land Economics* 40, 2:199–212. [5]

Hunter, Albert
1975   "The Loss of Community: An Empirical Test Through Replication." *American Sociological Review* 40, 5 (October):537–52. [9]

Hunter, Floyd
1953   *Community Power Structure.* Chapel Hill, N.C.: University of North Carolina Press. [10]

Institute for Juvenile Research
1976   *Youth and Society in Illinois.* 7 vols. Chicago: Institute for Juvenile Research (offset). [13]

Isard, Walter
1956   *Location and Space-Economy.* Cambridge, Mass.: M.I.T. Press. [4]

Jackson, Gregg
1975   "Reanalysis of Coleman's 'Recent Trends in School Integration.'" *Educational Researcher* (November):21–25. [14]

Jacobs, Jane
1961   *The Death and Life of Great American Cities.* New York: Random House, Inc. [5, 13]

Janowitz, Morris
1952   *The Community Press in an Urban Setting.* Glencoe, Ill.: Free Press. [2]

Jefferson, Thomas
1965   *Notes on the State of Virginia.* Chapel Hill, N.C.: University of North Carolina Press. [1]

Jencks, Christopher, and Brown, Marsha
1975 "The Effects of Desegregation on Student Achievement: Some New Evidence from the Equality of Educational Opportunity Survey." *Sociology of Education* 48 (Winter):126-40. [14]

Johnson, Earl S.
1971 "The Function of the Central Business District in the Metropolitan Community." In *The Social Fabric of the Metropolis,* edited by James F. Short, Jr., pp. 87-102. Chicago: University of Chicago Press. [4, 5]

Joroff, Sheila, and Navarro, Vincente
1971 "Medical Manpower: A Multivariate Analysis of the Distribution of Physicians in Urban United States." *Medical Care* 9, 5 (September 10):428-38. [11]

Kain, John F.
1970 "The Distribution and Movement of Jobs and Industry." In *The Metropolitan Enigma,* edited by James Q. Wilson, pp. 1-44. Garden City, N.Y.: Doubleday & Co., Inc. [8]
1973 "What Should America's Housing Policy Be?" *U.S. Department of Commerce, Economic Development Administration Program on Regional and Urban Economics,* Discussion Paper 82 (December 27). [11]

Kanter, Rosabeth Moss
1972 *Commitment and Community: Communes and Utopias in Sociological Perspective.* Cambridge: Harvard University Press. [2]

Kaplan, Robert S., and Leinhardt, Samuel
1973 "Determinants of Physician Office Location." *Medical Care* 11, 5 (September 10):406-15. [11]

Kasarda, John D.
1972 "The Theory of Ecological Expansion: An Empirical Test." *Social Forces* 51 (December):165-82. [5]
1976 "The Changing Occupational Structure of the American Metropolis: Apropos the Urban Problem." In *The Changing Face of the Suburbs,* edited by Barry Schwartz, pp. 113-36. Chicago: University of Chicago Press. [1, 5, 6, 8]

Kasarda, John D., and Janowitz, Morris
1974 "Community Attachment in Mass Society." *American Sociological Review* 39 (June):328-39. [2, 6, 8]

Kelley, Clarence
1974 *Crime in the United States (Uniform Crime Report) 1974.* Washington, D.C.: Government Printing Office. [13]

1975 *Crime in the United States (Uniform Crime Report) 1975.* Washington, D.C.: Government Printing Office. [13]

Kish, Leslie
1954 "Differentiation in Metropolitan Areas." *American Sociological Review* 19:388-98. [4, 5]

Kornhauser, William
1959 *The Politics of Mass Society.* New York: Free Press.
1973 "Power and Participation in the Local Community." In *Cities in Change,* edited by John Walton and Donald Carns, pp. 389-98. Boston: Allyn & Bacon, Inc. [10]

Kramer, John, ed.
1972 *North American Suburbs: Politics, Diversity, and Change.* San Francisco: Boyd and Fraser Publishing Company. [5]

Kramer, Judith
1970 *The American Minority Community.* New York: Thomas Y. Crowell Co., Inc. [9]

Krickus, Richard J.
1970 "White Ethnic Neighborhoods—Ripe for the Bulldozer?" *Middle America Pamphlet Series.* New York: American Jewish Committee. [9]

Lander, Bernard
1971 "Towards an Understanding of Juvenile Delinquency." In *Ecology, Crime, and Delinquency,* edited by Harwin L. Voss and David M. Petersen, pp. 161-75. New York: Appleton-Century-Crofts. [11, 13]

Lane, Roger
1976 "Criminal Violence in America: The First Hundred Years." *Annals* 423 (January):1-13. [13]

Langer, William L.
1973 "The Black Death." *Scientific American* (February 1964). In *Cities: Their Origin, Growth, and Human Impact,* edited by Kingsley Davis, pp. 106-11. San Francisco: W. H. Freeman & Company Publishers. [3, 11]

Laurenti, Luigi
1960 *Property Values and Race.* Los Angeles: University of California Press. [9]

Law Enforcement Assistance Administration, U.S. Department of Justice
1975 *Criminal Victimization Surveys in the Nation's Five Largest Cities.* Washington, D.C.: Government Printing Office. [13]

Lemert, Edwin
1971   "Deviance and Social Control." In *The Criminal in Society,* edited by Leon Radzinowicz and Marvin Wolfgang, pp. 30–43. New York: Basic Books, Inc., Publishers. [13]

Levy, Leo, and Rowitz, Louis
1973   *The Ecology of Mental Disorder.* New York: Behavioral Publications, Inc. [11]

Levy, Leo, and Visotsky, Harold M.
1969   "The Quality of Urban Life: An Analysis from the Perspective of Mental Health." In *The Quality of Urban Life,* edited by Henry J. Schmandt and Warner Bloomberg, pp. 255–68. Beverly Hills, Calif.: Sage Publications, Inc. [11]

Lewis, Oscar
1965   "Further Observations on the Folk Urban Continuum and Urbanization with Specific Reference to Mexico City." In *The Study of Urbanization,* edited by Philip M. Hauser and Leo F. Schnore, pp. 441–503. New York: John Wiley & Sons, Inc. [6]

Lieberson, Stanley
1961   "The Division of Labor in Banking." *American Journal of Sociology* 66:491–96. [4]
1962   "Suburbs and Ethnic Residential Patterns." *American Journal of Sociology* 67:673–81 [9]
1963   *Ethnic Patterns in American Cities.* New York: Free Press. [5, 9]

Lieberson, Stanley, and Silverman, Arnold R.
1965   "The Precipitants and Underlying Conditions of Race Riots." *American Sociological Review* 30 (December):887–98. [9]

Lindsay, A. D., tr.
1950   *The Republic of Plato.* New York: E. P. Dutton & Co., Inc. [2]

Lineberry, Robert L.
1975   "Suburbia and the Metropolitan Turf." *Annals* 422 (November):1–10 [4, 5]

Linsky, Arnold
1969   "Some Generalizations Concerning Primate Cities." In *The City in Newly Developing Countries: Readings on Urbanism and Urbanization,* edited by Gerald Breese, pp. 288–94. Englewood Cliffs, N.J.: Prentice-Hall, Inc. [4]

Linton, Ron M.
1972   "Breathing." In *The City in the Seventies,* edited by Robert K. Yin, pp. 140–44. Itasca, Ill.: F. E. Peacock Publishers, Inc. [12]

Lipset, Seymour Martin
1960   *Political Man.* New York: Doubleday & Co., Inc. [10]

Long, Larry H., and Glick, Paul C.
1976   "Family Patterns in Suburban Areas: Recent Trends." In *The Changing Face of the Suburbs,* edited by Barry Schwartz, pp. 39–68. Chicago: University of Chicago Press. [5, 6]

Loomis, W. F.
1973   "Rickets." *Scientific American* (December 1970). In *Cities: Their Origin, Growth, and Human Impact,* edited by Kingsley Davis, pp. 112–22. San Francisco: W. H. Freeman & Company Publishers. [11]

Lopata, Helena Znaniecki
1964   "The Functions of Voluntary Associations in an Ethnic Community: 'Polonia.' " In *Contributions to Urban Sociology,* edited by Ernest W. Burgess and Donald J. Bogue, pp. 203–23. Chicago: University of Chicago Press. [9]

Lord, J. Dennis, and Catau, John
1976   "School Desegregation, Busing, and Suburban Migration." *Urban Education* 11, 3 (October):275–94. [14]

Lynd, Robert S., and Lynd, Helen M.
1929   *Middletown.* New York: Harcourt, Brace & World, Inc. [1, 8, 10]
1937   *Middletown in Transition.* New York: Harcourt, Brace & World, Inc. [8, 10]

McAllister, Ronald J., et al.
1971   "Residential Mobility of Blacks and Whites: A National Longitudinal Survey." *American Journal of Sociology* 77, 3 (November):445–56. [9]

McCoy, Rhody
1969   "Introduction." In *Diary of a Harlem School Teacher,* edited by J. Haskins, pp. xi–xiii. New York: Grove Press, Inc. [14]

McDermott, Walsh
1973   "Air Pollution and Public Health." *Scientific American* (October 1961). In *Cities: Their Origin, Growth, and Human Impact,* edited by Kingsley Davis, pp. 132–40. San Francisco: W. H. Freeman & Company Publishers. [11]

McEntire, David
1960   "The Housing Market in Racially Mixed Areas." In *Residence and Race,* edited by David McEntire, pp. 157–71. Berkeley: University of California Press. [9]

Mack, Raymond W.
1968   *Race, Class, and Power.* New York: D. Van Nostrand Company. [9]

McKelvey, Blake
1963   *The Urbanization of America, 1860–1915.* New Brunswick, N.J.: Rutgers University Press. [9]

McKenzie, Roderick D.
1926   "The Scope of Human Ecology." *Publications of the American Sociological Society* 20:141–54. [5]

1933   *The Metropolitan Community.* New York: McGraw-Hill Book Company. [4]

1957   "The Rise of Metropolitan Communities." In *Recent Social Trends,* Research Committee on Social Trends. New York: McGraw-Hill Book Company, 1933. Reprinted in *Cities in Society,* edited by Paul K. Hatt and Albert J. Reiss, Jr., pp. 201–13. 2d ed. Glencoe, Ill.: Free Press. [4]

1971   "The Ecological Approach to the Study of the Human Community." *American Sociological Review* 30 (1924). In *The Social Fabric of the Metropolis,* edited by James F. Short, Jr., pp. 17–33. Chicago: University of Chicago Press. [5]

McKeon, Richard, ed.
1947   *Introduction to Aristotle.* New York: Random House, Inc. [2]

McLennan, Barbara N., and McLennan, Kenneth
1971   "Public Policy and the Control of Crime." In *Exploring Urban Problems,* edited by Melvin R. Levin, pp. 564–75. Boston: Urban Press. [13]

McNeill, William H.
1963   *The Rise of the West.* Chicago: University of Chicago Press. [2]

Mahood, H. R., and Angus, Edward L., eds.
1969   *Urban Politics and Problems.* New York: Charles Scribner's Sons. [8]

Mann, Peter H.
1970   "Descriptive Comparison of Rural and Urban Communities." In *Neighborhood, City, and Metropolis,* edited by Robert Gutman and David Popenoe, pp. 38–53. New York: Random House, Inc. [1]

Marden, Charles F., and Meyer, Gladys
1968   *Minorities in American Society.* New York: D. Van Nostrand Company. [9]

Marden, Parker G.
1966   "A Demographic and Ecological Analysis of the Distribution of Physicians in Metropolitan America." *American Journal of Sociology* 72:290–300. [11]

Marshall, Harvey
1973   "Suburban Life Styles: A Contribution to the Debate." In *The Urbanization of the Suburbs,* edited by Louis H. Masotti and Jeffrey K. Hadden, pp. 123–48. Beverly Hills, Calif.: Sage Publications, Inc. [6]

Martin, Walter
1956   "The Structuring of Social Relationships Engendered by Suburban Residence." *American Sociological Review* 21:445–53. [6]

Martindale, Don
1958   "Prefatory Remarks: The Theory of the City." In *The City* by Max Weber. Translated and edited by Don Martindale and Gertrud Neuwirth. New York: Free Press. [15]

Masotti, Louis H., ed.
1975   "The Suburban Seventies." *Annals* 422. [5]

Masotti, Louis H., and Hadden, Jeffrey K., eds.
1973   *The Urbanization of the Suburbs.* Beverly Hills, Calif.: Sage Publications, Inc. [6]

Meadows, Paul, and Mizruchi, Ephraim H., eds.
1969   *Urbanism, Urbanization, and Change.* Reading, Mass.: Addison-Wesley Publishing Co., Inc. [8]

Mehta, Surinda K.
1969   "Some Demographic and Economic Correlates of Primate Cities." In *The City in Newly Developing Countries: Readings on Urbanism and Urbanization,* edited by Gerald Breese, pp. 295–308. Englewood Cliffs, N.J.: Prentice-Hall, Inc. [4]

Melville, Keith
1972   *Communes in the Counterculture: Origins, Theories, and Styles of Life.* New York: William Morrow & Co., Inc. [2]

Merridew, Alan
1975   "Doctors Seeking Greener Suburb Pastures, Flee City." *Chicago Tribune* (November 20). [11]

1975   *Chicago Tribune,* December 18, sec. 7, p. 1. [5]

Merton, Robert K.
1957   "Social Structure and Anomie." In *Social Theory and Structure,* edited by Robert K. Merton, pp. 131–60. Rev. ed., Glencoe, Ill.: Free Press. [13]

Meyer, John R.
1970   "Urban Transportation." In *The Metropolitan Enigma,* edited by James Q. Wilson, pp. 40–75. Garden City, N.Y.: Doubleday & Co., Inc. [11]

Milgram, Stanley
1973   "The Experience of Living in Cities." *Science* 167 (March 13, 1970):1461–68. In *Cities in Change: Studies on the Urban Condition,* edited by John Walton and Donald Carns, pp. 159–76. Boston: Allyn & Bacon, Inc. [6]

Miller, Walter B.
1958   "Lower Class Culture as a Generating Milieu of Gang Delinquency." *Journal of Social Issues* 14, 3:5–19.[13]

Mills, C. Wright
1959   *The Power Elite.* New York: Oxford University Press. [10]

Mizruchi, Ephraim H.
1969   "Romanticism, Urbanism, and Small Town in Mass Society: An Exploratory Analysis." In *Urbanism, Urbanization, and Change,* edited by Paul Meadows and Ephraim H. Mizruchi, pp. 243–52. Reading, Mass.: Addison-Wesley Publishing Co., Inc. [1, 8]

Mladenka, Kenneth R., and Hill, Kim Quailie
1976   "A Reexamination of the Etiology of Urban Crime." *Criminology* 13, 4 (February):491–506. [11]

Moltoch, Harvey
1969   "Racial Change in a Stable Community." *American Journal of Sociology* 75, 2 (September):226–37.

Mowrer, Ernest R.
1958   "The Family in Suburbia." In *The Suburban Community,* edited by William Dobriner, pp. 147–64. New York: G. P. Putnam's Sons. [6]

Mumford, Lewis
1961   *The City in History.* New York: Harcourt, Brace & World, Inc. [3, 4, 11]

Munger, Frank J.
1973   "Community Power and Decision Making." In *Cities in Change,* edited by John Walton and Donald Carns, pp. 332–54. Boston: Allyn & Bacon, Inc. [10]

National Advisory Commission on Civil Disorders (Kerner Commission)
1968   *Report of the National Advisory Commission on Civil Disorders.* New York: Bantam Books, Inc. [9]

National Commission on Urban Problems
1972   *Building the American City.* Washington, D.C.: Government Printing Office. [1, 11]

National Resources Committee
1937   "The Process of Urbanization: Underlying Forces and Emerging Trends." In *Our Cities: Their Role in the National Economy,* National Resources Committee, pp. 29–41. Washington, D.C.: Government Printing Office. [4, 5]

Nelson, Howard J.
1969   "The Form and Structure of Cities: Urban Growth Patterns." *Journal of Geography* 68:75–83. [5]

Nelson, Wade
1977   "Crime Our No. 1 Concern." *Chicago Daily News,* 5 April 1977:1.

Niedercorn, John H., and Hearle, Edward F. R.
1964   "Recent Land Use Trends in Forty-Eight Large American Cities." *Land Economics* 40:105–9. [5]

Nisbet, Robert A.
1966   *The Sociological Tradition.* New York: Basic Books, Inc., Publishers. [2]

Novak, Michael
1971   "White Ethnic." *Harper's* (September). [9]

O'Connor, Edwin
1956   *The Last Hurrah.* Boston: Little, Brown and Company. [9, 10]

O'Connor, Len
1975   *Clout: Mayor Daley and His City.* Chicago: Henry Regnery Company. [10]

Ogburn, William F.
1937   *Social Characteristics of Cities.* Chicago: International Association of City Managers. [4]

Ornstein, Allen C.
1974   *Race and Politics in School/Community Organizations.* Pacific Palisades, Calif.: Goodyear Publishing Co., Inc. [14]

Palen, John J.
1975   *The Urban World.* New York: McGraw-Hill Book Company. [4]

Pappenfort, Donnell
1959   "The Ecological Field and the Metropolitan Community." *American Journal of Sociology* 64:380–85. [4]

Parenti, Michael
1967   "Ethnic Politics and the Persistence of Ethnic Identification." *American Political Science Review* 61, 3:717–26. [9]

Park, Robert E.
1925   "Suggestions for the Investigation of Human Behavior in the Urban Environment." In *The*

City, edited by Robert E. Park, Ernest W. Burgess, and Roderick D. McKenzie, pp. 1–46. Chicago: University of Chicago Press. [5]

1926 "The Urban Community as a Spatial Pattern and a Moral Order." In *The Urban Community,* edited by Ernest W. Burgess, pp. 3–18. Chicago: University of Chicago Press. [5, 13]

1936 "Human Ecology." *American Journal of Sociology* 42:1–15. [5]

Park, Robert E.; Burgess, Ernest W.; McKenzie, Roderick
1925 *The City.* Chicago: University of Chicago Press. [1]

Parsons, Talcott
1937 *The Structure of Social Action.* New York: Free Press. [2]

1960 "The Principal Structures of Community." In *Structure and Process in Modern Societies,* by Talcott Parsons, New York: Free Press. [2]

1967 "Durkheim's Contribution to the Theory of Integration of Social Systems." In *Sociological Theory and Modern Society,* by Talcott Parsons, New York: Free Press. [2]

Passow, A. Harry
1967 *Toward Creating a Model Urban School System.* New York: Teachers College Press. [14]

1971 "Urban Education in the 1970s." In *Urban Education in the 1970s,* edited by A. Harry Passow, pp. 1–45. New York: Teachers College Press. [14]

Pettigrew, Thomas F.
1968 "Race and Equal Educational Opportunity." *Harvard Educational Review* 38:66–70. [14]

Pettigrew, Thomas F., et al.
1973 "Busing: A Review of the Evidence." *The Public Interest* 29 (Winter):88–118. [14]

Pickard, Jerome P.
1972 "U.S. Metropolitan Growth and Expansion, 1970–2000, with Population Projections." In *Population Distribution and Policy,* edited by Sara Mills Mazie, pp. 127–82. U.S. Commission on Population Growth and the American Future, vol. 5 of Commission Research Reports. Washington, D.C.: Government Printing Office. [7]

Pirenne, Henri.
1952 *Medieval Cities.* Princeton, N.J.: Princeton University Press, 1969. [1]

1961 "Northern Towns and Their Commerce." In *History of Western Civilization: Medieval Europe,* Topic V. Selected Readings by the College History Staff, pp. 48–76. 2d ed. Chicago: University of Chicago Press. From *The Cambridge Medieval History,* vol. VI, pp. 505–27. Cambridge: Cambridge University Press, 1932. [3]

Plant, James S.
1930 "Some Psychiatric Aspects of Crowded Living Conditions." *American Journal of Psychiatry* 9, 5 (March):849–60. [11]

1960 "Family Living Space and Personality Development." In *A Modern Introduction to the Family,* edited by Norman W. Bell and Ezra F. Vogel, pp. 510–20. New York: Free Press. [11]

Plunkett, George Washington
1967 "How to Get a Political Following." In *Politics in the Metropolis,* edited by Thomas R. Dye and Brett W. Hawkins, pp. 266–72. Columbus; Charles E. Merrill Publishing Company. [10]

Polk, Kenneth
1967 "Urban Social Areas and Delinquency." *Social Problems* 14, 3 (Winter):320–25. [11, 13]

President's Commission on Law Enforcement and Administration of Justice
1967 *The Challenge of Crime in a Free Society.* Washington, D.C.: Government Printing Office. [13]

1967 *Task Force Report. Crime and Its Impact: An Assessment.* Washington, D.C.: Government Printing Office. [1, 13]

Quinney, Richard
1964 "Crime, Delinquency, and Social Areas." *Journal of Research in Crime and Delinquency* 1 (July):149–54. [13]

Real Estate Research Corporation
1974 *The Costs of Sprawl, Executive Summary.* Washington, D.C.: Government Printing Office. [11]

Reiss, Albert J., Jr.
1970 "The Sociological Study of Communities." In *Neighborhood, City, and Metropolis,* edited by Robert Gutman and David Popenoe, pp. 27–37. New York: Random House, Inc. [1]

1971 "Assessing the Current Crime Wave." In *Exploring Urban Problems,* edited by Melvin R. Levin, pp. 537–63. Boston: Urban Press. [13]

Reiss, Albert J., Jr., ed.
1964 *Louis Wirth on Cities and Social Life.* Chicago: University of Chicago Press. [6]

Ribicoff, Abraham
1971   "The Healthiest Nation Myth." *Saturday Review* 53 (22 August 1970). In *The Nation's Health,* edited by Stephen Lewin, pp. 12–19. New York: The H. W. Wilson Company. [11]

Richmond, Julius B.
1970   "Human Development." In *The Health of Americans,* edited by Boisfeuillet Jones, pp. 5–38. Englewood Cliffs, N.J.: Prentice-Hall, Inc. [11]

Ringer, Benjamin B.
1972   "Jewish-Gentile Relations in Lakeville." In *North American Suburbs,* edited by John Kramer, pp. 174–84. San Francisco: Boyd & Fraser Publishing Company. [9]

Roback, G. A.
1973   *Distribution of Physicians in the United States, 1972, Vol. II, Metropolitan Areas.* Chicago: American Medical Association Center for Health Services Research and Development. [11]

Roebuck, Janet
1974   *The Shaping of Urban Society.* New York: Charles Scribner's Sons. [11]

Rose, Arnold, and Rose, Caroline B., eds.
1965   *Minority Problems.* 2d ed. New York: Harper & Row. [9]

Rossi, Peter H.
1960   "Theory and Method in the Study of Power in the Local Community." Paper given at the meetings of the American Sociological Association. [4]

Rourke, Anthony J.
1971   "Small Town Doctor Needs More Than an Office," *Modern Medicine* 117, 5 (November):151. [11]

Rousseau, Jean Jacques
1950   *The Social Contract and Discourses.* New York: E. P. Dutton & Co., Inc. [2]

Royko, Mike
1971   *Boss: Richard J. Daley of Chicago.* New York: E. P. Dutton & Co., Inc.

Rubin, Lillian
1972   *Busing and Backlash.* Berkeley: University of California Press. [14]

Russell, Bertrand
1945   *A History of Western Philosophy.* New York: Simon & Schuster, Inc. [2]

Schmandt, Henry J., and Bloomberg, Werner, eds.
1969   *The Quality of Urban Life.* Beverly Hills, Calif.: Sage Publications, Inc. [8]

Schmandt, Henry J., and Goldbach, John C.
1969   "The Urban Paradox." In *The Quality of Urban Life,* edited by Henry J. Schmandt and Werner Bloomberg, pp. 473–98. Beverly Hills, Calif.: Sage Publications, Inc. [1, 8]

Schnore, Leo F.
1957   "Metropolitan Growth and Decentralization." American Journal of Sociology 63:171–80. [5]
1957   "Satellites and Suburbs." *Social Forces* 36:109–27. [5]
1958   "The Growth of Metropolitan Suburbs." In *The Suburban Community,* edited by William Dobriner, pp. 26–44. New York: G. P. Putnam's Sons. [6]
1961   "The Myth of Human Ecology." *Sociological Inquiry* 31:128–39. [5]
1963   "The Social and Economic Characteristics of American Suburbs." *Sociological Quarterly* 4:122–34. [5, 6]
1965   "On the Spatial Structure of Cities in the Two Americas." In *The Study of Urbanization,* edited by Philip M. Hauser and Leo F. Schnore, pp. 347–98. New York: John Wiley & Sons, Inc. [5]
1970   "Urban Form: The Case of the Metropolitan Community." In *Urban Life and Form,* edited by Werner Z. Hirsch. New York: Holt, Rinehart & Winston, 1963. Reprinted in *Neighborhood, City, and Metropolis,* edited by Robert Gutman and David Popenoe, pp. 393–414. New York: Random House, Inc. [4, 5]
1976   "Black Suburbanization 1930–1970." In *The Changing Face of the Suburbs,* edited by Barry Schwartz, pp. 69–94. Chicago: University of Chicago Press. [5]

Schorr, Alvin L.
1963   *Slums and Social Insecurity: An Appraisal of the Effectiveness of Housing Policies in Helping to Eliminate Poverty.* Washington, D.C.: Government Printing Office. [11]
1970   "Housing and Its Effects." In *Neighborhood, City, and Metropolis,* edited by David Gutman and Robert Popenoe, pp. 709–11. New York: Random House, Inc. [11]

Schwartz, Barry, ed.
1976   *The Changing Face of the Suburbs.* Chicago: University of Chicago Press. [1, 5, 6, 8]

Schwirian, Kent P., ed.
1974   *Comparative Urban Structure: Studies in the Ecology of Cities.* Lexington, Mass.: D. C. Heath & Company. [1, 5, 11]

Scribner, Jay D., and O'Shea, David
1974 "Political Developments in Urban School Districts." In *Uses of the Sociology of Education, the 73rd Yearbook of the National Society for the Study of Education, Part II,* edited by C. Wayne Gordon, pp. 380–408. Chicago: University of Chicago Press. [14]

Seeley, John R., et al.
1972 "The Home in Crestwood Heights." In *North American Suburbs: Politics, Diversity, and Change,* edited by John Kramer, pp. 116–36. Berkeley: Glendessary. [6]

Sellin, Thorsten
1971 "Conflicting Norms." In *Culture, Conflict and Crime,* edited by Thorsten Sellin. New York: Social Science Research Council, 1938. Reprinted in *The Criminal in Society,* edited by Leon Radzinowicz and Marvin Wolfgang, pp. 395–99. New York: Basic Books, Inc., Publishers. [13]

Sennett, Richard
1969 *Classic Essays on the Culture of Cities.* New York: Appleton-Century-Crofts. [6]

Severo, Richard
1965 "New York's Italians: A Question of Identity." *New York Times,* 8 November 1970. In *Minority Problems,* edited by Arnold Rose and Caroline B. Rose, pp. 70–75. 2d ed. New York: Harper & Row. [9]

Shaw, Clifford, and McKay, Henry D.
1967 *Juvenile Delinquency and Urban Areas.* Chicago: University of Chicago Press. [13]

Shaw, Clifford; Zorbaugh, Harvey; McKay, Henry D.; and Cottrell, Leonard S., Jr.
1929 *Delinquency Areas.* Chicago: University of Chicago Press. [13]

Shevsky, Eshref, and Bell, Wendell
1955 *Social Area Analysis.* Stanford, Calif.: Stanford University Press. [5]

Shevsky, Eshref, and Williams, M.
1948 *The Social Areas of Los Angeles.* Berkeley: University of California Press. [5]

Short, James F., Jr., ed.
1971 *The Social Fabric of the Metropolis.* Chicago: University of Chicago Press. [5, 6]

Short, James F., Jr., and Nye, F. Ivan
1958 "Extent of Unrecorded Juvenile Delinquency: Tentative Conclusions." *Journal of Criminal Law, Criminology, and Police Science* 49:296–302. [13]

Shyrock, Henry S.
1957 "The Natural History of Standard Metropolitan Areas." *American Journal of Sociology* 63:163–70. [4, 7]

Shyrock, Henry S., et al.
1973 *The Methods and Materials of Demography.* Vol. 1. 2d printing, rev. U.S. Bureau of the Census. Washington, D.C.: Government Printing Office. [7]

Siegel, Adrienne.
1975 "When Cities Were Fun: The Image of the American City in Popular Books, 1840-1870." *Journal of Popular Culture* 9 (Winter):573–83. [1]

Simmel, Georg
1969 "The Metropolis and Mental Life." In *The Sociology of Georg Simmel,* translated by Kurt Wolff. New York: Free Press, 1950. Reprinted in *Classic Essays on the Culture of Cities,* edited by Richard Sennett, pp. 47–60. New York: Free Press. [6]

Singleton, Gregory H.
1973 "The Genesis of Suburbia: A Complex of Historical Trends." In *The Urbanization of the Suburbs,* edited by Louis H. Masotti and Jeffrey K. Hadden, pp. 29–50. Beverly Hills, Calif.: Sage Publications, Inc. [5]

Sizer, Theodore B.
1970 "The Schools and the City." In *The Metropolitan Enigma,* edited by James Q. Wilson, pp. 342–66. New York: Doubleday & Co., Inc. [14]

Sjoberg, Gideon
1964 "The Rural-Urban Dimension in Preindustrial, Transitional, and Industrial Societies." In *Handbook of Modern Sociology,* edited by R. E. L. Faris, pp. 127–60. Chicago: Rand McNally & Company. [6]
1970 "The Preindustrial City." *American Journal of Sociology* 60 (March 1955):438–55. In *Neighborhood, City, and Metropolis,* edited by Robert Gutman and David Popenoe, pp. 167–76. New York: Random House, Inc. [3]
1973 "The Origin and Evolution of Cities." *Scientific American* (September 1965). In *Cities: Their Origin, Growth, and Human Impact,* edited by Kingsley Davis, pp. 19–27. San Francisco: W. H. Freeman & Company Publishers. [3]

Smith, Larry
1971   "Space for the CBD's Functions." *Journal of the American Institute of Planners* 6 (1961). In *Internal Structure of the City,* edited by Larry S. Bourne, pp. 352–60. New York: Oxford University Press. [5]

Smith, T. Lynn
1970   "The Changing Functions of Latin American Cities." *Studies of Latin American Societies,* pp. 372–89. Garden City, N.Y.: Doubleday & Co., Inc. [4]

Srole, Leo F., et al.
1975   *Mental Health in the Metropolis.* Torchbook enlarged edition, Book 1. New York: Harper & Row. [11]

St. John, Nancy
1970   "Desegregation and Minority Group Performance." *Review of Educational Research* 40 (February):111–33. [14]

Statistical Policy Division, Office of Management and the Budget
1973   *Social Indicators, 1973.* Washington, D.C.: Government Printing Office. [11]

Stevens, William K.
1976   "Detroit Facing Court Ordered Busing of 21,000 Students Remains Calm." *New York Times* (January 4):40. [14]

Stewart, George R.
1972   "Garbage." In *The City in the Seventies,* edited by Robert K. Yin, pp. 136–40. Itasca, Ill.: F. E. Peacock Publishers, Inc. [12]

Stewart, William H.
1970   "Health Assessment." In *The Health of Americans,* edited by Boisfeuillet Jones, pp. 39–64. Englewood Cliffs, N.J.: Prentice-Hall, Inc. [11]

Still, Bayard
1974   *Urban America: A History with Documents.* Little, Brown and Company. [1]

Still, Henry
1972   "Littered Land." In *The City in the Seventies,* edited by Robert K. Yin, pp. 130–36. Itasca, Ill.: F. E. Peacock Publishers, Inc. [12]

Stouffer, Samuel A.
1955   *Communism, Conformity, and Civil Liberties.* Garden City, N.Y.: Doubleday & Co., Inc. [10]

Suttles, Gerald
1968   *The Social Order of the Slum.* Chicago: University of Chicago Press. [2, 6, 9, 11]

1972   *The Social Construction of Communities.* Chicago: University of Chicago Press. [2, 8]

Sutton, Willis, and Munson, Thomas
1976   "Definitions of Community: 1954 through 1973." Paper presented at the meetings of the American Sociological Association, New York. [1]

Szymanski, Albert
1976   "Racial Discrimination and White Gain." *American Sociological Review* 41 (June):403–14. [9]

Taeuber, Irene B.
1972   "The Changing Distribution of the Population of the United States in the Twentieth Century." *Population Distribution and Policy,* edited by Sara Mills Mazie, pp. 31–108. U.S. Commission on Population Growth and the American Future, vol. 5 of Commission Research Reports. Washington, D.C.: Government Printing Office. [7]

Taeuber, Irene B., and Taeuber, Conrad
1971   *The People of the United States in the Twentieth Century* (Census Monograph). Washington, D.C.: Government Printing Office. [1, 4]

Taeuber, Karl
1964   "Negro Residential Segregation: Trends and Measurement." *Social Problems* 12:42–50. [9]
1975   "Racial Segregation: The Persisting Dilemma." *Annals* 422:87–96. [5]

Tallman, Irving, and Morgner, Ramona
1970   "Life Style Differences Among Urban and Suburban Blue Collar Families." *Social Forces* 48, 3:334–48. [6]

Theodorson, George A., ed.
1961   *Studies in Human Ecology.* New York: Harper & Row. [1, 5]

Thomlinson, Ralph
1969   *Urban Structure.* New York: Random House, Inc. [4, 5]

Tilly, Charles
1970   "Race and Migration to American Cities." In *The Metropolitan Enigma,* edited by James Q. Wilson, pp. 144–69. Garden City, N.Y.: Doubleday & Co., Inc. [8]

Timms, D. W. G.
1971   *The Urban Mosaic.* Cambridge, N.Y.: Cambridge University Press. [5]

Tobin, Gary A.
1976   "Suburbanization and the Development of

Motor Transportation: Transportation Technology and the Suburbanization Process.'' In *The Changing Face of the Suburbs,* edited by Barry Schwartz, pp. 95–112. Chicago: University of Chicago Press. [4, 5]

Tönnies, Ferdinand
1957   *Community and Society (Gemeinschaft and Gesellschaft).* Translated and edited by Charles Loomis. New York: Harper & Row for Michigan State University Press. [2]

Tyron, Robert
1955   *Identification of Social Areas by Cluster Analysis.* Berkeley: University of California Press. [5]

Ullman, Edward
1941   "A Theory of Location for Cities." *American Journal of Sociology* 46 (May):853–64. [4]

United Nations
1974   *Concise Report on the World Population Situation in 1970–1975 and Its Long-Range Implications.* New York: United Nations. [4]

United Nations Bureau of Social Affairs, Population Division
1973   "World Population Trends, 1920–1960." In *Cities in Change,* edited by John Walton and Donald Carns, pp. 62–90. Boston: Allyn & Bacon, Inc. [4]

U.S. Bureau of the Census
1970   "Trends in Social and Economic Conditions in Metropolitan and Non-Metropolitan Areas." *Current Population Reports, Series P-23, 33.* Washington, D.C.: Government Printing Office. [8]

1971   *Census of Housing, 1970: Final Report HC(1)-A1, United States Summary.* Washington, D.C.: Government Printing Office. [11]

1971   *Census of Population, 1970: General Population Characteristics, Final Report PC(1)-B1, United States Summary.* Washington, D.C.: Government Printing Office. [7]

1971   *Census of Population, 1970: Number of Inhabitants, Final Report PC(1)-A1, United States Summary.* Washington, D.C.: Government Printing Office. [1, 7, 11]

1972   *Census of Population, 1970: General Social and Economic Characteristics, Final Report PC(1)-C1, United States Summary.* Washington, D.C.: Government Printing Office. [7, 9]

1973   *Graphic Summary of the 1970 Housing Census.* Washington, D.C.: Government Printing Office. [8]

1975   *Historical Statistics of the United States, Colonial Times to 1970. Bicentennial Edition.* Vol. 1. Washington, D.C.: Government Printing Office. [1, 7]

1975   *Statistical Abstract of the United States: 1974.* Washington, D.C.: Government Printing Office. [4, 7, 8]

1975   "School Enrollment: Social and Economic Characteristics of Students, October 1974." *Current Population Reports, Series P-20.* Washington, D.C.: Government Printing Office. [14]

1975   "Social and Economic Conditions of the Metropolitan and Non-Metropolitan Population: 1974 and 1970." *Current Population Reports, Series P-23, 55.* Washington, D.C.: Government Printing Office. [7]

1975   "Some Recent Changes in American Families." *Current Population Reports, Series P-20, 52.* Washington, D.C.: Government Printing Office. [15]

1976   "Fertility History and Prospects of American Women: June 1975." *Current Population Reports, Series P-20, 288.* Washington, D.C.: Government Printing Office. [15]

1976   "Mobility of the Population of the United States March 1970 to March 1975." *Current Population Reports, Series P-20, 285.* Washington, D.C.: Government Printing Office. [7, 14]

1976   "Population Profile of the United States: 1975." *Current Population Reports, Series P-20, 292.* Washington, D.C.: Government Printing Office. [7]

1977a   "Geographical Mobility: March 1975 to March 1976." *Current Population Reports, Series P-20, 305.* Washington, D.C.: Government Printing Office. [15]

1977b   "Marital Status and Living Arrangements: March 1976." *Current Population Reports, Series P-20, 306.* Washington, D.C.: Government Printing Office. [15]

1977c   "Population Profile of the United States: 1976." *Current Population Reports, Series P-20, 307.* Washington, D.C.: Government Printing Office. [15]

U.S. Commission on Civil Rights
1967   *Racial Isolation in the Public Schools.* Washington, D.C.: Government Printing Office. [14]

U.S. Congress, House Committee on Banking and Currency
1970   *The Quality of Urban Life.* Hearings before the Subcommittee on Urban Growth, 30 September 1969 through 24 June 1970. [1]

U.S. Department of Health, Education, and Welfare, Office of Education
1973   *Digest of Educational Statistics.* Washington, D.C.: Government Printing Office. [14]

U.S. Department of the Interior
1973   *Mining and Minerals Policy.* Washington, D.C.: Government Printing Office. [12]

University of Chicago College History Staff, eds.
1961   *History of Western Civilization, Medieval Europe,* Topic V. Selected readings by the College History Staff. 2d ed. Chicago: University of Chicago Press. [2]

   a. Power, Eileen. "Peasant Life and Rural Conditions, 1100-1500." From *The Cambridge Medieval History,* vol. VII, pp. 716-50. Cambridge: Cambridge University Press, 1932. [2]
   b. "A Manor of the 13th Century, A.D. 1279." From *Translations and Reprints from the Original Sources of European History,* vol. III, no. 5, pp. 4-7. Philadelphia: University of Pennsylvania Press. [2]
   c. Pirenne, Henri. "Northern Towns and Their Commerce." From *The Cambridge Medieval History,* vol. VI, pp. 505-27. Cambridge: Cambridge University Press, 1932. [2]
   d. "Ordinances of the Gild Merchant." From *Translations and Reprints from the Original Sources of European History,* vol. II, no. 1, pp. 12-17. Philadelphia: University of Pennsylvania Press. [2]

Vance, Rupert, and Demerath, N. J., eds.
1954   *The Urban South.* Chapel Hill, N.C.: University of North Carolina Press. [4]

Vance, Rupert, and Sutker, Sara S.
1954   "Metropolitan Dominance and Integration." In *The Urban South,* edited by Rupert Vance and N. J. Demerath, pp. 114-34. Chapel Hill, N.C.: University of North Carolina Press. [4]

van der Haag, Ernest
1976   "No Excuse for Crime." *Annals* 423 (January):133-41. [13]

Vander Zanden, James W.
1966   *American Minority Relations.* New York: Ronald Press. [9]

Van Til, Jon, and Van Til, Sally Bould
1973   "Citizen Participation in Social Policy: The End of the Cycle." In *Cities in Change,* edited by John Walton and Donald Carns, pp. 75-102. Boston: Allyn & Bacon, Inc. [10]

Vidich, Arthur, and Bensman, Joseph
1958   *Small Town in Mass Society.* Garden City, N.Y.: Doubleday & Co., Inc. [1, 8]

Wainwright, Loudon
1970   "Dilemma in Dyersville." *Life* (May 29):47-50. [11]

Walton, John
1973   "The Bearing of Social Science Research on Public Issues: Floyd Hunter and the Study of Power." In *Cities in Change,* edited by John Walton and Donald Carns, pp. 318-32. Boston: Allyn & Bacon, Inc. [10]

Wanklin, J. M., et al.
1955   "Factors Influencing the Rate of First Admission to Mental Hospital." *Journal of Nervous and Mental Disease* 121:103-16. [11]

Ward, David
1974   "The Emergence of Central Immigrant Ghettoes in American Cities: 1840-1920." In *Comparative Urban Structure,* edited by Kent P. Schwirian, pp. 457-75. Lexington, Mass.: D. C. Heath & Company. [1]

Warren, Roland
1972   *The Community in America.* 2d ed. Chicago: Rand McNally & Company. [1, 2, 4, 8]

Ways, Max
1971   "How to Think about the Environment." In *Metropolis in Crisis,* edited by Jeffrey K. Hadden et al., pp. 314-25. Itasca, Ill.: F. E. Peacock Publishers, Inc. [11, 12]

Weber, Max
1947   *The Theory of Social and Economic Organization.* New York: Oxford University Press. [10]
1958   *The City.* New York: Free Press. [1, 3, 6]
1961   "Ethnic Groups." In *Theories of Society,* edited by Talcott Parsons et al., pp. 305-9. New York: Free Press. [9]
1961   "Types of Social Organization." In *Theories of Society,* edited by Talcott Parsons et al., New York: Free Press. [2]

Weiss, Theodore S.
1976   "On Removing $300 Plus Rental Limits." *New York Times* (March 12). [11]

Wheeler, Stanton; Cottrell, Leonard S., Jr.; and Romasco, Anne
1970   "Juvenile Delinquency: Its Prevention and Control." In *Delinquency and Social Policy,* edited by Paul Lerman, pp. 428-43. New York: Praeger Publishers, Inc. [13]

White, Lynn
1972   "Technology and Social Change." In *Social Change,* edited by Nisbet, Robert A., pp. 101-23. New York: Harper & Row. [3]

White, Morton, and White, Lucia
1961   "The American Intellectual Versus the American City." *Daedalus* 90, 1 (Winter):166-79. [1, 8]

Whyte, William F.
1943   *Street Corner Society.* Chicago: University of Chicago Press. [6, 9, 10, 11]

Whyte, William H.
1957   *The Organization Man.* New York: Doubleday & Company, Inc. [6]
1967   "Cluster Development." In *Taming Megalopolis, Vol. I: What Is and What Could Be,* edited by H. Wentworth Eldredge, pp. 462-77. San Francisco: Anchor Press. [6]

Wilkes, Judith A.
1967   "Ecological Correlates of Crime and Delinquency." In *Task Force Report. Crime and Its Impact: An Assessment,* President's Commission on Law Enforcement and Administration of Justice, pp. 138-56. Washington, D.C.: Government Printing Office. [13]

Williams, Robin M.
1964   "Ethnocentrism." In *Strangers Next Door: Ethnic Relations in American Communities,* edited by Robin M. Williams, pp. 17-29. Englewood Cliffs, N.J.: Prentice-Hall, Inc. [9]

Wilson, James Q.
1968   "The Urban Unease: Community vs. the City." *The Public Interest* 12 (Summer):25-39. [1, 2, 8, 9, 13]

Wilson, James Q., ed.
1970   *The Metropolitan Enigma.* Garden City, N.Y.: Doubleday & Co., Inc. [8]

Wirth, Louis H.
1938   "Urbanism as a Way of Life." *American Journal of Sociology* 44, 1 (July):1-24. [1, 6]
1964   "The Ghetto." In *Louis Wirth on Cities and Social Life,* edited by Albert J. Reiss, Jr., pp. 84-98. Chicago: University of Chicago Press. [9]

1964   "The Scope and Problems of the Community." *Publications of the American Sociological Society* 37 (1933):61-73. In *Louis Wirth on Cities and Social Life,* edited by Albert J. Reiss, Jr., pp. 165-77. Chicago: University of Chicago Press. [5]

Wisenbaker, Joseph
1976   "Desegregation and White Flight: A Case Study." *Educational Research Quarterly* 1, 2 (Summer):17-27. [14]

Wolfgang, Marvin
1970   "Urban Crime." In *The Metropolitan Enigma,* edited by James Q. Wilson, pp. 270-311. Garden City, N.Y.: Doubleday & Co., Inc. [13]

Wolman, Abel
1966   "The Metabolism of Cities." In *Cities,* edited by *Scientific American* editors, pp. 156-74. New York: Alfred A. Knopf, Inc. [12]

Yin, Robert K., ed.
1972   *The City in the Seventies.* Itasca, Ill.: F. E. Peacock Publishers, Inc. [9]

Yinger, Milton J.
1961   "Social Forces Involved in Group Identification or Withdrawal." *Daedalus* 90, 2 (Spring):247-63. [9]

Zimmer, Basil G.
1975   "The Urban Centrifugal Drift." In *Metropolitan America in Contemporary Perspective,* edited by Amos H. Hawley and Vincent P. Rock, pp. 23-91. New York: John Wiley & Sons, Inc. [1, 5]

Credits

Chapter 8

222 Courtesy of Mobil Oil Corporation / 224 *top* The Bettmann Archive; *bottom* Dan O'Neill from Editorial Photocolor Archives / 227 Docuamerica / 228 *top, left to right* Daniel S. Brody, Jean-Claude Lejeune, W. R. Grace and Company; *middle* Jean-Claude Lejeune; *bottom* Robert V. Eckert / 229 *top* Robert V. Eckert; *bottom* David S. Strickler / 230–231 *top* Owen Kent from Chicago Historical Society; *bottom left* Mildred Mead from Chicago Historical Society; *bottom right* Robert V. Eckert / 233 *top* Robert V. Eckert; *bottom* Jean-Claude Lejeune / 234–235 Bruce Anspach from Editorial Photocolor Archives / 240–241 Photography by Thomas D. Lowes / 243 *top left* Ralph E. Tower from Chicago Historical Society; *top right* Glenn E. Dahlby from Chicago Historical Society; *bottom* Sigmund J. Osty from Chicago Historical Society / 245 Chicago Aerial Survey

Chapter 9

252 Bob Combs / 256 Brown Brothers / 260–262 Photography by Thomas D. Lowes / 264 Docuamerica / 267 *top* UPI Photo; *bottom left* UPI Photo; *bottom right* UPI Photo / 268 *top* UPI Photo; *bottom* UPI Photo / 270 Docuamerica / 276 John R. Maher / 277 *top* Campaign for Human Development, U.S. Catholic Conference; *bottom* UPI Photo / 278–281 Photography by Thomas D. Lowes

Chapter 10

296 UPI Photo / 299 UPI Photo / 303 UPI Photo / 305 *top* Docuamerica; *bottom* UPI Photo / 308–309 *top* Photography by Thomas D. Lowes / 308 *bottom* Brown Brothers / 314 *top* Docuamerica; *bottom* Docuamerica

Chapter 11

322 Ann Kaufman Moon from Frederic Lewis / 326 *left* Paul S. Conklin; *right* Docuamerica / 329 Grant White from Freelancers Photography Guild / 330 *top* Department of Housing and Urban Development; *bottom* Docuamerica / 333 *top* Department of Housing and Urban Development; *bottom* Bob Combs / 340–341 *top left* Shel Hershorn from Black Star; *bottom left* Docuamerica; *top right* Steven Scher from Editorial Photocolor Archives; *bottom right* Docuamerica / 346 *top left* Wide World Photos; *center left* UPI Photo; *bottom left* Wide World Photos; *top right* UPI Photo; *center right* Wide World Photos; *bottom right* UPI Photo / 347 National Library of Medicine / 356–358 Photography by Thomas D. Lowes / 359 Wide World Photos

Chapter 12

366 Docuamerica / 368 *top* Daniel S. Brody from Editorial Photocolor Archives; *bottom* R. Rosen from Editorial Photocolor Archives / 372–375 Photography by Thomas D. Lowes / 376 Docuamerica / 378 The Washington Post / 379 *top* Docuamerica; *bottom* P. K. Anderson / 380 The Library of Congress / 383 *top left* Docuamerica; *top right* Bruce McAllister from EPA-Docuamerica; *bottom* Bill Shrout from EPA-Docuamerica / 384 Mary Jane Gauen, Evanston Recreation Department / 385 Commonwealth Edison Company / 386 Robert C. Holt, Jr., The St. Louis Post-Dispatch / 387 *top* Robert L. Purdy from Associated Photographers, Inc.; *bottom* UPI Photo / 390–391 Paul Sequeira from EPA-Docuamerica

Chapter 13

398 Paul Conklin / 400 *top left* Wide World Photos; *top right* UPI Photo; *bottom left* UPI Photo; *bottom right* Wide World Photos / 406–407 Wide World Photos / 416 *top* Wide World Photos; *bottom* UPI Photo / 418–419 Photography by Thomas D. Lowes / 420 Everett C. Johnson from Leo de Wys

Chapter 14

426 Jean-Claude Lejeune / 429 Jeanne Hamilton from Editorial Photocolor Archives / 430 *top* Barbara Van Cleve from Van Cleve Photography; *bottom* Louie Psihoyos / 432–433 Photography by Thomas D. Lowes / 438 *top* UPI Photo; *bottom* Daniel S. Brody / 440 David S. Strickler

Chapter 15

450 Jean-Claude Lejeune

Name Index

Subject Index